ARROGANCE

D1537164

and

SCHEMING

in the

BIG TEN

*Michigan State's Quest for Membership
and Michigan's Powerful Opposition*

DAVID
YOUNG

ISBN-13: 978-0615584195
ISBN-10: 0615584195

Cover:
November 14, 1953 *MSC Inaugural Big Ten Season,* UM vs. MSC
East Lansing, Michigan*

Back Cover:
October 11, 1924 *College Field Dedication Game,* UM vs. MSC
East Lansing, Michigan*

September 25, 1948 *Macklin Field Expansion-Dedication Game,* UM vs. MSC
East Lansing, Michigan*

October 9, 1948 *Series-Renewal Game,* MSC vs. ND
South Bend, Indiana**

November 14, 1953 *MSC Inaugural Big Ten Season,* UM vs. MSC
East Lansing, Michigan*

*Courtesy of Jack Briegel UM Ticket Collection
atrueblueguy@aol.com

**Courtesy of University of Notre Dame Archives

ADDITIONAL COPIES: createspace.com/3757162; amazon.com; kindle

To Andrew, Michael, and Christopher,

my three sons.

Never stop pursuing your dreams.

Contents

Acknowledgements

I MET Michigan State archivist Portia Vescio for the first time in September of 2008. She informed me that President John Hannah, a major character in this drama, had retained very few documents during his first decade in office. She felt I would have better success beginning my research by visiting the Bentley Historical Library at the University of Michigan. Her advice set me on the right track.

While driving back to Holland later that day, I recalled that Don Williams, professor emeritus of chemistry at Hope College (and a patient of mine),[1] had once told me that his son was employed as an associate archivist at the university. I contacted Don to confirm this and he agreed to arrange a meeting. Two weeks later, Brian Williams and I met for the first time at the Bentley.

As it turned out, the timing was propitious. Five months earlier, the Eileen Aigler estate had finally agreed to donate her husband's papers to the university. Brian informed me that I would be the first researcher to have access to Ralph Aigler's documents dating back a century. I soon discovered that the Michigan law professor's role in this story was as significant as John Hannah's. I am deeply indebted to Brian for his assistance over the past three years.

Portia Vescio was extremely helpful in gathering information pertaining to the Spartans of Michigan State. She also recommended that I scan the on-line State Board of Agriculture minutes. The documents, dating back to 1900, offered some clues to the Aggie/Spartan story. The board member packets, provided in advance of those monthly meetings, occasionally filled in the details.

David McCartney (University of Iowa, Iowa City), David Null (University of Wisconsin, Madison), Bryan Whitledge (University of Illinois), Bertha Ihnat (The Ohio State University), Peter Lysy (University of Notre Dame), Carrie Lynn Schwier (Indiana

---

[1] Permission to acknowledge this doctor-patient relationship was granted by Professor Williams.

University), Kevin Leonard (Northwestern University), Erin George and Karen Spilman (University of Minnesota), Eileen Ielmini (University of Chicago) and Kathryn Hensley (University of Pittsburgh), as archivists or associates, were very supportive of my endeavor.

Mary Hannah-Curzan, Thomas Hannah, and I enjoyed a Saturday brunch while looking out over Lake Michigan at Tom's home near Good Hart, Michigan. In sharing stories about their father, I gained a better appreciation of his character and leadership.

In November of 2009 I had the honor of interviewing the Reverend Theodore M. Hesburgh, C.S.C.,[2] president emeritus of the University of Notre Dame. What was intended to be a 20-minute visit with Father Ted, discussing his memories of John Hannah, turned into a four-hour encounter. At his suggestion, we continued our conversation while dining at the Morris Inn on campus. Despite my intention to pay for both meals, the highly respected academic leader and adviser to numerous U.S. presidents beat me to the check. Had I known he was going to pay for my $30 filet mignon, I would have ordered the fish!

Michigan President Emeritus James Duderstadt, during an interview a few years ago, offered insight into the collaborative relationship that actually exists between the state institutions when not competing on the gridiron.

Daryl Rogers and I communicated via telephone on two occasions. His recollection of that remarkable 1978 Spartan season was amazing. Dan Underwood, assistant to Rogers, shared memories of the real story behind the "arrogant asses" alliteration that ultimately became Coach Rogers' legacy to generations of Spartan faithful.

College Football Data Warehouse (www.cfbdatawarehouse.com) proved to be an invaluable web resource for verifying dates, schedules, and trends. I referred to it often while trying to figure out the complex story behind the 9/6/2 Western Conference scheduling scheme, especially as it applied to the State University of Iowa during the 1940s.

O.W. Mourer deeded his business papers to Lansing insurance agent David Chapman. Gartha Angus, his associate, was kind enough to forage through papers pertaining to the Fred Jenison estate settlement on my behalf. Steve Demos, a retired cardiovascular surgeon from Muskegon, cautiously repaired John Hannah's 1921-22 University of Michigan enrollment card–and did so without a scalpel! John and Eileen Nordstrom, George Guerre, and James Klunzinger reviewed my rough draft in advance of professional editing; Bryan Barron, Jeff Kinzel, and Scott Vitter read the final version. Thank you all for your comments.

Lakeshore Health Partners, of which I am a member, is a subsidiary of Holland Hospital. Because of the affiliation, I was offered access to its marketing department. Martha Slager's staff was extremely helpful in developing a strategy for promoting and distributing my work. The cover and portraits were formatted by Gwen Petroelje.

I ADMIT that I am not technologically proficient. Early on I was backing up my writings on a floppy disk; it remained my only copy. Six chapters into the book, the floppy went blank–and I panicked. A local computer store was unsuccessful in retrieving the information, so I contacted my close friend Kevin Nelis for advice. Lacking a solution, Kevin could only recommend that I call Raymond Aman, a patient of mine. Ray eagerly took up the challenge, and two days later, I had most of my manuscript back. But the patient scolded the doctor for not taking proper care of his data. I deserved it. But for his services in helping me

---

[2] Congregatio a Sancta Cruce (Congregation of Holy Cross)

out of a mess, I promised Ray a copy of my finished product. Sadly, he suddenly passed away a few months later.[3]

With Ray's and Kevin's prodding, I began to back up my work on the computer, a thumb drive, and in an email folder. But the practice was taxing on my limited time. I got lazy and would only occasionally transfer manuscript copies to those additional sites, gambling that the hard drive was sufficient. And then it happened. In early January of 2011, my laptop got infected with a virus–and it was not the flu. At 11:00 p.m. that night, while writing, I suddenly witnessed the disease overtake my computer screen. Margaret was in bed. I shouted out to her to hurry downstairs. Her first question was, "Have you backed everything up?" After acknowledging my major blunder, I literally wept for a few minutes. Despite the time, she suggested that I call Kevin at his home. For the next two hours, while I was cursing my stupidity under breath, he valiantly tried to salvage what remained.

Fortunately, a few days later, BestBuy Geek Squad employees were able to retrieve most of my manuscript. With my son Michael's help, I have finally learned to back things up properly. His approached clicked with me. He also guided me through some technical challenges during the final phases of manuscript preparation. It was a joy working with him.

Dick Holm, of D2words, LLC, edited the manuscript. We used Google Docs to interact on-line regarding his suggestions. I am a much better writer for the experience. Dick suggested footnotes rather than endnotes. He felt the "story" behind my research–the piecing together of a very complex puzzle–would be lost to the reader by placing hundreds of citations and a few commentaries at the end of the book. Debra Wierenga, also of D2words, was invaluable in formatting the manuscript for publication. Thank you both for your commitment–and patience.

My sons–Andy, Mike, and Christopher–were in college when I began this project. I could never have taken on so monumental a task had they remained at home. Early on I shared with them why I was undertaking this challenge at age 53. They seemed disinterested. I wrote it off to late adolescence. But about six months into my writings, while on spring break from Indiana University, Andy asked his mother, "Is dad really writing a book?" Her answer prompted his reply: "Cool!" If I have accomplished anything throughout this ordeal, it has been to demonstrate to my boys (and their friends Keenan and Drew) that you never stop pursuing your dreams–regardless of your age.

Margaret has stood beside me throughout this long journey. Not once did she complain about the thousands of hours I spent reading, documenting, and writing. After 27 years of marriage, she understood my passion for a project that became an obsession.

Mom and Dad passed away in 2002 and 2009 respectively.[4] I inherited a little money from their estate and spent much of it on this undertaking. My parents would be proud to know that their 18-year-old son–who had to be gently coaxed into attending Notre Dame–would one day use their gift to finance the pursuit of a dream. Without their subtle nudge in February of 1973, this historical exploration, prompted by a youthful encounter with Jack Breslin, would remain hidden among 13 archives throughout the upper Midwest.

David J. Young

---

[3] Permission to acknowledge this doctor-patient relationship was granted by Mrs. Raymond Aman.

[4] Sirach 3:12-14. *New American Bible,* New York-Oxford: Oxford University Press, 1990.

x

Prologue

IT WAS a gorgeous sunny Saturday afternoon in late May of 1976. I was between my junior and senior years at the University of Notre Dame. My younger brothers, Mike and Tim, were hanging out with me. We hadn't been together since Christmas break four months earlier. In one week I would be returning to South Bend for summer school. I planned to study organic chemistry.

Video games were years away. In 1976 kids spent time together in outdoor activities. With so beautiful a day, we decided to play a pick-up game of commando basketball on the driveway that separated us from the Breslins next door. Whoever controlled the ball was on offense. The other two played defense. There were no other rules.

Tim was the athlete. Tall, talented and confident, my youngest brother dominated any game we devised. Commando basketball was no exception. Lacking his skills, Mike and I always played like hooligans. We pushed, shoved, and taunted him. Even though this brotherly intimidation never worked, it didn't prevent us from trying!

Jack Breslin was mowing the grass in his backyard next door. It was part of the usual Saturday ritual for him. He would play golf in the morning at either Lansing Country Club or Forest Akers and attend to his lawn in the early afternoon.

It was the first game of commando basketball we had played since I had departed for school back in mid-August of 1975. Mr. Breslin was always intrigued with our intense competition, regardless of the seasonal sport we played. He cut a few strips of the yard and stopped for a moment. After briefly observing our play from a distance, he decided to wander over to watch the action more closely. The Yardboy remained idling in the background. Following a few more minutes of pushing and shoving, we took a break to visit with him.

Mom and Dad had acquired the house on Pebblebrook Lane four years earlier, and we got to know our neighbor soon thereafter. Jacweir Breslin was executive vice president of Michigan State University. He rose rapidly through the ranks after graduating from college in 1946. His mentor at Michigan State College of Agriculture and Applied Science was President John Alfred Hannah. Other than his love for Spartan athletics, that was about all we knew about him. He never mentioned his athletic prowess while attending school during the war years. It was typical of his character.

We grew up Spartan fans. With the university nearby, it was not unusual for my brothers and me to observe any sporting activity taking place near the Red Cedar River. We often attended football and basketball games. As both a Cub and Boy Scout, I ushered at many football games years earlier. By my teen years I was selling programs. In addition to being lucrative for a 14-year-old, the Saturday-morning job offered me free admission to many games at Spartan Stadium. Tim and Mike joined me in the small business venture. We dominated sales on the river bridge connecting north and south campus near the library.

During hot summer days, if bored at home, my brothers and I would bike over to Michigan State. There was always something to do. We climbed trees, walked across the Red Cedar shallows, and meandered about the botanical gardens. On many occasions we snuck into the men's Intramural Building near Jenison Fieldhouse. With Tim's basketball prowess, we found ourselves often participating in pick-up games with summer-session students.

So, being rabid fans of anything Green, it was only natural for our conversations to invariably turn to the Spartans. Jack Breslin shared many interesting tales about coaches, athletes, and special games with us during those brief interactions. It was a common bond. But on this particular Saturday in May the conversation was not about sports. Instead, Mike shared some exciting news. After one year of study at Michigan State, he had applied and recently been accepted at Notre Dame as a sophomore transfer student.

JACK BRESLIN graduated from Michigan State College with a Bachelor of Science degree in 1946. He earned six letters in three sports and was senior class president. Despite volunteering for military service, he was denied due to a minor physical ailment.[1] As a consequence, he remained on campus, finished his degree, and took a job at Chrysler Corporation in Allentown, Pennsylvania. Four years later, in 1950, he returned to Michigan State at the urging of John Hannah to take on the role of field secretary and assistant director of alumni relations.[2] Three years later he was promoted to a position in the Student Placement Office. Hannah recognized leadership potential. Mr. Breslin quickly advanced over the next decade while serving under the legendary president.

In 1957 he attained a Master's in Guidance and Counseling to complement his position as director of the Placement Bureau at the university. By 1961 he would be appointed secretary of the Board of Trustees, a university position equivalent to chief operating officer in corporate America. By 1969 Breslin was executive vice president of one of the largest research universities in the world.

In recognition of his dedication and commitment, the university bestowed on him an Honorary Doctorate of Law degree in the spring of 1986. "No one individual has done more to advance the significant best interests of MSU over the past quarter century than Jack Breslin."[3] Those were John Hannah's words. The $40 million Student Events Center, a magnificent edifice on west campus, was posthumously named after him. He had played a

---

[1] Breslin, Brian. 10 October 2009. Personal communication.
[2] MSU Information File: Biographical Information, Jacweir (Jack) Breslin. Michigan State University Archives, East Lansing: undated
[3] MSU Information File: Jack Breslin. Michigan State University Archives, East Lansing: 2 August 1988.

critical role in its planning and development over the previous decade. The building remains his legacy for over 40 years of service to his alma mater.[4]

Back at court side, as Mike commented on the acceptance letter from South Bend, Mr. Breslin seemed more excited about the news than Mom and Dad had been a day earlier. Of course he was not faced with private school tuition for two sons now attending the University of Notre Dame du Lac! Regardless, his reaction was sincere. He grabbed Mike's hand and congratulated him. Michigan State's loss was Notre Dame's gain.

And then he shared a story with us about the two schools. It had little to do with sports and much to do with special relationships. It was an honor to attend the University of Notre Dame, he told us. He maintained the highest respect for the school, its integrity, and its standards. He spoke of Fathers Theodore Hesburgh and Edmund Joyce as leaders of unquestionable character and honor. Due to John Hannah's friendship with the two priests, Breslin had gotten to know them well. He was especially familiar with Father Ted. He mentioned how the careers of Hannah and Hesburgh paralleled each other. Both were not only exceptional institutional leaders, they were also academic visionaries, eloquent speakers, public servants, and advisers to numerous U.S. presidents.

With the lawnmower still idling nearby, Breslin gave us a cursory history lesson. Through Hannah's friendship with Hesburgh and his predecessor, Father John Cavanaugh, a unique institutional relationship had developed that profoundly benefited Michigan State College of Agriculture and Applied Science. Without Notre Dame, he said, the college would not be the great university that it had become by 1976.

I was 21 at the time. Mike was 19, and Tim was a junior in high school. None of us were really interested in a lecture about institutional relationships. Our attention span was waning. We were more focused on resuming our commando game. And if he kept talking, I feared his lawnmower might run out of gas.

But Mr. Breslin was not done. He commented on the wonderful athletic relationship that had evolved between the schools since the late 1940s: "You know, had it not been for Notre Dame, Michigan State would never have been admitted into the Big Ten. Father Cavanaugh did us a huge favor in aiding our application." Cavanaugh Hall was an all-male dorm located on the north quad just east of the Golden Dome. That was all I knew about anyone with that Irish name. He never went into detail regarding what the distinguished president of Notre Dame had accomplished on behalf of the Spartans.

Realizing that we'd listened for about as long as was tolerable for three kids eager to resume a game, he started walking back to his lawnmower. But he was not quite done. "And despite Notre Dame's assistance, if the University of Michigan had had its way…" He was too close to the Yardboy by now. His words were muffled by the engine.

That was it. I never gave the truncated history lesson a second thought. He resumed his afternoon task. After grabbing the ball from Tim, we three resumed our commando play.

EAST LANSING was a great place to grow up during the 1960s and 70s. The university dominated the landscape of the town. Its faculty and staff had imprints throughout the community. Many of my friends at St. Thomas Aquinas grade school had family affiliated

---

[4] MSU Information File: Biographical Information, Jacweir (Jack) Breslin. Michigan State University Archives, East Lansing: undated

with the campus nearby. Some parents were administrators, others coaches, but most were prominent professors in various departments.

Duffy Daugherty lived directly behind us when we lived in the split level on Old Mill Road. He and his wife attended our parish. Mr. Daugherty was never home. The Spartan head football coach was in constant demand on the speaking tour. His knowledge of the game, his wisdom, and his self-deprecating humor made him a favorite at corporate engagements.

Our pastor, Father Jerome MacEachin, was a professor in the Religion Department at the university. He was instrumental in building St. John's Student Center for Catholic college students matriculating to Michigan State. Father Mac bled green blood. It was not Irish, however. Like our pastor, I too was a Spartan at heart. So it came as no surprise that in my senior year of high school I decided to apply to Michigan State. Most of my friends had similar plans.

But one day in the early fall of 1972 Dad asked, "Have you given Notre Dame any thought?" The question caught me off guard. I had no idea he had an interest in any school other than Michigan State. My father had 10 season tickets to all home football games. He shared them with business clients. Being naïve to marketing techniques, I had assumed Dad was a rabid Spartan fan. I was wrong.

MY FATHER grew up during the Depression. He experienced verbal and physical abuse while being raised a Catholic in times of religious intolerance. He and his family found consolation and pride in the success of the Fighting Irish on the gridiron.

My mother was raised in South Bend. From 1929 through 1934 her parents rented a home on East Wayne Street. Her best friend in grade school, Mary Jeanne Rockne, lived just down the street in a home her father purchased in 1930.

In March of 1931 Knute Rockne died in a plane accident in Kansas. Mother vividly recalled the day after the tragedy. The vacant lot adjacent to the Rockne home was filled with floral arrangements from dignitaries and prominent people the popular coach had befriended during his successful tenure at Notre Dame. Mary Jeanne and Mom skipped aimlessly about the arrangements while reading the notes and cards. Both were too young to fully appreciate the significance of a parent's death.

A few years later, Mother's father also passed away unexpectedly. After graduating from South Bend Central, she and Grandma moved back to Lansing to be near family. Mom never shared the Rockne story with any of us until my fourth year in South Bend.

So in the fall of 1972 I had no idea of the affection my parents held for Our Lady's university. At their prompting I had applied and been accepted. And four years later, in May of 1977, I graduated from the University of Notre Dame du Lac.

ON A Saturday 29 years later, following an exhausting night on-call at the hospital, I opted to sit in front of my television and watch Notre Dame play Michigan State in South Bend. It was September 17, 2005. I was tired enough to doze through much of the game but I was wide awake at the end, and what I saw astounded me.

After a hard-fought game that had gone into overtime, several members of the victorious Spartans were running onto the field carrying a huge block "S" flag that they had grabbed from their cheerleaders. Stopping at the 35-yard line, they thrust it into the turf, a spontaneous and defiant proclamation of victory amid an otherwise usual post-game celebration.

The announcers on television kept returning to the scene. Producers in NBC trailers adjacent to the west stadium entrances recognized a newsworthy controversy unfolding. The activity on the gridiron was good for additional advertising revenue. It was a coup for the national network.

As I watched, my thoughts suddenly and unexpectedly returned to Jack Breslin's history lesson 29 years earlier. How would he have responded to the scene on television? The defiant activity was absolutely contrary to his concept of sportsmanship. And for two schools sharing a special relationship dating back decades, I believe he would have been deeply disturbed by the disrespect displayed on the field.

The memory of September 17, 2005, haunted me for some time and it kept taking me back to Jack Breslin's court side talk in 1976. Why was the relationship between the two institutions so special? How had Notre Dame assisted Michigan State College in becoming Michigan State University? And perhaps of greatest intrigue for a kid growing up in East Lansing, what had Jack Breslin meant when he said, "… if the University of Michigan had had its way…" as he approached his idling lawnmower?

JOHN ALFRED Hannah was a visionary. His goal upon assuming the presidency of Michigan State in July of 1941 was to make the college a "distinguished university." His challenge lay in accomplishing that transformation. Relationships with various institutions and influential leaders would prove critical. He would also use athletics, football in particular, as a means towards an end. And as a consequence of that controversial tactic, Notre Dame, Michigan, Pittsburgh, Ohio State, Minnesota, Chicago, Illinois, Purdue, Wisconsin, Northwestern, and Iowa would all play some role in either aiding or hindering his dream.

In the early 1940s, it became apparent that if Hannah was to achieve his vision of transforming the college, he needed affiliation with an association of distinguished universities. He set his sight on the Western Conference.[5] The president's tenacious pursuit of that evolving dream has become folklore in East Lansing–at least for old grads. What really happened, though, differs greatly from the prevailing myth.

Jack Breslin's abbreviated rendition of Michigan State's quest for membership in a preeminent conference provided a small clue to an historical account much bigger and more complex than even he appreciated. And as it turns out–somewhat surprisingly–the actual story begins with a famous announcement by a renowned academician and iconoclast on December 21, 1939, in Chicago, Illinois.

---

[5] The minutes of the first gathering of faculty leadership on February 8, 1896 reference the "Intercollegiate Conference of Faculty Representatives." By default that would become the official title of the original association of seven schools. Some faculty, however, briefly referred to their organization as the Conference on Athletics. Other unofficial names included the Intercollegiate Conference, Western Conference, Big Seven, Big Nine, and Big Ten. In 1987 the presidents dropped the 1896 title in favor of The Big Ten Conference. Most of these names will be used interchangeably throughout this historical exploration.

Dramatis Personae

Ralph W. Aigler
University of Michigan professor, faculty representative 1917-1955
Charles Bachman
Michigan State College of Agriculture and Applied Science head football coach 1933-1946
Paul Blommers
State University of Iowa professor, faculty representative 1947-1955
John Gabbert Bowman
University of Pittsburgh chancellor 1921-1945
Paul Brechler
State University of Iowa athletic director 1947-1960
John Cavanaugh
University of Notre Dame du Lac president 1946-1952
Lotus Coffman
University of Minnesota president 1920-1938
Herbert Orin Crisler
University of Michigan head football coach 1938-1947, athletic director 1941-1968
James Crowley
Michigan State College of Agriculture and Applied Science head football coach 1929-1933
Lloyd Emmons
Michigan State College of Agriculture and Applied Science professor and dean, faculty representative 1949-1953
Rufus Fitzgerald
University of Pittsburgh provost 1938-1945, chancellor 1945-1955
John Griffith
Western Conference commissioner 1922-1944
James Hagan
University of Pittsburgh athletic director 1937-1948

Thomas Hamilton
United States Naval Academy athletic director 1948-1949
University of Pittsburgh athletic director 1949-1959
Virgil Hancher
State University of Iowa president 1940-1964
John A. Hannah
Michigan Agricultural College, Michigan State College of Agriculture and Applied Science,
Michigan State University College of Applied Science, Michigan State University
extension services specialist 1923-1935
secretary of the State Board of Agriculture 1935-1941
president 1941-1969
Theodore M. Hesburgh
University of Notre Dame du Lac executive vice president 1949-1952
Robert Maynard Hutchins
University of Chicago president 1929-1945
Frederick Cowles Jenison
The State Agricultural College student circa 1896-1900, insurance agent 1904-1939
Harry Kelly
State of Michigan governor 1943-1947
Lawrence Kimpton
University of Chicago professor, faculty representative 1944-1946
Harry Kipke
University of Michigan student-athlete 1920-1924
Michigan State College of Agriculture and Applied Science head football coach 1928-1928
University of Michigan head football coach 1929-1937
Frank Leahy
University of Notre Dame du Lac head football coach 1941-1943, 1946-1953
Karl Leib
State University of Iowa professor, faculty representative 1938- 1947
president of NCAA 1947-1949
Kenneth Little
University of Wisconsin professor, faculty representative 1947-1951
Frank McCormick
University of Minnesota athletic director 1932-1941, 1945-1950
James Lewis Morrill
University of Minnesota president 1945-1960
Justin Morrill
US Congress 1855-1866
US Senate 1867-1898
Clarence "Biggie" Munn
Michigan State College of Agriculture and Applied Science head football coach 1947-1953
Floyd Reeves
University of Chicago professor 1929-1953
consultant to President John Hannah of Michigan State College 1943-1953
Michigan State College of Agriculture and Applied Science professor 1953-1962

Frank Richart
University of Illinois professor, faculty representative 1936-1949
Henry Rottschaefer
University of Minnesota professor, faculty representative 1934-1957
Alexander Ruthven
University of Michigan president 1929-1951
Lynn St. John
The Ohio State University athletic director 1912-1947
Ernest Schroeder
State University of Iowa athletic director 1936-1947
Robert Sidey Shaw
Michigan State College of Agriculture and Applied Science president 1928-1941
R. E. Sherrill
University of Pittsburgh professor, athletic council member circa 1944-1948
Kenneth Wilson
Western Conference commissioner 1945-1961
Fielding Yost
University of Michigan head football coach 1901-1923, 1925-1926,
athletic director 1921-1940
Ralph Young
Michigan Agricultural College, Michigan State College of Agriculture and Applied Science
athletic director 1923-1954

Another Main Character
In this drama is a school that was founded in East Lansing, Michigan.
Over the years its name has changed several times.
This text remains true to those changes.
Here, as an aid to the reader, is a chronological list of those names:

Agricultural College of the State of Michigan 1855-1861
The State Agricultural College 1861-1909
Michigan Agricultural College 1909-1925
Michigan State College of Agriculture and Applied Science 1925-1955
Michigan State University of Agriculture and Applied Science 1955-1964
Michigan State University 1964-

xx

Chronology of Historical Events

1817: Catholepistemiad Michigania founded in Detroit

1837: University of Michigan (UM) relocates to Ann Arbor

1852: Henry Phillip Tappan arrives in Ann Arbor

1855: The Agricultural College of the State of Michigan (ACSM) founded

1862: Morrill Land-Grant Act; ACSM becomes The State Agricultural College (TSAC)

1863: Tappan resigns

1885: Ralph William Aigler born

1895: President James Smart invites seven university presidents to form a regional conference

1896: Intercollegiate Conference of Faculty Representatives founded; North Central Association on Accrediting (NCA) founded

1899: Indiana and Iowa join conference

1901: Fielding H. Yost arrives in Ann Arbor

1902: John Alfred Hannah born

1905: Roosevelt declaration; Intercollegiate Athletic Association of the United States (IAAUS) founded

1906: Intercollegiate/Western Conference revises Handbook

1907: faculty representatives approve the 'non-intercourse' (boycott) policy

1908: UM withdraws; Decade of Defiance begins; Nebraska Response; TSAC becomes an 'independent'

1909: TSAC becomes Michigan Agricultural College (MAC)

1910: IAAUS becomes National Collegiate Athletic Association; Yost Boycott of Notre Dame (ND) begins

1912: Ohio State joins conference; Lynn St. John becomes OSU athletic director (AD)

1917: UM rejoins conference; Ralph Aigler becomes UM faculty representative

1918: The Great War ends; War Department report on deconditioned recruits/advent of the physical education degree

1920: American Professional Football Association founded; Taylorville-Carlinville pay-for-play scandal

1921: Hannah attends UM law school; ND ends series with MAC

1922: John Griffith becomes first commissioner; Hannah transfers to MAC

1923: Hannah graduates from MAC; Hannah becomes extension service agent; Ralph Young becomes MAC coach and athletic director

1924: College Field dedication

1925: MAC becomes Michigan State College of Agriculture and Applied Science (MSC); Aggies/Spartans

1927: Michigan Stadium dedication; Young resigns as MSC football coach, remains AD

1928: MSC hires Harry Kipke as coach

1929: Robert Maynard Hutchins becomes Chicago president; Kipke resigns; UM hires Kipke as coach; MSC hires James Crowley as coach; Iowa probation

1932: Iowa/Crowley confidential negotiations; Yost-Young "scrimmage game" understanding

1933: NCA investigates MSC; Crowley resigns; MSC hires Charles Bachman

1934: Henry Rottschaefer becomes Minnesota faculty representative

1935: Hannah becomes secretary of the State Board (SBA); Southeastern Conference codifies the 'athletic' scholarship; Aigler Boycott; Macklin Field expansion; Kipke investigation begins

1936: Minnesota General College investigation by Aigler; Wisconsin Reynold's Plan; Pitt Boycott; MSC Huston Committee explores application to conference

1937: first MSC rejection; James Hagan becomes AD at Pitt; Tom Harmon enrolls at UM; UM fires Kipke

1938: St. John's "Buckeye Rule;" UM hires Herbert Orin Crisler

1939: Fred Jenison dies; Griffith contracts with Pitt; Aigler Boycott ends; Chicago withdraws from football (The Announcement); Blackstone Hotel cocktail party/'anonymous source' escapade

1940: 9/6/2 temporary scheduling format; the Michigan Rule; Yost retires; Crisler becomes AD; SBA closes Jenison estate; Harmon wins Heisman Trophy

1941: Hagan-Griffith-St. John scheme; Hannah becomes president; Faculty Senate Resolution of October; Ralph Aigler's respiratory illness; Pearl Harbor; Jenison Awards; first Pitt rejection

1942: Yost Series with ND; Crisler-Young scheduling debate; Hannah ghostwrites letters for Young

1943: second MSC rejection; War Department edict; MSC cancels 1943-44 contracts

1944: MSC announces plans to resume football; D-Day; GI Bill of Rights; Griffith dies; second Pitt rejection; Crisler Boycott of ND begins

1945: Kenneth Wilson becomes commissioner; third Pitt rejection; Jenison Awards expanded; WWII ends; faculty approves 9/6/2 scheduling format as Handbook policy

1946: Chicago withdraws from conference (The Second Announcement); Ruthven supports MSC's application; St. John recruits Wilson as insider; Aigler-Richart-Kimpton Scheme; fourth Pitt rejection; third MSC rejection; Spaghetti and Meatball contract; Board in Control policy on scrimmage game; contentious scheduling negotiations (MSC-UM) resume; Bachman resigns; MSC hires Clarence "Biggie" Munn as coach

1947: Jenison Awards expanded; fourth MSC rejection; faculty tentatively approves Rule 6 (academic scholarships for athletes) and Highland Park yardstick; Munn press conference/"weak sisters" incident; St. John retires; Wilson begins investigation of compliance with Rule 6; UM wins mythical national championship; Crisler retires from coaching, remains as AD

1948: Sanity Code approved; MSC drops Jenison Awards; Iowa-ND long-term contract; Morrill Plan; Wilson reveals Rule 6 violations; Richart-Aigler Motion; McCormick Miscue; fifth MSC rejection; revised Morrill Plan; Hovde/Purdue threat; Hagan resigns as AD; Macklin Stadium dedication; MSC-ND resume rivalry; Pitt announces Captain Tom Hamilton as next AD; Hamilton's 'delay' tactic; Rottschaefer Motion; Aigler Amendment; Iowa "no" vote; fifth Pitt rejection; MSC elected into conference; Purdue Boycott; MSC Boycott; Asterisk Motion

1949: Committee of Three; Crisler Scheme; Larkin Motion; MSC becomes member; Spoelstra article

1953: MSC probation; MSC inaugural season in Big Ten/co-champions/Rose Bowl selection

1954: MSC defeats UCLA in Rose Bowl; Young announces retirement; Munn resigns to become AD

1955: Aigler retires; MSC becomes Michigan State University of Agriculture and Applied Science (MSUAAS)

1964: MSUAAS becomes Michigan State University; Aigler dies

1969: Hannah retires

1978: Crisler Boycott of ND ends; the Underwood Alliteration/Daryl Rogers

1991: Hannah dies

2008: Bentley Historical Library receives Ralph W. Aigler Papers

Arrogance and Scheming in the Big Ten

*Michigan State's Quest for Membership
and Michigan's Powerful Opposition*

DECEMBER 21, 1939. The University of Chicago was on Christmas break. At most schools the holiday interlude marked the end of final exams and another grading period. A new semester typically followed shortly after New Year's Day. Chicago was different. Neither midyear exams nor semester transitions applied at this university. The school located on the Midway was a decade into a novel academic experiment unlike any other in the country.

Chicago students had to master a core curriculum. The focus for learning was independent study.[1] Attendance at classes was not mandatory and grades were nonexistent. Competency was measured by a comprehensive examination administered by a board of examiners. The program attracted only exceptional, highly motivated students. Their Christmas holiday did not signal the beginning or end of anything academic.

But if students at Chicago did need a break in late December of 1939, it was from the humiliation of yet another dismal football season in the Western Conference. For those few who followed the Maroons on the gridiron, it was a debacle.

The University of Chicago football team had struggled in the Intercollegiate Conference of Faculty Representatives for the past 10 years. The once-mighty collegiate football power, coached by the legendary Amos Alonzo Stagg until 1933, had declined in the past decade, and 1939 was a crowning disaster. Led by Coach Clark Shaughnessy, the Maroons finished the year with two wins and six losses. Within the conference, Chicago had lost three games. They had won none. The offense generated a total of 37 points for the season while the defense gave up 308 points.

Over the past decade Chicago had won 24 games, tied eight, and lost 49. Its record within the Western Conference over that stretch was seven wins, 38 losses, and one tie. Perhaps the only shining light in this dim decade was the play of Jay Berwanger.[2] In 1935 the Downtown Athletic Club of New York designated him the best player in the country, presenting him with a trophy depicting a football player running with his right arm extended

---

[1] McNeil, William H. *Hutchins' University: A Memoir of the University of Chicago 1929-1950.* Chicago and London: The University of Chicago Press, 1991. pp. 27-28
[2] Lester, Robin. *Stagg's University: The Rise, Decline & Fall of Big-Time College Football at Chicago.* Urbana and Chicago: University of Illinois Press, 1999. pp. 154-155

and his left arm cradling a football. Berwanger was the first ever to receive what would later be known as the Heisman Trophy.

So "The Announcement" of December 21, 1939, did not surprise most students, faculty, and administrators when it was proudly shared with the press by President Robert Maynard Hutchins. Many had anticipated it. But to the world of intercollegiate football it was shocking news.

Hutchins' statement was brief. The University of Chicago would end all football competition. It would no longer participate on the gridiron in the esteemed conference it helped found almost 40 years earlier. Chicago was the first school of any renown to cancel a football program purportedly based on principle alone. Hutchins anticipated that others would follow. The self-assured legal scholar would be disappointed.[3]

THE SIGNIFICANCE of Hutchins' announcement would be debated for months among college presidents, board members, academicians, students, alumni, and fans around the country. It was not your typical sports story. Newspaper editorials applauded the action almost universally; sports writers in those very same papers "deplored and ridiculed the decision."[4]

Poor performance on the gridiron for many college football enthusiasts was not a reason for abdicating the team sport. There were far more honorable gains from competition. As John Hannah of Michigan State College stated years later:

> There is something about team athletics that requires a degree of
> dependence on other members of the team, and thus teaches something
> worthwhile to those involved ... A shortcoming of formal education is that
> it fails to generate in young people an appreciation [that] one does not
> usually accomplish much working [alone]. One must rely on others to do
> their part ... This is one bit of learning that every young man and woman
> gains from team athletics.[5]

Others argued that team sports provided an identity for the college. "The competitions and contests, the delight in bodily activity, the loyalties, and the honor that form a part of that vast organism called college athletics are the reflection in our college life of characteristics that are common to the youth of the world."[6] Group or institutional identity brought together faculty, administrators, and students for a common pursuit. Victories were ultimately irrelevant. It was the esprit de corps that athletic competition generated that wedded graduates to their alma mater for life.

But in December of 1939 there were major reasons for Hutchins and his board to recuse Chicago from competitive football.

FIFTEEN YEARS earlier, in 1924, the University of Chicago had been acknowledged as

---

[3] McNeill, William H. *Hutchins' University: A Memoir of the University of Chicago 1929-1950*.
Chicago and London: The University of Chicago Press,1991. p. 98
[4] Ibid.
[5] Hannah, John A. *A Memoir*. East Lansing: Michigan State University Press, 1980. p. 114
[6] Savage, Howard J. *American College Athletics*. Boston: D.B. Updike-The Merrymount Press. 1929.
p. 33

the mythical Western Conference champions[7] by both the press and the public. The title substantiated a tradition of football excellence and innovation dating back to the school's founding in 1892.

Under the guidance of a young Amos Alonzo Stagg, the university football program would become a power in the association it helped found in 1895. Stagg's unique tenure as a member of the faculty was a first in college football. President William Rainey Harper wanted to assure him job security regardless of win-loss records.

Stagg's teams were dominant and competed at the level of other powers within the Intercollegiate Conference of Faculty Representatives. He was an ardent proponent, for the most part, of the rules of engagement and eligibility that defined the novel conference. Like so many coaches of that time, however, Stagg found ways around some of those very conference rules he professed adherence to in principle.[8] He liked winning, after all, as much as any other coach!

But all that would change within a few decades. Following the successful 1924 season, Stagg's program steadily declined. There were many reasons. Perhaps the most significant, however, involved concerns expressed by the faculty. The focus on athletics was superseding an institutional vision clearly defined by President William Rainey Harper and John D. Rockefeller in the early 1890s. A few professors at the university led the effort to return to that founding ideal. And with that development, the demise of a once-great football program became inevitable.

---

[7] Throughout the book the term "mythical" is juxtaposed to conference or national champion. Lacking a format to determine the best team in the Big Ten or about the country, the Associated Press (AP), through a survey of sportswriters, would begin declaring a conference as well as a national champion by the mid 1930s. The United Press (UP) polled coaches following the bowl season and announced its national champion beginning in the early 1950s. Regardless of the poll, opinion weighed-in heavily. The designation of a "mythical" title was used to reflect a controversial format based on win-loss percentage, margin of victory, schedules, and opinion.

[8] Lester, Robin. *Stagg's University: The Rise, Decline & Fall of Big-Time College Football at Chicago*. Urbana and Chicago: University of Illinois Press, 1999. pp. 89-90

From Chaos to Order: The Emergence of the Western Conference

B y the turn of the nineteenth century, college football had already gotten out of control. There were no eligibility requirements. Cheating was rampant. Games were violent and controlled by athletes and thugs recruited merely to play for the school on game day. None of these participants were enrolled and actively working toward a degree. Some were even paid for services rendered.[1]

In response to this situation, the Intercollegiate Conference of Faculty Representatives was founded in 1895 by seven universities at the request of President James Smart of Purdue. Sharing his idea with Cyrus Northrup of the University of Minnesota in November of 1894, they agreed to invite six prominent schools to meet in Chicago a few months later. The agenda centered on one concern: "Is it not about time for college officials to gather to relieve interstate collegiate athletics of some of their more objectionable features?"[2]

The two called together the presidents of Lake Forest College, Chicago, Northwestern, Wisconsin, and Illinois in January of 1895. The University of Michigan could not attend the meeting. The leadership voted on 12 rules that would guide the formation of a conference of members sharing similar convictions of fair play.[3] Faculty oversight was seen as critical to the success of the association. It would guarantee the integrity of the weekend game and the institutions sponsoring them.[4]

On February 8, 1896, faculty representatives from Purdue, Minnesota, Wisconsin, Illinois, Northwestern, Chicago, and Michigan met in Chicago to put into practice the concepts approved previously by the presidents.[5] Lake Forest opted out. The State

---

[1] Kryk, John. *Natural Enemies: Major College Football's Oldest, Fiercest Rivalry – Michigan vs. Notre Dame.* Lanham: Taylor Trade Publishing, 2007. pp. 11, 25-26

[2] Ratermann, Dale. *The Big Ten: A Century of Excellence.* Champaign: Sagamore Publishing, 1996. pp. 3-5

[3] Ibid., p. 7

[4] Ibid., p. 3

[5] Rules, Regulations and Opinions of the Intercollegiate Conference of Faculty Representatives, Revised 1930. University of Minnesota Archives. Department of Intercollegiate Athletics Papers;

University of Iowa and Indiana University became members in 1899. In the spring of 1912, The Ohio State University would be welcomed after a formal application.

The mandate from the presidents to their faculty was to restore integrity to intercollegiate athletic competition:

> The conference adopted a code of eligibility rules in order, first, to bring
> and keep intercollegiate athletics in their proper relationship to an
> educational institution, and, second, to attain up to certain point equality in
> competitive conditions.[6]

The seven intended to compete only against other members of the conference. The well-being of the student was their focus. Winning gridiron games was secondary. The rules drafted by the presidents would help ensure safe and fair play.

The Intercollegiate Conference of Faculty Representatives derived its official name from the title of the minutes of the first meeting.[7] It was mandatory that a board at each school, dominated by faculty, would oversee student athletic activities. Non-faculty, including a few students and alumni, could also serve. But ultimate control would now rest with the academicians in charge of student well-being.[8]

One academician-representative from each school would attend meetings in Chicago every May and December as a member of the Faculty Representatives Committee that ruled the conference. Officers and standing committees were selected to address matters pertaining to enforcement or interpretation of the sacrosanct Intercollegiate Handbook that defined all rules and regulations.[9]

The primary focus for the faculty representatives remained eligibility. An athlete had to meet academic entrance requirements to attend a college. He had to complete a full year of studies while in residence before he could participate in any sport, with competition limited to three years in the aggregate. Time devoted to football was limited to two hours per day, excluding Sundays.[10] Only two weeks of preseason practice was allowed. The season began the last Saturday of September and ended the weekend before Thanksgiving.[11] Subsidies, or pay-for-play, were strictly forbidden.

There were no postseason "bowl" games; qualifying for them would place too much

Box 13, folder: 1895-1908, 1930, 1941

[6] Aigler to Long. 18 September 1935. Bentley Historical Library, University of Michigan. Ralph W. Aigler Papers, 87406 Aa 2; Box 12, folder: athletic correspondence 1933-36 "L" misc.

[7] Aigler to Richart. 9 November 1944. Bentley Historical Library, University of Michigan. Ralph W. Aigler Papers, 87406 Aa 2; Box 8, folder: correspondence 1940-45 Richart

[8] Aigler to Stone. 5 November 1940. Bentley Historical Library, University of Michigan. Ralph W. Aigler Papers, 87406 Aa 2; Box 8, folder: correspondence 1940-45 "S" misc.

[9] Rules, Regulations and Opinions of the Intercollegiate Conference of Faculty Representatives, Revised 1930. University of Minnesota Archives. Department of Intercollegiate Athletics Papers; Box 13, folder: 1895-1908,1930, 1941

[10] Handbook of the Intercollegiate Conference of Faculty Representatives, Revised 1941. University of Minnesota Archives. Department of Intercollegiate Athletics Papers; Box 13, folder: 1895-1908,1930, 1941

[11] Small Handbook of the Intercollegiate Conference of Faculty Representatives. University of Minnesota Archives. Department of Intercollegiate Athletics Papers; Box 13, folder: small Handbooks 1895-1908, 1930, 1941

emphasis on winning during the regular season.[12] [13] A postseason of play would also interfere with studies prior to the Christmas break. The conference wanted to emphasize that academics took precedence over athletic endeavors during and following the closure of the season.[14]

The Intercollegiate Conference of Faculty Representatives, most commonly referred to as the Western Conference, had resolved most of the existing problems at the time. Subsidies, in particular, had been banned. But with the advent of professional football in the early 1920s, remuneration became an issue once again.

THE AMERICAN public was developing a passion for sports. By the early 1920s, fans were supporting professional baseball throughout the spring and summer and college football during the autumn. Professional football made its debut on the sports scene when the American Professional Football Association was organized in 1920. Two years later its name would be changed to the National Football League. Contests were held on Sundays to avoid competing against Saturday's much more popular college games. But the professional play, held in a few northern industrial cities, was slow to capture the attention and financial support already enjoyed by the colleges.

In smaller communities around the country, however, Sunday afternoon proved a popular time for competition between neighboring towns. Former college players were hired to compete. Dollars gained from gate receipts or passing the hat would be split among the players. Civic pride brought out crowds willing to finance the afternoon entertainment. Betting on outcomes was part of the activity enjoyed by the fans.

One such game–a November 27, 1921, contest between Taylorville, Illinois, and nearby Carlinville–put the amateur subsidy problem back in the spotlight. It also caught the faculty representatives of the Western Conference off guard.

The significance of the Taylorville-Carlinville scandal lay in what it revealed about professionalism creeping into amateur intercollegiate athletics. Taylorville had hired most of the University of Illinois team. Carlinville had acquired the services of some Notre Dame players. Following the game, a large sum of money was exchanged among the college players in clear violation of Handbook rules.

The moonlighting exploits received wide publicity in the newspapers. The Western Conference faculty representatives, embarrassed by the publicity, were forced to again address a daunting problem that threatened the integrity of its institutions of higher learning.[15] The challenge remained: how to monitor the in-season activities of football

---

[12] Text of Address, Nat'l Collegiate Athletic Ass'n. Morrill, J.L. 7 January 1947. University of Minnesota Archives. Department of Intercollegiate Athletics Papers; Box 6, folder: J.L. Morrill Papers

[13] Hannah, John A. "Speech of Dr. John A. Hannah at the Fortieth Annual Convention of the National Collegiate Athletic Association." 9 January 1946. Bentley Historical Library. University of Michigan. Herbert Orin Crisler Papers, 85823 AC UAm Aa2; Box 1, folder: topical correspondence Michigan State University clippings and misc.

[14] Rules, Regulations and Opinions of the Intercollegiate Conference of Faculty Representatives, Revised 1930. University of Minnesota Archives. Department of Intercollegiate Athletics Papers; Box 13, folder: 1895-1908, 1930, 1941

[15] Kryk, John. *Natural Enemies: Major College Football's Oldest, Fiercest Rivalry – Michigan vs. Notre Dame.* Lanham: Taylor Trade Publishing, 2007. p. 97

players as well as the off-season pursuits of baseball players enticed by dollars.[16] The athletic directors vowed greater vigilance in discouraging "the boys from playing professional football, at least so long as they were undergraduates."[17]

Within the Western Conference, students were obligated to sign a statement indicating they were fully in compliance under the letter and spirit of Handbook rules.[18] Any remuneration during four years of matriculation was grounds for ineligibility. The student played for the "pleasure and physical, mental, [and] social benefit … Sport [remained] nothing more than an avocation."[19]

DURING THE 1905 college football season 10 players died and 159 were seriously injured on gridirons across the country. President Theodore Roosevelt was greatly disturbed by the violence that pervaded the popular game. With his force of persuasion, the Intercollegiate Athletic Association of the United States (IAAUS) was created in December of that year. By 1910 the organization would be known as the National Collegiate Athletic Association or the NCAA. Its emphasis was on promoting reform and creating common rules to govern play. Violent acts were forbidden.[20]

The original association emphasized the importance of faculty control. The IAAUS sought to define standard rules, promote national tournaments, encourage the growth of conferences, and expand its presence. It was also charged with finding ways to control subsidization and recruitment, practices that promoted victories at any cost–clearly contrary to the spirit of amateurism.[21]

Conferences proliferated in response to Roosevelt's support of the new association. Using the Intercollegiate Conference of Faculty Representatives as a role model, all professed similar convictions of fair, honest play as outlined by the IAAUS. Reality, however, would dictate otherwise.

In the interest of growing the IAAUS, compromising language was included in its first constitution to meet the demands of those who focused more on victories than altruistic competition. Schools wanted to maintain "home rule" at their institutions, with "faculty control" left for individual or conference interpretation. Similarly, either a school or regional conference could set its own standards involving the three cardinal sins of eligibility, proselyting (recruiting) and subsidizing. The IAAUS was essentially powerless to act. Its mandate was neither to monitor nor enforce; that remained a regional concern.

Twenty years later, in 1929, a herculean study entitled *American College Athletics* was published. Written by Professor Howard Savage, it was better known as the "Carnegie Report Bulletin Twenty-Three." The highly controversial survey, which investigated athletic

---

[16] Griffith to Weaver. 22 October 1935. Bentley Historical Library, University of Michigan. Ralph W. Aigler Papers, 87406 Aa 2; Box 6, folder: correspondence 1934-39 Griffith 4/34-1/36

[17] Ibid.

[18] Small Handbook of the Intercollegiate Conference of Faculty Representatives. University of Minnesota Archives. Department of Intercollegiate Athletics Papers; Box 13, folder: small Handbooks 1895-1908, 1930, 1941

[19] Savage, Howard J. *American College Athletics*. Boston: D.B. Updike-The Merrymount Press, 1929. p. 35

[20] Falla, Jack. *NCAA: The Voice of College Sports*. Mission, Kansas: NCAA, 1981. p. 14

[21] Behee, John R. *Fielding Yost's Legacy to the University of Michigan*. Ann Arbor: Uhlrich's Books, Inc., 1971. p. 62

programs across the country, pointed out the pervasive problems of intercollegiate athletics. It singled out football in particular.

Savage's report ridiculed the specious claim by many institutions that faculty leadership controlled the game. It stated that many of the boards in control of athletics at colleges and universities (often dominated by non-faculty and zealot fans) were more intent on promoting victories than institutional integrity. As a result, the well-being of the student-athlete was being ignored.[22]

According to Savage, without faculty control, a commitment to the amateur code was "mere subterfuge." Many individual boards viewed the three cardinal sins as "venial" rather than "mortal." Winning football, after all, was profitable. Tickets became valued commodities at successful programs. Colleges and universities discovered that Saturdays were a necessary source of revenue to subsidize growing athletic departments and certain academic programs.[23] [24] [25] Such economic realities, prior to philanthropy funding institutions, made it easy to justify the commission of venial sins. It also legitimized the building of enormous stadia to meet the overwhelming demand for tickets by students, alumni and rabid fans willing to pay out dollars for weekend entertainment.[26]

The burgeoning presence of radio contributed to college football's growing popularity. Radio sales grew from $60 million in 1922 to more than $842 million in 1929, an increase of over thirteen hundred percent.[27] With garrulous play-by-play announcers, gifted in embellishing scenes on the field, radio allowed a larger segment of the public to experience live football action during the 1930s and 40s. Athletic directors, predictably, sought ways to capture revenues from this technology. Yale "took the plunge by agreeing to let Atlantic Refining broadcast its games for twenty thousand dollars." Others would follow.[28]

Radio, however, never became a meaningful source of income for most college football teams. It wasn't until the advent of live television broadcasts during the mid-1950s that advertising dollars assumed a role in the funding of athletic programs. Radio did help popularize the sport by allowing fans to enjoy games for free during the financially trying times of that era.

THE PHENOMENON of college football, both the pregame spectacle and the contest itself, was outpacing the ability of conferences and faculty boards to adjust. As certain programs succeeded, other schools sought to emulate them. The solution for many was hiring coaches

---

[22] Savage, Howard J. *American College Athletics.* Boston: D.B. Updike-The Merrymount Press, 1929. pp. 82, 100

[23] "Prof. Adams in Interview." *Wisconsin Cardinal* 24 January 1906. University of Wisconsin-Madison Archives. University Faculty, 5/21/2; Box 1, folder: athletic board and sports reports

[24] Soderstrom, Robert M. *The Big House: Fielding Yost and the Building of the Michigan Stadium.* Ann Arbor: Huron River Press, 2005. pp. 113, 175

[25] Lester, Robin. *Stagg's University: The Rise, Decline & Fall of Big-Time Football at Chicago.* Urbana and Chicago: University of Illinois Press, 1999. p. 125

[26] Watterson, John Sayle. *College Football: History-Spectacle-Controversy.* Baltimore & London: The Johns Hopkins University Press, 2000. p. 156

[27] Crowley, Joseph N. *In the Arena: The NCAA's First Century.* Indianapolis: NCAA, 2006. p. 61

[28] Watterson, John Sayle. *College Football: History-Spectacle-Controversy.* Baltimore and London: The Johns Hopkins University Press, 2000. p. 182

with football pedigrees. Contracted to fill stadiums and generate revenue, these highly paid coaches recognized that job security depended on Saturday-afternoon victories. And to achieve that success, they needed talent. Despite being bound by certain rules limiting contact with high school athletes, many coaches found ways to recruit them. In spirit, the NCAA amateur code was honorable. In practice, it was of little significance.

Overzealous alumni and fans were part of the problem for most programs obsessed with winning. Recognizing the role of these outside influences, the Western Conference faculty leadership, in April of 1927, drafted a code of honor for alumni to follow.[29] This code was meant to appease critics who claimed that the Intercollegiate Conference was an ineffective agent for enforcement. It was far easier, and less costly, to blame outsiders than to pursue an internal investigation.

Shortly after the enactment of the alumni code, in May of 1929, a funding scandal at the State University of Iowa was revealed. It forced the Faculty Representatives Committee to finally act on principle, discipline one of its own, and make a statement for the rest of college football. But following the Iowa incident, new rumors erupted about other programs within the conference. In April of 1931 Law Professor James Paige, faculty representative from the University of Minnesota, was disturbed by what was going on at Northwestern and Purdue. He charged Northwestern with flagrantly violating conference rules by permitting "legalized subsidizing and recruiting...." Paige claimed that the school offered scholarship and loan funds to athletes throughout most of the 1920s.[30]

Purdue, a few months earlier, was charged with allowing a small group of wealthy alumni out of Chicago to effectively take charge of its athletic department. They hired an aggressive coach, without faculty board approval, and agreed to assist him in recruiting and subsidizing athletes to attend school in West Lafayette. Their intent was to focus on football at the expense of all other sports.[31] [32] The Boilermakers, in essence, were emulating a very successful program a few hours away in Notre Dame, Indiana.[33] Despite these flagrant violations, the conference failed to penalize either school. Northwestern and Purdue were not the only ones guilty of purported violation of Handbook rules and regulations. To some

---

[29] Griffith to Aigler. 13 April 1927. Bentley Historical Library, University of Michigan. Ralph Aigler Papers, 87406 Aa 2; Box 2, folder: 1927 correspondence

[30] Paige to Aigler. 7 April 1931. Bentley Historical Library, University of Michigan. Ralph Aigler Papers, 87406 Aa 2; Box 4, folder: correspondence 1929-33 Paige

[31] Griffith to Paige, Aigler, French. 8 December 1930. Bentley Historical Library, University of Michigan. Ralph Aigler Papers, 87406 Aa 2; Box 4, folder: correspondence 1929-33 Paige

[32] Griffith to Paige, Aigler, French. 14 January 1931. Bentley Historical Library, University of Michigan. Ralph Aigler Papers, 87406 Aa 2; Box 3, folder: correspondence 1929-33 Griffith (1931)

[33] Griffith to Paige, Aigler, French. 8 December 1930. Bentley Historical Library, University of Michigan. Ralph Aigler Papers, 87406 Aa 2; Box 4, folder: correspondence 1929-33 Paige

extent, all members practiced subterfuge in pursuit of victories.[34 35 36 37 38 39 40 41 42]

Enforcement remained a major challenge for the Western Conference.

THE UNIVERSITY of Michigan holds the dubious distinction of being the first school in the history of the Intercollegiate Conference of Faculty Representatives to be penalized for violations of conference rules.

In January of 1906, partly in response to the Roosevelt mandate one month earlier, the conference had passed legislation intended to curb the violence permeating the game of football. President James Burrill Angell of the University of Michigan called the meeting in Chicago "to address the evils complained of..." in the college game.[43] A number of rules were agreed upon by the nine members, and the faculty representatives took them back to their boards in control of athletics for approval.

President Angell's football coach, Fielding Yost, was disturbed by this legislation. He and his loyal followers felt that certain regulations were aimed at his "point-a-minute" juggernaut that had dominated the Western Conference since his arrival in 1901.[44]

Yost suspected that his rival, Amos Alonzo Stagg of the University of Chicago, was the impetus behind many of those new rules. He would ultimately defy most of these restrictions. In response, the University of Chicago requested release from its contractual obligations to play the Wolverines during the fall of 1906.[45] The action by Chicago and Stagg prompted additional legislation to discipline Yost.

In April of 1907, in response to defiant steps taken by the University of Michigan during the previous season, a resolution was passed by the faculty representatives stating

---

[34] Griffith to Long. 23 November 1938. Bentley Historical Library, University of Michigan. Ralph W. Aigler Papers, 87406 Aa 2; Box 6, folder: correspondence 1934-39, Griffith 9/37-7/39

[35] Aigler to Long. 22 October 1935. Bentley Historical Library, University of Michigan. Ralph W. Aigler Papers, 87406 Aa 2; Box 12, folder: Athletics correspondence 1933-36 "L" misc.

[36] Aigler to Griffith. 26 May 1938. Bentley Historical Library, University of Michigan. Ralph W. Aigler Papers, 87406 Aa 2; Box 6, folder: correspondence 1934-39

[37] Behee, John. *Fielding Yost's Legacy to the University of Michigan.* Ann Arbor: Uhlrich's Books, 1971. pp. 88-89

[38] Aigler to Long. 28 November 1934. Ralph W. Aigler Papers, 87406 Aa 2; Box 12, folder: Athletics correspondence 1933-36 "L" misc.

[39] Aigler to Paige. 8 April 1932. Bentley Historical Library, University of Michigan. Ralph W. Aigler Papers, 87406 Aa 2; Box 4, folder: correspondence 1929-33 Paige

[40] Goodenough, et al. Exhibit "B." Athletic Department (University of Michigan), Bentley Historical Library, University of Michigan. 943 Bimu 2, Box 84, folder: Athletic Department, faculty representatives minutes (folder)

[41] Aigler to Wilson. 18 April 1947. Bentley Historical Library, University of Michigan. Ralph W. Aigler Papers, 87406 Aa 2; Box 3, folder: correspondence: 1929-33 Griffith, John (1930)

[42] Lester, Robin. *Stagg's University: The Rise, Decline & Fall of Big-Time Football at Chicago.* Urbana and Chicago: University of Illinois Press, 1999. pp. 89, 190-191

[43] Chicago Beach Hotel. Chicago, Ill., Jan. 19, 1906. University of Wisconsin-Madison Archives. University Faculty, 5/21/2; Box 1, folder: athletic board and sports reports

[44] Kryk, John. *Natural Enemies: Major College Football's Oldest, Fiercest Rivalry – Michigan vs. Notre Dame.* Lanham: Taylor Trade Publishing, 2007. p. 44

[45] Behee, John. *Fielding Yost's Legacy to the University of Michigan.* Ann Arbor: Uhlrich's Books Inc. 1971. p. 68

that "in the judgment of this conference there should be non-intercourse in athletics between members of the conference and any member that does not conform in full to the conference rules." Referred to as the "non-intercourse" rule, General Regulation #7 was license to collectively boycott a program in violation of Handbook policies pertaining to institutions.[46]

Aggressive attempts by Wolverine athletic leaders to rescind some of the rules proved unsuccessful. As a result, the University of Michigan's recently reconstituted Board in Control of Athletics, subservient to the successful Yost, opted to withdraw from the conference on January 13, 1908. Faculty control had been lost prior to that decision in a political ploy by university regents to repopulate the board with non-faculty members who were more focused on winning football.[47] The "Decade of Defiance" was the end result. The remaining eight members of the conference, mindful of the April 1907 resolution, "severally" agreed to boycott Michigan.

The non-intercourse rule lacked a clause mandating that all members adhere to the new Handbook policy indefinitely. As a consequence, the University of Minnesota defied the boycott for a home-and-home series with Michigan beginning in 1909. The two schools had maintained a rivalry over the "Little Brown Jug" since 1903. Minnesota had a solid football program during those years and wanted to challenge the Wolverines on the gridiron and regain control of the Jug. But Michigan, still a very formidable football team, soundly defeated the Golden Gophers in both games.

The conference leadership reacted to the Minnesota decision by revising the non-intercourse rule of April 1907. The Intercollegiate Conference Handbook now stated that "members of the Conference shall sever athletic relations with a member that does not conform in full to the Conference rules … [Schools] shall not hold athletic relations with universities or colleges that have been members of this Conference and have withdrawn … until reinstated."[48]

The final phrase, "until reinstated," was directed at the University of Michigan. The revised April 1907 statement essentially maintained an open invitation for Michigan to return to the conference should it reconcile its wayward practices and resume full faculty control at the university. The assumption that the Wolverines would eventually rejoin the group was critical in The Ohio State University decision to pursue admission to the conference in the late fall of 1911. Ohio State gambled that the Wolverines might one day return home. The football rivalry that ended with the 1912 game was lopsided in favor of Michigan. Since 1897 the Buckeyes had never defeated the Wolverines; two games had ended in ties. In 14 contests, Michigan outscored OSU by an average of 22 points.

The Wolverines ultimately returned to the conference in the summer of 1917. It was a crowning achievement for a young law professor named Ralph W. Aigler, raised in Ohio but educated at Michigan. Aigler's forensics had convinced the university regents and

---

[46] Small Handbook of the Intercollegiate Conference of Faculty Representatives. 10 September 1908. University of Minnesota Archives, Department of Intercollegiate Athletic Papers; Box 13, folder: small Handbooks 1895-1908, 1930, 1941

[47] Behee, John. *Fielding Yost's Legacy to the University of Michigan.* Ann Arbor: Uhlrich's Books Inc. 1971. p. 71

[48] Exhibit B: "Rules, Regulations, and Opinions of the Western Intercollegiate Conference of Faculty Representatives as Revised 1924." 6 June 1924. Bentley Historical Library, University of Michigan. Athletic Department, 943 Bimu 2; Box 84, folder: faculty representatives minutes

administrative leadership of the necessity of having tenured faculty guidance on the board.[49] Without his leadership in reinstating faculty control of Wolverine athletics, the school would not have been invited back into the conference.[50]

Michigan resumed participation in the conference in November of the same year. Ralph Aigler's reward was to serve as chair of the Board in Control through 1940. He also was selected as faculty representative for the University of Michigan. He would maintain that role until his retirement in 1955. Aigler's duration of service and legal acumen would give the university a dominant voice in conference politics and decisions for decades.

With Michigan's return, the membership was now set at ten. The Ohio State University gamble of May 1912 had paid off. Its nemesis from Ann Arbor was back home and actively participating in gridiron contests. The rivalry with the Buckeyes would resume in 1918 with another Michigan victory in Columbus.

---

[49] Behee, John. *Fielding Yost's Legacy to the University of Michigan.* Ann Arbor: Uhlrich's Books, 1971. pp. 79-81

[50] Ibid., pp. 81-84

Boycotts and Vigilante Justice

DURING THE early years of the Western Conference there were few ways to enforce rules other than by "non-intercourse," as sanctioned by General Regulation #7. The conference's disciplinary legislation, such as it was, reflected the influence of Fielding Yost and his displeasure with rules that he thought were aimed at his successful program.

Over the course of the next decade it became apparent that addressing individual violations by coaches was a cumbersome process. With a growing number of complaints filed by athletic directors, many based on rumor or innuendo, the three-man Eligibility Committee could not possibly handle the caseload. At the request of the athletic directors, the Faculty Representatives Committee approved the addition of a commissioner in June of 1922.[1]

Professional baseball, in response to the 1919 Black Sox scandal, had appointed Judge Kenesaw "Mountain" Landis as its first commissioner in 1920. Baseball's owners had voted to form a commission to oversee the national pastime, and that commission became "the commissioner," as the highly respected Landis agreed to serve only if absolute power was granted to him. The University of Michigan's Ralph Aigler, a passionate professional baseball fan, recommended the same title for the newly adopted position in the Western Conference. He later regretted his suggestion. It had turned out to be a misnomer.[2][3]

The intention of Western Conference leaders was to hire someone who would assist faculty representatives in fulfilling various responsibilities tied to three standing committees. In many ways, the job was a glorified secretarial position. It called for skills in scheduling and organizing meetings, gathering and summarizing information requested by faculty and directors, investigating accusations by coaches and disseminating findings to the appropriate committee. The commissioner would also provide public-relations services for

[1] Behee, John. *Fielding Yost's Legacy to the University of Michigan.* Ann Arbor: Uhlrich's Books, 1971. p. 107

[2] Aigler to Mantho. 13 March 1945. Bentley Historical Library. University of Michigan. Ralph W. Aigler Papers, 87406 Aa 2; Box: 8, folder: correspondence 1940-45 "L-M" misc.

[3] Aigler to Salsinger. 16 March 1945.Bentley Historical Library. University of Michigan. Ralph W. Aigler Papers, 87406 Aa 2; Box: 8, folder: correspondence 1940-45 "S" misc.

the conference, serving as a voice of reason to counter charges made by sometimes scurrilous newspaper reporters. The conference chose Major John Griffith, formerly of the University of Illinois Athletic Department and the U.S. Army, for the job.

The commissioner would work with, or for, three standing committees. The Colleges Committee decided which non-conference schools might compete against the membership; it also monitored whether those programs complied with Handbook rules. The Officials Committee, with its focus on fair play, oversaw the activities of those assigned to referee, umpire, or judge sporting engagements.

But it was the Eligibility Committee that held real power within the conference. With a membership consisting of three faculty representatives, the committee had final jurisdiction in all questions that athletic directors raised regarding eligibility. Since proselyting[4] and subsidizing were intimately intertwined with eligibility, the committee addressed those concerns as well. As commissioner, Griffith was to assist this group and to fully investigate all claims of wrongdoing. He had no other voice on the committee except when requested.[5]

On paper, the concept of improved enforcement with the assistance of a non-faculty employee gathering evidence and testimony in advance of adjudication by the committee was sound. In practice, enforcement remained a challenge. If, following Griffith's research, the committee felt an institution was in serious violation of conference standards, its solution was collective non-intercourse. The offending school would be denied the opportunity to schedule competitive games in the respective sport until the violation was rectified. For track and field, baseball, and a few other sporting endeavors of that era, the implications were minor. But if the wrongdoing pertained to football, the repercussions were profound. With enormous stadiums proliferating about the conference during the 1920s, huge gate returns were shared between competing schools. Lacking conference interaction, a school's athletic budget was at risk. It was this financial threat that in theory ensured institutional adherence to the Intercollegiate Conference Handbook.

In reality, the investigatory role of the commissioner added little to improve enforcement. The Eligibility Committee's oversight remained a burdensome process. The commissioner's lack of power only added to the ineffectiveness of the committee.

Ralph Aigler, of the University of Michigan, in a letter to law school professor and faculty representative James Paige of Minnesota pointed out the problem that Commissioner Griffith faced when investigating rumors:

> The thing we must remember is that when a person has no power to compel
> the attendance of witnesses and to make them talk with the threat of
> prosecution for perjury in case of failure to tell the truth, it is frequently
> exceedingly difficult to get the facts which others want to conceal.
> However, even with the power to compel testimony, you and I well know
> that it is not always an easy matter to uncover the facts.[6]

---

[4] Proselyte/proselyting" was often interchanged with recruit/recruiting during the era under study.
[5] Rules, Regulations and Opinions of the Intercollegiate Conference of Faculty Representatives-Revised 1930. University of Minnesota Archives, Department of Intercollegiate Athletic Papers; Box 13, folder: small handbooks 1895-1908, 1930, 1941
[6] Aigler to Paige. 26 December 1930. Bentley Historical Library, University of Michigan. Ralph W. Aigler Papers, 87406 Aa 2; Box 4, folder: correspondence 1929-33 Paige

The commissioner knew of many suspect practices provided him by the athletic directors, the coaches and on occasion the press. The problem was that he lacked persuasive power to even gather reliable evidence. At one point Major Griffith was so frustrated that he actually proposed hiring "spies to check on activities in every institution in the conference."[7] Griffith was a staunch anticommunist. He made his request during the Red Scare of the late 1930s.[8]

UNABLE TO effectively discipline coaches and programs, a frustrated athletic director turned to "vigilante justice;" he and his faculty representative would bypass due process and make a unilateral decision to punish a fellow member that they felt had violated the Handbook. The discipline meted out by this suspect practice of jurisprudence involved the powerful process of scheduling. President Lotus Coffman of the University of Minnesota described the ploy:

> The schedules of the conference … are used as a weapon in the hands of certain individuals to visit their views, their policies, and their forms of punishment on persons or institutions that offend them.[9]

In seeking to punish another program, an athletic director or coach might act on unverified evidence, rumors, or innuendo. They could side-step the ineffective Eligibility Committee process and either threaten or impose a solo boycott.

The University of Chicago, for example, demanded that Wisconsin play them in Chicago at Stagg Field for five consecutive years. Minnesota required Indiana to play three straight games in Minneapolis.[10] Either the accused would accept the conditions for competition or face boycott. Even if the school knew nothing of its alleged wrongdoing, it often quietly complied, avoiding both the financial consequences of non-intercourse and the bad press that public awareness might generate.

WESTERN CONFERENCE schedules were drawn up every other year. Athletic directors and coaches would meet in late May, often in Chicago, for this onerous process. Home-and-home series were desirable but not mandatory between two programs. The emphasis was on accommodating members before allowing non-conference schools to fill remaining dates. Vigilante justice made the task even more challenging. A singular boycott imposed by one school could wreak havoc on the overall process.

With biennial scheduling, a decision by a school to deny intercourse with a fellow Western Conference member potentially impacted relationships for up to 24 months. If reconciliation was reached in the meantime, contractual relations between the two might resume with the next scheduling meetings. However, if the accused lacked an explanation, a boycott might continue indefinitely. The University of Chicago avoided contracting with

---

[7] Griffith to Long. 23 November 1938. Bentley Historical Library, University of Michigan. Ralph W. Aigler Papers, 87406 Aa 2; Box 6, folder: correspondence 1934-39, Griffith 9/37-7/39
[8] Griffith to Aigler. 26 April 1939. Bentley Historical Library, University of Michigan. Ralph W. Aigler Papers, 87406 Aa 2; Box 6, folder: correspondence 1934-39
[9] Griffith to Aigler. 23 February 1931. Bentley Historical Library, University of Michigan. Ralph W. Aigler Papers, 87406 Aa 2; Box 3, folder: Griffith 1931
[10] Ibid.

Northwestern for years due to concerns with purported recruiting and subsidizing practices in Evanston.[11]

Law professor Aigler struggled with the concept of vigilante justice. The most effective means to discipline, in his opinion, remained due process as provided by the Handbook.

> Now, I am a strong believer in the efficacy of non-intercourse with institutions not deemed desirable as competitors. It is a pretty effective weapon to compel housecleaning, and I think any rule that makes such a weapon non-usable is at least questionable. One may say that the way to handle those difficulties is not by refusal to have relationships with the institution involved but to require an improvement in the situation that leads to … objections. I agree wholeheartedly that this latter weapon should be used before the former is invoked ... [If a school is in violation] and we can get reasonably good evidence to that effect, certainly the conference ought to do something about it, rather than to leave the problem to be handled by refusal to meet [another team without explanation].[12]

Aigler was arguing for a more effective, streamlined corrective-action process short of involving the Eligibility Committee. Communication with the accused was critical if reconciliation was to take place. The problem was that most members chose not to confront; it was far easier to boycott. Let the accused figure it out! In the meantime, the financial repercussions for non-intercourse would provide sufficient retribution.

In May of 1929 the athletic directors considered revising the biennial scheduling scheme. A resolution to extend contracts to four years was proposed. Under the existing process, in late May of every other year athletic directors would meet to draft commitments for the upcoming two seasons. The proposal would lessen the frequency of gatherings for the one- or two-day task involving chalk, a blackboard and constant deal-making.

After an ad hoc committee studied the proposal, it recommended maintaining the status quo. The current practice of vigilante justice would continue. It reasoned that if the scheduling process were extended to four years, those schools disciplined in this manner would now face a penalty far too harsh for the violation.[13] The proposal could force some members to abdicate the conference rather than risk financial ruin. It was concluded this was too draconian a penalty and too risky for the sustainability of the conference.

IT WOULD take an egregious violation, one revealed in early 1929, for the Western Conference to finally place a collective penalty on one institution. While vigilante justice was intended only for matters involving misdeeds of coaches and their staffs, concerns regarding institutional malfeasance required due process as defined in General Regulation

[11] Griffith to Paige, Aigler, French. 8 December 1930. Bentley Historical Library, University of Michigan. Ralph W. Aigler Papers, 87406 Aa 2; Box 4, folder: correspondence 1929-33 Paige

[12] Aigler to Griffith. 26 May 1938. Bentley Historical Library, University of Michigan. Ralph W. Aigler Papers, 87406 Aa 2; Box 6, folder: correspondence 1934-39

[13] Minutes of the Intercollegiate Conference of Faculty Representatives. 29 May 1929. Bentley Historical Library, University of Michigan. Athletic Department, 943 Bimu 2; Box 84, folder: UM Athletic Department, faculty representative minutes (folder)

#7. Disciplinary actions could include expulsion from the conference. The process would begin with the Eligibility Committee. At its recommendation, the institutional violation would be brought before the collective ruling body for adjudication.

The pivotal scandal involved the State University of Iowa, which had violated General Regulation #7 from the Handbook of the Intercollegiate Conference of Faculty Representatives.[14] It was only the second time since articles of incorporation were penned in 1896 that the rule would be cited against an institution. The first application had followed Michigan's departure from the conference in January of 1908. It was imposed after the university had withdrawn. The Wolverine Decade of Defiance was the end result.

The Iowa scandal involved the cardinal sin of subsidizing, sanctioned by the university's athletic department. The scheme took place during the latter part of the 1920s. It was operational just prior to the release of the Carnegie Report of 1929. Boosters, with the tacit approval of Athletic Director Paul Belting, were offering loans and direct subsidies to student-athletes. Commissioner Griffith pursued a full investigation, ultimately aided by Belting's input.[15] Forced to resign by Iowa, he sought vindication by eagerly cooperating with Griffith.[16] [17]

For years the Western Conference had been vilified by the press and non-conference schools for not practicing what it preached. The Iowa scandal finally offered the faculty leadership an opportunity to change that perception. Its decision to discipline a member would send a message to the amateur sporting world that the Intercollegiate Conference was still the vanguard of amateurism.[18]

This led to severe punishment of the State University of Iowa. The non-intercourse rule, applied severally, was imposed, banning the university from competing in the conference for two years.[19] The budgetary impact would prove to be devastating on the school's athletic department.[20] Of perhaps greater significance, the scandal was an embarrassment for an academic institution of Iowa's repute. Its integrity had been impugned.

The Eligibility Committee had never before applied General Regulation #7 of the Handbook proactively for institutional violations. As an employee of the university, Paul Belting's involvement in a booster scheme had indirectly implicated the entire institution. But the faculty leadership opted to keep the investigation confidential. Because full

---

[14] "Rules, Regulations and Opinions of the Intercollegiate Conference of Faculty Representatives-Revised 1930." University of Minnesota Archives, University of Minnesota Department of Intercollegiate Athletics Papers; Box 13, folder: small handbooks 1895-1908, 1930, 1941

[15] Kuever to Athletic Council. 7 May 1929. University of Iowa Archives, Iowa City, Iowa. Board in Control of Athletics. Box: BIC minutes, folder: 1929-34

[16] Griffith to Aigler. 3 December 1929. Bentley Historical Library, University of Michigan. Ralph W. Aigler Papers, 87406 Aa 2; Box 3, folder: Griffith, John 1930

[17] Griffith to Aigler, French, Paige. 3 March 1930. Bentley Historical Library, University of Michigan. Ralph W. Aigler Papers, 87406 Aa 2; Box 3, folder: Griffith, John 1930

[18] Griffith to Aigler. 5 February 1930. Bentley Historical Library, University of Michigan. Ralph W. Aigler Papers, 87406 Aa 2; Box 3, folder: Griffith, John 1930

[19] Aigler to Griffith. 14 December 1929. Bentley Historical Library, University of Michigan. Ralph W. Aigler Papers, 87406 Aa 2; Box 3, folder: Griffith, John 1930

[20] Williams to Moenkhaus. 25 January 1930. Bentley Historical Library, University of Michigan. Ralph W. Aigler Papers, 87406 Aa 2; Box 4, folder: correspondence: 1929-33, Moenkhaus

disclosure to the press was denied,[21] reporters were forced to piece the story together. Relying on insufficient or incorrect information, many claimed that Iowa, unlike other conference schools, had been merely unlucky in getting caught.[22] [23] As a consequence, the conference leadership remained a focal point for criticism by both the press and public.[24] [25]

The publication of the Carnegie Report of 1929 had preceded official revelation of the Iowa scandal in December. Howard Savage's detailed report and his charges against most of the institutions in the conference had been embarrassing.[26] [27] The State University of Iowa, however, had gotten off relatively easily. The survey had only briefly mentioned the university's "over-enthusiastic alumnus" subsidizing promising athletes.[28] The investigation by Commissioner Griffith and the Western Conference was not mentioned.

There may have been political reasons for this omission. The well-endowed Carnegie Foundation had recently granted Iowa almost three million dollars for construction of a medical research facility. Aware of Commissioner Griffith's concurrent investigation of his institution, State University of Iowa President Walter Jessup wanted to ensure that Carnegie investigator Professor Harold Bentley departed Iowa City with a favorable impression of the athletic program. President Jessup accompanied Savage's colleague throughout his one-day investigation, ensuring that access to damaging files was controlled. In contrast to Iowa's experience, Carnegie investigations at the other nine institutions lasted at least two days. Savage's team was allowed full exposure to critical data at each stop. Athletic and administrative personnel were encouraged to fully cooperate with the investigator.[29]

The University of Michigan was singled out in particular by the Carnegie Report.[30] Its faculty representative, Professor Ralph Aigler, challenged Savage's conclusions in several letters that followed the release of the three-year investigation. Aigler, obsessed with disproving charges that indirectly impugned his national reputation, went to great lengths to

---

[21] Ward, Arch. "Why Should Intellectuals Rule Sport?" Bentley Historical Library, University of Michigan. Ralph Aigler Papers, 87406 Aa 2; Box 4, folder: correspondence 1929-33 Paige

[22] Aigler to Griffith. 14 December 1929. Bentley Historical Library, University of Michigan. Ralph W. Aigler Papers, 87406 Aa 2; Box 3, folder: Griffith, John 1930

[23] Griffith to Aigler. 23 January 1930. Bentley Historical Library, University of Michigan. Ralph W. Aigler Papers, 87406 Aa 2; Box 3, folder: Griffith, John 1930

[24] Aigler to Moenkhaus. 21 December 1929. Bentley Historical Library, University of Michigan. Ralph W. Aigler Papers, 87406 Aa 2; Box 4, folder: correspondence 1929-33, Moenkhaus

[25] Griffith to Works. 3 March 1936. Bentley Historical Library, University of Michigan. Ralph W. Aigler Papers, 87406 Aa 2; Box 6, folder: correspondence 1934-39 Griffith 1/36-1/37

[26] Griffith to Aigler. 16 February 1932. Bentley Historical Library, University of Michigan. Ralph W. Aigler Papers, 87406 Aa 2; Box 3, folder: Griffith, John 1932

[27] Board in Control of Athletics: Annual Report. 1 September 1928 – 31 August 1929. Bentley Historical Library, University of Michigan. Ralph W. Aigler Papers, 87406 Aa 2; Box 13, folder 1933-1939 Athletics

[28] Savage, Howard. *American College Athletics*. Boston: D.B. Updike-The Merrymount Press, 1929. p. 260

[29] Griffith to Aigler. 6 November 1929. Bentley Historical Library, University of Michigan. Ralph W. Aigler Papers, 87406 Aa 2; Box 3, folder: Griffith, John 1930

[30] Savage to Aigler. 2 February 1930. Bentley Historical Library, University of Michigan. Ralph W. Aigler Papers, 87406 Aa 2; Box 4, folder: correspondence 1929-33 Savage

verify the integrity of the Michigan program.[31]

Many of Aigler's points were valid–others were dubious. Regardless of the accuracy of Savage's charges against the Wolverines, the study illustrated that even Michigan struggled with adherence to the rules and regulations drafted by the conference.[32]

THE UNIVERSITY of Michigan led the membership in condemning the actions of Iowa's former athletic director, Paul Belting. Fielding Yost, greatly angered by the Hawkeye's antics, insisted that all Iowa players involved in the payouts by boosters be declared ineligible for the remainder of their careers. Ralph Aigler's motion in support of his director's proposal was approved by the ruling Faculty Representatives Committee.[33] Iowa, lacking any recourse, accepted the decision of the conference.[34]

Yost's "hostile" position towards the State University[35] and its athletes was surprising. Back in 1920 the University of Michigan Club of Detroit was involved in "landing [summer] jobs" for current and incoming "star" athletes.[36] In early August, Coach Yost was made aware by Robert Clancy, the club's field secretary, that summer employment had been successfully offered to two highly sought after high school graduates. He assured the coach that both would enroll in September. For a few months of work, future All-Americans Harry Kipke and Doug Roby were each paid $1,000 by unscrupulous alumni eager to "influence" their decisions to become Wolverines.[37] [38] [39]

At issue was the money. In relative dollar value, Kipke and Roby earned $10,900 for no more than 10 weeks of unskilled labor.[40] The Intercollegiate Handbook stated that "While it is not possible or desirable to prevent alumni from taking an active part in the recruiting of athletic material from High School … athletic directors, coaches, and all persons connected directly with the University should remain entirely passive" in the

---

[31] Board in Control of Athletics: Annual Report. 1 September 1928 – 31 August 1929. Bentley Historical Library, University of Michigan. Ralph W. Aigler Papers, 87406 Aa 2; Box 13, folder: 1933-1939 Athletics

[32] Board in Control of Athletics: Annual Report. 1 July 1936 – 30 June 1937. Bentley Historical Library, University of Michigan. Ralph W. Aigler Papers, 87406 Aa 2; Box 13, folder: 1933-1939 Athletics

[33] Memorandum of the Meeting of the Big Ten at Chicago. 6-7 December 1929. University of Iowa Archives, Iowa City, Iowa. Board in Control of Athletics Minutes, RG 28.03.05, 1929-34

[34] Minutes of the Meeting of the Athletic Board. 11 December 1929. University of Iowa Archives, Iowa City, Iowa. Board in Control of Athletics Minutes, RG 28.03.05, 1929-34

[35] Memorandum of the Meeting of the Big Ten at Chicago. 6-7 December 1929. University of Iowa Archives, Iowa City, Iowa. Board in Control of Athletics Minutes, RG 28.03.05, 1929-34

[36] "Report of Field Secretary R. H. Clancy, June 16th, 1920, To University of Michigan Club of Detroit Through President J.M. O'Dea." 16 June 1920. Bentley Historical Library. University of Michigan, Board in Control of Athletics, 8729 Bimu F81 2; Box 3, folder: June

[37] Clancy to Yost. 5 August 1920. Bentley Historical Library. University of Michigan, Board in Control of Athletics, 8729 Bimu F81 2; Box 3, folder: August

[38] Bartelme to Yost. 31 December 1920. Bentley Historical Library. University of Michigan, Board in Control of Athletics, 8729 Bimu F81 2; Box 3, folder: December

[39] An athlete was not considered committed to a school until he officially registered for classes in September. A field secretary was obligated to remain in touch with "pledged stars" until that time.

[40] This calculation, derived from MeasuringWorth.com, was based on the 2010 Consumer Price Index (CPI).

process.[41] No Michigan employee, including Fielding Yost, was involved in the scheme. Despite the excessive payouts "leaving the impression that [athletes] were being improperly influenced" by alumni,[42] based on that vague Handbook rule, the head coach had no obligation to report the actions.

But four months later, the Michigan athletic leadership would find itself caught up in an embarrassing recruiting scandal involving Robert Clancy and his alumni club.[43] In early December, the *Detroit News* was about to publish an article about the organization's summer activities. After being forewarned of the muckraking report, Yost drove to Detroit and met with the investigators for a few hours of discussion. "I went over the matter thoroughly with these men and explained just what had been done, so far as I knew and assured them I did not believe that any boy had come to Michigan through the use of any money influences."[44] Damage control was on his mind.[45] Yost had apparently forgotten about the August letter from Clancy.

Faculty Representative Ralph Aigler's hard-line motion, in December of 1929, precluding any future eligibility for Hawkeye athletes receiving dollars from boosters, would seem disingenuous in the context of the Detroit Club's "influence" scheme nine years earlier. But in fairness to the professor, it appeared he never knew of the lucrative jobs given Kipke and Roby prior to their enrolling at Michigan in the fall of 1920.[46] Had he been aware of the scheme, it is unlikely the future All-Americans would have played football in Ann Arbor.[47]

SIX YEARS following the humiliating and financially devastating probation imposed on Iowa by the Western Conference, Ralph Aigler and the Michigan Board in Control would be addressing a scandal of comparable magnitude in Ann Arbor. It involved the unscrupulous practices of a young coach hired to replace a Wolverine legend.

Harry Kipke grew up in Lansing, Michigan, only a few miles from The State Agricultural College. He later attended Central High School where he excelled in all sports.[48] Dollars and high-pressure recruiting by Wolverine alumni out of Detroit led to his attending the University of Michigan in 1920. Kipke's football skills were critical in Yost's

---

[41] "A Digest of the Proceedings of the Intercollegiate Conference of Faculty Representatives, 1895-1920." 3rd revision-1920. Hathi Trust Digital Library (Full Text); http://hdl.handle.net/2027/mdp.39015071258787

[42] Yost to Bartelme. 17 December 1920. Bentley Historical Library. University of Michigan, Board in Control of Athletics, 8729 Bimu F81 2; Box 3, folder: December

[43] Ibid.

[44] Ibid.

[45] Yost to Aigler. 11 December 1920. Bentley Historical Library, University of Michigan. Board in Control of Intercollegiate Athletics, 8729 Bimu F81 2; Box 3, folder: December

[46] Aigler to Scroggs. 20 April 1922. Bentley Historical Library, University of Michigan. Ralph W. Aigler Papers, 87406 Aa 2; Box 1, folder: 1921 correspondence, P-Z misc.

[47] Clancy to Aigler. 13 December 1920. Bentley Historical Library, University of Michigan. Ralph W. Aigler Papers, 87406 Aa 2; Box 1, folder: 1921 correspondence, C-F misc. In an attempt at clearing his name as the scandal unfolded, Clancy wrote to the faculty representative and offered him copies of the March and June field secretary reports to the Alumni Club of Detroit. He did not include nor mention the August 5, 1920 letter to Yost.

[48] "Member Biography, Harry Kipke." College Football Hall of Fame. South Bend, Indiana. 13 March

winning two Big Ten titles and the 1923 mythical national championship. He and Doug Roby salvaged the Wolverine coach's career. Following graduation, Kipke would eventually end up in East Lansing as head coach of the Spartans for the 1928 season. A call from Michigan Athletic Director Yost, however, provided him an opportunity he could not pass up, and he returned to his alma mater in June of 1929. Yost, with the support of Ralph Aigler, hired his former All-American as head coach with a salary of $6,000 a year.[49]

After a very impressive start in Ann Arbor, Coach Kipke later struggled during the mid-1930s. His record against Michigan State College reflected that decline. MSC, an independent program since departing the Michigan Intercollegiate Athletic Association (MIAA) in 1908, had been dominated on the gridiron for years by Michigan. In a series dating back to 1898, the Aggies had won only two games and tied three while losing 23 times to Michigan through the 1933 season. Changing its nickname to Spartans in 1925 failed to alter the trend. The 1934 season marked a temporary turnaround. Michigan State proceeded to run up a four-game winning streak against the Wolverines. All these victories occurred in Michigan Stadium.

Yost had retired as head coach in 1923 following Kipke's last season of eligibility. But it was tough for the legend to turn coaching over to hand-picked successor George Little. Despite a record of six wins and two losses, Little failed to meet the athletic director's expectations. As a result, Yost resumed coaching in 1925 and 1926. After two more successful seasons, he again retired to become a full-time administrator. He chose Elton "Tad" Wieman as his replacement.

Wieman also did well, winning six and losing two his first year. His second year, however, was less successful. Coach Wieman would discover that Fielding Yost was an impatient man. As Ralph Aigler later stated, "eighty percent of the difficulty (in Wieman's lack of success) was due to Mr. Yost."[50] The legend was constantly criticizing his coach and staff. He reassigned Wieman elsewhere in the athletic department following the 1928 season while seeking another "Michigan Man" to lead the team.

Wieman was not satisfied with a desk job. He ultimately landed an assistant coaching position with a winner in Minneapolis by the name of Herbert Orin "Fritz" Crisler in 1930. A letter of recommendation from Ralph Aigler helped seal the job for the former Wolverine coach maligned by Yost.[51] Wieman was impressed with the leadership of the young Crisler, who was serving as both coach and athletic director at Minnesota. He shared his thoughts with the Michigan law professor who had helped salvage his own career.[52] Aigler felt Wieman was a good judge of character and decided to follow Crisler's career path at Minnesota and later Princeton.[53] Eight years later, Wieman's assessment would prove providential for the University of Michigan.

With Wieman gone, Harry Kipke was offered the job. He proved to be a winner

---

2010. http://collegefootball.org/famersearch.php?id=20079.

[49] Minutes of the Meeting of the Board in Control of Athletics. Bentley Historical Library, University of Michigan. Board in Control of Intercollegiate Athletics, 8729 Bimu F81 2; Box 49, folder: Board in Control minutes 1927-73.

[50] Aigler to Paige. 21 January 1930. Bentley Historical Library, University of Michigan. Ralph W. Aigler Papers, 87406 Aa 2; Box 4, folder: correspondence 1929-33 Paige

[51] Ibid.

[52] Ibid.

[53] Ibid.

during his first five seasons coaching the Wolverines. After leading Michigan to five wins, three losses and one tie in 1929, he would only lose one game and tie three over the next four seasons. During that time, the Wolverines won 31 games, four Big Ten titles and two mythical national championships. But the head coach would eventually appreciate the challenges his predecessors had faced in dealing with an intimidating and very critical Yost.[54]

FIELDING YOST was one of the most successful coaches in college football history. He was without a doubt a brilliant leader, strategist and motivator.[55] But he also violated the Handbook, like so many others, during the early years of his long stay in Ann Arbor.[56] [57] With the ascent of Ralph Aigler as faculty representative in 1917, that practice would no longer be acceptable. Despite Aigler's intolerance of any rule violation, and without Yost's foreknowledge, suspect activity took place following the disastrous 1919 season. The Wolverines had finished that campaign winning only three of seven games; within the conference Yost had one victory against four defeats. Perhaps of greater significance, especially to Buckeye fans, Michigan lost for the first time to Ohio State in a rivalry that had begun in 1897. Some alumni felt that a "modern coaching system" led by a new head coach was in order.[58] But for Yost supporters, a major reason for the substandard performance on the gridiron was due to the lack of eligible talent. Poor academic performance precluded many Wolverines from participating on Saturdays.[59]

Upon completion of the 1919 season, members of the University of Michigan Club of Detroit met for their annual "smoker" in late November. The group of Yost loyalists decided to assist the embattled coach in rejuvenating Michigan football by hiring alumnus Robert Clancy as field secretary. One of Clancy's many objectives was to assist current athletes in maintaining academic eligibility. Under his direction, student managers, fraternity members, tutors and professors all aided the cause.[60] [61]

The secretary was also charged with organizing the alumni into a formidable force to support the football program. Financial contributions to the school were solicited. Graduates were also encouraged to sell the Wolverine tradition to prospective athletes.[62] However, a small group of alumni under Clancy's oversight would exceed that directive and pursue actions contrary to the amateur code. Within short order, Michigan would be loaded

[54] Behee, John. *Fielding Yost's Legacy to the University of Michigan.* Ann Arbor: Uhlrich's Books, 1971. pp. 101-102

[55] Ibid., p. 94

[56] Ibid., p. 107

[57] Report of Directors Meeting at Iowa City, March 9 & 10, 1928. Bentley Historical Library. University of Michigan, Athletic Department, 943 Bimu 2; Box 2 folder: Faculty Representatives Meetings 1918-1940

[58] Behee, John. *Fielding Yost's Legacy to the University of Michigan.* Ann Arbor: Uhlrich's Books, 1971. p. 86

[59] "Report of Field Secretary R. H. Clancy, June 16th, 1920, To University of Michigan Club of Detroit Through President J.M. O'Dea." 16 June 1920. Bentley Historical Library. University of Michigan, Board in Control of Athletics, 8729 Bimu F81 2; Box 3, folder: June

[60] Ibid.

[61] Behee, John. *Fielding Yost's Legacy to the University of Michigan.* Ann Arbor: Uhlrich's Books, 1971. pp. 87-88

with talent.[63] [64] But in December of 1920, Fielding Yost became aware that some news reporters in Detroit planned to reveal the suspect practices of that group.[65] Realizing the potential repercussions for the university, Yost took a role in leadership and "issued a warning to the Detroit Club against over-indulging in recruiting."[66] Shortly after, Clancy resigned.[67]

Over the next three years Fielding Yost coached championship teams in large part due to Clancy's recruiting success. In the aftermath of the Detroit Club scandal, he would be named athletic director. And Ralph Aigler, as faculty representative, would become even more active in departmental oversight. By 1935 he would discover violations as serious as those committed in Iowa City a few years earlier.

Harry Kipke began fielding losing teams in 1934. In that season the Wolverines gained only one victory. The coach could do nothing right in the mind of the incorrigible Yost. Past success was irrelevant. Michigan football was present tense.

Ralph Aigler appreciated the challenges of coaching in the footsteps of a legend.[68] He recognized the pressure Yost placed on his successors. Aigler decided to cautiously inform the athletic director about proper ways of mentoring the young Kipke.

> I know perfectly well that not for one minute would you intentionally do anything that would undermine [Kipke's] leadership of his coaching staff and of the squad. I gather that there have been some occasions when he has felt that things that you have done or said did have an unfortunate effect along this line. I am sure you will not consider me presumptuous when I dare say that I hope that you will make every effort to avoid such instances.[69]

Unlike his approach with Yost, however, Aigler chose a different tactic for Kipke. He asked close friend and *Detroit News* sports editor H.L. Salsinger to meet with the coach and offer counsel in how to deal with Yost. Aigler wanted Salsinger to help Kipke regain control of his staff and the team. The meeting remained highly confidential. As Salsinger's notes to the professor pointed out, the newsman dominated the conversation. Kipke was

---

[62] "Report of Field Secretary R. H. Clancy, June 16th, 1920, To University of Michigan Club of Detroit Through President J.M. O'Dea." 16 June 1920. Bentley Historical Library. University of Michigan, Board in Control of Athletics, 8729 Bimu F81 2; Box 3, folder: June

[63] Clancy to Yost. 26 June 1920. Bentley Historical Library. University of Michigan, Board in Control of Athletics, 8729 Bimu F81 2; Box 3, folder: June

[64] Clancy to Yost. 5 August 1920. Bentley Historical Library. University of Michigan, Board in Control of Athletics, 8729 Bimu F81 2; Box 3, folder: August

[65] Yost to Bartelme. 17 December 1920. Bentley Historical Library. University of Michigan, Board in Control of Athletics, 8729 Bimu F81 2; Box 3, folder: December

[66] Behee, John. *Fielding Yost's Legacy to the University of Michigan.* Ann Arbor: Uhlrich's Books, 1971. p. 88

[67] Aigler to Yost. 21 January 1921. Bentley Historical Library. University of Michigan, Board in Control of Athletics, 8729 Bimu F81 2; Box 4, folder: January

[68] Aigler to Paige. 11 February 1930. Bentley Historical Library, University of Michigan. Ralph W. Aigler Papers, 87406 Aa 2; Box 4, folder: Athletics, correspondence 1929-33, Paige

[69] Aigler to Yost. 19 January 1937. Bentley Historical Library, University of Michigan. Ralph Aigler Papers, 87406 Aa 2; Box 7, folder: correspondence 1934-39, "X-Y-Z" misc.

surprisingly subdued as he listened to the respected reporter's advice:

> Now, about Yost. He is an old man. He has aged rapidly in the last two
> years. He hasn't much farther to go. He is vain, cantankerous, obstinate,
> petulant, quarrelsome ... But I want you to overlook his failings and I want
> you to go out of your way to be helpful to him ... You will have to make
> certain allowances for Yost. To him you will never be anything but a punk
> or a squirt ... The older they get the more disdainful they are of the younger
> generation.

Salsinger wanted Kipke to appreciate the power that Aigler held in the athletic
department. He told him that it was critical to seek out the law professor's counsel on how
to withstand the scrutiny and criticisms of the old coach.[70] [71] His job depended on it.

Short of briefly meeting with Aigler, Kipke failed to heed Salsinger's advice about
patronizing Yost. It became evident to Aigler that the young coach was incapable of
accepting advice.[72] In hindsight there may have been reasons. Harry Kipke had been
violating conference rules dating back to at least 1932.[73] By the close of the embarrassing
1934 campaign, which included a loss to Michigan State, Kipke was desperate. In an ironic
twist, he resorted to tactics used by the Clancy group to resurrect Yost's coaching career 13
years earlier.

The Lansing native was familiar with a few of those practices. During the summer
months of 1920, he had been inappropriately recruited by Robert Clancy and a few rabid
Michigan graduates. It was his indoctrination into the sordid side of intercollegiate athletics.

Kipke won four games and lost four in 1935. The following year he duplicated his
one and seven record of 1934. Coinciding with those substandard seasons, rumors within
the athletic department began to surface. The Board in Control and Ralph Aigler took the
comments seriously. There appeared some merit to the charges. A very confidential internal
investigation took place over the next few years while the board contemplated its options.

The 1937 season was relatively successful on the field. However, the ongoing
investigation of Coach Kipke's tactics off the gridiron proved intolerable for the Board in
Control. In a letter to President Alexander Ruthven, Aigler cited the board's concerns.

> I think you will be interested to know that at least two years ago [1935]
> various members of our Board [in Control of Athletics] began to question
> ... whether there should not be a change in the position of head football
> coach ... The Board conducted a long and thorough investigation ... it was
> concluded that we should go on with Mr. Kipke as head coach for another
> year. So far as the winning of games is concerned, the season of 1937 just

---

[70] Salsinger and Kipke conversation. (Confidential). Circa December 1936. Bentley Historical
Library, University of Michigan. Ralph W. Aigler Papers, 87406 Aa 2; Box 10, folder:
correspondence 1946-52 "S" misc.

[71] Aigler to Murfin. 10 November 1936. Bentley Historical Library, University of Michigan. Ralph
Aigler Papers, 87406 Aa 2; Box 12, Athletics, folder: correspondence 1935-36

[72] Aigler to Salsinger. 19 March 1938. Bentley Historical Library, University of Michigan. Ralph W.
Aigler Papers, 87406 Aa 2; Box 7, folder: correspondence 1934-39 "S" misc. (SA-SP)

[73] Aigler to Ruthven. 10 December 1937. Bentley Historical Library, University of Michigan. Ralph
Aigler Papers, 87406 Aa 2; Box 7, folder: correspondence 1934-39, Ruthven

finished was, of course, a distinct improvement over the last year. The members of the Board, however, have not felt that the only question to be considered was the percentage of wins and losses. Success as measured by games won is at most only possibly indicative of situations of much more importance.[74]

The law professor continued his explanation to President Ruthven regarding the reasons for severing Kipke's coaching contract. The findings of the two-year investigation were distressing.

… Mr. Kipke has indulged in practices which, had they been publicly known, might have caused the University the deepest embarrassment. I refer particularly to the fact that about five years ago [1932] the football team was called together for practice somewhere in the country a considerable length of time before the date set for the opening of football practice. It appears also that … a considerable number of members of the squad, [during the past few summers], engaged in practice that would clearly be a violation of the rules under which we operate.[75]

Aigler emphasized that Coach Kipke was aware of the illegal gatherings and had done nothing to stop them. The head coach had also violated the training-table rule. He would provide the meals on Monday evenings and charge the costs back to the Board in Control, a clear violation of a conference dictum dating back to 1906. Feeding the athletes was viewed as a subtle form of subsidizing.

Finally, the faculty representative revealed his greatest concern regarding the Michigan coach: Kipke was indirectly committing the three cardinal sins. The first involved financial aid. Commission by Kipke of the other two–lax adherence to eligibility requirements as well as recruiting infractions–became evident during his final years at Michigan. But it was pay-for-play that most troubled Aigler. The scheme was the antithesis of amateurism, a concept he had championed since taking on a role in athletic leadership in 1912.[76] The rumors of suspect violations in Ann Arbor that were spread by conference schools in the recent past had been validated.

As you know, we have had to deal with some problems of improper subsidization. We have found that while the offenses have not been really serious, nevertheless there have been violations of the rules. Our investigations do not warrant any statement … that the head coach actually was aware of these situations, though one cannot do less than wonder whether he did not have some acquaintance with them.[77]

Aigler's greatest fear was publicity. Any leak would compromise the integrity of the

---

[74] Aigler to Ruthven. 10 December 1937. Bentley Historical Library, University of Michigan. Ralph Aigler Papers, 87406 Aa 2; Box 7, folder: correspondence 1934-39, Ruthven

[75] Ibid.

[76] Behee, John. *Fielding Yost's Legacy to the University of Michigan.* Ann Arbor: Uhlrich's Books, 1971. pp. 79-80

[77] Aigler to Ruthven. 10 December 1937. Bentley Historical Library, University of Michigan. Ralph W. Aigler Papers, 87406 Aa 2; Box 7, folder: correspondence 1934-39, Ruthven

University of Michigan. Even Commissioner Griffith was unaware of the investigation. In early November of 1937, during board discussions about the fate of Harry Kipke, the professor wrote Griffith regarding innuendos being spread about the conference concerning Michigan and its current eligibility standards. All suspect activity seemed to revolve around the recent admission of future All-American Tom Harmon.

> I feel very happy that so far even as rumors are concerned there is no
> indication that Michigan has been represented by anyone not truly eligible.
> These rumors which have been so general have not touched anyone other
> than those who were dropped from college last year and some boys who are
> now enrolled as freshmen.[78]

Around this same time, Aigler was denigrating Michigan State among faculty leadership within the conference for purportedly violating the amateur code. The Spartans applied for admission to the conference in May of 1937. The previous autumn they had defeated Michigan for the third straight year in football. Aigler's backroom comments, based on innuendo, may have swayed the vote against Michigan State. The example illustrated just how well Michigan maintained confidentiality about its own infractions.

THOMAS DUDLEY Harmon grew up in Gary, Indiana, where his exploits as a football star at Horace Mann High School had caught the attention of many colleges and universities. He was not only a great football and basketball player, he also excelled in track as an all-state competitor in the high hurdles.[79] When Harmon was a high school senior in 1936, 18 institutions sought his skills; Michigan State was included in that group. Charlie Bachman had a winning program in East Lansing. He had completed four years as head coach with the close of the 1936 football season, winning 24 of 34 games during that stretch. But of perhaps greater significance, Bachman's Spartans had dominated the University of Michigan on the gridiron in Ann Arbor. Michigan State was a legitimate suitor for Harmon.

In early spring of 1937, MSC athletic director and track coach Ralph Young was guest speaker for a sports banquet at Horace Mann.[80] Young had driven to Gary, Indiana, for one purpose only: Michigan State wanted Harmon's services as a Spartan, potentially competing in three sports. During the 1920s and 1930s it was not unusual for coaches to speak at high school banquets. It was a subtle way of proselyting/recruiting when the practice was illegal. Fielding Yost was acknowledged as one of the best at this while coaching for 25 years in Ann Arbor.[81] Ralph Young may have given an inspiring speech, but he failed to land Tom Harmon, who had already narrowed his choice to Purdue and Michigan.[82]

---

[78] Aigler to Griffith. 11 November 1937. Bentley Historical Library, University of Michigan. Ralph W. Aigler Papers, 87406 Aa 2; Box 6, folder: correspondence: 1934-39 Griffith 9/37-7/39.

[79] "Indiana Basketball Hall of Fame," *2008 Hoops Hall*. New Castle, Indiana. 23 June 2010, http://www.hoopshall.com/hall/h/tom-harmon

[80] Minutes of the State Board of Agriculture. 14 June 1937. www.onthebanks.msu.edu

[81] Savage to Aigler. 14 February 1930. Bentley Historical Library, University of Michigan. Ralph W. Aigler Papers, 87406 Aa 2; Box 4, folder: correspondence 1929-33 Savage

[82] Watterson, John Sayle. *College Football: History-Spectacle-Controversy*. Baltimore and London: The Johns Hopkins University Press, 2000. p. 188

Doug Kerr, Harmon's football coach at Horace Mann, had originally steered him toward Ann Arbor, where he had played football for the Wolverines a few years earlier.[83] Although clearly a violation of proselyting standards for the conference and the NCAA, Kerr's activity was quite common.[84] [85] Because a college coach was not allowed to visit a prospect, alumni would often act on his behalf and personally market their alma mater. This subtle recruiting scheme worked very well. Based on the Carnegie Report findings, the University of Michigan was, at least in years past, quite adept at it.[86]

The alumnus/recruiter would encourage the student to write to the head coach of the program to request an interview. The coach was allowed to write back and offer a date and time.[87] Although it was the responsibility of the student to finance the travel, the costs were often covered by alumni, who would either provide transportation or reimburse expenses.[88] In Tom Harmon's case, however, no letters were exchanged. Coach Kerr drove the high school senior and three other Horace Mann prospects to Ann Arbor to visit with Athletic Director Fielding Yost in February of 1937. Harry Kipke was probably informed of Kerr's star athlete shortly after the visit. Aggressive recruiting followed.[89]

Harmon became a Wolverine following graduation from Horace Mann in the spring of 1937. The rumors from rejected suitors followed. Coaches and directors charged that Michigan had violated its trumpeted strict admission and eligibility standards in accepting Harmon.[90] [91] [92] Commissioner Griffith's office in Chicago was inundated with complaints.

The University of Michigan prided itself on maintaining the highest requirements for admission in the Western Conference. It obligated all applicants to graduate from an accredited high school. The student was also asked to provide a letter of recommendation from his principal. Only those finishing in the upper third of their graduating high school class were accepted. These requirements applied to all students regardless of athletic skills.[93]

---

[83] Kerr to Yost. 19 February 1937. Bentley Historical Library, University of Michigan. Board in Control of Athletics. 8729 Bimu F81; Box 21, folder: November 1935-March 1937

[84] Griffith to Aigler. 31 May 1938. Bentley Historical Library, University of Michigan. Ralph W. Aigler Papers, 87406 Aa 2; Box 6, folder: correspondence 1934-39, Griffith 9/37-7/39

[85] Griffith, John. "Report to the Faculty Conference Submitted by the Commissioner of Athletics of the Intercollegiate Conference." 2 December 1936. Bentley Historical Library, University of Michigan. Ralph W. Aigler Papers, 87406 Aa 2; Box 6, folder: correspondence:1934-39, Griffith 1/36-1/37

[86] Savage to Aigler. 13 November 1929. Bentley Historical Library, University of Michigan. Ralph W. Aigler Papers, 87406 Aa 2; Box 4, folder: correspondence 1929-33 Savage

[87] Ibid.

[88] Savage, Howard J. *American College Athletics*. Boston: D.B. Updike-Merrymount Press, 1929. p. 238

[89] Watterson, John Sayle. *College Football: History-Spectacle-Controversy*. Baltimore and London: The Johns Hopkins University Press, 2000. p. 188

[90] Griffith to Aigler. 13 January 1939. Bentley Historical Library, University of Michigan. Ralph W. Aigler Papers, 87406 Aa 2; Box 6, folder: correspondence1934-39, Griffith 9/37-7/39

[91] Griffith to Aigler. 14 August 1941. Bentley Historical Library, University of Michigan. Ralph W. Aigler Papers, 87406 Aa 2; Box 8, folder: Griffith, John

[92] Griffith to Aigler. 12 November 1937. Bentley Historical Library, University of Michigan. Ralph W. Aigler Papers, 87406 Aa 2; Box 6, folder: correspondence1934-39, Griffith 9/37-7/39

[93] Aigler to Long. 28 November 1934. Bentley Historical Library, University of Michigan. Ralph W.

Professor Aigler championed those benchmark standards. Others in the conference had more lax rules for admission. Only a year earlier, while writing to President Lotus Coffman of Minnesota, he had commented on the minimum requirements for acceptance maintained by members about the conference.[94] He later intimated that the demise of Wolverine football in the mid-1930s may have been due in part to excessively strict eligibility requirements.

> So many promising football players have tried to enter Michigan and been rejected, and then have gone elsewhere, that I think we are certain to have much more limited material than was formerly the case. While at many of our sister conference institutions, admission follows almost as a matter of course for anyone who has graduated from a reputable high school, with us the admission requirements are now such that if a student was not in the upper third of his class, he has precious little chance of getting in. I have observed that the type of boy who is apt to be keenly interested in athletics, particularly the type of sport represented by football, often is not overly enthusiastic about intellectual pursuits … I do not mean that all football players are necessarily dumb. What I mean to say simply is that the type of boy to whom football makes a strong appeal is not apt to have the keenest sort of interest in high scholarship [necessary for admission to Michigan].[95]

His pondering followed the 1934 season in which the Wolverines had won only one game. Three years later, the university would accept an athletic phenomenon finishing in the bottom 10 percent of his high school class.

Out of 261 seniors, Tom Harmon graduated 243rd at Horace Mann. He lacked acumen in "history, English, mathematics, and languages." Despite his academic deficiencies, the future All-American was accepted on probationary status.[96] Violation of well-defined admission criteria, for the services of an exceptional athlete, constituted Harry Kipke's commission of the third cardinal sin involving lax eligibility requirements. Harmon began varsity play during his sophomore year of 1938. He was crucial in rejuvenating Michigan football.

UPON COMPLETION of the 1937 season, the Board in Control encouraged Coach Kipke to resign with dignity. The investigation would remain confidential. The inquiring press would be kept in check. When Kipke refused the offer, the board had no choice but to fire him. It proved a very embarrassing moment for the university. Because Aigler declined comment on the dismissal, the public interpreted the action as "an indication that even the University of Michigan insists on a 'winner.'"[97] The press did its part to publicize an

Aigler Papers, 87406 Aa 2; Box 12, folder: Athletics, correspondence 1933-36
[94] Aigler to Coffman. 14 April 1936. University of Minnesota Archives, President's Office; Box 5, folder: 120
[95] Aigler to Griffith. 21 November 1934. Bentley Historical Library, University of Michigan. Ralph W. Aigler Papers, 87406 Aa 2; Box 6, folder: correspondence 1934-39, Griffith 4/34-1/36
[96] Griffith to Aigler. 13 December 1937. Bentley Historical Library, University of Michigan. Ralph W. Aigler Papers, 87406 Aa 2; Box 6, folder: correspondence 1934-39, Griffith 9/37-7/39
[97] Aigler to Ruthven. 10 December 1937. Bentley Historical Library, University of Michigan. Ralph W. Aigler Papers, 87406 Aa 2; Box 7, folder: correspondence 1934-39 Ruthven

inaccurate story. The public never learned the real reason for his termination.[98]

Kipke's career as a coach was ruined, but he moved on. In 1940 he was elected to the university Board of Regents and served for eight years. With the advent of the Second World War, he enlisted in the Navy in 1942. Following decommissioning, he returned to a career in private business.

Tom Harmon was awarded the Heisman Trophy in 1940 as the best college football player in the country during his senior year. Following graduation in 1941, he joined the Army Air Corps, where he earned the Purple Heart and the Silver Star for heroic acts in service to his country. Harmon remained a lifelong goodwill ambassador for the University of Michigan.

WITH THE Kipke scandal behind him, Ralph Aigler contemplated the future direction of Michigan athletics. Within four years, Fielding Yost, mentally and physically declining since 1936, would face mandatory retirement.[99] [100] Acknowledging the critical staffing needs of coach and director, Aigler politicked for a man who could ultimately fill both positions with Yost's departure in 1940.[101] His personal choice was Herbert Orin "Fritz" Crisler. The University of Chicago graduate was the current coach and athletic director at Princeton. His passion for the amateur code was not unlike the man who held office at Hutchins Hall in the Law Complex, Ralph Aigler.[102]

In December of 1937 numerous applications for the head coaching position arrived by mail in Ann Arbor. Aigler wasn't interested in any of the candidates. He wanted Crisler. At Tad Wieman's insistence back in 1930, the professor had kept track of the Stagg prodigy. Aigler decided to be proactive. He personally contacted Crisler in mid-December, but the Princeton coach expressed no desire for taking on the Michigan challenge. The faculty representative, however, remained doggedly persistent. Despite lacking letters of recommendation and also declining an interview in Ann Arbor, Crisler still ended up on the board's short list of two candidates.[103] It is noteworthy that Aigler composed that list. The other candidate was Lieutenant Thomas Hamilton of the Naval Academy. It was easy for the Michigan law professor to convince President Alexander Ruthven of his choice.[104] He faced a greater challenge with the Board in Control.

Responding to Aigler's unrelenting pursuit, Crisler sent his contractual demands to Ann Arbor. Perhaps this would finally silence the chairman of the group overseeing

---

[98] Aigler to Salsinger. 19 March 1938. Bentley Historical Library, University of Michigan. Ralph W. Aigler Papers, 87406 Aa 2; Box 7, folder: correspondence 1934-39 "S" misc. (SA-SP)

[99] Murfin to Aigler. 5 November 1936. Bentley Historical Library, University of Michigan. Ralph W. Aigler Papers, 87406 Aa 2; Box 12, Athletics, folder: correspondence 1935-36

[100] Aigler to Murfin. 10 November 1936. Bentley Historical Library, University of Michigan. Ralph W. Aigler Papers, 87406 Aa 2; Box 12, folder: Athletics, correspondence 1935-36

[101] Behee, John. *Fielding Yost's Legacy to the University of Michigan.* Ann Arbor: Uhlrich's Books, 1971. p. 103

[102] Aigler to Lorenz. 28 February 1945. Bentley Historical Library, University of Michigan. Ralph W. Aigler Papers, 87406 Aa 2; Box 10, folder: correspondence 1946-52 Personal

[103] Mackey to Aigler. 17 February 1947. Bentley Historical Library, University of Michigan. Ralph W. Aigler Papers, 87406 Aa 2; Box 10, folder: correspondence 1946-52

[104] Aigler to Ruthven. 5 February 1938. Bentley Historical Library, University of Michigan. Ralph W. Aigler Papers, 87406 Aa 2; Box 7, folder: correspondence 1934-39, Ruthven

Michigan athletics. The Board in Control was shocked by his stipulations. Crisler insisted that the appointment as head coach and ultimately athletic director be approved with nothing short of a unanimous vote of the board. He demanded an annual income of $10,000. Regardless of his win-loss record he was to assume the director of athletics position upon Yost's retirement in June of 1941. Faculty rank would be provided the coach to ensure job stability. All of his Princeton assistants must be hired by the Michigan athletic director. This included Tad Wieman, who had been fired as head coach by the Wolverine legend in 1928! Finally, Crisler insisted "there shall be no record of any kind referring to him." The process must remain confidential regardless of the outcome. Fritz Crisler knew he held the dominant card in this poker game.

Board member James Duffy "asked for a recorded Yea and Nay vote on the ... question, 'is the Board now willing to accept Mr. Crisler's terms?'" Aigler and four others voted yea. The remaining eight, including Yost, were troubled by the outrageous demands. This was, after all, one of the most storied football programs in the country. Why should the University of Michigan accommodate someone who had never even expressed an interest in the job?

"After prolonged discussion ... it was moved by Mr. Duffy ... that it was the consensus of this Board that Lieutenant Thomas J. Hamilton be recommended as head football coach ..." The vote was 11 in favor and two opposed to the motion.[105] It was easy to predict how the university faculty representative to the Western Conference had voted. Ralph Aigler was obsessed with hiring the Princeton athletic leader. He had previously met with President Ruthven and convinced him of the merits of one man for both positions. Crisler had acquired those skills while at Minnesota and now Princeton. Ruthven agreed to sell the university regents on the Aigler proposal.

Even though hiring a new coach remained a job obligation of the aging athletic director, Aigler essentially inherited the task. He had been intimately involved in athletic department operations over the previous few years at the request of university leadership. Yost's declining health had raised questions about his ability to manage during the final chapter of his career.[106] Aigler's office in Hutchins Hall became the athletic department for major decisions during that transitional period.

On the afternoon of December 23, 1937, the de facto athletic director called an "informal" meeting of the board in his office at the law school complex. With the exception of Yost and board member Alexander, all others were present. Aigler made the same convincing pitch to them that he had made to Ruthven the previous day.[107]

He now had to deal with Yost. In a deftly written letter to the director a few days after the board meeting in Hutchins Hall, Aigler cited the merits of Fritz Crisler. He also noted that President Ruthven had requested that Crisler be interviewed. Yost had no knowledge of Aigler's previous discussions with the university president. The law professor also wrote that Commissioner John Griffith, a trusted friend of Yost, rated the Princeton

---

[105] Minutes of the Meeting of the Board in Control of Physical Education. 31 January 1938. Bentley Historical Library, University of Michigan. Board in Control of Intercollegiate Athletics, 8729 Bimu F81 2; Box 49, folder: Board in Control minutes 1927-73

[106] Aigler to Murfin. 10 November 1936. Bentley Historical Library, University of Michigan. Ralph W. Aigler Papers, 87406 Aa 2; Box 12, folder: correspondence 1935-36

[107] Aigler to Yost. 23 December 1937. Bentley Historical Library, University of Michigan. Ralph W. Aigler Papers, 87406 Aa 2; Box 7, folder: correspondence 1934-39, "X-Y-Z" misc.

leader his personal choice for the head coach position.[108] The savvy faculty representative knew how to deal with a very complex personality.

A special meeting was called one week later on a Sunday afternoon at the Yost residence. Aigler told the membership of Ruthven's desire to have one man hold both positions. The board had no choice but to rescind the earlier action recommending Hamilton to the ruling regents. Its members then unanimously accepted Crisler's terms. Even Yost, a staunch supporter of the Navy lieutenant, supported the nomination in the spirit of unanimity.[109] [110] [111]

Aigler's strategy had been brilliant. Years later, he took full credit for bringing Crisler to Ann Arbor.[112] [113] Within a few years, the once-proud program that had declined to new lows during the shameful Kipke years would regain its winning ways and its reputation as a leader in amateur athletics.

THE LEGACY of Fritz Crisler at Michigan may have been very different if Harry Kipke 's contract was terminated in 1936. The Board in Control had contemplated that action but decided to offer him one more year to reconcile.[114] Had Crisler been hired head coach in the spring of 1937 it is unlikely that Tom Harmon would have attended the University of Michigan. The Horace Mann athlete did not meet the scholastic requirements for admission. Because Fritz Crisler played by the rules, no pressure would have been placed on the registrar to admit Harmon. As a consequence, the All-American would have probably played football in West Lafayette.

With the board's decision to retain Kipke, Harmon enrolled at Michigan in the fall of 1937. In his first season as head coach, Crisler inherited one of the greatest football players in the history of the university. A winning attitude returned to Michigan Stadium. By 1947 the Wolverines would again claim the mythical national championship. Despite leaving Michigan in ignominy, Harry Kipke's real legacy at the university may well have been the way he indirectly paved the path for Tom Harmon coming to Ann Arbor.

THE TOM Harmon rumors were not the only ones spread about the conference over the previous decade. The commissioner's office was inundated with various complaints from the conference's athletic directors.

---

[108] Aigler to Yost. 23 December 1937. Bentley Historical Library, University of Michigan. Ralph W. Aigler Papers, 87406 Aa 2; Box 7, folder: correspondence 1934-39, "X-Y-Z" misc.

[109] Behee, John. *Fielding Yost's Legacy to the University of Michigan.* Ann Arbor: Uhlrich's Books, 1971. pp. 103-104

[110] Minutes of the Meeting of the Board in Control of Physical Education. 31 January 1938. Bentley Historical Library, University of Michigan. Board in Control of Intercollegiate Athletics, 8729 Bimu F81 2; Box 49, folder: Board in Control minutes 1927-73

[111] Minutes of the Meeting of the Board in Control of Physical Education. 6 February 1938. Bentley Historical Library, University of Michigan. Board in Control of Intercollegiate Athletics, 8729 Bimu F81 2; Box 49, folder: Board in Control minutes 1927-73

[112] Mackey to Aigler. 27 January 1947. Bentley Historical Library, University of Michigan. Ralph W. Aigler Papers, 87406 Aa 2; Box 10, folder: correspondence 1946-52

[113] Aigler to Mackey. 11 February 1947. Bentley Historical Library, University of Michigan. Ralph W. Aigler Papers, 87406 Aa 2; Box 10, folder: correspondence 1946-52

[114] Aigler to Ruthven. 10 December 1937. Bentley Historical Library, University of Michigan. Ralph W. Aigler Papers, 87406 Aa 2; Box 7, folder: correspondence 1934-39, Ruthven

The boycott had become a very active tool of retribution beginning in the late 1920s. By 1931 Aigler, aware of recruiting tactics used by Purdue alumni out of Chicago,[115] suggested to Commissioner Griffith that "creating difficulties in schedule making" might be in order; he was implying a boycott.[116] Aigler also threatened non-intercourse with Minnesota due to inappropriate coaching antics of Clarence Spears,[117] putting the annual Little Brown Jug tradition in jeopardy. Coach Spears left Minnesota only to be courted by Wisconsin a few years later. The Wolverines, among others, contemplated not scheduling the Badgers if Wisconsin hired Spears.[118] Within a few years other controversies at Wisconsin and Ohio State would challenge the Office of the Commissioner and the faculty leadership.[119] [120] [121]

Chicago and Stagg boycotted Northwestern due to recruiting and subsidizing rumors that were later substantiated by John Griffith. The Wildcats had legitimized a financing scheme that had successfully lured talent to Evanston and away from the Midway well before the Iowa scandal of 1929.[122] Stagg was obsessed with disciplining the school that compromised his success during his waning years as the Maroons' head coach.

It became increasingly obvious to many college and university presidents that the game of football was again in trouble. The NCAA, created after the first crisis of 1905, was impotent to address the problems exposed by the Carnegie Report. Enforcement remained a conference matter. Most were derelict in upholding the national association's amateur code. But President Lotus Coffman of the University of Minnesota, recognizing the many defects in the rules governing the game,[123] decided to tackle the problem in early 1931. He felt it was appropriate, at least within the Western Conference, for the presidents to take control.[124] The academicians, in his opinion, clearly lacked the power to effectively enforce the Handbook.

The Carnegie Bulletin of October 1929 did little to help the faculty cause. Despite the Western Conference leadership's decision to discipline the State University of Iowa in May with non-intercourse,[125] the Savage report was damning in the eyes of the 10 presidents

---

[115] Paige to Elliott. 7 May 1931. Bentley Historical Library, University of Michigan. Ralph W. Aigler Papers, 87406 Aa 2; Box 4, folder: correspondence 1929-33 Paige

[116] Aigler to Griffith. 15 January 1931. Bentley Historical Library, University of Michigan. Ralph W. Aigler Papers, 87406 Aa 2; Box 3, folder: Griffith 1931

[117] Ibid.

[118] Aigler to Paige. 8 April 1932. Bentley Historical Library, University of Michigan. Ralph W. Aigler Papers, 87406 Aa 2; Box 4, folder: correspondence 1929-33 Paige

[119] Lorenz to Aigler. 2 June 1936. Bentley Historical Library, University of Michigan. Ralph W. Aigler Papers, 87406 Aa 2; Box 12, folder: athletic correspondence 1933-36 "L" misc.

[120] Aigler to Griffith. 14 October 1935. Bentley Historical Library, University of Michigan. Ralph W. Aigler Papers, 87406 Aa 2; Box 6, folder: correspondence Griffith, John 1934-39

[121] Aigler to Long. 22 October 1935. Bentley Historical Library, University of Michigan. Ralph W. Aigler Papers, 87406 Aa 2; Box 12, folder: athletics correspondence 1933-36 "L" misc.

[122] Griffith to Paige, Aigler, French. 8 December 1930. Bentley Historical Library, University of Michigan. Ralph W. Aigler Papers, 87406 Aa 2; Box 4, folder: correspondence 1929-33 Paige

[123] "The Conference and the North Central Association." Undated. Bentley Historical Library, University of Michigan. Ralph W. Aigler Papers, 87406 Aa 2; Box 3. (implied author Ralph Aigler).

[124] Aigler to Paige. 24 February 1931. Bentley Historical Library, University of Michigan. Ralph W. Aigler Papers, 87406 Aa 2; Box 4, folder: correspondence 1929-33 Paige

[125] Aigler to Griffith. 14 December 1929. Bentley Historical Library, University of Michigan. Ralph

mandated to uphold the integrity of their institutions. Ralph Aigler decided to write to Alexander Ruthven. His intent was to be proactive and educate the recently appointed president of the University of Michigan on the positive steps taken by the conference in the aftermath of the humiliating revelations.

Aigler, acknowledging the problem so disturbing to Coffman, cited the Iowa case to illustrate that the faculty-representative model was still effective in adjudicating and enforcing conference rules. Only six months earlier, the governing committee of academicians had unanimously imposed severe penalties on the Hawkeyes. Iowa could return to membership upon completion of a corrective-action plan outlined by the other nine leaders.[126] He also pointed out some positive steps taken by the Faculty Representatives Committee since Howard Savage's scathing expose.

> As you know, the Conference has been doing a lot, including spending of money, to find out what the conditions in the ten members really are and then to remedy whatever evils may be found. The publicity regarding these matters in the "Big Ten" should not be taken as showing that we are worse than others, or even as bad, but rather that we are trying to do something about them.[127]

One year later, in December of 1930, a more informed Ruthven wrote to Faculty Representative Aigler in a "personal and confidential" letter, his opinion regarding the state of affairs in college athletics. Through interactions with his peers in the interim, he had gained a more thorough appreciation of the challenges facing institutions striving to maintain integrity while sponsoring intercollegiate competition.

> A plain, bald statement of the situation is that we are facing a revolution in intercollegiate athletics. Every university president to whom I have talked agrees that the present plan of organization and other conditions, however effective in the past, are wrong. Some of us would like to see changes made which would correct what is wrong and save the game. In other words, we would like to see the revolution sane, quiet, and constructive, not noisy, irrational, and destructive … Administrative officers, faculties, students, educators generally, the great foundations, and others are disgruntled and we must both keep our heads and also face the situation frankly and honestly.[128]

The word "revolution" was probably quite disturbing for conservative Republican Aigler, especially when coming from the chief administrator of the University of Michigan. But the message was clear: The game was in transition and if there was any hope of salvaging amateurism, the proponents of that code must be amenable to change as well. The

---

W. Aigler Papers, 87406 Aa 2; Box 3, folder: Griffith

[126] Aigler to Griffith. 14 December 1929. Bentley Historical Library, University of Michigan. Ralph W. Aigler Papers, 87406 Aa 2; Box 3, folder: Griffith

[127] Aigler to Ruthven. 8 November 1929. Bentley Historical Library, University of Michigan. Ralph W. Aigler Papers, 87406 Aa 2; Box 4, folder: correspondence 1929-33 Ruthven

[128] Ruthven to Aigler. 12 December 1930. Bentley Historical Library, University of Michigan. Ralph Aigler Papers, 87406 Aa 2; Box 4, folder: correspondence 1929-33, Ruthven

current means of enforcement, predominantly vigilante justice, lacked any requirements for corrective actions that would lead to reconciliation and changed behavior.

That "sane, quiet, and constructive" revolution that Alexander Ruthven had anticipated did not take place. The status quo remained intact while rumors of wrongdoings continued among the schools in the conference. John Griffith pursued several investigations, and in three instances where accusations were proven accurate, justice prevailed despite the antiquated system under attack by Ruthven and many of his colleagues.

Instance one: The conference was successful in addressing a crisis in leadership at Wisconsin, where the faculty had lost control of athletics to outside influences.[129] The action was a violation of the basic tenet of the Intercollegiate Conference. A simple suggestion by Eligibility Committee member Ralph Aigler–that the general faculty at Wisconsin decide the question whether to remain within the conference–precluded the leadership from having to implement non-intercourse with the university.[130] [131]

Instance two: Minnesota was reputed to have eligibility problems with its General College. Aigler felt that the General College, a novel educational experiment, was being used to allow academically substandard students an opportunity to participate in football.[132] In strict confidence he reported those concerns to the commissioner. A controversial investigation proved the Michigan professor right, and Minnesota responded in a way that met conference standards.[133] [134]

Instance three: Ohio State was reportedly offering very cheap housing and kitchen equipment to athletes residing at the Towers Club at the stadium or the Buckeye Club at the gymnasium.[135] [136] The school was also supposedly subsidizing athletes by providing them jobs through the State of Ohio. Some athletes were rumored to be earning $1,100 a year for part-time jobs while carrying full academic loads.[137] Aigler again requested, in confidence, that the commissioner investigate the rumors. With a mistrust of the Buckeye program that dated back years,[138] the professor suggested a Michigan boycott of Ohio State if no

---

[129] Board in Control of Physical Education. December 1936. Bentley Historical Library, University of Michigan. Ralph W. Aigler Papers, 87406 Aa 2; Box 13, folder: athletics

[130] Griffith to Aigler. 2 March 1936. Bentley Historical Library, University of Michigan. Ralph W. Aigler Papers, 87406 Aa 2; Box 6, folder: correspondence 1934-39

[131] Griffith to Aigler. 3 March 1936. Bentley Historical Library, University of Michigan. Ralph W. Aigler Papers, 87406 Aa 2; Box 6, folder: correspondence 1934-39

[132] Griffith to McCormick. 7 October 1936. Bentley Historical Library. University of Michigan Archives. Ralph W. Aigler Papers, 87406 Aa 2; Box 6, folder: correspondence 1934-39

[133] Eurich to Coffman. 7 April 1936. University of Minnesota Archives. President's Office; Box 5, folder: 120

[134] Coffman to Aigler. 17 April 1936. University of Minnesota Archives. President's Office; Box 5, folder: 120

[135] Aigler to Weaver. 30 November 1934. Bentley Historical Library, University of Michigan. Ralph W. Aigler Papers, 87406 Aa 2; Box 12, folder: athletic correspondence 1933-38 "W" misc. (WA-WE)

[136] Aigler to Long. 28 November 1934. Bentley Historical Library, University of Michigan. Ralph W. Aigler Papers, 87406 Aa 2; Box 12, folder: athletic correspondence 1933-36 "L" misc.

[137] Aigler to Griffith. 14 October 1935. Bentley Historical Library, University of Michigan. Ralph W. Aigler Papers, 87406 Aa 2; Box 6, folder: correspondence 1934-39 Griffith 4/34-1/36

[138] Ibid.

disciplinary action was taken by the conference.[139]

Fortunately for Ralph Aigler, Ohio Governor Martin Davey unwittingly allowed the Wolverine to maintain his cover. In somewhat of a muckraking role, Davey revealed to the press that "most of the Ohio State football team [was] on the state payroll." An investigation was called for by the conference. As a close friend of long-serving Ohio State Athletic Director Lynn St. John, Commissioner John Griffith felt that it would be a conflict of interest for him to poke around Columbus. At Griffith's request, Professor B.S. Stradley of the North Central Association of Colleges and Secondary Schools (NCA)[140] carried out the task instead. The accrediting agency investigator found no inherent wrongdoing on Ohio State's part. The athletic department, he said, was not culpable since the jobs had been provided by State of Ohio employees unaffiliated with the university. Aigler, in a letter to fellow representative Floyd Long of Northwestern, conceded defeat. Although "[I am] still not wholly satisfied about [Stradley's decision] ... I know of no other way to get at the problem."[141] No scheduling boycott took place.

It was amid this setting of contention and mistrust among conference members that the University of Chicago made a momentous decision. That decision, which was the result of a confidential, months-long debate between the university's board and its iconoclastic president, was announced on December 21, 1939. The university's pronouncement that it would cease participating in football would have far-reaching implications for years to come in the Western Conference.

---

[139] Aigler to Griffith. 6 April 1936. Bentley Historical Library, University of Michigan. Ralph W. Aigler Papers, 87406 Aa 2; Box 6, folder: correspondence 1934-39 Griffith 1/36-1/37

[140] NCA was the acronym for a large Midwest academic accrediting agency. It had no affiliation with the National Collegiate Athletic Association (NCAA).

[141] Aigler to Long. 22 October 1935. Bentley Historical Library, University of Michigan. Ralph W. Aigler Papers, 87406 Aa 2; Box 12, folder: athletic correspondence 1933-36 "L" misc.

The University of Chicago: Education versus Football

"The question was seriously asked whether it was possible to have a great university without a football team; what the moral consequences of such a drastic action would be; and how the University could be expected to have any 'spirit' without the rallying point provided by a football team. I greatly fear that my administration will be remembered solely because it was the one in which intercollegiate football was abolished."

Robert Maynard Hutchins[1]

THE UNIVERSITY of Chicago was founded in 1890 by Baptist Hebrew scholar William Rainey Harper. The academician was brilliant, loquacious, and persuasive. His gift of personality sold one of the shrewdest businessmen of all time on a vision to create in Chicago a great graduate university focused on research. John D. Rockefeller had interest in a similar institution in New York. Harper convinced the oil baron Chicago would prove a better venue.[2] Backed by the financial support of the richest man in the world, the professor would build an infrastructure and acquire a faculty to fulfill that dream.

Rockefeller's original plan when buying into Harper's dream was to support a university system steeped in the Baptist tradition. A trust of "western colleges" would be created to spread the Baptist doctrine. Those schools would encourage exceptionally bright baccalaureates to attend the university for graduate studies on the Midway. One main undergraduate college in Chicago was to complement the university. A seminary would be positioned in New York as part of Rockefeller's novel academic vision. The trust of colleges was also intended to feed the seminary.

Harper's plan differed somewhat from his financier's. He envisioned a full-blown university for graduate studies and research in line with Johns Hopkins and Clark

---

[1] Hutchins, Robert. *The State of the University*. University of Chicago Archives, LD902.1; 1929-49. p. 37

[2] Lester, Robin. *Stagg's University: The Rise, Decline & Fall of Big-Time Football at Chicago.* Urban and Chicago: University of Illinois Press, 1999. p. 4

University. A college division in Chicago would come later.[3][4] But Rockefeller prevailed. His philanthropy served notice that he would have no small say in this grand scheme. The charter for the University of Chicago was adopted in May of 1890.[5] Harper assumed its presidency.

In planning the college, Harper sought innovative programs to complement the traditional didactics. One unique concept was a commitment to physical health and wellness for the matriculate. The visionary referred to this as "physical culture." It would be included in the core college curriculum. As part of the emphasis on maintaining health, intercollegiate football as an extracurricular activity would be encouraged at the University of Chicago undergraduate division.[6] Even in the early 1890s, Harper recognized the value a football team might bring to his fledgling school.

Football was already a growing phenomenon on college campuses in the East. Harper, having spent time in New York previously, was well aware of the game. A viable program could bring additional publicity to the Midway project and aid its growth. Revenue from football was not a factor during the early 1890s. Instead, the game offered a common identity for the students, faculty, administration, and community at-large.[7] The end result was loyalty that bound all to one common goal of pride in the school and its evolving tradition.

President Harper convinced a young Amos Alonzo Stagg, fresh out of Yale, to develop the Department of Physical Culture and Athletics. He enticed Stagg with a tenured position as associate professor and director. He would be both a coach and a teacher. "The arrangement was remarkable for its time because it reformed the prevailing noxious control of intercollegiate activity by students and alumni and gave stature to the new pedagogy of physical education."[8] Harper's move set a precedent.

As innovative as Harper's idea was in enticing Stagg to Chicago, the granting of tenure would come back to haunt the university years later as the college reassessed its curriculum and caliber of students during the 1920s.

IN 1895, three years after accepting its first students, the University of Chicago was invited by President Smart of Purdue to participate with six other prominent upper Midwest schools in discussions about the status of intercollegiate football. With no standard rules to ensure safe and fair competition for the students, the game had gotten out of control. Chicago signed on as a founding member of the Intercollegiate Conference of Faculty Representatives in 1896.

Rules of engagement and eligibility were formed. This was a conference, not a league.[9] As a consequence, win-loss records and championships were not the goals of

[3] Hutchins, Robert. *The State of the University.* University of Chicago Archives, LD902.1; 1929-49. p. 1

[4] Chernow, Ron. *Titan: The Life of John D. Rockefeller, Sr.* New York: Random House, 1998. p. 311

[5] Ibid., p. 317

[6] Lester, Robin. *Stagg's University: The Rise, Decline & Fall of Big-Time Football at Chicago.* Urbana and Chicago: University of Illinois Press, 1999. p.6

[7] Ibid., pp. 18-24

[8] Ibid., p. 17

[9] Annual Report of the Board in Control of Physical Education. 18 January 1940. Bentley Historical Library, University of Michigan. Ralph W. Aigler Papers, 87406 Aa 2; Box 32, folder: Board in

participation. The leadership merely sought comfort in knowing the teams adhered to "equality in competitive conditions."[10] The well-being of the student participant remained the focus for the faculty charged with overseeing intercollegiate athletics.

JANUARY OF 1906 marked the death of William Rainey Harper at the age of fifty. With his passing, new leadership assumed the task of advancing his unique model of higher education.

President Harper, during his brief tenure in office, much to the frustration of Rockefeller and his foundation, never adhered to a budget. The leaders that followed him shared that trait. In 1908, after donating $24 million to Harper's dream over almost two decades, the oil baron decided it was finally time to cut his financial ties with the university. The school would have to find ways to sustain itself without Rockefeller's largesse. Financial discipline was now in order.[11]

The challenge for the University of Chicago, in the aftermath of Rockefeller's decision, was how to raise money for an endowment to subsidize operations. Previous attempts at gaining donations from wealthy Chicagoans were compromised by Rockefeller's insistence that the school maintain its fundamentalist Baptist convictions. His foundation board and key advisors, however, eventually convinced the philanthropist to drop that requirement for doctrinal control in 1907. To keep his legacy afloat until dollars from non-Baptist sources could be raised, he agreed to gift an additional $10 million to the school. His financial contribution to the dream he shared with Harper now totaled $35 million.[12]

Between 1910 and 1932 Rockefeller philanthropies would add an additional $35 million to the coffers at the Midway. His son also donated $6 million to his father's academic legacy. The Rockefeller gifting ultimately totaled $76 million. In real dollars, the wealthiest man in the world and his family had contributed almost $1.5 billion to the university.[13] Despite this generosity, in keeping with his wishes, not one building would bear his name.[14] Following his death in 1937, however, the chapel was re-named in his honor.

THE EARLY years of Stagg's leadership found the football program in good hands. He was a successful innovator, motivator, and leader. As determined by the press and without the sanction of the conference, the Maroons won six mythical Western Conference championships from 1899 to 1924. Numerous athletes, following graduation, went on to coach at other schools. Perhaps the most famous was Herbert Orin "Fritz" Crisler, who coached at Minnesota, Princeton, and finally the University of Michigan.

Although not a graduate of the school on the Midway, a student-athlete named Ralph H. Young would attend Chicago for two years while playing under Stagg.[15] Young

---

Control Annual Reports

[10] Aigler to Long. 18 September 1935. Bentley Historical Library, University of Michigan. Ralph W. Aigler Papers, 87406 Aa 2; Box 12, folder: athletic correspondence 1933-36 "L" misc.

[11] Chernow, Ron. *Titan: The Life of John D. Rockefeller, Sr.* New York: Random House, 1998. p. 496

[12] Ibid., pp. 496-497

[13] An approximate number was arrived at by using MeasuringWorth.com and the 2010 CPI for the year 1910 ($35M) and 1932 ($41M).

[14] Chernow, Ron. *Titan: The Life of John D. Rockefeller, Sr.* New York: Random House, 1998. p. 497

[15] Stabley, Fred W. *The Spartans: Michigan State Football.* Tomball, Texas.: Strobe Publishers, 1975.

later transferred to Washington and Jefferson in Pennsylvania.[16] He would eventually become head football and track coach as well as athletic director at Michigan Agricultural College in 1923. Young resigned from gridiron coaching following the 1927 season but continued managing the athletic department. He retired from Michigan State College of Agriculture and Applied Science in 1954.

The Maroon football success intrigued Chicagoans. The weekend events drew reasonable crowds. With increasing demand and limited seating at Stagg Field, tickets were sold for the opportunity to witness a game. Football soon became an unexpected source of income for the university. After winning the mythical 1924 Big Ten championship, Stagg projected profits of a few hundred thousand dollars a year if the Board of Trustees would allow him either stadium expansion or construction of a new, larger facility.

The administrative leadership of the school was in a quandary over his proposal. They were not quite convinced that adding money to Stagg's program was in the best interest of the University of Chicago. Stagg, in their opinion, had outlasted his welcome. His football program was at odds with curricular changes that would emphasize intellectual rather than athletic pursuits.[17]

At about the same time that Stagg was petitioning for more seating capacity, a study performed by Dean of the Colleges Ernest Wilkins revealed some disturbing information about the coach's program. Wilkins' survey indicated that football players were generally not of the same intellectual caliber as non-athletes. It was a discovery not unique to Chicago. Eligibility requirements were lowered at most schools focused on victories. Dean Wilkins concluded that "drastic and extensive reform, but not abolition of football," was in order. He predicted that failure to reform would force schools such as Chicago to cease intercollegiate football competition.[18]

Chicago did not reform its athletics. Instead of confronting the football legend about the misaligned focus, the administrative leadership merely allowed the program to atrophy with time. Denying Stagg a great stadium to attract athletic talent was the beginning of the end for a once mighty program.

There were other factors that contributed to the demise of football on the Midway. One of great significance involved a novel curriculum that demanded motivated minds.

The administration sought to improve the college division at the university to complement the now highly regarded graduate program of the mid-1920s. The goal was to attract more intellectually gifted undergraduates. With the assistance of Dean Wilkins and Professor Chauncey Boucher, a unique educational model evolved at the University of Chicago. It became known as the "New Plan." The core curriculum included courses of one-year duration. Lectures by graduate program professors were offered. Mandatory attendance was not required. The only obligation for the student was passing the comprehensive six-hour examination upon mastering the subject matter.[19] [20] Only very

---

p. 58

[16] "Ralph H. Young." Find a Grave Photos. 12 July 2010. http://www.findagrave.com

[17] Lester, Robin. *Stagg's University: The Rise, Decline & Fall of Big-Time Football at Chicago.* Urban and Chicago: University of Illinois Press, 1999. p. 125

[18] Ibid., p. 126

[19] Ibid., p. 133

[20] Boyer, John W. *A Twentieth Century Cosmos.* University of Chicago Archives, LD 929.B694; 2007. p. 10

bright students could succeed in this model.[21]

Amos Alonzo Stagg struggled with selling the New Plan to talented athletes not quite fitting the scholarly mold of the typical student. Boucher's curricular experiment was not conducive to winning football. If anything, it played a major role in the decline of the game at the University of Chicago.

With substandard football talent, Stagg's teams could not compete, and fans stopped coming to games. Adding to the poor attendance was the presence of both Notre Dame and Northwestern in the weekend football market about Chicago. Only 90 miles away, Notre Dame considered Chicago a "home field" for the huge Catholic population of the area. Many games were played in Soldier Field in front of crowds often exceeding 100,000. The popularity of Knute Rockne with the press and the success of his teams lured fans and dollars away from Stagg's university. Northwestern, a fellow member of the Western Conference, often played home games on the same weekend as the Maroons. This too contributed to declining attendance figures at Stagg Field.[22]

The coach had been at Chicago since 1892. By 1925 Stagg was 63 years old. Fondly referred to as "the Old Man," the moniker may have worked against him during his final decade with the Maroons. Many argued that his penchant for innovation had long since passed. Some felt he no longer was in touch with the evolving game. His nemesis from the University of Michigan, Fielding Yost, was 54 at that time. He retired from coaching following the 1926 season and remained athletic director at Michigan until retirement in late 1940. Stagg, however, doggedly held on to both positions at Chicago despite Yost's example. Academic tenure kept him safely in place.

REGARDLESS OF the reasons for the demise of football on the Midway, it would take the hiring of Robert Maynard Hutchins as president in 1929 to bring closure to the embarrassing Wilkins' survey of five years earlier.

Hutchins arrived at Chicago as the precocious 29-year-old former dean of the School of Law at Yale. He was brilliant, pompous, eloquent, and iconoclastic. He was the right fit for the University of Chicago. He had the self-assurance and the ability required to reinvent the school and enhance its unusual academic model for undergraduate studies.

By 1937, a college education under the revised New Plan would commence during today's equivalent of junior year in high school.[23] Following four years in the college the student could opt to accept a diploma or continue on in university graduate studies. The intent of the program was to promote advanced degrees and develop researchers with a University of Chicago pedigree.[24]

The challenge for Amos Alonzo Stagg, and his successor Clark Shaughnessy, was to discover scholar-athletes able to compete at the Western Conference level of play. While the nine other member schools were finding subtle ways of circumventing Handbook rules and

---

[21] McNeill, William H. *Hutchins' University: A Memoir of the University of Chicago 1929-1950.* Chicago and London: The University of Chicago Press, 1991. p. 51

[22] Lester, Robin. *Stagg's University: The Rise, Decline & Fall of Big-Time Football at Chicago.* Urban and Chicago: University of Illinois Press, 1999. pp. 131-133.

[23] Hutchins, Robert. *The State of the University.* University of Chicago Archives, LD902.1; 10 September 1942. p. 7

[24] Annual Report to Board in Control. 18 January 1940. Ralph W. Aigler Papers. 87406 Aa 2; Box 32, folder: Michigan, University, Board in Control, annual reports.

regulations, the University of Chicago was raising its eligibility requirements due to the New Plan. In May of 1939 faculty representative George Works offered a memo to the conference proposing leniency in some rules that impacted athletic participation at Chicago.

In essence the Maroons were asking that all bona fide students, excluding freshmen, be allowed to participate in athletics. This would include transfer and graduate students.[25] Faculty representatives, dating back to 1932, were aware of the innovative educational model being advanced at the university. They understood the challenge it posed for the athletic department. But it was not within their purview to adapt the rules to accommodate the unique requests of one institution. The conference leadership was mandated only to ensure that eligibility standards adopted by each school were enforced. If Chicago could not compete because of a challenging academic program, it had two options: abide by the rules as stated or withdraw from the conference.[26]

The Western Conference did not allow freshmen to compete at the varsity level. In addition, it permitted student participation in any sport for only three consecutive years. The rule proved a major problem at Chicago. Due to its academic model, it was not unusual for a student to take a year off from gridiron play in order to meet an independent-study requirement unique to a particular course. At least one year of eligibility was lost depending on when that sabbatical from football took place.

The New Plan, by the mid-1930s, allowed younger kids to matriculate at the college on the Midway. As a consequence, the first year of gridiron eligibility was often two years earlier than for students attending other Big Ten schools. Physically undeveloped athletes only added to the challenges of coaching at the university. Injuries were an additional concern.[27] Needless to say, many parents opted to keep their sons in traditional high schools until they graduated.[28] A skinny 18-year-old playing against a well-toned Bronko Nagurski was a frightening thought for any mother!

Despite the challenges of attracting athletes to a school offering a novel academic format for learning, the administration noted a surprising increase in transfers from other schools by the late 1930s. The concept of independent study was apparently intriguing to certain gifted student-athletes from other institutions.[29] The conference rule of 1896, however, forbade participation for one year following transfer. The student, as a consequence, lost a season of eligibility.[30] [31]

---

[25] McCormick to Ford. 25 May 1939. University of Minnesota Archives, President's Office 1911-45; Box 5, folder 120: athletics

[26] French to Paige. 9 December 1932. University of Minnesota Archives, President's Office. Box 4, folder: 118 athletics

[27] Minutes of the Conference Athletic Directors' Meeting. 8-9 March 1940. Appendix A (April 4, 1940). Bentley Historical Library, University of Michigan. Athletic Department, 943 Bimu 2; Box 84, folder: faculty representatives minutes.

[28] Lester, Robin. *Stagg's University: The Rise, Decline & Fall of Big-Time Football at Chicago.* Urbana: University of Illinois Press, 1999. p. 158

[29] Ibid., pp. 158-159

[30] A Digest of the Proceedings of the Intercollegiate Conference of Faculty Representatives 1895-1908. 10 September 1908. University of Minnesota Archives, Department of Intercollegiate Athletics Papers; Box 13, folder: small Handbook 1895-1908, 1930, 1941

[31] "Minutes of the Meeting of the Directors of Athletic of the Intercollegiate Conference-Appendix A." 4 April 1940. Bentley Historical Library, University of Michigan. Athletic Department, 943

The antiquated rule of 1896 had been approved to prevent "tramp" athlete enrollment, a common practice around the turn of the century. The tramp would play out eligibility at one school only to apply elsewhere. He never intended to graduate. Some were playing football into their mid to late twenties.[32] [33] But with Western Conference rules later mandating progression toward a degree in an appropriate time frame, the tramp athlete became a footnote in the history of intercollegiate athletics. Even the athletic directors of the conference recognized that new legislation "obviated" the need for the obsolete rule.[34] Chicago was granted no leniency, however. The rule remained in the Handbook as revised in 1941.[35]

Thus, it was evident that the dismal decade of decline in football performance during the 1930s reflected Hutchins' emphasis on academics. Perhaps the only source of pride for the school took place following the 1935 season. Scholar-athlete John Jacob "Jay" Berwanger was awarded the first Downtown Athletic Club Trophy as the outstanding college football player for that year.

Four years later, in 1939, Chicago would lose to the University of Michigan 85-0. The Wolverines were led by a future Heisman Trophy winner named Tom Harmon. The defeat, one of many during that discouraging season, would culminate in The Announcement of December 21, 1939, alerting the sporting world of the University of Chicago's intention to terminate its football program.

Prior to The Announcement, however, Chicago athletic leaders were still attempting to convince the Western Conference faculty representatives of its need for leniency in the rules of participation. At the December 8, 1939, Intercollegiate Conference meeting held in Chicago, Dean George Works moved "that the request by the University of Chicago for waiver of the rules of eligibility in [regards to] the memorandum of May 14, 1939 be granted." The motion was soundly defeated.[36]

With the Faculty Representative Committee denying compromise while Chicago maintained its revised New Plan of 1937, Hutchins and his Board of Trustees had no recourse but to discontinue football competition in the Western Conference. The University of Chicago could no longer effectively compete at that level.[37] The board, however, planned to allow student participation in sports other than football. They had no desire to withdraw from the Western Conference.

Bimu 2; Box 84, folder:faculty representatives minutes

[32] McCormick to Ford. 25 May 1939. University of Minnesota Archives, President's Office 1911-45; Box 5, folder 120: athletics

[33] Lester, Robin. *Stagg's University: The Rise, Decline & Fall of Big-Time Football at Chicago.* Urban and Chicago: University of Illinois Press, 1999. p. 158

[34] Minutes of Joint Meeting of the Intercollegiate Conference of Faculty Representatives. 8 December 1945. University of Illinois Archives, Series 4/2/12; Box 2, folder: minutes 1945-46

[35] Handbook of the Intercollegiate Conference of Faculty Representatives-Revised 1941. University of Minnesota Archives, Department of Intercollegiate Athletic Papers; Box 13, folder: small handbooks 1895-1908, 1930, 1941

[36] Minutes of the Intercollegiate Conference of Faculty Representatives. 9 December 1939. University of Minnesota Archives, President's Office, Department of Physical Education; Box 44, folder: Intercollegiate Conference minutes 1927-45

[37] Works to Aigler. 22 December 1936. Bentley Historical Library, University of Michigan. Ralph W. Aigler Papers. 87406 Aa 2; Box 7, folder: correspondence 1934-39 NCAA

THE ANNOUNCEMENT made headlines. Traditionally December was not a month for significant sporting news, but the University of Chicago gave sportswriters and editors weeks of good material.

President Hutchins became a media darling as he defied conventional wisdom and spoke out against college football.[38] His eloquence and haughty demeanor captivated audiences. He was suddenly "the" expert on the challenges facing intercollegiate athletics. Hutchins basked in the limelight as a voice of reason and sanity as he commented on an amateur game that was purportedly out of control.[39] He confidently predicted others would soon follow his lead.[40][41]

The faculty representatives and athletic directors of the Western Conference were caught off guard by The Announcement. Unfortunately for the leadership, Professor Ralph Aigler would be on sabbatical in Hawaii for the remainder of the semester.[42] His wise counsel, gained from years of experience, was limited to occasional letters and telephone conversations with his colleagues.[43][44] It would be left to the eight remaining faculty leaders to work through the crisis.

The Announcement of December 21, 1939, proved a public-relations nightmare for the Western Conference. It was unable to offer a reasonable immediate response. Adding to the humiliation for Commissioner John Griffith, an anonymous authority at the University of Chicago made headlines one week later by charging the conference with duplicity in adherence to the Handbook.

The unnamed administrator quoted in press releases argued that violations were rampant and that all schools were guilty of noncompliance. But Chicago, in the opinion of the unnamed critic, merited canonization. The Maroons were without sin. The university abided by the strict amateur standards of eligibility, proselyting/recruiting, and subsidizing. The authority argued that Chicago could not possibly compete among a group of heathens!

The faculty representatives, athletic directors, and commissioner were obsessed with discovering the anonymous source. It was critical to know whether he spoke with true authority. Frustration mounted as the press continued to denigrate the conference following that scoop. It would take weeks of investigative snooping, but by early February the commissioner had reasonable evidence that the anonymous source was Robert Maynard

---

[38] McNeil, William H. *Hutchins' University: A Memoir of the University of Chicago 1929-1950.* Chicago: The University of Chicago Press, 1991. pp. 97-98

[39] "Football Handicap Asserts Hutchins." 12 January 1940." *New York Times*. University of Minnesota Archives, President's Office 1911-45; Box 5, folder 120: athletics

[40] McNeil, William H. *Hutchins' University: A Memoir of the University of Chicago 1929-1950.* Chicago: The University of Chicago Press, 1991. p. 98

[41] Griffith to Moenkhaus. 8 January 1940. The Ohio State University Archives, Director of Athletics, (RG 9/e-1/9), "Intercollegiate Conference: Commissioner: Correspondence (Griffith): 1939-1940 (Folder 2 of 2)."

[42] Aigler to Griffith. 25 April 1939. Bentley Historical Library, University of Michigan. Ralph W. Aigler Papers, 87406 Aa 2; Box 6, folder: correspondence 1934-39

[43] Crisler to Aigler. 15 April 1940. . Bentley Historical Library, University of Michigan. Ralph W. Aigler Papers. 87406 Aa 2; Box 12, folder: athletics: 1939-41, A-Z misc.

[44] Rottschaefer to Aigler. 18 March 1940. Bentley Historical Library, University of Michigan. Ralph W. Aigler Papers. 87406 Aa 2; Box 8, folder: correspondence 1940-45 Rottschaefer

Hutchins.[45] This was confirmed four weeks later on March 12 by *Chicago Tribune* columnist Arch Ward.[46] Hutchins' quotes had been made at the Blackstone Hotel during a cocktail party on December 27, 1939. He had invited the press with the understanding that all his comments would remain strictly anonymous.[47]

Over the next few years Hutchins would maintain his stance regarding the overemphasis on athletics and the hypocrisy of the current amateur rules.[48] He criticized the role intercollegiate athletics had assumed in tainting higher educational ideals.[49] The integrity of institutions, forced to violate rules of engagement in pursuit of victories and dollars, was being compromised by a society increasingly obsessed with sports.

CHICAGO HAD a right to withdraw from competitive football. There was no obligation that conference members must participate in all sporting endeavors.[50] What disturbed the faculty representatives and athletic directors, however, were Hutchins' anonymous claims of their schools' hypocrisy. They resented his implication that many universities were guilty of committing cardinal sins.

Commissioner John Griffith, in early January, went to great lengths to prove that all nine members were in compliance with policies regarding loans and scholarships. He said that athletes with intellectual gifts were not discriminated against. He also disproved claims by the unnamed source that Chicago offered no financial aid. Based on data gathered by Griffith, the Maroons actually gave out more assistance than any other institution.[51] [52]

Of greater concern to the representatives, however, was whether the faculty Board in Control at Chicago had actively participated in the decision to withdraw. If this was merely a unilateral action by Hutchins and his Board of Trustees, the action would be in violation of the basic conference tenet of faculty control of all athletic matters.[53] The faculty

---

[45] Griffith to St. John. 12 February 1940. The Ohio State University Archives, Director of Athletics (RG 9/e-1/9), "Intercollegiate Conference: Commissioner: Correspondence (Griffith): 1939-1940 (Folder 1 of 2)."

[46] Ward, Arch. "Wake of the News." 12 March 1940. *Chicago Tribune.* The Ohio State University Archives, Director of Athletics (RG 9/e-1/9), "Intercollegiate Conference: Commissioner: Correspondence (Griffith): 1939-1940 (Folder 1 of 2)."

[47] Crisler to Aigler. 15 April 1940. Bentley Historical Library, University of Michigan. Ralph W. Aigler Papers. 87406 Aa 2; Box 12, folder: athletics: 1939-41, A-Z misc.

[48] "Quit Football to Stay Honest, Asserts U. of C." 27 December 1939. *Chicago Daily News.* The Ohio State University Archives, Director of Athletics (RG 9/e-1/9), "Intercollegiate Conference: Commissioner: Correspondence (Griffith): 1939-1940 (Folder 2 of 2)."

[49] Griffith to St. John. 13 May 1944. The Ohio State University Archives, Director of Athletics (RG 9/e-1/10), "Intercollegiate Conference: Commissioner: correspondence (Griffith): 1943-1944 (folder 1 of 3)."

[50] Annual Report to the Board In Control. 18 January 1940. Bentley Historical Library, University of Michigan. Ralph W. Aigler Papers, 87406 Aa 2; Box 32, folder: Board In Control Annual Reports

[51] Griffith to St. John. 15 January 1940. The Ohio State University Archives, Director of Athletics (RG 9/e-1/9), "Intercollegiate Conference: Commissioner: correspondence (Griffith): 1939-1940 (folder 2 of 2)"

[52] Griffith to Rottschaefer. 8 January 1940. The Ohio State University Archives, Director of Athletics (RG 9/e-1/9), "Intercollegiate Conference: Commissioner: correspondence (Griffith): 1939-1940 (folder 2 of 2)"

[53] Richart to Aigler,Griffith. 23 January 1940. Bentley Historical Library, University of Michigan

representatives never pursued action against the school. There was no need to prolong the discussion on this embarrassing moment in conference history.

Instead, they decided to offer an olive branch to the Maroons. They wanted to point out to the press that Chicago remained a valued founding member of the conference and that it could continue participation in other sports.[54] Should the school maintain competition in those activities, however, there would be no compromise on conference rules as applied to the New Plan.

And in response to inquisitive reporters, the academic leadership emphasized that there was no need to replace the Maroons in football.[55] The Western Conference was not a league. The 1930 revised Conference Handbook allowed only eight contests a season. Of those weekends of play, a minimum of four games with fellow members was obligatory.[56] The faculty and directors anticipated no problem with meeting scheduling requirements. Expansion to 11 was not necessary.

So, in the opinion of the leadership,the Western Conference could easily survive with nine members competing in football. Eight years later that conviction would be challenged as scheduling became a very contentious issue for the weaker programs in the conference.

DESPITE THE faculty leadership offering an "olive branch" to the University of Chicago by late January of 1940, Robert Maynard Hutchins continued to embarrass the Western Conference by making unfounded charges. In response, the athletic directors decided to take matters into their own hands.

A special two-day meeting at the Sherman Hotel was called in early March. They "took exception to the following: first, the alleged statement by President Hutchins at a cocktail party as reported in the *Chicago Daily News* December 27th, 1939, concerning the Conference; second, to a brochure mailed by one, John Nuveen, containing statements derogatory to the Conference; third, the report that the University of Chicago authorities had collected information concerning alleged illegitimate subsidizing on the part of other Conference universities, which information had not been passed on in accordance with the directors' agreements."[57] Until answers were forthcoming, further scheduling in other sports would be put on hold.[58] But it was apparent to those in attendance that Chicago director T. Nelson Metcalf had not been involved in any discussions with the administration or board

---

Ralph W. Aigler Papers. Aa 2; Box 8, folder: correspondence 1940-45 Richart

[54] Richart to Aigler,Griffith. 23 January 1940. Bentley Historical Library, University of Michigan Ralph W. Aigler Papers. Aa 2; Box 8, folder: correspondence 1940-45 Richart

[55] Aigler, Ralph W. Annual Report to the Board In Control. 18 January 1940. Bentley Historical Library, University of Michigan. Ralph W. Aigler Papers, 87406 Aa 2; Box 32, folder: Board In Control Annual Reports

[56] Rules, Regulations and Opinions of the Intercollegiate Conference of Faculty Representatives-revised 1930. University of Minnesota Archives, Department of Intercollegiate Athletic Papers; Box 13, folder: small handbooks 1895-1907, 1930, 1941

[57] Crisler to Aigler. 15 April 1940. Bentley Historical Library, University of Michigan. Ralph W. Aigler Papers. Aa 2; Box 12, folder: athletics 1939-41, A-Z misc

[58] Minutes of the Meeting of the Directors of Athletic of the Intercollegiate Conference. 8-9 March 1940. Bentley Historical Library, University of Michigan. Athletic Department, 943 Bimu 2; Box 84, faculty representatives minutes. 1918-1940

over the past three months regarding The Announcement. He lacked answers to what all believed were Hutchins' charges. The leadership proposed that he approach the university administrators for names of Handbook violators.[59]

The majority then planned to release a statement to the press "which in substance stated that further sports schedules would be held in abeyance until the attitude of the [leadership] at the University of Chicago toward the Conference was made clear."[60] But in advance, John Griffith submitted a copy of the statement to the "authorities on the South Side before any publication was made." The courtesy was never acknowledged. The university offered no reply.[61]

The directors' press release was misinterpreted by reporters as "an ultimatum to Chicago." Either provide the commissioner with evidence supporting membership malfeasance or publicly retract the statement. And if the authorities chose to do neither, the Maroons would "... suffer the penalty of being refused games with Conference schools in all sports."[62] In other words, the directors were threatening a boycott. But as it turned out, the disciplinary action never entered into their discussion.[63]

Regardless of what transpired at the March meeting, Ralph Aigler was disturbed by the lack of faculty involvement. The misunderstanding by the press, in his opinion, could have been avoided had they been present. Henry Rottschaefer of Minnesota, in a letter written a week later, clarified the story for his colleague still on sabbatical in Hawaii. The representatives had been invited to those meetings. By a canvassed vote of 5-4 they elected not to participate. It was an unfortunate decision that ultimately led to further public humiliation for the conference.[64]

Despite the bad press, the directors again met in private session with Nelson Metcalf on April 4, 1940. To no one's surprise, he had "dodged" an encounter with his president.[65] He failed to offer information on the violations that Hutchins claimed profligate in the conference. Instead, Metcalf provided them with a memo citing reasons for the withdrawal.[66] The statement was clearly written by faculty representative George Works and a vice-president at the university.[67]

Needless to say, a number of directors were quite incensed by the persistent

---

[59] Crisler to Aigler. 15 April 1940. Bentley Historical Library, University of Michigan. Ralph W. Aigler Papers. Aa2; Box 12, folder: athletics 1939-41, A-Z misc

[60] Memorandum. 22 April 1940. Bentley Historical Library, University of Michigan. Athletic Department, 943 Bimu 2; Box 84, faculty representatives minutes. 1918-1940

[61] Long to Aigler. 2 April 1940. Bentley Historical Library, University of Michigan. Ralph W. Aigler Papers. Aa 2; Box 12, folder: athletics 1939-41 A-Z misc.

[62] Rottschaefer to Aigler. 18 March 1940. Bentley Historical Library, University of Michigan. Ralph W. Aigler Papers. Aa 2; Box 8, folder: correspondence 1940-45 Rottschaefer

[63] Ibid.

[64] Ibid.

[65] Crisler to Aigler. 15 April 1940. Bentley Historical Library, University of Michigan. Ralph W. Aigler Papers. Aa 2; Box 12, folder: athletics 1939-41, A-Z misc.

[66] Metcalf to Athletic Directors. 4 April 1940. Minutes of the Conference Athletic Directors' Meeting. (Appendix A). Bentley Historical Library, University of Michigan. Athletic Department. 943 Bimu 2; Box 84, folder: Faculty Representatives Minutes (folder)

[67] Crisler to Aigler. 15 April 1940. Bentley Historical Library, University of Michigan. Ralph W. Aigler Papers. Aa 2; Box 12, folder: athletics 1939-41, A-Z misc.

Chicago defiance. Fritz Crisler led the charge. He was ready for "aggressive" action against his alma mater. Fortunately, cooler heads prevailed at the follow-up April 8 gathering. John Griffith navigated a more appropriate course of action. Chicago was permitted participation in other conference sports.[68] There would be no boycott.[69] And the commissioner would pursue a public-relations offensive to counter negative press about the conference in the aftermath of the Blackstone affair.[70]

FOLLOWING THE Announcement of December 21, 1939, a few Midwest institutions quietly inquired about membership in the conference. It was rumored that the schools included Nebraska, Marquette, and Pittsburgh.[71] The Faculty Representatives Committee maintained its resolve of February 1940. In essence, they told the sporting world "… it is inexpedient to enlarge the conference at this time." That standard response, first given confidentially to Nebraska in 1908 following its application to replace a defiant Michigan, was now dusted off to quell public clamor for expansion.[72]

In December of 1940, a mid-sized land-grant college based in East Lansing, Michigan, would begin succession plans in light of the anticipated retirement of its long-serving president in July. The man chosen to assume the seat held by Robert Sidey Shaw had a vision for transforming the agriculturally based college into a major research university. Western Conference membership, especially in the context of the Chicago announcement of one year earlier, was deemed critical to attaining that goal.

---

[68] St. John to Griffith. 8 April 1940. The Ohio State University Archives, Director of Athletics (RG9/e-1/9), "Intercollegiate Conference: Commissioner: Correspondence (Griffith): 1939-1940 (folder 1 of 2)."

[69] Ibid.

[70] Griffith to Directors of Athletics of the Conference. 9 May 1940. The Ohio State University Archives, Director of Athletics (RG 9/e-1/9), "Intercollegiate Conference: Commissioner: Correspondence (Griffith): 1939-1940 (folder 1 of 2)."

[71] Frank, Stanley. "The Big Ten's Surprise Package." 14 October 1950. *Saturday Evening Post.* Michigan State University Archives, Ralph Young Papers; Box 903, folder: 68

[72] Minutes of the Inter-Collegiate Conference. 6 June 1908. University of Minnesota Archives. Intercollegiate Athletic Papers; Box 13, folder: Intercollegiate Conference Minutes 1907-1933

T HE COACH and his assistant were walking leisurely across the campus west of the stadium. Daryl Rogers and Dan Underwood had just finished an early-morning racquetball game at the nearby Intramural Building. Next on the agenda was a strategy session at the football offices in Jenison Fieldhouse. Monday afternoon practice was still hours away. The coaches needed time to plan offensive and defensive schemes for the Indiana Hoosiers visiting East Lansing that weekend.

The date was October 16, 1978. Michigan State University had just defeated a very talented Michigan football team led by Glen "Bo" Schembechler. It would be the Wolverines' only loss that season. But of greater significance for the Spartans, the victory marked a turning point in the team's fortunes.

In Michigan State's opener against Purdue, Eddie Smith, the team's prolific quarterback, had broken his wrist, putting him out of action for four weeks. In his absence, the Spartans had won just one game while losing three. Michigan was expected to dominate the intrastate rivalry on that fifth weekend of play.

By the day of the Wolverine game, Smith had recovered and was ready to play in Ann Arbor. His return would rejuvenate the Spartans. In front of over 105,000 fans the quarterback led MSU past Michigan 24-15. The team would remain undefeated following that upset, finishing the season with eight wins against three losses.

More impressive than their win-loss record, however, was the turn-around in team production. Michigan State scored an average of 49 points during the final eight games. The hibernating defense also awakened when Smith returned to action, allowing just 9.8 points, on average, per contest.

The University of Michigan soundly defeated all opponents remaining on its schedule. Schembechler's team completed the year with ten victories against the one loss. In conference play the Wolverines tied their rival from 60 miles away; both schools won seven and lost one.

Michigan State was in the final year of a devastating probation related to recruiting and subsidizing violations at the time. In 1976 the NCAA had imposed, among other penalties, a three-year restriction on scholarships. In response, the MSU administration released the coaching staff and hired Daryl Rogers of San Jose State to lead the Spartans.

As a consequence of the probation, the University of Michigan was chosen to represent the Big Ten in the Rose Bowl on New Year's Day. Despite defeating the Wolverines back in October, Michigan State would spend January 1, 1979, watching its rival lose to the University of Southern California.

If there was any satisfaction with the completion of the 1978 campaign, it was the lifting of the NCAA sanctions within a few months. Michigan State University would once again be a member in good standing within the conference.

Assistant Coach Dan Underwood had played football under Coach Hugh "Duffy" Daugherty during the early 1960s. The legendary coach would later lead the Spartans to the summit of college football in 1965 and 1966 with one of the greatest teams in the history of the game. But following that incredible 1966 season, ending with a shared national championship with Notre Dame, the program began to decline under his tenure. Within a few years, Michigan would hire Bo Schembechler. The arrival of the new coach in Ann Arbor in late 1968 would herald the resurgence of Wolverine football. The school would soon dominate the Spartans on the gridiron.

Daugherty was replaced in 1973 by Dennis Stolz, a very successful MIAA head coach at Alma College. Stolz struggled his first season, compiling only five victories against six defeats. His real success lay in recruiting two of the most sought-after high school football players in the country out of Youngstown, Ohio, shortly following that gridiron campaign. That "victory" over Woody Hayes, of Ohio State University, however, would prove to be Stolz's downfall. He had violated an old Buckeye tradition later ratified as General Regulation XIV in the revised 1948 Handbook.

The policy "strongly affirm[ed] that ... intercollegiate athletic teams should be truly representative of their student bodies." It also forbade any form of recruiting. Crossing state borders by coaches or college representatives in search of talent was illegal.[1] The regulation essentially codified the "Buckeye Rule," first proclaimed by long-serving Ohio State athletic director Lynn St. John back in 1938. In his opinion, since the OSU roster was typically dominated by native sons, "the state of Ohio belong(ed) to the University."[2] And consistent with his old decree, the student body reflected that composition.

Ohio State took the Buckeye Rule very seriously. St. John and his staff closely monitored the borders.[3][4] The state, after all, was traditionally loaded with talent.[5] If there was suspicion that coaches from other programs had lured kids away, as reflected in

[1] Four Hundred and Ninety-First Meeting of the Athletic Board of The Ohio State University. 12 October 1948. The Ohio State University Archives, Athletics: Director of (RG 9/e-1/1), " Athletic Board: Minutes: Jun 1946-Jun 1951."

[2] Griffith to Aigler. 31 May 1938. Bentley Historical Library, University of Michigan. Ralph W. Aigler Papers, 87406 Aa 2; Box 6, folder: correspondence 1934-39 Griffith 9/37-7/39

[3] St. John to Griffith. 10 February 1944. The Ohio State University Archives, Director of Athletics (RG 9/e-1/10), "Intercollegiate Conference: Commissioner: Correspondence (Griffith): 1943-44 (Folder 2 of 3)."

[4] Untitled (football rosters of Big Nine schools). circa 1946. The Ohio State University Archives, James E. Pollard Papers (RG 40/52/2/33), "Western Conference: 1931, 1938, 1945, 1950."

[5] Jacquin, Eddie. "In Perspective." *Champaign News-Gazette* 18 May 1941. The Ohio State University Archives, Director of Athletics (RG 9/e-1/9), "Intercollegiate Conference: Commissioner: Correspondence (Griffith): 1941-1942 (Folder 2 of 2)."

published roster demographics, he would charge a violation of his de facto rule. Indiana, in 1938, was threatened with a boycott for having six Ohioans on its team. St. John never disciplined the Hoosiers; he merely served notice. It was a classic example of vigilante justice.

Richard Larkins, upon St. John's retirement in 1947, assumed the directorship. Within short order, Purdue, with a new, aggressive coaching staff, was challenging the rule. Larkins was livid. In a flaming letter to head Coach Stuart Holcomb, he educated him on the Ohio tradition.

> Ohio State is limited to interesting only boys in the state of Ohio coming to [Columbus]. We are encroaching on no one else's territory and we feel that we have a prior claim to the scholastic youngsters in this state. We do not feel that Indiana, Purdue, Michigan, or any other Conference school, has much business within the state … we can not, or will not, sit idly by and be Boy Scouts while representatives of other Conference institutions are encroaching on our legitimate territory.[6]

Purdue learned a painful lesson months later. Larkins planned to boycott the Boilermakers for three years.[7]

Woody Hayes was hired to lead the Buckeyes in 1951. Despite the conference adopting new rules in the late 1950s, including acceptance of both athletic scholarships and recruiting beyond state borders, the irascible coach still insisted that all boys raised as Ohioans belonged to The Ohio State University. In his opinion, no outside coach or booster had any right entering his state to recruit home-grown talent. If an athlete wanted to play elsewhere, it had to be on the student's initiative only. Hayes was a firm believer in the Buckeye Rule, just like the man who hired him, Richard Larkins. And Woody also loved winning football games.

Denny Stolz and his staff violated the Buckeye Rule–still enforced by Hayes–in early 1974. The two Youngstown athletes were at the top of the list of talented players he wanted in Columbus. Later that year, an undefeated Ohio State team traveled to East Lansing in early November only to lose in the final seconds to the Spartans. It was a turnaround season for Stolz's program. MSU finished the year with seven wins against three defeats and one tie. And Wayne Woodrow Hayes was furious. The loss had cost him a shot at the national championship.

Within one year the NCAA began investigating rumors of improprieties in East Lansing. That investigation determined that an MSU booster had loaned the two Youngstown natives a credit card for their personal use. Numerous other violations were also discovered. A three-year probation, with profound limitations on football scholarships, followed in 1976. The old man had gotten his revenge!

So two years later, MSU's victory over the Wolverines was important not only because it spoiled their undefeated season; it also signified the return of Spartan football after its devastating probation. The Curse of Woody Hayes was finally over. The victory

---

[6] Larkins to Holcomb. 23 May 1947. The Ohio State University Archives, Director of Athletics (RG 9/e-1/10). "Intercollegiate Conference: Commissioner: Correspondence (Wilson): 1947-1951."

[7] Meeting of the Athletic Directors. 30 November 1948. University of Wisconsin-Madison Archives. Faculty Athletic Board, Series 5/21/6; Box 1, folder: Western Conference minutes 1947-51

was also sweet for former MSU President John Hannah. Win-loss records were always irrelevant for him.[8] His only desire each season was defeating the University of Michigan. And, as will be seen, he had his reasons.[9]

Daryl Rogers was not privy to this history of Spartan football. He failed to fully appreciate the significance of beating the Wolverines … anytime! So while "Danny" continued to ramble on about the recent game, Daryl was only marginally involved in the conversation. He shared little of Underwood's enthusiasm over the recent accomplishment of Michigan State. His focus was on the Indiana Hoosiers. The Californian, after all, had been hired to build a program.

But as the two approached the steps of Jenison Fieldhouse, Rogers caught himself chuckling over an Underwood comment. "And you know Daryl, what really makes that game on Saturday so special for me is that we beat those arrogant asses in Ann Arbor, right on their own turf!"

Dan Underwood would later claim no ownership of the verbiage. Biggie Munn and Duffy Daugherty both used the phrase commonly, intermixed with the usual coaches' expletives, at practices and team meetings during "Michigan Week" every year.[10]

Coach Rogers thought the Underwood Alliteration was a clever use of words, but Indiana was coming to town and he had a job to do.[11]

NEITHER DARYL Rogers nor Danny Underwood had any in-depth knowledge of the history of the intrastate rivalry dating back to 1898. The State Agricultural College lost to the Wolverines 39-0 in that first game. Despite the close proximity of the schools, the traditional game was held in Ann Arbor all but four times through the 1947 season. Other than two losses in 1913 and 1915, one tie in 1930, and a surprising four-game losing streak beginning in 1934, the Wolverines won all other contests against the Aggies/Spartans played at Regents Field, Ferry Field, and later Michigan Stadium. If the series proved anything over those years, it was the value of a home-field advantage.

Although he may not have known it, Underwood's comment to Rogers suggesting an air of superiority in Ann Arbor may have had some historical validity. While chairman of the University of Chicago Athletic Council in 1917, faculty representative Albion Small argued that there was no equity in college football scheduling. The stronger programs, with large stadiums and impressive gate receipts, dominated the weaker ones. Many conference and non-conference schools were willing to accept the terms of Big Ten powers such as the Wolverines. The return on investment for a visit to Ann Arbor, as an example, was well worth a passive position in contract negotiations. The phenomenon was later referred to as "athletic Darwinism."[12] Dates were "offered" to the weaker programs. There was little negotiation.

Ralph Young, athletic director at Michigan State, was obligated to balance his department's budget. With the completion of Michigan Stadium in 1927, the bus trip made

---

[8] Hannah, John A. *A Memoir.* East Lansing: Michigan State University Press, 1980. p. 124

[9] Hannah to Hovde. 17 September 1952. Michigan State University Archives. John A. Hannah Papers, UA2.1.12; Box 90, folder: 22 miscellaneous correspondence "H"

[10] Underwood, Dan. 30 July 2010. Personal communication

[11] Rogers, Daryl. 27 February 2009. Personal communication

[12] Lester, Robin. *Stagg's University: The Rise, Decline & Fall of Big-Time Football at Chicago.* Urbana and Chicago: University of Illinois Press, 1999, p. 1

even more sense.[13] Except for two games held in East Lansing–the 1924 and 1948 stadium dedication games–the Spartans would play the remaining 30 contests in Ann Arbor over those three decades. The Wolverine tradition and a 65,000 seat discrepancy made the difference.

Michigan Athletic Director Fielding Yost, as a Darwinist during the early 1930s, essentially mandated that the Spartans assume the opening weekend on his schedule every year. He had sound financial reasons for reserving that date. It guaranteed him a near-capacity crowd for the "scrimmage game." Nine out of 13 Michigan/Michigan State games since 1932 were scheduled for the Wolverine season opener.[14] And Ralph Young, in a passive negotiating role, accepted the long-term offer which assured the college direly needed shared revenue.[15]

With his appointment in July of 1941 as the president of Michigan State College of Agriculture and Applied Science, John Hannah recognized the importance athletic prominence in football might have in promoting his special vision for the school. Playing the annual intrastate rivalry in the later part of the season was a way of gaining national press.[16] He also felt contesting the game on occasion in East Lansing, regardless of venue capacity, was good for school spirit and campus culture.[17]

Beginning in December of 1942, under the directive of his new boss, Ralph Young sought later dates and, additionally, a contract for a home-and-home series with Michigan as of 1943.[18] Only two years earlier, in July of 1940, while reporting shared expenses for the 1939 football contest, Young had reminded Fielding Yost, "Our game has always been played at Ann Arbor and it goes without saying that it will be played there in the future, making it a home game for both of us."[19] Fritz Crisler maintained a copy of that communiqué for his personal records. He responded to the surprising new request–contrary to the 1932 Yost-Young understanding–by writing that the game being played later in the season and at alternating sites would not serve the people of the state any better. Attendance figures justified continuing the game in Ann Arbor.[20] It was a sound financial rebuttal to Young's overture.

Crisler knew he held the dominant position in the scheduling negotiations. In response to the additional home-and-home request, he made a preposterous suggestion that

[13] Crisler to Emmons. 4 February 1949. Bentley Historical Library, University of Michigan. Herbert Orin Crisler Papers, 85823 AC UAm Aa 2; Box 1, folder: topical correspondence, MSU 1947-49

[14] Michigan State Football Date. February 1949. Bentley Historical Library, University of Michigan. Herbert Orin Crisler Papers, 85823 AC UAm Aa 2; Box 1, folder: topical correspondence, MSU 1943-46

[15] Hannah to Ruthven. 24 September 1941. Bentley Historical Library, University of Michigan. Ralph W. Aigler Papers, 87406 Aa 2; Box 8, folder: correspondence "H" misc.

[16] Crisler to Ruthven. 13 January 1943. Bentley Historical Library, University of Michigan. Herbert Orin Crisler Papers, 85823 AC UAm Aa 2; Box 1, folder: topical correspondence, MSU 1943-46

[17] Hannah, John A. *A Memoir*. East Lansing: Michigan State University Press, 1980. p. 124

[18] Young to Crisler. 2 December 1942. Bentley Historical Library, University of Michigan. Herbert Orin Crisler Papers, 85823 AC UAm Aa 2; Box 1, folder: topical correspondence, MSU 1943-46

[19] Young to Yost. 8 July 1940. Bentley Historical Library. University of Michigan. Herbert Orin Crisler Papers, 85823 AC UAm Aa 2; Box 1, folder: topical correspondence, MSU 1943-46

[20] Crisler to Young. 16 December 1942. Bentley Historical Library, University of Michigan. Herbert Orin Crisler Papers, 85823 AC UAm Aa 2; Box 1, folder: topical correspondence, MSU 1943-46

undoubtedly upset Athletic Council members in East Lansing who were privy to it.

> If this [desire to hold some games at Macklin Field] is true, perhaps you would like to be released from the arrangement whereby you come to us each year in order to free Michigan State to negotiate for a game at home with some other institution. Rest assured we would understand if you proceeded to make such arrangements. We have a great many requests from other institutions for a football relationship with Michigan in Ann Arbor.

The somewhat condescending, perhaps arrogant tone was out of character for Crisler. He knew the Spartans needed the Wolverines on their schedule. His comments may have reflected frustration with the Spartan administration. The director, after all, suspected that someone else may have penned the letter.

By December 28, 1942, Young modified his initial "invitation" to Crisler. He cited various reasons for the college's desire to change past practices regarding scheduling contests.

> In all of the years since you have been head coach at Michigan we have been made the opening game on the University's home schedule with the exception of the last season when you played Great Lakes prior to the normal opening day. From our standpoint it was the same situation. We have requested from time to time that we be given a place later on your schedule other than at the opening of the season. The attendance figures cited in your letter are an ample indication that in the eyes of the public this annual game merits a place near the climax of the season rather than as an opener. From your standpoint it assures a good crowd at an opening game. From our standpoint we have been defeated for five successive years, and that is always likely to happen. After we have been beaten by the University early in the season, the remainder of our football schedule has had the luster removed. We do not believe that it helps the University or football in Michigan to have Michigan State relegated so early in the season to an "also ran" status.

The Spartan director pleaded reconsideration of past scheduling practices. Michigan State was clearly still in a passive relationship with the dominant species.

After acknowledging the University of Michigan as "one of the world's outstanding educational institutions, with a large body of distinguished alumni, a great athletic tradition and prestige," Young cautiously presented the grand college vision of President John Alfred Hannah.

> Michigan State is also an outstanding educational institution … For more than eighty years we have filled a legitimate place in the educational program of this state. The taxpaying public contributes through the state government millions of dollars annually to the support of our two institutions. If there is a place educationally for two good, state supported universities in Michigan, we believe there is a place for Michigan State College athletically. We do not expect or seek to usurp the high place the University occupies. The University of Michigan and Michigan State

College have enjoyed a long period of cooperative relations. Our athletic rivalry in all sports is very desirable from our standpoint, and we want them to continue. We feel, however, that we should have some small voice in formulating the basis upon which these relations are to continue.[21]

In Crisler's opinion, these were strange comments coming from an athletic director's pen.

Following receipt of Young's December 28 letter, he wrote to President Alexander Ruthven in mid-January of 1943 about his dilemma. Only a few days earlier, he had contacted Ralph Young about the unusual letters. To his surprise, Young, in confidence, admitted he personally remained committed to the traditional agreement between the two schools. That was enough evidence for Fritz Crisler.[22] He shared a copy of the two December communiqués with Ruthven, convinced now the author was President John Hannah, not Ralph Young.

> Whenever any athletic matters have relationship to a wide University policy ... I conclude that you and the Regents would like to be acquainted with it and even give us guidance so as to be consistent with general University policies ... Reading between the lines it is not difficult to deduct that the influence and hopes of President Hannah are reflected in [Young's] request ... There may be reasons, then, why this should not be treated purely as an athletic matter. We may have alliances with Michigan State and it may be wise to promote a cordial and pleasant relationship with the authorities of our sister institution. It may be even possible that we may have some working agreement with Michigan State so far as appropriations are concerned or other matters having to do with the State Legislature.
>
> You will observe that the original request in the letter of December 2, inviting us to play at Lansing, has been expanded considerably in the December 28 communication to include (1) a later date in the schedule and (2) Michigan sponsoring the membership of Michigan State College in the Western Conference. I have a notion President Hannah is strongly pressing the latter two points with his people ... If it is to be treated only as an athletic matter, I am of the strong conviction it would be unwise to play at Lansing on alternate years or to play the game on any Saturday other than the opening date of the season.[23]

President Ruthven met with his athletic director on January 27 to discuss the

---

[21] Young to Crisler. 28 December 1942. Bentley Historical Library, University of Michigan. Herbert Orin Crisler Papers, 85823 AC UAm Aa 2; Box 1, folder: topical correspondence, MSU 1943-46

[22] Michigan State Football Date. circa February 1949. Bentley Historical Library, University of Michigan. Herbert Orin Crisler Papers, 85823 AC UAm Aa 2; Box 1, folder: topical correspondence, MSU 1947-49

[23] Crisler to Ruthven. 13 January 1943. Bentley Historical Library, University of Michigan. Herbert Orin Crisler Papers, 85823 AC UAm Aa 2; Box 1, folder: topical correspondence, MSU 1943-46

matter.[24][25] The two arrived at a decision. Crisler could continue treating the Michigan State request as "an athletic matter." Ruthven saw no conflict with overall university policy at that time. The opening day of the season would be reserved for the college, at Michigan Stadium, for the foreseeable future.

Due to evolving international developments, however, that debate between the athletic directors would be held in abeyance for a number of years. A Faculty Senate resolution of October 1941, apparently forgotten by President Hannah while ghostwriting Ralph Young's letters in December of 1942, would add a new twist to the scheduling discussions that resumed in November of 1946.

THE THREAT of conflict with Germany pervaded the thoughts of Americans in early December of 1940. Even though Pearl Harbor was still a year away, there was an atmosphere of apprehension when the Western Conference athletic directors met in Chicago. Led by former Army Major John Griffith, they discussed ways to assist the military in preparing young men for service. Meetings with key leaders of the armed forces followed.

Approximately one-third of recruits called to arms during the First World War were unfit based on a military study following the conflict.[26] As a consequence, the 1918 War Department investigation recommended the development of physical education programs in high schools and colleges. At that time the Army was fully supportive of any sporting activity, including football, that promoted the conditioning of American youths who might someday be called to service.[27]

Due to its proactive stance, the Western Conference was later chosen in confidence by Navy and Marine Corps brass to participate in a program for military preparedness.[28] Most of the schools were awarded physical-fitness contracts to train seamen and marines. Intercollegiate athletics would continue as part of that program. The Navy felt that there was much to be gained from the entertainment and esprit de corps derived from competition.[29] The Army's War Department, for unclear reasons, was not included in the discussions.

In early 1942 conference leaders voted to expand the schedule from eight to ten

[24] Crisler to Ruthven, 13, January 1943. Bentley Historical Library, University of Michigan.
Alexander Grant Ruthven Papers, 86550 Ac Aa; Box 34, folder 27 "Physical Education (Board in Control)"
[25] Williams, Brian A. "Re. Ruthven's reply." E-mail to David J. Young. 20 July 2010.
[26] Minutes of the Meeting of the Stockholders and Directors of the Intercollegiate Conference Athletic Association. 7 December 1940. Bentley Historical Library, University of Michigan. Athletic Department, 943 Bimu 2; Box 84, folder: Athletic Director's Office, Big Ten Directors Committee minutes 1932-1940
[27] Annual Report of Board in Control. Circa January 1944. Bentley Historical Library, University of Michigan. Alexander Grant Ruthven Papers, 86550 Aa UAm; Box 36, folder:22
[28] Griffith to Conference Athletic Directors. 19 August 1942. Bentley Historical Library, University of Michigan. Athletic Department, 943 Bimu 2; Box 84, folder: Athletic Director's Office, Big Ten Directors Committee Minutes 1941-52
[29] Annual Report of the Board in Control of Intercollegiate Athletics. January 1944. Bentley Historical Library, University of Michigan. Alexander Ruthven Papers, 86550 UAm; Box 36, folder: 22 1944

games to accommodate service teams formed at various bases about the Midwest.[30] As part of the contract, the faculty representatives agreed to suspend all Handbook regulations; military athletic rule would apply for the duration of the war. Academic standing and years of participation in college would have no bearing on the ability to play. Football eligibility would not be impacted following decommissioning and return to collegiate life.[31]

Unlike many Western Conference schools, a military presence had been evident at Michigan State dating back decades. As the pioneer land-grant school under the Morrill Act of 1862, the college accepted federal lands to subsidize the institution. It also agreed to offer courses in "military tactics" to interested students. The Army secured a foothold at The State Agricultural College in 1885, when Lieutenant John Lockwood was assigned "to train farm boys who had volunteered to drill and do calisthenics twice a week."[32] By 1917 the Reserve Officers Training Corp (ROTC) was formed as the First World War erupted.[33] As a consequence of these historic developments, the Army was firmly entrenched on campus by the early 1940s. Michigan State's commitment to train soldiers in the spring of 1942 was in part due to that presence.[34]

But that relationship did not stop the Navy from considering use of the East Lansing campus. Shortly after Pearl Harbor, representatives stopped by Michigan State to investigate its facilities. They were interested in making the college a Navy preflight school. But due to the longstanding arrangement with the ROTC, President Hannah declined further overtures.[35] That decision would profoundly affect the football program within a year.

Subsequently, the War Department, "in a complete reversal of its [recommendations of] 1918, ruled that their trainees in the universities and colleges [would] not be allowed to participate in intercollegiate athletics, it being declared that they would not have sufficient free time."[36] Having no football in East Lansing during the war years was a shocking prospect for Michigan State.

In 1942, 135 Spartan athletes participated in various sports on campus. By the summer of 1943, all but one had been transferred to other sites for training in combat preparedness. Many of those athletes were football players. If inducted into the Navy they were allowed to continue participation at another school or base until deployment.[37]

---

[30] Minutes of the Meeting of the Directors of Athletics of the Intercollegiate Conference. 5-7 March 1942. Bentley Historical Library, University of Michigan. Athletic Department, 943 Bimu 2; Box 84, folder: Athletic Director's Office, Big Ten Directors Committee Minutes 1941-52

[31] Annual Report of the Board in Control of Intercollegiate Athletics. January 1944. Bentley Historical Library, University of Michigan. Alexander Ruthven Papers, 86550 UAm; Box 36, folder: 22 1944

[32] Widder, Keith. *Michigan Agricultural College: The Evolution of a Land-Grant Philosophy, 1855-1925.* East Lansing: Michigan State University Press, 2005. pp. 129-130

[33] Ibid., p. 411

[34] Bachman, Charles. "The Athletic Side of John A. Hannah." Circa 1970. Michigan State University Archives. Hannah Archives Project, UA 2.1.12.2; Box 34, folder: 2 Bachman

[35] Ibid.

[36] Annual Report of the Board in Control of Intercollegiate Athletics. January 1944. Bentley Historical Library, University of Michigan. Alexander Ruthven Papers, 86550 UAm; Box 36, folder: 22 1944

[37] Thomas, David. *Michigan State College: John Hannah and the Creation of a World University, 1926-1969.* East Lansing: Michigan State University Press, 2008. p. 78

So, as of late March 1943, it appeared Michigan State might be forced to void all football contracts for the foreseeable future.[38] And by August it was official; the 1943 and 1944 seasons were canceled.[39] In the absence of a football program competing against other schools, many Spartan coaches were recruited to assist in the war effort elsewhere, utilized either as instructors or coaches depending on the military's needs.

Ironically, the college was not lacking for manpower to form a team in East Lansing. The Army housed over 2000 men on campus.[40] Many were football players from other schools. Their physical training, however, would be limited to conditioning drills and marching in formation with the War Department edict in force.[41]

And so, lacking a team for intercollegiate competition, the discussions of December 1942 between Ralph Young and Fritz Crisler regarding scheduling future home-and-home contests were now irrelevant.

But by spring of 1944 the Michigan State administration was informed by the War Department that it could field a team beginning in the fall of that same year.[42] Projected manpower needs of the military had been met. On May 12, 1944, a fortnight before the Western Conference scheduling meetings, the Spartans revealed their plans to the University of Michigan as well as the press.[43] John Hannah wanted the college back on the Wolverines' schedule for the following season. Unfortunately, it was too little too late. As had been its practice for well over a decade, the University of Michigan had already scheduled its non-conference opponents well in advance of the May meeting in Chicago.[44] [45] There were no dates, including the scrimmage-game weekend, available for the Spartans in 1945 and 1946. Ralph Young had no alternative but to contract with a number of schools of little football repute. The annual state rivalry remained in abeyance.

Serendipitously, all this would change quite unexpectedly within months. On January 17, 1945, Penn's athletic director contacted Frtiz Crisler requesting to get out of a contractual obligation to play the Wolverines on the third weekend of that season in Ann Arbor. Michigan's Crisler offered the Spartans the Penn position. Ralph Young eagerly accepted.

A few months later, in May of 1945, "because of scheduling difficulties Navy asked

---

[38] Young to Crisler. 25 March 1943. Bentley Historical Library, University of Michigan. Herbert Orin Crisler Papers, 85823 AC UAm Aa2; Box 1, folder: Topical correspondence MSU 1943-46

[39] Annual Report of the Board in Control of Intercollegiate Athletics. January 1944. Bentley Historical Library, University of Michigan. Alexander Grant Ruthven Papers, 86550 UAm; Box 36, folder: 22 1944

[40] Thomas, David. *Michigan State College: John Hannah and the Creation of a World University, 1926-1969.* East Lansing: Michigan State University Press, 2008. pp. 287-288

[41] Annual Report of the Board in Control of Intercollegiate Athletics. January 1944. Bentley Historical Library, University of Michigan. Alexander Ruthven Papers, 86550 UAm; Box 36, folder: 22 1944

[42] Hannah, John A. "Intercollegiate Athletics." 11 August 1943. Northwestern University Archives, Franklyn Snyder Papers; Box 3, folder: 1

[43] Michigan State Football Date. February 1949. Bentley Historical Library, University of Michigan. Herbert Orin Crisler Papers, 85823 AC UAm Aa 2; Box 1, folder: topical correspondence MSU 1947-49

[44] Ibid.

[45] Yost to Griffith. 22 May 1934. Bentley Historical Library, University of Michigan. Ralph W. Aigler Papers, 87406 Aa 2; Box 7, folder: correspondence 1934-39 "X-Y-Z" misc.

to have the seventh game in '46 moved to '48." Crisler once again contacted Young with the option to take the academy's date for 1946. The Spartan athletic director's response was predictable.[46]

Regardless of Crisler's surprising gestures, lacking a football program for almost two years, the Spartans were crushed by the Wolverines in each contest. Despite Michigan's dominance on the field, the Spartans would remain a nuisance for its athletic director in the off seasons. Having now experienced two games in midseason, the college leadership could no longer tolerate the university's control over dates and venues.

MOST INSTITUTIONS utilize the semester format. Michigan State, until the fall of 1992, chose to operate under the quarter system. Its tradition as an agrarian-focused institution may have contributed to that unique academic calendar.

In the early 1870s two terms were listed in the college catalog. The first extended from February through the end of June. The second term began in July and finished in mid-November. At that time The State Agricultural College curriculum was focused primarily on agrarian science. The "model farm," just south of the Red Cedar River, was the practical laboratory used during those two terms for students planning careers in agriculture.

As the school grew, the curriculum evolved to allow studies unrelated to agriculture. Still under a calendar-year academic schedule, the college adapted to better meet the needs of all students by offering three terms. By 1878 they were designated spring, summer and autumn. The terms finally coincided with the traditional academic year beginning in 1896. Registration would begin in late September rather than February. Terms became quarters in 1912 when the administration offered a summer session.[47]

The University of Michigan, due to the semester format, began its academic year the third week of September. The college, on the other hand, with the shorter quarters, started classes in early October. Since most Western Conference schools also adhered to the semester scheme, football competition could commence the final weekend in September. The university, however, traditionally started its season with the Spartans the first Saturday in October. The week leading up to that game coincided with freshman orientation and college registration back in East Lansing.[48] The following Monday lecture halls were filled at Michigan State.

Needless to say, on game-day Saturday, chaos prevailed in East Lansing as students completed registering before rushing off to Michigan Stadium, 60 miles away, for the kick-off.

In early October of 1941 the College Faculty Senate approved a policy ostensibly to address the disruption brought on by the rivalry during that week.[49] It resolved that all future

---

[46] "Michigan State Football Date." February 1949. Bentley Historical Library, University of Michigan. Herbert Orin Crisler Papers, 85823 AC UAm Aa 2; Box 1, folder: topical correspondence MSU 1947-49

[47] Vescio, Portia. Personal communication. Email to David Young. 16 June 2010. Ms. Vescio, Public Services Archivist at the Michigan State University Archives, researched this poorly documented subject with the assistance of undergraduate Megan Badgley.

[48] Hannah to Ruthven. 24 September 1941. Bentley Historical Library, University of Michigan. Ralph W. Aigler Papers, 87406 Aa 2; Box 8, folder: correspondence "H" misc.

[49] Minutes from the All Faculty Meeting. 6 October 1941. Michigan State University Archives. Academic Senate Records, UA.14.1; volume 7

contests with the University of Michigan take place after the beginning of classes in East Lansing.[50] Fritz Crisler, as a consequence, would have no choice but to schedule the Spartans for a weekend later in the season.

The idea behind that policy came from the desk of John Hannah, who may have had an ulterior motive for pushing his agenda on the Faculty Senate. On September 18, 1941, he alerted the State Board of Agriculture, the college's governing body, of his plans to fix the problem.[51] Six days later, he wrote President Alexander Ruthven proposing his solution to the disruptive week in East Lansing.[52] Ruthven shared Hannah's letter with his faculty representative–he needed advice on how to respond to a question with athletic-policy implications. Based on his response, Ralph Aigler was skeptical of Hannah's intentions.

> Just between you and me, may I say that I have a very strong suspicion that
> back of President Hannah is a wish to have the Michigan-Michigan State
> game come later in the season, the theory being that if they have more time
> to prepare their team for the game they will stand a better chance of
> winning … In as much as the game with us is the high spot of their season,
> a loss in that game is a serious blow to the entire season which follows.
> They would like our game to come towards the end of the season so that
> they could build up through the preceding games to ours as a climax.

Aigler concluded his thoughts. "On this phase of the problem which I have last mentioned, our position is simply that the Michigan State game is a local affair with our Conference competition as the outstanding feature."[53] The president asked his faculty representative to offer a response on his behalf. Aigler's letter arrived in East Lansing three weeks later.

The tradition of the early October "scrimmage game" with Michigan, played every year in Ann Arbor, had begun in 1932. It assured Fielding Yost a large crowd during the Depression, when he had to meet onerous bond obligations on his legacy, Michigan Stadium. Ralph Young agreed to abide by his colleague's plan.[54]

In April of 1935 Young, on behalf of the Athletic Council, petitioned President Shaw to allow for a nine-game football season. "It is quite essential," he wrote, "for us to play one game preceding our University of Michigan game in order to iron out the rough spots on our team."[55] The Athletic Council's request was approved and Young signed up Wayne University, located in Detroit, for the upcoming four seasons. The Spartans, insisting that all contests be held in East Lansing, dominated the series with the smaller intrastate school.

---

[50] Minutes of the Meeting of the Board in Control of Intercollegiate Athletics. 15 November 1946. Bentley Historical Library. University of Michigan. Board in Control of Intercollegiate Athletics, 8729 Bimu F81 2; Box 49, folder: Board in Control minutes February 1938-June 1950

[51] Minutes of the State Board of Agriculture. 18 September 1941. www.onthebanks.msu.edu

[52] Hannah to Ruthven. 24 September 1941. Bentley Historical Library, University of Michigan. Ralph W. Aigler Papers, 87406 Aa 2; Box 8, folder: correspondence "H" misc.

[53] Aigler to Ruthven. 30 September 1941. Bentley Historical Library, University of Michigan. Ralph W. Aigler Papers, 87406 Aa 2; Box 8, folder: correspondence "H" misc.

[54] Hannah to Ruthven. 24 September 1941. Bentley Historical Library, University of Michigan. Ralph W. Aigler Papers, 87406 Aa 2; Box 8, folder: correspondence "H" misc.

[55] Young to Shaw. 18 April 1935. Michigan State University Archives. MSU Board of Trustees, UA1.0; Box 1882, folder: 6 supplementary materials 4/18/35

Michigan and Fielding Yost eventually figured out the scheme being used by the Spartans to counter those unanticipated consequences of the 1932 "scrimmage game" accord. On January 16, 1939, Yost, Crisler, and Aigler met in East Lansing with their counterparts, Ralph Young, Charlie Bachman, and Ralph Huston. The agenda centered on the college's noncompliance with certain Handbook regulations. One violation, in particular, involved the number of contests a non-conference school could schedule each season. Exceeding eight games, in theory, offered that program an unfair advantage over the Big Ten membership. The university insisted that Director Young end the practice. The college could contract only eight games a season if it wished to continue competing against Michigan.[56] The agreement with Wayne was cancelled shortly thereafter. And the scrimmage game with Michigan, held in Ann Arbor, resumed the first weekend in October the following season.

Regardless of this successful ploy by Michigan, the 1940 game was so disruptive to orientation/registration week in East Lansing that President Hannah decided to take action in mid-September of the following year. At least it appeared that way.

IN LATE November of 1936, as the young secretary of the State Board of Agriculture, John Hannah was asked to serve on a special committee charged with exploring the feasibility of a Spartan application for admission into the Western Conference. Although the school was eventually unsuccessful, the experience was enlightening for the college administrator. He gained a great deal of respect for the powerful influence Professor Ralph Aigler held over his nine colleagues from member institutions.

President Hannah, in mid-September of 1941, wrote directly to Alexander Ruthven. He had reasons for circumventing institutional protocol. Hannah wanted to bypass the Michigan athletic leadership–Ralph Aigler in particular–and appeal directly to Ruthven in changing the "customary" university practice of controlling game-date decisions.[57] But the renowned zoologist, much to Hannah's frustration, turned the matter over to his faculty representative.[58] Aigler's tardy reply of October 20 was unsympathetic to the Spartan plight.[59] His comments substantiated the college leader's convictions about the law professor gained from serving on the 1936 ad hoc Huston Committee. Ralph William Aigler was no friend of Michigan State.

Despite the university's delayed and disappointing response to Hannah's September request, the president already had plans firmly in place for change. The Faculty Senate, subservient to the desires of its popular new leader, passed his registration week policy on October 6. The rivalry must take place following the start of fall classes. At the time, however, there was no reason to alert the university of the Senate resolution. It held no significance as the next conference scheduling meeting was not planned until spring of 1943.

---

[56] Yost to Young. 20 January 1939. Bentley Historical Library, University of Michigan. Herbert Orin Crisler Papers, 85823 AC UAm Aa 2; Box 1, folder: topical correspondence "MSU" 1943-46

[57] Hannah to Ruthven. 24 September 1941. Bentley Historical Library, University of Michigan. Ralph W. Aigler Papers, 87406 Aa 2; Box 8, folder: correspondence "H" misc

[58] Aigler to Ruthven. 30 September 1941. Bentley Historical Library, University of Michigan. Ralph W. Aigler Papers, 87406 Aa 2; Box 8, folder: correspondence "H" misc.

[59] Aigler to Hannah. 20 October 1941. Bentley Historical Library, University of Michigan. Ralph W. Aigler Papers, 87406 Aa 2; Box 8, folder: correspondence "H" misc

One year later, during the Young/Crisler scheduling debate of December 1942, the resolution definitely merited comment. But President Hannah, in the guise of Ralph Young, found no need to mention it in his letters to the Michigan athletic director. Lacking awareness of the new college policy, Fritz Crisler's only concern, in even communicating with Ralph Young, was to confirm that the opening date for the next two seasons belonged to Michigan State.

In October of 1946, following completion of the war and the resumption of football in East Lansing, the old Spartan request for a home-and-home series later in the season came up again for discussion. But Crisler wanted nothing to do with this tedious debate. He had far greater concerns on his mind. The director anticipated a contentious conference-scheduling meeting in mid-December. He needed verification from Young that the old Yost understanding of 1932 was still in force. His complex agreements with inter-regional programs hinged on the Spartans' accepting that first Saturday of the football season.

The Spartans, however, were not about to give in so easily. John Hannah wanted out of the scrimmage game arrangement. And to do so, he would dust off the old Faculty Senate resolution of 1941. A few weeks later, as the debate heated up, Fritz Crisler, for the first time, would receive from Ralph Young a paraphrased version of that college policy.

> Because of the disruption of the registration procedures caused by the
> migration of its thousands of students, the Michigan State College Faculty
> took action … forbidding the scheduling of future football games in Ann
> Arbor between the University of Michigan and Michigan State College
> prior to the opening of fall quarter classes [in East Lansing].[60]

Crisler was blindsided by this new twist in his discussions with Ralph Young.[61]

Despite the Wolverine athletic leadership being frustrated by the apparent Spartan oversight, there may have been a valid reason why they had not been apprised of the Faculty Senate resolution previously: preparation for a two-front war.

In March of 1941, the athletic directors, meeting in West Lafayette, had agreed that it was "not desirable to schedule football games more than four years in advance." As a consequence, the 1945 and '46 schedules were "put over until the May meetings of 1942."[62] One year later, at that spring gathering, with military preparedness being the focus of the directors and coaches, "it was voted to table the suggestion that the 1945 and 1946 football schedules be drawn up at a near future date."[63] And by March of 1943, due to tentative directives from the War Department, Michigan State was anticipating no intercollegiate competition in football for at least two years. Lacking a team, Director Young had no

---

[60] Minutes of the Meeting of the Board in Control of Intercollegiate Athletics. 15 November 1946. Bentley Historical Library. University of Michigan. Board in Control of Intercollegiate Athletics, 8729 Bimu F81 2; Box 49, folder: Board in Control minutes June 1950

[61] Ibid.

[62] Meetings of the Conference Athletic Directors and Joint Meeting with the Conference Basketball Coaches.7-8 March 1941. Bentley Historical Library, University of Michigan. Athletic Department, 943 Bimu 2; Box 84, folder: Athletic Director's office, Big-Ten directors committee minutes 1941-52

[63] Minutes of the Meeting of the Directors of Athletics of the Intercollegiate Conference. 15-16 May 1942. Bentley Historical Library, University of Michigan, Ralph W. Aigler Papers, 87406 Aa 2; Box 14, folder: Athletics 1940-1942 meeting minutes

reason, in the interim, to meet with Fritz Crisler to discuss the 1941 Faculty Senate policy and its impact on future scheduling between the schools.

The conference directors would finally gather in the spring of 1944 to settle contracts for the 1945 and '46 seasons. The scheduling meeting served no useful purpose for Michigan State. It had already been denied contests with Michigan for the foreseeable future. In the absence of any need to negotiate with Crisler, Ralph Young, once again, had no reason to inform him of the 1941 Hannah decree.

The next conference scheduling meeting would not take place until December of 1946, when contracting for 1947 and '48 was on the agenda. By alerting Crisler to the resolution of 1941, Young was forewarning his counterpart that the college could no longer accept the scrimmage-game weekend.[64] There was now a valid reason, tied to academic policy, for demanding a later date to contest the rivalry. Having taken five years to develop, the strategy showed that John Hannah had both foresight and patience.

Regardless of the reasons for the college failing to inform the university about its 1941 policy, the Michigan Board in Control and its chairman, Fritz Crisler, cried foul. The Spartan ploy would severely hamper Crisler's intricate scheduling scheme for the next two years. The Wolverines had already contracted two weekend dates each season with non-conference programs from each coast. The practice, illegal by Handbook standards, had been abused by Michigan for years. In advance of biennial spring meetings, it was clearly stated that only one weekend per season could be set aside for competition with a nonmember.[65]

This rule had been adopted to assure weaker conference programs dates with the tier-one powers. Once members were accommodated, schools could sign up non-conference teams for home-and-home commitments on remaining Saturdays.

Theoretically, the annual Michigan State game, in the opinion of the other nine athletic directors, fulfilled the Handbook rule as applied to the University of Michigan. But Michigan found that interpretation unacceptable. In a somewhat defiant stance towards his fellow directors, Crisler would not officially ink MSC on the Wolverine schedule until all other dates were filled.[66] Instead, shortly after the meeting commenced, he would secure on the chalkboard pre-arranged dates he had promised non-conference schools well in advance

---

[64] Minutes of the Meeting of the Board in Control of Intercollegiate Athletics. 15 November 1946. Bentley Historical Library. University of Michigan. Board in Control of Intercollegiate Athletics, 8729 Bimu F81 2; Box 49, folder: Board in Control minutes February 1938-June 1950

[65] Handbook of the Intercollegiate Conference of Faculty Representatives, Revised 1941. University of Minnesota Archives. Department of Intercollegiate Athletics Papers; Box 13, folder: 1895-1908, 1930, 1941

[66] "1947-49 Western Conference Football Schedule." 12 December 1946. . Bentley Historical Library, University of Michigan. Board in Control of Intercollegiate Athletics, 8729 Bimu F81 2; Box 35, folder: football schedules 1944, 1946-1947

of the biennial scheduling meeting.[67] [68] [69] [70] It was an irritating practice that would ultimately be challenged by Paul Brechler, of the State University of Iowa, in December of 1948.[71] [72]

From past experience, Fielding Yost had learned that prominent inter-regional schools were unwilling to contract for the scrimmage game. Feeling that there was a better chance of defeating the Wolverines after warming up against weaker opponents, reputable programs would only agree to play in Ann Arbor later in the season.[73] [74]

Yost was well aware that the intrastate contest was mandated by the taxpayers of Michigan. There was no obligatory date, however, on which to hold the game each year. As a consequence, the athletic director, with Ralph Young's passive consent back in 1932, began offering the opening weekend to Michigan State on an annual basis. It was a brilliant financial scheme on his part.[75] No other program willing to play that first Saturday of the season could muster half the attendance brought in by the Spartans. And for Ralph Young, despite having little say in the discussion, it was well worth the trip to Ann Arbor. Fielding Yost sent a check to Young, on December 21, 1937, for $15,725.79. It covered the balance due Michigan State for the contest held a few months earlier. The Spartan director, in reply, "was pleased to note" the attendance of 63,311. No doubt Yost shared Young's enthusiasm for those figures during tough economic times. The Spartan director closed his letter of appreciation by writing, "This was a fine Xmas present for us."[76]

For years Yost, and later Crisler, had no problems dealing with Ralph Young. Their challenge, rather, was how to accommodate many of the schools in the Western Conference.

---

[67] Crisler to Young. 23 October 1946. Bentley Historical Library, University of Michigan. Herbert Orin Crisler Papers, 85823 AC UAm Aa 2; Box 1, folder: topical correspondence, MSU 1943-46

[68] Crisler to Fairman. 24 February 1947. Bentley Historical Library, University of Michigan. Board In Control of Intercollegiate Athletics, 8729 Bimu F81 2; Box 35, folder: football schedules 1944, 1946, 1947

[69] Crisler to Fairman. 4 April 1947. Bentley Historical Library, University of Michigan. Board In Control of Intercollegiate Athletics, 8729 Bimu F81 2; Box 35, folder: football schedules 1944, 1946, 1947

[70] Crisler to Wilkinson. 8 September 1947. Bentley Historical Library, University of Michigan. Board In Control of Intercollegiate Athletics, 8729 Bimu F81 2; Box 35, folder: football schedules 1944, 1946, 1947

[71] Minutes of the Intercollegiate Conference-Meeting of Athletic Directors. 1 December 1948. University of Wisconsin-Madison Archives. The University Faculty Athletic Board, Series 5/21/6; Box 1, folder: Western Conference minutes 1947-51

[72] Annual Meeting of the Stockholders and Directors-Intercollegiate Conference Athletic Association. 11 December 1948. University of Wisconsin-Madison Archives. The University Faculty Athletic Board, Series 5/21/6; Box 1, folder: Western Conference minutes 1947-51

[73] Fairman to Crisler. 25 March 1947. Bentley Historical Library, University of Michigan. Board in Control of Intercollegiate Athletics, 8729 Bimu F81 2; Box 35, folder: football schedules 1944, 1946, 1947

[74] Crisler to Fairman. 4 April 1947. Bentley Historical Library, University of Michigan. Board in Control of Intercollegiate Athletics, 8729 Bimu F81 2; Box 35, folder: football schedules 1944, 1946, 1947

[75] Michigan State Football Date. February 1949. Bentley Historical Library, University of Michigan. Herbert Orin Crisler Papers, 85823 AC UAm Aa 2; Box 1, folder: topical correspondence, MSU 1947-49

[76] Young to Yost. 21 December 1937. Bentley Historical Library, University of Michigan. Board in Control of Intercollegiate Athetics, Bimu F81 2; Box 22, folder: papers 1937 December

But due to Michigan's continuing violations of the Handbook rule on contracting non-conference games in advance of the May meetings, there were very few dates available for the weaker schools–Iowa, Indiana, and Purdue–to contest the Wolverines.[77] [78] With an eight-weekend season, only three slots were effectively open on Michigan's schedule. Since the mid-1930s, Ohio State had assumed the final weekend of the season. That rivalry was sacrosanct. The Little Brown Jug tradition required Minnesota being on the schedule every year. The Spartans took up a third date. The final two weekends were reserved for those prominent inter-regional programs.

It was difficult to discipline Michigan. The shared revenue from a game in Ann Arbor was critical to the financial well-being of many conference athletic departments. Even a full house in Bloomington, Iowa City, or West Lafayette would not offer dollars comparable to a poorly attended game in Ann Arbor.

The Announcement of December 1939, and the University of Chicago's withdrawal from football participation, was a wake-up call for the faculty leadership. The conference had to be more sensitive to the needs of its weaker members. A new scheduling format was necessary. There simply were not enough weekends to assure tier-two schools an opportunity to compete against those traditional powers that controlled huge gate receipts.

The temporary solution, as conceived by Fritz Crisler[79] and proposed by Ralph Aigler at the Western Conference spring meetings of 1940, was to expand the schedule to nine games. Six were mandated with conference schools. Two of those six had to be played at home sites. The remaining three weekends were open to nonmembers. The plan was to apply to the 1943 and '44 seasons only. The additional game was necessary to allow Michigan to fulfill previously arranged contracts with non-conference competition. Assuming the Wolverines would now abide by the Handbook policy and cease past practices, the directors agreed to resume the traditional eight game season in 1945 but with the understanding that six rather than four contests be held with conference members.[80] The latter stipulation was intended to accommodate the weaker programs.

The Crisler-Aigler proposal was also an experiment. Other conferences were extending play by one or two games a season. At issue for the leadership was how an additional contest might impact a student's classroom performance. Reassessment of that aspect of the 9/6/2 arrangement would take place upon completion of the 1944 season.[81] All parties seemed satisfied with the compromise. Unfortunately, with the advent of war, the temporary scheduling scheme was never fully implemented. A decision was made,

---

[77] Crisler to Wilkinson. 8 September 1947. Bentley Historical Library, University of Michigan. Athletic Department, 943 Bimu 2; Box 35, folder: football schedules 1944, 46, 47

[78] Crisler to Fairman. 24 October 1947. Bentley Historical Library, University of Michigan. Athletic Department, 943 Bimu 2; Box 35, folder: football schedules 1944, 46, 47

[79] Northshore Hotel, Evanston, Illinois. Friday Evening (Faculty Representatives Meeting). 24 May 1940. Bentley Historical Library, University of Michigan. Athletic Department, 943 Bimu 2; Box 84, folder: Big Ten Faculty Representatives minutes 1918-46

[80] Minutes of the Directors of Athletics of the Intercollegiate Conference. 24-25 May 1940. Bentley Historical Library. University of Michigan. Athletic Department, 943 Bimu 2; Box 84, folder: Athletic Director's office, Big Ten committee minutes 1932-40

[81] (Minutes of the Faculty Representatives of the Intercollegiate Conference). 24 May 1940. Bentley Historical Library. University of Michigan. Athletic Department, 943 Bimu 2; Box 84, folder: athletic director's office, Big-Ten directors committee minutes 1941-1952

nonetheless, in December of 1945 to officially adopt the 9/6/2 format. It would soon prove to be a highly contentious issue among certain members of the conference.

But in the fall of 1946, the Spartans had little concern with scheduling challenges facing Western Conference athletic directors regarding a decision made one year earlier. The college was more focused on how to gain a home-and-home series with the University of Michigan later in the season. The Faculty Senate resolution, perhaps coyly conceived years earlier, might finally be part of the answer for John Hannah.

IN EARLY October of 1946, President Hannah would successfully negotiate a long-term home-and-home contract with the University of Notre Dame. It was a major coup for the Spartan football program. Encouraged by the good news, Ralph Young could now resume the old debate on scheduling, held in check during the war years, with his counterpart from Ann Arbor. John Hannah stood nearby Young and his typewriter.

In November 1946 the Michigan State athletic director telegraphed Fritz Crisler stating that he could no longer accept the scrimmage weekend promised by the Wolverine director a few weeks earlier. He requested a home-and-home series as well as a Saturday later in the season. Crisler, no doubt, was irritated by the demand. The members of his conference would be meeting in four weeks to arrange football contracts for the first time since the war had ended. He needed reassurance from Young that the Spartans would maintain the first date on his schedule. Success of the recently approved 9/6/2 rule, at least for Michigan, was predicated on the college being fully cooperative with the traditional Yost-Young understanding. But now he faced a new challenge–a recalcitrant Michigan State.

A few weeks earlier, on October 23, Crisler had informed the Spartan director that Michigan was unable to offer any date other than the 27th of September for the 1947 season.

> Our Athletic Board reviewed our schedule policy very thoroughly and
> discovered that it is not very elastic. We are required to meet six
> Conference opponents. Some years in order to schedule six contests for
> each institution and retain old rivalries, Michigan is compelled from time to
> time to play seven. It is further the desire of the Board to maintain Eastern
> and Western relationships because of alumni and various other reasons ...
> As a result, the Board finds it difficult to free any date except the opening
> Saturday. This is not only true for 1947, but is likely to prevail for the
> immediate future. It is the hope of the Board that Michigan State will be
> able to conveniently make whatever adjustments are necessary to meet
> Michigan in the opening game.[82]

Ralph Young took his time responding, waiting until November 5. The delay was due, in part, to his sharing the content of the letter with his athletic council. No doubt many members were upset with Crisler's audacious request that the college accommodate his institution. It was time for Michigan State to take a stand. John Hannah's solution, with the approval of his council, was to resurrect the 1941 Faculty Senate policy. It was now Michigan's turn to "conveniently make whatever adjustments [necessary]" to accommodate

---

[82] Crisler to Young. 23 October 1946. Bentley Historical Library, University of Michigan. Herbert Orin Crisler Papers, 85823 AC UAm Aa 2; Box 1, folder: topical correspondence, MSU 1943-46

the college! Fritz Crisler and his Board in Control were unaware of the five-year old college resolution pertaining to registration and orientation week.[83] Young's reply went on to explain the reasoning behind the academic policy, even though it had never been implemented due to wartime developments.

But in the spirit of compromise, the Spartan alerted Crisler that the council would "recommend to its faculty the acceptance of the September 27 date in 1947 despite the conflict with registration, if assurance is given by the University of Michigan that in 1948 and future seasons thereafter the annual football game between the two schools will be scheduled on some date which follows the opening of fall quarter classes."[84]

The debate was starting to get very interesting.

Now it was Crisler's turn for a delayed response. The head Wolverine had to report the new developments to his Board in Control. Two weeks later, on November 18, the chairman wrote back to Young pointing out that "our Board has voted with regret that because of our existing schedule commitments and the regulations of the Conference regarding the making of advance football schedules it is impossible for us to give you the assurance for which you ask." Michigan suddenly found it convenient to abide by the Handbook policy it had clearly ignored for years.

The 9/6/2 compromise now offered a great counter to the Spartan surprise of November 5, 1946. But cooler heads ultimately prevailed on the board. The two schools, after all, were obligated to compete each year. As Crisler wrote to Young:

> Noting, however, the position taken by the Faculty of Michigan State
> College which will not permit you to schedule a game with the University
> of Michigan at Ann Arbor during Michigan State College's registration
> period, it was further voted that we express to you our willingness to come
> to East Lansing for the opening game of the 1947 season, September 27.

The olive branch offered by the Board in Control was a relative concession. There would be no compromise on a long-term home-and-home series so critical to the success of Hannah's grand plans for the college. Crisler would argue that even contractual relationships within the conference were restricted to two years.[85] Historical precedent limited commitments for a valid reason. Back in 1929, the directors had proposed four-year contracts, rather than the traditional two-year arrangements, to ease the cumbersome scheduling process that consumed so much of their time. The faculty representatives vetoed the proposal after an ad hoc committee reviewed the potential consequences of an extended schedule.[86]

Regardless of conference history on scheduling challenges, Michigan State was not ready to concede. It declined the Michigan offer. Five weeks later, on Christmas Eve, Ralph

---

[83] Ibid.

[84] Young to Crisler. 5 November 1946. Bentley Historical Library, University of Michigan. Herbert Orin Crisler Papers, 85823 AC UAm Aa 2; Box 1, folder: topical correspondence, MSU 1943-46

[85] Crisler to Young. 18 November 1946. Bentley Historical Library, University of Michigan. Herbert Orin Crisler Papers, 85823 AC UAm Aa 2; Box 1, folder: topical correspondence, MSU 1943-46

[86] Minutes of the Intercollegiate Conference of Faculty Representatives. 25 May 1929. Bentley Historical Library, University of Michigan. Athletic Department, 943 Bimu 2; Box 84, folder: Athletic Director's office, Big-Ten Faculty Representatives minutes 1918-1946

Young offered a counter proposal featuring Michigan State's plans to enlarge Macklin Field. The facility adjacent to the Red Cedar River would accommodate almost 52,000 when completed before the 1948 season, an increase of over 20,000 seats.[87] Macklin "Stadium" would become the sixth largest in the country behind Notre Dame, Michigan, Illinois, Ohio State, and Minnesota.[88] The Spartans were confident that this addition would make it financially more attractive for the Wolverines to visit East Lansing every other year.

The plan to expand the stadium was in large part due to the "Spaghetti and Meatball" contract John Hannah had just signed with the University of Notre Dame in early October. The Irish were willing to resurrect the relationship they had had with the college based on a promise by Hannah to construct a larger facility. A long-term home-and-home arrangement assured the school of one sell-out in its enlarged facility. President Hannah hoped that Michigan would follow that lead and sign a similar contract. He needed another program capable of filling Macklin Field in those years the college played the Irish in South Bend.

Fritz Crisler's arithmetic would still indicate a 35,000-seat discrepancy despite the Macklin expansion. That translated into significant lost revenue. Radio broadcasts contributed little to the annual bottom line for athletic directors. WWJ signed a contract with Michigan in 1940 to cover all home games in Ann Arbor; income from the arrangement was a mere $8,250.[89] Television rights, sold to major networks, were still years away. Ticket sales remained the main source of dollars for college programs in December of 1946.

Excited about the prospects of a stadium seating 52,000, however, Young pointed out that "with this [expansion] in mind, I would like to suggest that our 1947 game be played in Ann Arbor the last Saturday in September and that you open our new stadium by playing our dedication game in 1948, either on the last Saturday in September or the first Saturday in October." He reminded Crisler that a home-and-home long-term arrangement remained his athletic council's primary interest.

Ralph Young also acknowledged that the old Faculty Senate Policy of 1941 posed only a minor problem if the university agreed to the Spartan proposal. "In order to play in your stadium on the last Saturday in September in 1947, it will be necessary to ask our faculty to make an exception to their previous rule of not playing the games in your stadium while registration is in progress."[90] Young sounded optimistic that the college could work around the resolution. It helped, of course, that John Hannah was actively engaged in the writing of those letters.

Crisler declined the home-and-home proposal but accepted the stadium dedication game for 1948.[91] Even though his financial instinct told him this was a poor return on

---

[87] Young to Crisler. 24 December 1946. Bentley Historical Library, University of Michigan. Herbert Orin Crisler Papers, 85823 AC UAm Aa 2; Box 1, folder: topical correspondence, MSU 1943-46

[88] Thomas, David. *Michigan State College: John Hannah and the Creation of a World University, 1926-1969.* East Lansing: Michigan State University Press, 2008. p. 128

[89] Minutes of the Meeting of the Board in Control of Physical Education. 5 April 1939. Bentley Historical Library, University of Michigan. Board in Control Minutes, 8729 Bimu F81 2; Box 49, folder: February 1938-June 1950

[90] Young to Crisler. 24 December 1946. Bentley Historical Library, University of Michigan. Herbert Orin Crisler Papers, 85823 AC UAm Aa 2; Box 1, folder: topical correspondence, MSU 1943-46

[91] Crisler to Young. 27 January 1947. Bentley Historical Library, University of Michigan. Herbert

investment, he had no choice but to travel to East Lansing in 1948.[92] The State Capitol, after all, was only two miles from campus.

It had taken an enlarged stadium to convince the university to change its policy. The last time Michigan had seen the Red Cedar River was in 1924 when Michigan Agricultural College dedicated College Field.[93] Stadium construction or expansion was proving to be a very costly way to lure a Wolverine to East Lansing.

THE 1978 season ended for Michigan State University with a sound defeat of Iowa on November 25. Michigan's didn't end until after the Rose Bowl.

With the season over, the only unfinished obligation for Coach Daryl Rogers was to appear at "Spartan Busts" wherein the coaches traveled to certain larger cities about the state to honor Spartan football players from those regions. It was a way of saying thank you for their long hours and dedication to the program. The first bust was always celebrated in the greater Detroit area. Flint, Grand Rapids, Benton Harbor, and East Lansing would follow, with a meal and numerous speeches making up the agenda. Since there was nothing newsworthy about these celebrations, the press was not invited.

There was little professional sporting activity taking place the evening in Detroit when Rogers spoke to a large crowd at the first Spartan Bust of the postseason. Big Ten basketball was not yet in full swing. It was too early to begin hyping the Wolverine game in Pasadena a few weeks away. In short, there was little that merited sports-page coverage. As Rogers recalled, the evening started out fairly reserved for a celebration of a very successful season. Minor applause followed brief comments by various guests speakers.

Finally, it was Coach Rogers' turn to speak. He started out by recapping the season game by game. It was an easy task for the head coach. After quickly commenting about the first four contests he turned his attention to the Wolverines.

Rogers said that the turnaround moment for the season was the contest in Ann Arbor. With Eddie Smith back in uniform after an injury, the Spartans defeated a great Michigan crew. Even this wasn't getting much of a response from the crowd. Something needed to be done to raise the spirits of everyone in attendance.

So Coach Rogers decided to deviate from his format and take a gamble. Dan Underwood's comments two months earlier were on his mind. Continuing his discussion on the Wolverine game, the transplanted Californian suddenly raised his voice and blurted out the phrase that has remained associated with Daryl Rogers' brief, yet successful, tenure in East Lansing ever since. "And despite beating 'em on their own turf, those arrogant asses in Ann Arbor are taking our spot in Pasadena!"

The early-winter hibernation in the dining hall was over. Rogers recalled being momentarily surprised by the response. The audience stood up and exuberantly cheered for over five minutes. The Underwood phrase turned out to be the highlight of the evening.

Unknown to the organizers of the event, there were some sportswriters in attendance. The following morning the lead story in print was Coach Rogers' comment on the "arrogant asses in Ann Arbor." Veteran sports editor Joe Falls of the *Detroit Free Press,*

Orin Crisler Papers, 85823 AC UAm Aa 2; Box 1, folder: topical correspondence, MSU 1943-46

[92] Crisler to Mackey. 16 February 1948. Bentley Historical Library, University of Michigan. Herbert Orin Crisler Papers, 85823 AC UAm Aa 2; Box 35, folder: football schedules 1944, 46, 47

[93] Widder, Keith. *Michigan Agricultural College: The Evolution of a Land-Grant Philosophy, 1855-1925.* East Lansing: Michigan State University Press, 2005. p. 390

as paraphrased by Rogers, claimed "this comment will shake the very foundations of relations between these two great state institutions." He found humor in the hyperbole. "Busts are just a venue for having a good time, celebrating the season, and poking fun at our rivals."

Years later Daryl Rogers still encounters Michigan State alumni and fans. Invariably they bring up the Underwood Alliteration of 1978.[94] It took him three years of coaching in East Lansing, but that night in Detroit Daryl Rogers finally grasped the significance of the rivalry between the two schools.[95] He needed no history lesson to realize that this was one very unique intercollegiate athletic relationship.

---

[94] Rogers, Daryl. 27 February 2009. Personal communication.
[95] Underwood, Dan. 30 July 2010. Personal communication.

On the Origin of Arrogance

"CATHOLEPISTEMIAD OF Michigania" was chartered in 1817 by the United State Congress. It was a private secondary school modeled after Napoleon's imperial University of France founded a decade earlier.[1] Located in a small trading post known as Detroit, the school was founded by Father Gabriel Richard and Reverend John Monteith, one a Catholic priest, the other a Presbyterian Divine.[2] The school was initially financed by the sale of Indian lands granted through an act of the Northwest Territorial government. Within four years it would be renamed the University of Michigan.[3]

In 1837 it was relocated to Ann Arbor when the territory became the 26th state within the union.[4] Associated with that move, the school transitioned toward a state institution modeled after "the Prussian system, with programs in literature, science, and arts; medicine; and law—the first three academic departments of the new university."The revised state constitution of 1851 provided the university "an unusual degree of autonomy as a 'coordinate branch of state government' with full powers over all university matters granted to its governing Board of Regents."[5]

The university's operational independence, assured by the new constitution, allowed it a unique status among state schools. As part of a territorial possession, it was originally funded by the U.S. Congress. Federal lands granted to the institution were sold off to finance its early development. There was no taxpayer support for the University of Michigan prior to the Civil War. As a consequence, Michigan could "[regard] itself as much a national university as a state university … with some discretion when dealing with the

---

[1] Duderstadt, James J. *The View from the Helm.* Ann Arbor: The University of Michigan Press, 2007. p. 9

[2] Ibid., p. 8

[3] Kryk, John. *Natural Enemies: Major College Football's Oldest, Fiercest Rivalry-Michigan vs. Notre Dame.* Lanham, New York: Taylor Trade Publishing, 2007. p. 4

[4] Ibid., p. 4

[5] Duderstadt, James J. *The View from the Helm.* Ann Arbor: The University of Michigan Press, 2007. p. 9.

Michigan State Legislature [in later years]."[6]

Its vision, as a national university, ultimately took form in 1852 when the Board of Regents hired Henry Phillip Tappan as the school's first president. Professor Tappan, an academician from New York City, laid the groundwork for building "a university very different from those characterizing the colonial colleges of the 19th century America."

> Tappan articulated a vision of the university as a capstone of civilization, a
> repository for the accumulated knowledge of mankind, and a home to
> scholars dedicated to the expansion of human understanding. In his words,
> "a university is the highest form of an institution of learning. It embraces
> every branch of knowledge and all possible means of making new
> investigations and thus advances in knowledge."[7]

Tappan would accomplish all this by not focusing on utilitarian training in the vocations. That would soon become the task of certain state colleges with the passage of the Morrill Land-Grant Act of 1862. Nor would he emphasize traditional courses as taught by the early colonial colleges. Rather, the president "blended the classical curriculum with the European model that stressed faculty involvement in research … and the preparation of future scholars."[8]

Michigan would become "the first university in the West to offer a professional education by establishing a medical school in 1850, providing some engineering courses in 1854, and offering a legal education in 1859."[9] These were just a few examples of the innovative spirit that pervaded his tenure in Ann Arbor.

Prior to Tappan's arrival, however, state legislation, passed in 1837, "… required the university to set up branches throughout the state to function as preparatory schools for the university." Included in this was support for agrarian studies at those sites.

> Section 20 of the act provided that: 'In each of the branches of the
> University, there shall be a department of agriculture, with competent
> instructors in the theory of agriculture, including vegetable physiology and
> agricultural chemistry, and experimental and practical farming and
> agriculture …' The real significance of Section 20 was that the people of
> Michigan served notice at the beginning of statehood that they expected
> state government, relying in part upon federal resources, to provide
> agricultural education at an institution of higher learning.[10]

The university, for various reasons, would stop supporting the branches within 10 years. The decision was not popular among the farming establishment about the state.

In 1850 a state constitutional convention rewrote the original 1837 document. In acknowledging the failure of Section 20 in creating preparatory branches capable of training

---

[6] Duderstadt, James J. *The View from the Helm.* Ann Arbor: The University of Michigan Press, 2007. p. 9

[7] Ibid., p. 10

[8] Ibid., p. 11

[9] Ibid., pp. 11-12

[10] Widder, Keith R. *Michigan Agricultural College: The Evolution of a Land-Grant Philosophy, 1855-1925.* East Lansing: Michigan State University Press, 2005. pp. 22-23

farmers, the convention mandated the establishment of an agricultural school. It was not sufficient to have a department within the university devoted to agrarian interests. The powerful agricultural movement wanted a school to teach young men how to farm more efficiently. Practical research was paramount. Unfortunately, the authors of the new constitution remained vague on whether the university or a separate college would provide this service.[11]

Upon his arrival in Ann Arbor, Tappan was up to the challenge posed by the poorly worded document. He wanted his school to be the focal point for agrarian science research.

During the first three years of Tappan's presidency he argued that agricultural studies must remain in Ann Arbor. The president wanted "to make the University one of the first in our country, and if we can, second to none in the world; and therefore there is no branch of knowledge that we can lawfully omit…it is better to have one great institution than a half dozen abortions." Agrarian studies were no exception. In Tappan's opinion "an Agricultural Department belongs to the University."[12] He saw no purpose in the state operating a separate college dedicated only to farming interests.

The association of an air of superiority, or perhaps arrogance, with the University of Michigan may have originated with those early remarks by President Tappan.

The farmers gained a political victory over the academician when, in 1855, the state legislature passed an act creating an agricultural college separate from the university.[13] The model farm, a concept he opposed for its utilitarian purposes, was included in the legislation. It was intended "to be a place at the college where young men would learn to operate and manage a farm in the most efficient, profitable manner possible."[14] In the opinion of Henry Phillips Tappan, it was academic heresy.

During a subsequent speech on the natural order of academic institutions that he gave to colleagues in Albany, New York, Tappan noted "that normal schools and agricultural colleges should fall between primary schools and universities in the hierarchy of American education." He went on to state that "universities alone can multiply universities; universities alone can properly form and order all the subordinate institutions."[15]

In that same speech he failed to acknowledge the new agricultural college in East Lansing as being part of the state's "promising educational organization."[16] He wanted nothing to do with an institution promoting vocational training. The Agricultural College of the State of Michigan would remain a "subordinate institution" in the opinion of the university's first president. It is an attitude that appears to have persisted among future

---

[11] Widder, Keith R. *Michigan Agricultural College: The Evolution of a Land-Grant Philosophy, 1855-1925.* East Lansing: Michigan State University Press, 2005. p. 23

[12] Ibid., pp. 24-26

[13] Ibid., p. 29

[14] Ibid., p. 26

[15] Ibid., p. 27

[16] Ibid., p. 26

generations of Michigan graduates.[17] [18] [19]

Henry Tappan's stay in Ann Arbor was short lived. He was not well liked by the press. His aristocratic manner was not accepted by common folk of the area. He was even characterized by one writer as "a thorough and unmitigated ass."[20]

President Tappan was essentially run out of town. But despite being scorned by many, he had accomplished his mission. The foundation for a great national public university was created during his brief tenure in Ann Arbor. In decades to come, many Michigan graduates, trained under his educational model, would leave their marks on society through law, medicine, business, engineering, and the creative arts. Tappan's legacy lives on to this day.

But many Michigan alumni, appropriately proud of their school, might have also promoted the institutional arrogance that Dan Underwood referenced in the alliteration mentioned to Daryl Rogers years later. Law Professor Ralph Aigler described the origins of that pride in 1948, when writing to Commissioner Ken Wilson.

> With the possible exception of the University of California, I suppose
> Michigan is almost unique in the loyalty and enthusiasm of its alumni.
> Many years ago under the Presidency of Dr. Angell definite efforts were
> initiated to make the alumni feel that they were and are an integral part of
> the University "family" … That the efforts of the University have borne
> tangible fruit in respects much more important than athletics is shown by
> the large percentage of physical equipment here that is the gift of alumni …
> over one third of the University's plant has been provided by generous
> alumni … in this respect Michigan as a state institution is in a class by itself
> … It has often struck me that our associates would do better to try to
> emulate Michigan so far as the building up of alumni organizations is
> concerned rather than to throw verbal bricks at Michigan because she
> happens to be fortunate enough to have that sort of backing.[21]

Some conference schools, perhaps envious of the Michigan model, struggled to match the success of the Wolverines. Michigan State College, however, declined to "throw bricks" at its sister institution. It would passively accept the natural "subordinate" order, as outlined by President Tappan, during the first half of the twentieth century.

Tappan's vision was critical to defining the university. But the realization of that vision required the bringing together of a disparate group of intellectuals and successful alumni. The graduates may have gifted the bricks, but Michigan football, dating back to the late 1870s, provided the mortar that ultimately built one of the great centers of higher

---

[17] Kuich to Williams. 8 February 1954. Bentley Historical Library, University of Michigan. G. Mennen Williams Papers; Box 129, Boards and Commissions, 1954: colleges, state, MSU

[18] Kuich to Williams. 12 March 1955. Bentley Historical Library, University of Michigan. G. Mennen Williams Papers; Box 159, Boards and commissions, 1955:colleges, state, MSU rename

[19] Unnamed resolution. 29 March 1955. Herbert Orin Crisler Papers, 85823 AC UAm Aa2; Box 1, folder: topical correspondence: MSU 1954-60, 1965-66

[20] Coleman, Mary Sue. "Notre Dame Graduate School Commencement." 19 May 2007. www.umich.edu/pres/speeches/070519notredame.html.

[21] Aigler to Wilson. 11 June 1948. Bentley Historical Library, University of Michigan. Ralph W. Aigler Papers, 87406 Aa 2; Box 10, folder: correspondence 1946-52 Wilson, K.L.

learning in the world.

FIELDING YOST was born in Fairview, West Virginia, on April 30, 1871. After temporarily working with his father in business, he enrolled at West Virginia Law School in 1895. While studying law he was introduced to the game of football. Following a brief stint as a lineman, he went on to coaching in 1897. Over the next few years he was an itinerant football coach at a number of schools. Success followed him at each stop. Yost was respected as a gentleman, instructor, and leader of young men.

In 1901 he was recruited by Charles Baird to be a part-time coach at the University of Michigan. Four decades later, Fielding Yost would retire as athletic director from the school he made famous for athletic excellence. He set the standard for winning football that all his successors were measured against. In 25 years of coaching at Michigan, Yost won 165 games while losing 29 and tying 10. The Wolverines achieved six mythical national championships during his tenure.

As athletic director, the man was a visionary. The university golf course, designed by noted architect Alistair MacKenzie, was completed under his managerial oversight. Yost Fieldhouse, the first of its kind, served numerous athletes and their sports. His passion for a huge facility to meet the growing demand for season tickets by alumni and fans alike culminated in the dedication of Michigan Stadium in 1927. Yost's leadership was critical to the success of that controversial project,[22] which defined his legacy at the University of Michigan.

Recognized for its unique simplicity,[23] the bowl, and the huge crowds filling it on Saturday afternoons in the fall, proved an invaluable recruiting tool at a time when proselyting was illegal in the Western Conference. The opportunity to play in front of 85,000 people was quite a selling point for kids in the pre-television era. Yost's structure, and the tradition it engendered, would ensure Michigan's ongoing presence among the elite powers of college football.

Athletic Darwinism in Ann Arbor had its origins with Fielding Yost first walking the sidelines at Regents and later Ferry Field.[24] But the huge stadium, completed after his years in coaching, assured the dominance of the Wolverine species. Due to its seating capacity, and its proximity to an economically thriving Detroit, the structure guaranteed enormous gate receipts shared equally with competitors. Schools petitioned to play in Ann Arbor.[25] The income provided programs was a great return on investment for the trip to southeastern Michigan. The only stipulation, for non-conference schools, was adherence to Western Conference rules on eligibility.[26] Michigan State College knew that only too well.

Although canonized by alumni and fans of the university during his tenure on the

---

[22] Soderstrom, Robert M. *The Big House: Fielding H. Yost and the Building of Michigan Stadium.* Ann Arbor: Huron River Press, 2005. pp. 257-260, 261-279

[23] Ibid., pp. 277-279

[24] Griffith to Aigler. 25 February 1931. Bentley Historical Library, University of Michigan. Ralph W. Aigler Papers, 87406 Aa 2; Box: 3, folder: Griffith, John 1931

[25] Wilkinson to Crisler. 26 August 1947. Bentley Historical Library, University of Michigan. Herbert Orin Crisler Papers, 85823 AC UAm Aa 2; Box 35, folder: football schedules 1944, 46, 47

[26] Crisler to Mackey. 16 February 1948. Bentley Historical Library, University of Michigan. Herbert Orin Crisler Papers, 85823 AC UAm Aa 2; Box 35, folder: football schedules 1944, 46, 47

sidelines, Fielding Yost was no saint when it came to following the amateur code.[27] He manipulated rules and schedules for the benefit of Michigan football and his career as coach.[28] [29] But he wasn't alone. As the Carnegie Report of 1929 pointed out, sinners exceeded saints in the college coaching ranks of his era.

During his early years Yost, like so many other coaches, frequently violated rules and regulations of the Western Conference;[30] his obstinate stance opposing certain policies promoting a cleaner game led to Michigan's departure from the conference in 1908.[31]

The resulting Decade of Defiance would temporarily redefine the school's intercollegiate athletic philosophy. The faculty lost control over Michigan athletics. In the absence of its oversight, Michigan was no different from non-conference schools of that era. The Wolverines could apply the NCAA amateur code as it best suited Yost's penchant for winning football. Eligibility, subsidizing, and recruiting were left to the school's athletic board, dominated by alumni, students, and boosters, for interpretation. And yet despite no longer claiming membership in the Intercollegiate Conference, Michigan did abide by most Handbook rules practiced by the eight remaining institutions.[32] [33]

During that decade away from its conference home, a conservative young law professor by the name of Ralph W. Aigler politicked to realign Michigan's forlorn priorities; resumption of faculty control was critical to maintaining institutional integrity in academics and amateur athletics. Aigler's rhetoric and leadership would prove critical in the university regaining membership in the Western Conference by June of 1917.[34] His reward for the role he played was election as both chair of the Board in Control and faculty representative to the conference. These two positions provided him a pulpit for preaching his vision of evangelical amateurism.

With Ralph Aigler leading the congregation, Fielding Yost saw the light. He had no choice but to convert to Aigler's strict religion. But it was unclear whether he was a true believer.

> When Yost [became athletic director] in 1921, he resolved for Michigan to pursue what he termed "equality of competition." It was not that he had become a reform zealot–far from it. He just could not [tolerate playing] anybody who could get away with more than he could. The way Yost saw it, if he had to abide by harsh constraints, so should everybody … He [would soon make] it his goal to see every [Western Conference] member

---

[27] Kryk, John. *Natural Enemies: Major College Football's Oldest, Fiercest Rivalry – Michigan vs. Notre Dame.* Lanham: Taylor Trade Publishing, 2007. pp. 98-99

[28] Ibid., pp. 43-44

[29] Behee, John R. *Fielding Yost's Legacy to the University of Michigan.* Ann Arbor: Uhlrich's Books, Inc., 1971, pp. 86, 107, 110

[30] Ibid., p. 107

[31] Ibid., p. 72-74

[32] Kryk, John. *Natural Enemies: Major College Football's Oldest, Fiercest Rivalry – Michigan vs. Notre Dame.* Lanham, New York: Taylor Trade Publishing, 2007. p. 75

[33] Ibid., p. 86

[34] Behee, John R. *Fielding Yost's Legacy to the University of Michigan.* Ann Arbor: Uhlrich's Books, Inc., 1971. p. 79

play only those schools "hitched in the same harness."[35]

Upon retiring from coaching in 1926, Yost became Michigan's full-time athletic director for the remaining 15 years of his remarkable career. He would insist that his successors abide by "stringent scholastic standards for athletes."[36] Working closely with Aigler in crafting university athletic policies and practices, the former coach appeared aligned with Aigler's evangelical convictions. By December of 1929, he would take the leadership in condemning the State University of Iowa for violations of Handbook eligibility standards.[37] Brother Yost was clearly born again!

ON SEPTEMBER 24, 1938, the Board in Control of Athletics at the University of Michigan met at the Michigan Union. One week later the season would open with Michigan State playing in Ann Arbor for the 14th straight year.

During the meeting, Yost displayed concern over the misuse of the "Block M" by "non-athletic" organizations at the school. He moved that the board restrict use of the emblem to university athletics only. The motion unanimously carried.[38] This was the first acknowledgement on record of how valuable that bold single letter was to the athletic identity of the University of Michigan.

Years later Don Canham, the man asked to replace Fritz Crisler as athletic director, would realize the financial value of that copyrighted letter.[39] The former track coach, now administrator, earned millions of dollars for his athletic department through the marketing of the Block M during his 20 years in office. It remains one of the most recognizable symbols in college sports in large part due to the foresight of Fielding Yost.

MICHIGAN STADIUM will forever remain Yost's legacy to the University of Michigan. His greatest accomplishment during 40 years in Ann Arbor, however, might actually be his promotion of the University of Michigan as a special place for returning athletes and alumni. On October 28, 1939, he organized a "Round Up" of all former players. It was a sentimental time for the brilliant gridiron tactician. Most of his players gathered at the Michigan Union to "pay tribute to the Michigan Spirit."

Yost commented on those in attendance being "part of the great family of Michigan men, bound together by fadeless memories which, over a span of four decades or more, grow sweeter in retrospect." He described how they all had "so much to do with building that intangible, yet very real and actual thing that men and women the country over

---

[35] Kryk, John. *Natural Enemies: Major College Football's Oldest, Fiercest Rivalry – Michigan vs. Notre Dame.* Lanham, New York: Taylor Trade Publishing, 2007. p. 86

[36] Behee, John R. *Fielding Yost's Legacy to the University of Michigan.* Ann Arbor: Uhlrich's Books, Inc., 1971. p. 107

[37] "Memorandum of the Meeting of the Big Ten at Chicago." Lauer, Edward H. 6-7 December 1929. University of Iowa Archives, Iowa City, Iowa. Board in Control of Athletics, RG 28.03.05; minutes 1929-34

[38] Minutes of the Meeting of the Board in Control of Physical Education. 24 September 1938. Bentley Historical Library, University of Michigan. Board in Control Minutes, 943 Bimu 2; Box 49, folder:Board in Control minutes February 1938-June 1950

[39] Kryk, John. *Natural Enemies: Major College Football's Oldest, Fiercest Rivalry – Michigan vs. Notre Dame.* Lanham, New York; Taylor Trade Publishing, 2007. p. 311

recognize as the indomitable, fighting, militant Spirit of Michigan."

Yost was just beginning to warm up. "Everyone of you, have had a definite part in building that great spirit; you left it as a precious heritage to the Men of Michigan who have followed you."

The old coach closed with some very emotional words. It was a locker-room pep talk unlike any other during his 25 years on the sidelines in Ann Arbor.

> But do let me reiterate a fact of which you are all keenly aware at this
> moment. It pertains to the Spirit of Michigan. It is based upon a deathless
> loyalty to Michigan in all her ways; an enthusiasm that makes it second
> nature for Michigan men to spread the gospel of their university to the
> world's distant outposts; and conviction that nowhere is there a better
> university, in any way, than this Michigan of ours. The spirit that inspired
> "The Victors" and "Varsity" still lives."

The phrase "Michigan Man" was coined during those stirring remarks.[40] The designation would become an entitlement of honor and pride for future generations of athletes contributing to the school's famed athletic tradition.

ONE OF the first public mentions of Michigan's athletic arrogance was noted in a letter from *Detroit News* sports writer H. G. Salsinger to faculty representative Ralph Aigler in January of 1943. The two had struck up a close friendship over the years. The relationship was also symbiotic. Salsinger would use Aigler to gain scoops or confirm stories on Wolverine athletics.[41][42][43] In return, Aigler was offered free tickets to professional sporting events in Detroit;[44] the law professor was a rabid Tigers and Red Wings fan. And Ralph Aigler would often seek the sportswriter's opinion on controversial intercollegiate athletic policies.[45] He needed someone in the press he could trust in strictest confidence.[46] Salsinger was his man.

In mid-January of 1943, Salsinger wrote Aigler thanking him for sharing a copy of the annual report of the Board in Control of Athletics at the University of Michigan. This occurred during the time when Michigan State College had been politicking for admission to the Western Conference. Rumors in the press claimed the University of Michigan opposed it. In the annual report he had sent to his friend, Aigler had included a note

---

[40] Behee, John R. *Fielding Yost's Legacy to the University of Michigan.* Ann Arbor: Uhlrich's Books, Inc., 1971. pp. 111-119

[41] Salsinger to Aigler. 31 January 1943. Bentley Historical Library, University of Michigan. Ralph W. Aigler Papers, 87406 Aa 2; Box 8, folder:correspondence 1940-45 "S" misc.

[42] Salsinger to Aigler. 9 January 1945. Bentley Historical Library, University of Michigan. Ralph W. Aigler Papers, 87406 Aa 2; Box 8, folder:correspondence 1940-45 "S" misc.

[43] Salsinger to Aigler. 19 March 1945. Bentley Historical Library, University of Michigan. Ralph W. Aigler Papers, 87406 Aa 2; Box 8, folder:correspondence 1940-45 "S" misc.

[44] Salsinger to Aigler. 3 February 1937. Bentley Historical Library, University of Michigan. Ralph W. Aigler Papers, 87406 Aa 2; Box 7, folder:correspondence "S" misc. (SA-SP)

[45] Aigler to Salsinger. 10 January 1945. Bentley Historical Library, University of Michigan. Ralph W. Aigler Papers, 87406 Aa 2; Box 8, folder:correspondence 1940-45 "S" misc.

[46] Aigler to Griffith. 14 February 1939. Bentley Historical Library, University of Michigan. Ralph W. Aigler Papers, 87406 Aa 2; Box 6, folder:correspondence 1934-39

mentioning the problem the university was having with its perception about the state. He used the word "snobbishness" to describe how both the press and public viewed the university regarding its stance on the Spartan initiative. Salsinger responded to the professor's concerns.

> You say that it is not snobbishness that keeps Michigan State out of the
> Western Conference but I repeat that it is. At the same time I want to
> emphasize that it is not snobbishness on Michigan's part because Michigan
> State's schedule absolutely proves that it is not, but there are a few other
> members of the Western Conference that are not quite in line with
> Michigan, a few others who pursue the holier-than-thou attitude.[47]

Regardless of the sportswriter's comments, Aigler's raising the subject about institutional arrogance suggests it was a major concern for the university.

One decade later, in early October of 1953, Governor G. Mennen Williams, anticipating the inaugural Big Ten season for Michigan State, proposed a trophy to honor the winner of the annual Michigan-Michigan State game. But the University of Michigan was vehemently opposed to sharing any trophy with the Spartans. Its leadership wanted nothing to do with elevating the intrastate rivalry to a game comparable to the Ohio State or Minnesota contests held each year.

A special Board in Control of Intercollegiate Athletics meeting was called in Ann Arbor to devise a plan to counter the initiative from the State Capitol. Arthur L. Brandon, director of University Relations, was invited to the gathering. Apparently his skills were needed in addressing the politically delicate matter promoted by a very popular governor. Fritz Crisler summarized his recommendations.

> Mr. Brandon's opinion … was that he thought we were dealing with a
> pretty warm subject …he thought the matter should not be decided by this
> Board [in control] at this time because if we took the responsibility, we
> would again be considered the snooty University of Michigan and were not
> cooperative with the other institution.[48]

Brandon's comments implied that there was some history behind this perception of being "snooty" or "snobbish."

THE UNDERWOOD Alliteration, "arrogant asses in Ann Arbor," was a phrase that Biggie Munn and Duffy Daugherty used to charge up the troops during Michigan week in East Lansing. Daryl Rogers borrowed it, not to denigrate the University of Michigan, as implied by certain sportswriters, but to "poke fun" at a sister institution sharing a very intense intrastate rivalry.[49]

Despite maintaining a perception–at least in the opinion of many Spartan faithful–

---

[47] Salsinger to Aigler. 31 January 1943. Bentley Historical Library, University of Michigan. Ralph W. Aigler Papers, 87406 Aa 2; Box 8, folder:correspondence 1940-45 "S" misc.

[48] Minutes of the Meeting of the Board in Control of Intercollegiate Athletics. 16 October 1953. Bentley Historical Library, University of Michigan. Herbert Orin Crisler Papers, 85823 AC UAm Aa 2; Box 6, folder: The University Board in Control of Intercollegiate Athletics 1953-54

[49] Rogers, Darryl. 27 February 2009. Personal communication.

of institutional arrogance towards Michigan State, the University of Michigan has collaborated with the school for well over a century.[50] Ralph Aigler, Fritz Crisler, and John Hannah (on Ralph Young's stationary) acknowledged that conviction at various times during the 1940s.[51] [52] [53] The schools complement each other in fields of research and education. Each institution has its unique interests at the regional, national and international levels.[54] Missions are clearly defined in both Ann Arbor and East Lansing; they reflect the vision and dedication of gifted leadership, both past and present.

One of those brilliant leaders arrived in Ann Arbor back in 1852. Henry Phillip Tappan's vision still guides the University of Michigan. Another leader returned to East Lansing on January 1, 1935, as secretary of the State Board of Agriculture.[55] Within six years John Hannah would assume the presidency of Michigan State. His vision and leadership ultimately proved him a giant, not only in academia, but in service to his country and to the world.

---

[50] Duderstadt, James J. 1 May 2009. Personal communication.

[51] Aigler to Wilson. 8 August 1945. Bentley Historical Library, University of Michigan. Ralph W. Aigler Papers, 87406 Aa 2; Box 8, folder: correspondence 1940-45 misc. Wilson

[52] Young to Crisler. 28 December 1942. Bentley Historical Library, University of Michigan. Herbert Orin Crisler Papers, 85823 AC UAm Aa2; Box 1, folder: MSU correspondence 1943-46

[53] Crisler to Ruthven. 13 January 1943. Bentley Historical Library, University of Michigan. Herbert Orin Crisler Papers, 85823 AC UAm Aa2; Box 1, folder: MSU correspondence 1943-46

[54] Duderstadt, James J. 1 May 2009. Personal communication.

[55] Minutes of the State Board of Agriculture. 22 November 1934. www.onthebanks.msu.edu.

John Hannah: Visionary on a Mission

"John Hannah and I worked together for many years to achieve civil rights in this country. I cherish his memory as one of the finest persons I have ever met."

Theodore M. Hesburgh[1]

HENRY PHILLIP Tappan arrived in Ann Arbor in 1852. His vision was that the University of Michigan would become a great research institution focused on the sciences and the professions, including medicine and law. His university was to be the "home for scholars dedicated to the expansion of human understanding."[2] Unlike the prominent colleges out east that catered to a certain class of people, the only obligation for matriculating at Michigan was an intellectual penchant for question and discovery. Graduate studies were emphasized.

Justin Smith Morrill maintained a very different vision for higher education. For the practical congressman from Vermont, a utilitarian education was of greater significance to young men and women during a time when the United States was advancing westward, territories were transitioning to statehood, and former trading posts, such as Detroit and Chicago, were evolving into major cities.

In 1857 the congressman proposed what would become known as the Morrill Act. The intent of the legislation was to create colleges capable of educating "those vocational groups which existing colleges and universities were neglecting in their devotion to the learned professions."[3] It became law with President Abraham Lincoln's signature on July 2, 1862.

---

[1] Hesburgh, Theodore M. "John Hannah." E-Mail to David J. Young. 4 January 2010
[2] Duderstadt, James J. *A View From the Helm.* Ann Arbor: The University of Michigan Press, 2007. p. 11
[3] Kuhn, Madison. *Michigan State: The First One Hundred Years-1955.* East Lansing: Michigan State University Press, 1955. p. 287

The Morrill Land-Grant Colleges Act "specified that its 'leading object shall be, without excluding other scientific and classical studies, and including military tactics, to teach such branches of learning as are related to agriculture and the mechanic arts, in order to promote the liberal and practical education of the industrial classes in the several pursuits and professions of life.'"[4] The decree, of sorts, called for one institution in each state to be dedicated to this mission. Financial support for the schools would be provided by federal lands granted to the states. An endowment fund, based on the sale of those tracts, would support operations at the institution. The infrastructure costs remained the obligation of the taxpayers.[5]

The significance of Justin Morrill's vision lay in its focus on economic development.

> The Morrill Act generated support for a system of higher education that dramatically expanded American democracy, which helped to lead the way for economic growth in the United States. Land-Grant universities trained engineers, agriculturalists, and scientists who made possible the "managerial revolution" that built the American economy in the late nineteenth and twentieth centuries. Men and women applied skills learned in their study of science, mathematics, agriculture, domestic science, economics, literature, and history to provide leadership in all realms of life … No longer would higher education be limited primarily to the children of the nation's social and economic elite.[6]

Agriculture still commanded a large percentage of the gross domestic product at the time; non-agrarian enterprises, enabled by the Industrial Revolution, were gradually assuming a greater share of that measure of economic growth. The Morrill Act addressed both through its emphasis on practical or vocational education.

THE AGRICULTURAL College of the State of Michigan was founded in 1855. Recently passed legislation mandated a school dedicated to agrarian sciences. Land was set aside along the Red Cedar River adjacent to the small town of East Lansing. A few buildings were constructed for instruction and laboratory research. Students learned skills necessary for efficient and productive farming. Farmland just south of the river banks was toiled over for use in practical research. It became the model farm that Henry Phillip Tappan disdained.

Seven years later the United States Congress passed the Morrill Act of 1862. The small agricultural college was almost broke. Fully aware of the innovative legislation passed by Congress, its administrators applied for the federal grants necessary to sustain operations. Legally chartered and operational at the time Lincoln penned his name to Morrill's bill, the college was first in line to receive 250,000 acres of federal property. It became the pioneer land-grant institution. Tracts of heavily wooded northern Michigan

---

[4] Kuhn, Madison. *Michigan State: The First One Hundred Years-1955.* East Lansing: Michigan State University Press, 1955. p. 287

[5] Widder, Keith R. *Michigan Agricultural College: The Evolution of a Land-Grant Philosophy, 1855-1925.* East Lansing: Michigan State University Press, 2005. p. 2

[6] Ibid., pp. 47-48

property would eventually be sold off for college revenue.[7] The Agricultural College of Pennsylvania, Ohio State, Purdue, Illinois, Wisconsin, and Minnesota followed the lead set by The State Agricultural College.

Early on the school struggled with its original mission while pursuing the land-grant mandate. The addition of mechanics, later known as engineering, was controversial. The college had been created to meet the unique needs of agriculture.[8] The Morrill Act altered the intent of that state legislation. But in accepting the federal grant, the faculty was obligated to "teach such branches ... related to agriculture and the mechanic arts ..." The farmers had no choice; their school desperately needed the endowment.[9]

As the college continued to grow under the Morrill mandate, administrators sought more accurate school-related names to reflect curricular changes taking place. It was "difficult to interest high school graduates in studying mechanical engineering or home economics in an 'agricultural college.'" A degree in non-agrarian studies from such a college, some reasoned, might hinder employment opportunities. So what started as the Agricultural College of the State of Michigan in 1855 became The State Agricultural College in 1861, with initial emphasis on State as opposed to Agricultural. By 1909 the school adopted the title Michigan Agricultural College. Sixteen years later the legislature approved changing the name once again to Michigan State College of Agriculture and Applied Sciences. That designation remained for 30 years.[10]

In 1955, following a very contentious legal battle with the University of Michigan over the proprietary rights of the words "university" and "Michigan," the name was changed to Michigan State University of Agriculture and Applied Science.[11] [12] [13] [14] The college had been offering advanced degrees for years; the designation was fitting. With the new state constitution ratified in the early 1960s, the original land-grant college was finally acknowledged as Michigan State University.

By comparison, Catholepistemiad of Michigania went through just one name change since its founding in 1817. The parochial school became the secular University of Michigan in 1821.

Michigan State, on the other hand, with six different school names on its diplomas during its first 100 years, appeared to struggle with its identity. This may have reinforced the perception of it being "subordinate" to the university–an institution based in East

---

[7] Kuhn, Madison. *Michigan State: The First One Hundred Years-1955*. East Lansing: Michigan State University Press, 1955. pp. 73-75

[8] Widder, Keith R. *Michigan Agricultural College: The Evolution of a Land-Grant Philosophy 1855-1925*. East Lansing: Michigan State University Press, 2005. p. 138

[9] Kuhn, Madison. *Michigan State: The First One Hundred Years-1955*. East Lansing: Michigan State University Press, 1955. pp. 47-49

[10] Ibid., p. 303

[11] Hatcher to Williams. 27 January 1954. Bentley Historical Library, University of Michigan. G. Mennen Williams Papers; Boards and Commissions, 1954: colleges, state, MSU

[12] "Letter to Michigan Alumni." February 1954. Bentley Historical Library. University of Michigan. G. Mennen Williams Papers; Boards and Commissions, 1954: colleges, state, MSU

[13] Stason to Hatcher. 25 February 1955. Bentley Historical Library. University of Michigan, Harlan Hatcher Papers. Aa2 Ac; Box 53: MSU name and letters to Blythe Stason

[14] Stason to Hatcher. 10 May 1955. Bentley Historical Library. University of Michigan, Harlan Hatcher Papers. Aa2 Ac; Box 53: MSU name and letters to Blythe Stason

Lansing that was uncertain of its purpose–validating Michigan's claim of superiority that had originated with Henry Phillip Tappan. It would take a new president at Michigan State to ultimately change that perception.

JOHN HANNAH was born in Grand Rapids, Michigan, on October 9, 1902. His childhood years were atypical. Early on he displayed a zeal for hard work, a commitment to assist his parents in the family business, an interest in self-directed education, and a penchant for leadership.

John was the oldest of four children raised by Wilfred and Mary Hannah. His father's primary business was owning and operating Grand Rapids Floral Company. Wilfred maintained gardens and greenhouses adjacent to the family home. He also bred poultry. Due to constraints on his time, the elder Hannah turned the operational responsibility for the small poultry business over to his son at the age of six. He handled the task with surprising aplomb. The younger Hannah developed interests in breeding unusual birds and showed his prizes at state and county fairs about the region. Leadership skills followed. By his high school years he had become secretary of the West Michigan Poultry Association, which led to a position in the State Poultry Association. He ultimately became superintendent of the Poultry Department at the West Michigan State Fair in Grand Rapids and later the Michigan State Fair in Detroit.[15]

Needless to say, John Hannah had little interest in athletics as a boy. He was too busy with his work in scientific agriculture to devote time to games and competition with other students.

Following graduation from high school, at age 16, John attended Grand Rapids Junior College, intent on becoming a lawyer. In 1920, after two years there, he transferred to the University of Michigan to study law. At that time Michigan offered an undergraduate LL.B, as well as a graduate LL.M and LL.D legal degree.[16]

After one year in law school he questioned continuing studies in Ann Arbor. Finances were limited.[17] But he had also become disenchanted with certain aspects of the legal training he was receiving. Years later, Hannah's University of Chicago consultant on curriculum development, Floyd Reeves, shared some of young John's idealistic reasons for departing the university.

> He did not like [legal studies] because schools [like Michigan] trained so
> many [students] to fight for narrow interpretations of the law rather than for
> a broader idea of securing justice for people.[18]

Hannah's experience at the University of Michigan would shape his character and remain a creedal compass throughout his life.

Professor Reeves noted how Hannah often used that "compass" while serving Michigan State as secretary of the State Board of Agriculture and later as president.

---

[15] Hannah, John A. *A Memoir.* East Lansing: Michigan State University Press, 1980. pp. 9-14

[16] Williams, Brian. "Re; history of law school, stadium capacities." Email to David J. Young. 15 November 2010.

[17] Hannah, John A. *A Memoir.* East Lansing: Michigan State University Press, 1980. p. 15

[18] Reeves, Floyd. 11 June 1970. Michigan State University Archives, Hannah Archives Project, UA2.1.12; Box 34, folder 37

I found … his philosophy on the relationship of justice to the letter of the law … carry right over to his operation of [the college]. Before I decided to come [to Michigan State] on a full-time basis in 1953, I had learned that Hannah [always sought] justice … he would lean over backward–he would be willing to violate the letter of the law if necessary in order to carry out the spirit of the law.[19]

This concept of justice or fairness would ultimately shape his thoughts on how colleges and universities should recompense student-athletes. His convictions proved extremely controversial among certain amateur purists including Ralph Aigler and Herbert Orin Crisler of the University of Michigan.

On January 9, 1946, Hannah gave an eloquent and honest keynote address at the Fortieth Annual Convention of the NCAA in St. Louis, Missouri. He denounced the utter hypocrisy of institutions professing adherence to the amateur code of the NCAA while practicing otherwise. Schools were condoning illicit subsidies to their athletes in pursuit of victories on the gridiron. The same colleges and universities that were charged with forming the character of future leaders in government, industry, and academia were compromising their own institutional integrity.

Hannah spoke of "securing justice" at two levels in intercollegiate athletics. On one level, institutions had to compete fairly by adhering to a code of sportsmanship and ethics. On another, if compatible with their missions, institutions must financially assist athletes in a transparent manner comparable to that offered the non-athletes. Faculty scholarship committees would service both the athlete and non-athlete alike; names of all beneficiaries should be published by the college. The integrity of the institution and its leadership, he said, would be assured through public scrutiny.[20]

The speech was well received–and his recommendations were ignored. A few years later, in January of 1948, the NCAA would adopt the Sanity Code. A faction of purists, including Ralph Aigler of the University of Michigan, promoted the code in response to the growing practice of offering athletic, rather than academic, scholarships to athletes. But because it lacked any effective means of enforcement, the code was essentially rescinded in January of 1950.

In late 1951 Hannah was asked to chair an ad hoc committee of the Association of College Educators (ACE) charged with defining acceptable financial aid for athletes. Institutional presidents had taken it upon themselves to deal with the subsidy problem in the aftermath of the Sanity Code debacle. In his influential position as chair, Hannah was charged with manipulating the ACE recommendations. The purists of amateurism, including Ralph Aigler, argued that he pushed his own agenda for legally sanctioning grants or awards for athletes.[21]

---

[19] Reeves, Floyd. 11 June 1970. Michigan State University Archives, Hannah Archives Project, UA2.1.12; Box 34, folder 37

[20] Hannah, John A. "Speech of Dr. John A. Hannah at the Fortieth Annual Convention of the National Collegiate Athletic Association." 9 January 1946. Bentley Historical Library, University of Michigan Archives. Herbert Orin Crisler Papers, 85823 AC UAm Aa 2; Box 1, folder: topical correspondence, Michigan State University clippings and misc.

[21] Watterson, John Sayle. *College Football: History-Spectacle-Controversy.* Baltimore: The Johns Hopkins University Press, 2000. pp. 227-240

By the mid to late 1950s the athletic scholarship would become a legitimate means of subsidizing student-athletes. It coincided with the retirement of long-serving faculty representative Ralph Aigler from the University of Michigan in 1955.

A YOUNG John Hannah, studying law at Michigan during the winter months of 1921-1922, was visited by Professor E. C. Foreman. Still active in state poultry leadership, the student was well known to the director of the innovative extension service program at Michigan Agricultural College. Privy to Hannah's financial plight, Foreman encouraged him to transfer and pursue a degree in agriculture. He promised him a job as an outreach agent serving poultry breeders about the state upon graduation.[22] This concept of continuing education, first explained to Hannah by Foreman while the two met in Ann Arbor, would guide his educational philosophy throughout his career.

Although spending only one year at the University of Michigan, the experience was not in vain for the young Hannah. He became enamored with athletics and, in particular, college football. The heightened excitement about campus during the week leading up to the 1921 Ohio State game in Ann Arbor left an indelible mark on him.[23] He was impressed with how football promoted esprit de corps. Years later he would comment on the value of intercollegiate sport.

> Athletics unify a university probably more than any other feature of the institution. They merge the enthusiasm of students, alumni, faculty, friends and supporters of the university, and all to the university's good.[24]

Hannah moved to East Lansing and completed requirements for his degree in one year. With the support of Dean Robert Sidey Shaw of the Agriculture Department, he was able to test out of many classes. Shaw merely required rigorous oral exams verifying scholastic competency; Hannah's years of self-directed study had gained him the proficiency in the agrarian sciences that he needed.[25] He graduated in the late spring of 1923, having taken on a heavy credit load to complete his degree. There was no time to attend Aggie football games during the demanding year.

After graduation, Professor Foreman hired the 20-year-old Hannah and, as promised, offered him a position as a poultry science specialist in the extension service at the college. These agents were expected to instruct farmers on recent developments in their area of agrarian interest. With the emphasis on providing a practical outreach education for the farmer, any problems or difficulties that became apparent during regional visits to the farms were to be researched by the extension service and the professors back in East Lansing. Dean Shaw's department oversaw the work. All agents ultimately reported to him.

Hannah proved a very popular and successful agent. One of his assets was "an uncanny ability to appraise the knowledgability of his audience and to accordingly set a pattern of presentation that was understood." Hannah "impressed [the farmers] with his quiet handsomeness, his modesty, his serious manner, and his quick understanding of the

---

[22] Hannah, John A. *A Memoir*. East Lansing: Michigan State University Press, 1980. p. 16

[23] Ibid., p. 15

[24] Ibid., p. 124

[25] Ibid., p. 17

reasons that could prompt a listener's questions"[26] While serving breeders about the state, he continued activities in regional and national poultry associations. He was gaining a reputation.

The job was taxing. Hannah spent over 200 days a year off campus. Despite being away from East Lansing for days at a time, he captured the attention of a few critical administrators at the college. The poultry expert displayed characteristics and keen intellect that the school sought in future leaders.

There were four significant events early in John Hannah's career that marked his rise to prominence at Michigan State. The first involved Dean Robert Shaw being asked to assume the presidency of the college in June of 1928. Dr. Shaw was an extremely well liked and capable leader. His unique relationship with Hannah, first as mentor and then as boss, would prove fortuitous seven years later, in the summer of 1934.

The second critical event in Hannah's rise was his being offered the managing director position with National Poultry Breeders and Hatchery Code based in Kansas City, Missouri. President Shaw granted him a leave of absence in 1932 to assume this role in the federal government. At age 30, Hannah was given the authority to formulate and implement policy for the entire poultry industry. A second leave was approved the following year. But despite being successful in this position, Hannah found the work unfulfilling. The private agricultural concerns that he dealt with, however, were impressed with his intelligence, knowledge, and management skills; one large Chicago food-packaging company offered him a salary three times his current income to "head up [its] produce department or that part of it [dealing] with poultry, eggs, and butter."[27] He declined the offer.[28] His real interest, by late fall of 1933, was a return to East Lansing and employment with the college.[29]

In November of 1932, the State Board of Agriculture, the oversight body for Michigan State College, mandated that the "responsibility for the administration of the College [fall] under the direct supervision of the State Board of Agriculture and the President …" No longer would the secretary of the board–the business manager for the college–act independent of the president in daily operations. He was now obligated to report directly to that office.[30] This became official state law in late 1933,[31] promoting a close working relationship between the president and secretary. Unknown to John Hannah at the time, this change in college operations would profoundly impact his ascent to the presidency.

The final event leading to Hannah's advancement at Michigan State came with the retirement of Board Secretary Herman Halladay. It led President Shaw, in late summer of 1934, to personally drive to Chicago to visit with Hannah, who was still on leave from the college while serving the federal government. Shaw asked Hannah to assume the position vacated by Halladay. The Grand Rapids native was 32 at the time.

---

[26] Thomas, David. *Michigan State College: John Hannah and the Creation of a World University, 1926-1969.* East Lansing: Michigan State University Press, 2008. p. 11

[27] Hannah, John A. *A Memoir.* East Lansing: Michigan State University Press, 1980. p. 20

[28] "University Presidents: Exit Methuselah." *Time* 21 March 1969: 42. Hannah was reportedly offered $18,000 per year to assume the position in Chicago. His salary as secretary of the State Board was $4,500.

[29] Hannah, John A. *A Memoir.* East Lansing: Michigan State University Press, 1980. pp. 19-20

[30] Special Meeting of the State Board of Agriculture. 25 November 1932. www.onthebanks.msu.edu

[31] Minutes of the State Board of Agriculture. 19 October 1933. www.onthebanks.msu.edu

Becoming secretary of the board would, in essence, make Hannah the chief operating officer of the college under Shaw's oversight. He would be in charge of all matters unrelated to academics. President Shaw proved persuasive. John Hannah accepted the position. On January 1, 1935, he assumed the administrative role. Due to the 1933 state law, he would work closely with the president on a daily basis. The experience, under the adept mentoring of Shaw, ultimately proved invaluable.

Over the next six years Hannah would serve with distinction, gaining the respect of colleagues and State Board members.

At the board meeting of December 21, 1940, President Shaw announced his desire to retire by the end of the academic year. The members approved his request. Following that decision, the board met in executive session. It was moved by Melville McPherson and seconded by Lavina Masselink to tender the position to John Alfred Hannah effective July 1, 1941. The vote was unanimous. Secretary Hannah was summoned back to the board room where he accepted the call to serve his alma mater.[32]

THE PRESS release, approved by the State Board of Agriculture on December 21, 1940, announced the surprising promotion of a man lacking a doctorate to the presidency of Michigan State. Of perhaps comparable intrigue, the statement also included a very nearsighted vision for the college following the departure of Robert Shaw.

> The Board is aware of the splendid progress that has been made in the fields of Engineering, Home Economics, Veterinary Medicine, Applied Sciences and Liberal Arts but feel the President of the College should be a man with a keen appreciation of the importance of maintaining and increasing the effectiveness of the services of the College to the agricultural interests of Michigan. Mr. Hannah is a graduate of the Agricultural Division of the College. He served for ten years as an extension poultry man and is internationally known for his work in this field. He was engaged in special work for the U.S.D.A. when he was asked to become Secretary of the College and gave up a more lucrative position to take over that position where his conduct has made him a natural selection for promotion to the office of the presidency of Michigan State College.[33]

That statement by the board supported the status quo at Michigan State College of Agriculture and Applied Science. The vision for the school would remain agrarian. The views of the man they chose to lead the school, however, would be much farther sighted.

JOHN ALFRED Hannah, upon assuming leadership of the college, envisioned Michigan State evolving into a huge land-grant research institution. He foresaw the school expanding its influence, through the extension-service concept, to all corners of the world.

In his position of prominence, he would take on issues of social justice. The new president instituted international studies with the plan of allowing peoples of all faiths, traditions, cultures, and skin colors to matriculate at Michigan State. A man of character and

---

[32] Minutes of the State Board of Agriculture in Executive Session. 21 December 1940. www.onthebanks.msu.edu

[33] Ibid.

openness, Hannah wanted to serve all people.

The new president was actively involved in civil and human rights well before such involvement became politically and socially correct. He publicly supported allowing black teachers to instruct at Michigan State. He integrated the dormitories years before other colleges did. Hannah "… struck racial identification from student records, refused [athletic] games where Negroes would suffer discrimination, and rejected a Negro 'quota' for the faculty on the ground that 'it is not the policy [nor] practice of the university to examine the color of a man's skin for the purpose of either qualifying or disqualifying him from employment.'"[34]

During his tenure in the Eisenhower administration as assistant secretary of defense for manpower and personnel in 1953-54, Hannah "ordered integration of remaining all-Negro fighting units and the all-white elementary schools on the southern bases."[35] His leadership earned President Dwight Eisenhower's respect. Hannah was later asked to assume the secretary of defense position in July of 1957. After "going through a soul-searching experience," he opted to remain at Michigan State University of Agriculture and Applied Science.[36]

But President Eisenhower recognized his talent and remained persistent. He again sought Hannah's services later that year for what turned out to be a task of historic proportions. John Hannah accepted Eisenhower's call to be the first chair of the U.S. Commission on Civil Rights, a position he held from 1957 until 1969.

The commission was originally formed by the Congress to appease liberal factions disturbed with racial injustice pervasive in the Deep South. "There was no desire for legislation on the part of Eisenhower … and Jack Kennedy knew the bill we ultimately proposed would harm his chances for re-election."[37] It would take the tragedy of November 1963 and the transition of presidential power to Lyndon Johnson for the Civil Rights Act of 1964, as drafted by Hannah, Reverend Theodore Hesburgh of Notre Dame, and the commission, to be signed into law. It remains one of the most significant legislative enactments in the history of the country.

John Hannah led in other ways as well during his storied tenure at Michigan State. In his inaugural address of 1949, President Harry Truman outlined his vision for foreign policy in the postwar era. Called the "Four Points," it would guide U.S. diplomacy in the evolving Cold War years.

> "… a fourth point in foreign policy: 'to help the free peoples of the world, through their own efforts, to produce more food,' clothing, housing, [and] power to 'realize their aspiration for a better life' [was announced by the newly elected president]. Mr. Hannah immediately volunteered the 'full cooperation' of the Land Grant schools. Here, he pointed out, was an opportunity to carry out the extension service to the world's troubled

---

[34] Kuhn, Madison. Circa 1976. Michigan State University Archives. Hannah Archives Project, UA2.1.12.2; Box 34, folder: 27 "John Hannah"

[35] Ibid.

[36] Hannah to Morrill. 12 July 1957. University of Minnesota Archives, James L. Morrill; Box 1, folder: correspondence A-L HA-HE

[37] Hesburgh, Theodore M. Personal communication. 17 October 2008

areas."[38]

Truman subsequently nominated President Hannah to the advisory board for the "Four Points." Hannah used that appointment to "[urge] universities to accept their greatest opportunity in history ... he asked business groups to see in this, not another costly give-away program, but a thrifty investment in helping underdeveloped areas [to] grow by their own efforts."[39]

The college president, once again, was ahead of his time. His experience as an extension service agent for Michigan Agricultural College, a few decades earlier, had led him to envision applying a similar concept at a global level. Senator John Kennedy, perhaps unwittingly, would borrow on Hannah's adaptation of Truman's Four Points, and propose the Peace Corps, late at night on October 14, 1961, on the steps of the Michigan Union Building in Ann Arbor. Instead of using professors and support staff from colleges and universities, Kennedy's election-year proposal, essentially based on the land-grant concept of extension service, would encourage graduates of those institutions to volunteer their skills to peoples around the globe.

John Hannah built on the foundation of an agricultural college, signed into law in 1855, and created a great university by his retirement in 1969. Students and alumni have been challenged to continue his vision of extending service beyond family to include neighbors, communities, regions, country, and the world.

---

[38] Kuhn, Madison. Circa 1976. Michigan State University Archives. Hannah Archives Project, UA2.1.12.2; Box 34, folder: 27 "John Hannah"
[39] Ibid.

Application Denied!

FOOTBALL WAS introduced to The State Agricultural College in June of 1886, seven years after the game was adopted by the University of Michigan. It was rough going at first, with losses to Olivet and Albion, two small denominational colleges in mid Michigan. But by 1908, the Aggies dominated all athletics, including football, within the Michigan Intercollegiate Athletic Association (MIAA), a conference it helped found 20 years earlier. Out of frustration, in large part due to an inability to compete, the six fellow members–Hillsdale, Olivet, Albion, Kalamazoo, Alma, and the Normal School at Ypsilanti–banded together and expelled the much larger state institution. The small, predominantly private schools demonstrated their collective power. The practice of athletic Darwinism, based on control of large gate receipts, was still a decade away.

The Aggies found victories difficult to achieve against more formidable opponents as an independent. Coach John Macklin had some success during his tenure from 1911 to 1915, but the next seven seasons were inconsistent and disappointing. With its program in steady decline, and Old College Field still seating only 4,000,[1] the school found scheduling competition for home-and-away games an onerous task. At a time when money had begun entering the game, competitors bypassed East Lansing for sites offering a greater return on investment for weekend travel.[2] The Aggies were left with contests against old foes from the MIAA and far-off institutions lacking football traditions.

Notre Dame severed its relationship with the Aggies following the 1921 season. Over the course of 25 years the schools had competed 14 times. It was a good rivalry, but the modest gate receipts in East Lansing, shared between the two institutions, made the Irish decide against renewing the biennial contract.[3] It was a devastating loss for MAC.

This occurred during the early years of coach Knute Rockne's successful reign in

---

[1] Widder, Keith. *Michigan Agricultural College: The Evolution of a Land-Grant Philosophy, 1855-1925.* East Lansing: Michigan State University Press, 2005. p. 382

[2] Soderstrom, Robert M. *The Big House: Fielding H. Yost and the Building of Michigan Stadium.* Ann Arbor: Huron River Press, 2005. pp. 108-109

[3] Bachman, Charles. "The Athletic Side of John Hannah." Circa 1970. Michigan State University Archives. Hannah Archives Project, UA 2.1.12.2; Box 34, folder: 2 Bachman

South Bend. Due to its denominational identity, Notre Dame had developed a national following among the large Catholic immigrant population inhabiting major northern cities at the turn of the century. A few large venues were considered home games for the Irish. The 1925 Notre Dame-Navy game drew 125,000 spectators to Soldier Field in Chicago, most of them Irish supporters. In the pre-television era, that translated into an enormous gate return for both schools.[4] Notre Dame Stadium, back home in South Bend, had a capacity of 55,000 when completed in 1930. There was little logic, from a financial perspective, in maintaining the series with the Michigan college.

The Irish agreed to welcome the Aggies back on their schedule if and when shared receipts justified a home-and-home series, but that would require a stadium in East Lansing seating well over 30,000.[5] Until that time, in the opinion of Notre Dame Athletic Board Chairman Dean James E. McCarthy, the rivalry with the college would be held in abeyance.[6]

So the Aggies faced a conundrum in the early 1920s. In order to attract quality opponents necessary to resurrect its program, a larger-capacity facility, capable of generating significant dollars, was needed on campus. But to justify enlarging Old College Field, or even building a new stadium, the State Board of Agriculture demanded numbers that would make bond sales to finance the project feasible.

With the loss of the Irish contract, the State Board, in March of 1922, finally agreed to build a new facility.[7] In June, the administration secured a loan for $160,000 to finance a 15,000 seat stadium.[8] With bleachers, College Field could accommodate almost 20,000 ticket holders.[9]

Construction was completed in time for the 1923 season. The potential revenue, however, failed to meet Notre Dame's requirements. Other prominent athletic institutions, including most Western Conference schools with much larger stadiums, followed the Irish lead and declined contracts with the Aggies.

SIXTY MILES away, in Ann Arbor, the University of Michigan faced a very different challenge. Despite a seating capacity more than twice that found in East Lansing, Ferry Field proved inadequate for Wolverine ticket demands of the mid-1920s. Athletic Director Fielding Yost proposed to his Board in Control and the university regents a stadium that could accommodate up to 85,000 with bleachers included. The controversial plan would at least double the capacity at Ferry Field. With numbers to support his audacious vision, Yost successfully sold his idea to the regents despite many naysayers, including Professor Ralph Aigler.[10] Bonds totaling $1.5 million funded the project.

---

[4] Lester, Robin. *Stagg's University: The Rise, Decline & Fall of Big-time College Football at Chicago.* Urbana and Chicago: University of Illinois Press, 1999. p. 132

[5] Bachman, Charles. "The Athletic Side of John Hannah." Circa 1970. Michigan State University Archives, Hannah Archives Project, UA2.1.12.2;. Box 34, folder: 2 Bachman

[6] Ibid.

[7] Widder, Keith. *Michigan Agricultural College: The Evolution of a Land-Grant Philosophy, 1855-1925.* East Lansing: Michigan State University Press, 2005. p. 390

[8] Meeting of the State Board of Agriculture. 16 June 1923. www.onthebanks.msu.edu

[9] Widder, Keith. *Michigan Agricultural College: The Evolution of a Land-Grant Philosophy, 1855-1925.* East Lansing: Michigan State University Press, 2005. p. 390

[10] Soderstrom, Robert M. *The Big House: Fielding H. Yost and the Building of Michigan Stadium.*

Yost's stadium would prove much more valuable than its projected cost, offering shared revenue far in excess of that gained from smaller stadia about the conference. It reaffirmed the decisive political role the university held within the Western Conference. And, for its state rival, an hour away by bus, the facility also defined the dominant relationship the university held over Michigan State College for the next three decades. The Spartans, maintaining a facility seating at most 20,000, clearly valued that shared revenue attained with the sales of an additional 65,000 tickets.

Michigan Stadium rarely filled to capacity during its early years. A major reason was that its 1927 completion closely correlated with the stock market crash of 1929 and the onset of the Great Depression. By 1940, the university had paid off only one-third of its debt obligation, well below projections. Attendance figures in Ann Arbor averaged only 40,000 per game.[11] Ferry Field sat 41,000 when Yost proposed the bowled stadium. Ralph Aigler's objections, back in October of 1923, appeared prescient, in hindsight.[12] But no one could have predicted the Great Depression and its effect on ticket sales and debt obligations during the 1930s.[13]

Yost's gamble ultimately paid off. The bonds were retired in the years following the Second World War in large part due to his successor, Herbert Orin Crisler. The new director was the quintessential numbers cruncher. Attendance figures were closely monitored. It was critical for the financial viability of the athletic department that near capacity was achieved for two or three games each year. His records indicated those big draws included Ohio State, Minnesota, and Michigan State College. Crisler, like any good manager, was focused on ticket sales.[14] That obsession would impact his decisions on scheduling, for the most part, throughout his long tenure as athletic director.

Crisler's data also proved that another school, boycotted by Fielding Yost since 1910, was an even greater draw than the other traditional rivalries. Much to his financial frustration, however, the university was based in South Bend, Indiana.

Fielding Yost despised Notre Dame. His reasons appeared to date back to a game scheduled for November of 1910. A few months before the contest, Michigan insisted that two Irish athletes be declared ineligible and Notre Dame refused. A contentious debate followed, with no resolution. Within 24 hours of kickoff, Michigan pulled out of the game. The Yost Boycott would follow. It lasted 32 years.[15]

Despite press, alumni, and fan demand for games with the Irish, Yost would find reasons not to compete. His relationship with Coach Knute Rockne during the 1920s only added to that intransigence. Yost felt that the Irish legend and his school did not pursue fair play consistent with the Handbook policies of the Western Conference.[16] The coach was also troubled by a de facto national recruiting network that the Irish maintained in all major

Ann Arbor: Huron River Press, 2005. pp. 112-113

[11] Soderstrom, Robert M. *The Big House: Fielding H. Yost and the Building of Michigan Stadium.* Ann Arbor: Huron River Press, 2005. p. 354

[12] Ibid., pp. 112-113

[13] Ibid., p. 354

[14] Stadium attendance data. Bentley Historical Library, University of Michigan. Herbert Orin Crisler Papers, 85823 AC UAm Aa; Box 1, folder: topical correspondence MSU 1947-49

[15] Kryk, John. *Natural Enemies: Major College Football's Oldest, Fiercest Rivalry – Michigan vs. Notre Dame.* Lanham: Taylor Trade Publishing, 2007. p. 62

[16] Ibid., pp. 85-92

northern cities. Amos Alonzo Stagg of Chicago shared similar concerns.[17] They both felt that the network gave Rockne an unfair advantage in acquiring talent from well-organized Catholic school systems. Yost was consumed with competing on a "relatively" level playing field every Saturday in his later years.[18] That field, in his opinion, tilted towards Rockne and the Irish.

A year prior to his retirement in June of 1941, however, the athletic director, finally agreed to play Notre Dame in a home-and-home series for two years beginning in 1942. In addition to a great outcry by the press and fans to resume the rivalry around that time, the withdrawal of Chicago from football had conveniently opened a few weekend dates on the Wolverine schedule.[19] Following the second game of the Yost Series, Fritz Crisler would better understand why his predecessor had maintained the boycott for so many years.[20] But the former Princeton coach's opinions about the Irish may have been formed well before that controversial 1943 game.

Ralph Aigler's disdain for the athletic department and the football program at Notre Dame dated back years.[21] [22] [23] [24] No doubt, upon Crisler's arrival in Ann Arbor, the faculty representative and his athletic director educated the new coach on various reasons for having maintained the Yost Boycott since 1910.

The short-lived Michigan-Notre Dame series began in South Bend on November 14, 1942. The Wolverines defeated a very talented Irish team led by Frank Leahy in front of a full house. The following year the schools met in Ann Arbor. Attendance was 86,408, surpassing official capacity records for that time. Ticket sales totaled $189,658.11. That same year, Ohio State visited Ann Arbor the weekend prior to Thanksgiving. The Buckeye game drew 39,139 customers. Gross receipts were $69,879.62. Clearly Notre Dame was very good for business.[25]

The 1943 game was vindication for Leahy. The Irish crushed an ill-prepared Michigan team. Crisler was very diplomatic following the contest while heaping praise on the winner. In private, however, he had been plotting for one year to forego any future contact with Notre Dame.[26] As concurrent athletic director, he vowed to never let another

---

[17] Lester,Robin. *Stagg's University: The Rise, Decline & Fall of Big-Time Football at Chicago.* Urbana and Chicago: University of Illinois Press, 1999. p. 137

[18] Kryk, John. *Natural Enemies: Major College Football's Oldest, Fiercest Rivalry – Michigan vs. Notre Dame.* Lanham: Taylor Trade Publishing, 2007. p. 86

[19] Ibid., pp. 114-123

[20] Ibid., p. 142

[21] Ibid., p. 118

[22] Aigler to Griffith. 26 October 1932. Bentley Historical Library, University of Michigan. Ralph W. Aigler Papers, 87406 Aa 2; Box 3, folder: correspondence 1929-32 Griffith (1932)

[23] Aigler to Long. 12 May 1936. Bentley Historical Library, University of Michigan. Ralph W. Aigler Papers, 87406 Aa 2; Box 12, folder: athletic correspondence 1933-36 "L" misc.

[24] Aigler to Griffith. 13 January 1932. Bentley Historical Library, University of Michigan. Ralph W. Aigler Papers, 87406 Aa 2; Box 3, folder: correspondence Griffith 1932

[25] Untitled. 15 February 1949. Bentley Historical Library, University of Michigan. Herbert Orin Crisler Papers, 85823 AC UAm Aa 2; Box 1, folder: topical correspondence MSU 1943-46

[26] Kryk, John. *Natural Enemies: Major College Football's Oldest, Fiercest Rivalry – Michigan vs. Notre Dame.* Lanham: Taylor Trade Publishing, 2007. pp. 140-141

revenue-generating Wolverine team compete against the Irish.[27] It was a surprising decision for so savvy a businessman.

The dollars generated from games with the Irish were difficult to ignore. Crisler was still managing the enormous stadium debt he had inherited from Yost. Full-capacity crowds paid bills, including past-due bond obligations.[28]

In 1946 Crisler pleaded with Pittsburgh Athletic Director James Hagan to contract a game in Ann Arbor. "We should be able to make quite a bit of money … our ticket sales are amazing."[29] It was a surprising prediction. Just five years earlier, Pitt drew only 33,848 fans to a game in Michigan Stadium.[30] With its program still in disarray, the Panthers could not possibly draw a crowd comparable to a contest with the Irish.[31]

Likewise, Guy Mackey was encouraged to move the Boilermaker-Wolverine game to Michigan Stadium in 1948. Based on Crisler's calculations, a full house at Ross Ade Stadium could generate $70,000. If the game was played in Ann Arbor, he projected $185,000 split between the programs. "It is a matter of simple arithmetic … I don't know how your finances are but we certainly could use that money."[32] Of course the Wolverine director's predictions were based on a Purdue team capable of filling Michigan Stadium. But the attendance records he kept over the years failed to support those optimistic projections. His data indicated that the 1944 and 1945 contests, both played in Ann Arbor, had averaged only 46,402 fans.[33] Mackey didn't buy into the logic. The game remained in West Lafayette.

As an athletic director focused on balancing the Wolverine budget,[34] it must have pained Fritz Crisler to overlook the revenue that a Notre Dame contract would generate. But Crisler was also a man of conviction. He purportedly had numerous reasons for evading Irish requests for continuing the relationship with the Wolverines following the Yost Series.[35] The Crisler Boycott began in 1944. In essence, revealed only to his Board in

---

[27] Kryk, John. *Natural Enemies: Major College Football's Oldest, Fiercest Rivalry – Michigan vs. Notre Dame.* Lanham: Taylor Trade Publishing, 2007. pp. 140-141p. 153

[28] Crisler to the President, the Honorable Board of Regents and the University Council. January 1944. Bentley Historical Library, University of Michigan. Alexander Ruthven Papers, 86550 Aa, Uam; Box 36, folder: 22

[29] Crisler to Hagan. 7 October 1946. Bentley Historical Library, University of Michigan. Herbert Orin Crisler Papers, 85823 AC UAm Aa 2; Box 35, folder: Football Schedule: 1944, 46, 47

[30] Crisler to the President, the Honorable Board of Regents and the University Council. January 1945. Bentley Historical Library, University of Michigan. Ralph W. Aigler Papers, 87406 Aa 2; Box 13, folder: athletics 1940-48 Board in Control

[31] Wallace, Francis. 4 November 1939. "The Football Laboratory Explodes: The Climax in the Test Case at Pitt." *The Saturday Evening Post.* University of Pittsburgh Archives, 9/10-A; Box 1, folder: FF 772

[32] Crisler to Mackey. 16 February 1948. Bentley Historical Library, University of Michigan. Board in Control of Intercollegiate Athletics, 8729 Bimu F81 2; Box 35, folder: football schedules 1944, 1946, 1947

[33] MSC/Minnesota/Ohio. 15 February 1949. Bentley Historical Library, University of Michigan. Herbert Orin Crisler Papers, 85823 AC UAm Aa 2; Box 1, folder: topical correspondence MSU 1947-1949

[34] Ibid.

[35] Kryk, John. *Natural Enemies: Major College Football's Oldest, Fiercest Rivalry – Michigan vs. Notre Dame.* Lanham: Taylor Trade Publishing, 2007. pp. 153-157

Control of Intercollegiate Athletics, it became official university athletic policy a few years later. Serendipity played no small part in that evasive maneuver.

The temporary 9/6/2 scheduling agreement of 1940, proposed to accommodate the tier-two programs struggling for weekend dates with the powers of the conference, unexpectedly became official Handbook policy as of mid-December 1945. As long as all competition was completed by the Saturday before Thanksgiving, faculty leaders would permit the additional game. [36]

With one more weekend of play, however, the shrewd director and his board realized a unique opportunity to silence critics clamoring for an ongoing Notre Dame series. On October 4, 1946, the Board in Control unanimously approved a motion by Ralph Aigler that it "shall be the policy of this Board" that an east and west coast team, in addition to Michigan State, be guaranteed spots on its schedule every year. The reason for the proposal was to appease the university's national alumni base as well as assure an annual game with the Spartans on opening day.[37] As a consequence, Crisler could tactfully argue that university athletic policy, in concert with the 9/6/2 conference rule, precluded any additional contracts with non-conference regional schools. [38] [39] The Crisler Boycott would last 34 years.

Herbert Orin Crisler retired from the University of Michigan in the spring of 1968. Don Canham, chosen as his successor, inherited a projected budget deficit for the upcoming year. In reviewing both attendance and financial data, he noted that the Wolverines averaged only 67,000 paying customers in a stadium capable of accommodating over 100,000. He reassigned the current coach, Chalmers "Bump" Elliott, and hired Glen "Bo" Schembechler to revive the program.[40]

Canham also noted a lack of sellouts. To enhance the sale of season tickets, he alternated the years Michigan State and Ohio State came into town, but he also needed another school that could fill his stadium. Notre Dame was the answer. With the prodding of his friend, Irish Athletic Director Edward "Moose" Krause, Canham decided to terminate the Crisler Boycott in December of 1968.[41] For almost seven decades, other than the Yost Series of 1942-43, the schools had not met on the gridiron due to the staunch convictions of two very stubborn Michigan legends.[42] But finally, on September 23, 1978, the programs would resume a rivalry that dated back to 1887. Scheduling commitments precluded any competition prior to that date.[43]

---

[36] Minutes of the Joint Meeting of the Intercollegiate Conference of Faculty Representatives and Athletic Directors. 8 December 1945. Bentley Historical Library, University of Michigan. Athletic Department, 943 Bimu 2; Box 84, folder: Big 10 records 1941-52

[37] Minutes of the meeting of the Board in Control of Intercollegiate Athletics of the University of Michigan. 4 October 1946. Bentley Historical Library, University of Michigan. Board in Control of Intercollegiate Athletics, 8729 Bimu F81 2; Box 49, folder: BIC minutes Feb 1938-June 1950

[38] Crisler to Emmons. 28 September 1948. Bentley Historical Library, University of Michigan. Ralph W. Aigler Papers. 87406 Aa 2; Box 9, folder: correspondence 1946-52 "C" misc

[39] Kryk, John. *Natural Enemies: Major College Football's Oldest, Fiercest Rivalry – Michigan vs. Notre Dame.* Lanham: Taylor Trade Publishing, 2007. pp. 140-142

[40] Ibid., pp. 159-160

[41] Ibid., p. 160

[42] Ibid., pp. 85-103, 140-142

[43] Ibid., p. 161

The significance of Canham's business moves would, unwittingly, promote a unique relationship among three schools. His decision to resume play with Notre Dame introduced the "Tripartite Rivalry" to intercollegiate football.[44] Michigan, Notre Dame, and Michigan State have competed against each other on three separate weekends, in the early fall, almost every year since that historical match-up in September of 1978. The popularity of these games continues unabated.

UNLIKE HIS boycott against Notre Dame, Fielding Yost was obligated to continue the annual contest with Michigan State. He and his successor would mandate that the game be played in Ann Arbor every year, typically the first weekend of the autumn campaign.[45]

The scrimmage game was traditionally a poor draw for the Wolverines. But by "offering" the Spartans that date, rather than to other non-conference schools, Yost was assured of decent ticket sales for the season opener during the Depression years. Only Ohio State and Minnesota routinely exceeded the attendance figures from a Spartan visit.[46]

Prior to the College Field dedication game of 1924, the Wolverines had played the Aggies 17 times with only three games contested in East Lansing. Following that visit, it would be 24 years before Michigan would again compete on the gridiron adjacent to the Red Cedar River.

DURING AN earlier time, in July of 1914, Michigan Agricultural College had retained John Macklin as coach by offering him the added responsibilities of the athletic directorship. The board approved a shocking $4,000 salary with an "additional five hundred dollars to be paid from Athletic Association funds."[47] A winning coach, even back in 1914, was well worth the expenditure for a school struggling to maintain a viable program.

Macklin was very successful in East Lansing. During his five-year tenure, beginning in 1911, he won 29 games and lost only five. Included in that impressive record were two victories over the University of Michigan. Never before, since the series began in 1898, had the Aggies defeated the Wolverines.

The fact that Michigan was in the midst of its Decade of Defiance may have benefited Macklin. Fielding Yost's teams were not quite up to par with those he had led while in the Western Conference. The non-intercourse rule, implemented by the conference faculty representatives, proved an effective boycott against Michigan.[48] Lacking quality Midwest teams to schedule, Yost turned eastward.

In this ten year span, the Wolverines had compiled a dismal 11-13-3 record

---

[44] Yost, Fielding H. Untitled. Circa 1931. Bentley Historical Library, University of Michigan. Fielding Harris Yost Papers, 86327 Aa 2; Box 8, folder: miscellaneous. In a talk delivered later in his career, Yost commented on old rivalries. One in particular, the "Triangular Rivalry," involved Nebraska, Kansas and Missouri back when he coached the Lincoln school in 1898.

[45] Hannah to Ruthven. 24 September 1941. Bentley Historical Library, University of Michigan. Ralph W. Aigler Papers, 87406 Aa 2; Box 8, folder: correspondence 1940-45 "H" misc.

[46] Untitled. 15 February 1949. Bentley Historical Library, University of Michigan. Herbert Orin Crisler Papers, 85823 AC UAm Aa 2; Box 1, folder: topical correspondence MSU 1943-46

[47] Minutes of the State Board of Agriculture. 15 July 1914. www.onthebanks.msu.edu

[48] Behee, John. *Fielding Yost's Legacy to the University of Michigan.* Ann Arbor: Uhlrich's Books, 1971. p. 77

against its three principal archrivals: Penn, Syracuse, and Cornell. While Michigan had continued to adopt almost all of the evolving Big Ten guidelines, these Eastern schools did not. And for Yost, who probably took football rules more seriously than anyone in history, these numerous defeats rankled his very soul.[49]

By June of 1917, the University of Michigan was invited back into the Western Conference. Under the leadership of Ralph Aigler, the school reconciled its wayward past and resumed faculty control of athletics. Fielding Yost was a relieved man. He no longer had to compete against teams unwilling to abide by the conference rules he maintained adherence to, in principal, during his years of independence.[50]

Michigan Agricultural College's success during the Macklin years, against Yost and others, raised concerns regarding compliance with the NCAA amateur code in East Lansing. Eligibility was a major one. Similar to so many institutions of that time, the Aggies pursued questionable tactics in attracting talented athletes to the East Lansing. Itinerants participated in games. Academic requirements for matriculation were marginal. Rumors of payouts by boosters were pervasive.[51]

President Jonathan Snyder's response to those accusations was to offer Macklin the directorship of athletics in 1914. Snyder was a fan of football and enjoyed the success like everyone else. But as leader of the college, he was concerned about suspect practices that might impact the integrity of the school.[52] In granting him the new position, and salary increase, Snyder reminded Macklin of the vital role he played in maintaining the reputation of MAC. It appeared to be a discreet, yet effective, way of disciplining his coach.

> Your department is just as important as any other department in this institution and in some respects even more so. There is no one connected with the institution whose personal influence will count for more than your own.[53]

Snyder even "encouraged Macklin to hire a tutor for a football player who was having academic problems."[54] He wanted the program to continue its successful ways but with more oversight on Macklin's part. The president would not tolerate booster activities. Only qualified students could participate in athletics.

One year later Macklin resigned his two positions at the college to pursue business interests.[55] It may have just been an excuse. His departure, after all, coincided with the strengthening of the Athletic Council. The faculty and administration were granted more supervision over college athletics while student oversight and influence were profoundly

---

[49] Kryk, John. *Natural Enemies: Major College Football's Oldest, Fiercest Rivalry – Michigan vs. Notre Dame*. Lanham: Taylor Trade Publishing, 2007. p. 86

[50] Ibid.

[51] Widder, Keith. *Michigan Agricultural College: The Evolution of a Land-Grant Philosophy, 1855-1925*. East Lansing: Michigan State University Press, 2005. p. 377

[52] Ibid.

[53] Ibid.

[54] Ibid.

[55] Kuhn, Madison. *Michigan State: The First Hundred Years*. East Lansing: Michigan State University Press, 1955. p. 259

weakened.[56] Institutional integrity, for President Snyder, would not be compromised in pursuit of victories. Perhaps the burden of adhering to Snyder's dictum, and the enhanced faculty oversight, proved untenable for a coach hired to win football games in East Lansing.

In the absence of John Macklin, the football fortunes of Michigan Agricultural College languished over the next seven years. The State Board of Agriculture opted for change, feeling that a new direction in the athletic department and football program was necessary. Perhaps all that was required was an innovative leader willing to abide by Snyder's rules.

To that end, Knute Rockne was offered a three-year contract to coach Michigan State following the 1921 season. He was guaranteed $4,500 per year with incremental annual increases while coaching in East Lansing.[57] After much thought, Rockne opted to stay in South Bend.

In the meantime, Old College Field gave way to a new structure by 1923. With that achievement, the school soon changed its nickname from "Aggies" to "Spartans" in 1925. The latter designation evoked the tenacity of ancient Greek warriors.[58] [59] It also coincided with the adoption of a new name for the college, reflecting additional curricular offerings for students. The land-grant school was now known as Michigan State College of Agriculture and Applied Science.[60]

But changing the institution's name and moniker would not improve the performance of its football players on Saturday afternoons in East Lansing. Quality coaches, such as Rockne, and talented athletes were essential for a winning football tradition.

In March of 1923, Ralph Young was hired as head football coach and athletic director at Michigan Agricultural College at an annual salary of $6,000. His predecessor, Albert Barron, was no Knute Rockne. Only able to defeat former MIAA associates, he was relieved of his duties after just two seasons.

A few years later, certain alumni pushed for a more aggressive program. The Snyder dictum of 1914, and the introduction of faculty control in athletics, may have forced the issue. Ever since John Macklin's departure, it had been difficult for the college to win games against formidable opponents. Expressing concerns with "various aspects of the athletics of the college," the Detroit Club of Michigan State College Alumni approached President Kenyon Butterfield in March of 1926 and requested a reorganization of the Athletic Council. The implication was that the club wanted more involvement of non-faculty in deciding the course of athletics at Michigan State. (Just prior to its withdrawal from the Western Conference in 1908, the University of Michigan had lost faculty control to

[56] Widder, Keith. *Michigan Agricultural College: The Evolution of a Land-Grant Philosophy, 1855-1925*. East Lansing: Michigan State University Press, 2005. p. 388

[57] Stabley, Fred W. *The Spartans: Michigan State Football*. Tomball, Texas: Strode Publishers, 1988. pp. 53-55

[58] Widder, Keith. *Michigan Agricultural College: The Evolution of a Land-Grant Philosophy, 1855-1925*. East Lansing: Michigan State University Press, 2005. p. 393

[59] "Michigan State Official Athletic Site: Traditions." *Michigan State Official Website of Spartan Athletics*. 12/26/2009. www.msusports.com

[60] Widder, Keith. *Michigan Agricultural College: The Evolution of a Land-Grant Philosophy, 1855-1925*. East Lansing: Michigan State University Press, 2005. p. 79

outside influences in a somewhat similar manner.[61]) A State Board of Agriculture committee was appointed to study alumni grievances in greater detail.[62]

Despite no record in the board minutes of an ad hoc committee's recommendations, difficult decisions were made at the highest level. With a record of 18 wins, 22 losses, and one tie through 1927, Ralph Young was relieved of his football coaching duties but was retained as athletic director and track coach. Gridiron coaching was turned over to a young Harry Kipke in September of 1928. His arrival heralded a major transition in how the college would approach athletics. For $6,000 a year, the Spartans wagered a bet that the 28-year-old, with a Wolverine pedigree, would turn the college's football fortunes around.[63] Although Kipke was head coach in East Lansing for only 18 months, there was no suggestion of malfeasance prior to his resignation on June 20, 1929 to accept Fielding Yost's offer in Ann Arbor.[64] No requests for dollars from the State Board to finance recruiting trips or suspect speaking engagements were documented in board minutes. Kipke appeared to be compliant with the NCAA amateur code during his first job as a head coach. James Crowley, his successor, was another story.

"SLEEPY JIM" Crowley graduated from the University of Notre Dame du Lac in the spring of 1925. He excelled in an offensive backfield later immortalized as the "Four Horsemen." All-American status was one of his many accomplishments while being coached by Knute Rockne. Crowley later played some professional football before returning to the collegiate ranks as an assistant coach at the University of Georgia.

The 27-year-old Crowley signed on as head coach of the Spartans in late July of 1929; he began work on the first day of September. His guaranteed income was $6,000 per year.[65] Using the talent gathered by former coaches Kipke and Ralph Young, the Notre Dame great would lead the Spartans to five wins against three losses. His second season would be the most successful in 15 years for the Spartans. His overall record was five wins, one loss, and two ties–including one with eventual Big Ten co-champion Michigan. The talk on campus was all about Jim Crowley, his leadership, and his coaching style.[66]

Michigan State administrators, perhaps unwittingly, provided him with the tools necessary for attracting skilled ballplayers to East Lansing. Coinciding with the success of that first season, the State Board of Agriculture, concerned with maintaining enrollment figures during the early years of the Depression, agreed to establish a "fund from the accrued interest on the M.S.C. Fund, for the loaning of money to students who are unable to meet payment of fees on the first day of registration ... loans would be made on a one to ninety day basis subject to the approval of the Secretary of the College."[67]

The loan fund was intended for all students[68] but Crowley found it quite useful for

[61] Behee, John. *Fielding Yost's Legacy to the University of Michigan.* Ann Arbor: Uhlrich's Books Inc., 1971. p. 71

[62] Minutes of the State Board of Agriculture. 17 March 1926. www.onthebanks.msu.edu

[63] Minutes of the State Board of Agriculture. 19 November 1927. www.onthebanks.msu.edu

[64] Minutes of the State Board of Agriculture. 29 June 1929. www.onthebanks.msu.edu

[65] Minutes of the State Board of Agriculture. 17 July 1929. www.onthebanks.msu.edu

[66] Thomas, David. *Michigan State College: John Hannah and the Creation of a World University, 1926-1969.* East Lansing: Michigan State University Press, 2008. p. 36

[67] Minutes of the State Board of Agriculture. 18 December 1929. www.onthebanks.msu.edu

[68] Ibid.

his own purposes. Many student-athletes would avail themselves of the money. Most would pay the school back through work-study programs. Others were delinquent. A few never reimbursed the college.[69]

Loans to athletes, considered contrary to the amateur code regardless of academic acumen, were viewed as a subtle way of acquiring the services of talented young men. Many schools outside the Western Conference, however, offered them; most never required payback. The State University of Iowa had been severely penalized by the Intercollegiate Conference of Faculty Representatives for offering financial assistance from boosters. But the Michigan State loan program differed from others. College administrators controlled all subsidies. Boosters were not welcomed.

Michigan State made efforts at collecting payments from all students borrowing dollars from the college. But athletes unable or unwilling to meet obligations were treated differently. In response to a growing delinquency problem, a loan-guarantee program was put in place for them. And in the interest of maintaining institutional integrity, the college leadership set up an arrangement with local insurance agent Fred Jenison of nearby Lansing. He was asked to underwrite loans to needy kids gifted in certain sports.[70] By dealing with only one man the comptroller could trust, the school maintained control over boosters too eager to buy talent for the school.

In addition to assuring loans to athletes, the college also provided Jim Crowley with travel money.[71] [72] With it, the coach could visit large cities to deliver a speech at either an alumni club or a high school sports banquet. Alumni and fans would introduce talented athletes to Crowley following his presentation. The ruse was a common practice during that era as a way to meet football prospects. "Sleepy Jim" could, in theory, offer no discussion about the specifics of playing in East Lansing. To do so was considered recruiting, a violation of the amateur code. But the practice–including subtle comments, perhaps with a wink–was difficult to monitor. Boosters in attendance would later encourage the high school seniors to write the coach and request a visit. Fielding Yost, during his coaching years, was acknowledged as one of the best at this recruiting ploy.[73] Jim Crowley made hundreds of talks in his four years at Michigan State College.[74] The tactic was critical for building and maintaining a football tradition.

Availing himself of all resources provided by the college, Crowley's program proceeded on schedule. With competitive football finally a reality in East Lansing under the new coach, Michigan State administrators decided to push forward with an aggressive strategic plan for the school that would also benefit its coach. The State Board approved travel expenses for a small contingency of athletic personnel to attend the annual Western Conference meetings, held in Chicago, in December of 1929. It was a first for the college. The intent was ostensibly to promote good will. In point of fact, the Spartans wanted to

---

[69] Outstanding Notes: 1931-32. Circa 1940. MSU Board of Trustees, UA1.0. Supplementary Material; Box 1885, folder: 17 7/5/40.

[70] Hannah to Jenison. 28 October 1937. Michigan State University Archives. Jenison Family Papers, Collection 12; Box 1, folder: 10

[71] Minutes of the State Board of Agriculture, 18 January 1930. www.onthebanks.msu.edu

[72] Minutes of the State Board of Agriculture, 16 January 1931. www.onthebanks.msu.edu

[73] Behee, John. *Fielding Yost's Legacy to the University of Michigan.* Ann Arbor: Uhlrich's Books, 1971. p. 101-2

[74] Minutes of the State Board of Agriculture, 16 March 1933. www.onthebanks.msu.edu

contract games with the membership. The more reputable universities inked on its schedule, the better chance MSC had in creating ticket demand to justify additional stadium expansion necessary to solidify those relationships. It might also serve as a recruiting tactic for enticing young men wanting to compete against traditional regional powers.

Athletic Council Chairman Joseph Cox, Athletic Director Ralph Young, and Assistant Director Lyman Frimodig were offered stipends to attend the meetings. Head baseball coach John Kobs and basketball coach Ben Van Alstyne also accompanied Crowley's contingent from East Lansing.[75] It would prove the first of many unsuccessful trips for the athletic program. Michigan would remain the Spartans' only Big Ten opponent.

In October of 1931, Michigan State College defeated Georgetown University in East Lansing. Jim Crowley was impressed with an intense assistant on the sidelines for the Hoyas. Following that season, he hired Frank Leahy, age 23 at the time, to be his line coach in East Lansing.[76] His one-year tenure at the college allowed him time to develop a friendship with an agricultural extension service specialist by the name of John Hannah.[77] That relationship with the recent Notre Dame graduate would prove providential 15 years later for both Michigan State and Hannah.[78]

IN DECEMBER of 1930 Jim Crowley requested a new contract with a pay raise. It was an audacious move following one very successful season. The State Board asked President Shaw to meet with Crowley and work out details.[79] They were pleased with the coach's gridiron results and wanted to avoid losing his services. The Harry Kipke experience was still fresh in their collective recall.

One month later Shaw reported consummation of a three-year agreement. As of September 1, 1931, Crowley's salary was increased to $7,500. For each of the following two years he would be compensated $8,000. The State Board approved of the contract.[80]

James Harold Crowley was the precursor of the modern day "celebrity coach."[81] He used one year of gridiron success, in combination with his growing popularity on campus, to hold the college hostage for a huge salary increase. The "Crowley Tactic" remains a very effective ploy eight decades later for many college coaches in revenue-generating sports.[82]

With his new contract in hand, the former member of the Four Horseman was now eager to gallop off to Spartan alumni clubs about the Midwest. He needed talent to ensure his winning ways. Crowley, after all, had greater ambitions than spending his career in East Lansing. The coach would ultimately reveal those intentions in February of 1932.

The State University of Iowa had been censored in May of 1929 for egregious violations of conference rules on subsidizing and recruiting. Following a financially devastating scheduling boycott by the remaining nine conference members, the Hawkeye

---

[75] Minutes of the State Board of Agriculture, 16 November 1929. www.onthebanks.msu.edu

[76] Hannah, John A. *A Memoir.* East Lansing: Michigan State University Press, 1980. p. 110

[77] Ibid.

[78] In his memoirs, John Hannah mistakenly stated that Crowley hired Leahy following a Spartan visit to Washington, D.C. in October of 1930. Leahy was in his senior year in South Bend at the time.

[79] Minutes of the State Board of Agriculture, 19 December 1930. www.onthebanks.msu.edu

[80] Minutes of the State Board of Agriculture, 16 January 1931. www.onthebanks.msu.edu

[81] Duderstadt, James J. *Intercollegiate Athetics and the American University.* Ann Arbor: The University of Michigan Press, 2000. pp. 152-159

[82] Ibid., pp. 152-159

athletic administration sought a coach able to turn around their program using honorable practices. Their man was Jim Crowley.

Iowa had just cleaned house in the athletic department, with exception of Coach Burton Ingwersen, who was untainted by the scandal. But in December of 1931, Ingwersen found the current environment in Iowa City intolerable for developing a program. He resigned following an embarrassing season with only one victory. His decision was unanimously accepted by the Board in Control of Athletics.[83] Crowley was soon contacted by a member of the board. On January 21, 1932, one year after signing a revised contract with a significant salary increase, Crowley snuck off to Iowa City in violation of a clause in the agreement. He later telegraphed Professor E. H. Lauer, faculty representative at Iowa, indicating his desire to stay in East Lansing. To his credit he had met with President Shaw upon his return from Iowa. The college leader, and savvy negotiator in his own right, reminded Crowley of his contractual obligations to Michigan State; two years remained on that agreement.[84]

Iowa's Board in Control was unmoved by his telegram. They planned to send a committee to East Lansing to meet with the celebrity coach and President Shaw. Crowley was encouraged to keep all further conversations confidential.[85]

One day later, on January 24, Crowley again telegraphed the Iowa leadership expressing his intention to remain in East Lansing. The Hawkeyes were undeterred by his refusal. The board met following this second rejection; they were now ready to use money to entice the Spartan coach. Defying Crowley's wishes, a few members were asked to travel to Michigan State and meet with administrators. They were also authorized to offer the coach $9,000 annually to live in Iowa City.[86]

The financial inducements were tempting. But it was not enough for him to walk away from his contract with Michigan State. The Board in Control gathered on February 20, 1932, one month after Crowley had informed Shaw of his initial rendezvous with the Hawkeyes in Iowa City, and passed a unanimous motion to up the ante to $10,000 a year in order to secure his services. A board member planned to call the coach and set up a confidential meeting in Chicago within the next few days to consummate the agreement.[87]

"Sleepy Jim" was suddenly wide awake. The money was impressive. He met with the Iowa officials in Chicago on February 22, 1932, once again in violation of his agreement with Shaw. Lawyers were now involved as the State University of Iowa was contemplating legal means to release the Horseman from a binding contract.[88]

By this time, Crowley, realizing that Iowa was quite serious about retaining his services, decided to take charge of the negotiations. He demanded a five-year contract and a

[83] Minutes of the Athletic Board Meeting. 12 December 1931.The University of Iowa Archives. Iowa City, Iowa. Board in Control of Athletics Minutes, RG 28.03.05; 1929-34

[84] Special Meeting of the Athletic Board. 23 January 1932. The University of Iowa Archives. Iowa City, Iowa. Board in Control of Athletics Minutes, RG 28.03.05; 1929-34

[85] Ibid.

[86] Meeting of the Athletic Board. 25 January 1932. The University of Iowa Archives. Iowa City, Iowa. Board in Control of Athletics Minutes, RG 28.03.05; 1929-34

[87] Meeting of the Athletic Board. 20 February 1932. The University of Iowa Archives. Iowa City, Iowa. Board in Control of Athletics Minutes, RG 28.03.05; 1929-34

[88] Meeting of the Athletic Board. 22 February 1932. The University of Iowa Archives. Iowa City, Iowa. Board in Control of Athletics Minutes, RG 28.03.05; 1929-34

salary close to $11,000 per year. The board consented on the 24th of February.[89]

The coach was now in a real predicament. He had promised Shaw his allegiance to the college only one month earlier. He could have easily ended all further Hawkeye advances. Instead, the former All-American cautiously continued conversations with the Iowa officials. Any semblance of integrity Jim Crowley may previously had was now gone.

The Rockne protégé, torn by greed, had to make a decision. Michigan State had been very good to him. The board had agreed to his demands for contract renegotiation and a salary increase after his second successful year in East Lansing. But to accept the Iowa proposal would entail lawyers, confrontation, and bad press. Iowa gave him until the 25th of February to make up his mind.

Crowley requested time to sleep on it; the board granted him a 48-hour extension.[90] Two days later, the coach contacted the school and informed its leadership of his desire to remain in East Lansing.[91]

As it turned out, the former Irish star had no choice. His discussions with the State University of Iowa during most of February were held in confidence until he had to once again confront his boss in East Lansing about the latest Iowa offer. The president remained unmoved by Crowley's predicament. But to assist his coach, he agreed to wire the revised contract to the Iowa attorneys. Finally realizing that they had no legal recourse, the Hawkeyes stopped hovering over their prey. And the State Board of Agriculture, in the person of Robert Sidey Shaw, again reminded Crowley of his legal obligations for the duration of the agreement.[92]

"Sleepy Jim" Crowley resumed his duties recruiting, perhaps illegally, and coaching, while remaining an ambassador of good will for Michigan State College. The coach also continued to work at signing up Western Conference teams to compete against his Spartans while attending the December 1932 gathering of the membership in Chicago.[93] In return for contractual compliance, Crowley would be immune from salary cuts demanded of all other college employees during that financially challenging year.[94] Perhaps the board's gesture, in the early years of the Depression, was intended to keep him around for a few more seasons.

The gesture proved futile. Jim Crowley resigned as head coach of Michigan State College on February 28, 1933, with one year left on his contract to assume a similar position at Fordham University in New York.[95] An editorial commentary in the State News "indicated that the students [felt] that he [had] used his position to advance his own success ..."[96] It was an accurate assessment of an unconscionable act. Fortunately, the Iowa

---

[89] Meeting of the Athletic Board. 24 February 1932. The University of Iowa Archives. Iowa City, Iowa. Board in Control of Athletics Minutes, RG 28.03.05; 1929-34

[90] Meeting of the Athletic Board. 25 February 1932. The University of Iowa Archives. Iowa City, Iowa. Board in Control of Athletics Minutes, RG 28.03.05; 1929-34

[91] Meeting of the Athletic Board. 27 February 1932. The University of Iowa Archives. Iowa City, Iowa. Board in Control of Athletics Minutes, RG 28.03.05; 1929-34

[92] Minutes of the State Board of Agriculture, 27 February 1932. www.onthebanks.msu.edu

[93] Minutes of the State Board of Agriculture, 15 December 1932. www.onthebanks.msu.edu

[94] Minutes of the State Board of Agriculture, 1 June 1932. www.onthebanks.msu.edu

[95] Minutes of the State Board of Agriculture, 16 February 1933. www.onthebanks.msu.edu

[96] Stradley, B.S. "Michigan State College of Agriculture and Applied Science-1933." 26 April 1933. Michigan State University Archives. Robert Shaw Papers, UA2.1.11; Box 840, folder: 71

enticement remained in confidence. The students never learned of his selfish antics of one year earlier.

Following Crowley's announcement, Frank Leahy expressed interest in the vacancy at Michigan State. Extension service specialist John Hannah recognized the potential in his friend. With some temerity, he approached President Shaw about hiring the Irishman. Shaw, however, felt that Leahy was too young and inexperienced for the position.[97] He had already made up his mind, with the assistance of Ralph Young, to hire Charles Bachman, at a salary of only $6,500.[98] Leahy would later assume the head coaching position at his alma mater in South Bend. But the gesture of support by Hannah, as will be seen, was probably not forgotten by the future Hall of Fame coach.

DURING CROWLEY'S early years in East Lansing, the administration would become aware of an additional subsidizing practice encouraged by the coach. In the early 1930s, Crowley had been instrumental in growing the Downtown Coaches Club,[99] a booster organization that funneled money illegally to athletes. Robert Shaw was not opposed to the school assisting athletes out of a sense of fairness.[100] What concerned him, however, was non-college money funding athletes. Shaw, like so many other college presidents, feared losing control of disbursements.[101] In the absence of institutional oversight, the integrity of the school was always at risk.

It was primarily for this reason that the president supported loans for athletes. His program would assure an honorable distribution of money commensurate with the cost of a college education. He wanted no play-for-pay scheme at Michigan State. It was assumed most players would reimburse the school. Those unwilling or unable to honor a promise would have their loans forgiven.

In September of 1932, Michigan State asked the school's comptroller to become an ex officio member of the Athletic Council, with voting privileges.[102] The financial administrator was in charge of all student loans, including those granted athletes. His presence on the council would assure Crowley legitimate dollars necessary to recruit talent to East Lansing. The State Board agreed to support the president's plan guaranteeing institutional oversight of all subsidies. This was Shaw's attempt at reining in the Horseman and his Lansing boosters.

In hindsight it was probably fortuitous that the State University of Iowa had not hired Jim Crowley. A North Central Association (NCA)[103] investigation of Michigan State, in early 1933, found the former coach in violation of a number of amateur rules while under

[97] Hannah, John. *A Memoir*. East Lansing: Michigan State University Press, 1980. p. 110
[98] Minutes of the State Board of Agriculture. 16 February 1933. www.onthebanks.msu.edu
[99] Devine, Tommy. "Michigan State Challenges the Big Ten to Clean House." 18 June 1949. *Sports Illustrated.* Michigan State University Archives. John Hannah Papers, UA2.1.12; Box 80, folder: 13
[100] Bachman, Charles."The Athletic Side of John Hannah." circa 1970. Michigan State University Archives, Hannah Archives Project, UA 2.1.12.2; Box 34, folder: 2 Bachman
[101] Meeting of the Joint Group of the Intercollegiate Conference, "Report of Special Committee on Rules Revisions." 28-29 May 1953. University of Wisconsin-Madison Archives. The University Faculty Athletic Board, Series 5/21/6; Box 1, folder: Western Conference Minutes 1947-51
[102] Minutes of the State Board of Agriculture, 15 September 1932. www.onthebanks.msu.edu
[103] The NCA was the accrediting agency for most Midwest colleges and universities. The NCAA (National Collegiate Athletic Association) had no ties to the organization.

its employ.[104] This put the college at risk of losing academic accreditation. But with his departure for Fordham just a few months earlier,[105] the NCA granted leniency. It would only request, in confidence, minor corrective actions.[106] Its published report gave the college a passing grade. Ralph Aigler was appalled by the findings. He was convinced that Crowley was corrupt.[107] The law professor, however, was not privy to the confidential reprimand of 1933.[108] [109]

But regardless of Aigler's conviction, one year earlier Iowa's Board in Control was certain "Sleepy Jim" Crowley was the right man for the job. It had no idea of his suspect practices in East Lansing. The last thing the State University needed, in the aftermath of its 1929 scandal, was the hiring of an unscrupulous winner. The NCA monitored most Midwest schools, including Iowa. The coach, had he been hired by the Hawkeyes, would have been a marked man by the accrediting agency. Any new infractions discovered by the NCA, while periodically investigating Iowa, could have decimated a football program struggling to regain credibility.

Fortunately for Crowley, Fordham had used the Middle State Commission for accrediting its institution since 1921.[110]

IN FEBRUARY of 1932, one year before Charlie Bachman's arrival on campus, the State Board approved, for the first time, academic scholarships to assist gifted students in financial need during the Depression. The MSC Scholarship Fund was reserved for those with the highest scholastic records. The small endowment monies were limited to eligible juniors and seniors.[111]

One month later the Alumni Scholarship Plan was proposed. It was comparable to one in operation at Michigan. The proposal was felt to be "… safe-guarded … and desirable for this institution."[112] The administration intended the Alumni Scholarship to bring in students who would otherwise be unable to attend the school. It would "probably result in no loss of revenue to the college" due to the anticipated interest that would be generated among friends and associates with financial means to also matriculate at the institution. The focus of the plan, intended for students with scholarly acumen,[113] was on maintaining enrollment numbers. Although athletic skill was not to be considered, there would be no

---

[104] Stradley, B. S. "Michigan State College of Agriculture and Applied Science-1933." 26 April 1933. Michigan State University Archives. Robert Shaw Papers, UA2.1.11; Box 840, folder: 71

[105] As will be seen, Crowley may have been asked to resign rather than finish his remaining year under contract.

[106] Stradley, B. S. "Michigan State College of Agriculture and Applied Science-1933." 26 April 1933. Michigan State University Archives. Robert Shaw Papers, UA2.1.11; Box 840, folder: 71

[107] Aigler to Griffith. 1 October 1935. Bentley Historical Library, University of Michigan. Ralph W. Aigler Papers, 87406 Aa 2; Box 6, folder: correspondence 1934-39, Griffith 4/34-1/36

[108] Works to Shaw. 26 April 1933. Michigan State University Archives. Robert Shaw Papers, UA2.1.11; Box 840, folder: 71

[109] Stradley, B.S. "Michigan State College of Agriculture and Applied Science-1933." 26 April 1933. Michigan State University Archives. Robert Shaw Papers, UA2.1.11; Box 840, folder: 71.

[110] Di Bari, Joseph J. "Question on football tenure of Jim Crowley." E-Mail to David J. Young. 2 May 2011.

[111] Minute of the State Board of Agriculture. 18 February 1932. www.onthebanks.msu.edu

[112] Minutes of the State Board of Agriculture. 17 March 1932. www.onthebanks.msu.edu

[113] Minutes of the State Board of Agriculture. 17 March 1932. www.onthebanks.msu.edu

discrimination against an athlete with intellectual promise.

By October the school provided scholarships for violin, voice, piano, and clarinet.[114] Eight months later competitive band scholarships were offered students with both musical and scholarly gifts.[115] The college, in doing so, wanted to acknowledge non-scholastic acumen. The grants, and the means of overseeing them, would one day provide John Hannah with a formidable argument for justifying athletic awards to students bringing a different type of talent to the institution.[116] [117]

With the scholarship plans in place, prospective students began evaluating Michigan State with greater interest. The president and the State Board of Agriculture, seeking financial stability in the mid-1930s, wanted to create an environment that would sustain enrollment and support an expanding infrastructure. Having a good football team was part of that strategy.

From 1933 through 1937, Coach Bachman won 32 games, lost 11 and tied four. But of greater significance, he defeated the University of Michigan four straight years. Beginning with the 1934 season, the Spartans offense put up 81 points on the scoreboard in Ann Arbor. The defense allowed only 27. The school was making news on sports pages. For the administration and the State Board, it signified progress. But a few more items on the board's agenda still needed attention before the college could achieve its overall strategy of financial stability during tough economic times.

WITH BACHMAN'S program now firmly in place it was time for the Spartans to address competitive relationships and scheduling issues. Reputable opponents were needed to enhance ticket demand in East Lansing and thereby justify another expansion of College Field beyond its current capacity of 20,000 seats. The challenge, however, was how to entice these schools to visit East Lansing during the fall. The State Board wanted hard data–evidence of sustainable ticket sales–before supporting further construction.

Attention was first directed to South Bend. Michigan State had never gotten over the Irish divorce of 1921. Jim Crowley's tenure had been too short to develop a renewed relationship with his alma mater. Hiring Charlie Bachman, also a Notre Dame graduate, immediately following Crowley's departure, may have been intended to help promote a reconciliation between the two schools.[118]

Beginning in early 1934, Bachman, Ralph Young, and other Spartan administrators made a habit of attending the annual Notre Dame Football Banquet.[119] In advance of that first trip to South Bend, Young wrote to President Shaw announcing their intentions. He

---

[114] Minutes of the State Board of Agriculture. 19 October 1933. www.onthebanks.msu.edu

[115] Minutes of the State Board of Agriculture. 11 June 1934. www.onthebanks.msu.edu

[116] Hannah, John A. "Speech of Doctor John A. Hannah at the Fortieth Annual Convention of the National Collegiate Athletic Association." 9 January 1946. Bentley Historical Library, University of Michigan. Herbert Orin Crisler Papers, 85823 AC UAm Aa 2; Box 1, folder: topical correspondence, Michigan State University clippings and misc.

[117] In the State Board minutes, the term "scholarship" was used to describe non-scholastic grants provided students with gifts in the arts. Hannah chose to designate subsidies provided athletes as "awards." As will be seen, he had reasons for this terminology.

[118] Bachman, Charles."The Athletic Side of John Hannah." Circa 1970. Michigan State University Archives, Hannah Archives Project, UA2.1.12.2; Box 34, folder: 2 Bachman

[119] Minutes of the State Board of Agriculture. 18 January 1934. www.onthebanks.msu.edu

reminded Shaw that "Father O'Hara is slated to become the president of Notre Dame next spring and we intend to see him regarding our future football relations with Notre Dame."[120] The board approved the travel expenses.

The practice of courting Notre Dame continued for years. In late May of 1946, Irish Coach Frank Leahy responded to Spartan line coach Al Kawal's letter inquiring about a visit to South Bend. He encouraged Kawal and a few colleagues to attend the Old Timer's Game closing out the spring football drills in South Bend. John Hannah eagerly approved monies for the trip.[121] [122]

A few months earlier, in mid-January, Hannah had a brief encounter with Leahy during the annual NCAA convention in St. Louis. Lacking the time to begin a meaningful dialogue regarding athletic relations, Hannah promised to write his friend. But he didn't follow up on that promise until nearly five months later, when Kawal's request for reimbursement reminded him of it. Hannah's June communiqué to Leahy would ultimately prove to be historically significant, in terms of both athletics and academics, for Michigan State College.

But in 1934 Notre Dame remained uninterested in returning to East Lansing. Capacity at College Field, still only 20,000 with 6,000 bleacher seats added, was not sufficient to justify a home-and-home series. The following year, with the financial support of alumni, the facility was increased to approximately 29,000 including temporary seating.[123] The State Board, with encouragement from those donors,[124] agreed to re-name the upgraded stadium Macklin Field in recognition of the former coach.[125] It was hoped that the expansion might finally interest Notre Dame.[126] Despite the potential for increased ticket sales, however, the Irish remained noncommittal. The shared revenue was still not large enough to meet its financial needs as a private school lacking taxpayer support.

NOTRE DAME was not the only school on the Spartan list of potential competitors. In the spring of 1935 the Athletic Council "adopted a plan to attempt to secure at least one Western Conference game for our stadium each fall …" Ralph Young proposed asking the University of Illinois to travel to East Lansing for a future game in advance of the biennial scheduling meeting in May. He was willing to guarantee the Illini $10,000 for the trip.[127] Any revenue exceeding that guarantee would be evenly split after expenses were covered.

---

[120] Young to Shaw. 8 January 1934. Michigan State University Archives. Michigan State Board of Trustees, Supplementary Material, UA1.0; Box 1881, folder: 52 1/18/34

[121] Leahy to Kawal. 27 May 1946. Michigan State University Archives. MSU Board of Trustees, UA1.0; Box 1892, folder: 3 supplementary material 6/20/46

[122] Young to Hannah. 29 May 1946. Michigan State University Archives. MSU Board of Trustees, UA1.0; Box 1892, folder: 3 supplementary material 6/20/46

[123] Kuhn, Madison. *Michigan State: The First Hundred Years.* East Lansing: Michigan State University Press, 1955. pp. 360-361

[124] Thomas, David. *Michigan State College: John Hannah and the Creation of a World University, 1929-1969.* East Lansing: Michigan State University Press, 2005. p. 42

[125] Minutes of the State Board of Agriculture. 21 March 1935. www.onthebanks.msu.edu

[126] Bachman, Charles. "The Athletic Side of John Hannah." Circa 1970. Michigan State University Archives. Hannah Archives Project, UA 2.1.12.2;. Box 34, folder: 2 Bachman

[127] Young to Shaw. 18 April 1935. Michigan State University Archives. Michigan State Board of Trustees, Supplementary Material, UA1.0; Box 1882, folder: 6 4/18/35

Much to the surprise of Young, the Illini declined his offer. But it was not the typical rejection he had become accustomed to in recent years from Western Conference schools. Athletic Director George Huff wanted nothing to do with the powerful Spartans. He cited various reasons.

> I have just talked with [Coach] Zuppke and without being diplomatic or evasive, I will say that we don't want to play Michigan State in 1937–the only reason for that being that you are too good. We always play five Conference games, and for the last two years we have played the Army. We will play Southern California for the next two years, and while Southern California and the Army are strong they are no stronger than Michigan State in my judgment, yet there is the matter of trips which appeals to our players. To go to California means a lot to them – to go to East Lansing, it wouldn't mean much … But to get back to the original proposition, I am sure that we cannot arrange a game with Michigan State for the reason stated at the beginning of this letter; namely, that you are too good … This is a compliment, whether you take it that way or not.[128]

Director Young then tried to secure a game with Ohio State, Purdue, or Northwestern with similar guarantees. He was again unsuccessful.[129]

At about the same time, in January of 1935, a seemingly inconsequential transition took place in East Lansing. With the resignation of Herman Halladay, John Hannah, of the agricultural extension services, was selected secretary of the State Board.[130] Over the next six years, Secretary Hannah, learning how costly it was to lack conference affiliation, actively participated in strategic planning to address the problem.

In May of 1936, Ralph Young requested approval from the State Board to arrange football games in East Lansing with some prominent programs for the 1938 season. The rejections of 1935 had not swayed the Athletic Council's long-term strategic plans. The enlarged Macklin Field was not on the order of Michigan Stadium but, with appropriate financial inducements, the council was confident its athletic director could sign a few contracts with some regional powers.

Young was allowed to offer Notre Dame a $20,000 guarantee for meeting the Spartans in East Lansing in 1938. Ohio State, Minnesota, Illinois, and Northwestern were enticed with $15,000 promises. Wisconsin, Iowa, and Purdue carried a $10,000 price tag. Indiana and the University of Chicago were valued at $8,000 for that year. The board approved a motion to support the Athletic Council's plan but preferred that Young focus on the first two groups of schools.[131]

The Spartans were rebuffed by all.

The good will of attending the annual Notre Dame Football banquet for was still not paying off. The Irish remained uninterested; the expanded Macklin Field still failed to meet

---

[128] Huff to Young. 11 April 1935. Michigan State University Archives. Michigan State Board of Trustees, Supplementary Material, UA1.0; Box 1882, folder: 6 4/18/35

[129] Young to Shaw. 18 April 1935. Michigan State University Archives. Michigan State Board of Trustees, Supplementary Material, UA1.0; Box 1882, folder: 6 4/18/35

[130] Minutes of the State Board of Agriculture. 22 November 1934. www.onthebanks.msu.edu

[131] Minutes of the State Board of Agriculture. 22 May 1936. www.onthebanks.msu.edu

their seating capacity requirements. The Western Conference schools, likewise, expressed no desire to contract with the Spartans despite the impressive dollar guarantee. Young was dumbfounded.

As it turned out, Ralph Aigler may have played a subtle role in those rejections. During the mid 1930s Michigan State was dominating the Wolverines on the gridiron. Aigler, in letters shared with colleagues, offered his reasons for the Spartan success. The school was not adhering to Handbook eligibility requirements for competition with a member program (Michigan). His comments, based on rumors, were not complimentary towards the athletic and administrative leadership at the school.[132] His opinion may have swayed contracting decisions among schools unfamiliar with the East Lansing program. A four year de facto boycott resulted. Ironically, at the same time he was denigrating the Spartans, a highly confidential internal investigation of Harry Kipke's suspect practices, also in violation of the Handbook, was taking place in Ann Arbor. Two years later the coach would be forced to resign. But the Kipke scandal did not stop Ralph Aigler from criticizing the Wolverine's intrastate rival among his colleagues.

In November of 1936, following another successful season under Bachman, the State Board, at the request of the Athletic Council, authorized Ralph Young to continue offering impressive guarantees on an annual basis to those regional programs.[133] The board and council, however, were unaware of the Aigler Boycott. The Spartan leadership was convinced that sooner or later a director would succumb to the dollars.

At that same meeting, the State Board also approved a motion, drafted by the Athletic Council, to "authorize the President to appoint a committee to represent Michigan State College in petitioning the athletic organization known as the Western Conference for admission and to take such steps as are necessary to secure favorable consideration on the part of the Western Conference schools for this application."[134] With three wins in a row over the Wolverines, the Spartans were confident they could now compete with many of the Big Ten powers.

As a member of the prestigious conference, the college would no longer face the daunting challenge of scheduling. Being affiliated with regional schools would also lessen travel time for the students and save on transportation costs for the athletic department. President Shaw appointed faculty representative Dean Ralph Huston, board member Gilbert Daane, and Secretary John Hannah to the special committee.[135]

Based on a letter sent to Ralph Aigler by Dean Huston in December of 1936, it was apparent the Huston Committee anticipated formidable resistance to a successful application. Noting the pattern of rejections by every school Ralph Young petitioned for contracts, the three members were convinced someone in the Western Conference had been quietly campaigning against the college.[136] It appeared that person resided in Ann Arbor. In a politically tactful way, however, Huston avoided directly implicating the powerful Aigler.

With the intent of countering Aigler's influence on conference members, and to

---

[132] Aigler to Long. 7 October 1935. Bentley Historical Library, University of Michigan. Ralph W. Aigler Papers, 87406 Aa 2; Box 12, folder: correspondence 1933-36 "L" misc.

[133] Minutes of the State Board of Agriculture. 23 November 1936. www.onthebanks.msu.edu

[134] Ibid.

[135] Ibid.

[136] Huston to Aigler. 4 December 1936. Bentley Historical Library, University of Michigan. Ralph W. Aigler Papers, 87406 Aa 2; Box 7, folder: correspondence 1934-39 NCAA

present the positive attributes of the institution, the State Board authorized Huston to visit five conference schools in February of 1937.[137] The ultimate goal was to win votes for the May meeting in Chicago. Handbook rules, after all, only required a simple majority for admission into the conference.

ON MAY 22, 1937, the Intercollegiate Conference of Faculty Representatives met at the University of Michigan Union in Ann Arbor, Michigan. All members of the Western Conference, with the exception of Chicago, were present. Item 7 on the agenda involved a request for admission from Michigan State College.

> After discussion it was moved, seconded and unanimously carried that it was the sense of the Conference that it was inexpedient to increase the size of the Conference at this time. (Professor Aigler, representing the University of Michigan, was temporarily absent from the meeting when the application for membership was discussed and…action…taken).[138] [139]

The reason for the rejection was essentially the same as that provided the University of Nebraska in June of 1908 following Michigan's withdrawal from the conference. That succinct reply had been provided every suitor since.[140] [141] The diplomatic verbiage was intended to offer a "graceful refusal" to a fellow institution.[142] Notre Dame tried gaining a seat in December of both 1912 and 1919.[143] [144] It tried again in May of 1926.[145] The convenient "Nebraska Response" was provided each time.[146] [147]

Ralph Aigler's recusing himself while the discussion and vote on Michigan State

[137] Minutes of the State Board of Agriculture. 18 March 1937. www.onthebanks.msu.edu

[138] Minutes of the Intercollegiate Conference of Faculty Representatives. 22 May 1937. Bentley Historical Library, University of Michigan. Athletic Department, 943 Bimu2; Box 84, folder: Faculty Representative minutes (folder)

[139] The parentheses were included in the meeting minutes.

[140] Minutes of the Intercollegiate Conference. 6 June 1908. University of Minnesota Archives, Intercollegiate Athletic Papers; Box 13, folder: Intercollegiate Conference minutes 1907-1933

[141] Aigler to Rottschaefer. 18 February 1944. Bentley Historical Library, University of Michigan. Ralph W. Aigler Papers, 87406 Aa 2: Box 8, folder: correspondence 1940-45 Rottschaefer

[142] Rottschaefer to Aigler. 13 September 1944. Bentley Historical Library, University of Michigan. Ralph W. Aigler Papers. 87406 Aa 2; Box 8, folder: correspondence 1940-45 Rottschaefer

[143] Minutes of the Intercollegiate Conference of Faculty Representatives. 6 December 1912. Bentley Historical Library, University of Michigan. Athletic Department, 943 Bimu2; Box 84, folder: Faculty Representative minutes 1918-1940

[144] Minutes of the Intercollegiate Conference of Faculty Representatives. 6 December 1919. Bentley Historical Library, University of Michigan. Athletic Department, 943 Bimu2; Box 84, folder: Faculty Representative minutes 1918-1940

[145] Minutes of the Intercollegiate Conference of Faculty Representatives. 28 May 1926. Bentley Historical Library, University of Michigan. Athletic Department, 943 Bimu2; Box 84, folder: Faculty Representative minutes 1918-1940

[146] Minutes of the Inter-Collegiate Conference of Faculty Representatives. 6 June 1908. University of Minnesota Archives. Intercollegiate Athletic Papers; Box 13, folder: Intercollegiate Conference minutes

[147] Aigler to Rottschaefer. 18 February 1944. Bentley Historical Library, University of Michigan. Ralph W. Aigler Papers. 87406 Aa 2; Box 8, folder: correspondence 1940-45 Rottschaefer

took place was a politically wise move. His opinions about the Spartans were well known to his colleagues by now.[148] The Aigler Boycott, still in force, reflected his influence over conference decisions. But mindful of potential leaks, despite the tradition that all meetings remain confidential,[149] he was unwilling to risk embarrassing his university should the decision and unanimous tally be revealed to the press.

Michigan State administrators were provided no data on the voting outcome. And respectful of Michigan State's desire for confidentiality, the application was never revealed to the press by the commissioner.

But the State Board of Agriculture and its young secretary, smarting from the rejection, remained suspicious of the role Ralph Aigler had played in both the scheduling boycott and now the application denial. It was becoming apparent that any future interactions with the conference would require working adeptly around the most powerful man in the Western Conference.

PRIOR TO the vote of May 22, 1937, Professor Huston had undertaken good will visits to West Lafayette, Indianapolis, Bloomington, Champaign-Urbana, Iowa City, and Madison to meet with faculty representatives at each school. He began his five-day trip on the 14th of February.[150]

In a visit to the University of Illinois, Huston met with faculty representative Professor Frank Richart "in order that we may discuss certain athletic policies and problems we have at Michigan State College."[151] In a follow-up note he included a glossy brochure on Michigan State College for Richart's perusal.[152] Huston was clearly selling the college's attributes in trying to win votes for membership. As the unanimous decision three months later indicated, he was not only unsuccessful in swaying Richart, but also every other faculty representative he visited during his travels.

John Hannah's evolving mistrust of the University of Michigan athletic leadership probably originated with Huston's discoveries during that five-day expedition.[153] [154] It was only logical to the secretary of the State Board that Ralph Aigler had to be the source denigrating Michigan State. The Spartans had maintained minimal athletic interaction with other programs over the past decade. The question for Hannah and his fellow administrators remained: Why was Aigler taking this seemingly defiant stance? The answer, in hindsight,

---

[148] Aigler to Long. 7 October 1935. Bentley Historical Library, University of Michigan. Ralph W. Aigler Papers, 87406 Aa 2; Box 12, folder: correspondence 1933-36 "L" misc.

[149] Rules, Regulations and Opinions of the Intercollegiate Conference of Faculty Representatives-Revised 1930. University of Minnesota Archives, Department of Intercollegiate Athletics Papers; Box 13, folder: 1930

[150] Richart to Aigler. 14 May 1946. Bentley Historical Library, University of Michigan. Ralph W. Aigler Papers. 87406 Aa 2; Box 9, folder: correspondence: 1946-52 "H" misc.

[151] Huston to Richart. 4 February 1937. University of Illinois Archives. Series 4/2/12; Box 2, folder: Western Intercollegiate Conference 1936-37

[152] Huston to Richart. 25 February 1937. University of Illinois Archives. Series 4/2/12; Box 2, folder: Western Intercollegiate Conference 1936-37

[153] Hannah, John A. *A Memoir.* East Lansing: Michigan State University Press, 1980. p. 119

[154] In September of 1941, Hannah bypassed Fritz Crisler (and thus Ralph Aigler) and communicated directly with President Ruthven regarding the university's "customary" control over scheduling. Having served on the Huston Committee, he was well aware of Aigler's influence over athletic policy at the university and within the conference.

appeared to involve the professor's own feelings of impotence in dealing with the college.

Ralph Aigler was totally powerless to discipline the Spartans. Vigilante justice was not feasible against a school the university was mandated to interact with every fall. Boycotting was politically impossible in a state demanding the annual rivalry.

Adding to his frustration, there was no legitimate way Aigler could ask outside organizations to investigate the East Lansing program. The NCAA lacked that authority; it would be years before it would assume a role in investigation and discipline. The North Central Association on academic accrediting had already inspected Michigan State in 1933. To the professor's limited understanding, it had found no violations. He could not trust the NCA to perform another in-depth investigation.

Surprisingly, despite being an attorney, the professor chose not to entertain dialogue with his nemesis from East Lansing. A meeting with Robert Shaw, Ralph Huston, and Ralph Young to discuss rumored violations might have been beneficial. Confrontation, without valid evidence to support claims, could prove embarrassing, however, for a man steeped in forensics. So Aigler chose subterfuge. All he could do was share his opinion about rumored violations in East Lansing.

By January of 1939, he finally realized the value of a face-to-face encounter. The troika of Aigler, Fritz Crisler, and Fielding Yost traveled to East Lansing to confront Huston, Young, and Coach Charlie Bachman on purported conference Handbook violations.[155] [156] Although that meeting did not satisfactorily answer all his questions about eligibility, recruiting, and subsidizing, Ralph Aigler was impressed by the Spartans' empathic treatment of students in need of financial aid during the Depression. The encounter had a positive impact on his formerly intransigent stance on all forms of financial aid for athletes.[157]

In hindsight, it was probably naïve for Michigan State to have even applied for membership in May of 1937. The conference had no reason to expand to 11 members. But since all previous applications by suitors were kept in confidence, the Spartan leadership had no knowledge of the failed attempts by other institutions over the preceding three decades. The Nebraska Response that was provided in 1937 was merely a reflection of a long-held conviction to maintain the status quo.

Regardless of the recent events impacting the college athletic department, Bachman, Young, and others continued their annual attendance at the December Western Conference meetings. Their intent was to develop relationships that might prove profitable in upcoming years. They also patiently sat outside the Sherman Hotel meeting room, in Chicago, every other year in late May, while scheduling took place behind closed doors.

Persistence finally paid off. The Spartans were successful in landing a four-year commitment with Purdue beginning in the late 1930s.[158] The college was also able to sign

---

[155] Yost to Young. 20 January 1939. Bentley Historical Library, University of Michigan. Herbert Orin Crisler Papers, 85823 AC UAm Aa2; Box 1, MSU correspondence: 1943-46

[156] Bachman, Charles. "The Athletic Side of John Hannah." Circa 1970. Michigan State University Archives, Hannah Archives Project, UA2.1.12.2;. Box 34, folder: 2 Bachman. The former coach confused college subsidies of the late 1930 with the Jenison Awards of December, 1941. But his recollection of the agenda was consistent with other documents of that time.

[157] Aigler to Griffith. 17 January 1939. Bentley Historical Library, University of Michigan. Ralph W. Aigler Papers, 87406 Aa;. Box 6, correspondence: 1934-39 Griffith 9/37-7/39

[158] Bachman, Charles. "The Athletic Side of John Hannah." Circa 1970. Michigan State University

up Indiana in June of 1939 for a game in East Lansing. The Hoosiers agreed to a $3,500 guarantee.[159] (Athletic Director Zora Clevenger should have taken the $8,000 offered by Ralph Young one year earlier. Indiana's value had apparently depreciated during the interim!)

Michigan State, lacking conference affiliation, continued its eligibility practices, allowable under NCAA rules at the time.[160] It would also recruit and offer legitimate subsidies, in defiance of no one other than Ralph Aigler.[161] [162]

AS IT turned out, there were two announcements in the year of 1939. The one in late December, as delivered at a press conference by Robert Maynard Hutchins of the University of Chicago, shocked the sporting world. The other, revealed only in the privacy of a college-administration board room in East Lansing just nine months earlier, would remain confidential for a few years.

That announcement, however, would profoundly impact the course of events at Michigan State just as a transition in leadership was to take place. The bequest, totally unexpected, would allow the new president the wherewithal to ultimately achieve not only the Shaw strategy, but the Hannah vision.

Archives. Hannah Archives Project. UA2.1.12.2; Box 34, folder 2 Bachman

[159] Minutes of the State Board of Agriculture. 1 June 1939. www.onthebanks.msu.edu

[160] Falla, Jack. *NCAA: The Voice of College Sports.* Mission, KA: National Collegiate Athletic Association, 1981. pp. 20-23

[161] Minutes of the State Board of Agriculture. 10 June 1940. www.onthebanks.msu.edu

[162] Young to Shaw. 20 May 1940. Michigan State University Archives. MSU Board of Trustees, UA1.0. Supplementary Material; Box 1885, folder: 15 7/5/40

A Unique Bequest Funds a Grand Vision

PHILANTHROPY IN America had its origins in the country's transition from an agrarian to an industrial economy. That change ultimately enabled small groups of monopolists and robber barons to achieve vast stores of wealth. Known as either financiers or industrialists, some of them would later seek the more honorable title of philanthropist. Posterity, they hoped, would look more kindly on a benefactor than an opportunist.

John D. Rockefeller, the wealthiest man in the world in the late 19th and early 20th centuries, exemplified this transformation of identity. Ruthless in his younger years, he would discover spiritual fulfillment decades later while giving away an unfathomable fortune to special charities and civic-development programs. One of his most significant projects was the creation of the University of Chicago. Over the course of almost two decades he would give $35 million to the university,[1] an amount equivalent to well over $829 million today.[2]

Horace H. Rackham would also become a philanthropist. Although his fortune paled in comparison to Rockefeller's, his gifting would profoundly impact the development of two state institutions.

Rackham's wealth was obtained through serendipity. Born in June of 1858, he grew up in the farming community of Leslie, Michigan. At the age of 21 he moved on to Detroit, where the rapidly expanding economy offered opportunity for a bright young man uncertain of his path in life. His first job: working for a paint and varnish company. Along the way, Rackham became intrigued by the law. With no education beyond high school, at age 26 he began studying jurisprudence under the tutelage of Adolph Sloman and Edward Kane. One year later, following completion of his apprenticeship, Rackham was admitted to the Bar on June 4, 1884.

Nineteen years later, the lawyer would have a fortuitous encounter with a young man obsessed with a novel idea: building an affordable motorized buggy to replace the

[1] Chernow, Ron. *Titan: The Life of John D. Rockefeller.* New York: Random House, 1998. p. 497
[2] This value was arrived at by using MeasuringWorth.com and the CPI for 2010. It assumes all $35M was gifted in 1910, the last year Rockefeller personally donated dollars to the school.

horse and benefit the common man. In June of 1903, Henry Ford sought legal counsel in drafting documents to incorporate the fledgling Ford Motor Company. A close associate advised he contact the law firm of Rackham and Anderson. For $50, the two lawyers did the work. In appreciation for their services, Ford also offered them an opportunity to invest in the new company.[3]

The inventor planned to sell 890 shares at $100 each in a private offering limited to 12 business contacts and friends. Against the counsel of others, including his banker, Rackham and his partner agreed to each buy 50 shares valued at $5,000. In 1919 Henry Ford repurchased the shares for $12.5 million. During his 16 years owning the stock, Rackham received over $2 million in dividends. At age 55, Horace and Mary Rackham were exceptionally wealthy. In today's standard, their fortune was equivalent to almost $180 million.[4]

The lawyer would subsequently resign from his firm and devote the remainder of his life to philanthropy. He insisted on remaining anonymous. He died in 1933 at age 75, with no children.[5] Following his death, a board was formed to divest the estate within five years to the Rackhams' directed charities. "It was no mere happenstance that the University became the major beneficiary … of the five Rackham trustees only two had advanced education, both at the University of Michigan."[6] In 1935 President Alexander Ruthven approached the Rackham Board for financial assistance in maintaining the graduate school that Henry Phillip Tappan had created nearly 80 years ago.

The trustees proceeded to endow the university with $4 million to sponsor research initiatives. The ease in receiving the money prompted Ruthven to ask for more, which he got–$2.5 million for a state-of-the-art building dedicated to graduate studies. The building and the graduate school were both named in his honor.[7] The trustees also gave endowed monies for the creation of the Rackham Scholarships to assist gifted undergraduates. Almost 70 percent of the $14.2 million fund was ultimately granted to the University of Michigan.

Michigan State College also benefited from Rackham's generosity; its grants, however, were significantly smaller than the university's. During the mid-1930s, the foundation acknowledged the college's role in specific areas of agricultural research. The study of brucellosis, an often fatal disease of livestock, appeared to be one particularly significant interest of the Rackham Board. In the spring of 1937 the foundation provided a grant of $6,000 to Professors Ward Giltner and Forest Huddleson for research on the bacteria.[8] The school would eventually acquire patent rights for two vaccines, brucellin and brucellogen, in large part due to the funding.[9]

In October of that same year a letter from Clarence E. Wilcox, a Rackham trustee, was read to the State Board of Agriculture. The foundation planned to grant "… funds for

---

[3] Brazier, Marjorie Cahn. "Biography of an Endowment." *Michigan Historical Collections,* Bulletin 34: May 1985. pp. 1-5

[4] This number was arrived at by using MeasuringWorth.com and the 2010 CPI.

[5] Ibid., pp. 1-5

[6] Ibid., p. 9

[7] Biderman, John O. "History of the Rackham Building." *University of Michigan 2010.* 8 February 2010 <http://www.rackham.umich.edu/rackham_building/history_of_the_rackham_building/>

[8] State Board of Agriculture Minutes. 14 June 1937. www.onthebanks.msu.edu

[9] Gardner to McDonel. 29 November 1948. Michigan State University Archives. Michigan State Board of Trustees, UA1.0. Supplementary Material; Box 1895, Folder 14 12/16/48

scientific, chemical and experimental research in agricultural chemurgy, and farm, soil, crop and agricultural research and on allied subjects." The trust was to be known as the Horace H. Rackham Research Endowment of the Michigan State College of Agriculture and Applied Science. It was consistent with the utilitarian philosophy of the Land Grant Act of Justin Morrill. The trustees intended to offer the school $500,000 for the program.[10] Needless to say, the State Board approved a resolution graciously accepting the terms of the contract. The college, like the university, was financially struggling during the Depression,[11]

The Rackham gift would be the largest provided to the agricultural college since its origins in 1855.[12] Ransom E. Olds previously held the distinction. He donated $100,000 in 1916 to rebuild the engineering building destroyed in a devastating fire.[13] His beneficence to Michigan Agricultural College was the first of its kind for the school. It assured the continuation of a critical program, necessary for land-grant status, that some college leaders feared might implode in the aftermath of the conflagration.[14]

Dating back to the early 1900s, most gifting to the school had been in very small increments. A company or benefactor would offer a gift for a scholarship that rarely exceeded a few hundred dollars in value. On occasion an estate would bequeath the school money or property. The Kellogg Foundation donated forest land and a bird sanctuary for research.[15] Many years later it would fund the Kellogg Center for Continuing Education. The program, consistent with the land-grant mission, provided the foundation for the college's commitment to lifelong learning.

As it grew, Michigan State offered research and development services to businesses with an agricultural focus. These companies would provide professors at the college with grants to investigate a production or distribution problem. The practice was consistent with the Morrill Act. Land-grants were in existence not only to educate the young but to service the utilitarian needs of the economy as well.

But, up until 1937, endowment money was not a significant line item on the balance sheets at the college. Philanthropy was the exception rather than the rule at Michigan State.

ON MARCH 8, 1939, two years following the Rackham gift, another benefactor bequeathed an unexpected large sum of money to the college.[16] The gift, following a year and a half in probate, would surpass the amount provided by the Rackham Foundation. The benefactor was a man with a very unique will.

Frederick Cowles Jenison was born on November 26, 1881, to Nelson F. and Alice Cowles Jenison. He was their only child. The Jenisons lived in Lansing, Michigan, and owned and operated the Lansing Dry Goods Store on N. Washington Avenue. Nelson also

---

[10] "Research: Michigan State University."*Michigan State University*. 2009. East Lansing. 16 February 2010. <http://www.msu.edu>

[11] Kuhn, Madison. *Michigan State: The First Hundred Years 1855-1955*. East Lansing: Michigan State University Press, 1955. p. 333

[12] Thomas, David. *Michigan State College: John Hannah and the Creation of a World University, 1926-1969*. East Lansing: Michigan State University Press, 2008. p. 3

[13] Kuhn, Madison. *Michigan State: The First Hundred Years 1855-1955*. East Lansing: Michigan State University Press, 1955. pp. 266-268

[14] Ibid., pp. 266-268

[15] Minutes of the State Board of Agriculture. 1 June 1932. www.onthebanks.msu.edu

[16] Minutes of the State Board of Agriculture. 8 March 1939. www.onthebanks.msu.edu

maintained some interest in various investments.[17] On January 19, 1884, two years after the birth of his son Jenison bought property in downtown Lansing from Hiram H. Smith of Jackson, Michigan. The parcel at the southwest corner of Ottawa and Washington Avenue was acquired for $7,500 on a land contract at 7 percent interest per annum.[18] Almost 60 years later the appreciated value of that property alone would profoundly benefit the small agricultural college a few miles east of downtown Lansing.

Fred Jenison attended The State Agricultural College and graduated around the turn of the century.[19] [20] In 1904, at age 23, he started the Frederick C. Jenison Insurance Agency and sold general insurance and surety bonds. When his father passed away three years later, the family business was maintained by his mother. In 1909, Fred married Amy Prudden. The couple lived in Lansing. With his mother's death in 1915, the only child would inherit the stocks and properties that his father had acquired over the years.[21] After nine years of marriage, Fred divorced Amy and married Edith Thompson two months later. Both marriages were childless.[22]

The Fred C. Jenison Agency thrived. The owner's investments, primarily attained through inheritance, also did very well. In April of 1925, F.W. Woolworth Company signed a 19-year lease for his three-story building in downtown Lansing on the Hiram H. Smith property his father had acquired 41 years earlier. That lease offered him an annual revenue of $27,000 by 1937.[23] The profits allowed Fred to invest in a few subdivision properties in East Lansing and some large tracts of land about the state. Fred was also quite proficient at buying stocks and bonds. The investor rarely experienced losses, even during the Great Depression years.[24] He and Edith maintained a very comfortable lifestyle in downtown Lansing.

ALTHOUGH NOT an athlete, Fred Jenison loved sports. Football was a particular passion. In addition to attending games at Old College Field, he routinely watched practices on campus.[25] Jenison made some invaluable contacts with college administrators during many spring and fall afternoons standing on the sidelines. Those connections, he probably anticipated, might one day benefit his agency.

John Hannah, secretary of the State Board of Agriculture as of January 1935, shared a similar liking for football. Unmarried at the time, he would occasionally meander

---

[17] Harms, R. "Inventory of Jenison Papers." Michigan State University Archives. East Lansing: August 2002

[18] Jenison-Smith Land Contract. Michigan State University Archives. Jenison Family Papers, Collection 125: Box 6, folder: 47

[19] Hannah, John A. *A Memoir*. East Lansing, Michigan State University Press, 1980. p. 121

[20] The Michigan State archives could not verify Jenison's dates of attendance.

[21] Harms, R. "Inventory of Jenison Papers." Michigan State University Archives. East Lansing: August 2002

[22] Ibid.

[23] Jenison-Woolworth Lease. 15 April 1927. Michigan State University Archives. Jenison Family Papers, Collection 125; Box 6, folder: 47

[24] Harms, R. "Inventory of Jenison Papers." Michigan State University Archives. East Lansing: August 2002

[25] Bachman, Charles. "The Athletic Side of John A. Hannah." Circa 1970. Michigan State University Archives. Hannah Archives Project, UA2.1.12; Box 34, folder 2 Bachman

over to observe practice. Despite lacking any adolescent interest in football, he became a student of the game in later years.[26] So it came as no surprise that Jenison and the young administrator would strike up a friendship while observing Charlie Bachman run practices during the mid 1930s.

ON SEPTEMBER 1, 1929, James Crowley, one of the famed Four Horsemen of Notre Dame, took the coaching reins at the college. In pursuit of victories for the Spartans, he was provided the financial means by Michigan State to accomplish his goals.

A student-loan program was approved by the State Board to assist all matriculates in December of 1929.[27] Theoretically any student, with documented need, could apply for the financial assistance. The loan committee was staffed by three college employees: the comptroller and two faculty members. By mandate, the Athletic Council, in the guise of a faculty representative, held one of those positions.[28] This assured the athletic department, and indirectly the coaches, a presence in the financial aid process. The committee composition, as it turned out, proved very helpful for Jim Crowley in luring young men to Michigan State.

The school also instituted a scholarship program for students with academic gifts. Athletes were not excluded, but they had to meet strict scholastic requirements to receive a grant.[29][30][31][32] No athlete was found eligible during the Crowley years.[33]

The loans and academic scholarships were not sufficient for an aggressive young head coach charged with building a successful program. Crowley needed additional money to entice talented athletes to East Lansing.

The Horseman was head coach during the era of play-for-pay as popularized by certain reprobate schools. The University of Pittsburgh, for example, under Jock Sutherland, was rumored to hire athletes for its highly successful football team. The rumors proved true when the university's payment scheme was exposed in a two-part investigative article published in the *Saturday Evening Post,* a major embarrassment for the chancellor and his administration. Sutherland would eventually lose his job, in the late 1930s, for the practice that violated the amateur code.[34]

Shortly after his arrival in East Lansing, Crowley helped promote a booster organization to provide somewhat similar sustenance for special athletes. The Downtown Coaches Club, a group of local businessmen and fans, many of whom were alumni, raised

---

[26] Bachman, Charles. "The Athletic Side of John A. Hannah." Circa 1970. Michigan State University Archives. Hannah Archives Project, UA2.1.12; Box 34, folder 2 Bachman

[27] Minutes of the State Board of Agriculture. 18 December 1929. www.onthebanks.msu.edu

[28] Stradley, B.S. "Michigan State College of Agriculture and Applied Science-1933." 26 April 1933. Michigan State University Archives. Robert Shaw Papers, UA2.1.11; Box 840, folder: 71

[29] Minutes of the State Board of Agriculture. 18 February 1932. www.onthebanks.msu.edu

[30] Minutes of the State Board of Agriculture. 17 March 1932. www.onthebanks.msu.edu

[31] Minutes of the State Board of Agriculture. 12 January 1933. www.onthebanks.msu.edu

[32] Minutes of the State Board of Agriculture. 19 October 1933. www.onthebanks.msu.edu

[33] Stradley, B.S. "Michigan State College of Agriculture and Applied Science-1933." 26 April 1933. Michigan State University Archives. Robert Shaw Papers, UA2.1.11; Box 840, folder: 71

[34] Wallace, Francis. "The Football Laboratory Explodes: The Climax in the Test Case at Pitt." *Saturday Evening Post.* 4 November 1939. University of Pittsburgh Archives, 9/10-A; Box 1, folder: FF 772

money and disbursed it to students. The college leadership was unaware of the scheme.

With no accountability, boosters were free to pay out sums far in excess of college costs to acquire the services of highly sought after athletes. In appreciation for their endeavors, the financiers gained exposure to the coaches and athletic policy makers.[35] [36] Since Crowley was an employee, the integrity of Michigan State College of Agriculture and Applied Science was in jeopardy with his tacit approval of the illegal practice. Just a few years earlier the State University of Iowa's reputation had been tarnished over activities of a similar nature. President Robert Shaw was no doubt well aware of it.

Four months before Crowley assumed coaching responsibilities in East Lansing, the subsidizing scandal in Iowa City was a major sports story. Among the charges: alumni and boosters had gained control of the athletic department while working closely with its director; Handbook rules had been ignored in pursuit of a winning program; athletes had been provided loans by local businessmen with no obligation for payback. Following an investigation, the Western Conference imposed severe penalties. The institution was humiliated over its failure to monitor athletic department practices.[37] Its integrity was seriously damaged.

The greatest fear for President Shaw, a few years into the Crowley tenure at the college, was a similar scandal in East Lansing. His concern was best expressed to Sports Information Director George Alderton. The dictum became known as "Shaw's Law."

> Remember always that no player, no team, no coach, no sport is ever more important than the good name of Michigan State College.[38]

Years later John Hannah cited that quote often as a reminder to his athletic director, faculty representative, coaches, and athletes. The integrity of the school exceeded all other interests, including winning football.[39]

Sometime during the early winter of 1933, the North Central Association investigated the athletic program at Michigan State. The accrediting organization, as part of its overall assessment of an academic institution, had only recently begun evaluating athletic departments. The practice was based on the theory that these departments, like others at a school, held influence over the character development of young people.[40] Although many colleges and universities didn't agree with it, they had no choice but to

---

[35] Devine, Tommy. "Michigan State Challenges the Big Ten to Clean House." *Sports Illustrated* June 1949:15-17, 68-69. Michigan State University Archives. John Hannah Papers, UA2.1.12; Box 80, folder: 13

[36] Devine, Tommy. "The Michigan State Construction Job." *Sport* December 1953: 15-17, 66-67. Michigan State University Archives. Ralph Young Papers, UA17.114; Box 903, folder: 72

[37] Aigler to Houston. 29 September 1953. Bentley Historical Library, University of Michigan. Ralph W. Ailger Papers, 87406 Aa 2; Box 9, folder: correspondence 1946-52 Houston

[38] Hannah to Emmons. 19 February 1953. Michigan State University Archives. John A. Hannah Papers, UA2.1.12; Box 69, folder: 38

[39] Hannah to Munn, Scott. 21 May 1956. Michigan State University Archives. John A. Hannah Papers, Hannah Administrative Files: Intercollegiate Athletics, director's office, UA2.1.12; Box 41, folder: 5

[40] Paige to Coffman. 21 May 1931. University of Minnesota Archives, President's Office; Box 4, folder: 118 athletics

cooperate with the NCA investigators.[41] [42] [43]

Michigan State was not in compliance with many of the accrediting agency's standards. The association cited the college for offering loans, providing free training-table meals, and supplying tutoring services to student-athletes in direct violation of the new NCA policies on additional financial aid. Crowley was guilty of "solicit[ing] athletes by correspondence and in person." The investigator also felt the coach was overpaid as a faculty member. His salary reflected an "over emphasis on winning teams ... rather than any educational value the students [might] receive from contact with a man who is [far too often] absent from campus." Fortunately for Michigan State, Jim Crowley, in mid-February, asked to be released from his contract to accept a job at Fordham University.[44] Had he not resigned, a more serious reprimand by the NCA might have placed the college's academic accreditation at risk.[45] Robert Shaw's greatest fear would have become a reality.

The significance of the investigation, however, was its revelation that Michigan State had been favoring athletes over students in awarding loans for tuition and fees. The accrediting report noted that the college claimed that "... the loan committee [had] no information [regarding] the students to indicate whether they are or are not athletes except that they may know the individual students personally."[46]

The NCA countered by citing statistics that implied just the opposite was taking place. Five percent of men at the college were classified as athletes. Of all the loans given out to students in 1931-32, however, 11 percent had gone to athletes; in the following year this increased to 12 percent.[47] Michigan State and President Shaw were advised to address the discrepancy or face another inspection the following year.[48]

Charlie Bachman recalled the incident somewhat differently many years later. As paraphrased by the now-retired coach, President Shaw had been blunt and to the point with Professor B. S. Stradley from the NCA.

> 'Our country is in a depression and money is hard to get. Many of our
> students come from average or low-income homes ... we [ask] some boys
> to attend a full schedule of classes [while] demanding they make passing
> grades, and advance with their class. Some of these boys in addition give
> two hours a day to football and play games at home and away for which the
> College makes money. Many of our players work a 3-hour shift in the
> evening in the Buildings and Grounds Department. This makes for a long

---

[41] Long to Aigler. 7 March 1931. Bentley Historical Library, University of Michigan. Ralph W. Aigler Papers, 87406 Aa 2; Box 4, folder: correspondence 1929-33 Long, O.F.

[42] Scott,Walter Dill. "Who is in Control of the Conference Universities?" 18 March 1931. University of Minnesota Archives, President's Office; Box 4, folder: 118 athletics

[43] Griffith to Aigler. 12 May 1931. Bentley Historical Library, University of Michigan. Ralph W. Aigler Papers, 87406 Aa 2; Box 3, folder: Griffith 1931

[44] Stradley, B.S. "Michigan State College of Agriculture and Applied Science-1933." 26 April 1933. Michigan State University Archives. Robert Shaw Papers, UA2.1.11; Box 840, folder: 71

[45] Ibid.

[46] Ibid.

[47] Ibid.

[48] Works to Shaw. 26 April 1933. Michigan State University Archives. Robert Shaw Papers, UA2.1.11; Box 840, folder: 71

day… if a boy is willing to do all these things then the College should at least see that he go to bed at night with a warm dinner in his stomach, provided by the College, and that [it] also provide tutoring for those players [that] need help.' … The [NCA] group agreed with him and the matter was closed. I think that the President's statement that our players were required to make passing grades and advance with their classes was a determining factor in their acceptance of Dr. Shaw's new amateur rules.[49]

Bachman's statement regarding "Shaw's new amateur rules" was not quite accurate. Michigan State had only recently begun the practice of awarding 32 scholarships to outstanding students during the Depression era.[50] To qualify, a student had to have graduated within the upper fifth of his high school class and to have completed a comprehensive set of examinations. The NCA's detailed investigation of the school's practices indicated that MSC had not awarded scholarships to an athlete unless he met those stringent requirements. Consistent with those rules, no athlete had ever qualified![51]

Loans, however, were another matter. Professor George Works of the University of Chicago, in response to Stradley's investigative report, demanded corrective action in a letter to President Shaw. Works was secretary of the NCA at the time.[52] The challenge for Michigan State, with Works' mandate in mind, was how to comply while balancing the fairness concept rooted in Robert Shaw's "new amateur rules." Shaw did not want to penalize the hard-working student-athlete. His apparent solution was loan guarantees. Enter Frederick Cowles Jenison.

CHARLES O. Wilkins was comptroller of the college. By design, he was a member of the committee of three overseeing all borrowing requests. The faculty had a majority presence, but it was Wilkins who ultimately approved all contracts with students. Educational loans were a problem for the school from the outset of the program. Economic times required timely paybacks for a college profoundly impacted by limited state funding. The school could not afford defaults. So it was no surprise that collections remained an ongoing struggle for the business office. By 1938 there were 180 outstanding notes dating back to at least 1931.[53] And as of 1950 the school was still trying to collect on loans from 1929. The comptroller, at that time, recommended that they finally be written off.[54]

Athletes were a notable exception. None were cited on those lists maintained by the business office. Their delinquent notes were always paid back.

In March of 1930 the Athletic Council had petitioned the State Board for "the

---

[49] Bachman, Charles. "The Athletic Side of John A. Hannah." Circa 1970. Michigan State University Archives, Hannah Archives Project. UA2.1.12; Box 34, folder: 2 Bachman

[50] Minutes of the State Board of Agriculture. 18 February 1932. www.onthebanks.msu.edu

[51] Stradley, B.S. "Michigan State College of Agriculture and Applied Science-1933." 26 April 1933. Michigan State University Archives. Robert Shaw Papers, UA2.1.11; Box 840, folder: 71

[52] Works to Shaw. 26 April 1933. Michigan State University Archives. Robert Shaw Papers, UA2.1.11, Box 840, folder :71

[53] Outstanding Notes: 1931-32. Circa 1940. Michigan State University Archives. Michigan State University Board of Trustees, UA1.0. Supplementary Material; Box 1885, folder: 17 7/5/40

[54] May to Hannah. 11 April 1950. Michigan State University Archives. Michigan State University Board of Trustees, UA1.0. Supplementary Material; Box 1897, folder: 2 4/18/50

appointment of the Comptroller of the College to act as an ex officio member of the Council" with voting privileges. Two and a half years later, the board finally approved the request.[55] Charles Wilkins assumed his seat with that group shortly thereafter. The council was seeking financial advice from the administration on matters pertaining to athletic department operations when it first proposed the action in late winter of 1930. There may have been other, perhaps strategic, reasons for this unique request however.

By attending Athletic Council meetings, the comptroller would be privy to the talented athletes Crowley was recruiting with promises of subsidies. Wilkins could then share those names with the student loan committee. In the interest of assisting the football program, Wilkins' committee would merely rubber-stamp requests for aid from the head coach. Assuming that was the case, the statement by Michigan State to Professor Stradley in 1933 that "… the loan committee [had] no information [regarding] the students to indicate whether they are or are not athletes except that they may know the individual students personally," was not quite accurate. But in fairness to the college, Charles Wilkins only assumed the seat on the council after the State Board approved the request in September of 1932. That late action by the governing body implied Wilkins' impact on loan promises to athletes extended no more than five months before Stradley's investigation of the college in the early spring of 1933.

The original petition by the Athletic Council in March of 1930 coincided with aggressive recruiting efforts by Coach Crowley. During that era most high school seniors made enrollment decisions by late spring. Crowley was the first coach on record at Michigan State to travel about the Midwest in pursuit of senior athletes during the winter months. He visited the Chicago and Milwaukee Alumni Clubs in January and was reimbursed by the college for expenses.[56]

But in the spring of 1930, speeches alone were not sufficient to attract a boy to East Lansing. Crowley needed readily available money to acquire talent. The State Board failed to act on the Athletic Council's request that the comptroller sit-in on its meetings. As a consequence, Crowley may have encouraged the Downtown Coaches Club to fund his plan. John Hannah later commented that "… the club raised a lot of money, spent a lot of money and it wasn't long before good athletes [began to appear] on our campus." The State Board secretary, however, opposed the practice.[57]

"Sleepy Jim" Crowley appeared to be an impatient man. Student loans, approved in December of 1929, were not sufficient for the aggressive Crowley. A pay-for-play scheme, supported by the boosters, expeditiously accomplished what he wanted to be done during his early tenure in East Lansing.

Robert Shaw eventually became aware of Crowley's scheme. There were rumors reported to him that alumni and boosters were promising athletes financial support and later reneging on those agreements. The school, much to his dismay, had no control over the activity.[58] It was only a matter of time before some upset athlete or parent might reveal the illegal practices to the press.

---

[55] Minutes of the State Board of Agriculture. 15 September 1932. www.onthebanks.msu.edu

[56] Minutes of the State Board of Agriculture. 18 January 1930. www.onthebanks.msu.edu

[57] Devine, Tommy. "The Michigan State Construction Job." *Sport* December 1953. Michigan State University Archives. Ralph Young Papers, UA17.114; Box 903, folder: 72

[58] Ibid.

The State Board's delayed approval of the comptroller becoming an ex officio member of the Athletic Council in September of 1932–first proposed a few years earlier–may have been in part President Shaw's response to Crowley's involvement with the booster club. Wilkins would assure the coach loans, referenced in Stradley's investigation, necessary to attract talented football players. But the loans would originate from Michigan State College. There would be no need for outside sources offering the coach illegal dollars to lure a talented athlete to East Lansing. Accountability, to protect the "good name of Michigan State College," would be assured.

The challenge was how to collect on delinquent loans offered athletes incapable or unwilling to make payments in good faith. The college could not afford providing free educations during the Depression years. The solution to the comptroller's dilemma lay in having one guarantor for those notes. It was a means of ensuring Shaw's Law. Wilkins' choice for the role was businessman Fred Jenison.

The insurance agent probably knew Charles Wilkins well before 1934. The comptroller would have been the administrator Jenison dealt with directly while soliciting college business for his agency. Their association may have prompted the request that Jenison be that guarantor for student-athlete loans.

Jenison agreed to offer the service. It conveniently provided him a firmer foothold in Wilkins' office at Michigan State College. It also was a way of fortifying his passion for Spartan football. Wilkins turned delinquent notes over to Jenison on a periodic basis. Subsequently, the college would be reimbursed. The practice appeared to begin shortly after the 1933 NCA investigation.[59]

Despite providing the unusual service to his alma mater, it was unlikely that Fred Jenison's agency benefited by selling new products to the school. Bids were requested for any project, acquisition or service necessary for college operations. Insurance products sold to the college were no exception. Agents were encouraged to offer proposals for specific coverage sought by the administration.[60] As a consequence of this business practice, Michigan State maintained no cohesive insurance plan for protection of its growing infrastructure during most of the 1930s.

THE LOAN-GUARANTEE program was closely monitored by Michigan State and President Shaw. On October 28, 1937, Secretary Hannah wrote to Fred Jenison regarding some unpaid notes he had overlooked. "For your information there are … in the Treasurer's Office notes signed by (11) athletes for fees that have long been past due …" Hannah boldly underlined the word "fees" twice.[61]

Charles Wilkins reported directly to Hannah. The comptroller had been unsuccessful in gaining reimbursement from Jenison for some delinquent payments. The total amount was $444.95. A statement from the second in command at the college probably prompted a hasty response from the agent. As will be seen, however, there might have been another reason for Hannah's terse note to the agent.

---

[59] Hannah to Jenison. 28 October 1937. Michigan State University Archives. Jenison Family Papers; Collection 125; Box 1, folder: 10

[60] Wilkins to Hannah. 18 October 1937. Michigan State University Archives. Michigan State Board of Trustees, UA1.0. Supplementary Materials: 10/21/37; Box 1883, folder: 18

[61] Hannah to Jenison. 28 October 1937. Michigan State University Archives. Jenison Family Papers, Collection 125; Box 1, folder: 10

During the summer of 1937, Comptroller Wilkins made a presentation before the State Board regarding his concerns with inadequate fire protection on current campus buildings. Michigan State was in the early phases of enormous infrastructure growth, with numerous construction projects in progress. Wilkins was asked to report back in a few months with his recommendations. In October of 1937 he advised purchasing comprehensive fire insurance for all campus buildings.[62] Bids were requested, and 14 agencies responded. After reviewing all proposals, Wilkins recommended the Fred C. Jenison Agency plan.[63] Hannah supported his business manager's logic.

Jenison had clearly done a professional job in assessing the insurance needs of the college. In a confidential letter to Hannah and Wilkins, he presented an impressive proposal. The agent made an argument for Michigan State to simplify its insurance coverage and work with one agent rather than many (as had been its past practice). He also suggested acquiring the product from Queen Insurance Company based out of New York. That company was involved with the Great Chicago Fire and the San Francisco Earthquake decades earlier. It had received accolades for its timely and equitable loss adjustments in both catastrophes.[64]

The board accepted Wilkins' recommendations. Michigan State consummated the agreement on October 28, 1937, one week following that State Board meeting.[65] The annual premium for the blanket policy on fire coverage was $19,838.90.[66] Fred Jenison's commission for landing the business was $2,080.17. Realizing the financial gain for the agent, it was understandable, in hindsight, why a perturbed John Hannah, earlier that same day, wrote Jenison expressing his ire over the agent failing to reimburse the college $444.95 for delinquent loans dating back three years. No doubt, upon receiving the letter, Jenison immediately wrote out a check made payable to Michigan State College!

THE QUEEN Insurance contract was one of two major policies sold by Fred Jenison in 1937. A few months earlier, he had been successful in selling to the college surety bonds in the amount of $10,000 as well as a blanket bond to cover employees in the business office.[67] In gratitude for gaining that business, Jenison provided a gift of $100 to the State Board for the acquisition of two large flags for the military band on campus.[68]

Jenison's courtship of the college proved well worth the time and effort. He received almost $3,000 per year in payouts for his business accomplishments.[69] An executive from Queen Insurance Company personally congratulated him on his success. He offered the independent agent the company's full services for any future needs of the

---

[62] Minutes of the State Board of Agriculture. 21 October 1937. www.onthebanks.msu.edu

[63] Wilkins to Hannah. 18 October 1937. Michigan State University Archives. Board of Trustees, UA1.0. Supplementary Materials; Box 1883, folder: 18 10/21/37

[64] Jenison to Hannah and Wilkins. 19 October 1937. Michigan State University Archivers. Board of Trustees, UA1.0. Supplementary Materials; Box 1883, folder: 19 10/21/37

[65] Queen Insurance Company of America: receipt. 9 February 1938. Michigan State University Archives. Jenison Family Papers, Collection 125; Box 8, folder: 14

[66] Chapman, David A. 6 May 2010. Personal communication. O.W. Mourer acquired the Jenison Agency in 1939. Mourer's personal papers were donated to Chapman.

[67] Minutes of the State Board of Agriculture. 15 June 1936. www.onthebanks.msu.edu

[68] Minutes of the State Board of Agriculture. 14 June 1937. www.onthebanks.msu.edu

[69] Chapman, David A. 6 May 2010. Personal communication.

college.[70]

Six months after selling the large policy to Michigan State College, Jenison, at the age of 56, experienced personal tragedy when his wife, Edith, passed away unexpectedly in April of 1938. Her death probably forced him to contemplate estate planning. Fred and Edith had no heirs.

FREDERICK COWLES Jenison would survive his wife by only 10 months. On February 12, 1939, he died suddenly. At the March 8, 1939, board meeting Secretary Hannah announced that Jenison, having no living relatives, had bequeathed his entire estate to Michigan State College. Hannah was to be the executor of his will.

The initial estimate of that estate was $125,000.[71] In a gesture of appreciation for his support of Spartan athletics over the years, the State Board of Agriculture approved naming the new Gymnasium and Field House after Fred C. Jenison.[72] It was only the second time in school history that a facility had been named after a benefactor. The honor was traditionally reserved for former presidents, board members, or prominent faculty.

A decade later, the president's residence on central campus, following renovation with Jenison estate money, would be named in honor of Fred's mother, Alice Cowles Jenison.

Stocks, bonds, and property made up most of the assets of the Jenison estate. His agency, with prominent clients and receivable commissions, had value as well. Michigan State, being a state-owned facility, posed challenges for the executor. There were legal implications for the college selling what were now considered state-owned properties on the open market. A ruling by the state attorney general was required. Hannah, being well connected with state government, successfully cleared the hurdle.[73]

The Jenison's housekeeper, Matilda Walker, had been under their employ for over 17 years. Hannah used $4,000 from the estate, in line with Fred's wishes, to acquire an insurance policy for the German immigrant. She was guaranteed a monthly income of $40 after age 65.[74]

The business assets were sold for $20,000 to the O.W. Mourer Agency in Lansing just a few months following Jenison's death.[75] [76] Ogle Mourer was one of the 14 agents vying for the Michigan State contract that Jenison had ultimately been awarded. In acquiring the Fred C. Jenison Agency assets, he gained access to the college business office for future insurance needs of the expanding school. Mourer also assumed management of

---

[70] EWH to Jenison. 10 January 1939. Michigan State University. Jenison Family Papers, Collection 12; Box 8, folder: 16

[71] Minutes of the State Board of Agriculture. 8 March 1939. www.onthebanks.msu.edu

[72] Minutes of the State Board of Agriculture. 20 April 1939. www.onthebanks.msu.edu

[73] Read to Hannah. 31 January 1940. Michigan State University Archives. Board of Trustees, UA1.0. Supplementary Materials; Box 1885, folder: 6 10/21/37

[74] Minutes of the State Board of Agriculture. 21 December 1939. www.onthebanks.msu.edu

[75] Chapman, David. 5 May 2010. Personal communication. Chapman '56 worked for Mourer while attending MSC. Mourer acquired all Jenison Agency assets.

[76] Angus, Gartha. 5 May 2010. Personal communication. Mourer sold his agency to Mourer-Foster in the mid 1950s but retained both the MSC and John Hannah accounts until he formally retired.

all current policies.[77] [78]

On August 8, 1946, the agent made his final payment with interest to the college. Mourer would extend his appreciation to Michigan State for continued business by periodically gifting the State Board. Confidentiality was always requested, and monies were to be used at the discretion of the board.[79] For the next 16 years he would gift the institution over $62,000.[80]

Other assets were dealt with shortly after Jenison's death. Michigan State sold the stocks and bonds immediately. The Jenison home at 403 Seymour in downtown Lansing, valued at $14,500, was acquired by the Michigan TB Association.[81] One of the lots in the Chesterfield subdivision sold for $1,200.[82] East of Eagle, Michigan, the college opted to maintain 94 acres of virgin land for use by the forestry department. Professors sought the tract for research and educational purposes.[83]

But the asset of greatest significance in the estate was the property, first acquired by Nelson Jenison in 1884, located at the corner of Ottawa and Washington Avenue in downtown Lansing. Fred Jenison was quite aware of the value of the building sitting on that land. The leasing agreement he had negotiated with the F.W. Woolworth Company back in April of 1927 was currently earning the estate $27,000 a year. By May of 1947 the annual rental would provide the future owner of the property $35,820 in gross revenue.[84]

A few years before his death, Jenison had been contacted by a real estate agent from New York representing a client interested in acquiring Woolworth-leased properties about the country. A quick negotiation and sale "at a fair price" was promised. Jenison, however, never followed through on the offer.[85] It was far too valuable an asset at the time.

After Fred Jenison's death, the value of the Woolworth property was estimated at $300,000 by real estate agents in the Lansing area.[86] The closing took place within two months of the appraisal. The final price was never revealed.

ON JULY 5, 1940, the State Board of Agriculture met in executive session to review Hannah's report as the executor of the Jenison estate. Secretary Hannah submitted an audited summary of each financial transaction. All claims against the estate had been settled. He then recommended that the matter be closed and that all dollars be turned over to Michigan State College.[87] The final value of the bequeathal was $625,552.61.[88]

---

[77] Treasurer of Michigan State Board of Agriculture to Michigan Inspection Bureau. 5 May 1939. Personal papers of David Chapman

[78] Hannah to Mourer. 1 April 1939. Personal papers of David Chapman

[79] Minutes of the State Board of Agriculture. 16 October 1947. www.onthebanks.msu.edu

[80] Mourer to Pierson, M.R. 19 August 1959. Personal papers of David Chapman

[81] Minutes of the State Board of Agriculture. 21 December 1939. www.onthebanks.msu.edu

[82] Minutes of the State Board of Agriculture. 22 February 1940. www.onthebanks.msu.edu

[83] Minutes of the State Board of Agriculture. 18 April 1940. www.onthebanks.msu.edu

[84] Jenison-Woolworth Lease 15 April 1927. Michigan State University Archives. Jenison Family Papers, Collection 125; Box 6, folder: 47

[85] Phelps to Jenison. 29 July 1936. Michigan State University Archives. Jenison Family Papers, Collection 125; Box 7, folder: 2

[86] Minutes of the State Board of Agriculture. 22 February 1940. www.onthebanks.msu.edu

[87] Minutes of the State Board of Agriculture. 5 July 1940. www.onthebanks.msu.edu

[88] Minutes of the State Board of Agriculture. 28 August 1941. www.onthebanks.msu.edu

The State Board had one final obligation before closing the estate. On a motion by Melville McPherson, and supported by his colleague Forest Akers, "it was voted to recommend that Mr. Hannah be allowed the customary legal fee for handling the executorship of (the) Estate ..." John Hannah was awarded $6,330 for his impeccable services over the preceding 15 months.[89]

As executor, the secretary of the board was privy to a parcel of property Jenison had owned in northern Michigan: a quarter mile of Lake Michigan frontage on 40 acres that included a cabin and a small farm.[90] Hannah requested that the fee be used to acquire the land in Good Hart near the Straits of Mackinac. Having married Robert Shaw's daughter Sara in 1938, Hannah wanted the property as a summer vacation residence for his wife and family. The appraised value was $5,000. The State Board granted approval without dissent. With that action completed, a motion for final closure of the estate was approved.[91]

THE FREDERIK Cowles Jenison will mandated that his estate be used by the president of the college and the State Board for "improvement of the university with particular emphasis on athletics."[92] Twelve months following legal closure of the bequeathal, John Hannah would succeed the retiring Robert Shaw as the twelfth president of Michigan State College. Fully aware of Jenison's intentions, the new head of the college would use income derived from the gift to offer financial aid to athletes attending the school. That subsidy, extremely controversial for its time, would prove critical for Hannah in achieving his vision of transforming the pioneer land-grant college into an institution offering extension services to the world.

---

[89] Minutes of the State Board of Agriculture. 28 August 1941. www.onthebanks.msu.edu

[90] Hannah to Morrill. "Hannah Summer Cabin at Good Hart, Michigan." 2 September 1948. University of Minnesota Archives. Morrill J.L.; Box 1, folder: correspondence A-L, Ha-He

[91] Minutes of the State Board of Agriculture. 18 April 1940. www.onthebanks.msu.edu

[92] Hannah, John A. *A Memoir.* East Lansing, Michigan State University Press, 1980. p. 121

Oxymoron: The Athletic Scholarship

A THLETICS BECAME a significant part of the collegiate experience with the advent of intramural sports in the mid-1800s. Baseball, football, track and field, and later basketball evolved, each reflecting the competitive American spirit. Club sports, played on campuses, gradually transitioned beyond those boundaries with institutions agreeing to sponsor their own teams. The phenomenon of intercollegiate athletics was not far off. Football, by the turn of the 20th century, became *the* collegiate game. By the early 1920s, it captivated the public as a form of entertainment.

As a growth industry, football spawned many new careers. Coaches, administrators, support staff, athletic trainers, and vendors were just a few of many. One profession, the sportswriter, would proliferate with the growing popularity of athletic competition. Newspapers needed writers to fill sports pages capable of generating additional advertising dollars. Beyond assuring financial success for publishers, these men further impacted the popularity of the collegiate game. The Carnegie Report of 1929 devoted an entire chapter to those gifted with the pen.[1] The power of written words, often embellished, was profound. Heroes, institutional legends, and storied traditions were created with the typewriter.[2]

Regardless of accuracy, these reporters helped sustain a nation during periods of war or economic duress.

With the rising popularity of football, in no small part due to sportswriters such as Grantland Rice, the controversial role of academic institutions as entertainers for the mass public became more pervasive.[3] [4] Fans gained an identity with a regional home team. Victories boosted community pride. Gridiron success ultimately became the only goal on Saturday afternoons in the fall. In more and more homes, Sunday mornings were devoted to church attendance and the sports page.

---

[1] Savage, Howard. *American College Athletics*. Boston: D.B. Updike/The Merrymount Press, 1929. pp. 266-290

[2] Sperber, Murray. *Onward to Victory*. New York: Henry Holt and Company, 1998. p. 53

[3] Lester, Robin. *Stagg's University: The Rise, Decline & Fall of Big-Time Football at Chicago.* Urbana and Chicago: University of Illinois Press, 1995. pp. 127-28

[4] Ruthven to Griffith. 19 December 1930. Bentley Historical Library, University of Michigan. Ralph W. Aigler Papers, 87406 Aa 2; Box 4, folder: correspondence 1929-33 Ruthven

Tickets for games with limited seating were soon valued commodities. With this increasing demand, successful programs built enormous stadiums of concrete and brick during the early 1920s. The challenge for athletic directors, charged with balancing their budgets, was meeting mortgage payments. A winning football program made the job easier.

Originally a part-time position, college football coaching became a full-time job with the influx of money into the game from ticket sales. Coaches took on roles as surrogate father figures. They were encouraged to develop men of character and integrity, but they were also expected to achieve victories on the field. Incomes reflected that growing pressure. A coach with a pedigree, and past success, was highly sought after.

James Crowley considered resigning from Michigan State in February of 1932 to take on the State University of Iowa job. The inducement was a salary close to $11,000. Only one year earlier, he had renegotiated his contract with the Spartans, following one successful season, for a 33 percent pay increase. If not for a binding clause, craftily included in the revised agreement by President Robert Shaw, Crowley would have been coaching in Iowa City during the fall of 1932.

Some schools gave coaches faculty positions, with tenure, to mitigate the pressures of winning. It was seemingly a noble practice that had its origins at the University of Chicago. In 1892, Amos Alonzo Stagg was hired by President William Rainey Harper. As an enticement to sign-on, Harper offered the coach faculty status. Stagg's academic title was "Associate Professor and Director of Physical Culture and Athletics." Harper's "innovation" marked the beginning of the professionalization of college coaching in America.[5]

Crowley, too, was hired by Michigan State as an associate professor in physical education.[6] But a faculty position with tenure was minor reassurance in the opinion of most coaches. As Howard Savage commented in the Carnegie Report, "A coach who trusts to faculty status and fair words for safety in the hour of disapproval leans upon a broken reed."[7] Job security, as a coach on Saturday afternoons, still depended on winning football games.

Despite Savage's pessimistic assessment of contracted promises, Michigan State did have a history of abiding by the tenure guarantee. If a Spartan coach lost his job on the gridiron, tenure always assured him a teaching position with faculty status in the department of physical education.[8] When Crowley's successor, Charlie Bachman, was asked to resign as head coach in 1946, he remained on the faculty while teaching at the college until retiring in 1954.[9]

In the late fall of 1963 another head coach at Michigan State, Hugh "Duffy" Daugherty, was under immense pressure to step down. The success of his predecessor, Biggie Munn, a Spartan legend, was still haunting him. With unrelenting criticism from the public and press, Daugherty was contemplating an offer from Notre Dame. President John

---

[5] Lester, Robin. *Stagg's University: The Rise, Decline & Fall of Big-Time College Football at Chicago.* Urbana and Chicago: University of Illinois Press. p. 17

[6] Minutes of the State Board of Agriculture. 17 July 1929. www.onthebanks.msu.edu

[7] Savage, Howard. *American College Athletics*. Boston: D.B. Updike/The Merrymount Press, 1929. p. 189

[8] Hannah to Members of Athletic Council and Members of the Council of Deans. 29 October 1963. Michigan State University Archives. John Hannah Papers, UA2.1.12; Box 41, folder 4: Intercollegiate athletics, D. Daugherty

[9] Minutes of the State Board of Agriculture. 22 November 1954 . www.onthebanks.msu.edu

Hannah reassured the embattled coach.[10] He devised a plan to circumvent the criticism and assuage his coach's concerns.

> A few years ago, the University adopted the policy of appointing chairmen of academic departments for five-year periods, their appointments being subject to review at the end of each five-year period ... The recommendation to the Trustees in the case of Mr. Daugherty is that the policy in the academic departments be extended to athletics, and that he be appointed head football coach for a five-year period ... This would put him on the same basis as chairmen of academic departments; he will continue as full professor, and retain the tenure protection as such.[11]

John Hannah made it very clear this was not a contract extension. Professor Daugherty maintained faculty status. Similar to chairs in other college departments, a review of his leadership skills and accomplishments as department head would take place in five years. If it was determined he was no longer an effective leader, the professor could return to "teaching status" in the physical education department. But in the meantime, Daugherty had the full support of the president and the Board of Trustees. Win-loss records would not impact his job security at Michigan State University of Agriculture and Applied Science.

Hannah effectively silenced the critics. Professor Duffy Daugherty ultimately coached two of the most talented and successful football teams in college football history. The Notre Dame-Michigan State contest of 1966 remains, in the opinion of many, the most famous intercollegiate game of all time. Sociological and cultural reasons for that claim far exceed points of contention regarding the unsatisfactory 10-10 outcome.[12]

ALL SCHOOLS professed adherence to the amateur code promoted by an impotent NCAA, but, in practice, most failed to abide by it. As money became a significant factor in college football, the three cardinal sins–recruiting, subsidizing, and suspect eligibility requirements for either admission or continued play–were often committed by men hired to succeed on Saturday afternoons. Rumors of violations permeated the game. Quite often they were valid.[13] [14]

Many Southern schools, including those within the Southeastern Conference, maintained no real standard for eligibility.[15] In the absence of rules, any athlete, regardless

---

[10] Thomas, David. *Michigan State College: John Hannah and the Creation of a World University, 1926-1969.* East Lansing: Michigan State University Press. p. 328

[11] Hannah to Members of Athletic Council and Members of the Council of Deans. 29 October 1963. Michigan State University Archives. John Hannah Papers, UA2.1.12; Box 41, folder 4: Intercollegiate athletics, D. Daugherty

[12] Celizic, Mike. *The Biggest Game Of Them All: Notre Dame and Michigan State and the Fall of '66.* New York: Simon and Schuster, 1992. pp. 309-321

[13] Griffith to Aigler. 14 August 1941. Bentley Historical Library, University of Michigan. Ralph W. Aigler Papers, 87406 Aa 2; Box 8, folder: correspondence 1940-45 Griffith

[14] "Report on Directors Meeting Held at Iowa City, March 9 & 10, 1928." Wieman, E.E. Bentley Historical Library, University of Michigan. Athletic Department, 943 Bimu 2; Box 84, faculty representatives minutes.

[15] Griffith to Conference Athletic Directors and Football Coaches. 5 September 1944. The Ohio State

of his qualifications for higher education, could participate in football. Recruiting was closely tied to controversial "athletic" scholarships offered to finance attendance at the schools. North of the Mason-Dixon Line the University of Pittsburgh maintained similar institutional practices. It won mythical national championships with a policy that essentially employed athletes during the 1930s. "Salaries," more accurately "fixed subsidies," were assured by the "go-and-get-'em brigade" of recruiters openly searching out talent to maintain Pitt's highly successful program.[16]

But Pittsburgh was not alone. As the Carnegie Report pointed out, athletic scholarships were pervasive even during the 1920s. Disguised as "awards for leadership, all-around performance or based on committee or personal recommendations," Savage concluded they still were "frankly and unequivocally ... athletic scholarships." A number of northern schools were implicated.[17]

The Western Conference proudly professed a higher standard than others. Recruiting and subsidies were strictly forbidden if offered "on the basis of athletic skill." Short of qualifying under closely monitored academic scholarship criteria, the phrase essentially forbade any form of loan, grant, or job offering typically available for the non-athlete. With the increasing popularity of the game and the inherent pressure to win, however, coaches and their representatives found ways to circumvent the regulations.

Various revisions of the Intercollegiate Handbook attempted to address these practices. In the 1930 version, "athletic directors and coaches shall not, by the distribution of literature, or by personal interviews of their own seeking, endeavor to recruit athletes." They could, however, as representatives of the institution, make speeches at high school banquets, which became a subtle way of selling a program and meeting talented athletes. The coach or director might also "... [respond] to inquiries, or in casual conversation ... point out what they believe to be the advantages of attending [their] institution ... but further they shall not go." The policy went on to forbid associates of the school, including field secretaries, alumni, students, and fans, from any form of recruiting.[18]

The 1941 revision of the Handbook was less vague. Recruiting was clearly becoming a problem in the prewar years. "It shall not be permissible for any member of the athletic department to participate in recruiting or subsidizing." The section went on to forbid any open correspondence "or initiative in making personal contact with any prospective athlete with the view to influencing him in his choice of college."[19] In essence, speeches at awards banquets or alumni gatherings (that might include high school students) were now unacceptable unless the coach followed strict policy guidelines.

By tradition, especially within the Western Conference, the athlete was obligated to initiate communication with a coach. It usually was in the form of a letter requesting an

---

University Archives, Director of Athletics (RG 9/e-1/10), "Intercollegiate Conference: Commissioner: Correspondence (Griffith): 1944-45."

[16] Wallace, Francis. "Test Case at Pitt: The Facts about College Football Play for Pay." *The Saturday Evening Post,* 28 October 1930. University of Pittsburgh Archives, 9/10-A; Box 1, folder: FF772

[17] Waterson, John Sayle. *College Football: History-Spectacle-Controversy.* Baltimore and London: The Johns Hopkins University Press, 2000. pp. 166-167

[18] Handbook of the Intercollegiate Conference of Faculty Representatives-Revised 1930. University of Minnesota Archives, Department of Intercollegiate Athletics Papers; Box 13, folder: small handbook 1895-1907, 1931, 1941

[19] Ibid.

interview on campus; the high school senior, through that correspondence, was also permitted to market himself.[20] The coach was not allowed to travel to the student. Their conversations were to be informational only. Inducements, including potential jobs, were strictly forbidden.[21] The player, while visiting the campus, could not demonstrate athletic skills.[22] [23] If the coach remained interested in the athlete, all he could offer was a tryout during the fall, assuming the student gained admission to the college. The three-member Faculty Representatives Committee on Eligibility closely monitored practices about the conference.

In reality, certain coaches did travel to meet athletes. Ohio, loaded with high school football talent, was raided by coaches for decades. By the late 1930s, OSU Athletic Director Lynn St. John decided to make a stand. He proclaimed what might be called the "Buckeye Rule." In St. John's opinion, Ohio boys belonged to the large school based in Columbus. His edict essentially forbade coaches, at least those employed by member institutions, from invading the state in search of skilled players. There would be scheduling repercussions for anyone caught crossing his borders.[24] [25]

The NCAA, with the assistance of a number of amateurism purists, including Ralph Aigler and Karl Leib, of Iowa, drafted in 1947 what would be known as the Sanity Code. It was intended to end the lunacy in recruiting and subsidizing. The code allowed academic scholarship dollars for athletes entering college with demonstrable high school proficiency in valid course work. It was officially passed by the membership in January of 1948. Punishment for violation of the code was harsh; expulsion from the NCAA and its sponsored tournaments was mandatory. The greater penalty, however, was institutional embarrassment.

Anticipating passage of the Sanity Code, the Western Conference revised its Handbook during the spring of 1947. As part of that revision, General Regulation XIV included a phrase that essentially codified the Buckeye Rule. "This Conference strongly affirms that intercollegiate athletic teams should be truly representative of their student bodies" in terms of the percentages of in-state and out-of-state matriculates.[26] Any deviation from that ratio would raise suspicions about illegal recruiting outside home state

---

[20] Waterson, John Sayle. *College Football: History-Spectacle-Controversy.* Baltimore and London: The Johns Hopkins University Press, 2000. p. 168

[21] Handbook of the Intercollegiate Conference of Faculty Representatives-Revised 1941. University of Minnesota Archives, Department of Intercollegiate Athletics Papers; Box 13, folder: small handbook 1941

[22] Rules, Regulations and Opinions of the Intercollegiate Conference of Faculty Representatives-Revised 1930. University of Minnesota Archives, Department of Intercollegiate Athletics Papers; Box 13, folder: 1930

[23] Handbook of the Intercollegiate Conference of Faculty Representatives-Revised 1941. University of Minnesota Archives, Department of Intercollegiate Athletics Papers; Box 13, folder: small handbook 1941

[24] Untitled (football rosters of all Big Nine schools). Circa 1946. The Ohio State University Archives, James E. Pollard Papers (RG 40/52/2/33), "Western Conference: 1931, 1938, 1945, 1950."

[25] Griffith to Aigler. 31 May 1938. Bentley Historical Library, University of Michigan Archives. Ralph W. Aigler Papers, 87406 Aa 2; Box 6, folder: correspondence 1934-39 Griffith 9/37-7/39

[26] "Records of Proceedings and the Official Minutes of the 491st Meeting of the Athletic Board of The Ohio State University." 12 October 1948. The Ohio State University Archives, Director of Athletics (RG 9/e-1/1), "Athletics Board: minutes: June 1946-June 1951."

boundaries.[27]

Despite the Handbook regulations on recruiting, many coaches, over the years, found ways to draw students to their programs. Alumni were encouraged to steer prospects to their alma mater and ultimately the coach's office.[28] [29] High school talent was often provided means to visit the school.[30] [31]

Boosters offered another form of financial assistance to help a school's recruiting efforts. In the Midwest, jobs off campus were provided by those fans owning local businesses.[32] Quite often the athlete performed little if any work. And it was not unusual for remuneration to exceed what the non-athlete received for a similar work.[33]

In some regions of the country, fans and alumni created slush funds to pass dollars, under the table, to athletes needing assistance.[34] There was no need for repayment. Loans provided by boosters were another means to subsidize the student; guaranteed forgiveness was often implicit.[35]

AS AN unsanctioned hand-out from colleges, the athletic scholarship probably had its origins in the 1920s, as the Carnegie Report noted. It first became an officially legitimate subsidy in the Deep South during the Depression. The Southeastern Conference codified the practice in 1935. Unlike the East and Midwest, opportunities for a student to legitimately finance an education, through jobs, were sparse in that region of the country.[36]

The SEC resolution of 1935 was very carefully worded. "Be it resolved: That athletes may receive for their services any aid, such as scholarships, work, or other financial assistance, such as any other student may receive for participation in any other activity … such aid, however, shall not be in excess of the legitimate expenses of attending the institution … "[37] The statement was noxious to many Western Conference purists.

But Fielding Yost of Michigan, when asked to render an opinion on behalf of his

---

[27] Aigler to Mullendore. 14 July 1945. Bentley Historical Library, University of Michigan. Ralph W. Aigler Papers, 87406 Aa 2; Box 8, folder: correspondence 1940-45 "L-M" misc.

[28] Behee, John. *Fielding Yost's Legacy to the University of Michigan.* Ann Arbor: Uhlrich's Books, Inc., 1971. p. 88

[29] Griffith to Crisler. 8 April 1944. . The Ohio State University Archives, Director of Athletics (RG 9/e-1/10), "Intercollegiate Conference: Commissioner: Correspondence (Griffith): 1943-44 (Folder 1 of 3)."

[30] Griffith to Yost. 27 July 1937. Bentley Historical Library, University of Michigan Archives. Ralph W. Aigler Papers, 87406 Aa 2; Box 6, folder: correspondence 1934-36 Griffith 1/52-8/37

[31] Griffith to Yost. 18 October 1935. Bentley Historical Library, University of Michigan Archives. Ralph W. Aigler Papers, 87406 Aa 2; Box 6, folder: correspondence 1934-39

[32] Aigler to Long. 22 October 1935. Bentley Historical Library, University of Michigan Archives. Ralph W. Aigler Papers, 87406 Aa 2; Box 12, folder: correspondence

[33] Waterson, John Sayle. *College Football: History-Spectacle-Controversy.* Baltimore and London: The Johns Hopkins University Press, 2000. pp. 169-170

[34] Ibid., p.167

[35] Savage, Howard. *American College Athletics.* Boston: D.B. Updike/The Merrymount Press, 1929. p. 251

[36] Waterson, John Sayle. *College Football: History-Spectacle-Controversy.* Baltimore and London: The Johns Hopkins University Press, 2000. p. 183

[37] Yost to Griffith. 26 May 1936. Bentley Historical Library, University of Michigan. Ralph W. Aigler Papers, 87406 Aa2; Box 7, correspondence: 1934-39, "X-Y-Z" misc.

fellow directors and Commissioner Griffith, was not so troubled. "When all five paragraphs [outlining the rules for awarding scholarships to athletes] are read and considered, the resolution is entirely different from what one might be led to believe by reading only the first paragraph."[38] A native West Virginian, Yost may have also been sensitive to the economic plight of the southern states. He found little to criticize.

Regardless of Yost's conclusions, what ultimately mattered, at least for the directors and the commissioner, was the opinion of the powerful and influential Ralph Aigler. He vehemently opposed the SEC policy. The Western Conference discouraged members from competing against schools offering any financial assistance at that time.[39] Aigler believed that maintaining contracts with the SEC schools would only condone the illegal practice.[40]

The law professor was a stickler for rules and regulations. During his 38-year tenure as Big Ten faculty representative for the University of Michigan, he heard numerous proposals by member institutions planning to offer legitimate scholarships to athletes. With his oversight as a long-serving member of the Eligibility Committee, however, the real intent of such programs was invariably discovered.

The University of Wisconsin, for example, had proposed a clever way of recruiting and subsidizing young men of "superior academic and athletic attainments." The Reynolds Plan involved a summer training school for 100 in-state boys meeting this requirement. Upon completion of the program, the university would grant a certain number of scholarships to attend Wisconsin.[41] Faculty and coaches were involved.

Aigler opposed the proposal. He questioned condoning a program that "frankly permits subsidization and recruitment to a certain point." He predicted others would soon emulate the Reynolds scheme but "… each one would try to work out a plan that would be just a little more attractive than the Wisconsin plan." The professor noted that "the problems involved in … recruiting and subsidizing are difficult ones and I doubt whether any plan, [including the Wisconsin proposal] … can solve them all." He expressed "sympathy" for students struggling to finance a college education while competing in athletics. But the law professor was a realist, too. He concluded that "we may [strive towards eliminating the evils of intercollegiate competition], but with human nature as it is the hope that we shall attain complete success is in my humble opinion a vain one."[42]

Professor Robert Reynolds' innovative proposal was vetoed by the Faculty Representative Committee. It was another victory for the most powerful man in the Western Conference.

AS BIG Ten commissioner and public relations front man, John Griffith found it difficult to

---

[38] Yost to Griffith. 26 May 1936. Bentley Historical Library, University of Michigan. Ralph W. Aigler Papers, 87406 Aa2; Box 7, correspondence: 1934-39, "X-Y-Z" misc.

[39] Rules, Regulations and Opinions of the Intercollegiate Conference of Faculty Representatives – Revised 1930. University of Minnesota Archives. Department of Intercollegiate Athletics Papers; Box 13, folder: small handbooks 1895-1908, 1930, 1941.

[40] Aigler to Griffith. 17 January 1939. Bentley Historical Library, University of Michigan. Ralph W. Aigler Papers, 87406 Aa2; Box 6, correspondence: 1934-39 Griffith 9/37-7/39

[41] Griffith to Lorenz. 9 June 1936. Bentley Historical Library, University of Michigan. Ralph W. Aigler Papers, 87406 Aa2; Box 6, correspondence 1934-39

[42] Aigler to Lorenz. 1 July 1936. Bentley Historical Library, University of Michigan. Ralph W. Aigler Papers, 87406 Aa2; Box 12, Athletic Correspondence: 1933-36 "L" misc.

justify the conference's hard-line stance on recruiting and subsidizing. The SEC policy on athletic scholarships challenged him in particular. He had to craft a cautious reply to avoid claims of insensitivity to the plight of the student struggling to meet college expenses during tough economic times.[43]

By the late 1930s, that intransigent position, primarily promoted by Ralph Aigler, was gradually yielding to common sense. Certain financing options appeared to be plausible if managed properly by the institution.[44] [45] Surprisingly, Michigan State College played a role in that conversion.

On January 16, 1939, Professor Aigler, Athletic Director Fielding Yost, and Head Coach Herbert "Fritz" Crisler drove to East Lansing to meet with their Michigan State counterparts, Dean Ralph Huston, Ralph Young, and Charlie Bachman. The encounter took place at the Student Union.[46]

Michigan called for the meeting, in large part, to remind the Spartans of their need to comply with Handbook policies.[47] Failure to do so, they warned, could potentially result in the termination of future contracts with the Wolverines. It was an impotent threat. The intrastate rivalry would survive the January confrontation. Taxpayers would not tolerate a Michigan boycott of what they considered a state classic.[48]

The Michigan Troika had a very specific agenda. Aigler did not believe that the college abided by the revised 1930 Handbook rule on eligibility—one of the three cardinal sins.[49] [50] [51] Only a few years earlier, in 1935, he wrote in confidence to a fellow faculty representative that "any high school graduate can get into Michigan State ..."[52] Both Crisler and the aging Yost were present to offer examples of the other sin committed by MSC—subsidies. Rumors of loans, scholarships, and free training-table meals were at issue.[53] [54]

---

[43] Aigler to Lorenz. 1 July 1936. Bentley Historical Library, University of Michigan. Ralph W. Aigler Papers, 87406 Aa2; Box 12, Athletic Correspondence: 1933-36 "L" misc.

[44] Aigler to Owens. 23 January 1939. Bentley Historical Library, University of Michigan. Ralph W. Aigler Papers, 87406 Aa 2; Box 6, folder: correspondence 1934-39

[45] Aigler to Griffith. 26 January 1939. Bentley Historical Library, University of Michigan. Ralph W. Aigler Papers, 87406 Aa 2; Box 6, folder: correspondence 1934-39

[46] Yost to Young. 20 January 1939. Bentley Historical Library, University of Michigan. Herbert Orin Crisler Papers, 85823 AC UAm Aa2; Box 1, MSU correspondence: 1943-46

[47] Ibid.

[48] Aigler to Long. 7 October 1935. Bentley Historical Library, University of Michigan. Ralph W. Aigler Papers, 87406 Aa 2; Box 12, folder: athletics correspondence 1933-36 "L" misc.

[49] Handbook of the Intercollegiate Conference of Faculty Representatives-September 10, 1908. University of Minnesota Archives, University of Minnesota Department of Intercollegiate Athletics Papers; Box 13, folder: A Digest of the Proceedings of the Intercollegiate Conference of Faculty Representatives 1895-1908, 1930, 1941

[50] Yost to Young. 20 January 1939. Bentley Historical Library, University of Michigan. Ralph W. Aigler Papers, 87406 Aa 2; Box 1, folder: topical correspondence "MSU 1943-46"

[51] Aigler to Long. 7 October 1935. Bentley Historical Library, University of Michigan. Ralph W. Aigler Papers, 87406 Aa 2; Box 12, folder: athletics correspondence 1933-36 "L" misc.

[52] Ibid.

[53] Yost to Young. 20 January 1939. Bentley Historical Library, University of Michigan. Herbert Orin Crisler Papers, 85823 AC UAm Aa2; Box 1, MSU correspondence: 1943-46

[54] Bachman, Charles. "The Athletic Side of John A. Hannah." Circa 1970. Michigan State University Archives. Hannah Archives Project, UA2.1.12; Box 34, folder: 2 Bachman

Somewhat to the surprise of the Ann Arbor contingency, Michigan State was compliant with most Western Conference standards on eligibility for game-day competition.[55] The remaining violations pertaining to scholastic requirements would be addressed by Faculty Representative Huston.

The second agenda item, subsidies for athletes, proved to be highly contentious. The college representatives denied offering a training-table. But Michigan was more interested in other forms of financial aid provided students in violation of the Handbook.

Years later Charlie Bachman recalled the discussions in detail.[56] Yost, early on, took the offensive and charged the Spartans with granting scholarships to athletes. Dean Ralph Huston quickly retorted with a question to the legend from Ann Arbor. "Before we go into the details on our scholarships, would he ... explain what would happen if on good authority he learned that one of their alumni was subsidizing one of Michigan's top football players?"[57] In January of 1939, Huston was undoubtedly referring to Tom Harmon. The commissioner's office had been inundated with rumors of the future Heisman Trophy winner being supported by boosters about Ann Arbor.[58]

Yost answered Huston's question by stating, "We do not have any control over our alumni." The quick-thinking Huston caught the old man off guard with his reply: "We do have control over our [financial assistance]." Huston was referring to President Robert Shaw's dictum following the North Central Association investigation of the college back in 1933.[59] Shaw maintained it was ethically proper to assist athletes whose skills were benefiting the school's coffers, especially during the Depression years. His only requirement was that all grants, jobs, and loans from the school fall under the auspices of faculty and administrators. The president's experience with Bachman's predecessor, Jim Crowley, had taught him an invaluable lesson.[60]

Ralph Aigler departed the meeting enlightened by some of Dean Huston's responses. He wrote to Commissioner Griffith the following day. In that note, Aigler, referring to a small group of NCAA purists–including himself–who wanted to prohibit athletic scholarships, jobs, and loans, stated that their hard-line stance was "lacking in sympathy with the needy boy," and might lose "the general support" of the membership. "The compromise I have in mind would be to recognize frankly that we will get little, if any, public support for a movement that rests upon the illegality, so to speak, of honest jobs or even of aid in getting honest jobs for athletes."[61]

---

[55] Bachman, Charles. "The Athletic Side of John A. Hannah." Circa 1970. Michigan State University Archives. Hannah Archives Project, UA2.1.12; Box 34, folder: 2 Bachman

[56] Bachman's statement, written 30 years later, was not chronologically accurate. Nonetheless, it offers an account of what took place during the meeting.

[57] Bachman, Charles. "The Athletic Side of John A. Hannah." Circa 1970. Michigan State University Archives. Hannah Archives Project, UA2.1.12; Box 34, folder: 2 Bachman

[58] Griffith to Crisler. 1 March 1939. Bentley Historical Library, University of Michigan. Ralph W. Aigler Papers, 87406 Aa2; Box 6, folder: correspondence 1934-39

[59] Stradley, B.S. "Michigan State College of Agriculture and Applied Science-1933." Circa April 1933. Michigan State University Archives. Robert Shaw Papers, UA 2.1.11; Box 840, folder 71

[60] Devine, Tommy. "The Michigan State Construction Job." *Sport* December 1953: 15-17, 66-67. Michigan State University Archives. Ralph Young Papers, UA 17.114; Box 903, folder: 72

[61] Aigler to Griffith. 17 January 1939. Bentley Historical Library, University of Michigan. Ralph W. Aigler Papers, 87406 Aa2; Box 6, correspondence: 1934-39 Griffith 9/37-7/39

Aigler was willing to accept certain forms of financial assistance. He found no real conflict with an alumnus or fan subsidizing an individual student-athlete with a loan or outright gift. He acknowledged that the concept was not "as free of criticism as the employment type of aid," but it was a subsidy that he could accept. "Aid given by an individual, generally speaking, is exceedingly difficult to uncover, and besides, it is usually explained by some rather natural interest in the boy himself." He felt it a rare case where a fan, for "love of alma mater," would subsidize numerous young men.[62]

For Aigler, sinning lay in athletic scholarships supported by pooling contributions from many anonymous sources. He wanted to focus efforts on eliminating booster funds that lacked institutional oversight.

> I am not foolish enough to think that there are no possible evils in the other
> types of subsidization to which I have referred, but I do think that they are
> relatively simple and inoffensive as compared with the ones I have
> emphasized for condemnation, and I wonder whether our efforts to keep
> real professionalism out of our college athletics will not be aided if we
> center our efforts at elimination upon these more vicious types of aid.[63]

A few days later, with legitimate subsidies still on his mind, he wrote to Professor William Owens of Stanford Law School. Aigler shared some of his ideas mentioned in the Griffith letter. He emphasized, once again, that maintaining "too quixotic and idealistic" a stance on all aid or assistance would hurt the amateur cause. "I think we have got to look at it from a practical point of view, taking into account ... the attitude of the public." The Michigan law professor concluded by stating, "I, for one, am ready to compromise a bit on a matter like this."[64]

Ralph W. Aigler, as will be seen, was no longer opposed to providing scholarship dollars to an intellectually gifted athlete. What troubled the professor, however, was offering an "athletic scholarship" merely for proficiency in a sport.[65] The juxtaposition of the two words was an oxymoron.[66]

ON JULY 1, 1941, John Hannah took over the office of Robert Shaw after having served as secretary of the State Board for six years. Among his previous responsibilities while managing operations at the college, Hannah had overseen a loan program intended for all enrolled students. A three-man committee, including the comptroller and two faculty members, determined which students merited aid.

Other than loans, Michigan State College had very little it could offer students during the Depression. The school, like so many others, was struggling financially. The budget for 1933-34 alone was reduced by 11 percent; individual salaries were lowered by

---

[62] Aigler to Griffith. 17 January 1939. Bentley Historical Library, University of Michigan. Ralph W. Aigler Papers, 87406 Aa2; Box 6, correspondence: 1934-39 Griffith 9/37-7/39
[63] Ibid.
[64] Aigler to Owens. 23 January 1939. Bentley Historical Library, University of Michigan. Ralph W. Aigler Papers, 87406 Aa2; Box 6, correspondence: 1934-39 Griffith 9/37-7/39
[65] Ibid.
[66] Duderstadt, James J. *Intercollegiate Athletics and the American University*. Ann Arbor: The University of Michigan Press, 2000. p. 191

almost seven percent.[67] President Hannah commented on those challenging years when he served as secretary.

> We had no scholarship funds, no gifts or blandishments of any economic value. It was the depth of the Depression and all Michigan State could offer was an opportunity for a young man to come to college. If he had no funds or family help, he might be able to borrow enough to pay his tuition and we might be able to help him get a part-time job.[68]

John Hannah was not quite accurate. For the first 60 years of its existence there were no scholarships offered at Michigan Agricultural College.[69] By 1932, however, the college administration finally had no choice but to assist students. The State Board of Agriculture established 32 "alumni scholarships," one from each senatorial district. Students had to finish in the top 20 percent of their high school class to be eligible for the grants. Aid was unrelated to athletic skills.[70]

Regardless of Hannah's recollections, during the 1930s Ralph Aigler was convinced that Michigan State College provided athletic scholarships. He shared that conviction with Commissioner Griffith in anticipation of the intrastate rivalry scheduled for October 5, 1935. Charlie Bachman's team had soundly defeated Harry Kipke's the year before. It was the first Spartan victory over the Wolverines in two decades of play in Ann Arbor.

> I am afraid we shall be in for a bad time of it next Saturday. Michigan State is pretty strong. They ought to be ... I understand that they are very liberal with scholarships for athletes. One thing I have had difficulty in understanding is how the North Central [NCA] people ever let Michigan State get by [their inspection of 1933].[71]

As it turned out, Aigler's impression of Spartan practices, and of the confidential NCA findings, was wrong. No athlete qualified for the special academic scholarships passed by the State Board of Agriculture in 1932. The only aid Michigan State offered athletes in 1933 was through a loan fund. The practice continued after NCA investigator Professor B.S. Stradley departed East Lansing. The only difference, however, was that the school would now be assuring administrative accountability.

Besides offering financial support through a loan program, Michigan State openly recruited talented athletes to the college. The practice, at that time, was not unique to the Spartans.

RECRUITING WAS a major concern in Professor Howard Savage's controversial report commissioned by the Carnegie Foundation. Proselyting was closely tied to subsidizing and,

[67] Kuhn, Madison. *Michigan State – The First Hundred Years.* Chicago: The Lakeside Press, R.R. Donnelley & Sons, 1955. pp. 333-341

[68] Hannah, John A. *A Memoir.* East Lansing, Michigan State University Press, 1980. p. 111

[69] Kuhn, Madison. *Michigan State – The First Hundred Years.* Chicago: The Lakeside Press, R.R. Donnelley & Sons, 1955. p. 341

[70] Minutes of the State Board of Agriculture. 17 March 1932. www.onthebanks.msu.edu

[71] Aigler to Griffith. 1 October 1935. Bentley Historical Library, University of Michigan. Ralph W. Aigler Papers, 87406 Aa2; Box 6, correspondence: 1934-39 Griffith 4/34-1/36

by implication, was in violation of the NCAA code defining amateurism. "An amateur athlete is one who participates in competitive physical sports only for the pleasure and the physical, mental, moral and social benefits directly derived therefrom."[72] The key phrase in the code was "participates ... only for the pleasure ..." Offering financial aid to gain a commitment from a high school athlete was not consistent with the national policy agreed upon by member colleges and universities.

Despite institutions vowing adherence to the NCAA code, Savage discovered otherwise. His investigation revealed that recruiting was commonly practiced by coaches with the assistance of alumni and boosters.[73]

Michigan State, without a doubt, recruited during the 1930s. Its subsidies, used in enticing athletes, were limited to loans with guarantees. The integrity of the institution, however, was protected by the secretary of the college, the comptroller, and the student loan committee. That oversight would ultimately assure adherence to Shaw's Law. There would no longer be boosters from the Downtown Coaches Club indirectly affiliated with the agricultural college. Fred Jenison, by an agreement with the college, would provide the necessary accountability.

In overseeing the school's financial aid program, John Hannah developed a sensitivity, in particular, to the plight of athletes. He struggled with how these students found time to study and attend classes, maintain a part-time job, and participate in practices and games.[74] The secretary of the State Board was way ahead of his time. It would eventually require a graduate student from the State University of Iowa, in 1953, to confirm what seemed so obvious to Hannah almost two decades earlier. In his master's thesis entitled "How Male College Students Use Their Time," Charles Andre Jacot published his survey results.[75]

> ... athletes are able to devote 18.2% or 13.08 hours per week less to study, leisure and work than students not engaged in an extracurricular activity ... If time for rest, meals, personal grooming, transportation and leisure are arbitrarily added to the totals ... the activity participant has only 11 to 14 hours a week at the most to hold a job and contribute to the cost of his education. This implies that economic status may influence activity participation, and justifies consideration of some type of institutional aid to the activity participant from a lower economic level.[76]

Hannah's response to the "obvious," back in the mid-1930s, was to assist all students, not just athletes, during those financially challenging times. He played a pivotal role in organizing a co-op boarding club in the basement of Wells Hall, an inexpensive

---

[72] Falla, Jack. *NCAA: The Voice of College Sports*. Mission, KA: National Collegiate Athletic Association, 1981. p. 52

[73] Savage, Howard. *American College Athletics*. Boston: D.B. Updike/The Merrymount Press, 1929. pp. 224-240

[74] Hannah, John A. *A Memoir*. East Lansing: Michigan State University Press, 1980. p. 114

[75] McCartney, David. "Masters thesis author." E-mail to David Young. 16 April 2011.

[76] "Minutes of the Conference Joint Group," Appendix 1: Report of Rules Revision Committee #2. 10-12 December 1953. Bentley Historical Library, University of Michigan. Athletic Department, 943 Bimu 2; Box 84, 1952-1957

means of remaining in college for men needing a bed and three meals.[77]

He also allowed student-athletes to room in his residence on Sunset Avenue. Their only obligation was to "… keep the furnace going and do some of the housework."[78]

FOUR MONTHS after John Alfred Hannah assumed the presidency of Michigan State College, Japan attacked Pearl Harbor. The onset of World War II supported his evolving conviction that the institution, in the spirit of the Justin Morrill Act, must change to meet the needs of a student population about to inherit a far more complex world upon cessation of hostilities.[79] No longer could the college just provide utilitarian services for the state of Michigan. Instead, Hannah was convinced that it must transition into a land-grant research institution capable of greater synergy.

To accomplish that goal, the president needed academicians and researchers capable of enhancing the reputation of Michigan State. The college budget, however, restricted that talent search. He could not interest, let alone hire, renowned intellectuals to move to an institution unable to match current salaries elsewhere. So Hannah adopted another strategy: aggressively (and more affordably) recruiting bright young minds, from prominent graduate programs, willing to gamble on his vision.[80] [81]

Enticing doctoral candidates and young, idealistic thinkers to an agriculturally based land-grant college required a unique campus culture and institutional identity; idyllic grounds covered with oaks and elms, spliced by a meandering river, were not enough. Hannah gambled that post-doctorate researchers were more likely to buy into his vision if weekend entertainment was included in the package. Such a diversion could promote an esprit de corps among faculty, students, administrators, and community supporters.[82] His experience at the University of Michigan two decades earlier, during the week-long build-up to the 1921 Ohio State game, supported his conviction.[83] The president's formula for institutional growth via athletics would one day be copied by other institutions, including UCLA, Florida State, Houston, and North Carolina State.[84]

Football, in particular, would be the focus of weekend entertainment for the short term.[85] But to create that culture on campus, even with a competitive team, the Spartans needed rivalries comparable to Ohio State-Michigan. The challenge for the administration, in the early 1940s, was attracting prominent schools to East Lansing capable of generating that game-day excitement. The Shaw administration had been unsuccessful in its attempt during the previous decade for a few reasons. Michigan State's reprobate reputation, as promoted by Ralph Aigler, played a major role. So, too, did the de facto boycott that Aigler

[77] Hannah, John A. *A Memoir*. East Lansing: Michigan State University Press, 1980. p. 111

[78] Ibid., p. 112

[79] Ibid., p. 54

[80] Ibid., p. 43

[81] Thomas, David. *Michigan State College: John Hannah and the Creation of a World University, 1926-1969*. East Lansing: Michigan State University Press, 2008. p. 103

[82] Hannah, John A. *A Memoir*. East Lansing: Michigan State University Press, 1980. p. 124

[83] Ibid., p. 24

[84] Duderstadt, James. *Intercollegiate Athletics and the American University*. Ann Arbor: The University of Michigan Press, 2000. p. 259

[85] Thomas, David. *Michigan State College: John Hannah and the Creation of a World University, 1926-1969*. East Lansing: Michigan State University Press, 2008. p. 294

initiated. In addition, the seating capacity of Macklin Field, approximately 29,000, limited potential shared revenue for visiting schools also in need of dollars.

John Hannah's solution turned out to be quite simple. Well aware of Fred Jenison's directive in his will, the president would use income from that fund to subsidize players attending Michigan State. He would end the loan-guarantee program. With a competitive team on campus, he anticipated improved ticket demand. Shared revenue from larger crowds at Macklin, in combination with guarantees, might encourage some Western Conference schools to reconsider travel to East Lansing.

The end result would be favorable press for the school. There was no better publicity, after all, than making headlines in Sunday morning sports pages.[86]

On December 18, 1941, just six months into his presidency, Hannah proposed the creation of the Jenison Awards. The following day he defined his plan in a memo to the administrative staff. "The Jenison Awards were established as grants in aid to worthy and deserving students … possessing unusual qualities of leadership who have demonstrated mental ability and physical strength and vigor." A special committee, "consisting of the Chairman of the Faculty Committee on Scholarships, the Registrar, the Director of Physical Education for Men, the Head Football Coach, and one other to be appointed by the President," would select those qualified to receive the awards. The final say on all nominees rested with John Hannah. The award included "waiving of tuition and college fees and a grant of $120 per term." All funding was to derive from income gained from the Fred Jenison bequeathal. Only 12 grants per class year were allowed; the total could not exceed 40 at any one time. A student was eligible for a maximum of four years of assistance. The awards were renewable on an annual basis. Hannah closed his memo by emphasizing this was for a trial period of five years. The program would commence with the 1942-43 academic year.[87]

These were not academic scholarships. Hannah made that very clear. The Jenison Awards were grants to cover collegiate expenses for athletes playing football while working towards a degree. It was just recompense for services that ultimately benefited the college on Saturday afternoons.

The Alumni Scholarships would remain available for those students, including certain athletes, graduating in the top 20 percent of their high school class or attaining a level of academic distinction during their collegiate years.

Hannah emphasized that "leadership, mental ability, and physical strength and vigor" had a value as much as intellectual prowess. He recognized that the practice field and gridiron were classrooms for the athlete, as much as the concert room for the musician and the lecture hall for the mathematician. Team concepts and focused goals were lessons all athletes would learn at afternoon practices and meetings. The experience of working together might better prepare each student-athlete for eventual careers away from campus.[88]

It was the president's intention to be totally open about the Jenison Awards. The college catalogue on scholarships and loans, published annually, listed the names of those

---

[86] Kuhn, Madison. "John Hannah." Michigan State University Archives. Circa 1970. Hannah Archives Project; UA2.1.12.2; Box 34, folder: 27

[87] "Members of the Administrative Group." 19 December 1941. Michigan State University Archives. Hannah Presidential Papers, UA2.1.12; Box 63, folder 7: Scholarships-Jenison 1942-45

[88] Hannah, John A. *A Memoir.* East Lansing: Michigan State University Press, 1980. p. 114

receiving athletic grants.[89]

IN 1956, seven years after Michigan State had finally become a member of the Big Ten, President Hannah expressed his desire to reform the conference's outdated stance on financial aid to athletes. Ralph Aigler had retired in April 1955[90] so his influence on controversial issues, such as subsidies, was no longer a factor. Hannah, as the newest member, could now comfortably promote an agenda he had first espoused in January of 1946, when he spoke at the NCAA annual convention. Iowa grad student Charles Jacot's 1953 survey offered him valuable data to support his proposal. He clarified his thoughts to faculty representative Leslie Scott.

> As you know, I have given this matter a good deal of thought over the years and would like to suggest for whatever consideration it is worth that the Big Ten adopt the general policy now in effect in most other conferences permitting the equivalent of tuition, board, room , and books to a definite number of athletes on each campus … This procedure would eliminate the hypocrisies in the present work programs which require the creation of jobs for athletes where they cannot possibly put in the required number of hours during the athletic seasons and carry their academic load programs at the same time. With this system I would absolutely ban all kinds of aid administered by alumni or others in excess of the board, room, tuition, and books figure. Having sat on all sides of the table, I am sure that the present rules are so unrealistic that every institution is in violation of them, and rigid enforcement would embarrass everyone; and for that reason there is no desire for enforcement or compliance.[91]

His intentions were honorable in the spring of 1956. But back in December of 1941, it appeared John Hannah had more self-serving reasons for promoting a similar concept known as the Jenison Awards. In May of 1945, he wrote Athletic Director Ralph Young about his reasons for wanting to double the number of Jenison Awards to 80 per year. Hannah had previously discussed with the State Board "some of the problems of maintaining intercollegiate athletic teams to compete creditably with other institutions …" The board approved his recommendation.[92] He now needed Young's support in implementing the changed policy.[93]

Based on this statement about competing creditably, it appeared Hannah had originally proposed the Jenison Awards to attract talent and develop a football power.[94] With

[89] "A Bulletin of Michigan State College," Volume 38, number 13:March 1944." Michigan State University Archives. John Hannah Presidential Records, UA2.1.12; Box 63, folder: 6 scholarships 1941-55

[90] Crisler to McEwen. 26 April 1955. Bentley Historical Library, University of Michigan. Herbert Orin Crisler Papers, 85823 AC UAm Aa 2; Box 6, folder: Board in Control athletic papers 1955-56

[91] Hannah to Scott. 22 May 1956. Michigan State University Archives. John A. Hannah Papers, UA2.1.12; Box 69, folder: 38 Athletic Council, general 1954-58

[92] Minutes of the State Board of Agriculture. 17 May 1945. www.onthebanks.msu.edu

[93] Hannah to Young. 19 May 1945. Michigan State University Archives. Hannah Presidential Papers. UA2.1.12, Box 63, folder 7: Scholarships-Jenison 1942-45

[94] Bachman, Charles. "The Athletic Side of John A. Hannah." Circa 1970. Michigan State University

over one year of varsity football action held in abeyance in East Lansing due to the War Department's edict forbidding Army recruits to compete in intercollegiate sports, he needed to quickly jump start his program. But the original 40 Jenison grants were not sufficient in 1945 to accomplish that objective. If others, such as the University of Michigan, had the power to control game sites and dates, Hannah would try to level the playing field by subsidizing additional talent.

In keeping with Fred C. Jenison's testamentary directives, the president chose to use the awards "for the improvement of the university with particular emphasis on athletics."[95] For John Hannah, that phrase implied using football to gain acceptance into the Western Conference.[96] The strategy, if successful, would enhance Michigan State's ability to attract those young doctorates necessary for transforming the institution into a land-grant university serving the world.

Prior to the Jenison Award announcement of December 1941, the president established tuition scholarships for "financially embarrassed students" possessing unique talents. The Thomas Gunson Scholarship, named in honor of the popular horticulture professor and grounds superintendent, was intended for students fulfilling very specific requirements. In addition to financial duress, the individual had to maintain a satisfactory academic record and possess qualities in leadership, mental strength, and physical vigor. The grants focused on those "demonstrating leadership in extracurricular activities including student publications, student government, athletics, et cetera." The candidates were to be nominated by a small group appointed by the president, subject to the approval of the Scholarship Committee; Hannah sat on the committee. Fifty were awarded each year to worthy students.[97]

The scholarships were not limited to athletes. Students gifted in band, orchestra, or writing were eligible as well. But an athlete provided with Gunson money was generally participating in non revenue-generating sports, whereas Jenison Awards, as originally intended, were reserved for football players.[98][99] By 1945, however, due to expansion of the program, coaches in baseball, basketball, swimming, track, and wrestling were each offered three grants per year to share with athletes.[100]

John Hannah, years later, was vilified for his promotion of these athletic awards by those who saw them as merely another name for an athletic scholarship.[101] Michigan State, as an independent, was viewed much like the schools of the Deep South that had pioneered

Archives. Hannah Archives Project, UA2.1.12; Box 34, folder: 2 Bachman

[95] Hannah, John A. *A Memoir*. East Lansing: Michigan State University Press, 1980. p. 121

[96] Ibid.

[97] Minutes of the State Board of Agriculture. 23 October 1941. www.onthebanks.msu.edu

[98] Hannah to Members of the Administrative Group. 19 December 1941. Michigan State University Archives. Hannah Presidential Papers, UA2.1.12; Box 63, folder 7: Scholarships-Jenison 1942-45

[99] Guerre, George. 5 February 2010. Personal communication. Guerre '49 and his family were neighbors during my childhood in East Lansing. He shared with me recollections of his collegiate years as a student and Jenison Award athlete during the late 1940s at Michigan State.

[100] Hannah to Young. 19 May 1945. Michigan State University Archives. Hannah Presidential Papers, UA2.1.12; Box 63, folder 7: Scholarships-Jenison 1942-45

[101] Watterson, John Sayle. *College Football: History-Spectacle-Controversy*. Baltimore and London: The Johns Hopkins University Press, 2000. pp. 227-240

the practice almost a decade earlier.[102] The difference was that Hannah refused to call these grants "scholarships" and insisted on institutional transparency on all financial aid packages.

The president would argue, in defense, that other conferences and schools permitted grants in excess of the aid provided by the Jenison Awards or Gunson Scholarships. "In the Big Eight and in the Southeast and Southern Conferences, made up largely of state supported institutions, athletic scholarships generally included board, room, tuition, books, laundry and sometimes spending." Michigan State mandated that the student meet his own living expenses. Additionally, unlike other schools, "If the award holder continued his interest in athletics, but could not compete successfully due to injury or lack of ability, he could not lose the award on either basis." The only requirements were that "recipients had to have graduated in the top third of their high school classes, and to hold their award they had to make a full year's progress toward their degrees each academic year." Finally, the student was required to maintain a "C" average in all academic subjects.[103]

Hannah's statement, quoted years later following his retirement, was not quite accurate. Neither the Jenison Award nor the Gunson Scholarship, as originally proposed and later revised, had high school class-standing requirements. Jenison and Gunson students were obligated only to "maintain [their] college work at a satisfactory level" or face revocation of the grant. There was no minimal grade point average required to continue the financial aid.[104] [105] [106] With a group that included "the Chairman of the Faculty Committee on Scholarships, the registrar, the director of physical education, the head football coach, and one other [member] appointed by the president," the committee could easily modify enrollment/eligibility requirements for gifted athletes. And if decisions were not to the satisfaction of the football coach, the president always had the final say.[107]

Ralph Aigler, by the late 1940s, would challenge those requirements. Through confidential sources in the greater Lansing area, he kept a list of Jenison awardees who did not meet the vague academic requirements. His claims appeared to have credibility.[108]

JOHN HANNAH was asked to give the keynote address at the January 9, 1946, annual convention of the NCAA. He was chosen, in large part, because of his controversial stance on subsidizing student-athletes. It was unfortunate that he was not given the honor four years earlier. His critics, including Ralph Aigler and Fritz Crisler, would have better

---

[102] Aigler to Little/Blommers/Wilson. 30 March 1949. Herbert Orin Crisler, AC UAm Aa2; Box 1, topical correspondence: 1947-49

[103] Hannah, John A. *A Memoir.* East Lansing: Michigan State University Press, 1980. p. 121

[104] "Members of the Administrative Group." 19 December 1941. Michigan State University Archives. Hannah Presidential Papers, UA2.1.12; Box 63, folder 7: Scholarships-Jenison 1942-45

[105] Hannah to Young. 19 May 1945 (attachment). Michigan State University Archives. Hannah Presidential Papers, UA2.1.12; Box 63, folder 7: Scholarships-Jenison 1942-45

[106] "A Bulletin of Michigan State College," Volume 38, number 13:March 1944." Michigan State University Archives. John Hannah Presidential Records, UA2.1.12; Box 63, folder: 6 scholarships 1941-55

[107] "Members of the Administrative Group." 19 December 1941. Michigan State University Archives. Hannah Presidential Papers, UA2.1.12; Box 63, folder 7: Scholarships-Jenison 1942-45

[108] Untitled. Circa 1948. Bentley Historical Library, University of Michigan. Ralph W. Aigler Papers, 87406 Aa 2; Box 9, folder: correspondence 1946-52 "E" misc.

understood the rationale behind his December 1941 proposal creating the Jenison Awards. Regardless of poor timing, Hannah was finally provided an opportune moment to wax eloquent about justice and institutional integrity.

> The responsibilities of our colleges and universities is not limited to presenting educational opportunities to those on our campuses … We have a greater responsibility to ourselves and to the nation to [ensure] that we never lose sight of a fundamental obligation to emphasize always those qualities that, for want of a better description, we term character. Our first obligation is to build men and women of character with an undying respect for certain standards of moral behavior, right living, and common decency … Certainly the public has a right to expect and demand the highest standards of behavior and performance from its public universities. If there is not to be the highest degree of honor, and ethics, and integrity … on the part of our publicly and church supported colleges and universities, where in the name of heaven is such integrity to be found?[109]

The president then argued that "if intercollegiate athletics are defensible, they are defensible only because of their contribution as a part of the greater educational experience."[110] The leader of the University of Chicago, the school Michigan State would one day replace in the conference, held a different opinion. Robert Maynard Hutchins felt that athletic competition brought little value to the serious student's academic experience.[111]

The problem with intercollegiate athletics, Hannah said, lay in the loss of control by institutions sponsoring sporting programs for students. He found absurd the obsession that purists of amateurism had for unenforceable rules and regulations governing colleges and universities. He also noted "the rules are very carefully worded to provide ample loopholes for individuals and agencies not officially connected with the college to do what the college agrees [in principle] not to do."[112]

The president of Michigan State then begged the question: why the need for complicated regulations? "I would perfectly willingly have thrown into the wastebasket all of the rules pertaining to proselyting, subsidizing and the like, provided there could be two simple statements adhered to and complied with by all …" His first requirement was that "all scholarships, grants in aid, remuneration for employment either actual or implied for athletes be administered by the same faculty organization or committee or procedure as for non-athletes." He then added a statement consistent with the Jenison Awards being provided to athletes in East Lansing at the time. "I would not require that athletes be eligible only to

---

[109] Hannah, John A. "Speech of Doctor John A. Hannah at the Fortieth Annual Convention of the National Collegiate Athletic Association." 9 January 1946. Bentley Historical Library, University of Michigan. Herbert Orin Crisler Papers, AC UAm Aa2; Box 1, folder: topical correspondence Michigan State University, clippings and misc.

[110] Ibid.

[111] Lester, Robin. *Stagg's University: The Rise, Decline & Fall of Big-Time Football at Chicago.* Urbana and Chicago: University of Illinois Press, 1999. p. 163

[112] Hannah, John A. "Speech of Doctor John A. Hannah at the Fortieth Annual Convention of the National Collegiate Athletic Association." 9 January 1946. Bentley Historical Library, University of Michigan. Herbert Orin Crisler Papers, AC UAm Aa2; Box 1, folder: topical correspondence Michigan State University, clippings and misc.

the same grants as are non-athletes, but I would require that all grants and scholarships and payments either of a gratuitous nature or for services be handled by the same officer or committee of faculty that administers the same programs for non-athletes, and all such records be available upon request to any recognized accrediting association or to the officers of this association."[113]

Hannah's second requirement was "an assurance from every college or university that it will not permit membership on any team ... except full-time students who have completed at least one year of residence, and have completed in that year the equivalent of one full year's work toward a college degree." With that commitment by institutions, "... then I shall be satisfied ..." The president then concluded his thoughts on this matter. "I am not going to worry too much about rules and regulations that bind colleges but have no effect on alumni groups, downtown coaches organizations, booster clubs, et cetera." If a school adhered to these "two simple statements," there would be no need for complex handbooks defining conference and NCAA rules for engagement.

He went on to argue that integrity, above all else, must pervade institutions educating the next generation of leaders.

> There may be corruption in business, there may be corruption in government, and in other places, but certainly there is no excuse for corruption in our colleges and universities. They must be institutions of high purpose, public examples for ethical behavior and for fundamental honesty where there is always an appreciation of the fundamentals of good character.[114]

This address essentially summarized Hannah's creedal convictions. A main reason he had departed the University of Michigan Law School was his struggle with the way it dealt with the concept of justice. He felt law schools, in general, trained "people to fight for narrow interpretations of the law rather than for a broader idea of securing justice for persons."[115] University of Chicago consultant Professor Floyd Reeves pointed out years later, "... [if] Hannah wanted to [gain] justice ... he would be willing to violate the letter of the law if necessary in order to carry out the spirit of the law."[116] Reeves' comments help explain why President Hannah had, in part, authorized the Jenison Awards and Gunson Scholarships back in 1941.[117] He was merely "securing justice" for young men providing services that benefited the college.

John Hannah felt it hypocritical for institutions of higher learning to profess conviction to an amateur code that encouraged duplicity. From 1908 until 1930, the

---

[113] Hannah, John A. "Speech of Doctor John A. Hannah at the Fortieth Annual Convention of the National Collegiate Athletic Association." 9 January 1946. Bentley Historical Library, University of Michigan. Herbert Orin Crisler Papers, AC UAm Aa2; Box 1, folder: topical correspondence Michigan State University, clippings and misc.

[114] Ibid

[115] "Statement of Floyd W. Reeves." 11 June 1970. Michigan State University Archives. Hannah Archives Project, UA2.1.12.2; Box 34, folder 37, p. 18

[116] Ibid., p. 19

[117] Acknowledging Reeves' laudable comments, Hannah had financial reasons for departing Ann Arbor as well.

Conference Handbook, despite revisions, had remained 23 pages long. The updated version of 1941 almost doubled in size to 44 pages.[118] [119] Even Hannah's most ardent critics, Ralph Aigler and Fritz Crisler, often struggled with interpreting the complex rules they helped create.[120] [121]

In Hannah's opinion, which was shared by a few faculty representatives in the Western Conference, too much time and money was being spent in oversight and enforcement.[122] He felt this responsibility should be the obligation of all institutions charged with a "higher purpose" and that public scrutiny would prove the ultimate judge. For John Hannah, on January 9, 1946, in St. Louis, Missouri, it was all about justice.

---

[118] "Handbook of the Intercollegiate Conference of Faculty Representatives: 1908." University of Minnesota Archives, Department of Intercollegiate Athletics Papers; Box 13, folder: small handbooks 1895-1908, 1930, 1941

[119] "Handbook of the Intercollegiate Conference of Faculty Representatives: Revised 1941." University of Minnesota Archives, Department of Intercollegiate Athletics Papers; Box 13, folder: small handbooks 1895-1908, 1930, 1941

[120] Aigler to Wilson. 8 August 1945. Bentley Historical Library, University of Michigan Ralph W. Aigler Papers, 87406 Aa2; Box 8, correspondence: 1940-45 "Wilson" misc.

[121] Aigler to Wilson. 19 February 1952. Bentley Historical Library, University of Michigan Ralph W. Aigler Papers, 87406 Aa2; Box 10, correspondence: 1946-52 Personal

[122] Richart to Pollard. 11 March 1949. University of Illinois Archives, Series No.4/2/12; Box 3, folder: Western Intercollegiate Conference 1948-49.

The Second Rejection: Competing for an Uncertain Spot

MICHIGAN STATE first applied for a position in the Western Conference in May of 1937. It would not be the last time. Over the next 12 years the Spartans would try on five occasions to join the exclusive club. If John Hannah had done a quick study of the Big Ten history he might not have been so persevering. Many schools sought admission. Most were denied. Three institutions, however, found the path to Chicago with little difficulty.

Expansion of the conference was never explicitly addressed in early Handbooks. Since the faculty representatives were mandated legislative responsibilities, it was understood that they alone determined membership size. The presidents, beyond drafting the original bylaws, held no further role in the operations of the conference. Simple majority ruled in all decisions, including requests for admission.[1]

The first Western Conference experience with expansion, beyond the original seven, coincided with an unusual invitation sent out by President Charles Adams of the University of Wisconsin to institutions about the Midwest. In November of 1896, Adams intended to form the Northwestern College Baseball League. He mailed letters to fellow conference presidents as well as those at Missouri, Kansas, Nebraska, Ohio State, Indiana, and Iowa.[2] The would-be baseball league was poorly organized and lacked any governance. At one point, President Andrew Sloan Draper of Illinois even denied its existence.[3] Adams argued otherwise while struggling to sustain the group.[4] Regardless of the debate, the invitation allowed both Indiana University and Iowa to form relationships with schools affiliated with a new association referred to as the "Conference on Athletics" but officially recognized as the Intercollegiate Conference of Faculty Representatives.

In early December of 1897, Indiana University President Joseph Swain, interested

---

[1] Rules, Regulations and Opinions of the Intercollegiate Conference of Faculty Representatives-Revised 1930. University of Minnesota Archives. Department of Intercollegiate Athletics Papers; Box 13, folder:small handbooks 1895-1908, 1930, 1941

[2] Davis to Swain. 25 November 1896. Indiana University Archives; Folder: Athletics-Big Ten

[3] Draper to Swain. 10 November 1897. Indiana University Archives; Folder: Athletics-Big Ten

[4] Elsom to Swain. 10 December 1897. Indiana University Archives; Folder: Athletics-Big Ten

in joining the conference, sent out letters of inquiry to a few members regarding the application process. President Adams of Wisconsin handed his letter over to Physical Education Director Dr. James Elsom. The physician encouraged Swain to communicate with Professor Amos Alonzo Stagg of Chicago. The chairman of the University of Michigan's Board in Control, Law Professor James Knowlton, was asked by his president to also respond to Swain's request. Knowlton, on December 11, pointed out that the annual meeting had already taken place. But he was quite interested in Indiana pursuing membership. He asked that President Swain write Stagg; as current chairman of the conference, he "is the only person authorized to invite [guests to the meeting]."[5] [6]

For unclear reasons, Indiana failed to make a presentation at the 1898 gathering. In anticipation of the next conference meeting, the head Hoosier penned letters to President Adams of Wisconsin and faculty representative Professor Clarence Waldo of Purdue in mid-November of 1899. He was politicking the two leaders. Swain indicated that "two or three other institutions" were already in favor of his application, and he was seeking additional support. With seven members, he needed only four votes to gain membership.[7]

As it turned out, he got those votes plus three more. Following a motion by Michigan's Professor Albert Pattengill, Indiana was unanimously admitted into the Intercollegiate Conference of Faculty Representatives on December 1, 1899.[8] The affiliation with the conference offered the university more regional recognition of its athletic accomplishments, and most importantly, participation in an organization committed to faculty control of athletics.[9] [10]

The State University of Iowa was also admitted on the same date.[11] President George MacLean had recently written to Stagg requesting membership; he pointed out that the school had "adopted and enforced (the) platform" on amateurism promoted in the Handbook. He referenced Iowa's undefeated 1899 season as an additional reason for its "representation in the conference."[12] Following a unanimous vote selecting the Hawkeyes as the ninth member, the faculty representatives approved a motion that there be no further expansion of their association.[13]

Almost one decade later, on January 13, 1908, the University of Michigan withdrew

---

[5] Elsom to Swain. 10 December 1897. Indiana University Archives; Folder: Athletics-Big Ten

[6] Knowlton to Swain. 11 December 1897. Indiana University Archives; Folder: Athletics-Big Ten

[7] Swain to Waldo. 16 November 1899. Indiana University Archives; Folder: Athletics-Big Ten

[8] Minutes of the Fifth Intercollegiate Conference of Faculty Representatives. 1 December 1899. *Proceedings of the Intercollegiate Conference of Faculty Representatives of the Athletic Committees or Boards in Control.* Minneapolis: The University Press, 1901. Bentley Historical Library, University of Michigan

[9] "The Student – Special Football Supplement." 2 December 1899. Indiana University Archives; Folder: Athletics-Big Ten

[10] Sampson to The Chairman (Faculty Committee on Athletics). 11 November 1899. University of Chicago Archives. Amos Alonzo Stagg Papers; Box 90, folder: 4

[11] Minutes of the Fifth Intercollegiate Conference of Faculty Representatives. 1 December 1899. *Proceedings of the Intercollegiate Conference of Faculty Representatives of the Athletic Committees or Boards of Control.* Minneapolis: The University Press, 1901. Bentley Historical Library, University of Michigan.

[12] MacLean to Faculty Board in Control (of Athletics at the University of Chicago). 15 November 1899. University of Chicago Archives. Amos Alonzo Stagg Papers; Box 90, folder: 4

from the Intercollegiate Conference. Nebraska, on the heels of Michigan's departure, applied for the vacated seat in June. The faculty, however, felt it too soon to consider a replacement for the Wolverines. In rejecting the Cornhuskers, they resolved "that it is the sense of the Conference that it is inexpedient to enlarge the membership at this time."[14]

Policies passed by the eight members in December of 1910, now almost three years after Michigan departed, would suggest that hope still remained for the Wolverines' return. The faculty leaders resolved during the meeting that they all "agree not to hold athletic relations with universities or colleges that have been members ... and have withdrawn ... until reinstated."[15] That recent motion, the earlier Nebraska rejection, and the fact that Michigan was ultimately "invited" to "resume membership" in June of 1917 without reapplying, implied that Michigan's departure was expected to be short-lived by the faculty.[16][17]

But a little over one year later, in January of 1912, The Ohio State University applied for admission to the Western Conference. This overture challenged the conference leadership still hoping for Michigan's return. The faculty representatives were aware of the contentious debates taking place in Ann Arbor as the academicians struggled to regain control of athletics.[18] But with four years having lapsed, optimism for a favorable resolution was waning. Sooner or later a decision about a replacement had to be made. Ohio State, a large land-grant school with admirable qualities, was a viable candidate.

Michigan's departure had been a great loss for the Western Conference. The school attracted large crowds, whether at home or away. The loss of ticket-sale revenue was felt by some of the smaller members such as Northwestern.[19] When completed in 1902, Michigan's Ferry Field could seat up to 18,000 with temporary bleachers, a large capacity by conference standards.[20] With the Wolverines gone, the conference needed another school with comparable drawing power. Ohio State appeared to be the one. Football had become a passion in Columbus. Ohio Field in 1909 sat 6,500 spectators,[21] and attendance figures on game day were impressive when compared to other Western Conference schools.

---

[13] Minutes of the Fifth Intercollegiate Conference of Faculty Representatives. 1 December 1899. *Proceedings of the Intercollegiate Conference of Faculty Representatives of the Athletic Committees or Boards of Control.* Minneapolis: The University Press, 1901. Bentley Historical Library, University of Michigan.

[14] Minutes of the Intercollegiate Conference of Faculty Representatives. 6 December 1912. University of Wisconsin Archives-Madison. President Van Hise Papers, Series 4/10/1; Box 36, folder: 549 Ehler, George

[15] Minutes of the Intercollegiate Conference. 3 December 1910. University of Minnesota Archives, Athletics #953; Box 13, folder: Intercollegiate Conference minutes 1907-1933

[16] Minutes of the Intercollegiate Conference of Faculty Representatives. 9 June 1917. University of Minnesota Archives, Intercollegiate Athletics Papers; Box 13, folder: 1907-1933

[17] Aigler to Shaw. 27 September 1947. Bentley Historical Library. University of Michigan, Ralph W. Aigler Papers, 87406 Aa 2: Box 10, folder: correspondence 1946-52 "S" misc.

[18] Behee, John. *Fielding Yost's Legacy to the University of Michigan.* Ann Arbor: Uhlrich's Books, Inc., 1971. pp. 77-79

[19] Ibid., p. 83

[20] "The Michigan Stadium Story," Bentley Historical Library. 15 April 2007. Ann Arbor: University of Michigan. 9 August 2010, www.bentleyref@umich.edu

[21] Pollard, James E. *Ohio State Athletics: 1879-1959.* Columbus: The Athletic Department of Ohio State University, 1959. p. 91

Beyond revenue gains from robust ticket sales, an Ohio State membership might also benefit the other eight schools still longing for a Wolverine return. Due to the rule forbidding institutions from contracting with former associates, the Wolverines would be denied gridiron play with the Buckeyes if The Ohio State University were admitted to the Western Conference. The implications for Michigan were profound. It had three traditional rivals. Minnesota and Chicago were unable to contract with Yost's club due to Handbook policy. If Ohio State joined the Western Conference, the game with the Buckeyes would be curtailed as well. That left only Michigan Agricultural College as an annual competitor. The Aggies were not considered a rival in the same context as the other three.

By admitting Ohio State, the faculty representatives may have indirectly influenced the debate on faculty control taking place in Ann Arbor among regents, administrators, faculty, alumni, local fans, students, and athletic department representatives. The gamble ultimately paid off.

THE MICHIGAN-Ohio State rivalry began innocently enough with a baseball game in the spring of 1895. The score was 4-4 in the bottom of the ninth inning. The Buckeyes had a runner on second base due to a questionable call by the umpire. The Michigan fans in attendance were livid. As the scene was later described, "Rowdyism, mistaken for college enthusiasm, prevailed to such an extent that the policemen and a few sensible alumni of the university alone, prevented a conflict which would undoubtedly have resulted disastrously for both sides ..."[22] The Wolverines walked off the diamond without completing the game.

The first football game between the schools took place two years later. The Wolverines crushed the Buckeyes 34-0 on October 16, 1897, in Ann Arbor. The historical significance of the game, at least for the Buckeyes, lay in the institution competing against a prominent university outside the Ohio Intercollegiate Athletic Association (OIAA). The contest introduced The Ohio State University to big-time college football.

During the first 14 years of the series, the Wolverines totally dominated the Buckeyes. Ohio State could muster only two ties, but the Buckeyes considered tied games as moral victories when competing against Michigan. The scoreless 1900 battle, contested in Ann Arbor, was one of those successes.[23]

Because the OIAA was not providing sufficient competition, Ohio State was beginning to consider affiliation with another conference. A somewhat skewed version of that first moral victory, reported in the *Columbus Dispatch*, also suggested that there was talk of joining the Western Conference as early as 1900.

> Another star has risen on the western football horizon. No longer can the
> "Big Nine" be referred to in western football discussion to the exclusion of
> the great Buckeye state. Hereafter it will be the "Big Ten" for it will be
> impossible to ignore the Ohio State University, whose football team scored
> a triumph on Regents field this afternoon by playing the great Michigan
> eleven to a standstill and successfully defended their goal against the attack
> of the heavy Michigan backs through two bitterly contested twenty-five

---

[22] Pollard, James E. *Ohio State Athletics: 1879-1959*. Columbus: The Athletic Department of Ohio State University, 1959. pp. 27-28

[23] Ibid., p. 77

minute halves.[24]

Even though the winless streak against Michigan continued, the Columbus faithful were undaunted. On October 16, 1909, following another crushing defeat to the Wolverines, the Ohio State *Lantern* headlined the game, "Wolverines Return Home Humbled by Score–Practical Victory for Varsity." The student paper boasted that "for the first time in years Michigan faced a score against her … and for six and a half minutes they were a defeated team."[25]

"Triumphs" and "practical" victories were important to Ohio State in those early years of the unusual rivalry. Their first legitimate win against the Wolverines, however, would not take place until 1919, when Ohio State outscored Michigan 13-3 in Ann Arbor. This victory marked the beginning of a three-game winning streak. The Ohio State University could finally claim real success.

THE BUCKEYES had first contemplated officially applying to the Intercollegiate Conference of Faculty Representatives in 1910. Joining the association and playing more prominent institutions would calm the clamoring of students, alumni,[26] and the press. Non-conference games, with competition more challenging than that offered in the OIAA, were scheduled with some eastern and southern programs, but travel proved expensive or impractical for the school and its loyal following. The solution to Ohio State's dilemma, in the opinion of law school Professor George Rightmire, was to change directions, literally.[27] Transportation by bus or train was more feasible to regional schools affiliated with the Western Conference.[28] Years later, in 1936, President Robert Shaw and the State Board of Agriculture would arrive at similar conclusions while considering an application for admission to the conference.

The problem for OSU, in joining the Intercollegiate Conference, was concern over the status of the University of Michigan. The Wolverines were in the midst of their Decade of Defiance. The rivalry Ohio State maintained with Michigan would come to a halt, due to conference rules, if the Buckeyes successfully gained membership. For a few months in advance of finally requesting an application, Ohio State authorities debated the conundrum.

Professor H.W. Johnstone of Indiana University, president of the Faculty Representatives Committee at the time, visited Columbus just prior to the Buckeye administration voting on whether to apply. Clearly the Western Conference was interested in Ohio State. After reviewing its sporting facilities and meeting with key athletic leadership, Johnstone returned home impressed with what the university could bring to his conference. Prior to departure, however, he reminded the Buckeyes of the conference rules on eligibility and faculty leadership necessary for membership.[29]

Johnstone's comments were persuasive. On January 22, 1912, the OSU Athletic Board unanimously decided to tender an application. The rivalry with the University of

---

[24] Pollard, James E. *Ohio State Athletics: 1879-1959*. Columbus: The Athletic Department of Ohio State University, 1959. p. 79

[25] Ibid., p. 83

[26] Ibid., p. 92

[27] Ibid., p. 71

[28] Ibid., p. 69

[29] Ibid., p. 107

Michigan would be held in abeyance; strategically, it was far more important to gain membership. But the board remained hopeful that the wandering Wolverines would soon rejoin the association. The Buckeyes desperately wanted to renew their rivalry and finally earn that first victory.[30]

Ohio State sent Professor Rightmire and two colleagues to the Palmer House, in Chicago, on January 26, 1912, to make a formal presentation for membership. A two-man committee was formed to investigate and make recommendations on the application. Professors Thomas Moran of Purdue and R. E. Wilson of Northwestern were assigned the task.[31] Approximately two months later the group met again and accepted their recommendation.[32] Ohio State was unanimously voted into the Intercollegiate Conference of Faculty Representatives. On May 31, it would be officially welcomed as the newest member.[33]

Ohio State's success apparently intrigued Nebraska, a school that had applied on numerous occasions since 1899.[34] On December 6, 1912, it petitioned for admission four years after its last rejection. Notre Dame and Marquette followed. The faculty resolved, however, "that it is the sense of the Conference that it is inexpedient to enlarge the membership at this time."[35] Unlike the two small Catholic schools, the Cornhuskers were quite familiar with the response; the same reasoning had been provided them in June of 1908 when they sought to fill the void left by Michigan's withdrawal. The Nebraska Response would become a conference standard reply for the next four decades.

There was no apparent desire to increase the conference to an even ten. With Ohio State now a member, the Big Nine would patiently await the return of its former member from Ann Arbor. That event finally took place on June 9, 1917, when a young Ralph W. Aigler made a presentation before the Western Conference leadership in Chicago. He announced that faculty control of intercollegiate athletics had resumed in Ann Arbor. It was a major achievement for the law professor who passionately led the coalition striving to regain that oversight.[36]

The Faculty Representatives Committee subsequently extended an invitation to Michigan to resume membership. The university accepted the offer and officially began competing again in the Big Ten on the 20th of November 1917.[37] The "Ohio State Tease"

---

[30] Pollard, James E. *Ohio State Athletics: 1879-1959*. Columbus: The Athletic Department of Ohio State University, 1959. p. 113

[31] Minutes of the Intercollegiate Conference. 26-27 January 1912. University of Minnesota Archives, Athletics # 953; Box 13, folder: Intercollegiate Conference Minutes 1907-1933

[32] Minutes of the Intercollegiate Conference. 6 April 1912. University of Minnesota Archives, Athletics # 953; Box 13, folder: Intercollegiate Conference Minutes 1907-1933

[33] Minutes of the Intercollegiate Conference. 31 May 1912. University of Minnesota Archives, Athletics # 953; Box 13, folder: Intercollegiate Conference Minutes 1907-1933

[34] Kryk, John. "The Door Opens." *Maple Street Press: Wolverines Kickoff 2011*. July 2011. pp. 17-19

[35] Minutes of the Intercollegiate Conference of Faculty Representatives. 6 December 1912. University of Wisconsin-Madison Archives. President Van Hise Papers, Series 4/10/1; Box 36, folder: 549 Ehler, George

[36] Linotyper's Copy Sheet: Aigler, Ralph William. Bentley Historical Library, University of Michigan. Ralph W. Aigler Papers, 87406 Aa 2; Box 8, folder: correspondence 1940-45 R. Aigler Bio. etc.

[37] Behee, John. *Fielding Yost's Legacy to the University of Michigan*. Ann Arbor: Uhlrich's Books,

might have hastened the return.

UNLIKE OHIO State, which sought membership in the Western Conference primarily for athletic reasons, Michigan State longed for a seat in Chicago, in large part, to enhance its academic reputation.[38] The school needed affiliation with other preeminent universities if a great land-grant research institution was to evolve in East Lansing. With the University of Chicago's withdrawal from football, John Hannah, like so many others, predicted the conference would eventually require an eleventh school. Scheduling football games with only nine participants would be a logistical challenge. For Hannah, 1943 seemed like an opportune time to aggressively pursue admission.

During the summer of 1941, however, in anticipation of applying two years later, the recently inaugurated Hannah had two pressing concerns: fixing the inherently unfair control that Michigan held over rivalry game dates and expanding media coverage of the school. Both would enhance the college's chances for a successful application.

In late September of 1941, Hannah wrote to President Alexander Ruthven regarding the impact of Michigan's dominance over the college in football-game contracting. "As you undoubtedly know, this community [of East Lansing], including the student body, faculty, employees, and townspeople, practically moves to Ann Arbor on the day of the game." He explained how disruptive scheduling the contest during orientation/registration week was for Michigan State. Hannah requested that Ruthven "suggest to the proper athletic authorities ... that in the future this game be scheduled at a date after the opening of classes here."[39] It was a wise move to write directly to Ruthven and circumvent both Fritz Crisler and Ralph Aigler. What Hannah did not anticipate, however, was Ruthven's response. Adhering to administrative protocol, the Michigan president turned the letter over to his faculty representative for his opinion. He would not impose a change in university athletic policy that rightfully remained a responsibility of Aigler and his Board in Control.

Ralph Aigler was sensitive to Hannah's plight as chief administrator at the college. He understood the disruption caused by playing in Ann Arbor during orientation/registration week in East Lansing. But he countered by pointing out to Ruthven that there were no good dates for holding the annual rivalry.

> I am not familiar with the daily programs in East Lansing, but on the assumption that they have lectures and classes up to Saturday noon, as we do here, it seems to me pretty clear that those Saturday exercises after the regular college work has started must be pretty badly shot to pieces. I can only wonder whether the interference with the program on the Saturday preceding the opening of college is any more serious in its effects than in the case of a Saturday after college is open.[40]

Inc., 1971. p. 84

[38] There is no doubt President Hannah wanted to promote athletics early on in his tenure. But by the mid 1940s, due to two separate studies-a survey of alumni and an investigation of the graduate program by the NCA-he would focus on academics: athletics would serve as a means to an end.

[39] Hannah to Ruthven. 24 September 1941. Bentley Historical Library, University of Michigan. Ralph W. Aigler Papers, 87406 Aa 2; Box 8, folder: correspondence 1940-45 "H" misc.

[40] Aigler to Ruthven. 30 September 1941. Bentley Historical Library, University of Michigan. Ralph W. Aigler Papers, 87406 Aa 2; Box 8, folder: correspondence 1940-45 "H" misc.

The law school professor then educated his boss on the politics behind Hannah wanting the date changed. It was not about the chaotic registration week after all. The Spartans would have a better chance of defeating the Wolverines later in the season. And the publicity of beating a national power like Michigan would benefit the Spartan football program. Aigler, based on his opinion of the athletic leadership in East Lansing, wanted nothing to do with aiding that cause.[41] He lacked any knowledge of Hannah's ultimate reason for promoting athletics: attaining university status for the college.

Aigler reassured his president that the Board in Control of Physical Education would address the matter.[42] He would also personally compose a response to Hannah's inquiry. One month later, Hannah received it. Aigler apologized for the delay; it had taken time to meet with his board before replying to the special request. He reminded the college president that disruption in student life was bound to occur regardless of what weekend was chosen for the intrastate contest held annually in Ann Arbor. He concluded by noting that "… the Michigan State game is an attractive feature on our schedule, but despite that, I am sure you recognize that after all the really big objective in our football season is to make the best possible showing in the Conference."[43]

In the meantime, lacking a timely response from Alexander Ruthven, the Faculty Senate went ahead and approved its president's proposal[44] on how to fix the problems of orientation/registration week in East Lansing. It would "[forbid] the scheduling of future football games in Ann Arbor … prior to opening of fall quarter classes [at the college]."[45]And with that October 1941 resolution, John Hannah now had in hand an institutional policy, as mandated by academicians, that would finally address the university's control over football scheduling. It was utter brilliance. But due to various circumstances, Michigan's athletic leadership was never apprised of the Faculty Senate's intentions until the fall of 1946.[46] The resolution, at that time, would unexpectedly impact contentious negotiations taking place between the intrastate rivals over annual football dates.

President Hannah, while reading Aigler's tardy reply, was probably perturbed by his low opinion of the state rivalry, but he brushed it aside. He wrote back five days later expressing a desire to "sit down and visit with you about some of our problems that are of mutual interest." Hannah also noted that 20 years earlier he had been a law student of the professor's while attending the University of Michigan.[47] That reminder of a previous academic relationship, in the context of his latest letter, seemed out of place. But John Hannah had his reasons. He was probably trying to develop a rapport with the longstanding occupant of 320 Hutchins Hall.

---

[41] Aigler to Ruthven. 30 September 1941. Bentley Historical Library, University of Michigan. Ralph W. Aigler Papers, 87406 Aa 2; Box 8, folder: correspondence 1940-45 "H" misc.

[42] Ibid.

[43] Aigler to Hannah. 20 October 1941. Bentley Historical Library, University of Michigan. Ralph W. Aigler Papers, 87406 Aa 2; Box 8, folder: correspondence 1940-45 "H" misc.

[44] Minutes of the State Board of Agriculture. 18 September 1941. www.onthebanks.msu.edu

[45] Minutes of the Meeting of the Board in Control of Intercollegiate Athletics. 15 November 1946. Bentley Historical Library. University of Michigan. Board in Control of Intercollegiate Athletics, 8729 Bimu F81 2; Box 49, folder: Board in Control minutes February 1938-June 1950

[46] Ibid.

[47] Hannah to Aigler. 25 October 1941. Bentley Historical Library, University of Michigan. Ralph W. Aigler Papers, 87406 Aa 2; Box 8, folder: correspondence 1940-45 "H" misc

Five years earlier, in December of 1936, while serving on the ad hoc Huston Committee,[48] Secretary Hannah and his two colleagues first suspected a Western Conference boycott of the school. The three members concluded that it was probably orchestrated by Professor Aigler. The reasons remained a mystery. And now, with receipt of the faculty representative's letter from Ann Arbor, it was quite obvious to Hannah who controlled athletic policy in Ann Arbor and also influenced conference politics in Chicago. If the president was to accomplish some long-term visionary plans for his college, he needed his old professor's assistance.

The former student continued his note by pointing out to Aigler that "Michigan State, as you know, has grown into a great university and is rather universally regarded." He encouraged him to "drop in" sometime when in central Michigan for a personal visit.[49]

Aigler responded graciously a few days later. He was surprised that Hannah had been a student of his back in the 1921-22 academic year. The Hannah tactic had worked! Aigler expressed a willingness to take him up on the offer to visit the Red Cedar Campus.[50] The last time he had been there was February of 1939 when he, Fielding Yost, and Fritz Crisler met with Spartan athletic leaders regarding concerns over potential Handbook violations on Michigan State's part.

AT ABOUT the same time the college Faculty Senate was debating its president's proposal regarding registration week, John Hannah was also at work formulating policies for subsidizing student-athletes. Not only did he feel that this was "serving justice" for kids donating hours of practice in revenue-generating sports that benefited the school, he also felt that it might assist Coach Charlie Bachman's football program. Quality athletes, enticed by subsidies to choose East Lansing for college, would bring prominence to Michigan State. The national media attention, through athletic success on the gridiron, would also lead to favorable press coverage of other aspects of the growing institution. The exposure, in the president's opinion, could only aid his campaign for admission into the Western Conference. Affiliation with 10 other highly regarded research institutions might further his strategy to make Michigan State a great center of higher education and research.

At the October 23 State Board meeting President Hannah proposed the Gunson Scholarships. Those 50 grants were intended for any student, including athletes, meeting two criteria: dire financial need and demonstrable leadership in certain extracurricular activities. Satisfactory classroom achievement was a minor requirement.[51] The policy, other than the academic stipulations, was quite similar to the University of Iowa Club of Greater Chicago scholarships approved by the conference faculty representatives in 1936.[52] The $400 grants from alumni donors met conference standards for disbursement of aid to athletes. Awards were based on the student's academic and extracurricular achievements.

---

[48] The committee was charged with exploring an application for admission of the college into the Western Conference.

[49] Hannah to Aigler. 25 October 1941. Bentley Historical Library, University of Michigan. Ralph W. Aigler Papers, 87406 Aa 2; Box 8, folder: correspondence 1940-45 "H" misc

[50] Aigler to Hannah. 1 November 1941. Bentley Historical Library, University of Michigan. Ralph W. Aigler Papers, 87406 Aa 2; Box 8, folder: correspondence 1940-45 "H" misc

[51] Minutes of the State Board of Agriculture. 23 October 1941. www.onthebanks.msu.edu.

[52] Griffith to French. 7 March 1939. Bentley Historical Library. University of Michigan. Ralph W. Aigler Papers, 87406 Aa;. Box 6, correspondence: 1934-39 Griffith 9/37-7/39

Athletic skills were not excluded. The State University of Iowa Scholarship Committee, composed of faculty, had the final say on all grants. That feature had satisfied the skeptical Aigler;[53] he had voted in favor of the Hawkeye proposal five years earlier.[54]

The Gunson Scholarship plan probably went unnoticed by the law professor from Ann Arbor. It was consistent with the revised Intercollegiate Handbook of 1941.[55] There was little controversy in a plan modeled after the Iowa policy. But the Jenison Awards, to be proposed to and rubber-stamped by the State Board in mid-December,[56] would undoubtedly gain Ralph Aigler's attention. John Hannah knew that only too well.

In late November of 1941, a few weeks in advance of that board meeting, Hannah quite suddenly requested a "few minutes in Ann Arbor the early part of next week" with Aigler.[57] He had a brief agenda: "intercollegiate athletics."[58] As a courtesy, he wanted to alert the faculty representative of his subsidy program that would soon be sanctioned by the State Board. At the very least, it would afford Hannah the opportunity to justify his proposal without the influence of hearsay and misguided press releases.

Unfortunately for John Hannah and Michigan State, shortly after that communiqué Aigler became ill with a throat infection that required hospitalization.[59] His secretary, Mary Pearce, relayed the news to Hannah. She noted that he anticipated being well within a few days. A rain-check for the upcoming Tuesday, December 1, was arranged.[60]

Ralph Aigler may have been a renowned legal expert in properties, but he was a poor diagnostician. He was seriously ill. The professor would spend the next five months in the University Hospital before heading southwest to recuperate in Arizona.[61] He remained in Tucson through the fall to fulfill a visiting professorship at the University of Arizona Law School. Aigler's wife became terminally ill near the end of that sabbatical. The couple returned to Ann Arbor in late December. Helen Aigler passed away in mid-January of 1943.[62]

Aigler's protracted illness and recovery, the semester in Tucson, and his wife's final days were events that precluded John Hannah from making any further contact with him. However, just prior to his departure for Arizona in early spring, out of respect to the man leading a sister state institution, Aigler asked a good friend to relay to President Hannah that

---

[53] Aigler to Griffith. 8 March 1939. Bentley Historical Librar,. University of Michigan. Ralph W. Aigler Papers, 87406 Aa2; Box 6, correspondence: 1934-39 Griffith 9/37-7/39

[54] Ibid.

[55] Handbook of the Intercollegiate Conference of Faculty Representatives-Revised 1941. University of Minnesota Archives, Department of Intercollegiate Athletics Papers; Box 13, folder: small handbooks 1895-1907, 1930, 1941

[56] Minutes of the State Board of Agriculture. 18 December 1941. www.onthebanks.msu.edu.

[57] Hannah to Aigler. 27 November 1941. Bentley Historical Library, University of Michigan. Ralph W. Aigler Papers, 87406 Aa 2; Box 8, folder: correspondence 1940-45 "H" misc.

[58] Hannah to Aigler. 13 April 1943. Bentley Historical Library, University of Michigan. Ralph W. Aigler Papers, 87406 Aa 2; Box 8, folder: correspondence 1940-45 "H" misc.

[59] Hannah to Aigler.27 November 1941. Bentley Historical Library, University of Michigan. Ralph W. Aigler Papers, 87406 Aa 2; Box 8, folder: correspondence 1940-45 "H" misc.

[60] Pearce to Hannah. 28 November 1941. Bentley Historical Library, University of Michigan. Ralph W. Aigler Papers, 87406 Aa 2; Box 8, folder: correspondence 1940-45 "H" misc.

[61] Aigler to Hannah 30 March 1943. Bentley Historical Library, University of Michigan. Ralph W. Aigler Papers, 87406 Aa 2; Box 8, folder: correspondence 1940-45 "H" misc.

[62] Ibid.

he was "still not seeing people."[63] The message, unfortunately, was never delivered.

The law professor returned to teaching in Ann Arbor shortly after the death of his wife. In late March of 1943, Aigler "… learned from [his messenger friend] that he had not seen [Hannah at that time] … and therefore had not given [him] the message." The professor was chagrined by the miscue. He wrote his former student offering an apology. Aigler was more than willing to meet with the president but anticipated that "whatever it was that was on your mind a year ago last November has long since been ironed out."[64]

The professor's assumption seemed logical. Hannah's brief agenda regarding "intercollegiate athletics" in late November of 1941 most likely involved future scheduling arrangements between the two schools. After all, it was the reason that the college president wrote to Alexander Ruthven in September. And now, in the early spring of 1943, with Michigan State's affiliation with the War Department probably precluding intercollegiate participation in sports, all scheduling with Michigan had to be put on hold for the foreseeable future. With all of this in mind, he anticipated no reason to arrange a visit at the time.[65] So Ralph Aigler probably had no clue as to what was John Hannah's actual intention for requesting a meeting just prior to his illness one and a half years earlier.

A good sense for timing had always been one of the president's strongest attributes in the opinion of his valued consultant, Professor Floyd Reeves.[66] But in the final month of 1941, due to circumstances beyond his control, that attribute failed him. Lacking an opportunity to debate the merits of his proposed subsidy program with his former law school professor, the president had no choice but to move ahead with the Jenison Awards. He would subsidize athletes to fulfill Fred Jenison's directive of using the estate "for the improvement of [the college] with particular emphasis on athletics."[67] Ralph Aigler would learn of the controversial plan secondhand.

One year later, in December of 1942, the college requested Michigan's sponsorship of an application for membership into the Western Conference in advance of the upcoming spring meetings. The confidential reply would prove as disappointing as the rejection of May 1937. But unlike that unanimous decision by the Faculty Representatives Committee, the second rejection of the Spartans required no vote of the conference membership.

DURING THE early part of December 1942 athletic directors Ralph Young and Fritz Crisler were carrying on a debate over scheduling future football contests. Young "cordially" invited Michigan to play the 1943 game in East Lansing as the start of a home-and-home series. The War Department edict, forbidding intercollegiate football on campuses training Army recruits, was still months away. Although the game had been previously inked in for Ann Arbor back in May of 1940, the Spartan director wanted to change venues.[68] He was under pressure by his Athletic Council and President Hannah to

---

[63] Aigler to Hannah 30 March 1943. Bentley Historical Library, University of Michigan. Ralph W. Aigler Papers, 87406 Aa 2; Box 8, folder: correspondence 1940-45 "H" misc.

[64] Ibid.

[65] Ibid.

[66] Reeves, Floyd W. "Statement of Floyd Reeves." Michigan State University Archives. Hannah Archives Project, UA2.1.12.2; Box 34, folder: 37

[67] Hannah, John A. *A Memoir*. East Lansing: Michigan State University Press, 1980. p.121

[68] Minutes of the Meeting of the Directors of Athletics of the Intercollegiate Conference. 24-25 May 1940. Bentley Historical Library, University of Michigan. Athletic Department, 943 Bimu 2; Box 84,

force Crisler's hand on this matter.[69]

Fritz Crisler responded a few weeks later, again taking the familiar dominant role. Ralph Aigler, on sabbatical in part for health reasons, was finishing up lecture obligations at the University of Arizona Law School. In the meantime the new athletic director was fully in control back in Ann Arbor.

Crisler argued the discrepancy in stadium seating did not justify holding the game in East Lansing. "I am not informed as to the exact seating capacity of your stadium but I raise the question whether or not you think the people in the State can best be served by playing the game here each year or on a home and home arrangement." He cited attendance figures averaging 62,992 paying customers over the past five years to support his argument.[70] Macklin Field, even at full capacity, would accommodate less than half that number.

The Wolverine director, with an air of Michigan arrogance, then suggested that the Spartans back out of the annual game if dissatisfied with the long-term agreement first proposed by Fielding Yost in 1932. Perhaps the college could arrive at a more favorable contract with another school. "Rest assured we would understand if you proceeded to make such [an arrangement]." Crisler reminded Young that the Wolverines had many requests from other institutions for a football relationship ..."[71] What he failed to mention was that none of those competitors would agree to the scrimmage game date. And no other program could guarantee him comparable ticket sales for the opener in Ann Arbor. Crisler was playing poker with Ralph Young. He appeared to be winning this hand.

Twelve days later Michigan State's athletic director responded with a single spaced two-page letter contesting Crisler's comments. Young had shared that December 16, 1942, communiqué with his council and John Hannah. His response, on athletic department letterhead, was written by John Hannah. The college president went into detail about the unfair advantage the scheduling arrangement had given the Wolverines over the years.

> After we have been beaten by the University early in the season, the
> remainder of our football schedule has had the luster removed. We do not
> feel it helps ... to have Michigan State relegated so early in the season to an
> "also ran" status.[72]

The president, oddly enough, then proceeded to describe the college as an outstanding educational institution. In point of fact, the school was struggling.

Soon after assuming the presidency, Hannah had questioned the effectiveness of pedagogy on campus. A few years later, in November of 1943, "an all-college committee on the improvement of ... teaching was established ..."[73] One of its mandates was to analyze

---

folder: Big Ten Directors Committee minutes 3/41-7/52

[69] Young to Crisler. 2 December 1942. Bentley Historical Library, University of Michigan. Herbert Orin Crisler Papers, 85823 AC UAm Aa 2; Box 1, folder: topical correspondence MSU 1943-46

[70] Crisler to Young. 16 December 1942. Bentley Historical Library, University of Michigan. Herbert Orin Crisler Papers, 85823 AC UAm Aa 2; Box 1, folder: topical correspondence MSU 1943-46

[71] Ibid.

[72] Thomas, David A. *Michigan State College: John Hannah and the Creation of a World University, 1926-1969.* East Lansing: Michigan State University Press, 2008. p. 295

[73] Combs, William H. Untitled statement on academics. 11 January 1971. Michigan State University Archives. Hannah Archives Project, UA2.1.12.2; Box 34, folder: 7

an alumni survey on the quality of instruction at Michigan State that had garnered poor marks. And to substantiate Hannah's concerns, the North Central Association, involved with accreditation of the school, reported a survey on faculty credentials in December of 1945. Michigan State ranked in the 61st percentile among peer institutions. The graduate program, in particular, was at risk for probation over the findings.[74]

But in December of 1942, President Hannah, in the guise of Ralph Young, waxed eloquent about the legitimate place the college held in higher education within the state. Quite boldly, despite being aware of teaching inadequacies at the college, he proclaimed that Michigan State merited admission into the Western Conference. But to gain that membership required the cooperation of the university. "We are not likely to be admitted to the Conference unless or until you and the University of Michigan are willing actively to sponsor our cause."[75]

Crisler, assuming the letter was written with Ralph Young's typewriter, thought it a strange request. Political relationships between the two institutions remained the purview of governing bodies at the highest level. Athletic directors completed schedules, hired coaches, and balanced departmental budgets. Sponsorship of Michigan State, let alone any institution, for membership in the conference was not a part of the job description.

By then Ralph Aigler was back in Ann Arbor caring for his dying wife. The director turned to President Alexander Ruthven, rather than his faculty representative and friend, for counsel on a response to the unusual letter from East Lansing. That discussion, held in Ruthven's office on January 27, 1943, allowed Crisler to comfortably decline the request for university sponsorship of a Spartan application.[76] [77] He should focus instead on "athletic matter(s)" strictly pertaining to scheduling of the intrastate rivalry. After all, the name on the letterhead belonged to Athletic Director Ralph Young, not President John Hannah.

The Michigan athletic director then addressed Hannah's reason for ghostwriting the letter. He informed Ruthven that "even if we did sponsor her membership in the Western Conference, we could not get enough support from our colleagues representing the other nine universities."[78]

The second attempt at an admission into the Intercollegiate Conference of Faculty Representatives ended on that note. Michigan State had once again been stymied by the apparent prejudice of its Wolverine neighbors. In East Lansing there was a growing belief that certain athletic leaders in Ann Arbor could no longer be trusted. There were now two men at the University of Michigan seemingly opposed to the Spartan cause. And, unfortunately for Michigan State, both Ralph Aigler and Frtiz Crisler maintained positions of influence within the Western Conference.

---

[74] Combs, William H. Untitled statement on academics. 11 January 1971. Michigan State University Archives. Hannah Archives Project, UA2.1.12.2; Box 34, folder: 7

[75] Crisler to Young. 28 December 1942. Bentley Historical Library, University of Michigan. Herbert Orin Crisler Papers, 85823 AC UAm Aa 2; Box 1, folder: topical correspondence MSU 1943-46

[76] Crisler to Ruthven. 13 January 1943. Bentley Historical Library, University of Michigan. Alexander G. Ruthven Papers, 86550 AC Aa 2; Box 34, folder: 27

[77] Michigan State Football Date. Circa 1946. Bentley Historical Library, University of Michigan. Herbert Orin Crisler Papers, 85823 AC UAm Aa 2; Box 1, folder: topical correspondence Michigan State University 1940-42

[78] Crisler to Ruthven. 13 January 1943. Bentley Historical Library, University of Michigan. Herbert Orin Crisler Papers, 85823 AC UAm Aa 2; Box 1, folder: topical correspondence MSU 1943-46

HAVING EXPERIENCED two rejections in six years, and aware by April of 1943 that intercollegiate athletics in East Lansing, due to a War Department edict, would be held in abeyance "for the duration,"[79] John Hannah was free to direct his attention to equally pressing concerns, particularly the growing problem of substandard instruction at the college.

His first decision was to hire Professor Floyd Reeves of the University of Chicago. The Roosevelt Democrat and the West Michigan Republican found common ground in discussing innovative educational models to improve the academic experience at Michigan State. Hannah and Reeves began to change the curriculum in 1943.[80]

The president's academic vision included providing freshmen and sophomores with a general education necessary in the evolving postwar world followed by specialized study for specific degrees after the successful completion of the core-curriculum requirements.[81] Surprisingly, Hannah succeeded where others had failed. With Reeves' counsel and a faculty willing to embrace Hannah's academic vision, the Basic College was created.[82]

President Hannah trumpeted his achievement to most of the Western Conference presidents. It was a brilliant strategy on his part. Athletic accomplishments alone would not get the college into the Big Ten. He needed to prove that Michigan State belonged in the same company as Michigan, Wisconsin, Purdue, the University of Chicago, and others.[83]

In May of 1944 Hannah shared a copy of the Basic College program with his counterpart Arthur Willard of the University of Illinois. Willard was thoroughly impressed and passed it on to his academic leadership team. The dean in charge of developing a similar model at Illinois commented in a return memo, "looks like our [program]; but it must be admitted that they have gone about it in a much better way than we have here ... I have asked Bob Fischer to go to East Lansing ... [to study their program]."[84] The provost returned to Champaign-Urbana amazed at how Michigan State was transforming its curriculum. He shared his assessment with President Willard.[85]

The Illinois leader wrote back to Hannah congratulating him "for having accomplished what I attempted to do at the University of Illinois ten years ago with no success." He went on to comment, "It is a wonderful achievement to have convinced any faculty, especially one in the technical fields of Agriculture and Applied Science, of the fundamental importance of providing such a program of basic education ... I am afraid it will be a long time before this University will take such a step."[86]

Despite the accolades coming into East Lansing about Hannah's successful

---

[79] Hannah to Aigler. Bentley Historical Library, University of Michigan. Ralph W. Aigler Papers, 87406 Aa 2; Box 8, folder: correspondence 1940-45 "H" misc.

[80] Hannah, John A. *A Memoir*. East Lansing, Michigan State University Press, 1980. p. 48

[81] Ibid., pp. 48-52

[82] Ibid., p. 50

[83] Ibid., p. 117

[84] Herrick to Willard. 6 June 44. University of Illinois Archives. General Correspondence, 1934-1946. Series 2/9/1; Box 104, folder: Mi

[85] Harno to Willard. 29 May 1944. University of Illinois Archives. General Correspondence, 1934-1946. Series 2/9/1; Box 104, folder: Mi

[86] Willard to Hannah. 29 May 1944. University of Illinois Archives. General Correspondence, 1934-1946. Series 2/9/1; Box 104, folder: Mi

curricular initiative, he still had to address the quality of teaching at the college. It was only five years earlier that the State Board acknowledged Robert Shaw for his leadership in gaining Michigan State the highest grade from its accrediting agency.[87] But a breakdown had occurred in the meantime. The alumni survey and the NCA assessment of faculty qualifications were reminders of work yet to be accomplished. Hannah vowed, in confidence to his core leadership team, that "the College must never again be embarrassed in such a manner."[88]

President Hannah appointed a group to address the problem, with Floyd Reeves intimately involved. Lacking funds to attract prominent professors, the school set out to hire the best and the brightest out of graduate schools from premier programs around the country.[89] Teaching skills were emphasized. With his eloquence and personality, the president proved to be a persuasive recruiter and successful salesman.[90][91]

He also promoted a program to enhance the faculty's lecture-hall skills, which the alumni surveys had said were lacking. Through a newly appointed Committee on Exchange of Professors, Michigan State would offer a sabbatical program with other schools willing to participate after the war. To that end, Hannah's representative, chemistry professor Ralph Huston, wrote to President Edwin B. Fred of Wisconsin. Although Fred showed interest in the concept of an exchange, Wisconsin politely declined. In the immediate postwar years a great shortage of professors was anticipated, and, with the return of so many veterans, enrollment was predicted to be at an all-time high. Wisconsin's leadership feared the sabbatical program might further deplete their pool of academicians.[92][93][94] Others shared this feeling. No exchanges were arranged.

But communicating with the University of Wisconsin leadership was not in vain. Hannah was able to develop a close friendship with Edwin B. Fred. He would soon be added to the Michigan State president's "blueberries and maple syrup" list.

Since his promotion to the presidency, Hannah would annually present certain people with blueberries grown on the agricultural extension services farms in South Haven, Michigan.[95] Each year, in midsummer, Stanley Johnston, research professor of horticulture, was instructed to send the finest berries to a list of university presidents and state

---

[87] Minutes of the State Board of Agriculture. 21 December 1940. www.onthebanks.msu.edu

[88] Combs, William H. Untitled 11 January 1971. Michigan State University Archives. Hannah Archives Project, UA2.1.12.2; Box 34, folder: 7

[89] Thomas, David. *Michigan State College: John Hannah and the Creation of a World University, 1926-1969.* Michigan State University Press: East Lansing, 2008. p. 104

[90] Ibid.

[91] Denison, James H. Untitled. 24 June 1970. Michigan State University Archives. Hannah Archives Project, UA2.1.12.2; Box 34, folder: 8

[92] Huston to Dykstra. 8 November 1945. University of Wisconsin-Madison Archives. Chancellors and Presidents, Series 4/16/1; Box 39, folder: General Correspondence Files 1945-46 Ma-Mo. Huston erroneously addressed the letter to Clarence Dykstra. The former president assumed the provost position at UCLA earlier that year.

[93] Herriott to Fred. 14 November 1945. University of Wisconsin-Madison Archives. Chancellors and Presidents, Series 4/16/1; Box 39, folder: General Correspondence Files 1945-46 Ma-Mo

[94] Fred to Huston. 28 December 1945. University of Wisconsin-Madison Archives. Chancellors and Presidents, Series 4/16/1; Box 39, folder: General Correspondence Files 1945-46 Ma-Mo

[95] Hovde to Hannah. Michigan State University Archives. President Files, UA2.1.12; Box 90, folder: 27 1952, 58-59

politicians.[96] Hannah would also send a gallon of award-winning maple syrup, produced by the Forestry Department from trees on campus, to those same people in late spring.[97] Once on the list, the gifting continued for decades. Fred was one of many presidents about the conference enjoying Spartan agricultural products.[98] [99]

The relationships that Hannah developed in this way would serve him well throughout his distinguished career.

ON DECEMBER 28, 1942, John Hannah, by way of a letter he penned for Ralph Young, expressed in detail to Herbert Orin Crisler various reasons for Michigan State becoming a member of the Intercollegiate Conference.

> We are the only large, state supported university in Western Conference territory not holding membership in the Conference. In enrollment, in equipment, in academic standing, and in geographic location we are not inferior to many members of the Western Conference. We believe that our membership in the Western Conference would be advantageous to Michigan State College and that it would not be harmful to the University of Michigan.[100]

Regardless of his convictions on the college's qualifications for membership, one week later Hannah would learn that another school had applied for an expansion seat in the conference and been rejected by the faculty representatives a year earlier. Although he knew he had some competition for that eleventh spot, Hannah was surprised when he found out who the competition was.

The University of Pittsburgh had one of the most successful football programs in the country during the 1920s and 30s. The school won mythical national championships by openly committing the cardinal sins: recruiting, subsidizing, and admitting/playing ineligible students. But the play-for-pay practice, as promoted by Head Coach Jock Sutherland, ultimately caught up with the institution. Schools were no longer willing to contract with Pitt. Chancellor John Gabbert Bowman decided it was time to address the problem. In 1939 Commissioner John Griffith was hired by the athletic program at Pitt to assist its new athletic director in enforcing the NCAA amateur code.[101] The former major in the US Army would now serve as compliance officer for 11 schools about the Midwest.

[96] Johnston to Hannah. 25 July 1966. Michigan State University Archives. President Files, UA2.1.12; Box 44, folder: 20 blueberry gifts

[97] Hovde to Hannah. Michigan State University Archives. President Files, UA2.1.12; Box 64, folder: 44 maple syrup

[98] Hannah to Foster. 5 March 1960. Michigan State University Archives. President Files, UA2.1.12; Box 64, folder: 44 maple syrup

[99] Fred to Hannah. 20 August 1948. University of Wisconsin-Madison Archives. Chancellors and Presidents, Series 4/16/1; Box 82, folder: President E. B. Fred, general correspondence files 1947-48 Fl-Hi

[100] Young to Crisler. 28 December 1942. Bentley Historical Library, University of Michigan. Alexander G. Ruthven Papers, 86550 Ac Aa 2; Box 34, folder: 27 "Physical Education (BIC)"

[101] Wallace, Francis. "The Football Laboratory Explodes-The Climax in the Test Case at Pitt." *The Saturday Evening Post*, 4 November 1939. The University of Pittsburgh Archives, 9/10-A; Box 1, FF 772.

Bowman brought on Griffith for one purpose: to regain the integrity of a great institution compromised by illicit athletic practices. For alumni and students, however, his hiring of Griffith as a consultant signaled the end of winning football at Pittsburgh. Some sportswriters suspected that the Bowman plan was merely a means for Pitt to gain admission into the Western Conference.[102] Affiliation, after all, would offer a quick fix to the mess created by an unscrupulous football coach.

Surprised by the outcry in Pittsburgh, Griffith was forced to deny to the press any conference dalliance with the university.[103] At no time, he said, had he been approached by the chancellor, the provost, or Athletic Director James Hagan regarding assistance in applying to the conference. The commissioner was well aware that it was not within his purview to recruit members for the conference. In point of fact, prior to assuming the consultant role at Pittsburgh, he had sought the approval of all athletic directors as well as the chairman of the Faculty Representatives Committee.[104] [105] Griffith wanted to reassure his bosses that he was not exceeding his job description. Despite that precaution on his part, the Panther uproar briefly challenged the commissioner's integrity.

John Griffith, however, would soon develop a good working relationship with Pitt's athletic director. The leaders, after collaborating for two years, concluded there might be some merit in the Panthers joining the conference after all. In February of 1941, the commissioner called upon his friend Lynn St. John, of Ohio State, to join him in a highly confidential meeting at the Schenley Hotel in Pittsburgh. They continued discussion back at the Hagan household into the late evening hours.[106] [107] [108]

The meeting proved to be very helpful for Pitt's strategic planning. Including St. John was a wise decision on the commissioner's part. His influence during future scheduling meetings undoubtedly contributed to the Panthers signing up most conference schools for short series over the next 10 seasons. By 1947, the university had become a de facto member of the conference. Most of its games were against Western Conference institutions that year. Less than a decade earlier, the Intercollegiate Conference had effectively boycotted that same school over the Sutherland payment scheme.[109]

---

[102] Wallace, Francis. "The Football Laboratory Explodes-The Climax in the Test Case at Pitt." *The Saturday Evening Post,* 4 November 1939. The University of Pittsburgh Archives, 9/10-A; Box 1, FF 772.

[103] Griffith to The Directors of Athletics of the Conference. 30 September 1939. The Ohio State University Archives, Director of Athletics (RG 9/e-1/9), "Intercollegiate Conference: Commissioner: Correspondence (Griffith): 1939-40 (Folder 2 of 2)."

[104] Griffith to St. John. 1 March 1940. The Ohio State University Archives, Director of Athletics (RG 9/e-1/9), "Intercollegiate Conference: Athletic Director's Correspondence: 1938-1940."

[105] Minutes of the Meeting of the Directors of Athletics of the Intercollegiate Conference. 6-7 December 1940. Bentley Historical Library, University of Michigan. Athletic Department, 943 Bimu 2; Box 84, folder: Big Ten Directors Committee minutes 1932-40

[106] Griffith to St. John. 6 February 1941. The Ohio State University Archives, Director of Athletics (RG 9/e-1/9), "Intercollegiate Conference: Commissioner: Correspondence (Griffith): 1940-41 (Folder 1 of 2)."

[107] Griffith to St. John. 12 February 1941. The Ohio State University Archives, Director of Athletics (RG 9/e-1/9), "Intercollegiate Conference: Commissioner: Correspondence (Griffith): 1940-41 (Folder 1 of 2)."

[108] Ibid.

[109] Wallace, Francis. "The Test Case at Pitt-The Facts about College Football Play for Pay." *The*

With probable encouragement from both Griffith and St. John, a confidential petition for application to the conference was placed before the Faculty Representatives Committee in December of 1941. No action was taken.[110] It would prove to be the first of five attempts by Pitt at seeking admission to the conference; the others included December of 1944, May of 1945, May of 1946, and December of 1948.

Regardless of its first rejection, Pittsburgh's presence on the schedule of so many Western Conference teams over the next decade could only serve it well in pursuing the highly confidential Hagan-Griffith-St. John plan.

JOHN HANNAH first learned of the Panther interest in conference membership in early January of 1943. President Virgil Hancher of Iowa, also on the "blueberries and maple syrup" list, wrote of it in response to Hannah's mid-December letter regarding conference expansion plans. Hancher indicated that Pittsburgh had applied sometime within the previous few years. He could not recall the specific date.[111] His revelation probably shocked Hannah. Pittsburgh had a terrible reputation. Coach Jock Sutherland had recently lost his job, in part, over egregious recruiting and subsidizing practices.[112]

When Hannah received the letter, Michigan State had yet to hear from Fritz Crisler about whether Michigan would sponsor a Spartan application for admission into the Western Conference. While awaiting that word from Ann Arbor, Hannah probably wondered which conference institution had the audacity to sponsor Pittsburgh in December of 1941. The Panther rejection, however, proved to Hannah how important institutional support was to an applicant's success. And for Michigan State, that success required the cooperation of the University of Michigan. No other school, in Hannah's opinion, could offer meaningful sponsorship comparable to that of a sister institution. The two schools, after all, had maintained a wonderful working relationship away from the gridiron.[113] [114] The conference faculty representatives, out of courtesy to a fellow member, would defer to Michigan's position on allowing a neighbor, 60 miles away, into the association.[115] [116] [117]

Two weeks later, following his discussion with President Ruthven, Crisler would

---

Saturday Evening Post, 28 October 1939. The University of Pittsburgh Archives, 9/10-A; Box 1, FF 772

[110] Hancher to Hannah. 31 December 1942. University of Iowa Archives, Iowa City, Iowa. Virgil Hancher Papers, RG 05.01.11; Box 60, file: 91

[111] Ibid.

[112] Wallace, Francis. "The Test Case at Pitt-The Facts about College Football Play for Pay." *The Saturday Evening Post,* 28 October 1939. The University of Pittsburgh Archives, 9/10-A; Box 1, FF 772.

[113] Aigler to Wilson. 8 August 1945. Bentley Historical Library, University of Michigan. Ralph W. Aigler Papers, 87406 Aa 2; Box 8, folder: correspondence 1940-45 misc. Wilson

[114] Young to Crisler. 28 December 1942. Bentley Historical Library, University of Michigan. Herbert Orin Crisler Papers, 85823 AC UAm Aa2; Box 1, folder: MSU correspondence 1943-46

[115] Morrill to Rottschaefer. 16 September 1948. University of Minnesota Archives, President's Office; Box 238, folder: physical education 1948-49

[116] Morrill to Hannah. 21 March 1946. University of Minnesota Archives, President's Office; Box 238, folder: physical education 1945-47

[117] Morrill to Rottschaefer. 17 May 1946. University of Minnesota Archives, President's Office; Box 238, folder: physical education 1945-47

decline sponsorship of the college. It was not within his purview as athletic director, he said, to promote the application of another program. The message was devastating for the Spartans. John Hannah had no idea that Alexander Ruthven had made the decision.[118] In his mind, Fritz Crisler was responsible for the second rejection.

A few months later, in March of 1943, President Hannah received a note of apology from Ralph Aigler. Prior to his departure for the Arizona desert one year earlier, he had requested that a close friend communicate to Hannah that he was "still not accepting visitors" while recovering from a serious respiratory illness. And now, back in Ann Arbor, Hannah's former professor had just learned that the message was never delivered.[119] Aigler's letter regarding a matter Hannah had probably long since forgotten was somewhat surprising. Was there more to the note than just extending an apology?

On the 13th of April, Hannah wrote back, excited over the communication with the powerful Aigler, especially in the aftermath of the recent Crisler rejection. He seized the moment and made a sales pitch for Michigan State, which, in his opinion, was now a "great university." The president concluded his letter by stating, "If the opportunity ever presents itself when you can without embarrassment sponsor a program that will result in the admission of this College to membership in the Western Conference, it will be very much appreciated."[120]

Aigler's reply was disappointing. He informed Hannah that there had been numerous applications by many institutions over the years. "Each time the question has come up the vote was decisively in the negative." He implied that Michigan had little influence in the application process that involved 10 voting members.[121] [122]

But Hannah detected a ray of hope in Aigler's response. His former professor described his conundrum as a representative to the Western Conference. On the one hand, he agreed with his nine colleagues. There was no reason for expansion in 1943. But he was also torn by a "desire to do something that is wanted by a sister State institution."[123] The optimist from East Lansing probably interpreted that comment favorably. Maybe he was making some headway in his relationship with Ralph Aigler after all.

PITTSBURGH AGAIN applied to the Western Conference in late 1944.[124] Because it requested no publicity regarding its intentions,[125] Commissioner Griffith cautiously

---

[118] Crisler to Ruthven. 13 January 1943. Bentley Historical Library, University of Michigan. Alexander G. Ruthven Papers, 86550 AC Aa 2; Box 34, folder: 27

[119] Aigler to Hannah. 30 March 1943. Bentley Historical Library, University of Michigan. Ralph W. Aigler Papers, 87406 Aa 2; Box 8, folder: correspondence 1940-45 "H" misc.

[120] Hannah to Aigler. 13 April 1943. Bentley Historical Library, University of Michigan. Ralph W. Aigler Papers, 87406 Aa 2; Box 8, folder: correspondence 1940-45 "H" misc.

[121] Aigler to Hannah. 15 April 1943. Bentley Historical Library, University of Michigan. Ralph W. Aigler Papers, 87406 Aa 2; Box 8, folder: correspondence 1940-45 "H" misc.

[122] Crisler to Young. 20 July 1945. Bentley Historical Library, University of Michigan. Herbert Orin Crisler Papers, 85823 AC UAm Aa 2; Box 6, folder: 1941-49, undated

[123] Aigler to Hannah. 15 April 1943. Bentley Historical Library, University of Michigan. Ralph W. Aigler Papers, 87406 Aa 2; Box 8, folder: correspondence 1940-45 "H" misc

[124] Sherrill to Richart. 23 May 1946. University of Pittsburgh Archives, Collection 9/2, FF1; Box 1

[125] Aigler to Rottshaefer. 31 July 1944. Bentley Historical Library, University of Michigan. Ralph W. Aigler Papers, 87406 Aa 2: Box 8, folder: correspondence 1940-45 Rottschaefer

advanced the Pitt agenda throughout the year. Minnesota's Henry Rottschaefer and Ralph Aigler, however, had become suspicious of Griffith's motives back in September.[126] The influential faculty leaders were probably not privy to Lynn St. John's involvement in the scheme. But the fact that the Ohio State athletic director had confidentially worked with Griffith in 1941 would imply there was collaboration.

In August Griffith sent a memo to the athletic directors of the conference informing them that Pittsburgh was insisting that all games held with the Eastern Intercollegiate Football Association be played under NCAA rules.[127] Griffith's announcement seemed to serve no purpose other than alerting the Western Conference that Pitt was truly cleaning house. But he may have trumpeted the statement for another reason as well. Aware of Panther plans for applying in December, the former Army major's memo may have reassured conference leadership that a sincere revival had taken place under Jimmy Hagan's leadership. The university would not only abide by the NCAA code, it insisted that other contracted schools do so as well.

Lynn St. John had written to Hagan in March of 1944 reminding him of the need to abide by the concepts of amateurism in collegiate sports. St. John provided Griffith with a copy, and the commissioner wrote back applauding him for taking the initiative with Hagan.[128] The confidential communication suggested that the two were still working together behind the scenes for the Panther cause.

Regardless of whether Griffith and St. John played a role in that application process of 1944, somebody had coached the Panthers on who held power among the faculty representatives. Those few influential leaders could sway the voting process in favor of a Pitt admission.

Throughout much of that year Henry Rottschaefer of the University of Minnesota communicated confidentially with Aigler about Pittsburgh's intent to apply for admission to the conference. Rottschaefer and Aigler had both been politicked by Panther representatives during the spring and summer months.[129] [130] [131] Each had separately concluded, however, that it was not the right time for expansion. Both feared that accepting an eleventh member would "produce many more applications and increase the difficulty of graceful refusal of any or all of them." Rottschaefer, in particular, disliked rejecting quality institutions while invoking the 1908 Nebraska Response.[132] But the Minnesota professor did acknowledge that

---

[126] Rottschaefer to Aigler. 13 September 1944. Bentley Historical Library, University of Michigan. Ralph W. Aigler Papers, Aa 2; Box 8, folder: Correspondence 1940-45 Rottschaefer

[127] Griffith to Conference Athletic Directors. 21 August 1944. Memorandum. The Ohio State University Archives, Director of Athletics (RG 9/e-1/10), "Intercollegiate Conference: Commissioner: Correspondence (Griffith): 1944-45."

[128] Griffith to St. John. 21 March 1944. The Ohio State University Archives, Director of Athletics (RG 9/e-1/10), "Intercollegiate Conference: Commissioner: Correspondence (Griffith): 1943-44 (Folder 2 of 3)."

[129] Aigler to Rottschaefer. 18 February 1944. Bentley Historical Library, University of Michigan. Ralph W. Aigler Papers, 87406 Aa 2: Box 8, folder: correspondence 1940-45 Rottschaefer

[130] Aigler to Rottschaefer. 31 July 1944. Bentley Historical Library, University of Michigan. Ralph W. Aigler Papers, 87406 Aa 2; Box 8, folder: correspondence 1940-45 Rottschaefer

[131] Rottschaefer to Aigler. 14 October 1944. Bentley Historical Library, University of Michigan. Ralph W. Aigler Papers, 87406 Aa 2; Box 8, folder: correspondence 1940-45 Rottschaefer

[132] Rottschaefer to Aigler. 13 September 1944. Bentley Historical Library, University of Michigan. Ralph W. Aigler Papers, 87406 Aa 2; Box 8, folder: correspondence 1940-45 Rottschaefer

expansion would eventually need to be addressed by the faculty.[133]

Pittsburgh's second application was tabled in December. John Griffith's unexpected death one day prior to the annual meetings probably contributed to that decision. It was moved that "final action" on the Panther request would take place at the May 1945 spring meetings. The minutes also noted, however, that "all faculty members present expressed a favorable reaction to the admission of the applicant as a member of the Conference."[134] The role Rottschaefer and Aigler had in the motion to table the request was never mentioned.

With the death of Commissioner Griffith on December 10, 1944, Pittsburgh lost a good friend and invaluable advocate. His insider information had greatly assisted the Panther cause. The athletic department, at least for the time being, could only depend on Lynn St. John for assistance. But the Buckeye director had some plans in mind. He had yet to give up on the Hagan-Griffith-St. John initiative.

WHILE THE Panthers were making confidential plans for an application that December, Michigan State made a surprising announcement in early May of 1944. It came subsequent to the War Department's determination that intercollegiate athletic competition was no longer "incompatible with [its] war training program."[135] Schools contracted to assist the Army were now allowed to interact with other institutions in various sports. Aware that the Western Conference scheduling meetings were two weeks away, the Spartan administration revealed plans to resume intercollegiate football later that fall. It would field predominantly civilian freshman; the underclassmen, due to a shortage of athletes, were permitted to play during the war years while conferences were governed by military rules. It would also use "older players who [were] either 4Fs in the draft or … discharged veterans."[136] [137]

Ralph Young alerted Fritz Crisler of the good news and inquired about weekend dates with the Wolverines for the upcoming two seasons.[138] Although the ink on the 1944 schedule had dried a few years earlier, Young had assumed that the 1945-46 campaigns were still up for grabs; he anticipated no problems with resuming the rivalry. But, to his dismay, "Michigan let it be known that there was no assurance that they would reopen their schedule to Michigan State [for the foreseeable future]."[139] Unknown to Ralph Young, the Wolverine director had already signed up three non-conference games for those two years.

---

[133] Rottschaefer to Aigler. 3 August 1944. Bentley Historical Library, University of Michigan. Ralph W. Aigler Papers, 87406 Aa 2; Box 8, folder: correspondence 1940-45 Rottschaefer

[134] Four Hundred and Forty-Fourth Meeting of the Athletic Board of The Ohio State University. 4 April 1945. The Ohio State University Archives, Director of Athletics (RG 9/e-1/1), "Athletic Board: Minutes: September 1940-May 1946."

[135] Hannah, John A. "Intercollegiate Athletics." 11 August 1943. Northwestern University Archives, Franklyn Snyder Papers; Box 3, folder: 1

[136] Alderton, George. "Spartans Return to Grid Saturday." *Lansing State Journal,* 29 September 1944. Michigan State University Archives. Madison Kuhn Collection, UA12.107; Scrapbook 108, folder: 5

[137] Alderton, George. "State Resumes Football-Bachman has 60 Candidates on 1944 Squad." *Lansing State Journal,* 10 September 1944. Michigan State University Archives. Madison Kuhn Collection, UA12.107; Scrapbook 108, folder: 5

[138] Michigan State Football Date. February 1949. Bentley Historical Library, University of Michigan. Herbert Orin Crisler Papers, 85823 AC UAm Aa 2; Box 1, folder: topical correspondence MSU 1947-49

[139] Hannah, John A. *A Memoir*. East Lansing: Michigan State University Press, 1980. p. 120

Even the scrimmage game date was unavailable for the intrastate rival.

Hannah, now aware of these developments, concluded that as long as Aigler and Crisler were in command of athletic policy at the University of Michigan there would be no cooperation from Ann Arbor.[140] But this assessment was unfair. Despite his personal disgust with certain practices taking place in East Lansing, including overt subsidies, Crisler had valid reasons for claiming he could not provide dates for the college on such short notice.

Due to alumni demands for games with prominent east and west coast schools, biennial scheduling for the Wolverines always proved to be a very complicated process. The simple solution, arrived at by Fielding Yost years earlier, was to make contractual promises with two non-conference programs well in advance of the spring meetings.[141] And to make it all work out, since 1932, there was an understanding between Yost and Ralph Young that the Spartans always held the scrimmage weekend.

Fritz Crisler continued the Yost practice. Despite clearly violating Conference Handbook rules passed in 1940, Crisler had arranged non-conference games years prior to the May meetings.[142] But with Hannah's announcement, in April of 1943, that the college would be unable to participate in intercollegiate athletics "for the duration of the war,"[143] the Wolverine director had decided to schedule that Spartan date with other programs in advance of the conference meeting. He had no reason to suspect that Michigan State would be resuming football in 1944.

DESPITE A successful 1944 autumn campaign under Coach Charlie Bachman, John Hannah remained concerned over strategically significant matters that were beyond his control as the college president. He was now well aware of Pittsburgh's recent advances toward admission to the conference. Unlike Michigan State, which years earlier had failed to contract games with conference members despite impressive financial guarantees, the Panthers had little trouble signing them up. The membership's actions made no sense to Hannah. Lacking insider information, the president could only speculate about why Pittsburgh was getting favorable treatment. Did they have a sponsor? Were others promoting their cause? And when would they apply again?

In addition to the Pitt concern, Hannah knew that the University of Nebraska had succeeded in signing up three conference teams for 1944 just a few years earlier. Rumors were rife that the Cornhuskers would soon be applying for admission to the conference as well.[144]

Regardless of his competition, President Hannah maintained that Michigan State was the most appropriate choice for an expansion spot in the Western Conference. But the question for him still remained: how to earn a position in the Big Ten while Michigan was actively working against his cause?

---

[140] Hannah, John A. *A Memoir*. East Lansing: Michigan State University Press, 1980. p. 119

[141] Yost to Griffith. 22 May 1934. Bentley Historical Library, University of Michigan. Ralph W. Aigler Papers, 87406 Aa 2; Box 7, folder: correspondence 1934-39

[142] Crisler to Wilkinson. 8 September 1947. Bentley Historical Library, University of Michigan. Athletic Department, 943 Bimu 2; Box 35, folder: football schedules 1944, 46, 47

[143] Hannah to Aigler. 13 April 1943. Bentley Historical Library, University of Michigan. Ralph W. Aigler Papers, 87406 Aa 2; Box 8, folder: correspondence 1940-45 "H" misc.

[144] Leib to Hancher. 8 January 1943. University of Iowa Archives, Iowa City, Iowa. Virgil Hancher Papers, RG 05.01.11; Box 60, folder: 91

DUE TO a chance invitation to join a baseball league, Indiana and Iowa had found gaining membership in the Intercollegiate Conference a simple process: write a letter of inquiry and show up at the December 1899 meeting. The Ohio State University, despite a requirement to end its peculiar, one-sided rivalry with the University of Michigan, had also found admission an easy task 13 years later. Michigan State College's experience, however, was quite the opposite.

John Hannah was now into his eighth year of trying to achieve a seat at the annual Chicago meetings in the Sherman Hotel. Decisive action was needed. The years 1945 and 1946 would prove critical, in his opinion, as he contemplated a way to counter an uncooperative leadership in Ann Arbor.

Suspect Sincerity–and Further Disappointment

WITHIN THREE days of John Griffith's death in early December of 1944, Lynn St. John met in confidence with Fritz Crisler during a brief interlude between meetings at the Sherman Hotel. The Intercollegiate Handbook mandated that the athletic directors hire the next commissioner. The very influential Buckeye leader wanted Crisler to assume the position–at least it seemed that way. Should he decline, St. John would promote Kenneth "Tug" Wilson of Northwestern for the job.[1]

The dean of Western Conference athletic directors played his cards well. At the special directors meeting in February to determine the next commissioner, Crisler was the unanimous choice of the group. He politely turned their offer down. In Ralph Aigler's opinion the position was ill-suited for a man with Crisler's talents.[2]

> I think he was tempted by a sort of evangelistic notion that in the office of Commissioner he could do something for the betterment of intercollegiate athletics generally. I am sure that if he had taken the position and had tried to realize his ideals, he would have been a terribly disappointed man.[3]

St. John probably anticipated Crisler's response. He held more influence, both regionally and nationally, as athletic director of the University of Michigan.

The directors, following a motion by Crisler that was, to no surprise, seconded by St. John, tendered the position to Wilson. The Northwestern director, a close friend of St. John's over the past 20 years, would accept the job. No one in attendance, including Wilson, was privy to the backroom discussion on December 10 between the two men from Ohio State and Michigan.

Tug Wilson was no Herbert Orin Crisler. A number of faculty representatives

---

[1] St. John to Crisler. 27 December 1944. Bentley Historical Library, University of Michigan. Board In Control of Intercollegiate Athletics, 8729 Bimu F81 2; Box 30, folder: papers 1944 January

[2] Lorenz to Aigler. 23 February 1945. Bentley Historical Library, University of Michigan. Ralph W. Aigler Papers, 87406 Aa 2; Box 12, folder: athletics 1941-45 correspondence A-Z misc.

[3] Aigler to Lorenz. 28 February 1945. Bentley Historical Library, University of Michigan. Ralph W. Aigler Papers, 87406 Aa 2; Box 10, folder: correspondence 1946-52 personal

questioned the decision of the athletic directors. Dr. William Lorenz of Wisconsin privately disapproved of the selection. In his opinion the Wildcat athletic leader was not deserving of the office.[4] While acknowledging Ken Wilson as a fine man, Lorenz noted to Ralph Aigler that "he does not impress me as being strong in his convictions; on the contrary ... he is rather easily influenced by more dominating personalities."[5] Although the law school professor lacked the diagnostic skills of the psychiatrist from the University of Wisconsin medical school, he also expressed doubt about Wilson's qualifications.[6]

Regardless of the concerns of a few faculty leaders, the committee officially rubber-stamped the athletic directors' selection on March 10, 1945. It was a unanimous decision.[7]

Following the vote, Aigler and Professor Frank Richart of Illinois were asked to serve on a committee to revise the duties of the commissioner.[8] The Michigan faculty representative, actively involved in defining the original job description back in 1922, would once again play a significant role in revising the responsibilities of that position to meet the needs of the conference in the postwar years.

Both Lorenz and Aigler would prove prescient in their assessment of Tug Wilson's leadership. Over the next several years, the commissioner's job description would undergo a few more iterations, including additional authority for adjudication and enforcement. But Wilson was not up to the task. Perhaps acknowledging his own inadequacies, he frequently sought Professor Aigler's counsel;[9] he needed all the help he could get during those early years.[10] [11] And by mid-1952, in the midst of a complex investigation of the latest member of the conference, he would really require the law professor's confidential assistance.

THE WARS in Europe and the Pacific were progressing favorably for the allied forces by the spring of 1945. Michigan State's decision to resume intercollegiate competition in the fall of 1944 proved wise in hindsight. Ralph Young was able to forge a makeshift schedule for that year. Despite being rebuffed by Fritz Crisler in May, the Spartan athletic director succeeded in arranging schedules for the 1945-46 seasons. There were no marquee programs on his chalkboard, however, back in East Lansing. Kentucky, Wayne State, Marquette, Mississippi State, Maryland, Missouri, and a weakened Pittsburgh would generate little national, let alone regional, press coverage.

John Hannah, as president of the college, was more concerned with the implications

---

[4] Lorenz to Aigler. 23 February 1945. Bentley Historical Library, University of Michigan. Ralph W. Aigler Papers, 87406 Aa 2; Box 10, folder: correspondence 1946-52 Wilson, Tug

[5] Lorenz to Aigler. 2 January 1945. Bentley Historical Library, University of Michigan. Ralph W. Aigler Papers, 87406 Aa 2; Box 12, folder: athletics 1941-45 correspondence 1940-45 A-Z misc.

[6] Aigler to Lorenz. 28 February 1945. Bentley Historical Library, University of Michigan. Ralph W. Aigler Papers, 87406 Aa 2; Box 10, folder: correspondence 1946-52 personal

[7] Minutes of the Intercollegiate Conference of Faculty Representatives. 9-10 March 1945. Bentley Historical Library, University of Michigan. Athletic Department, 943 Bimu 2; Box 84, folder: faculty representatives minutes 1941-1957

[8] Ibid.

[9] Wilson to Aigler. 24 October 1949. Bentley Historical Library, University of Michigan. Ralph W. Aigler Papers, 87406 Aa 2; Box 10, correspondence 1946-52 personal

[10] Wilson to Aigler. 6 September 1945. Bentley Historical Library, University of Michigan. Ralph W. Aigler Papers, 87406 Aa 2; Box 10, correspondence 1946-52 Wilson, K.L.

[11] Aigler to Wilson. 7 September 1945. Bentley Historical Library, University of Michigan. Ralph W. Aigler Papers, 87406 Aa 2; Box 10, correspondence 1946-52 Wilson, K.L.

of the apparent scheduling snub by Michigan. Aware of competition from Pittsburgh, and presumably Nebraska, for a seat in the Western Conference, he decided to take on an aggressive strategy. If his vision for the school was to become reality, it was critical he act to forestall those suitors.

In June of 1945 he wrote Commissioner Ken Wilson. He wanted to educate the new leader, whom he did not know, on Michigan State and its predicament.

> I would like to point out to you … as Commissioner of the Western
> Conference, the unfortunate position in which Michigan State College finds
> itself. This College has grown into a great university with a prewar,
> undergraduate enrollment of more than 7,000 students, with facilities,
> equipment, and staff fully comparable to the great universities that make up
> the Western Conference. We believe that we are entirely honorable and
> ethical in everything that we do athletically and otherwise, and I am
> personally certain that our administration of athletic matters is on a much
> sounder, more sensible basis than at many other institutions.[12]

The final statement was perhaps a subtle reminder to Wilson of Pittsburgh's recent unscrupulous intercollegiate practices. Michigan State, the president implied, lacked that ignominious reputation.

Hannah also commented on the challenges of scheduling as an independent. "Sending an athletic team in a single season from the Atlantic to the Pacific to the Gulf may be good laboratory for a course in geography, but one such long trip in a single season should be enough and certainly would entail much less loss of academic time."[13]

The president then announced Michigan State's desire to become a member of the Western Conference, saying he wanted "to be reasonably certain that the application will be considered on its merits and that there is some possibility of favorable action before the formal application is made."[14] Hannah was trying a different tactic. Lacking Michigan's willingness to sponsor his school, as decided by Fritz Crisler in late January of 1943,[15] he planned to approach the commissioner. The president felt that the new leader held a position of influence in the application process. But, at the same time, John Hannah desired confidentiality. "We do not wish to be embarrassed, however, by having a lot of publicity given to a formal application for admission should the application be turned down for preconceived reasons that we are not now acquainted with."[16]

The president had his reasons for wanting to avoid publicity. At about the same time he was writing to Wilson, Hannah and a small core of advisors, including Dean William

---

[12] Hannah to Wilson. 28 June 1945. Bentley Historical Library, University of Michigan. Herbert Orin Crisler Papers, 85823 AC UAm Aa 2; Box 6, folder: 1941-49, undated

[13] Ibid.

[14] Ibid.

[15] Crisler to Ruthven, 13, January 1943. Bentley Historical Library, University of Michigan. Alexander Grant Ruthven Papers, 86550 Ac Aa; Box 34, folder 27 "Physical Education (Board in Control)" On January 27, 1943 President Ruthven determined that John Hannah's request for university sponsorship of a Spartan application was a matter for the Board in Control rather than the regents to decide. Hannah was not aware of Ruthven's role. He assumed Crisler made the decision.

[16] Hannah to Wilson. 28 June 1945. Bentley Historical Library, University of Michigan. Herbert Orin Crisler Papers, 85823 AC UAm Aa 2; Box 6, folder: 1941-49, undated

Combs, were very quietly addressing some disturbing data derived from an alumni survey on the "effectiveness of teaching on campus."[17] And by December of 1945, the North Central Association on accrediting would reveal its humbling, but fortunately confidential, survey on the qualifications of many faculty members on campus. It also determined that the college barely met standards for granting advanced degrees.[18] Hannah desperately needed affiliation with the Western Conference institutions to enhance recruitment of professors with qualified credentials and research interests. A public rejection for admission at the annual meetings in either December of 1945 or May of 1946 could profoundly compromise his efforts.

Hannah, as noted in his statement to Wilson, also had concerns regarding "preconceived reasons that we are not now acquainted with." He was probably alluding to the Jenison Awards subsidy program. In May of 1945 the president received permission from the State Board to double the number of awardees to 80.[19] He discussed with his board "some of the problems of maintaining intercollegiate athletic teams to compete creditably with other institutions."[20] The president was gambling that subsidizing 40 additional athletes in sports other than football, was a means to an end: advancement of his college's reputation as a center of higher learning.

Hannah knew that his recommendations to expand the financial aid program would be controversial for two residents of Ann Arbor–Ralph Aigler and Herbert "Fritz" Crisler. The president, due to a number of unfortunate circumstances, had never had an opportunity to discuss with his former law professor the reasons for his proposal to openly subsidize student-athletes in December of 1941. A private debate would serve no purpose now; opinions had been formed long ago.

In an apparent attempt at being proactive, however, Hannah decided to go public with his plan to expand the Jenison Awards. He wrote to Ralph Young, immediately following approval of the proposal by the board, and requested "… that this item … be given to the press as it might avoid possible future embarrassment by placing this policy clearly on record …"[21] Very strict guidelines, comparable to the original 1941 policy, were to be followed. All athletes were required to live on campus and eat in college-operated dining halls. Jobs were prohibited.[22] The president wanted both Aigler and Crisler to fully understand, in no uncertain terms, what the grant entailed for an athlete at Michigan State College. The Jenison Awards were not athletic scholarships. They were one of many subsidies offered by the college to students with unique, but not necessarily scholarly, skills.[23]

Regardless of how the athletic leadership in Ann Arbor perceived the expansion

---

[17] Combs, William H. Untitled statement on academics. Michigan State University Archives, Hannah Archives Project, UA2.1.12.2; Box 34, folder: 7

[18] Ibid.

[19] Hannah to Young. 19 May 1945. Michigan State University Archives. John A. Hannah Papers, UA2.1.12; Box: 63, folder: 7 scholarships-Jenison 1942-45

[20] Minutes of the State Board of Agriculture. 17 May 1945. www.onthebanks.msu.edu

[21] Hannah to Young. 23 May 1945. Michigan State University Archives. John A. Hannah Papers, UA2.1.12; Box: 63, folder: 7 scholarships-Jenison 1942-45

[22] Ibid.

[23] "Scholarships and Prizes: Effective January 1, 1944." Michigan State University Archives, John A. Hannah Papers, UA2.1.12; Box 63, folder: 6 scholarships 1941-55

of the Jenison program, in June of 1945 John Hannah decided he now needed the support of the new commissioner of the Western Conference. Unfortunately, the president had no idea on the limits of power and influence held within that office. He was also unaware of Ken Wilson's ignorance of the Spartan subsidy program. "We naturally expect," he wrote to Wilson, "that the Western Conference will want to satisfy itself as to the policies and soundness of this institution and could have no objection to any such investigation ... but if the policy has already been settled that the Western Conference is not to be enlarged or if the schools to be admitted have been selected so that there is no possibility of favorable consideration, we should prefer to be so informed at the outset."[24]

Hannah was again referencing the potential admission of the University of Pittsburgh–his major concern in the late spring of 1945. He concluded by inviting Wilson to visit East Lansing and meet with appropriate staff and administrators.[25]

Fritz Crisler received a copy of the Hannah-Wilson letter on August 8, 1945, which Hannah had instructed Ralph Young to share with his counterpart in Ann Arbor.[26] It was important to him that the university be fully aware of his intentions in approaching the commissioner. Despite lacking a willing Wolverine to sponsor his college, John Hannah still needed Michigan's vote if an application was eventually tendered. Adherence to protocol was crucial.

COMMISSIONER KEN Wilson took up the offer to visit Michigan State that summer. Ralph Aigler, having been shown Crisler's copy of the Hannah-Wilson letter, wrote to the commissioner that same day. In his letter, Aigler educated Wilson on the history of Spartan athletic leadership and policy dating back to the 1937 application. He then explained the current state of affairs in East Lansing.

> One aspect of their desire to become a member is embarrassing to us here. I
> refer to the fact that some of the men over there seem to have the notion
> that Michigan stands in their way. To put it otherwise, they think that if
> Fritz and I would really advocate and urge their election that the result
> would come about. Somehow or other, they cannot grasp the fact that
> Michigan has only one vote out of ten, and that the other nine votes are not
> subject to anybody's direction.[27]

In stating this, Aigler minimized the influence that he had over other conference representatives who lacked knowledge on matters within the state, even though the May 1937 rejection of a Spartan application suggested otherwise. "You can readily see that if they were to make an application for membership, Fritz and I would be put in a position where it would be terribly difficult to adhere to what both of us have heretofore felt clearly

---

[24] Hannah to Wilson. 28 June 1945. Bentley Historical Library, University of Michigan. Herbert Orin Crisler Papers, 85823 AC UAm Aa 2; Box 6, folder: 1941-49, undated.

[25] Ibid.

[26] Young to Crisler. 8 August 1945. Bentley Historical Library, University of Michigan. Herbert Orin Crisler Papers, 85823 AC UAm Aa 2; Box 1, folder: MSU correspondence 1943-46 topical

[27] Aigler to Wilson. 8 August 1945. Bentley Historical Library, University of Michigan. Ralph W. Aigler Papers, 87406 Aa 2; Box 8, folder: correspondence 1940-45 Wilson, K.L.

desirable policy for the Conference, viz., to keep its membership at no more than ten."[28] He then pointed out to Wilson that the two institutions maintained a "very close and cordial" relationship.[29] However, "at the same time I feel absolutely certain that if they were to make an application, an adverse vote would be given [by the other nine] even though Michigan [was] to vote in favor of the action."[30]

He then brought up the Jenison Awards. He wanted Wilson to gain an understanding of the subsidy that, in his opinion, was contrary to the amateur code. The shrewd professor offered a subtle scheme for Wilson to use in discussions with the college administrators. "If Fritz has talked to you, he probably has suggested that you indicate that you have heard somewhere about their awarding certain scholarships pretty freely to athletes."[31] This cautious ploy avoided implicating Michigan in any scheme that would potentially embarrass President Hannah.

In explaining his understanding of the subsidy, Aigler intermixed "awards" with "scholarships," undercutting Hannah's intentions when he created the program in 1941. He also either hadn't read or didn't acknowledge the recent press release from the office of Ralph Young stating that the overt subsidy was to assist "worthy and deserving" students, "young men possessing unusual qualities of leadership who have demonstrated mental ability and physical strength and vigor."[32] If dollars had been provided to gifted musicians and singers for attending the college since the early 1930s, the president could easily justify similar largesse for skilled athletes benefiting the school in a different way.[33] [34] [35] [36]

Aigler then shared rumors with the commissioner about the process involved in gaining an award. "As a matter of fact, it is our information here that [Coach] Charlie Bachman himself either awards or at least is in position to promise these scholarships–awards which are quite comparable to those made by southern institutions."[37] He then suggested to Wilson that "you might well pretend that you do not know the name of the scholarships, but they are called 'Jennison [sic].'"[38]

Knowing that Tug Wilson's daughter was considering attending Michigan as an undergraduate, Aigler made a pitch for the school; it afforded him another opportunity to denigrate Michigan State's athletic leadership–and perhaps its president. "As in the case of athletes, we feel that Michigan has so much to offer prospective students that it is not

[28] Aigler to Wilson. 8 August 1945. Bentley Historical Library, University of Michigan. Ralph W. Aigler Papers, 87406 Aa 2; Box 8, folder: correspondence 1940-45 Wilson, K.L.

[29] Ibid.

[30] Ibid.

[31] Ibid.

[32] Hannah to Members of the Administrative Group. 19 December 1941. Michigan State University Archives. John A. Hannah Papers, UA2.1.12; Box: 63, folder: 7 scholarships-Jenison 1942-45

[33] Minutes of the State Board of Agriculture, 19 October 1933. www.onthebanks.msu.edu

[34] Minutes of the State Board of Agriculture, 5 July 1934. www.onthebanks.msu.edu

[35] Minutes of the State Board of Agriculture, 11 June 1934. www.onthebanks.msu.edu

[36] Hannah, John A. "Speech of Dr. John A. Hannah at the Fortieth Annual Convention of the NCAA." 9 January 1946. Bentley Historical Library, University of Michigan. Herbert Orin Crisler Papers, 85823 AC UAm Aa2; Box 1, folder: topical correspondence, Michigan State University clippings and misc.

[37] Aigler to Wilson. 8 August 1945. Bentley Historical Library, University of Michigan. Ralph W. Aigler Papers, 87406 Aa 2; Box 8, folder: correspondence 1940-45 Wilson, K.L.

[38] Ibid.

necessary to engage in high-pressure 'proselyting' or 'subsidizing!'" With such a partisan perspective from Aigler, Ken Wilson would arrive in East Lansing with a very tainted view of Michigan State College of Agriculture and Applied Science.[39]

THREE DAYS before President Hannah invited Kenneth Wilson to visit East Lansing, Ralph Young had communicated with Fritz Crisler. He referred to a conversation the two had had a few weeks earlier. The timing of the letter in juxtaposition to Hannah's, the optimistic tone and style of writing, and the strategic policy references regarding the college, would suggest that the president contributed to the delayed response.

> Our Athletic Council and College Administrative officials would be thrilled to have Michigan State College accepted for membership in the Western Conference and I have been instructed to tell you that we shall be very glad to have you follow through along the lines suggested in our talk at Ann Arbor the first of this month ... If Ralph Aigler is also willing to boost our cause, I shall be glad to have a small typewritten brochure prepared, setting forth the details concerning our college and physical education plant ... On behalf of the Administrative officials of Michigan State I want to sincerely thank you for the fine suggestions which you gave me and for your willingness to "go to bat" for us.[40]

Young, but more than likely Hannah, had misunderstood some major points in the discussion the director had with Crisler on June 1, 1945. His exuberance over any positive gesture from the Wolverines, in the aftermath of the 1944 scheduling snub, may have contributed to the confusion. In late July the Michigan athletic director pointed out a few of those misconceptions. He reminded his colleague that, "I think you and your people can recognize it would be inappropriate for the authorities at Michigan to go before the Conference with this matter if there is nothing of a formal nature presented by Michigan State to the Faculty Representatives."[41]

Crisler then offered a brief history lesson on applications to the conference over the past four decades. Ralph Aigler probably provided the background information. Crisler explained that many schools had applied, some repeatedly, and all had been turned down. The consensus had been that there was no need for expansion.[42] He pointed out that "even if the Michigan authorities supported the petition it would not necessarily follow that it would be acted upon favorably."[43] And, responding to outsiders who claimed the solution to conference scheduling woes lay in expanding to 11 members, the Michigan director noted that the general opinion of conference directors was "that an additional member would not relieve this [problem] but contribute more to the undesirable situation."[44] Fritz Crisler

---

[39] Aigler to Wilson. 8 August 1945. Bentley Historical Library, University of Michigan. Ralph W. Aigler Papers, 87406 Aa 2; Box 8, folder: correspondence 1940-45 Wilson, K.L.
[40] Young to Crisler. 25 June 1945. Bentley Historical Library, University of Michigan. Herbert Orin Crisler Papers, 85823 AC UAm Aa 2; Box 1, folder: MSU correspondence 1943-46 topical
[41] Crisler to Young. 20 July 1945. Bentley Historical Library, University of Michigan. Herbert Orin Crisler Papers, 85823 AC UAm Aa 2; Box 1, folder: MSU correspondence 1943-46 topical
[42] Ibid.
[43] Ibid.
[44] Crisler to Young. 20 July 1945. Bentley Historical Library, University of Michigan. Herbert Orin

closed his discouraging letter by suggesting a meeting be held that included Professor Aigler and President Hannah. The four could discuss aspects of the application process in greater detail if necessary.[45]

Young wrote back to Fritz Crisler a few weeks later, on August 8, expressing excitement over the proposal to meet. The Spartan director had recently visited with his president, probably just back on the job after a July vacation with his family at the Good Hart cabin, and "recommended [to him] that we place our official application for membership in the Big Ten in your hands for presentation whenever you thought the time was propitious."[46] Most likely that statement was also suggested by the man who now clearly formulated all academic and athletic strategy in East Lansing. John Hannah was ecstatic. Based on either his or Young's misinterpretation of Crisler's earlier comments, the president was convinced that he finally had his sponsor.

Four months later, the meeting proposed by Fritz Crisler had yet to take place. Young wrote back to his colleague in early November reminding him of the probable oversight. He noted that there had been speculation in major newspapers that President Hannah was no longer interested in conference membership and that the delay was a sign that the college was pursuing a new strategy. "Personally," Young wrote, "I am wondering why the article was ever printed when it was just opposite the truth, unless someone had evil designs to injure the chances of Michigan State receiving favorable consideration in the Big Ten."[47]

WHILE PATIENTLY awaiting a meeting with Michigan leadership to discuss what still appeared to him to be the university's willingness to sponsor the college, John Hannah delivered the keynote address at the annual NCAA convention in St. Louis on January 9, 1946. In that speech, Hannah spelled out his controversial philosophy on subsidies for athletes. Ralph Aigler, in attendance at that meeting, finally learned of his student's rationale for justifying the Jenison Awards.[48]

But by the end of January, six months after Fritz Crisler had made his proposal to meet, there was still no word from Ann Arbor. Ralph Young, at the insistence of his president, again wrote his counterpart and offered to gather anywhere–East Lansing, Detroit, or Ann Arbor to discuss the application process and the role Michigan might play in it for the Spartans.[49]

The president of Michigan State was frustrated. In his opinion, the university was no longer interested in assisting his cause. Following the NCAA convention, Hannah and Commissioner Tug Wilson had "exchanged letters" regarding a Spartan membership in the

---

Crisler Papers, 85823 AC UAm Aa 2; Box 1, folder: MSU correspondence 1943-46 topical

[45] Crisler to Young. 20 July 1945. Bentley Historical Library, University of Michigan. Herbert Orin Crisler Papers, 85823 AC UAm Aa 2; Box 1, folder: MSU correspondence 1943-46 topical

[46] Young to Crisler. 8 August 1945. Bentley Historical Library, University of Michigan. Herbert Orin Crisler Papers, 85823 AC UAm Aa 2; Box 1, folder: MSU correspondence 1943-46 topical

[47] Ibid.

[48] Minutes of the 126th Meeting of the Intercollegiate Conference of Faculty Representatives, 8 December 1945. Bentley Historical Library, University of Michigan. Athletic Department, 943 Bimu 2; Box 84, folder: Faculty Representatives minutes 1941-57

[49] Young to Crisler. 31 January 1946. Bentley Historical Library, University of Michigan. Herbert Orin Crisler Papers, 85823 AC UAm Aa 2; Box 1, folder: MSU correspondence 1943-46 topical

conference.[50] On the 26th of January, a few days in advance of Young's letter to Crisler, Hannah, now displaying some atypical pessimism on his part, had penned a plea to Wilson for assistance. Hannah still felt that Wilson, due to his title, held influence within the conference. He again requested that Ralph Young, in line with past protocol, provide a copy of the letter to Fritz Crisler.[51]

President Hannah reminded Wilson of the predicament the college faced in scheduling athletic competition. He then described the options for Michigan State in the postwar era.

> It is our first desire that if possible we be admitted to the Western
> Conference. If that is not possible, then we better recognize that fact and
> proceed on a long-time program as an isolated independent. It is simple
> enough to group together Notre Dame, Marquette, Pittsburgh, and
> Michigan State College, but for many reasons that we need not go into
> there are wide differences in fundamental philosophies between Michigan
> State College and the others in this grouping. I think it would be better to
> have the matter raised with the Conference now even though it means that
> we are refused admission than to continue on the present basis of hoping
> for eventual consideration. When the matter is disposed of by the
> Conference, we will know what our future athletic policies must be.[52]

John Hannah, in essence, was describing what would become his latest strategy for advancing the academic reputation of the college through athletic prominence. He might as well have designated them "Plan A" and "Plan B." He asked that Wilson "lay before [the Faculty Representatives Committee] our request for consideration for admission." In the absence of any viable chance with Plan A, the president would pursue long-term contracts with regional powers while maintaining independence from a conference affiliation.[53]

Having revealed his strategy to Ken Wilson, all Hannah could do was await a reply. He was confident that the commissioner would convey the message. But in the meantime, another newsworthy surprise was being debated by President Robert Maynard Hutchins and his board at the University of Chicago. The announcement, revealed to the press in early March of 1946, would profoundly impact the current relationship between Michigan State College of Agriculture and Applied Science and the University of Michigan.

JOHN HANNAH finally had his meeting, promised by Fritz Crisler back in July, regarding the application process. The long-anticipated encounter proved to be a brief, and perhaps disappointing, interaction with Ralph Aigler and Crisler in mid-February of 1946.[54] Aigler encouraged the president to send a note to the current faculty committee chairman, Dean

---

[50] Young to Crisler. 31 January 1946. Bentley Historical Library, University of Michigan. Herbert Orin Crisler Papers, 85823 AC UAm Aa 2; Box 1, folder: MSU correspondence 1943-46 topical
[51] Ibid.
[52] Hannah to Wilson. 26 January 1946. Bentley Historical Library, University of Michigan. Herbert Orin Crisler Papers, 85823 AC UAm Aa 2; Box 1, folder: MSU correspondence 1943-46 topical
[53] Ibid.
[54] Aigler to Richart. 21 December 1948. University of Illinois Archives. Series 4/2/12; Box 3, folder: Western Intercollegiate Conference 1948-49

Larry Kimpton of Chicago. The notice could serve as a formal application for admission into the conference.[55]

The president followed through on the common-sense advice. In addition to alerting Kimpton of the college's intentions, he also encouraged the Chicago professor to seek out Floyd Reeves. Hannah's consultant, a tenured faculty member at the university on the Midway, could answer any questions the dean might have regarding "the general attitudes and policies of [the] institution."[56] John Hannah felt that the chairman had some influence over his fellow nine members. Kimpton, with Reeves' input, might prove a valuable asset. Unknown to the president, however, the position held no additional power in conference governance. The chairman's role was merely to set agendas and run meetings.

President Hannah also typed a note to Professor Reeves that same day regarding his plans. Assuming Kimpton was too busy to seek him out, Hannah asked his consultant to schedule the meeting. He informed him that he had decided "to place our case in the hands of the officers and rely upon their presenting the matter in the hope that the application will be weighted upon its merits."[57]

Floyd Reeves greatly admired John Hannah. During his distinguished career in public service and academia, he had interacted with many prominent leaders including Herbert Hoover and Franklin Roosevelt. Yet he considered Hannah in a class by himself as both a visionary and leader.[58] He eagerly agreed to assist the president.

On March 21, in a confidential letter to President Hannah, Reeves penned his findings. Having discovered that Pittsburgh, Nebraska, and Michigan State were the three institutions interested in admission, Reeves impressed on Kimpton that he had done survey work at all three schools. He spoke highly of the leadership and innovative academics at Michigan State. He had very few positive comments to share regarding Pittsburgh. Nebraska was an admirable institution but, in Reeves' opinion, not on the same level as Michigan State. "I believe I made a strong case for Michigan State College, and I did so entirely on the basis of objective evidence."[59]

Professor Reeves then provided detailed comments from Kimpton.

> On the basis of geographical reasons only, at least one Conference
> institution and possibly two others prefer Pittsburgh. However, the record
> of Pittsburgh is so unsavory–operating as it does in an environment where
> athletic practices are so out of accord with those of the Western
> Conference–that it will probably not be selected. It appears that some
> objection to Michigan State College has been made on the basis of its past
> "policy with reference to athletic scholarships" concerning which point I
> have no information and also concerning which point the record of other

[55] Hannah to Kimpton. 27 February 1946. Michigan State University Archives. Floyd Reeves Papers, UA 21.12.1; Box 115, folder: 21

[56] Ibid.

[57] Ibid.

[58] Reeves, Floyd W. "Statement of Floyd W. Reeves." Michigan State University Archives, Hannah Archives Project, UA 2.1.12.2; Box 34, folder: 37 Reeves

[59] Reeves to Hannah. 21 March 1946. Michigan State University Archives. Floyd Reeves Papers, UA 21.12.1; Box 115, folder:21

Western Conference institutions is, by no means, in the clear.[60]

Kimpton's implication was that Ohio State, Indiana, and possibly the University of Michigan were the schools favoring Pittsburgh.

Although that insider information would prove to be very misleading within a few months, for the time being it offered some hope for Michigan State. Pittsburgh had no guaranteed seat at the Sherman Hotel after all.

Something else gave the Spartans reason for hope. After The Announcement of December 21, 1939, the University of Chicago soon found that competing in sports other than football was challenging within the conference. About all the Maroons could excel at was fencing; it was pointless to maintain membership over that one sporting event.[61]

The university's novel academic program was clearly not conducive to big-time intercollegiate athletics. The faculty representatives of the other nine schools had all anticipated a formal withdrawal from the conference for some time.[62] That Second Announcement finally took place on March 8, 1946. The University of Chicago would end its five decades of affiliation with the Intercollegiate Conference at the close of the academic year in late June. Athletic Director T. Nelson Metcalf read the statement at the Conference Directors' meeting. University of Chicago graduate Herbert Orin Crisler made a motion that they all regrettably accept the decision of his alma mater. It was unanimously approved.[63]

Following that announcement, with Reeves' confidential letter of March 21 in mind, President Hannah, reinvigorated with his old optimistic ways, was now ready to move forward with Plan A. Michigan State would petition for the seat soon to be vacated by Chicago. Fritz Crisler's previous comments regarding the historical reluctance by conference members to expand was now irrelevant. The membership, in Hannah's opinion, had no choice but to name a replacement. Based on Reeves' comments, he was quite optimistic about Michigan State's chances.

John Hannah immediately went to work. On March 18 he sent letters to all presidents within the conference expressing his desire to become a member; he cited various reasons why Michigan State merited the honor.[64] [65] Many of these institutional leaders were on his "blueberries and maple syrup" list. The college president anticipated follow-up letters supporting his initiative. He would be disappointed.

President Edwin Fred, of Wisconsin, in line with protocol, requested the opinion of

---

[60] Reeves to Hannah. 21 March 1946. Michigan State University Archives. Floyd Reeves Papers, UA 21.12.1; Box 115, folder:21

[61] McNeil, William H. *Hutchins' University: A Memoir of the University of Chicago 1929-1950.* Chicago: The University of Chicago Press, 1991. p. 155

[62] French to Paige. 9 December 1932. University of Minnesota Archives, President's Office; Box 4, folder: 118 athletics

[63] Minutes of the Western Conference Athletic Directors. 8 March 1946. Bentley Historical Library, University of Michigan. Athletic Department, 943 Bimu 2; Box 84, folder: Big Ten Directors Committee minutes 1941-52

[64] Hannah to Morrill. 18 March 1946. University of Minnesota Archives. President's Office; Box 238, folder: Physical Education 1945-47

[65] Hannah to Ruthven. 18 March 1946. Bentley Historical Library, University of Michigan. Herbert Orin Crisler Papers, 85823 AC UAm Aa 2; Box 6, folder: Board in Control of Intercollegiate Athletics 1941-49, undated

his faculty representative.[66] Psychiatry Professor William Lorenz, of the medical school, recommended only acknowledging the notice. He reminded his president that the Faculty Representatives Committee made all decisions on membership.[67] The Handbook was very clear on that point.

The University of Illinois offered a similar response. President Arthur Willard, who was so impressed with the accomplishments of Hannah's college in achieving a basic curriculum for all students, sought the counsel of Professor Frank Richart. He too advised restraint. In confidence, Richart did offer his personal opinion. He felt Michigan State was a "logical choice for new member, from considerations of geographical location, facilities, athletic standards and general reputation ... I have heard several reports of the fine and progressive leadership of President Hannah."[68] Willard composed a polite, restrained note to his friend in East Lansing.[69]

John Hannah had been pursuing a relationship with President Franklyn Snyder of Northwestern for years. The private university had little in common with the land-grant institution, but that did not stop the college leader from ultimately befriending Snyder. He put Snyder on his "blueberries and maple syrup" list and typically received a gracious note of appreciation each year.[70] Hannah periodically shared information with Snyder on curricular accomplishments at Michigan State achieved with the help of consultants like Floyd Reeves.[71] [72]

In early spring of 1945 the Spartan president asked the Northwestern leader to make the June commencement address at Michigan State.[73] Snyder agreed and, after his speech, departed East Lansing impressed with the leadership, the campus, and the vision of the school.[74] After receiving Hannah's recent letter, Snyder immediately wrote back to his friend a note of encouragement. "The Conference would be better in every way if Michigan State College were a member of it."[75] Unlike his fellow colleagues in leadership, he had

---

[66] Hannah to Fred. 18 March 1946. University of Wisconsin-Madison Archives. Chancellors and Presidents. President E.B. Fred, Series 4/16/1; Box 39, folder: general correspondence files 1945-46 Ma-Mo

[67] Lorenz to Fred. 26 March 1946. University of Wisconsin-Madison Archives. Chancellors and Presidents. President E.B. Fred, Series 4/16/1; Box 39, folder: general correspondence files 1945-46 Ma-Mo

[68] Richart to Willard. 25 March 1946. University of Illinois Archives. General Correspondence, 1934-46, Series 2/9/1; Box 104, folder: Mi

[69] Willard to Hannah. 26 March 1946. University of Illinois Archives. General Correspondence, 1934-46, Series 2/9/1; Box 104, folder: Mi

[70] Snyder to Hannah. 30 July 1945. Northwestern University Archives. Franklyn Snyder Papers; Box 13, folder: 20 NWU

[71] Snyder to Hannah. 31 March 1942. Northwestern University Archives. Franklyn Snyder Papers; Box 13, folder: 20 NWU

[72] Snyder to Hannah. 14 June 1945. Northwestern University Archives. Franklyn Snyder Papers; Box 13, folder: 20 NWU

[73] Geil to Snyder. 14 June 1945. Northwestern University Archives. Franklyn Snyder Papers; Box 13, folder: 20 NWU

[74] Snyder to Hannah. 12 February 1946. Northwestern University Archives. Franklyn Snyder Papers; Box 13, folder: 20 NWU

[75] Snyder to Hannah. 19 March 1946. Northwestern University Archives. Franklyn Snyder Papers; Box 13, folder: 20 NWU

apparently failed to communicate with his faculty representative.

One unexpected reply came from James Lewis Morrill of the University of Minnesota. The two leaders had been good friends since the early 1940s.

> Until your letter came I did not know that Michigan State College was at all interested in membership in the Big Ten. I'm sending copies of your letter to our Director of Athletics and to our faculty representative in the Intercollegiate Conference with an expression of my interest in the application … I suppose the Conference, frankly, will be inclined to pay a good deal of attention to the attitude of the University of Michigan. I'd be curious to know, if you want to tell me confidentially, whether you have any intimation of that attitude.[76]

Lew Morrill had just been inaugurated as president of Minnesota a year earlier. Prior to that appointment, he led the University of Wyoming from 1941 through the summer of 1945. Morrill graduated from Ohio State in 1913. After a brief stint as editor of a Cleveland newspaper, he returned to Columbus to serve as professor in the schools of journalism and education. His leadership skills were quickly recognized. Morrill was promoted to vice president of the large land-grant university, and after serving as an administrator for nine years, he departed for Wyoming.[77] His reputation was impeccable at all three institutions. Within a few years at Minnesota, Morrill would become a leader among the Council of Nine.

The request for confidential gossip about Michigan's stance on the Spartan initiative was expected from a man who spent the greater part of his career in Columbus. Morrill had graduated during the era when "practical victories" over Fielding Yost's juggernaut were all the Buckeyes could claim. Despite having moved away from central Ohio, he maintained a keen interest in all aspects of scarlet and gray athletics.[78]

John Hannah responded on March 23. Ralph Aigler of Michigan had "indicated not only his support of our application but a willingness and desire to speak for us when the matter is up for consideration." He pointed out that Fritz Crisler had invited Ralph Young and Hannah to dinner to discuss the admission process in greater detail. "Their attitude at that time was surprisingly friendly and agreeable to our cause."[79] But appearances can be deceiving. There had been a major shift at Michigan in institutional, not athletic, policy. In mid-March of 1946, President Ruthven announced his support of a Spartan application for admission into the Western Conference.[80] The statement from Ann Arbor occurred shortly after the University of Chicago had revealed its plans to withdraw from the conference.

Hannah's excitement over the news from Ann Arbor was short lived. Morrill, who

---

[76] Morrill to Hannah. 21 March 1946. University of Minnesota Archives, Presidents Office; Box 238, folder: Physical Education 1945-47

[77] "Dr. James Lewis Morrill." University of Minnesota News Service. 3 June 1957. University of Minnesota Archives, University Relations; Box 64, folder: President J. L. Morrill 1944-57

[78] Morrill to Pollard. 1 December 1947. University of Minnesota Archives, Morrill, J.L. Box 2, folder: PO-PZ

[79] Hannah to Morrill. 23 March 1946. University of Minnesota Archives, Presidents Office; Box 238, folder: Physical Education 1945-47

[80] Ruthven to Hannah. 23 March 1946. Bentley Historic Library, University of Michigan. Herbert Orin Crisler Papers, 85823 AC UAm Aa 2; Box 1, folder: MSU topical correspondence 1943-46

never trusted a Wolverine, contacted his faculty representative, Henry Rottschaefer, for his opinion on Ruthven's comments. Rottschaefer, a onetime law student of Ralph Aigler, was not as optimistic.[81] "It will be of interest to you to learn that, in informal discussions with Professor Aigler of Michigan, he intimated that Michigan might change its former position with respect to Michigan State's membership in the Big Ten, but carefully avoided making any definite statement."[82] The professor occupying room 320 in Hutchins Hall was not totally in line with his president's support of Michigan State College.

PRESIDENT ALEXANDER Ruthven's position regarding Michigan State had evolved over the course of three years. In early January of 1943 Fritz Crisler had written to him requesting an opinion on a letter ostensibly written by Ralph Young of Michigan State. During a meeting with Ruthven a few weeks later, Crisler was advised to ignore Young's unusual request that the university sponsor a Spartan application for membership in the Western Conference.[83] In Ruthven's opinion, matters pertaining to institutional relations and university policy resided within his office. The politically sensitive request raised by Ralph Young–with the stroke of John Hannah's pen–was not for Michigan's athletic leadership, including Ralph Aigler, to decide.

Shortly after The Second Announcement from Chicago, as anticipated, President Ruthven received a letter from John Hannah expressing his desire to replace the University of Chicago within the conference. Ruthven wrote back, "As I am sure you know, I would favor the granting of your request." The simple reply heralded a cataclysmic shift in university policy. Michigan would officially support a Spartan application for admission to the Western Conference.

> I have recently ascertained also that our faculty representative, Professor
> Ralph Aigler, and Mr. Herbert O. Crisler would approve of adding
> Michigan State College to the group if ten institutions are to be included in
> the future. Under our current system, intercollegiate athletics are entirely
> under the direction of a faculty board, and all I can do is to express my
> interest and transmit your letter to the Board [in Control of Intercollegiate
> Athletics]."[84]

President Ruthven had to make a decision in the best interests of the University of Michigan. He was responsible for institutional policy, after all.[85] Whether Ralph Aigler and Fritz Crisler agreed, in private, was of marginal significance. Based on his carefully worded reply, however, Ruthven made it clear to John Hannah that Michigan athletic policy was not

---

[81] Minutes of the Intercollegiate Conference of Faculty Representatives. 4-6 December 1952. Bentley Historical Library, University of Michigan. Ralph W. Aigler Papers, 87406 Aa 2; Box 14, folder: athletics meeting 1952 minutes

[82] Rottschaefer to Morrill. 27 March 1946. University of Minnesota Archives, Presidents Office; Box 238, folder: Physical Education 1945-47

[83] Crisler to Ruthven. 13 January 1943. Bentley Historic Library, University of Michigan. Alexander Grant Ruthven Papers, 86550 Ac Aa 2; Box 34, folder: 27 "Physical Education (Board in Control)"

[84] Ruthven to Hannah. 23 March 1946. Bentley Historic Library, University of Michigan. Herbert Orin Crisler Papers, 85823 AC UAm Aa 2; Box 1, folder: MSU topical correspondence 1943-46

[85] Crisler to Ruthven. 13 January 1943. Bentley Historical Library, University of Michigan Archives. Alexander Grant Ruthven Papers, 86550 AC Aa 2; Box 34, folder: 27

his responsibility.

Nevertheless, Hannah was ecstatic over the pronouncement. But four days later, in the context of Henry Rottschafer's report to Lew Morrill, he was forced to reconsider the sincerity of that commitment from Aigler and Crisler. President Ruthven's statement was valuable but it was no guarantee of membership in the Western Conference. Hannah still had to deal with the two men that influenced all athletic policies and decisions at the University of Michigan.

THE UNIVERSITY of Pittsburgh continued to maneuver behind the scenes for a position in the conference. It had been denied consideration for admission the previous year. But Ohio State's Lynn St. John was still interested in aiding the Panther strategic plan. Timing was critical, however. He was facing mandatory retirement in another year.

Based on a letter dated May 20, 1946, it was apparent St. John had successfully courted an ally for his cause: Commissioner Ken Wilson agreed to sign on. His office was privy to confidential discussions with all faculty representatives. That information could prove valuable for the Hagan-Griffith scheme drafted years earlier with the assistance of the old Buckeye.

Neither the commissioner nor St. John had any say in membership. But that did not dissuade the Ohio State athletic director from trying to influence the process. In his note to Wilson he laid out a strategy for John Griffith's successor to follow in guiding the Pittsburgh leadership behind the scenes. Wilson followed the advice of his old friend.[86]

In his confidential letter, the dean of athletic directors stated that Michigan State College offered nothing of value for the conference. The University of Pittsburgh, in his opinion, was a far better choice. Its large stadium and loyal fan base would surely benefit the financial bottom line for many members visiting Pittsburgh, Pennsylvania.[87] Although St. John didn't mention it, Ohio State stood to gain another rival, in addition to Michigan and Illinois, certain to guarantee capacity crowds regardless of venue.

The biennial scheduling meetings for late May were coming up in a few weeks. The faculty representatives typically gathered to address conference concerns as well. In the aftermath of The Second Announcement by Chicago, the question on the minds of Michigan State and Pittsburgh leadership was whether this might be the critical caucus to decide a replacement for the Maroons. Both had their insider connections. Professor Floyd Reeves had earlier convinced John Hannah this meeting was the relevant one. Pittsburgh, with a far more ornate network of insiders willing to proffer information, was less certain.

In early May, Panther Athletic Director James Hagan updated his Faculty Committee on Athletic Policies on membership status after its failed attempt one year earlier. With the death of John Griffith, St. John had successfully recruited the support of Tug Wilson. Hagan would now benefit from the insider information provided by the new commissioner. Wilson was in constant contact with faculty leaders by mail or telephone. His confidential counsel could prove invaluable to Pitt as it struggled to regain athletic prominence while maintaining academic integrity in line with "Code Bowman." St. John would continue his role as an undercover resource while working out of Columbus.

---

[86] Wilson to St. John. 20 May 1946. The Ohio State University Archives, Director of Athletics (RG 9/e-1/10), "Intercollegiate Conference: Commissioner: Correspondence (Wilson): 1945-47."

[87] St. John to Wilson. 13 May 1946. The Ohio State University Archives, Director of Athletics (RG 9/e-1/10), "Intercollegiate Conference: Commissioner: Correspondence (Wilson): 1945-47."

Hagan pointed out to the Faculty Committee on Athletic Policies that his sources recommended no formal application at the time. A letter expressing continued interest was adequate for the moment.[88]

The Pittsburgh group met again on May 23. Hagan had consulted with Ken Wilson, who confirmed that Michigan State was applying for admission to the conference in a few days. The commissioner noted that Michigan would profess allegiance in spirit only during the meeting. State politics obligated Aigler's statement of support.[89] It was a mere formality for a university sharing legislative dollars with the college.

James Hagan had also contacted Lynn St. John. The old athletic director, experienced in many conference political battles over the years, suggested a more aggressive tactic than a letter expressing interest. But Hagan, citing other confidential sources who felt a tamer approach was in order, decided it was not necessary for Pitt to be present at the meeting.[90] The Panther Faculty Committee agreed; it informed the conference leadership that Pittsburgh still remained highly interested in membership.[91]

The May minutes of the Faculty Committee on Athletic Policy were significant for two reasons. They suggested the existence of a faction among the Western Conference leadership interested in a Pitt admission. St. John and Wilson may not have been acting alone. One or two others appeared to be cooperating with Hagan as well. It was also apparent that the conference leadership had no intention of deciding a replacement at that time. The information that Professor Reeves had provided to President Hannah, as obtained through faculty chairman Larry Kimpton in late March, could no longer be considered accurate. Political machinations were in the works since Reeves had received that misguided advice.

A FEW key Western Conference faculty leaders were confronted with a challenging problem in anticipation of the spring meeting in Chicago. Chairman Dean Kimpton had received a letter from John Hannah, two weeks in advance of The Second Announcement of March, requesting an application for membership should the conference choose to expand to eleven. Hannah volunteered appearing before the committee at the May meetings to answer any questions. He was merely following the recommendations provided him by Ralph Aigler back in mid-February.

Based on recent tradition, the suitor was always invited to an upcoming conference meeting. Pittsburgh had been granted the opportunity in December of 1944 when Professor R. E. Sherrill and a colleague made a presentation.[92] It was considered only fair that Michigan State College be provided the same opportunity. On May 14, Professor Frank Richart wrote Ralph Aigler about the courtesy offered institutions seeking membership. Richart was secretary of the Faculty Representatives Committee; he assisted the chairman in setting the agenda for each meeting. He sought Aigler's opinion since the Hannah request

---

[88] Minutes of the Meeting of the Faculty Committee on Athletic Policies. 2 May 1946. University of Pittsburgh Archives, Collection 9/2; FF1; Box 1

[89] Minutes of the Meeting of the Faculty Committee on Athletic Policies. 23 May 1946. University of Pittsburgh Archives, Collection 9/2, FF1; Box 1

[90] Ibid.

[91] Sherrill to Richart. 23 May 1946. University of Pittsburgh Archives, Collection 9/2, FF1; Box 1

[92] Minutes of the Intercollegiate Conference of Faculty Representatives. 8 December 1944. University of Illinois Archives, Series 4/2/12; Box 2, folder: Conference Minutes 1944-45

had political implications for the law professor back in the state of Michigan.

Richart felt that since Pitt and Michigan State had forwarded applications before the committee, both schools should be offered an appearance in late May.[93] He was not convinced, however, that the directors were of one mind on expansion or replacement. The faculty would rely on their collective opinion before deciding whether to approve either school for membership.

Ralph Aigler concurred. "… [But] before any consideration is given to possible election of any new member, a decision should be reached on the general question as to whether we think it better to keep the number at nine."[94] Aigler was not convinced that the conference needed 10 members. Scheduling of football contests, with his 9/6/2 experiment now official policy as of December, should work–at least in theory.[95] [96] [97]

He suggested that the faculty could merely offer the standard 1908 Nebraska Response to Hannah–"It is not deemed expedient or desirable to increase the membership of the Conference [at this time]."[98] If they all agreed to remain a group of nine, following the directors' recommendation, "that stock resolution would be the answer to the applicant."[99] It would also allow Aigler to save face back home. There were some in the press that questioned his public commitment of support for Michigan State.[100] [101] "Assuming the application is turned down, I wonder whether [Hannah] and his institution would not have a little better feeling if we had followed the usual procedure."[102]

Aigler appeared confident that the request would be tabled. After all, his influential athletic director shared similar convictions with him on scheduling; Fritz Crisler was also

[93] Richart to Aigler. 14 May 1946. Bentley Historical Library, University of Michigan. Ralph W. Aigler Papers, 87406 Aa 2; Box 9, folder: correspondence 1946-52 "H" misc.

[94] Aigler to Richart. 15 May 1946. Bentley Historical Library, University of Michigan. Ralph W. Aigler Papers, 87406 Aa 2; Box 9, folder: correspondence 1946-52 "H" misc.

[95] North Shore Hotel, Evanston, Illinois. 25 May 1940. Bentley Historical Library, University of Michigan. Athletic Department, 943 Bimu 2; Box 84, folder: Athletic Director's office, Big-Ten Faculty Representatives minutes 1918-1946

[96] Minutes of the Joint Meeting of the Intercollegiate Conference Faculty Representatives, Athletic Directors, and Football Coaches, 6 December 1945. Bentley Historical Library, University of Michigan. Athletic Department, 943 Bimu 2; Box 84, folder: Athletic Director's office, Big-Ten committee minutes 1941-52

[97] Minutes of the 126th Meeting of the Intercollegiate Conference of Faculty Representatives, 8 December 1945. Bentley Historical Library, University of Michigan. Athletic Department, 943 Bimu 2; Box 84, folder: Faculty Representatives minutes 1941-57

[98] Aigler to Richart. 15 May 1946. Bentley Historical Library, University of Michigan. Ralph W. Aigler Papers, 87406 Aa 2; Box 9, folder: correspondence 1946-52 "H" misc.

[99] Ibid.

[100] Aigler to Editor of the *Michigan Daily*. 1 December 1948. Bentley Historical Library, University of Michigan. Ralph W. Aigler Papers, 87406 Aa 2; Box 10, folder: correspondence 1946-52 personal

[101] Aigler to Emmons. 6 December 1948. Bentley Historical Library, University of Michigan. Ralph W. Aigler Papers, 87406 Aa 2; Box 9, folder: correspondence 1946-52 "E" misc.

[102] Aigler to Richart. 15 May 1946. Bentley Historical Library, University of Michigan. Ralph W. Aigler Papers, 87406 Aa 2; Box 9, folder: correspondence 1946-52 "H" misc.

convinced that the 9/6/2 concept remained feasible.[103] [104] There was no reason, in the spring of 1946, for a return to 10 members merely for football scheduling.

Aigler concluded his remarks by reminding Professor Richart, "Please do not misunderstand me … it is not for me to make the decision on this matter, nor do I want to appear to be fighting the battles of Michigan State."[105] He did not want to be accused of manipulating the outcome of a very sensitive issue for both the public and press back in his state.

In deference to Aigler's concerns, the two decided to approach Dean Larry Kimpton of Chicago. Despite being a lame duck, he remained acting chairman of the Faculty Representatives Committee until the end of June. Protocol would dictate that he had the final say on the question originally posed by Frank Richart. The chairman, after all, determined the meeting agenda. Aigler was assigned the task of contacting Kimpton.[106]

Only two months earlier Professor Kimpton had met with Floyd Reeves and acknowledged that "action is likely to be taken …" to replace Chicago.[107] The take-home message Reeves relayed to President Hannah was that a vote would take place in May. With that knowledge in mind, the college president desperately needed to make a presentation in Chicago. John Hannah was confident he could sway votes away from both Pittsburgh and Nebraska and gain a seat for Michigan State College.

To the relief of Ralph Aigler, after presenting the Richart concern to Dean Kimpton on whether President Hannah should be allowed a presence at the spring meeting, the chairman of the Faculty Representatives Committee made the executive decision not to offer an invitation. Kimpton agreed it was pointless to do so if the directors were undecided on whether to replace his school. Aigler and Richart, of course, would guarantee that no vote would take place among the faculty as long as the athletic directors opposed returning to a 10-member association. And if Fritz Crisler was informed of the Richart-Aigler plan, his influence could virtually assure that outcome.

At Aigler's request, Kimpton then called John Hannah in East Lansing. He carefully explained "that it had been the custom [in] the past for institutions making application for the Conference to be represented [at the meeting]." He informed the president, however, that there was "no vital reason for his attendance at the meeting …" There would be no vote by the faculty until the athletic directors could decide whether to replace the University of Chicago. He did not mention that Professors Richart and Aigler had essentially predetermined there would be no action taken at that meeting.

---

[103] Minutes of the Meeting of the Directors of Athletics of the Intercollegiate Conference, 24-25 May 1940. Bentley Historical Library, University of Michigan. Athletic Department, 943 Bimu 2; Box 84, folder: Athletic Director's office, Big-Ten committee minutes 1932-1940

[104] Minutes of the Joint Meeting of the Intercollegiate Conference Faculty Representatives, Athletic Directors, and Football Coaches, 6 December 1945. Bentley Historical Library, University of Michigan. Athletic Department, 943 Bimu 2; Box 84, folder: Athletic Director's office, Big-Ten committee minutes 1941-52

[105] Aigler to Richart. 15 May 1946. Bentley Historical Library, University of Michigan. Ralph W. Aigler Papers, 87406 Aa 2; Box 9, folder: correspondence 1946-52 "H" misc.

[106] Kimpton to Aigler. 20 May 1946. Bentley Historical Library. University of Michigan. Ralph W. Aigler Papers, 87406 Aa 2; Box 9, folder: correspondence 1946-52 "H" misc.

[107] Reeves to Hannah. 21 March 1946. Michigan State University Archives. Floyd Reeves Papers, UA21.12.1; Box 115, folder:2

Kimpton, in a follow-up letter to Professor Aigler, noted that Hannah "was very gracious about the whole thing ..." The college president did promise the chairman that should the need arise for immediate presence at the meeting, "a phone call would bring him or someone else there in a matter of several hours."[108]

Aigler was relieved. He complimented Larry Kimpton on his handling of the delicate issue. And once again, perhaps revealing his ambivalence about a Michigan State admission, he commented, "I think you know that I had no personal desire to have Hannah in attendance."[109] Aigler was well aware of the persuasive powers of the man from East Lansing.

After being declined a spot on the agenda for the upcoming spring meeting, Hannah wrote to Professor Aigler on the 25th of May. Assuming that the Michigan faculty representative was now supporting Michigan State's initiative, he wanted to share his disappointment regarding the decision made by the chairman.[110] The president had no idea that Professor Aigler was already aware of Kimpton's telephone conversation with Hannah.

The Spartan leader remained convinced that a decision might still be made regardless of Kimpton's phone call. He still trusted Floyd Reeves' assessment from late February. Without being allowed a chance to personally influence votes, Hannah feared losing out to either Pittsburgh or Nebraska. So the president made a plea to Ralph Aigler just prior to his departure for the May meetings at the Lincoln Hotel in Urbana.

> Our cause is entirely in your hands, and I hope that you will see fit to press it at this time. We have tried to be ethical and have not contacted the faculty advisers of the various universities. Some months ago I wrote to the presidents ... and received very favorable replies from all of them. Most of them were of course noncommittal, but at least three of the presidents indicated that their schools are enthusiastically favorable to our cause which of course means nothing.[111]

He was referring to Northwestern, Minnesota, and Purdue.

On June 1, 1946, Dean Kimpton, in executive session, presented Michigan State's application to the membership. Professor Aigler "spoke briefly, mentioning Michigan State's qualifications."[112] He did what he had promised the college leadership and the public back home.

Following Aigler's presentation, Secretary Frank Richart "called attention to a telegram from Professor Sherrill from the University of Pittsburgh, indicating that the institution would welcome membership in the Conference ..." Not to be outdone, Professor Karl Leib of the State University of Iowa indicated that "a representative of the University

---

[108] Kimpton to Aigler. 20 May 1946. Bentley Historical Library. University of Michigan. Ralph W. Aigler Papers, 87406 Aa 2; Box 9, folder: correspondence 1946-52 "H" misc.

[109] Aigler to Kimpton. 25 May 1946. Bentley Historical Library. University of Michigan. Ralph W. Aigler Papers, 87406 Aa 2; Box 9, folder: correspondence 1946-52 "H" misc.

[110] Hannah to Aigler. 25 May 1946. Bentley Historical Library. University of Michigan. Ralph W. Aigler Papers, 87406 Aa 2; Box 9, folder: correspondence 1946-52 "H" misc.

[111] Ibid.

[112] Minutes of the Intercollegiate Conference of Faculty Representatives. 31 May-1 June 1946. University of Minnesota Archives, Presidents Office; Box 238, folder: Physical Education 1945-47

of Nebraska had expressed that institution's interest in membership."[113] He wanted all to be aware that the Cornhuskers remained intrigued with the Chicago seat despite their current passive position.

Nebraska had sought admission to the association on a number of occasions since 1899.[114] Perhaps its most historically significant attempt took place 38 years earlier, five months after Michigan's departure from the conference. Four years later, aware of Ohio State's successful application in the spring of 1912, the university tried once again in December. The same response given Professor R. G. Clapp in 1908 was again provided the Cornhuskers: It was not expedient to enlarge at that time.

Leib's reminder in May 1946 suggested that this was at least the third time Nebraska had considered membership since 1908. It was in Iowa's interest to support a Cornhuskers' application. They desperately needed an end-of-year rival of some regional interest. Michigan had Ohio State. Wisconsin competed against Minnesota. Illinois had played Northwestern since the Chicago withdrawal. And the Indiana-Purdue contest closed out the season for those intrastate programs.

IN A gesture of respect to the president, following conclusion of the Urbana meetings, Ralph Aigler wrote John Hannah on June 3 to sum up the agenda item pertaining to the college. The athletic directors had recommended, at least for the time being, that no action be taken on replacement of Chicago.[115] Whether Fritz Crisler played any role in that decision is left to conjecture. Lynn St. John, as an ardent supporter of Pitt, might have impacted the outcome as well. His faculty representative, Professor James Pollard, made the motion "that no further change be made at this time in membership ..." in deference to the directors' wishes.[116] It would have been inappropriate for Frank Richart, and most certainly Ralph Aigler, to make that proposal. The faculty approved the motion.

Professor Aigler knew nothing about the St. John-Wilson collaboration. But he was undoubtedly aware of some relationship that the commissioner maintained with Pittsburgh. Two weeks prior to the May conference meetings, Wilson had informed Pitt's athletic director, James Hagan, of Michigan's lukewarm support for the Spartan application. He emphasized that the Wolverine leadership would not influence a vote on the college application.[117] His statement implied that there had been a discussion with either Aigler or Crisler in advance of that annual gathering regarding the subject; Wilson needed to clarify the Wolverines' true intentions. This insider information was no doubt reassuring to the Panthers.

Perhaps violating the code of confidentiality inherent in executive sessions, Aigler shared with President Hannah his explanation of the story behind the de facto rejection of the college.

---

[113] Minutes of the Intercollegiate Conference of Faculty Representatives. 31 May-1 June 1946. University of Minnesota Archives, Presidents Office; Box 238, folder: Physical Education 1945-47

[114] Kryk, John. "The Door Opens." *Maple Street Press* July 2011: 117-19.

[115] Joint Minutes of the Faculty Representatives and Athletic Directors. 31 May 1946. Bentley Historical Library, University of Michigan. Athletic Department, 943 Bimu 2; Box 84, folder: Big Ten Directors Committee minutes 1941-52

[116] Ibid.

[117] Minutes of the Meeting of the Faculty Committee on Athletic Policies. 23 May 1946. University of Pittsburgh Archives, Collection 9/2; Box 1, folder: FF1

There was then, as you notice, no definite vote on your application. When the matter came before the Faculty Representatives, I made a statement to the effect that I hoped the Conference would see its way clear to elect Michigan State, but I did not press for a vote, realizing…the temper of the group was to approve the Directors' recommendation. I thought it better to leave the matter thus more or less in suspense.[118]

In an attempt at softening the disappointment, the professor encouraged Hannah to notify Frank Richart that the Spartan application should remain "in a live file." Pittsburgh maintained a similar file.[119] "After a little more time has gone by, one will be able to tell better what the long range disposition of the group is … you can readily understand that the informal application by Pittsburgh is a definite complication."[120]

Regardless of Ralph Aigler's intent, which John Hannah still failed to appreciate, this was now the third rejection he had experienced while serving in an administrative role at Michigan State. Although "very gracious" in accepting Dean Kimpton's request not to attend the May meeting, Hannah suspected that the Wolverines were once again behind this latest disappointment.[121]

The University of Michigan could no longer be trusted.[122] Its sincerity was suspect. Its promises were made and later broken. The failure of Crisler and Aigler to meet with Hannah and Young during the fall of 1945 illustrated that point only too well. Henry Rottschaefer's comment to Lew Morrill back in March, regarding Ralph Aigler's equivocal support for the Spartan initiative, seemed accurate in hindsight.[123] If Michigan truly professed a commitment to the college cause, Ralph Aigler should have used all his rhetorical clout in gaining a seat for Michigan State. Instead, the powerful faculty representative appeared to soft pedal his way around an application he could not support in private.[124]

Plan A, so promising only two months earlier following the Ruthven announcement, appeared no longer viable. As Hannah stated in his letter to Ken Wilson in January of 1946, if conference membership was not a viable option, "… we better recognize that fact and proceed on a long-time program as an isolated independent."[125] In early June of 1946, it was time to consider Plan B.

---

[118] Aigler to Hannah. 3 June 1946. Bentley Historical Library, University of Michigan. Ralph W. Aigler Papers, 87406 Aa 2; Box 9, folder: correspondence 1946-52 "H" misc.

[119] Ibid.

[120] Ibid.

[121] Thomas, David. *Michigan State College: John Hannah and the Creation of a World University, 1926-1969.* East Lansing: Michigan State University Press, 2008. p. 289

[122] Ibid.

[123] Rottschaefer to Morrill. 27 March 1946. University of Minnesota Archives. Presidents Office; Box 238, folder: Physical Education 1945-47

[124] Morrill to Rottschaefer. 16 September 1948. University of Minnesota Archives, President's Office; Box 238, folder: physical education and athletics 1948-49

[125] Hannah to Wilson. 26 January 1946. Bentley Historical Library, University of Michigan. Herbert Orin Crisler Papers, 85823 AC UAm Aa 2; Box 1, folder: MSU correspondence 1943-46 topical

The Spaghetti and Meatball Contract

MICHIGAN STATE, since the amicable divorce of 1921, had made it a practice for years to attend various Notre Dame athletic events celebrating either the end of a season or spring training. It was no secret why: The Spartans wanted to regain a football relationship with the Fighting Irish. The deterrent to a renewed relationship remained College Field and its capacity for only 20,000 seats.[1] Even the expansion of 1935, adding almost 9,000 paying customers into the stadium,[2] was insufficient by Notre Dame standards.

On May 29 of 1946, Athletic Director Ralph Young wrote to President John Hannah seeking approval for assistant coaches Al Kawal and Louis Zarza to attend the "Old Timers Game" closing out the spring football drills in South Bend, Indiana. The two Bachman assistants had written head coach Frank Leahy seeking tickets a few days earlier.[3] [4] The request for reimbursement of the trip must have reminded John Hannah of some unfinished business he had overlooked while actively pursuing Plan A since February.

Five months earlier Hannah had delivered his keynote address to the annual NCAA convention in St. Louis. During that brief stay in Missouri he ran into Frank Leahy. The Irish athletic director was an old friend of Hannah's. He had also been an assistant to Jim Crowley at Michigan State College in 1932.[5] Leahy was now the very successful head coach at Notre Dame.

President Hannah was pressed for time and unable to share his thoughts with the Irishman about "intercollegiate relationships." They had planned to get together "for a longer visit" but the opportunity never availed itself.[6] Upon returning to East Lansing in

---

[1] Untitled press release. 17 October 1946. University of Notre Dame Archives, [UPCC 6/13]

[2] Kuhn, Madison. *Michigan State: The First Hundred Years.* East Lansing: Michigan State University Press, 1955. p. 360

[3] Young to Hannah. 29 May 1946. Michigan State University Archives. Board of Trustees Records, UA1.0. Supportive materials; Box 1892, folder: 3 6/20/46

[4] Leahy to Kawal. 27 May 1946. Michigan State University Archives. Board of Trustees Records, UA1.0. Supportive materials; Box 1892, folder: 3 6/20/46

[5] Hannah, John A. *A Memoir.* East Lansing: Michigan State University Press, 1980. p. 110

[6] Hannah to Leahy. 3 June 1946. Michigan State University Archives. John A. Hannah Papers,

mid-January, Hannah forgot to follow up with Leahy. He was more focused on whether Fritz Crisler and Ralph Aigler would ever agree to a meeting regarding an application process for the college. The third rejection followed a few months later on the 1st of June. And so Ralph Young's note, in reference to the Old Timer's Game, probably reminded Hannah of the St. Louis encounter. A few days later, shortly after the Urban rejection, Coach Leahy received a long letter from the president of Michigan State.

John Hannah was fully in control of athletic policy and operations at the college; he essentially assumed command in December of 1942 while ghostwriting letters for Ralph Young to his counterpart in Ann Arbor regarding scheduling issues. The encounter with Frank Leahy made him realize the role that the Irish athletic director might play in the college achieving Plan B. So the president, wanting to discuss the future of his athletic program, invited his old friend to visit East Lansing. In his proposal, he referenced the decision by the conference faculty representatives two days earlier.

> It was necessary for us to learn whether or not there was any likelihood of our being admitted to the Western Conference, and an application was recently filed with them in the proper form. Their failure to act favorably upon it answers our question. It is now necessary for us to plan a long time program as a strong independent without further regard to the Western Conference. To accomplish this objective, the cooperation of Notre Dame University could aid us greatly; and I would like to talk to you frankly with all the cards face up on the table about the possibility of a long time football relationship.[7]

Hannah proposed a home-and-home series. He intimated that plans might be in the works for a stadium expansion certain to meet Notre Dame's expectations. But in the short term the Spartans would request playing home games in East Lansing despite not meeting the Notre Dame seating capacity requirement. That remained a critical feature to his proposal. If the Irish were interested in renewing a relationship, the president would petition his board for dollars to expand Macklin Field. Assuming he succeeded in gaining that approval, he had a few suggestions to offset financial losses for the Irish in the meantime.

Michigan State was willing to provide a very generous guarantee with options on gate receipts. This would come with the understanding that home games intended for South Bend might be switched to Detroit. With the large Catholic population about the metropolitan area, the game was a certain sellout in Briggs Stadium, which had undergone expansion in 1937 and could seat up to 53,000 fans.

Hannah needed Plan B to succeed. Admitting that it might be "somewhat unethical," he offered Notre Dame 100 percent of the proceeds of the games played in either South Bend or Detroit; the Spartans would cover their own expenses. And for games held in East Lansing, the college would assume all revenue from a facility seating only 29,000 ticket holders. From an accountant's perspective, it was a very generous deal.[8]

Frank Leahy punted the letter to the leadership on campus. The Holy Cross Order

---

UA2.1.12; Box 61, folder: 56

[7] Hannah to Leahy. 3 June 1946. Michigan State University Archives. John A. Hannah Papers, UA2.1.12; Box 61, folder: 56

[8] Ibid.

was in total control at Notre Dame. This was a matter for Father Hugh O'Donnell, the current president, and his administrative team to contemplate. Leahy's job was to turn out winners. Complicated financial arrangements were for those wearing priestly garb to address.

John Hannah was raised Catholic;[9] his mother's maiden name was Malone.[10] With Irish blood in him, he may have experienced a bit of luck in November of 1942 with the election of Republican Harry F. Kelly as governor of Michigan. The leader of the state (1943-47) was a 1917 graduate of the University of Notre Dame. The Irishman also happened to serve as president of the national Notre Dame Alumni Association during his tenure in state government.[11] Kelly's positions, as it turned out, would greatly aid the president's cause within a few years.

Shortly after assuming office, the politician and the educator became close friends. The relationship was symbiotic. Kelly, aware of Hannah's connections throughout the state, had used him in "rallying support" for his Victory Building Program legislation of 1944. The landmark law was critical to the economic stability of the state in the early postwar years.[12] Likewise, the president had taken advantage of his friendship with the governor. He used his connections with the office to gain dollars, through the Victory program, to develop the evolving infrastructure for Michigan State. Kelly was very impressed with Hannah as a leader. "We have a man in command at Michigan State who is second to none in the nation in meeting [the postwar problems in higher education]."[13]

Father O'Donnell's five-year tenure as president of Notre Dame was about to end when Leahy first received the Hannah letter in June. O'Donnell's replacement, as of early August, would be Reverend John J. Cavanaugh. As fate would have it, Governor Kelly was a very good friend of Father Cavanaugh's. They had worked together on alumni matters while Cavanaugh served in the O'Donnell administration. And if this additional Irish luck was not enough for the college president, John Cavanaugh was a native of Owosso, Michigan–30 minutes from downtown Lansing. He still maintained family in the area and visited them often. The Cavanaugh's became close with the Kelly's in large part due to the friendship between the two men.[14]

In mid-August Harry Kelly wrote a brief note to Cavanaugh. He congratulated him on the promotion to presidency of "du Lac."[15] He also mentioned interest in "seeing you sometime this fall."[16] That visit, as will be seen, would greatly impact the history of Michigan State College of Agriculture and Applied Science.

On September 25, 1946, the governor wrote John Cavanaugh confirming plans for a luncheon engagement at the Kelly household on October 1. The new Notre Dame president

[9] Kuhn, Madison. "John A. Hannah." Michigan State University Archives. Hannah Archives Project, UA 2.1.12.2; Box 34, folder: 27 "John Hannah"

[10] Hannah, John A. *A Memoir.* East Lansing: Michigan State University Press, 1980. p. 11

[11] Kelly-Hagopian, Joanne. "Harry Kelly." E-mail to David J. Young. 16 October 2008. Joanne, the eldest of the Kelly children, was kind enough to share background information on her father.

[12] Denison, James H. "Untitled." 24 June 1970. Michigan State University Archives. Hannah Archives Project, UA2.1.12.2; Box 34. folder: 8 Denison

[13] Kelly to Cavanaugh. 25 September 1946. University of Notre Dame Archives, [UPCC 17/4]

[14] Kelly to Cavanaugh. 16 August 1946. University of Notre Dame Archives, [UPCC 17/4]

[15] "The University of Notre Dame du Lac" (Our Lady of the Lake) is the official name of the school.

[16] Kelly to Cavanaugh. 16 August 1946. University of Notre Dame Archives, [UPCC 17/4]

was planning a drive over to Owosso that day to visit with his mother. Aware of Father John's plans, Harry and Anne invited him to make a stop in Lansing and spend a few hours at their home on West Genessee, just blocks from the State Capitol.[17]

Since assuming his position as president in early August, the Holy Cross priest was actively involved in negotiations with John Hannah and Michigan State College.[18] Kelly, undoubtedly aware of remaining impediments in contract discussions, alerted Cavanaugh of his plans to also invite President Hannah to the luncheon. The governor's agenda included "allowing a little time with the thought that you might like to take a ride in my car around the Michigan State College campus and see the marvelous postwar job that is being done there."[19] Kelly wanted his friend to witness firsthand what the college leader had accomplished in infrastructure development in only five years on the job in East Lansing. The governor's ulterior motive, however, was to close the deal. He was convinced a long-term agreement to compete on the gridiron, as proposed by Hannah a few months earlier, would serve both schools well.[20]

At that time, expansion of Macklin Field, critical to any successful negotiations with Notre Dame,[21] had not yet been approved by the State Board of Agriculture.[22] Cavanaugh, in the governor's opinion, had to be made aware that a promise from John Hannah for a stadium seating almost 52,000 fans, by September of 1948, would be a fait accompli.

On Tuesday, October 1, 1946, the two presidents met in the home of Harry Kelly. Family members recalled the event well. Father Cavanaugh was wearing his black cassock. Mrs. Kelly prepared spaghetti and meatballs for her six children. After clean-up, the adults, including Anne, retired to the dining room and shared in the same meal. With Harry Kelly facilitating the discussion, John Hannah addressed any remaining concerns that Notre Dame and Cavanaugh had. The "Spaghetti and Meatball" contract was consummated that afternoon.[23] [24] [25] [26]

The trip to the campus proved to be a formality. It confirmed for the new Notre Dame president that Harry Kelly's impressions of John Hannah were accurate. The stadium-expansion promise would become a reality with Hannah in leadership. All that remained was approval of the contract by the Faculty Board in Control of Athletics at Notre Dame. Cavanaugh assured the two of a favorable vote. The official announcement would take place simultaneously in South Bend and East Lansing on the 17th of October. The dedication game for the "new stadium" in East Lansing would be played with Notre Dame on the last

---

[17] Kelly to Cavanaugh. 25 September 1946. University of Notre Dame Archives, [UPCC 17/4]

[18] Ibid.

[19] Ibid.

[20] Ibid.

[21] Hannah to Cavanaugh. 2 October 1946. University of Notre Dame Archives, [UPCC 6/13]

[22] Ibid.

[23] Hannah, John A. *A Memoir.* East Lansing: Michigan State University Press, 1980. p. 120

[24] Kelly-Hagopian, Joanne. "Harry Kelly." E-mail to David J. Young. 16 October 2008. In high school at the time, Joanne recalled the luncheon and also her father's comments, years later, that a special agreement was reached that day between the two institutions.

[25] Hannah to Cavanaugh. 2 October 1946. University of Notre Dame Archives, [UPCC 6/13]

[26] Contract. 2 October 1946. University of Notre Dame Archives, [UPCC 6/13/]

Saturday in September 1948.[27]

On October 10, 1946, Father John Murphy, vice president of Notre Dame, presented the Hannah proposal to the Faculty Board in Cavanaugh's absence; he was out of town on university business. Lacking his input, the faculty unanimously rejected the contract![28]

Later that evening, after learning of the decision from Murphy by telephone, Cavanaugh "requested" that his vice president immediately petition the board for "reconsideration."[29] The following day Murphy sent off a highly confidential memo regarding the contract. Michigan State was willing to make concessions including "giving us 80% of the gross receipts"[30] for Notre Dame home games. Acknowledging the unusual offer as inadvisable from Notre Dame's vantage point "for a number of obvious reasons," Murphy went on to explain in great detail matters previously privy only to his president. "In view of these considerations, may I ask whether you, [the board], would be willing to reverse your decision of yesterday...?"[31] They were. With a few minor revisions, the Hannah proposal was approved.[32]

In an effort at trumpeting his major accomplishment, on Wednesday October 16, Hannah disclosed to the press that "an announcement of considerable public interest and pertaining to athletics would be made tomorrow."[33] The big tease worked. The following day Ralph Young revealed to a large press gathering, on the Red Cedar campus, that Notre Dame and Michigan State had agreed to renew football relations in 1948 after a 27-year lapse. The first game would take place in East Lansing. He also mentioned plans to enlarge Macklin Field. The schools signed a long-term contract to assure the ongoing rivalry.[34] One year later, on October 16, 1947, the State Board of Agriculture finally approved plans for expansion of the stadium. Hannah's critical promise to Father Cavanaugh would become reality.[35]

The Spaghetti and Meatball contract was a renewable two-game home-and-home series between the schools. Hannah and Cavanaugh had originally intended a long-term contractual relationship. The short series was agreed upon, temporarily, to appease skeptics in South Bend.[36] [37] [38] Other than a brief interruption during the 1995-96 seasons, the game has remained an annual classic for over 60 years. But contrary to Ralph Young's press conference statement, the first game would be held on October 9, 1948 in South Bend, not East Lansing. Ironically, the Faculty Senate Policy of 1941, presumably drafted by President Hannah, played a major role in that game-date change.

---

[27] Hannah to Cavanaugh. 2 October 1946. University of Notre Dame Archives, [UPCC 6/13]

[28] Ibid.

[29] Ibid.

[30] Ibid.

[31] Ibid.

[32] Murphy to members of the Faculty Board in Control of Athletics. 11 October 1946. University of Notre Dame Archives, [UUPCC 6/13]

[33] "Announcement Pending." *South Bend Tribune*, 16 October 1946: Sports Section

[34] "Michigan State, Notre Dame to Resume on Grid." *South Bend Tribune*. 17 October 1946: Sports Section.

[35] Minutes of the State Board of Agriculture, 16 October 1947. www.onthebanks.msu.edu

[36] Hannah to Cavanaugh. 2 October 1946. University of Notre Dame Archives, [UPCC 6/13]

[37] Cavanaugh to Hannah. 12 October 1946. University of Notre Dame Archives, [UPCC 6/13]

[38] Murphy to members of the Faculty Board in Control of Athletics. 11 October 1946. [UPCC 6/13]

Six days following the joint announcement regarding the renewed rivalry with the Irish, Fritz Crisler "regretfully" informed Ralph Young that, due to "various schedule commitments ... we are unable to clear any date except September 27, 1947, for the Michigan State-Michigan football game."[39] Unknown to the Spartan athletic director, Michigan's Board in Control, earlier in the month, unanimously approved a motion by Professor Ralph Aigler "[since] it is impracticable to carry out ... a schedule with a Conference team or [East /West coast] team on the first date [of the season] ... that it shall be the policy of this Board to invite Michigan State College to fill the opening date on the football schedule" indefinitely. Crisler, in his letter to Young, noted that his board "reviewed our schedule policy very thoroughly and discovered that it is not very elastic." He could only offer the college the opening Saturday each year.[40] The board's latest action essentially codified the Yost-Young understanding of 1932. The Wolverines would continue their dominant position in all scheduling matters.

On November 5, in response to Crisler's pronouncement, the college Athletic Council, perhaps with President Hannah's reminder, decided to conveniently dust off the old Faculty Senate policy of October 1941.[41] In a telegram to Fritz Crisler, Young alerted the university's athletic officials for the first time of that resolution "forbidding the scheduling of future football games in Ann Arbor between the University of Michigan and Michigan State College prior to the opening of fall quarter classes" in East Lansing.[42] The proposed Saturday was not in compliance with the Spartan policy. But, in the spirit of compromise, the director noted that "the Athletic Council ... will recommend to its faculty the acceptance of the September 27 date in 1947 despite the conflict with registration, if assurance is given by the [university] that in 1948 and future seasons thereafter the annual football game ... will be scheduled on some date which follows the opening of fall quarter classes at Michigan State College."[43] President Hannah, for a few reasons, wanted the rivalry held later in the season.

The Wolverines were caught off guard. Ralph Aigler, probably upset over the Spartan ploy–resurrecting an old academic policy never before revealed to the university–made a motion at the November 15 board meeting "that because of our existing schedule commitments and the regulations of the Conference regarding the making of advance football schedules, we regret to have to advise Michigan State ... that we cannot give them the assurance asked for in [their November 5] telegram."[44] But Michigan did offer an olive

---

[39] Crisler to Young. 23 October 1946. Bentley Historical Library, University of Michigan. Herbert Orin Crisler Papers, 85823 AC UAm Aa 2; Box 1, folder: MSU correspondence 43-46 topical

[40] Minutes of the meeting of the Board in Control of Intercollegiate Athletics. 4 October 1946. Bentley Historical Library, University of Michigan. Board in Control of Intercollegiate Athletics, 8729 Bimu F81 2; Box 49, folder: minutes Feb. 1938-June 1950

[41] It is unknown whether the Spartan leadership, by November 5, 1946, was aware of the latest university athletic policy to reserve the scrimmage date for MSC indefinitely. If that decision had been revealed to the college, it may have offered another reason for a Spartan retaliation.

[42] Young to Crisler. 5 November 1946. Bentley Historical Library, University of Michigan. Herbert Orin Crisler Papers, 85823 AC UAm Aa 2; Box 1, folder: MSU correspondence 43-46 topical

[43] Ibid.

[44] Minutes of the meeting of the Board in Control of Intercollegiate Athletics. 15 November 1946. Bentley Historical Library, University of Michigan. Board in Control of Intercollegiate Athletics, 8729 Bimu F81 2; Box 49, folder: minutes Feb. 1938-June 1950

branch. Acknowledging the "position taken by the faculty of [MSC] which does not permit [the school] to schedule a game with the [university in] Ann Arbor during [its] registration period, we express to them our willingness to come to East Lansing [instead] for the opening game of the 1947 season, September 27."[45] The Spartans temporarily acquiesced.

One month later, Young wrote his counterpart asking that the 1947 game in East Lansing be held in 1948 instead. He offered the dedication game for the expanded Macklin Stadium as an enticement.[46] Crisler, mindful of state politics, agreed to the new request. The 1947 contest would remain in Ann Arbor after all.[47] Notre Dame graciously agreed to the scheduling change. Thus, the first game of the renewed series would take place in South Bend.

John Hannah probably orchestrated the latest game date changes. With the Wolverines agreeing to compete at Macklin Stadium, their first visit since the College Field dedication of 1924, Hannah would not only gain national sports page headlines for that event but also for Notre Dame's return to East Lansing the following season after a 28-year hiatus. The publicity was good for the program–and for Michigan State College.

With Notre Dame on the schedule, the first phase of Plan B was complete. The second phase of Hannah's strategy was all that remained. It would prove to be an unenviable task.

MICHIGAN STATE, after almost two years of hibernation, resumed football action in the fall of 1944. It finished the season with six wins against one loss while playing civilian freshmen, 4Fs deemed physically ineligible for military service (such as future MSU Executive Vice President Jack Breslin),[48] and discharged veterans.[49] [50] Impressive though the record might seem, all competitors contracted with the Spartans had losing records that season. The following year the college achieved five wins, one tie, and three losses. With Jenison Awards attracting talented athletes, the team still failed to play up to expectations. The 1946 squad's performance proved even more discouraging, with only five victories in 10 games. The University of Michigan, as anticipated, soundly defeated the Spartans those two seasons at contests held in Ann Arbor.

Spartan coach Charlie Bachman was 54 years old. Many fans, alumni, and sports pundits felt that the game had passed him by. Innovative young coaches were creating new formations and schemes. The old "Notre Dame Box," for example, was being replaced by the T-formation. But Bachman refused to change with the times.[51]

---

[45] Ibid.

[46] Young to Crisler. 24 December 1946. Bentley Historical Library, University of Michigan. Herbert Orin Crisler Papers, 85823 AC UAm Aa 2; Box 1, folder: MSU correspondence 43-46 topical

[47] Crisler to Young. 27 January 1947. Bentley Historical Library, University of Michigan. Herbert Orin Crisler Papers, 85823 AC UAm Aa 2; Box 1, folder: MSU correspondence 43-46 topical

[48] Breslin, Brian. 10 August 2009. Personal communication.

[49] Alderton, George. "Spartans Return to Grid Saturday." *Lansing State Journal,* 29 September 1944. Michigan State University Archives. Madison Kuhn Collection, UA12.107; Scrapbook 108, folder: 5

[50] Alderton,, George. "State Resumes Football-Bachman has 60 Candidates on 1944 Squad." *Lansing State Journal,* 10 September 1944. Michigan State University Archives. Madison Kuhn Collection, UA12.107; Scrapbook 108, folder: 5

[51] Thomas, David. *Michigan State College: John Hannah and the Creation of a World University, 1926-1969.* East Lansing: Michigan State University Press, 2008. p. 277

Facing intense pressure in late November of 1946, following a second season of mediocre play, Bachman decided to tender his resignation to John Hannah. Some speculated the coach had been fired, but Hannah argued otherwise.[52] Regardless of how it was handled, the president assured him a dignified departure in mid-December of that year.[53] There appeared to be no involvement of Athletic Director Ralph Young or the Athletic Council in the process. This was a decision made from the top. Confidentiality was crucial to protect the reputation of a loyal employee and trusted friend.

For 13 years Charlie Bachman had been an ambassador for Michigan State College. He had also been a very successful coach. His record of 70 wins against 34 losses and 10 ties was impressive. But of greater significance for most Spartan faithful was his four-game winning streak over the Wolverines during the mid-1930s. Never before had the Aggies or Spartans even gained two consecutive victories in Ann Arbor.

Phase two of Plan B was intended not only to address the Bachman matter but also to acquire a first-rate young coach capable of developing a nationally respected program with the talent being made available through the Jenison Awards.

At the December 19, 1946, State Board of Agriculture meeting the president of the college officially announced the resignation of Charles Bachman as head football coach. Consistent with Michigan State policy, he would maintain tenure as professor of Physical Education, Health and Recreation for Men until his retirement in November of 1954.[54] John Hannah also alerted his board that he had hired Clarence Munn from Syracuse University to assume the vacated position. Munn's starting salary would be $11,000. He would also be guaranteed tenure as a professor.

Three assistants from Syracuse joined the new coach. A Wolverine influence was evident: Forest Evashevski and Laverne "Kip" Taylor were former gridiron greats during their years in Ann Arbor. The third assistant was a recent Syracuse graduate. Nicknamed "Stubby," he was better known as Hugh "Duffy" Daugherty while living in East Lansing.[55]

The new coaches began off-season recruiting on January 1, 1947. To assist his football staff in those efforts, Hannah authorized an additional 12 Jenison Awards.[56]

Plan B was now fully in place. The college would maintain its independence.

PRESIDENT HANNAH had essentially been in control of the athletic department and its oversight athletic council since December 1942. His decision to assume that leadership position, by 1947, would prove critical in forestalling a Pittsburgh advance. Unfortunately, in taking charge of the department, he may have set the stage for one of the most embarrassing moments in Michigan State sporting history.

Long before Hannah's rise to the presidency, Ralph Young had been hired as athletic director; he had also assumed the head coaching positions in football and track.

---

[52] Alderton, George. "State Squad Ridden with Injuries; Campus Factions Seek Bachman's Job." *Lansing State Journal,* 17 October 1946. Michigan State University Archives. Madison Kuhn Collection, UA12.107; Scrapbook 108, folder: 5

[53] Thomas, David. *Michigan State College: John Hannah and the Creation of a World University, 1926-1969.* East Lansing: Michigan State University Press, 2008. p. 276

[54] Minutes of the State Board of Agriculture. 27 November 1954. www.onthebanks.msu.edu

[55] Thomas, David. *Michigan State College: John Hannah and the Creation of a World University, 1926-1969.* East Lansing: Michigan State University Press, 2008. p. 281

[56] Minutes of the State Board of Agriculture. 16 January 1947. www.onthebanks.msu.edu

After a few lackluster years, he turned the football job over to Harry Kipke in 1928. He remained track coach for a number of years. Young retired from the athletic department in July of 1954.

As athletic director, Young maintained a significant role in operations during his early years. He and the Athletic Council were intimately involved in decisions regarding coaching personnel.[57] [58] [59] Ralph Young would inform President Robert Shaw of his recommendations. James Crowley was hired following a search coordinated by the athletic director.[60] With Crowley's resignation as head coach in 1933, Charlie Bachman was offered the position.[61] Young played a pivotal role in hiring the coach. The president and the State Board merely approved his decision.[62]

When Coach Crowley requested renegotiation of his contract after the first year, Ralph Young was not involved. President Robert Shaw managed the entire process at the request of the State Board. The political leadership of the school felt this matter was too confidential for the athletic director's involvement. His competency, otherwise, was never questioned during the Shaw years.

As part of scheduling responsibilities, Young was charged with signing up prominent programs for the Spartans to compete against in home-and-home series. Despite offering guarantees to Notre Dame and many Western Conference schools, he proved unsuccessful. No one on the board or the Athletic Council could fault his efforts; unknown to all, the Aigler Boycott was in force. Despite those failures, Ralph Young remained steadfast in courting relationships and promoting good will with coaches and directors of other institutions. He attended Western Conference meetings and annual Notre Dame postseason events.

Young's hard work finally paid off in the spring of 1939. Purdue accepted a generous guarantee to compete against the Spartans in a home-and-home series.[63] The Boilermakers were so pleased with the financial arrangement that a five-year renewal was inked in November of 1940.[64] Indiana University also agreed to play Michigan State with a similar–although far less generous–contract beginning in the fall of 1939. The Hoosiers must have been as desperate as the Spartans; the announcement was made three months before the start of the season.[65]

---

[57] Young to Shaw. 19 June 1929. Michigan State University Archives. Board of Trustees Records, UA1.0; Box 1880, folder: 27 6/20/1929

[58] Wilson to Young. 15 June 1929. Michigan State University Archives. Board of Trustees Records, UA1.0; Box 1880, folder: 27 6/20/1929

[59] Stewart to Shaw. 11 June 1929. Michigan State University Archives. Board of Trustees Records, UA1.0; Box 1880, folder: 27 6/20/29

[60] Young to Shaw. 16 July 1929. Michigan State University Archives. Board of Trustees Records, UA1.0; Box 1880, folder: 28 7/29/29

[61] Young to Shaw. 16 February 1933. Michigan State University Archives. Board of Trustees Records, UA1.0; Box 1881, folder: 38 2/16/33

[62] Stewart to Shaw. 11 June 1929. Michigan State University Archives. Board of Trustees Records, UA1.0; Box 1880, folder: 27 6/20/29

[63] Bachman, Charles. "The Athletic Side of John A. Hannah," Circa 1970. Michigan State University Archives. Hannah Archives Project, UA2.1.12.1; Box 34, folder: 2 Bachman

[64] Minutes of the State Board of Agriculture. 22 November 1940. www.onthebanks.msu.edu

[65] Minutes of the State Board of Agriculture. 1 June 1939. www.onthebanks.msu.edu

With the obligatory Wolverine contest in Ann Arbor, the director could now claim three Western Conference schools on his 1939 and 1940 schedules. The de facto Aigler Boycott had finally been broken through his persistent efforts. But Purdue and Indiana were not of the caliber of Illinois and Notre Dame. There was no assurance that either tier-two school would fill the 29,000 seats at Macklin Field.

The decline in confidence in Ralph Young's leadership probably began in December of 1942. At that time he was involved in a scheduling debate with Fritz Crisler. Failing to sway the Michigan director's stance regarding later dates and future home-and-home series with the Spartans, President John Hannah decided to intervene for Ralph Young in the negotiations. The University of Michigan's intransigence was compromising Hannah's long-term plans.[66][67]

Young was an affable, well-liked gentleman. He took pride in maintaining a good working relationship with Fritz Crisler. That desire to accommodate the Wolverine administrator may have contributed to his loss in stature at Michigan State. Young failed to push the Spartan agenda as aggressively as his president desired. He had valid reasons, however. As athletic director he was charged with balancing the budget. The Michigan game, played annually in Ann Arbor, was critical to the financial viability of the Spartan sports program. In the midst of this contentious debate now involving President Hannah, Ralph Young confided to Crisler that his personal preference remained holding the contest in Ann Arbor. He also had no problem with competing the first weekend of the season. The scrimmage game with Michigan suited him just fine.[68]

That confidential nod to Fritz Crisler was all that the Wolverine needed to stave off a relentless John Hannah. It is doubtful that the president ever learned of Ralph Young's comments to his colleague in Ann Arbor. But the fact that his athletic director had failed to assume a strong posture in contract negotiations in 1942 (and also in 1948 while the Spartan Athletic Council was aggressively challenging Crisler's dominance in scheduling matters) may have convinced Hannah that Young was no longer the right man for the job.

John Hannah's sudden involvement in matters reserved for an athletic director proved an epochal moment in athletic policy formation and operations at Michigan State. Most college presidents, including all within the Western Conference, typically deferred such matters to their faculty representatives and directors. From late December 1942 onward, however, it was apparent that at Michigan State Hannah was going to lead. He could not afford to let Ralph Young, as an employed manager, impede the transformation of the college into a major center of academic excellence and research.

Perhaps the most significant event in Spartan athletic history took place in early June of 1946 when John Hannah wrote to coach Frank Leahy of his interest in a long-term contract with Notre Dame.[69] Acknowledging Hannah's friendship with the Irish coach

---

[66] Young to Crisler. 2 December 1942. Bentley Historical Library, University of Michigan. Herbert Orin Crisler Papers, 85823 AC UAm Aa 2; Box 1, folder: topical correspondence MSU 1943-46

[67] Crisler to Ruthven. 13 January 1942. . Bentley Historical Library, University of Michigan. Alexander G. Ruthven Papers. 86550 Ac Aa 2; Box 34, folder: 27 "Physical Education (BIC)"

[68] Michigan State Football Date. Circa February 1949. Bentley Historical Library, University of Michigan. Herbert Orin Crisler Papers, 85823 AC UAm Aa 2; Box 1, folder: topical correspondence, MSU 1947-49

[69] Hannah to Leahy. 3 June 1946. Michigan State University Archives. John A. Hannah Papers, UA2.1.12; Box 61, folder: 56

dating back to 1932, it required only one letter from the president to accomplish what had evaded the Spartan athletic director since January of 1934.[70]

During the same time that Young was losing favor as a leader in East Lansing, Fritz Crisler was gaining a reputation as a very active manager in Ann Arbor. Alexander Ruthven remained on the sidelines. The president of the University of Michigan was placed in the game only once, in late January of 1943. At issue was how Crisler should respond to a letter he suspected was composed by John Hannah on Ralph Young's behalf. The director felt that the request for Michigan to sponsor a college application for admission into the conference involved institutional–not athletic–policy. Coach Crisler needed Ruthven's wisdom for that one special play against the Spartans. The president pulled it off just as the coach intended!

For 26 straight years Ralph Aigler had been re-elected chairman of the Board in Control of Physical Athletics. In February of 1942, due to by-laws revisions approved by the regents, Crisler's official title became "Director of Physical Education and Athletics." By virtue of his office he would assume chairmanship of what was now designated the Board in Control of Intercollegiate Athletics.[71] The regent's and Ruthven's action confirmed their confidence in the man chosen by Ralph Aigler to one day run the department.

Herbert Crisler was a respected manager. He made critical decisions in concert with the counsel of his board. At the March 15, 1948, meeting it was his recommendation alone that Bennie Oosterbaan be appointed the next head football coach. The proposal was approved by the board and later, as a formality, by the regents.[72] Unlike Ralph Young, Crisler was in complete control of his department at the University of Michigan.

FOLLOWING THE embarrassing loss to the University of Michigan on November 9, 1946, President Hannah probably decided it was the right time for a coaching change.[73] He and fellow administrators arrived at three names: Clarence "Biggie" Munn, Charles "Bud" Wilkinson, and Wesley Fesler.[74] With Charlie Bachman's resignation on December 6,[75] all was in place for John Hannah to take charge.

Over the course of the following week, the president was in total control of the interviewing process for the next head coach of Michigan State College.[76] Biggie Munn was his first choice;[77] Hannah had personally made the phone call inviting him to the Statler Hotel in Detroit. The two met in private for an extended period of time. Hannah then invited

---

[70] Minutes of the State Board of Agriculture. 18 January 1934. www.onthebanks.msu.edu

[71] Minutes of the Meeting of the Board in Control of Physical Education. 28 February 1942. Bentley Historical Library, University of Michigan. Board in Control of Intercollegiate Athletics, 8729 Bimu F81 2; Box 49, folder: Board in Control minutes Feb 1938-June 1950

[72] Minutes of the Meeting of the Board in Control of Physical Education. 15 March 1948. Bentley Historical Library, University of Michigan. Board in Control of Intercollegiate Athletics, 8729 Bimu F81 2; Box 49, folder: Board in Control minutes Feb 1938-June 1950

[73] Thomas, David. *Michigan State College: John Hannah and the Creation of a World University, 1926-1969.* East Lansing: Michigan State University Press, 2008. pp. 275-277

[74] Hannah, John A. *A Memoir.* East Lansing: Michigan State University Press, 1980. p. 115

[75] Thomas, David. *Michigan State College: John Hannah and the Creation of a World University, 1926-1969.* East Lansing: Michigan State University Press, 2008. p. 276

[76] Hannah, John A. *A Memoir.* East Lansing: Michigan State University Press, 1980. p. 115

[77] Thomas, David. *Michigan State College: John Hannah and the Creation of a World University, 1926-1969.* East Lansing: Michigan State University Press, 2008. p. 277

the ad hoc committee of the State Board, waiting outside the room, to join in the discussions. That same day Munn was offered the job.[78] At the December 16 board meeting, the president announced that the current Syracuse head coach had accepted the position in East Lansing.[79]

After hiring Biggie Munn, Hannah provided the new coach with the tools necessary to build a program capable of competing with Michigan. One tool he failed to provide him, however, was an occasional home-field advantage in the series with the Wolverines. After the 1924 College Field dedication-game, the Spartans traveled to Ann Arbor for the next 23 years. Hannah wanted an end to this scheduling dominance. In the fall of 1948, with his president's encouragement, Ralph Young got involved in another debate with Fritz Crisler regarding contractual fairness. He was unsuccessful in persuading the Wolverine to change the university's position on the matter.[80]

Quite suddenly the affable director was replaced, and Professor Lloyd Emmons was assigned the task of confronting the recalcitrant director from Ann Arbor. Emmons appeared to be the tough negotiator that Hannah wanted–someone who would not accept anything short of a home game in East Lansing in the near future.[81] [82] Emmons ultimately prevailed despite a defiant stance by the Board in Control of Intercollegiate Athletics.[83] Michigan finally agreed to visit the Red Cedar campus in 1953.[84] [85]

John Hannah was undoubtedly pleased with at least gaining the one home date. For Ralph Young, however, the writing had been on the wall. He had six years left as an apparent lame duck administrator before his retirement in 1954.

In an interview many years later, George Alderton, the *Lansing State Journal* sportswriter who promoted "Spartans" as the new moniker for the college in 1925, acknowledged that both Hannah and Biggie Munn held little regard for Ralph Young.

> I recall sitting in the baseball dugout next to Dr. Hannah, just the two of us, talking about Michigan State sports. We both looked up and spotted Ralph Young strolling across the field toward us. Analyzing the likelihood that Young would be joining us, the president turned to me and described his athletic director in a very unsavory way. I was shocked. It was so unlike

[78] Hannah, John A. *A Memoir*. East Lansing: Michigan State University Press, 1980. pp. 115-116

[79] Minutes of the State Board of Agriculture. 16 December 1946. www.onthebanks.msu.edu

[80] Minutes of the Meeting of the Board in Control of Physical Education. 15 November 1946. Bentley Historical Library, University of Michigan. Board in Control of Intercollegiate Athletics, 8729 Bimu F81 2; Box 49, folder: Board in Control minutes Feb 1938-June 1950

[81] Emmons to Crisler. 9 August 1948. Bentley Historical Library, University of Michigan. Ralph W. Aigler Papers, 87406 Aa 2; Box 9, folder: correspondence "C" 1946-52

[82] Emmons to Crisler. 25 January 1949. Bentley Historical Library, University of Michigan. Herbert Orin Crisler Papers, 85823 AC UAm Aa 2; Box 1, folder: topical correspondence MSU 1947-49

[83] Minutes of the Meeting of the Board in Control of Intercollegiate Athletics. 8 December 1948. Bentley Historical Library, University of Michigan. Board in Control of Intercollegiate Athletics, 8729 Bimu F81 2; Box 49, folder: Board in Control minutes Feb 1938-June 1950

[84] Crisler to Emmons. 28 September 1948. Bentley Historical Library, University of Michigan. Ralph W. Aigler Papers, 87406 Aa 2; Box 9, folder: correspondence "C" 1946-52

[85] McDonel to Emmons. 19 November 1948. Bentley Historical Library, University of Michigan. Ralph W. Aigler Papers, 87406 Aa 2; Box 9, folder: correspondence "C" 1946-52

John Hannah, but it was obvious he had little respect for Mr. Young.[86]

Hannah family members recalled their father as being much more diplomatic in commenting on others. They pointed out that "dad respected his athletic director but did not consider him a close associate."[87]

DURING HIS 30-year tenure as athletic director of Michigan State, Ralph Young maintained a seat on the Spartan Athletic Council. In theory the faculty and members of the council formed the college's athletic policies, and the director implemented them. Professor Lloyd Emmons, as faculty representative, sat on the council from 1948 through the early part of 1953.

A Hannah loyalist, Emmons served in various capacities at the college with distinction over a long career. And now, while maintaining a position on the Athletic Council as faculty representative, John Hannah had a trusted colleague in place to oversee all athletic practices. He could count on the Dean of Liberal Arts to keep him well informed.

Lacking any significant role in management during the waning years of his career, Young became derelict in certain duties.[88] [89] Both Fritz Crisler, in 1949, and Tug Wilson, four years later, would make comments about his inadequacies in running the athletic department. The lack of credible daily leadership since 1943 would culminate in a yearlong investigation into the Spartan athletic program in 1952. By February of 1953, the inaugural year of football competition in the Intercollegiate Conference of Faculty Representatives, President Hannah and Michigan State would be humiliated when the college was placed on probation for booster activities. It was not the way John Alfred Hannah had planned to celebrate the historic season.

While serving in the Eisenhower administration during an 18-month sabbatical that began in January of that year, President Hannah charged current faculty representative Dean Edgar Harden with investigating the root cause of the embarrassing probation. In March of 1954, Harden shared with his boss a discussion he recently had with the commissioner. The announcement of Ralph Young's retirement and Biggie Munn's promotion was less than six weeks old.

> My more immediate reason for writing you this letter is to inform you as to
> the feelings that Tug [Wilson] has concerning the makeup of our Athletic
> Council ... Now that we have a change in the Director of Athletics it seems
> appropriate that other changes might also be made ... It is my judgment
> that a great deal more responsibility has to be placed upon the Athletic
> Director, and that the Council should be only concerned in the broad
> policies which are developed and should have no more administrative

---

[86] Siebold, Jack. *Spartan Sports Encyclopedia: A History of the Michigan State Men's Athletic Program.* Canada: Sports Publishing, L.L.C., 2003. p. 717

[87] Mary Hannah-Curzan and Thomas Hannah. 7 August 2010. Personal communication. The comments were made in an interview with the Hannah's at Good Hart, Michigan.

[88] Crisler to Little. 30 March 1949. Bentley Historical Library, University of Michigan. Herbert Orin Crisler Papers,1922-1978; AC UAm Aa 2, Box 1, folder: topical correspondence MSU 1947-49

[89] Wilson to Aigler. 11 March 1953. Bentley Historical Library, University of Michigan. Ralph W. Aigler Papers, 87406 Aa 2; Box 10, folder: correspondence 1946-52 Wilson, K.L. 1952

responsibilities whatsoever.[90]

Implicit in Harden's comments was his belief that the athletic department lacked credible leadership.

It was unfortunate that during his early years guiding Michigan State, John Hannah had not confronted the long-serving athletic director about his job performance and management style; instead he chose to personally take charge of the department. His failure to either mentor or terminate a loyal Spartan, in hindsight, may have been the root cause of the probation of 1953.

FOLLOWING THEIR shared letters of March 1946, John Hannah had quickly forged a close friendship with President Lew Morrill of the University of Minnesota. Morrill was sincerely interested in helping his friend succeed in transforming the college. Despite Hannah's acceptance of Plan B by late summer of 1946, the head Golden Gopher with Buckeye blood had not yet given up on Plan A. He loved challenges; this one intrigued him if for no other reason than the University of Michigan was involved.

On December 10, 1946, Morrill wrote to Henry Rottschaefer expressing an interest in attending the annual conference joint meeting of faculty and directors taking place in three days at the University Club in Chicago. Morrill probably wanted to do some good old-fashioned politicking for Michigan State.[91] Unfortunately, the following day he discovered that his last-minute flight out of Minneapolis would not arrive in time for him to attend the Friday-evening dinner meeting. Morrill wrote a quick note to Rottschaefer asking if "it would not be an intrusion for me to sit in on the luncheon of the Faculty Representatives and the Commissioner, Saturday noon, at the University Club in Chicago … I don't want to be where I'm not supposed to be!"[92]

But Professor Rottschaefer failed to take notice of Morrill follow-up letter until December 20, when he was sifting through his campus mail. The annual Chicago meeting was long since over. As a consequence of the miscommunication, the president never made his pitch before the ruling body critical to admitting an institution into the conference.[93]

With President Morrill failing to meet with the faculty representatives to argue his case for John Hannah, the year ended with Plan B still the apparent future course for Michigan State athletics. However, Morrill, a powerful personality in the John Hannah mold, was not quite ready to acquiesce. He would soon recommend to the college president a novel strategy certain to gain membership. Plan A was still viable. But first Morrill had to deliver a major address to NCAA delegates in early January of 1947 regarding his solution to the decaying status of intercollegiate amateur athletics in the aftermath of the Second Great War. Once done with that project, he would go to bat for Michigan State College.

---

[90] Harden to Hannah. 4 March 1954. Michigan State University Archives. John Hannah Papers, UA2.1.12; Box 69, folder: 38

[91] Morrill to Rottschaefer. 10 December 1946. University of Minnesota Archives, President's Office; Box 238, folder: Physical Education and Athletics 1945-47

[92] Morrill to Rottschaefer. 11 December 1946. University of Minnesota Archives, President's Office; Box 238, folder: Physical Education and Athletics 1945-47

[93] Rottschaefer to Morrill. 20 December 1946. University of Minnesota Archives, President's Office; Box 238, folder: Physical Education and Athletics 1945-47

The Hannah-Morrill Alliance

JAMES LEWIS Morrill and John Alfred Hannah probably developed a professional relationship prior to the Buckeye relocating to Minneapolis in 1945. Both were quite active in the American Association of Land Grant Colleges and State Universities during the early 1940s. A few years later, Morrill would assume the presidency of the organization (1947-48). While serving in that role, the Minnesotan often turned to his colleague for assistance in carrying out "important committee chairmanships...." He "admired [Hannah's] philosophy and greatly respect[ed] his administrative leadership."[1] The feeling was mutual. They soon became close friends.

In August of 1948, the two discovered another common interest–northern Michigan. President Morrill owned a cottage on Otsego Lake, about an hour from the Hannah summer residence on the shores of Lake Michigan near Good Hart.[2][3] During the next 12 years they would make it an annual ritual to get together sometime in July and have some "… [good] old-fashioned chat sessions" at Hannah's cabin while enjoying sunsets over the great lake.[4]

The Morrill residence first appeared on Hannah's "blueberries and maple syrup" list in April of 1946.[5] The traditional gifting would continue throughout John Hannah's tenure in East Lansing. Lew Morrill struggled every year with how to reciprocate.[6] That first year he sent his friend a can of blue cheese produced at the research dairy science facility on the

---

[1] Morrill to Rottschaefer. 16 September 1948. The University of Minnesota Archives, President's Office; Box 238, folder: Physical Education and Athletics 1948-49

[2] Hannah to Morrill. 2 September 1948. University of Minnesota Archives, Morrill, J.L.; Box 1, folder: correspondence HA-HE

[3] Morrill to Hannah. 24 April 1947. University of Minnesota Archives, Morrill, J.L.; Box 1, folder: correspondence HA-HE

[4] Hannah to Morrill. 12 July 1957. University of Minnesota Archives, Morrill J. L. ; Box 1, folder: correspondence A-C, HA-HE

[5] Morrill to Hannah. 15 April 1946. University of Minnesota Archives, Morrill J. L. ; Box 1, folder: correspondence A-C, HA-HE

[6] Morrill to Hannah. 10 April 1950. University of Minnesota Archives, Morrill, J.L.; Box 1, folder: correspondence HA-HE

St. Paul campus.[7] But as Hannah soon realized, his seasonal gifts paled in comparison to what the University of Minnesota president would provide him in December of 1948.

PRESIDENT MORRILL, in early January of 1947, delivered the keynote address at the annual NCAA convention held in New York. His message was simple. It was time to clean up intercollegiate athletics. Athletic recruiting and financial aid had gotten out of control in the aftermath of the Second Great War. His solution involved the faculty representatives. Morrill felt it was critical that these leaders regain control of campus athletic programs. "Only the regular faculty, which carries the long-range burden of institutional policy and integrity and whose tenure is superior to passing passions, enjoys the great gift of freedom from fear and foolishness … it is time they take a hand in this crisis … "[8] He then referenced John Hannah's "brass-tacks" talk in St. Louis one year earlier.[9] "Like the football coach, the president is responsible to too many people–people … who have only a one-sided and seasonal interest in the university and who, for the most part, actually have no legal responsibility for any control of the university whatsoever."[10] The president's role, as chief executive, was merely to support his faculty leadership in assuring compliance with the amateur code.

Morrill shared the same passion for amateurism as Ralph Aigler and Fritz Crisler. Like these two Michigan leaders, he argued that the answer to the postwar demise of amateurism was having all "constituent members [of the NCAA] stand up and be counted on the issue of honest adherence to its constitution." He encouraged those who could not adhere to "decently withdraw, and be barred thereby from participation in the various so-called championship games and meets conducted by the Association." He emphasized his point with some colorful language. "In all sincerity I think that steps should be taken … to separate the sheep from the goats, to corral the men from the mice, to cull the college-minded from those who don't mind having their teams considered 'ball clubs,' in the professional vernacular of the sports pages." The NCAA, in his opinion, must set up "some means and machinery for the enforcement of its standards, possibly through inspection or accreditation, like that required by the best professional associations in the academic world or the regional collegiate and secondary school associations."[11]

Morrill's speech was intended to lay the groundwork for the Sanity Code of January 1948. The legislation, defining acceptable financial aid for athletes and penalties for institutions violating the new rules, was drafted, in part, by some influential leaders of the Big Nine including Karl Leib, Ralph Aigler, Ken Wilson, and Fritz Crisler.

By late August, however, the Minnesota leader's faith in most of the academicians

---

[7] Morrill to Hannah. 15 April 1946. University of Minnesota Archives, Morrill, J.L.; Box 1, folder: correspondence HA-HE

[8] Morrill, J.L. "Text of Address Nat'l Collegiate Athletic Ass'n." 7 January 1947. University of Minnesota Archives, Department of Intercollegiate Athletics Papers; Box 6, folder: J. L. Morrill – President

[9] Ibid.

[10] Ibid.

[11] Ibid.

within his conference charged with that responsibility would be greatly shaken.[12] [13] He was convinced, in reading faculty committee minutes provided him by his representative from a May gathering, that the leadership was soon to approve "athletic scholarships."[14] It was a major misunderstanding on his part–the debate pertained to "academic scholarships" for athletes meeting rigid scholastic requirements.[15] The implications of Morrill's misreading of those minutes would profoundly impact John Hannah's quest for membership in the Intercollegiate Conference of Faculty Representatives.

One week following Lew Morrill's presentation in New York, President Hannah announced plans to expand his Jenison program to help newly appointed Coach Biggie Munn in his recruiting efforts.[16] President Morrill was adamantly opposed to all athletic subsidies. He even disapproved of academic scholarships, as ultimately defined by the Sanity Code, for athletes with proven scholastic acumen.[17] [18] Yet Morrill fully appreciated his friend's convictions on assisting athletes based on his concept of justice and fairness.[19] Those views were clearly spelled out in Hannah's keynote NCAA address one year earlier.[20] It is unknown how Ralph Aigler reacted to the news. But based on his past practices, dating back to at least 1935, he probably shared it with a few of his close colleagues in athletic leadership about the conference. It was unlikely that Professor Henry Rottschaefer, Lew Morrill's faculty representative at Minnesota, was a member of that group.

HENRY RATTSCHAFFER was born on September 10, 1889, in the Netherlands. Four years later, the Rattschaffers–William, Gertie, and their children–immigrated to Holland, Michigan. Shortly afterwards, William changed the spelling of his family name to Rottschaefer to be phonetically accurate.[21] After graduating from the public school system, Henry attended Hope College, a small Christian liberal arts institution located just blocks away from the family residence on West 14th Street. Following graduation in 1909, with degrees in mathematics and philosophy, he served briefly as a high school principal and teacher. After two years, he decided to move to Ann Arbor to study jurisprudence at the University of Michigan. To finance his education, he taught undergraduate economics at the

---

[12] Morrill to Nunn. 27 August 1947. University of Minnesota Archives, President's Office; Box 238, folder: Physical Education and Athletics 1945-47

[13] Morrill to Rottschaefer. 16 September 1947. University of Minnesota Archives, President's Office; Box 238, folder: Physical Education and Athletics 1945-47

[14] Ibid.

[15] Rottschaefer to Morrill. 3 September 1947. University of Minnesota Archives, President's Office; Box 238, folder: Physical Education and Athletics 1945-47

[16] Minutes of the State Board of Agriculture. 16 January 1947. www.onthebanks.msu.edu

[17] Rottschaefer to Morrill. 3 September 1947. University of Minnesota Archives, President's Office; Box 238, folder: Physical Education and Athletics 1945-47

[18] Morrill to Rottschaefer. 16 September 1947. University of Minnesota Archives, President's Office; Box 238, folder: Physical Education and Athletics 1945-47

[19] Ibid.

[20] Hannah, John A. "Speech of Doctor John A. Hannah at the Fortieth Annual Convention of the National Collegiate Athletic Association." 9 January 1946. Bentley Historical Library, University of Michigan. Herbert Orin Crisler Papers, AC UAm Aa2; Box 1, folder: topical correspondence Michigan State University, clippings and misc.

[21] "Twelfth Census of the United States." AncestoryLibrary.com. 8 June 1900. <http://search.ancestorylibrary.com/cgi-bin/sse.dll?rank=1&gsfn=henry+&gsln_rottschaefer...>

school. Rottschaefer graduated in 1915 with a degree in jurisprudence. Harvard was his next stop. In 1916 he earned a doctorate (S.J.D.) while focusing on tax law.[22]

After a brief stint serving in World War I, Rottschaefer returned to New York City to take a position with a large firm. His career in private law ended in 1922, when he accepted a position at the University of Minnesota law school. Twelve years later, following the retirement of long-serving faculty representative and fellow law school associate James Paige, Rottschaefer–a football and basketball player at Hope College in his earlier years[23]– was asked by his fellow faculty to assume the role in the spring of 1934. He represented Minnesota in the Intercollegiate Conference for the next 23 years.

In May of 1937, Henry Rottschaefer voted against a Michigan State College application for admission into the Big Ten. Despite being a native of Michigan, Rottschaefer had been away from the state for years. He probably lacked knowledge of the recruiting and subsidizing practices during the "Sleepy Jim" Crowley tenure at the college. But the Minnesotan and his eight colleagues were undoubtedly aware of Ralph Aigler's opinion about suspect activities still taking place in East Lansing. Aigler's disdain for the college's athletic leadership, and its lack of commitment to conference Handbook policies, was well known among faculty associates and the commissioner.[24] [25] [26] The question remained, however, whether the strong-willed Rottschaefer could have been influenced by Aigler to cast a no vote at the time.

Rottschaefer had been a student of Aigler's at the University of Michigan law school.[27] During his early years on the Faculty Committee, the Minnesotan was probably influenced by his old professor's command of the group. His prominent role as president of the Association of American Law Schools, his reputation as a highly regarded and published academician, and his leadership in national amateur athletic policy were impressive credentials. But by the fall of 1936, any feeling of awe would give way to anger.

Minnesota President Lotus Coffman, back in 1933, had taken great pride in enacting the General College program, which would become his legacy as an educator.[28] Consistent with the land-grant philosophy of Justin Morrill, it was to serve the utilitarian needs of certain youth seeking a basic education lasting no more than two years. The focus was on gaining marketable skills for students lacking an interest or ability in rigorous

---

[22] "Rottschaefer to Retire." April 1957. University of Minnesota Archives, Rottschaefer; Box: Bio, folder: 4/57 law school news

[23] Brewer, Gordon M. *"But How You Played the Game!" – A History of Intercollegiate Athletics at Hope College 1862-1955.* Holland: Hope College Publishing, 1992. pp. 32, 34

[24] Aigler to Long. 7 October 1935. Bentley Historical Library, University of Michigan. Ralph W. Aigler Papers, 87406 Aa 2; Box 12, folder: correspondence 1933-36 "L" misc

[25] Aigler to Griffith. 1 October 1935. Bentley Historical Library, University of Michigan. Ralph W. Aigler Papers, 87406 Aa 2; Box 6, folder: correspondence 1934-39, Griffith 4/34-1/36

[26] Aigler to Griffith. 4 October 1935. Bentley Historical Library, University of Michigan. Ralph W. Aigler Papers, 87406 Aa 2; Box 6, folder: correspondence 1934-39, Griffith 4/34-1/36

[27] Minutes of the Intercollegiate Conference of Faculty Representatives. 4-6 December 1952. Bentley Historical Library. University of Michigan, Ralph W. Aigler Papers, 87406 Aa 2; Box 14, folder: athletics 1952, meeting minutes

[28] Coffman, Lotus D. "Coffman Welcomes Inquiry." *Minneapolis Daily.* 18 February 1936. University of Minnesota Archives, President's Office; Box 4, folder: 120

scholarly study.[29] A student could transfer from the college into the university, following completion of the less-challenging academic program, if "their work [was] satisfactory and they later [decided] to work for a degree."[30]

Despite the admirable features of the Coffman model, Ralph Aigler was suspicious from the beginning. He foresaw the program as a means to enroll academically subpar, yet gifted, athletes into the university system. Aigler informed Commissioner Griffith of his concerns.[31] The two then approached Thomas French of Ohio State, chairman of the Faculty Representatives Committee. In February of 1936, in a somewhat surprising decision, French appointed Aigler to investigate the program. It was an audacious move on the Buckeye's part. Who would suspect that the man filing the grievance was also the one investigating it? French was convinced that the Minneapolis press and university officials would never implicate the law professor under such arrangements.[32]

Because only the commissioner was privy to the grievance and French's plan, leaks would be minimized. The Michigan professor would summarize the results of his investigation to the Eligibility Committee following his visit to Minneapolis.[33]

Professor Aigler, out of courtesy to Coffman, reported his findings to the highly regarded academician in a series of letters over the early spring of 1936. The law professor was "shocked" by the minimal eligibility standards at the University of Minnesota. He was disturbed by the poor graduation rate for athletes attending the school. And in a move to also protect his cover, Aigler informed Coffman, "I am sure you can understand why it is that some members of the Conference have [raised] some questions with reference to Minnesota [practices]." The ploy was unsuccessful. The Minneapolis press, early on, implicated him as the source of the grievance.[34] Years later, Aigler would still maintain his cover while recalling the 1936 General College story with a fellow faculty representative.[35]

Despite being unwelcome in the Twin Cities, the legal scholar continued his investigation. He discovered that almost 50 percent of athletes unaffiliated with the General College majored in physical education. The evangelist of pristine amateurism felt "college teams should be truly representative of the undergraduate student bodies."[36] In Minnesota's case, "taking [physical education], the professional course in athletics," was not consistent with what most serious students studied at the university.[37] And what really troubled

---

[29] Cullum, Dick. "Big Ten Questions Eligibility of Gopher Stars." *Minneapolis Journal*. 16 February 1936. University of Minnesota Archives, President's Office; Box 5, folder: 120

[30] Ibid.

[31] Griffith to McCormick. 7 October 1936. Bentley Historical Library, University of Michigan. Ralph W. Aigler Papers, 87406 Aa 2; Box 6, folder: correspondence 1934-39

[32] Griffith to Aigler. 22 October 1936. Bentley Historical Library, University of Michigan. Ralph W. Aigler Papers, 87406 Aa 2; Box 6, folder: correspondence 1934-39

[33] Cullum, Dick. "Big Ten Questions Eligibility of Gopher Stars." *Minneapolis Daily*. 2 February 1936. University of Minnesota Archives, President's Office; Box 5, folder: 120

[34] Ibid.

[35] Aigler to Richart. 22 May 1947. University of Illinois Archives. Series: 4/2/12; Box 3, folder: Western Intercollegiate Conference 1946-47

[36] Aigler to Griffith. 23 October 1936. Bentley Historical Library, University of Michigan. Ralph W. Aigler Papers, 87406 Aa 2; Box 6, folder: correspondence 1934-39 Griffith 1/36-1/37

[37] Aigler to Griffith. 23 October 1936. Bentley Historical Library, University of Michigan. Ralph W. Aigler Papers, 87406 Aa 2; Box 6, folder: correspondence 1934-39 Griffith 1/36-1/37

Professor Aigler was that "with only two or three exceptions, every one…considered [in] their starting line-up is in Physical Education."[38]

Part of the problem with Ralph Aigler's confidential reporting to Coffman might have been how he presented his findings. His choice of words appeared to impugn the integrity of the president and the school. The law professor discovered that few football players graduate. He subtly chastised Coffman for that finding. He compared Minnesota's overall admission standards for athletes with those of the University of Michigan and found them unacceptable. Aigler was also troubled by the grading system applied to those athletes.[39] [40] The allowances in Minneapolis were inexcusable, in his opinion, for an institution of Minnesota's repute. Coffman, however, was confident that following a formal investigation, Aigler's "surmises [about graduation rates] will all be just surmises and that my doubts will vanish into thin air when the report is completed." He was also certain that the Michigan professor's comments about grading were in error.[41]

In the meantime, Ralph Aigler had discovered that other schools maintained questionable eligibility standards as well. "…We [at Michigan] have unduly handicapped our own teams in insisting upon a grade of scholarship that is not demanded at the institutions with which we compete."[42] On April 7, Dean Alvin Eurich reported back to Coffman some very disturbing trends. Hee substantiated Aigler's findings.[43] Ten days later the president of the University of Minnesota essentially pleaded guilty as charged.[44] [45]

Professor Aigler's investigation had merit after all. As a respected scholar in the field of education, Coffman was humiliated by the football staff manipulating his model for the benefit of the gridiron program.[46] A full report of the law professor's findings was provided to the collective Faculty Representatives Committee in October of 1936. But in the meantime, both Aigler and Coffman discovered that double-standards for athletes

---

[38] Aigler to Griffith. 23 October 1936. Bentley Historical Library, University of Michigan. Ralph W. Aigler Papers, 87406 Aa 2; Box 6, folder: correspondence 1934-39 Griffith 1/36-1/37

[39] Aigler to Coffman. 30 March 1936. University of Minnesota Archives, President's Office; Box 5, folder: 120

[40] Aigler to Coffman. 10 April 1936. University of Minnesota Archives, President's Office; Box 5, folder: 120

[41] Coffman to Aigler. 6 April 1936. University of Minnesota Archives, President's Office; Box 5, folder: 120

[42] Aigler to Coffman. 14 April 1936. University of Minnesota Archives, President's Office; Box 5, folder: 120

[43] Eurich to Coffman. 7 April 1936. University of Minnesota Archives, President's Office; Box 5, folder: 120

[44] Aigler to Coffman. 14 April 1936. University of Minnesota Archives, President's Office; Box 5, folder: 120

[45] Coffman to Aigler. 17 April 1936. University of Minnesota Archives, President's Office; Box 5, folder: 120

[46] Aigler to Griffith. 18 October 1936. Bentley Historical Library, University of Michigan. Ralph W. Aigler Papers, 87406 Aa 2; Box 6, folder: correspondence 1934-39 Griffith 1/36-1/37

existed at other conference schools as well.[47] [48] [49] At issue was whether to discipline the Golden Gophers, especially when so many others in the Big Ten were equally culpable.[50]

From 1933 through 1938 the University of Minnesota was one of the premier football programs in the country. Under Coach Bernie Bierman the Golden Gophers won 39 games, lost five, and tied four. In those six seasons the school claimed five Big Ten mythical titles. The 1934-35 teams were undefeated. They were crowned the mythical national champion in each season.

Coinciding with football success in Minneapolis was the discovery by Aigler and his Board in Control of serious violations of Handbook rules in Ann Arbor under Harry Kipke's oversight. With "the deliberate flaunting of Conference rules and ideals by Minnesota … " in pursuit of victories, it was understandable why the professor was obsessed with illicit eligibility practices in Minneapolis.[51]

The conference leaders decided to declare ineligible a few stellar Minnesota athletes. Perhaps of greater political significance, however, was the damage to Ralph Aigler's reputation among Minnesota's athletic leadership.[52] Henry Rottschaefer was one of those leaders.[53] [54] [55] He was incensed over the treatment of the Minnesota student-athletes. And as Coffman's faculty representative, he was undoubtedly aware of the somewhat condescending tone behind the words in Aigler's letters.

The relationship between Aigler and Rottschaefer remained strained for years.[56] In early July of 1941 Commissioner Griffith wrote to the Michigan faculty representative requesting his opinion on a matter involving a transfer student to the University of Minnesota from DePaul. Aigler determined the football player ineligible based on conference rules. Mindful of Professor Rottschaefer's lingering feelings over the General College decision five years earlier, he was very cautious in his remarks to Griffith.

---

[47] Aigler to Griffith. 6 April 1936. Bentley Historical Library, University of Michigan. Ralph W. Aigler Papers, 87406 Aa 2; Box 6, folder: correspondence 1934-39 Griffith 1/36-1/37

[48] Coffman to Aigler. 17 April 1936. University of Minnesota Archives, President's Office; Box 5, folder: 120

[49] Aigler to Griffith. 28 July 1936. Bentley Historical Library, University of Michigan. Ralph W. Aigler Papers, 87406 Aa 2; Box 6, folder: correspondence 1934-39 Griffith 1/36-1/37

[50] Aigler to Griffith. 23 October 1936. Bentley Historical Library, University of Michigan. Ralph W. Aigler Papers, 87406 Aa 2; Box 6, folder: correspondence 1934-39 Griffith 1/36-1/37

[51] Aigler to Griffith. 18 October 1936. Bentley Historical Library, University of Michigan. Ralph W. Aigler Papers, 87406 Aa 2; Box 6, folder: correspondence 1934-39 Griffith 1/36-1/37

[52] Griffith to St. John. 11 September 1941. The Ohio State University Archives, Director of Athletics (RG 9/e-1/9), "Intercollegiate Conference: Commissioner: Correspondence (Griffith): 1941-1942 (Folder 2 of 2)."

[53] Ibid.

[54] Aigler to Richart. 24 October 1941. Bentley Historical Library, University of Michigan. Ralph W. Aigler Papers, 87406 Aa 2; Box 8, folder: correspondence 1940-45 Richart

[55] Richart to Aigler. 27 October 1941. Bentley Historical Library, University of Michigan. Ralph W. Aigler Papers, 87406 Aa 2; Box 8, folder: correspondence 1940-45 Richart

[56] Griffith to St. John. 11 September 1941. The Ohio State University Archives, Director of Athletics (RG 9/e-1/9), "Intercollegiate Conference: Commissioner: Correspondence (Griffith): 1941-1942 (Folder 2 of 2)."

> The question is one of no little importance and of considerable delicacy,
> and because of that I have written thus fully [a three page response] ... I
> wish, therefore, that you would keep this matter to yourself until we have
> the judgment of more than one member of the Eligibility Committee.[57]

Professor Frank Richart of Illinois, who also sat on the Eligibility Committee, arrived at a similar conclusion. Ralph Aigler corresponded with his colleague from Illinois about the DePaul transfer student question. His comments reflected how sensitive Rottschaefer remained regarding any matter challenging the integrity of the University of Minnesota and its athletic practices.

> I realize the delicacy of this situation [as well]. I realize that if we declare
> [this student] ineligible for the next year at least Rottschaefer will rear up
> on his hind legs and protest.[58]

By late September of that same year Aigler felt a need to write the Dutch Minnesotan about the "delicate" case. "It has come to my attention that you people at Minnesota were inclined to blame Michigan for stirring up the question of eligibility regarding the [boy] whose [case was] recently under examination."[59] Aigler wanted to set the record straight. The University of Michigan was not the perpetrator of charges against Minnesota.

But in a confidential letter from John Griffith to Lynn St. John of Ohio State, the commissioner revealed just the opposite. He also confirmed that Rottschaefer was still incensed over the treatment of the university back in 1936. The current case involving the DePaul student only added to his ire. The Minnesotan was convinced Aigler was behind both grievances. Griffith was so concerned about sharing the information involving the powerful Ralph Aigler that he requested that St. John shred the letter.[60] Needless to say, the Ohio State athletic director failed to honor that special request!

The two grievances regarding the University of Minnesota, one in 1936 and the other in 1941, illustrated the tense relationship that existed between the pre-eminent legal scholars. As a consequence, Ralph Aigler no longer held any influence over his former student. But in May of 1937, six months after closure on the General College affair, the Minnesota representative's decision to deny a Michigan State application for admission probably had little to do with evolving impressions of his professor. Henry Rottschaefer simply felt that there was no valid reason to expand to 11 members.[61] [62]

---

[57] Aigler to Griffith. 7 July 1941. Bentley Historical Library, University of Michigan. Ralph W. Aigler Papers, 87406 Aa 2; Box 8, folder: correspondence 1940-45 Griffith

[58] Aigler to Richart. 15 July 1941. Bentley Historical Library, University of Michigan. Ralph W. Aigler Papers, 87406 Aa 2; Box 8, folder: correspondence 1940-45 Griffith

[59] Aigler to Rottschaefer. 27 September 1941. Bentley Historical Library, University of Michigan. Ralph W. Aigler Papers, 87406 Aa 2; Box 8, folder: correspondence 1940-45 Rottschaefer

[60] Griffith to St. John. 11 September 1941. The Ohio State University Archives, Director of Athletics (RG 9/e-1/9), "Intercollegiate Conference: Commissioner: Correspondence (Griffith): 1941-1942 (Folder 2 of 2)."

[61] Rottschaefer to Aigler. 13 September 1944. Bentley Historical Library, University of Michigan. Ralph W. Aigler Papers, 87406 Aa 2; Box 8, folder: correspondence 1940-45 Rottschaefer

[62] Rottschaefer to Aigler. 3 August 1944. Bentley Historical Library, University of Michigan. Ralph W. Aigler Papers, 87406 Aa 2; Box 8, folder: correspondence 1940-45 Rottschaefer

And so, a decade after that vote, the January 1947 press release from East Lansing indicating John Hannah's intention to expand the Jenison Awards–illegal subsidies in the opinion of both Ralph Aigler and Henry Rottscaefer–was probably never revealed to the Minnesota faculty representative. Lacking a close relationship with his colleague from Minneapolis, Aigler had no reason to share gossip on so provincial a concern involving the University of Michigan.

IN HIS January 1946 address to the NCAA, John Hannah spoke of hypocrisy in intercollegiate athletics. He found it duplicitous for institutions to profess a conviction opposing subsidies while practicing otherwise.[63] The following year Lew Morrill delivered his address to the association in New York. President Hannah was in attendance. At some point during those sessions, the college leader approached his friend. He had some damning information he wanted to share with the Minnesotan regarding an athletic scholarship program evolving at Michigan. A few months later, after receiving a copy of the incriminating evidence from Hannah, Morrill shared it with his executive assistant, William Nunn, and his athletic director, Frank McCormick.[64]

Back in September of 1946 the University of Michigan's M Club president, C.L. Peaman, sent out a note to all varsity sport members imploring support for a scholarship drive. The letterhead included as vice presidents of the organization the assistant alumni secretary and the college hockey coach. Both were employees of the university. By implication Michigan was supporting a measure seemingly in violation of the Intercollegiate Conference Handbook rules on subsidies.[65]

The communiqué mentioned that Wolverine athletics were at a critical crossroads. There were only so many students that the school could accommodate each year. A certain percentage, in deference to taxpayers, had to be Michigan residents. With returning veterans, previously in attendance at Michigan, wanting to complete their degrees in Ann Arbor, there remained limited positions available for out-of-state applicants.[66]

In 1946, 75 percent of the football team was composed of players residing outside Michigan borders. This was not unusual for the school. The university traditionally gathered much of its talent from around the country. The challenge for the M Club was how to ensure the school continued to attract that football talent when nonresident spots for athletes were so few in the postwar era.[67]

By September of 1946, Michigan, in the guise of a few former varsity letter-winners, felt that it had to participate in some subsidizing program if it wished to remain competitive. Handicapped by limited enrollment for nonresident athletes, the football program needed assurance that those students choosing to attend the university were certain to aid the Wolverine cause. The school could not waste enrollment spots held by the

---

[63] Hannah, John A. "Speech of Doctor John A. Hannah at the Fortieth Annual Convention of the National Collegiate Athletic Conference." 9 January 1946. Bentley Historical Library, University of Michigan. Herbert Orin Crisler Papers, 85823 AC UAm Aa 2; Box 1, folder: topical correspondence Michigan State University clippings and misc.

[64] Morrill to McCormick. 4 March 1947. University of Minnesota Archives, Department of Intercollegiate Athletic Papers; Box 6, folder: Michigan "M" policy

[65] Ibid.

[66] Ibid.

[67] Ibid.

registrar for Fritz Crisler's program. With the bidding by coaches around the country becoming more and more intense for veteran talent returning to the states, the only solution, in the mindset of the M Club leadership, was money. Tradition alone was no longer sufficient to attract quality players to Ann Arbor. A plea for contributions to a scholarship fund to be maintained by club members was sent out. Dr. Peaman's note emphasized that the school would abide by a code of honor to ensure its integrity.

> The University has approved the idea. No man will be admitted whose
> scholarship is not of the proper grade. Because he is an athlete, he will not
> be admitted just for that reason only ... Many of the prospective athletes
> are now on the G.I. program and will not need subsistence. We are sure that
> the whole program will be handled in a very wholesome manner, and we
> will not be criticized in any way. You can see that this means much to the
> Michigan Athletic Program.[68]

Although the essence of the program was not contrary to how John Hannah viewed financial aid, he found it hypocritical coming from a university denigrating his transparent subsidy program. Michigan, under the leadership of Professor Aigler, had opposed most financial support in the past.

The Minnesota president penned a note on the copy of the Hannah evidence and sent it off to his athletic director McCormick.

> President Hannah of Michigan State thinks Michigan is off on a
> tremendous "athletic scholarship" recruiting program. He talked to me
> about it in N.Y.–and sent me this....[69]

In July, Chet Roan, of the Minnesota Athletic Department, typed a memo to Morrill's executive secretary, William Nunn, alerting him that "athletic scholarships are just around the corner in the Western Conference."[70] He described a proposal made at the May faculty representatives meeting allowing scholarships for certain intellectually gifted athletes. The programs at each school would be monitored by the commissioner's office utilizing a measure soon to be known as the Highland Park Yardstick. Violation of the tool might impose eligibility penalties on the student. The inherent financial repercussions and tarnished reputation would prove painful for an institutional offender. The concept was approved in principle; the final draft would be forthcoming later in the year.[71]

Roan noted that Michigan, Iowa, and Purdue already had plans in operation. Indiana, Northwestern, and Illinois were about to initiate funds to legally subsidize intellectually gifted athletes meeting yardstick requirements. Only Ohio State and Minnesota lacked a program.

---

[68] Morrill to McCormick. 4 March 1947. University of Minnesota Archives, Department of Intercollegiate Athletic Papers; Box 6, folder: Michigan "M" policy

[69] Ibid.

[70] Roan to Nunn. 29 July 1947. University of Minnesota Archives, Department of Intercollegiate Athletic Papers; Box 6, folder: J.L. Morrill President

[71] Minutes of the Intercollegiate Conference of Faculty Representatives. 29-31 May 1947. University of Minnesota Archives, President's Office, Physical Education and Athletics; Box 238, folder: Physical Education and Athletics 1945-47

The administrator feared that if the May proposal passed "we here at Minnesota are going to be caught with our pants down, so to speak." He mentioned President Morrill's keynote address of six months earlier placing the university in peril of public criticism if no definite stance opposing the scholarships was taken.

Roan concluded that " … in view of the actions of many of the universities in setting up scholarship funds already, we are fairly sure that [the faculty proposal] will receive favorable action unless the presidents step into the picture."[72]

Consistent with past practice, Henry Rottschaefer sent President Morrill the minutes from the May conference meeting held in Highland Park, Illinois. Morrill failed to read them. He was too busy with other pressing concerns at the time.[73] In late August a memo from secretary William Nunn regarding Roan's comments on athletic scholarships crossed his desk. Morrill was blindsided by the report. [74] [75] [76] [77]

The president immediately retrieved the minutes of the Highland Park meeting of May 31, 1947. Quickly scanning through Rottschaefer's copy, he came across the faculty proposal prompting Roan's memo to Nunn. Agenda item 17 pertained to a motion permitting incoming freshmen academic scholarships based on scholastic performance– something Morrill viewed as "starting down a path which will only [lead to athletic scholarships]."[78] And of perhaps equal concern, the president discovered that the author of that proposal was the national evangelist of pure amateurism–Ralph W. Aigler of the University of Michigan!

Morrill's confidence in the Faculty Representative Committee upholding the integrity of the game and its amateur code was probably stunned when he read item 17. It appeared his eloquent words, delivered seven months earlier, in support of faculty as the vanguard for institutional integrity had been for naught. On August 27 he wrote to Henry Rottschaefer and Frank McCormick that he could no longer idly sit by and watch the demise of the game he loved.

> My own attitude, of course, is well known, and was re-expressed as
> earnestly and forcefully as I could express it in the NCAA Convention in
> New York last January. I think the country and the Conference can
> reasonably expect some leadership from Minnesota in this situation.
> Certainly if it gets out of hand somehow, I should be strongly inclined to go

---

[72] Roan to Nunn. 29 July 1947. University of Minnesota Archives, Department of Intercollegiate Athletic Papers; Box 6, folder: J.L. Morrill President

[73] Morrill to McCormick and Rottschaefer. 27 August 1947. University of Minnesota Archives, President's Office; Box 238, folder: Physical Education and Athletics 1945-47

[74] Morrill to Nunn. 27 August. University of Minnesota Archives, President's Office; Box 238, folder. Physical Education 1945-47

[75] Nunn to Willey. 4 August 1947. University of Minnesota Archives, President's Office; Box 238, folder: Physical Education and Athletics 1945-47

[76] Willey to Morrill. 7 August 1947. University of Minnesota Archives, President's Office; Box 238, folder: Physical Education and Athletics 1945-47

[77] Morrill to McCormick and Rottschaefer. 27 August 1947. University of Minnesota Archives, President's Office; Box 238, folder: Physical Education and Athletics 1945-47

[78] Morrill to Rottschaefer. 16 September 1947. University of Minnesota Archives, President's Office; Box 238, folder: Physical Education and Athletics 1945-47

to bat directly with my fellow presidents of the Big Ten ... [79]

Morrill was even prepared to take on the most influential man in Western Conference politics, a man whose commitment to fundamental Handbook rules was now in question. He wrote Rottschaefer on September 16 expressing skepticism about Ralph Aigler's intentions.

> Professor Aigler's proposal looks dangerous to me. It seems to me a
> somewhat oblique approach toward the legitimizing of athletic scholarships
> ... Of course it can be construed as a means of protection against the abuse
> of regular scholarships in their too frequent and illegitimate award to
> athletes. Possibly this is what Aigler had in mind–but I doubt it.[80]

As it turns out, Morrill's assessment of the motion by the dean of faculty representatives was totally wrong. Aigler had only become realistic about the need to offer assistance to students with scholastic as well as athletic gifts. A young man qualifying for an academic scholarship should not be discriminated against for consistently punting a football 45 yards on Saturday afternoons during the fall.[81]

The transition in Aigler's philosophy on limited financial aid had begun in mid-January of 1939 when he, Fielding Yost, and Frtiz Crisler drove over to East Lansing to meet with Spartan faculty representative Ralph Huston, coach Charlie Bachman, and director Ralph Young. They planned to discuss, among other matters, Spartan violations of Western Conference regulations. Subsidies and lax eligibility requirements were Aigler's main concerns that day. Through discourse with Professor Huston, however, he realized that there might be legitimate forms of financial assistance after all.[82] Robert Shaw's concept of fairness did have merit under certain circumstances.

Professor Aigler's motion, in May of 1947, was in some ways a response to that enlightening encounter eight years earlier. But he was also proposing an academic scholarship policy for the conference consistent with the Sanity Code–financial aid rules certain to be approved in January of 1948 at the annual NCAA convention.

Regardless of Aigler's sincere intentions at the Highland Park meeting, Lew Morrill interpreted the motion regarding item 17 in a different context and from a different viewpoint. He had not been privy to the discussions among national leaders of the amateur movement–Ralph Aigler included–that went into crafting that cautiously worded Sanity legislation. All Morrill could conclude was that the law professor was not to be trusted. In the context of the M Club letter that John Hannah had given him in March, it was clear to Morrill that the integrity of Michigan's athletic leader was in doubt. If the Wolverines were already offering scholarships well in advance of a formal vote on the final version of the Aigler proposal, it was only logical that most members would follow Michigan's lead.[83]

---

[79] Morrill to McCormick and Rottschaefer. 27 August 1947, University of Minnesota Archives. President's Office; Box 238, folder: Physical Education and Athletics 1945-47

[80] Morrill to Rottschaefer. 16 September 1947. University of Minnesota Archives, President's Office; Box 238, folder: Physical Education and Athletics 1945-47

[81] Rottschaefer to Morrill. 3 September 1947. University of Minnesota Archives, President's Office; Box 238, folder: Physical Education and Athletics 1945-47

[82] Aigler to Griffith. 17 January 1939. Bentley Historical Library, University of Michigan. Ralph W. Aigler Papers, 87406 Aa 2; Box 6, folder: correspondence 1934-39

[83] Nunn to Willey. 4 August 1947. University of Minnesota Archives, President's Office; Box 238,

Chet Roan's memo of July, in Morrill's opinion, was quite accurate: " … While it may be true that they may not call this [financial aid] an athletic scholarship…no matter what it is called, in its true form it will act as an athletic scholarship."[84]

Acknowledging his dismay with the nascent scholarship movement, Morrill was also frustrated with the ineffectiveness of the Office of the Commissioner. Instead of the current cumbersome faculty committee process, he felt an empowered leader was needed to swiftly investigate, adjudicate, and, if necessary, mete out punishment. The antiquated rules, rarely updated since 1896, were no longer effective in the postwar era.[85]

Having become a powerful voice among his peers after just two years of leading Minnesota, Morrill decided that it was time to take control of the situation.[86][87] He airmailed a memo to all Western Conference presidents on December 10, 1947, spelling out his intentions to shake up the staid operations of the nine-member conference. He was going to challenge the fundamental leadership role granted to the faculty since 1896.[88]

President Morrill's "alarmed" realization in late August of an evolving subsidy movement was historically significant for the Intercollegiate Conference. It would lead to a more active role by the Council of Nine in conference governance–a responsibility traditionally reserved for the faculty.[89] And as will be seen, that grab for power, as orchestrated by the Minnesotan, would ultimately benefit John Hannah as the presidents, at least temporarily, assumed a role in the membership-selection process during the fall of 1948.[90] In hindsight, it appeared that Plan A remained a viable option as long as Lew Morrill controlled the agenda for the council.

MICHIGAN STATE and the University of Pittsburgh continued politicking for membership in the conference throughout 1947. The faculty let it be known, however, that they had more pressing concerns than replacing the University of Chicago. Legalizing academic scholarships for athletes–the Aigler proposal–was the major topic of debate during the spring and summer months. The loss of talent to non-conference programs offering financial assistance with few scholastic requirements was necessitating some adaptation of conference standards if the membership was to remain competitive.[91]

folder: Physical Education and Athletics 1945-47

[84] Roan to Nunn. 29 July 1947. University of Minnesota Archives, Department of Intercollegiate Athletic Papers; Box 6, folder: J.L. Morrill President

[85] Morrill to the Presidents of the Western Conference Universities. 10 December 1947. University of Minnesota Archives, President's Office; Box 238, folder: Physical Education and Athletics 1945-47

[86] Morrill to Nunn. 27 August. University of Minnesota Archives, President's Office; Box 238, folder. Physical Education 1945-47

[87] Morrill to McCormick and Rottschaefer. 27 August 1947. University of Minnesota Archives, President's Office; Box 238, folder: Physical Education and Athletics 1945-47

[88] Morrill to the Presidents of the Western Conference. 10 December 1947. University of Minnesota Archives, President's Office; Box 238, folder: Physical Education and Athletics 1945-47

[89] Morrill to Nunn. 27 August 1947. University of Minnesota Archives, President's Office; Box 238, folder: Physical Education and Athletics 1945-47

[90] Aigler to Richart. 14 December 1948. Bentley Historical Library, University of Michigan. Ralph W. Aigler Papers, 87406 Aa 2; Box 10, folder: correspondence 1946-52 "R" misc.

[91] Richart to Breneman. 14 July 1947. University of Illinois Archives. Series 4/2/12; Box 3, folder: Western Intercollegiate Conference 1946-47

But the leadership's reluctance to address expansion did not dissuade one suitor. In December of 1946, John Hannah had composed a letter to the faculty representatives of the conference requesting that Michigan State's application for membership previously submitted in May be considered an ongoing one. Ralph Aigler had recommended that action in a letter of condolence following the third Spartan rejection.[92]

President Hannah wrote again in March of 1947 to new chairman Verne Freeman of Purdue. Hannah was aware that the faculty representatives were planning to meet in a few days to finish leftover business from December. The Spartan leader reiterated his request of December. He also expressed interest in meeting with the committee "if that was considered desirable."[93]

Hannah, one year earlier, had been denied a presentation before the faculty by Dean Larry Kimpton at the request of Ralph Aigler and Frank Richart. But at a special March 1947 gathering Freeman agreed to allow the college president time in May. Common courtesy ruled since Pittsburgh had been granted a similar opportunity previously.[94] [95]

The president appeared before the faculty representatives in Highland Park, Illinois, on May 29. The weekend visit coincided with the controversial decision by the faculty to support academic scholarships for qualified student-athletes. Hannah put on quite a performance and was very well received.[96] He was then escorted out of the conference room. At the request of the chairman, the athletic directors were polled on the question of expansion. "A majority … indicated no disposition to increase the membership" at that time. No further action was taken.[97]

At the same meeting it was announced that three athletic directors and one faculty representative would be retiring or transitioning away from conference leadership roles. One retirement, in particular, would have a significant impact on the Pittsburgh Panthers' initiative.

Lynn St. John had been employed by The Ohio State University from 1912, shortly after it joined the conference, until the early summer of 1947.[98] At the age of 70, declining health had finally caught up with him. Three years earlier, in June of 1944, Fritz Crisler had expressed concern over the mental status of the athletic director.

> St. John began to show signs of age when he talked at length and random
> about various things. As Chairman he monopolized most of the [athletic

---

[92] Aigler to Hannah. 3 June 1946. Bentley Historical Library, University of Michigan. Ralph W. Aigler Papers, 87406 Aa 2; Box 9, folder: correspondence 1946-52 "H" misc.

[93] Minutes of the Intercollegiate Conference of Faculty Representatives. 7-8 March 1947. University of Illinois Archives, Series 4/2/12; Box 3, folder: conference minutes 1946-47

[94] Ibid.

[95] Freeman to Richart. 22 April 1947. University of Illinois Archives, Series 4/2/12; Box 3, folder: Western Intercollegiate Conference 1946-47

[96] "First Session 10:30 Thursday" (Frank Richart personal notes). 29 May 1947. University of Illinois Archives. Series 4/2/12; Box 3, folder: conference minutes 1946-47

[97] Joint Minutes of the Western Conference Faculty and Athletic Directors. 29-30 May 1947. University of Illinois Archives. Series 4/2/12; Box 3, folder: conference minutes 1946-47

[98] "Lynn W. St. John." Circa July 1947. The Ohio State University Archives. Biography Files, Lynn St. John.

directors' May] meeting outside of schedule making.[99]

Crisler's clinical assessment might have offered an explanation for some politically impolite comments the old man later penned to his friend Commissioner Ken Wilson in the spring of 1946 about a school seeking admission to the conference. A derogatory phrase in his letter would foment a controversy that temporarily compromised any progress Hannah had achieved with his stellar performance in late May.

LYNN ST. John was an ardent advocate for the University of Pittsburgh's admission into the Western Conference. Ohio State could mine gold with the Pennsylvania school included in the nine-member association. But there was one additional benefit gained with the Panthers assuming that vacated Chicago seat. His football coaches might legitimately secure talent out of the Allegheny regions of western Pennsylvania. Kiski County was full of skilled players attending either Pennsylvania State College or the University of Pittsburgh. St. John, dating back years, was convinced a Pitt membership might steer some Keystone State players toward Columbus, Ohio.[100]

In early May of 1946, the Buckeye director wrote to the man he had personally politicked for as commissioner of the Western Conference, Ken Wilson. He was aware that John Hannah wanted to make a presentation at the upcoming faculty committee meeting.[101]

The old director was concerned about the president's recent political success back in the state of Michigan.[102] Alexander Ruthven had made a public announcement in March supporting a Spartan application for admission into the Western Conference. Michigan State was now a legitimate contender, along with the Panthers, for a tenth seat in the organization. Lacking knowledge of the backroom machinations taking place between Ralph Aigler, Frank Richart, and, ultimately, committee chairman Larry Kimpton to deny Hannah a presence at the upcoming gathering,[103] St. John had decided to pursue his own plan to salvage a Pitt initiative. But to do so, he needed the new commissioner's assistance.

Based on a letter dated May 13, 1946, it appeared that St. John had recently been successful in recruiting Ken Wilson to proffer confidential insider information to the Panthers on conference matters impacting their application process.

> In telephone conversation with James Hagan of Pittsburgh this afternoon, he indicated that he was expecting some advice and counsel from you bearing on the question of what move, if any, the University of Pittsburgh should make at this time with reference to following up the application they made a year ago for membership in the Western Conference.[104]

---

[99] Crisler to Aigler. 8 June 1944. Bentley Historical Library, University of Michigan. Ralph W. Aigler Papers, 87406 Aa 2; Box 12, folder: athletic correspondence 1940-45 Crisler

[100] Griffith to Aigler. 31 May 1938. Bentley Historical Library, University of Michigan. Ralph W. Aigler Papers, 87406 Aa 2; Box 13, folder: athletics, Board in Control 1940

[101] St. John to Wilson. 13 May 1946. The Ohio State University Archives, Director of Athletics (RG 9/e-1/10), "Intercollegiate Conference: Commissioner: Correspondence (Wilson): 1945-1947."

[102] Ibid.

[103] Aigler to Richart. 15 May 1946. Bentley Historical Library, University of Michigan. Ralph W. Aigler Papers, 87406 Aa 2; Box 9, folder: correspondence 1946-52 "H" misc

[104] St. John to Wilson. 13 May 1946. The Ohio State University Archives, Director of Athletics (RG 9/e-1/10), "Intercollegiate Conference: Commissioner: Correspondence (Wilson): 1945-1947."

Acknowledging his successful recruitment of Wilson to the Pitt cause, the Ohio State athletic director commented in his note that "we obviously found no time to discuss such a subject [regarding a strategy for Hagan] at our recent get-together [with other conference directors]."[105]

St. John was writing now to offer some suggestions, based on his limited knowledge of the Spartan application status, which the commissioner might provide the Pitt director. He encouraged Wilson to be forthright with any insider information that might aid the cause. "I know from my telephone conversation with Jim Hagan that he is expecting to hear from you ... This letter is an effort on my part to help you in making up your mind as to what you may justifiably say to [him] now."[106] He was well aware that Wilson, as commissioner, was in constant communication with the leading faculty representatives about the conference including Aigler, Richart, and Rottschaefer. Perhaps one of them had shared critical information about Michigan State that might benefit Hagan and Pittsburgh.

St. John, quite possibly in the interest of reassuring Wilson that his covert revelations were legitimate if considered in the context of what was good for the conference, shared his personal reasons for opposing a Spartan admission.

> Frankly and confidentially with you, I have no hesitation in saying that I
> see no justification whatever for the Conference taking on Michigan State.
> They would fundamentally and of necessity be another more or less weak
> sister, trying to "keep up with the Joneses" in their conference competition
> and definitely do not have anything of particular value to add to the
> Conference. Pittsburgh, because of its location and facilities, is the only
> institution that can possibly add anything to the Western Conference.[107]

Within one week Ken Wilson would be sharing confidential information with Pitt athletic director James Hagan about Michigan State and its relationship with the University of Michigan.

Unanticipated by St. John, his remark about "weak sisters" (tier-two programs) would ignite a tirade by the new head coach at MSC one year later. The outburst would prove to be a great embarrassment for Hannah and his college.

IN LATE May of 1947, John Hannah eagerly accepted Dean Verne Freeman's offer to meet with the faculty in Highland Park, Illinois.[108] His presentation provided plenty of background information, but his chief intent was to press for action on a vote to replace Chicago—now or in December.

> [The president] described the origin of his institution as the original of the
> Land Grant colleges, traced its development and growth to the present time,
> described its athletic facilities and staff and mentioned some of its

---

[105] St. John to Wilson. 13 May 1946. The Ohio State University Archives, Director of Athletics (RG 9/e-1/10), "Intercollegiate Conference: Commissioner: Correspondence (Wilson): 1945-1947."
[106] Ibid.
[107] Ibid.
[108] Devine, Tommy. "Junking of Grants Aided MSC Cause." 14 December 1948, *Detroit Free Press.* Michigan State University Archives. Madison Kuhn Collection, UA12.107; Scrapbook 108, folder: 5

difficulties in scheduling athletic meets, particularly in football. He noted that the institution followed rules and regulations essentially identical with those of the Conference, described its system of scholarships, and stated that if any time his institution was invited to join the Conference, it would follow strictly all Conference requirements ... [109]

The "principal topic discussed, [however], was the Jenison [Awards]."[110] [111] Hannah's answers to numerous questions about those grants were consistent with the NCAA keynote address he had given over a year earlier.[112] After extending appreciation to Hannah for his presentation, the faculty "agreed to take no action–but to take up the matter with the Directors."[113]

At the joint meeting that followed, "a majority of the directors indicated no disposition to increase membership at this time."[114] The academicians, ultimately responsible for membership decisions, would respect that wish. The Nebraska Response was provided the current suitor.[115] But regardless of the rejection, essentially the fourth in 10 years,[116] Hannah finally had an opportunity to sell his school and personally petition for admission to the conference. His rapport with the audience was exceptional in the opinion of those in attendance.[117] [118] Within a few days of the Highland Park presentation, however, a public-relations faux pas back in East Lansing would challenge all the good will achieved by the president that weekend.[119]

That gaffe occurred on June 6, 1947, when Coach Clarence Munn "was scheduled for a talk on hunting and fishing, [two of his passions], before the Kiwanis Club in Lansing."[120] But instead of sharing his outdoor experiences, he offered an "impromptu" response to the recent Highland Park rejection. Members of the press were in attendance.

---

[109] Minutes of the Intercollegiate Conference of Faculty Representatives. 29-31 May 1947. University of Wisconsin-Madison. The University Faculty Athletic Board, Series 5/21/6; Box 1, folder: Western Conference minutes 1947-54

[110] Devine, Tommy. "Junking of Grants Aided MSC Cause." 14 December 1948, *Detroit Free Press.* Michigan State University Archives. Madison Kuhn Collection, UA12.107; Scrapbook 108, folder: 5

[111] "First Session 10:30 Thursday" (Frank Richart personal notes). 29 May 1947. University of Illinois Archives. Series 4/2/12; Box 3, folder: conference minutes 1946-47

[112] Ibid.

[113] Ibid.

[114] Joint Meeting of the Western Conference Faculty Representatives and Athletic Directors. 29-30 May 1947. Bentley Historical Library, University of Michigan. Athletic Department, 943 Bimu 2; Box 84, folder: Faculty Representatives minutes 1941-1957

[115] "Munn Answered: No Pay for Play; Charge Seen Hurting 'S' Chances." 6 June 1947. *Lansing State Journal.* Michigan State University Archives. Madison Kuhn Collection, UA12.107; Scrapbook 108, folder: 5

[116] Ibid.

[117] Aigler to Hannah. 6 June 1947. Bentley Historical Library, University of Michigan. Ralph W. Aigler Papers, 87406 Aa 2; Box 9, folder: correspondence 1946-52 "H" misc

[118] Devine, Tommy. "Junking of Grants Aided MSC Cause." 14 December 1948, *Detroit Free Press.* Michigan State University Archives. Madison Kuhn Collection, UA12.107; Scrapbook 108, folder: 5

[119] Aigler to Hannah. 6 June 1947. Bentley Historical Library, University of Michigan. Ralph W. Aigler Papers, 87406 Aa 2; Box 9, folder: correspondence 1946-52 "H" misc.

[120] "MSC Coach Blasts Big 9 Tactics." 6 June 1947. *Detroit Free Press*. Michigan State University Archives. Madison Kuhn Collection, UA12.107; Scrapbook 108, folder: 5

Munn began what would become a diatribe by pointing out that "... Michigan State had been refused admittance to the conference because of its 'above-the-board' athletic scholarship system."[121]

> They dislike our Jenison [Awards] ... But why should we have to do like a hell of a lot of them do–pay athletes under the table ... In some Big Nine schools it is a practice to hand it to the players under the table and then take them into another room and make them sign a paper to the effect [that] they haven't received anything.[122]... We're not going to push the issue any further. I don't believe we'll get anywhere by apple polishing. If they want us, they'll ask us now.[123]

The press took advantage of the opportunity to goad him on further. They sought Munn's response to a Big Nine official's comment about the Highland Park rejection. The anonymous source had been widely quoted for stating that Michigan State was only a "weak sister using this as [his] reason for opposing MSC's membership application."[124] Coach Munn shot back, "I don't think that the gentleman who said that had any knowledge of Michigan State College."[125]

The damage was done. There was no turning back now. A few hours later Munn himself was feeling the full recoil from his talk. He told the *Detroit Free Press* that "certain things I said have been emphasized out of proportion. I neither lashed nor blasted the Western Conference. I was just explaining a few things."[126]

Munn had been the line coach at Michigan from 1938 through early 1946 before accepting the head job at Syracuse. Due to his long association with Fritz Crisler, it was implied in that newspaper article that the former Wolverine was privy to some rules violations taking place at the University of Michigan.[127]

The news traveled fast back to Ann Arbor. Michigan alumni had been in attendance during the Kiwanis tirade.[128] That very same day, Ralph Aigler found time to compose a note to John Hannah.

> Last Friday evening I would have said that the chances of your institution becoming a member of the Conference in the course of time were better than they had been up to that date. In other words you made an excellent impression and helped the cause of your institution ... During the evening following your meeting with us, the general matter of increase of our

[121] "Munn Answered: No Pay for Play; Charge Seen Hurting 'S' Chances." 6 June 1947. *Lansing State Journal*. Michigan State University Archives. Madison Kuhn Collection, UA12.107; Scrapbook 108, folder: 5

[122] Ibid.

[123] "MSC Coach Blasts Big 9 Tactics." 6 June 1947. *Detroit Free Press*. Michigan State University Archives. Madison Kuhn Collection, UA12.107; Scrapbook 108, folder: 5

[124] Ibid.

[125] Ibid.

[126] Ibid.

[127] Ibid.

[128] Wilson to Aigler. 9 June 1947. Bentley Historical Library, University of Michigan. Ralph W. Aigler Papers, 87406 Aa 2; Box 10, folder: correspondence 1946-52 Wilson, K.L. 1/2

numbers above nine was discussed with the Directors. Although no vote was taken, it was perfectly evident that a majority favored waiting a longer time before arriving at a definite decision. While no vote was taken electing your institution, it is significant, it seems to me, that no vote in the opposite direction was taken.

But then Aigler turned his attention to Munn's charges, which he felt had been directed at the University of Michigan. He wanted John Hannah to fret over the remarks he found noxious.

As I have told you, I have favored in our group your application; therefore, you can readily understand why it is that I am distressed and discouraged to find a prominent member of your organization popping off publically [sic]. It may be, of course, that Mr. Munn was incorrectly quoted but knowing him as well as I do (and liking him) I am quite prepared to believe that under the influence of his own verbal intoxication addressing the group, he may have said just about what was reported. Frankly, I fear that this has undone all the good that was accomplished by your meeting with us.[129]

The president had no option but to respond. Plan B was well in place. The Spartans would begin playing Notre Dame in 1948. But Plan A remained his ultimate goal.

Hannah's first obligation, however, was to make sure that Munn didn't exacerbate the situation. Not coincidentally, the new coach was "reported out of the city and not expected back for several days."[130]

The president then composed a note to Aigler indicating his sincere hope that "the faculty representatives will not give undue weight to this incident." He expressed regret over the choice of words of "one of our coaches who was irked at some newspaper comments to the effect that the Conference did not need another 'weak sister.'" The president claimed that the remarks "were somewhat distorted and widely publicized that as printed created unfortunate inferences." Hannah closed the brief letter by stating, "It is my own opinion that when and if we get into the Conference rests pretty largely with you and Mr. Crisler." He planned to send a more complete statement to other faculty representatives regarding Munn's comments. A copy of that letter was enclosed for Aigler's perusal. The commissioner would receive one as well.[131]

The concept of a de facto division within the conference was news to the press and public. The anonymous official's inference was quickly understood: The "weak-sister" schools included Iowa, Indiana, and Purdue.[132] The three, traditionally poor draws in

---

[129] Aigler to Hannah. 6 June 1947. Bentley Historical Library. University of Michigan. Ralph W. Aigler Papers, 87406 Aa 2; Box 9, folder: correspondence 1946-52 "H" misc.

[130] Devine, Tommy. "Key Figures Go 'into Hiding' After Munn's Slap at Big Nine." 7 June 1947, *Detroit Free Press*. Michigan State University Archives. Madison Kuhn Collection, UA17.107; Scrapbook 108, folder: 5

[131] Hannah to Aigler. 11 June 1947. Bentley Historical Library, University of Michigan. Ralph W. Aigler Papers, 87406 Aa 2; Box 9, folder: correspondence 1946-52 "H" misc.

[132] "Munn Answered: No Pay for Play; Charge Seen Hurting 'S' Chances." 6 June 1947. *Lansing State Journal*. Michigan State University Archives. Madison Kuhn Collection, UA12.107; Scrapbook 108, folder: 5

Columbus, Ann Arbor, Minneapolis, and Champaign-Urbana, were offered limited dates for contracts with the powerful tier-one schools during the biennial spring scheduling meetings. The Spartans, now proclaimed a substandard program, would merely join their ranks.

Hannah closed his letter to the conference leaders by expressing his hope that the spirit of good will that was evident during his May 29th presentation would lead to a Spartan admission sometime soon. He invited each representative to visit East Lansing and "see at first hand the kind of institution [Michigan State] has become."[133] After receiving the letter, Dean Kenneth Little of Wisconsin responded graciously and indicated that "I am sure ... this incident did not detract from the very excellent presentation which you made on behalf of Michigan State College.[134] [135] He understood who Munn was implicating. This was an intrastate squabble best kept within the borders.

Hannah was undoubtedly relieved by the words from Professor Little. Perhaps Ralph Aigler's comment that Munn's choice of words may have "undone all the good that was accomplished by your meeting with us" was an overstatement.

Granted an unplanned vacation by President Hannah, Biggie Munn had plenty of time to reflect on his inappropriate verbiage. Based on Hannah's comments, the "weak sisters" remark was particularly upsetting to the very intense, highly competitive Munn. He probably wanted to know the origin of the statement; it might prove helpful in rallying his players some day against the perpetrator's team. He could easily exclude Indiana, Purdue, and Iowa. Based on Ken Little's reply to Hannah, Wisconsin was clearly not the source of the comment. The University of Minnesota was Munn's alma mater, and President Morrill was a main proponent of the Spartan initiative. That left Northwestern, Ohio State, Illinois, and Michigan.

There was no obvious reason to suspect either the Wildcats or the Buckeyes. President Snyder of Northwestern had delivered the commencement address at Michigan State in the spring of 1945.[136] Following the Ruthven announcement of March 1946, Snyder professed full support of John Hannah's intentions.[137] Since he became athletic director in 1912, Lynn St. John and Ohio State had literally no interaction—at least on the gridiron—with Michigan State. There was no reason why anyone at Ohio State would be the source of such a denigrating comment.

The University of Illinois also had no relationship with the Spartans despite Ralph Young trying to arrange a contract with them on numerous occasions during the 1930s. Professor Frank Richart was actually convinced, in confidence to President Willard, that Michigan State was the logical replacement for Chicago back in March of 1946.[138] A few

---

[133] Hannah to Aigler. 11 June 1947. Bentley Historical Library, University of Michigan. Ralph W. Aigler Papers, 87406 Aa 2; Box 9, folder: correspondence 1946-52 "H" misc.

[134] Hannah to Little. 11 June 1947. University of Wisconsin-Madison. The University Faculty Athletic Board, Series 5/21/7; Box 1, folder: Western Conference General Files

[135] Little to Hannah. 16 June 1947. University of Wisconsin-Madison. The University Faculty Athletic Board, Series 5/21/7; Box 1, folder: Western Conference General Files

[136] Geil to Snyder. 14 June 1945. Northwestern University Archives, Franklyn Snyder Papers; Box 3, folder:1

[137] Snyder to Hannah. 19 March 1946. Northwestern University Archives, Franklyn Snyder Papers; Box 13, folder:20

[138] Richart to Willard. 25 March 1946. University of Illinois Archives, Series 2/9/1; Box: 104, folder: general correspondence, 1934-46

months later, however, he did collaborate with Ralph Aigler in convincing the Faculty Committee Chairman Larry Kimpton not to offer John Hannah time to make a presentation at the spring meetings. He was sensitive to Aigler's political plight back home and wanted to help. Of course Biggie Munn had no knowledge of either matter. Regardless, there appeared no reason to suspect the Illini.

That left only Michigan. Munn was probably indoctrinated by Spartan leadership, shortly after moving to East Lansing, about the role the Wolverines had played in blocking the college's application for membership. In his tirade, the new coach had implied that the Jenison Award program was the main reason for the recent rejection by the conference. The grants, at least at that time, were of only parochial interest for Michigan and Ralph Aigler. Prior to his June 6 "press conference," Biggie Munn was probably convinced that the law professor directed the debate following Hannah's presentation that ultimately led to the Nebraska Response.

As a former assistant to Fritz Crisler, Munn was likely privy to past booster activity in Ann Arbor prompting his comments about "under-the-table" monies. He moved to southeast Michigan immediately following the Harry Kipke tenure. Although Kipke's replacement, Crisler, was a strict adherent to the amateur code, there was little even he could do to curtail handouts by rabid fans and alumni. The constant rumors regarding subsidies provided Tom Harmon, a player Munn assisted in coaching, might have further strengthened his convictions that Michigan was as guilty as everyone else.

In Biggie Munn's opinion, it was only logical that the originator of the "weak sister" comment resided in Ann Arbor.

Commissioner Wilson, signed on by Lynn St. John as a confidential Panther proponent one year earlier, wrote to Ralph Aigler two days before John Hannah sent out his apologies. His letter may have overstated the significance of Munn's comments. But it was a show of support for the powerful representative. And for a man who some, including Aigler, considered a weak leader, it offered an opportunity to display some tough talk.

Wilson ran into Biggie Munn and Ralph Young at a track meet in Milwaukee a few days following the incident in East Lansing. The new Spartan coach offered his side of the story. The commissioner, in his "tough talk" note to Aigler, failed to buy the explanation.

> I told him very frankly that misquoted or not, he had done a great deal of harm to Michigan State. I was so burned up about it that I had dictated a rather stern letter to President Hannah. I told [Biggie] very frankly that he was grown up now and that he never could make public utterances that could be twisted in such a fashion … I refrained from answering the charge to the papers until I had a chance to investigate and can tell you very frankly that they are a very sick bunch up at Michigan State about the whole affair … I told [Biggie] it was up to Michigan State to rectify.[139]

Aigler responded to the Wilson letter by describing his written reaction to the Munn faux pas.

> I wrote President Hannah quite frankly. I felt warranted in doing this

---

[139] Wilson to Aigler. 9 June 1947. Bentley Historical Library, University of Michigan. Ralph W. Aigler Papers, 87406 Aa 2; Box 10, folder: correspondence 1946-52 Wilson, K.L. 1/2

because, as you know, he was at one time a student of mine ... I told him that I was very much disappointed and distressed by the remarks attributed to Clarence. Further, that the chances of his institution being elected to membership had probably been hurt more by that talk than he had helped by his personal presentation.[140]

Aigler writing in somewhat a paternalistic manner towards a former student and now respected college president seemed strange for so politically polished a man. The same tactic had gotten him into trouble with Henry Rottschaefer a decade earlier during the controversy over President Lotus Coffman's General College program at Minnesota. Regardless, the law professor at least had the support of the commissioner. It appeared he could not make the same claim about fellow faculty leadership.

Lynn St. John retired from Ohio State shortly after the Munn outburst. Even though he was showing signs of aging in those final years, the old man proved wise enough to find a way to effectively slow the Spartan initiative. St. John passed away September 30, 1950. Sixty-four years later, hidden in folder RG 9/e-1/10 at the archives in Columbus, the answer to Biggie Munn's question was found–and it exonerated both Ralph Aigler and Fritz Crisler!

THE UNIVERSITY of Pittsburgh refrained from applying to the conference in 1947. The message gained from the Michigan State rejection of May 1946 was clear: There were too many other pressing issues for the leadership to devote discussion time on a replacement for Chicago.

The short-term strategy developed by director James Hagan, his athletic board, and the Faculty Committee on Athletic Policy at Pitt was simple. The upcoming gridiron campaign of '47 included six Western Conference teams. It would afford the school's athletic leadership a great opportunity to interact with faculty and directors throughout the Big Nine. Even Michigan was on the Panther's schedule. The political payoff would prove invaluable.

Pittsburgh's Big Nine experience was a disaster. It lost all but one game that season. Ironically, the only victory on its nine-game schedule was achieved at the expense of Lynn St. John's Ohio State.

In the aftermath of the humiliating 1947 campaign, Chancellor Rufus Fitzgerald decided that it was time for different leadership in the athletic department. He was under immense pressure by irate alumni to renew the past glories of Panther football. By June of 1948 Hagan would resign and Frank Carver of the Sports Information Department would take over as interim director.[141] The school took its time in deciding on a replacement. It needed the right man to quell the uproar over the Hagan plan that essentially destroyed a winning tradition.

Unfortunately for the university, with the athletic department in turmoil in late 1947 there was no interim leadership directing the school's conference-affiliation strategy. That had been Hagan's responsibility. He had lost interest in pursuing the Pitt cause knowing it was only a matter of time before he would be forced out. Carver lacked the personal

---

[140] Aigler to Wilson. 12 June 1947. Bentley Historical Library, University of Michigan. Ralph W. Aigler Papers, 87406 Aa 2; Box 10, folder: correspondence 1946-52 Wilson, K.L. 1/2

[141] Alberts, Robert C. *Pitt: The Story of the University of Pittsburgh 1787-1987*. Pittsburgh: University of Pittsburgh Press. pp. 222-224

connections that Jimmie Hagan had nurtured over the previous seven years. His role was to keep the department operational until a new director was hired.

Adding to the Panther's woes, the athletic department also lost the powerful presence of Lynn St. John as its sub rosa advocate within the conference. In his absence, the commissioner remained the lone confidential insider aiding the university's cause.

DESPITE OFFERING full support for Michigan State College becoming a member of the Western Conference in mid-March of 1946, Minnesota President Lew Morrill felt a need to abide by protocol. He would profess allegiance to Hannah's cause only if the University of Michigan agreed that a replacement for the University of Chicago was in order.[142] With Michigan President Alexander Ruthven's statement a few days later in support of John Hannah's plan, Morrill was finally satisfied.[143] [144]

Both Ralph Aigler and Herbert Crisler publicly lined up behind their president and his decision. They had no choice. Ruthven, after all, signed their paychecks! But with all Michigan leadership officially sanctioning support for a Spartan application, Lew Morrill was ready to offer his as well. In July of 1947 the Minnesota president expressed his wish that Henry Rottschaefer and Frank McCormick promote the admission of Michigan State College among their respective colleagues.

> I am very sympathetic with the plea–for two reasons: (1) the Michigan
> State athletic plant, which I recently visited, is one of the finest in the
> nation, and (2) I am completely convinced of the soundness and integrity of
> President Hannah's views and influence upon the administration of athletics
> at Michigan State.[145]

Lew Morrill's visit to the campus earlier that spring to deliver the commencement address and receive an honorary degree may have paid off for Hannah.[146] Morrill departed East Lansing even more impressed with the accomplishments of the college president and fully convinced that Michigan State belonged in the Western Conference.

But in that same letter the Minnesota president showed he was still suspicious of the commitment by the Michigan athletic leadership.

> This [support] has been nominally given, I understand–whereas privately
> both Professor Aigler and Athletic Director Crisler have explained to their
> friends in the Conference that the move would not be so good. It is my own
> feeling that Michigan State is more likely to observe both the law and the
> spirit of eligibility requirements than Ann Arbor does![147]

[142] Morrill to Rottschaefer and McCormick. 17 May 1946. University of Minnesota Archives, President's Office; Box 238, folder: Physical Education and Athletics 1945-47

[143] Ruthven to Hannah. 23 March 1946. Bentley Historical Library, University of Michigan. Herbert Orin Crisler Papers, 85823 AC UAm Aa 2; Box 1, folder: topical correspondence MSU 1943-46

[144] Morrill to Rotschaefer. 9 July 1947. University of Minnesota Archives, President's Office; Box 238, folder: Physical Education and Athletics 1948-49

[145] Ibid.

[146] Morrill to Hannah. 24 April 1947. University of Minnesota Archives, Morrill, J.L.; Box 1, folder: correspondence A-L, Ha-He

[147] Morrill to Rotschaefer. 9 July 1947. University of Minnesota Archives, President's Office; Box

Clearly Morrill did not trust the University of Michigan–but he shared that opinion with only a few associates. John Hannah was one of them.

IN NOVEMBER of 1947 President Hannah wrote his friend in Minneapolis requesting a football relationship with the Golden Gophers. He stated that "a series of games with Minnesota will give us more of a lift in our dealings with some of our 'mutual friends' than anything I can think of." He was, of course, referring to the University of Michigan. Morrill, forever a Buckeye at heart, could never turn down an opportunity that might impact the fortunes of the Wolverine athletic program. He sent the request on to Frank McCormick. But unfortunately for Michigan State, scheduling conflicts precluded any series for the foreseeable future.

President Hannah had one more request for Morrill. "Your help in ferreting out any information that you think will be helpful to me in connection with our desire for admission to the Intercollegiate Conference will be appreciated."[148] He desperately needed Lew Morrill's insider connections if Plan A was to succeed on the college's fifth attempt. As Professor Floyd Reeves of the University of Chicago pointed out years later, John Hannah's greatest strength was his sense of timing.[149] The upcoming year of 1948 would prove critical if the college was to achieve its goal.

LIKE JOHN Hannah, Lew Morrill also understood the importance of timing, as his close colleagues acknowledged.[150] In early December, just prior to the annual meetings in Chicago, Morrill wrote to his fellow presidents expressing his concerns over conference governance and operations. The faculty representatives, in his opinion, were failing to fulfill their responsibilities as clearly spelled out in his keynote address to the NCAA in January.[151] The revelation in late August that implied they were condoning athletic scholarships was disturbing. He also felt the committee that ruled the conference was not effectively performing its job in adjudicating and disciplining.[152] He was convinced that a stronger commissioner was necessary.[153]

During the first session of the two-day meetings at the University Club in Chicago, the presidents, led by Morrill, argued for a more active role in the administration of intercollegiate athletics within the conference. A joint meeting including athletic directors, faculty representatives, and the presidents was proposed and accepted.[154] The faculty had no

238, folder: Physical Education and Athletics 1948-49

[148] Hannah to Morrill. 17 November 1947. University of Minnesota Archives, President's Office; Box 238, folder: Physical Education and Athletics 1948-49

[149] Reeves, Floyd W. 11 June 1970. Michigan State University Archives. Hannah Archives Project, UA2.1.12.2; Box 34, folder: 37 Statement of Floyd W. Reeves

[150] Patterson to Morrill. 17 December 1947. University of Minnesota Archives, Morrill, J.L.; Box 1, folder: correspondence 1945-47

[151] Aigler to Rottschaefer. 3 March 1948. Bentley Historic Library, University of Michigan. Ralph W. Aigler Papers, 87406 Aa2; Box 10, folder: correspondence 1946-52 Rottschaefer

[152] Morrill to Presidents of the Western Conference Universities. 10 December 1947. University of Iowa Archives, Iowa City, Iowa. Virgil Hancher Papers RG 05.01.11; Box 209, folder: 171

[153] Aigler to Rottschaefer. 3 March 1948. Bentley Historic Library, University of Michigan. Ralph W. Aigler Papers, 87406 Aa2; Box 10, folder: correspondence 1946-52 Rottschaefer

[154] Minutes of the Intercollegiate Conference of Faculty Representatives. 12-13 December 1947. University of Illinois Archives, Series 4/2/12; Box 3, folder: December '47 meeting

choice but to comply.[155] The meeting would take place after the holidays.

The Morrill motion could not have occurred at a more opportune time. During that same conference meeting, the representatives were obligated to elect members of the powerful Eligibility Committee. As expected, the old guard maintained their seats. Ralph Aigler and Frank Richart were re-elected, and Henry Rottschaefer was selected for the first time.

There had been a significant turnover of faculty representatives in recent years. The junior representatives were disturbed by the hold on power of the three long-serving leaders. Frank Richart concurred with their assessment.

> The senior members of the group should not be allowed to dominate the
> general proceedings of the Conference. There may have been some
> tendency in that direction in recent years, but I don't believe there will be in
> the future, since most of the newer members have shown a very healthy
> independence of thought which is a very good sign.[156]

In defense of the recent election, however, Richart pointed out that "the Conference has always been very free from any behind-the-scenes politics or cloakroom lobbying."[157] His assessment was not quite accurate. Backroom politicking had taken place 10 years earlier in May of 1937. It had also occurred in May of 1946, when Richart was actively involved with Ralph Aigler in manipulating the outcome of the third Spartan try for membership. And within five months, in May of 1948, the practice would be repeated again.

But regardless of Richart's assessment of conference operations, it was apparent that as the New Year was approaching the Intercollegiate Conference of Faculty Representatives was experiencing some internal turmoil unknown to the public and press. The presidents and junior members in leadership recognized some of those problems. As John Hannah had sensed months earlier, the timing was now right to make an aggressive move.

---

[155] Aigler to Richart. 14 December 1948. Bentley Historical Library, University of Michigan. Ralph W. Aigler Papers, 87406 Aa 2; Box 10, folder: correspondence 1946-52 "R" misc.
[156] Richart to Little. 23 December 1947. University of Wisconsin-Madison Archives. The University of Wisconsin Faculty Athletic Board, Series 5/21/7; Box 1, folder: Western Conference General Files
[157] Ibid.

McCormick's Miscue and the Final Rejection

THE G.I. Bill of Rights made available millions of dollars in federal funds for ex-servicemen planning to complete undergraduate degrees. Certain coaches and athletic directors, realizing that many of these veterans had athletic eligibility remaining, used the government aid for de facto athletic scholarships. Boosters, always willing to help out, provided the additional dollars needed to entice students returning home to change school colors and play for their favorite program. Competitive bidding for talent very quickly pervaded the college scene. It was a buyer's market for many young men lacking allegiance to any school.[1] [2]

The competition for talent was forecasted well in advance of the end of hostilities overseas.[3] Western Conference leaders, as early as May of 1945, expressed interest that the NCAA draft policies to curb the unsavory practices emanating from the "south, southwest, southeast, and west."[4] The Sanity Code, debated over the next few years, was the end result. Athletes, to remain eligible, were obligated to progress toward a degree in a timely fashion. Financial aid was only to be awarded for scholarship, not athletic skill. Recruiting by any means was strictly forbidden.[5] The penalty for noncompliance was banishment from the association. Participation in NCAA tournaments and championships would be denied to an offending school, now classified as an outsider. In January of 1948 the code was approved.

---

[1] Wilson to Aigler. 9 July 1946. Bentley Historical Library, University of Michigan. Ralph W. Aigler Papers, 87406 Aa 2; Box 10, folder: correspondence 1946-52 Wilson, K.L.

[2] Minutes of the Joint Meeting of the Athletic Directors and Football Coaches of the Intercollegiate Conference. 24 May 1945. Bentley Historical Library, University of Michigan. Athletic Department, 943 Bimu 2; Box 84, folder: Athletic Directors office, Big Ten Directors Committee minutes 1941-52

[3] Minutes of the Meetings of the Athletic Directors, Football Coaches and Basketball Coaches at the Hotel Sherman. 25-26 May 1944. Bentley Historical Library, University of Michigan. Athletic Department, 943 Bimu 2; Box 84, folder: Athletic Directors office, Big Ten Directors Committee minutes 1941-52

[4] Minutes of the Joint Meeting of the Athletic Directors and Football Coaches of the Intercollegiate Conference. 24 May 1945. Bentley Historical Library, University of Michigan. Athletic Department, 943 Bimu 2; Box 84, folder: Athletic Directors office, Big Ten Directors Committee minutes 1941-52

[5] Falla, Jack. *NCAA: The Voice of College Sports.* Mission: National Collegiate Athletic Association, 1981. p. 132

The Intercollegiate Conference, represented by a number of prominent leaders, held a significant role in drafting the new document.[6]

As planned back in December, the presidents, faculty representatives, and athletic directors gathered for a special meeting in February of '48.[7] The agenda was drafted by James Lewis Morrill. The Minnesota president was disturbed by suspect faculty leadership on matters of policy formation and enforcement of conference rules. Even though the Faculty Representatives Committee had been working for over a year revising the current Handbook in anticipation of Sanity Code approval, Morrill wanted the final draft to be consistent with his keynote address to the NCAA given one year earlier. The meeting was precedent. Not since the founding of the Intercollegiate Conference of Faculty Representatives in January of 1895 had the presidents been so actively involved.

The first order of business was redefining the role of the commissioner.[8] Morrill envisioned an office able to adjudicate and mete out justice quickly under the auspices of the Faculty Representatives Committee.

Virgil Hancher, president of the State University of Iowa and a law professor, had concerns with the plan. He shared his thoughts with Lew Morrill in advance of the special February meeting.

> I do not recall the exact basis upon which our commissioner is appointed. Unless he has a life time appointment, however, I fear that vesting more authority in him will not improve conditions substantially. It seems to me that freedom of action will only come when he is beyond the wrath of a majority of the institutions in the conference ... So many influential interests have a stake in a winning team that the assignment is very difficult. There is the highly paid coach, the sports writer (and editor beyond him), the Saturday alumni, and the huge gate receipts. There are times when each of these can make it difficult to maintain a simon-pure amateurism.[9] [10]

In line with Morrill's intentions, the group agreed to expand the investigative powers of the commissioner. In deference to Hancher's concerns regarding "influential interests," however, the faculty was given additional responsibilities. The commissioner would now answer to both the athletic directors and the academicians. The representatives would jointly share the task of hiring and firing him and monitoring his operations. This was seen as a means of protecting the directors from the influence of outside parties—alumni and overly zealous fans—more intent on victories than academic reputations. It was all

---

[6] Wilson to Faculty Representatives and Athletic Directors. 22 January 1948. Bentley Historical Library, University of Michigan. Ralph W. Aigler Papers, 87406 Aa 2; Box 10, folder: correspondence 1946-52 Wilson, K.L.

[7] Wilson to Presidents of Conference Institutions. 11 February 1948. University of Minnesota Archives, President's Office; Box 238, folder: Physical Education and Athletics 1948-49

[8] Hovde to Morrill. 29 September 1948. University of Minnesota Archives, President's Office; Box 238, folder: Physical Education and Athletics 1948-49

[9] Hancher to Morrill. 12 December 1947. University of Minnesota Archives, President's Office; Box 238, folder: Physical Education and Athletics 1945-47

[10] Rottschaefer to Morrill 26 February 1948. University of Minnesota Archives, President's Office; Box 238, folder: Physical Education and Athletics 1948-49

consistent with President Morrill's conviction, clearly defined in his 1947 NCAA keynote address, that only those assured tenure could effectively guarantee institutional integrity. The revision was a brilliant plan–at least in theory.

The commissioner was granted power, with some limitations, to enforce the Handbook, and the process therein was streamlined. An institution still had the right, however, to appeal to the Eligibility Committee if in disagreement with a ruling by the commissioner.[11]

With the direct backing of the presidents, the faculty had no choice but to approve the legislation that empowered the commissioner. But having the current officeholder carry out those new duties was another matter. In the opinion of many faculty and a few presidents, Ken Wilson lacked the fortitude and the focused interest necessary to perform the challenging tasks.[12] [13] [14] But others, such as Hancher of Iowa, acknowledged that the demands placed on the commissioner were beyond any one man's capabilities.[15] As events unfolded, however, on April 29, 1948, Wilson would temporarily silence those skeptics with his presentation of a very controversial investigation that embarrassed most members of the conference.

IN MAY of 1947 the faculty group met in Highland Park, Illinois, to debate Ralph Aigler's agenda item 17. The Michigan professor was keenly aware of developments in the Sanity Code draft. His proposal regarding academic scholarships for athletes was intended to be consistent with the NCAA code. But Aigler and his colleagues sought a far stricter version. His core group wanted the Intercollegiate Conference to remain the benchmark for pure amateurism–its standard would surpass any national code approved by the NCAA.[16] [17]

Over the summer months that followed the tentative approval of the Aigler proposal,[18] rules were drafted to permit academic scholarships for incoming freshmen. "Rule 6" allowed financial aid, beginning in the fall of 1947, for athletes graduating in the top 20 percent of their high school class.[19] The commissioner, with his newly granted

[11] Rottschaefer to Morrill 26 February 1948. University of Minnesota Archives, President's Office; Box 238, folder: Physical Education and Athletics 1948-49

[12] Hovde to Morrill. 29 September 1948. University of Minnesota Archives, President's Office; Box 238, folder: Physical Education and Athletics 1948-49

[13] Wilson to Faculty Representatives and Athletic Directors. 22 January 1948. Bentley Historical Library, University of Michigan. Ralph W. Aigler Papers, 87406 Aa 2; Box 10, folder: correspondence 1946-52 Wilson, K.L.

[14] Aigler to Rottschaefer. 3 March 1948. Bentley Historical Library, University of Michigan. Ralph W. Aigler Papers, 87406 Aa 2; Box 10, folder: correspondence 1946-52 Rottschaefer, Henry

[15] Hancher to Morrill. 12 December 1947. University of Minnesota Archives, President's Office; Box 238, folder: Physical Education and Athletics 1945-47

[16] Wilson to Faculty Representatives. 22 January 1948. Bentley Historical Library.,University of Michigan. Ralph W. Aigler Papers, 87406 Aa 2; Box 10, folder: correspondence 1946-52 Wilson, K.L.

[17] Crisler to the President, the Honorable Board of Regents and the University Council. January 1948. Bentley Historical Library, University of Michigan. Ralph W. Aigler Papers, 87406 Aa 2; Box 10, folder: athletics 1940-48 Board in Control

[18] Rottschaefer to Morrill. 3 September 1947. University of Minnesota Archives, President's Office; Box 238, folder: Physical Education and Athletics 1945-47

[19] Minutes of the Intercollegiate Conference of Faculty Representatives. 29-31 May 1947. University

powers, was asked to use a "tool" to determine institutional compliance with the financial-aid rule. Since the concept was agreed upon at the May meeting, it became known as the "Highland Park yardstick."[20]

In the fall of 1947, Commissioner Wilson was asked to investigate for the first time compliance with Rule 6. Using the 20 percent yardstick measure, he found seven of the nine schools in the conference were in violation, having provided scholarships to athletes inappropriately. Of greater concern to Wilson, however, was his discovery of serious institutional violations of Rule 6, section 4 by Purdue. He previewed his findings with the athletic directors on April 29, 1948, four weeks in advance of the annual spring meetings.[21] He wanted their feedback before reporting to the faculty.[22]

Wilson met with the faculty representatives in late May. Only Ohio State and Minnesota were unscathed by his investigation. Twenty-five athletes from seven schools had failed to meet the standards for an academic scholarship. He also presented the institutional infractions committed by the Boilermakers. Due to his "voluminous" report, no immediate action was taken on either matter. The representatives requested an opportunity to critically review the findings about the students before making decisions regarding future eligibility. In addition, the separate charges against Purdue required time to contemplate.[23] Wilson's findings, after all, had serious repercussions for the West Lafayette school. Disciplinary actions could involve a probation or collective conference boycott.[24]

The faculty and directors gathered in executive session the following day, with the focus on Purdue. A special three-member committee was formed "to meet immediately to consider infractions of rules or regulations as revealed in the Commissioner's report, with power to assess penalties."[25] Dean Freeman of Purdue, Professor Little of Wisconsin, and Professor Richart of Illinois were charged with the task. Freeman was included to ensure fair treatment of Purdue.

On May 29 the ad hoc committee presented its report.

> The Committee as a whole felt that under Rule 6, Section 4 the athletic administration of Purdue University is in error on three counts and that said administration has failed to administer its program under the spirit and

---

of Minnesota Archives, President's Office; Box 238, folder: Physical Education and Athletics 1945-47

[20] Minutes of the Intercollegiate Conference of Faculty Representatives. 29-31 May 1947. University of Minnesota Archives, President's Office; Box 238, folder: Physical Education and Athletics 1945-47

[21] Wilson to Aigler. 8 April 1948. Bentley Historical Library, University of Michigan. Ralph W. Aigler Papers, 87406 Aa 2; Box 10, folder: correspondence 1946-52 Wilson, K.L.

[22] Wilson to Aigler. 21 April 1948. Bentley Historical Library, University of Michigan. Ralph W. Aigler Papers, 87406 Aa 2; Box 10, folder: correspondence 1946-52 Wilson, K.L.

[23] Minutes of the Intercollegiate Conference of Faculty Representatives. 27-29 May 1948. University of Wisconsin-Madison. The University Faculty Board, Series 5/21/6; Box 1, folder: Western Conference minutes 1947-51

[24] Wilson to Aigler. 21 April 1948. Bentley Historical Library, University of Michigan. Ralph W. Aigler Papers, 87406 Aa 2; Box 10, folder: correspondence 1946-52 Wilson, K.L.

[25] Joint Meeting of the Faculty Representatives and Athletic Directors. 28 May 1948. Bentley Historical Library, University of Michigan. Athletic Department, 943 Bimu 2; Box: 84, folder: Faculty Representatives minutes 1941-1957

correct interpretation of the Conference Rules. Therefore, said athletic administration should be severely reprimanded and correction made immediately.[26]

Section 4 dealt specifically with financial aid provided by an institution. "No scholarships, loans or remissions of tuition shall be awarded on the basis of athletic skill, and no financial aid shall be given to students by individuals or organizations, alumni or other [sic], with the purpose of subsidizing them as athletes or of promoting the athletic success of a particular University." [27] Violation of the rule would cost the student at least a year of athletic eligibility.

The commissioner charged that the athletic department and the Purdue Alumni Scholarship Foundation had been providing monies to incoming athletes without involving the school administration and the Committee on Scholarship. He had evidence to support those claims.[28] He concluded that this was a breach of the controversial Rule 6, section 4.

Since the Purdue misdeeds involved institutional compliance, the faculty was obligated to determine the punishment.[29] An initial motion by Professor Little of Wisconsin and seconded by Dean Freeman of Purdue to accept the special committee's recommendation was summarily defeated. Both academicians served on that committee. The representatives, led by one man in particular, felt a "severe reprimand" and corrective action was not sufficient.

The violation by Purdue was an opportunity for the conference to demonstrate its commitment to the recently approved Sanity Code and "the cause of clean athletics in general."[30] The national press had questioned the sincerity of that latter conviction on numerous occasions in the past.[31] The faculty also wanted to demonstrate to the Council of Nine, including chief critic Lew Morrill, its resolve to enforce and discipline wayward members.

Ralph Aigler reworded the recommendation of the special committee. He moved that they also deny one year of eligibility to the freshman athletes of 1947-48 financed inappropriately by the university scholarship fund program. Unlike his faculty colleagues, the Michigan representative was well aware of the Purdue misdeeds; the commissioner had kept Aigler updated on his findings since early spring.[32] [33] As a consequence, the law

---

[26] Joint Meeting of the Faculty Representatives and Athletic Directors. 29 May 1948. Bentley Historical Library, University of Michigan. Athletic Department, 943 Bimu 2; Box: 84, folder: Faculty Representatives minutes 1941-1957

[27] Conference Athletic Handbook Revisions. 11 February 1948. University of Minnesota Archives, President's Office; Box 238, folder: Physical Education and Athletics 1948-49

[28] Crisler to Wilson. 4 May 1948. Bentley Historical Library, University of Michigan. Board In Control of Intercollegiate Athletics, 8729 Bimu F81 2; Box 31, folder: papers 1948, May

[29] Minutes of the Intercollegiate Conference Meeting of the Athletic Directors. 16 May 1948. University of Wisconsin-Madison. The University Faculty Athletic Board, Series 5/21/6; Box 1, folder: Western Conference minutes 1947-54

[30] Aigler to Lundquist. 12 August 1948. Bentley Historical Library, University of Michigan. Ralph W. Aigler Papers, 87406 Aa 2; Box 10, folder: correspondence 1946-52 "L" misc

[31] Ibid.

[32] Wilson to Aigler. 8 April 1948. Bentley Historical Library, University of Michigan. Ralph W. Aigler Papers, 87406 Aa 2; Box 10, folder: correspondence 1946-52 Wilson, K.L.

[33] Wilson to Aigler. 21 April 1948. Bentley Historical Library, University of Michigan. Ralph W.

professor had time to contemplate disciplinary actions well before the special committee recommendation. The Aigler motion passed.[34] Needless to say, the Boilermakers were steaming.

By mid-July Purdue President Fred Hovde was alerted to the "special censure." The entire investigation, in his opinion, was flawed. Hovde felt that "rules were to a certain extent in flux" between August and December of 1947;[35] it was not until June of 1948 that the boards in control of athletics at each member school finally sanctioned the scholarship policy and allowed the ink to dry on the revised Handbook. The retroactive penalty, he said, was "unfair and discriminatory."[36] But what really disturbed Hovde was the commissioner's plan to expose Purdue to the public. That decision, made by an employee of the conference no less, would impugn the integrity of the university.[37] The former Minnesota engineering student, football player, and highly regarded professor felt that this was going well beyond Wilson's revised job description.

So President Hovde decided to fight back. In a confidential letter to Professor G.R. Lundquist, chairman of the faculty ruling body for that year, he threatened retaliation.

> Should the Faculty Committee itself or through the Commissioner release
> any story singling out Purdue University for censure or unfavorable
> publicity in this matter, then I as President of Purdue University will be
> forced to release a story in defense of the University and give our critical
> comments about the Conference actions in order to explain the matter to the
> Faculty, student body, alumni, and citizen constituencies.[38]

The representatives felt obligated to stand behind their commissioner; to acquiesce to Hovde's threat would only weaken Wilson's development as a leader.[39] He needed to appear decisive if the group was to maintain a principled stance on enforcement.[40] In private, however, a number of those same men were empathetic to Hovde's concerns.[41] [42] [43]

The controversial decision regarding Purdue posed serious consequences for the school months later. Its purported violation of Rule 6, section 4 would also profoundly

---

Aigler Papers, 87406 Aa 2; Box 10, folder: correspondence 1946-52 Wilson, K.L.

[34] Minutes of the Intercollegiate Conference Joint Meeting of the Faculty Representatives and Athletic Directors. 29 May 1948. University of Illinois Archives. Series 4/2/12; Box 3, folder: Western Intercollegiate Conference 1947-48

[35] Hovde to Lundquist. 23 July 1948. Bentley Historical Library, University of Michigan. Ralph W. Aigler Papers, 87406 Aa 2; Box 10, folder: correspondence 1946-52 "L" misc.

[36] Ibid.

[37] Ibid.

[38] Ibid.

[39] Crisler to Wilson. 4 May 1948. Bentley Historical Library, University of Michigan. Board In Control of Intercollegiate Athletics, 8729 Bimu F81 2; Box 31, folder: papers 1948, May

[40] Aigler to Lundquist. 12 August 1948. Bentley Historical Library, University of Michigan. Ralph W. Aigler Papers, 87406 Aa 2; Box 10, folder: correspondence 1946-52 "L" misc

[41] Ibid.

[42] Little to Lundquist. 17 August 1948. University of Wisconsin-Madison. The University Faculty Athletic Board, Series 5/21/7; Box 1, folder: Western Conference General Files

[43] Richart to Lundquist. 15 August 1948. University of Illinois Archives. Series 4/2/12; Box 1, folder: Western Intercollegiate Conference minutes 1947-48

complicate football scheduling during the December meetings in Chicago. Three schools–Ohio State, Michigan, and Illinois–threatened to boycott the Boilermakers.[44] Lacking those programs to compete against on the gridiron would severely impact the athletic budget for Purdue University for the foreseeable future.[45]

As an association of nine members, Western Conference football contracting for game dates remained a challenge throughout the decade. The 9/6/2 rule, approved in December of 1945, made scheduling an even more onerous task for the directors. Purdue notwithstanding, the recent experiences of Iowa demonstrated just how frustrating that could be for a tier-two program in the aftermath of The (Chicago) Announcement of December 1939.

IN THE absence of plans for conference expansion to 11 schools, the State University of Iowa struggled to find a non-conference rival to end its season.[46] In the early 1940s, following Robert Maynard Hutchins' announcement on the Midway, they were fortunate to contract with a few schools from the Big Six; Oklahoma and Kansas State partially filled the void. But what director Ernest Schroeder probably wanted most was a long-term season-ending rivalry game with the University of Nebraska.

Iowa and Nebraska had a football relationship that dated back to 1891. By 1939 the schools had competed on the gridiron 27 times; 14 of those contests closed out the season for the Hawkeyes. But most were played before 1921. By that time, conference rivalries were developing in response to a growing demand by fans. They also assured directors of full stadiums and large gate receipts. Iowa and Northwestern, for example, had begun competing on the last weekend before Thanksgiving starting in November of 1921. Over the next 19 seasons, nine of the Hawkeyes' final games involved the Wildcats.[47]

After a 10-year hiatus from competition, Iowa and Nebraska had resumed their series in 1930. Over the next decade, the schools played each other seven times–four of those contest ended the Big Ten campaign for Iowa. Following a one-year break in 1939, the institutions met again on the gridiron in 1940 and continued competing through the 1946 season.

Iowa's difficulty with scheduling games–season finales in particular–had its origin following that 1921 Big Ten season. At the time, Michigan's Ralph Aigler "began advocating [with athletic director Lynn St. John] that the Michigan-Ohio State game should be the final one of the schedule for the two teams."[48] Earlier in the fall campaign, Ohio State had defeated the Wolverines for the third straight time. Aigler felt that the contest had

---

[44] Minutes of the Intercollegiate Conference. Meeting of the Athletic Directors. 30 November 1948. University of Wisconsin-Madison. The University Faculty Athletic Board, Series 5/21/7; Box 1, folder: Western Conference General Files

[45] Wilson, Kenneth. Memorandum. 12 May 1948. Bentley Historical Library, University of Michigan. Board In Control of Intercollegiate Athletics, 8729 Bimu F81 2; Box 31, folder: papers 1948, May

[46] Wilson to Faculty Representatives. 5 August 1947. University of Illinois Archives. Series 4/2/12; Box 3, folder: Western Intercollegiate Conference 1946-47

[47] Due to the 1929 Iowa scandal, the conference boycotted the Hawkeyes in 1930. Nebraska assumed the spot reserved for Northwestern that season. Iowa and Northwestern resumed their rivalry the following season.

[48] Aigler to Laylin. 7 October 1933. Bentley Historical Library, University of Michigan. Ralph W. Aigler Papers. 87406 Aa 2; Box 12, athletic correspondence: 1933-36 "L" misc.

become such a rivalry that it merited the Saturday date before Thanksgiving. But St. John ignored the request and maintained a relationship with the University of Illinois as its last opponent of the season. By June of 1932, however, the Buckeye had a change of heart.[49] He and Fielding Yost agreed to begin contracting in line with the old Aigler proposal. The agreement was consummated with gridiron action on November 23, 1935.

A ripple effect followed. Illinois asked the University of Chicago to assume the weekend previously shared with Ohio State. But when Chicago dropped football in December of 1939, the Illini turned to their other intrastate rival, Northwestern. As a consequence of decisions made by tier-one powers, by the fall of 1940, Iowa would lose its season finale with the Wildcats.

Athletic Director Ernest Schroeder was in a bind. The eight conference members still participating in football had well-established relationships for their final games. Recognizing the value of its old rivalry with Nebraska, Schroeder sought help from Lincoln. The Cornhuskers eagerly signed up; competing against Iowa offered them an unparalleled opportunity to gain membership in the Western Conference. From 1940 through 1945 the two schools contracted on an annual basis—three of those Saturdays with Nebraska ended the season for Iowa. But by the spring of 1944 the Cornhuskers' interest in seeking admission into the conference was waning. Although an application was considered in March of 1946[50] it was probably promoted more by Iowa and its faculty representative, Karl Leib, than by advocates from Lincoln.[51]

With Nebraska appearing uninterested in admission, there was no longer a need for it to collaborate with Iowa on scheduling. As a consequence, the State University struggled to find a program willing to close out its 1946-47 campaigns.[52] During those two years the Hawkeyes ended their seasons one week earlier than required by Handbook policy.[53] Although a point of frustration for director Schroeder and his Board in Control, all would change by the summer of 1948. Due to some very adept negotiations by new athletic director Paul Brechler, Iowa signed up a school out of South Bend, Indiana, willing to fill the date. The renewable contract signed with the marquee program assured Iowa a game certain to capture national interest and fill its 44,000 seat stadium.[54]

THE LIST of 25 students charged with violating the Highland Park yardstick was too

---

[49] Aigler to Laylin. 7 October 1933. Bentley Historical Library, University of Michigan. Ralph W. Aigler Papers. 87406 Aa 2; Box 12, athletic correspondence: 1933-36 "L" misc.

[50] Reeves to Hannah. 21 March 1946. Michigan State University Archives. Floyd Reeves Papers, UA21.12.1; Box 115, folder: 21

[51] Minutes of the Intercollegiate Conference of Faculty Representatives. 31 May-1 June 1946. University of Minnesota Archives, Presidents Office; Box 238, folder: Physical Education 1945-47

[52] Wilson to Faculty Representatives. 5 August 1947. University of Illinois Archives. Athletic Committee Chairman and Faculty Representatives File 1907-1949, Series 4/2/12; Box 3, folder: Western Intercollegiate Conference 1946-47

[53] 1947-48 Western Conference Football Schedule. 12 December 1946. Bentley Historical Library, University of Michigan. Board In Control of Intercollegiate Athletics, 8729 Bimu F81 2; Box 35, folder: football schedules 1944, 1946, 1947

[54] Smith, Lyall. "As of Today: MSC Prepared to Pass Big Nine Entrance Test." *Detroit Free Press* 9 November 1948. Smith was comparing seating capacity at various stadiums in the conference at the time. He cited Iowa's at 44,000 at the time.

lengthy for the faculty to address during the 1948 May meetings. The attendees at the joint gathering decided to reconvene on June 5 in Chicago. This allowed a few weeks for registrars and scholarship committees to investigate claims made by the Office of the Commissioner.

Upon returning to the Sherman Hotel in early June, the nine leaders were able to winnow Wilson's list down to 15 students. It was an arduous two-day process; all 15 were declared ineligible for one year of competition.[55] But Northwestern petitioned for additional time in order to locate data on its suspect students. With a complex scholarship program in place for years, the Wildcats claimed some athletes might have received legitimate monies for reasons unrelated to academic performance measured by the yardstick.[56] By early September Northwestern had verified that four of its five students were in compliance. The committee subsequently closed its review of Wilson's original investigation. Of the 25 students implicated back in May, only 11 were declared ineligible for one year of football competition.[57]

Due to the Northwestern delay, the commissioner's report remained filed for over two months in his office within the Sherman Hotel. Finally, in mid-September, the names of the schools found in violation of the scholarship rule as well as the 11 students declared ineligible were released to the press. Illinois, Michigan, Purdue, Wisconsin, and Northwestern were all cited.[58] [59]

But the Purdue reprimand was never disclosed to the public. That finding remained confidential in deference to Fred Hovde. His vow to go public had weighed heavily on the leadership.[60] [61] [62] It was a major victory for the president. His institution had avoided embarrassing publicity. Purdue's integrity was unscathed by the flawed investigation.

Frustrated by Hovde's threat, certain conference leaders continued their search for another program to one day publicly censure.[63] [64] Decisive action of that nature would make

[55] Minutes of the Intercollegiate Conference of Faculty Representatives. 5-6 June 1948. University of Wisconsin-Madison. The University Faculty Board, Series 5/21/6; Box 1, folder: Western Conference minutes 1947-51

[56] Ibid.

[57] Minutes of the Intercollegiate Conference of Faculty Representatives. 12 September 1948. University of Wisconsin-Madison. The University Faculty Board, Series 5/21/6; Box 1, folder: Western Conference minutes 1947-51

[58] Lundquist to Richart. 1 September 1948. University of Illinois Archives. Series 4/2/12; Box 3, folder: Western Intercollegiate Conference 1947-48

[59] Minutes of the Intercollegiate Conference of Faculty Representatives. 12 September 1948. University of Wisconsin-Madison. The University Faculty Board, Series 5/21/6; Box 1, folder: Western Conference minutes 1947-51

[60] Lundquist to Richart. 11 August 1948. University of Illinois Archives. Series 4/2/12; Box 3, folder: Western Intercollegiate Conference 1947-48

[61] Richart to Lundquist. 13 August 1948. University of Illinois Archives. Series 4/2/12; Box 3, folder: Western Intercollegiate Conference 1947-48

[62] Lundquist to Richart. 1 September 1948. University of Illinois Archives. Series 4/2/12; Box 3, folder: Western Intercollegiate Conference 1947-48

[63] Aigler to Blommers. 8 December 1952. Bentley Historical Library, University of Michigan. Ralph W. Aigler Papers, 87406 Aa 2; Box 9, folder: correspondence 1946-52 "B" misc.

[64] Aigler to Reed. 19 May 1952. Bentley Historical Library, University of Michigan. Ralph W. Aigler Papers, 87406 Aa 2; Box 10, folder: correspondence 1946-52 Reed, William

a statement to the press and public that the Intercollegiate Conference of Faculty Representatives took the Sanity Code very seriously.

ONE WEEK before the May 1948 meeting of the faculty and directors, Henry Rottschaefer had penned a note to Frank Richart of Illinois. The Minnesota law school professor requested that "the matter of expanding the Conference membership to include Michigan State" be placed on the agenda.[65] Rottschaefer was following the plans drafted by his president. Lew Morrill was intent on forcing a vote on Michigan State. He was convinced that the college, led by a man of the highest integrity, was fully compliant with conference rules.[66]

In anticipation of that joint meeting, the athletic directors met on May 16 in Chicago. Ken Wilson, at the time, was not privy to Rottschaefer's intention to promote Michigan State's application in the near future. He began the meeting by updating the directors on scholarship violations previously reported to them during a special gathering on the 27th of April. The commissioner then "requested the directors ... consider Michigan State's pending application for membership in the Conference."[67] He knew that the faculty, at the joint meeting scheduled in two weeks, would make no decision on an application without input from the directors regarding expansion back to 10 members. But Wilson's request was puzzling. The Spartans had no intention of applying in May. Hannah was more focused on December.

Wilson was undoubtedly aware of the turmoil in the athletic department in Pittsburgh. The 1947 gridiron experiment of competing against six conference schools, a plan devised by James Hagan, had been a disaster. By late November it was understood that Hagan was a lame duck. He would tender his resignation in early June of 1948. In the meantime, coordination of a plan for Western Conference affiliation–a responsibility given the athletic director–was held in abeyance at Pitt. Anything the commissioner could do, as a covert Panther advocate, to forestall a Spartan advance would be greatly appreciated by both administrators and faculty. Membership in the Intercollegiate Conference, after all, would not only benefit the struggling athletic program but also help the school regain academic integrity lost during the humiliating Jock Sutherland tenure in Pittsburgh.[68]

So following Wilson's surprising inquiry to the group, "An extended discussion was held and it was the sense of the directors that the Conference should determine in what manner Michigan State is adhering to the Conference regulations before final action be taken on the application."[69] Fritz Crisler might very well have played a major role in that decision. The requirement was consistent with Ralph Aigler's (and Crisler's) February 1946

---

[65] Rottschaefer to Richart. 20 May 1948. University of Illinois Archives. Series 4/2/12; Box 3, folder: Western Intercollegiate Conference 1947-48

[66] Morrill to Rottchaefer and McCormick. 9 July 1947. University of Minnesota Archives, President's Office; Box 238, folder: Physical Education and Athletics 1948-49

[67] Minutes of the Intercollegiate Conference Meeting of the Athletic Directors. 16 May 1948. University of Wisconsin-Madison Archives. The University Faculty Athletic Board, Series 5/21/6; Box 1, folder: Western Conference minutes 1947-54

[68] Sherrill to Fitzgerald. 10 April 1946. University of Pittsburgh Archives, 2/10; Box 4, folder: FF24

[69] Minutes of the Intercollegiate Conference Meeting of the Athletic Directors. 16 May 1948. University of Wisconsin-Madison Archives. The University Faculty Athletic Board, Series 5/21/6; Box 1, folder: Western Conference minutes 1947-54

conversation with John Hannah[70] that Michigan State must be in full compliance with the Handbook before Michigan would support any application for admission.[71]

Two weeks later, on May 29, the representatives and directors met in Madison, Wisconsin. After debating Aigler's motion on disciplining Purdue, Rottschaefer's proposal requesting a vote on admitting Michigan State was addressed. In a counter motion that would have profound political significance many months later, Frank Richart requested that the faculty "… take no action on that institution's application for … membership until it can be shown that Michigan State is adhering to the spirit and wording of all phases of Conference Rules."[72]

Ralph Aigler's apparent influence (with the assistance of Fritz Crisler) in the athletic directors' decision not to expand the group–and the representatives' vote to honor that desire–was now without a doubt. Based on its similar verbiage, the author of the Richart motion was the faculty representative from the University of Michigan.[73] It was the second major victory for the law professor during that morning session; the severe reprimand imposed on Purdue was the other.

The decision by the directors and faculty was undoubtedly gratifying for Professor Aigler. Four months earlier, following passage of the Sanity Code, President John Hannah had announced to the State Board of Agriculture his intention to revise the entire financial aid program at Michigan State. The Jenison Awards, in particular, would be rescinded. The Sanity Code permitted only academic scholarships to athletes. The Spartan subsidies were not consistent with that edict.[74] [75]

Ralph Aigler, shortly after hearing of Hannah's decision, congratulated the president in supporting the NCAA policy. But there remained a subtle hint of skepticism in his letter regarding the president's apparent conversion to Aigler's concept of amateurism; years of dealing with rumors from East Lansing were hard to forget. In commenting on the historic amendment, he noted that its success will depend on "…the attitude of the member institutions and those representing them. If a considerable percentage of the membership should start out with the idea of circumventing the new rules in every possible way, then the whole movement will fail…I am proceeding on the assumption that [most] will make an honest effort to respect the rules."[76] The Michigan scholar was privy to a number of suspect activities still taking place at MSC in violation of conference policies for schools competing against its membership. Training tables for non-gridiron sports and aggressive recruiting by

---

[70] Hannah to Kimpton. 27 February 1946. Michigan State University Archives. Floyd Reeves Papers, UA 21.12.1; Box 115, folder: 21

[71] Aigler to Richart. 21 December 1948. University of Illinois Archives. Series 4/2/12; Box 3, folder: Western Intercollegiate Conference 1948-49

[72] Minutes of the Intercollegiate Conference Joint Meeting of the Faculty Representatives and Athletic Directors. 29 May 1948. Bentley Historical Library, University of Michigan. Athletic Department, 943 Bimu 2; Box 84, folder: Big-Ten directors meeting 3/41-7/52

[73] Aigler to Richart. 21 December 1948. University of Illinois Archives. Series 4/2/12; Box 3, folder: Western Intercollegiate Conference 1948-49

[74] Minutes of the State Board of Agriculture. 15 January 1948. www.onthebanks.msu.edu

[75] Hannah would honor promises made to athletes already receiving financial aid. This decision was ruled acceptable by the NCAA for all schools offering similar assistance.

[76] Aigler to Hannah. 26 January 1948. Bentley Historical Library, University of Michigan. Ralph W. Aigler Papers, 87406 Aa 2; Box 9, folder: correspondence 1946-52 "H" misc.

Spartan coaches were among a few examples.[77] Aigler would not support the college's admission until it was in full compliance with the Intercollegiate Handbook; "mere promises to comply" by John Hannah were not sufficient.[78] It appeared that the professor still could not trust his former student.

The morning meeting of May 29 was adjourned shortly after that vote. At the request of the faculty leadership, the commissioner would notify President Hannah of its decision not to consider a Spartan application until full compliance with the Western Conference rules and regulations was verified. The directors' vote of May 16 weighed heavily in that determination. Michigan State College of Agriculture and Applied Science had just received its fifth rejection in 11 years. And it all took place without John Hannah's awareness.

DESPITE COMMISSIONER Wilson being a covert advocate for Pittsburgh, in hindsight he probably had no private agenda when he "requested the directors … consider Michigan State's pending application for membership in the Conference" at the May 16 meeting. As it was later revealed, the source of that request was Frank McCormick, athletic director at the University of Minnesota. Acting without the knowledge or the approval of Lew Morrill, McCormick "made a formal endeavor to get action on the Michigan State application" by the athletic directors. It would not be until mid September–much to the surprise of his boss–that McCormick would reveal his independent action to the president.[79]

Wilson was merely carrying out the Minnesota director's request. Aware of McCormick's intentions well in advance of the May 16 meeting, the commissioner probably informed both Ralph Aigler and Fritz Crisler of the plan. He was in constant communication with the two influential athletic leaders during his tenure in office. The scoop would give the them ample time to strategize prior to the meeting. With Fritz Crisler's influence among the directors, a "no" vote on conference expansion was a certainty. The faculty would honor their decision.

The original Morrill Plan was to have Rottschaefer make a motion to the faculty and bypass any director involvement. The Minnesota president was well aware of Article I, section 1 defining the process for attaining membership. It remained a faculty decision alone; there was no need for the athletic directors' input.[80] Henry Rottschaefer's request, on May 20, for a spot on the agenda of the upcoming faculty meeting was consistent with that plan. McCormick, acting independently, was uninformed of the Morrill-Rottschaefer strategy. The miscommunication among the three men proved an invaluable lesson for Lew Morrill. He would soon announce a revised plan to fix that problem. If Michigan State and John Hannah were to succeed at a later date, it would require collaborative strategic planning between the two institutions.

THE HONEST miscue of Frank McCormick notwithstanding, the unexpected phone call

---

[77] Aigler to Richart. 21 December 1948. University of Illinois Archives. Series 4/2/12; Box 3, folder: Western Intercollegiate Conference 1948-49

[78] Ibid.

[79] Morrill to Rottschaefer. 16 September 1948. University of Minnesota, President's Office; Box 238, folder: Physical Education and Athletics 1948-49

[80] Rottschaefer to Morrill. 26 February 1948. University of Minnesota Archives, President's Office; Box 238, folder: Physical Education and Athletics 1948-49

from the commissioner, alerting John Hannah of the conference leadership's decision, was another disappointment for him. Fortunately for the president and Michigan State, the fifth rejection remained confidential.

Unaware of Lew Morrill's strategy, Hannah wrote his friend a few days following the telephone conversation with Ken Wilson. After learning of the circumstances predating the faculty vote, Hannah expressed suspicions to Morrill that Michigan's Fritz Crisler was probably behind the directors' decision not to expand–at least as long as a Spartan was the suitor. He was convinced, more than ever, that its athletic leadership was too powerful and influential.

> Our people all feel ... that with the continuous opposition of our friends at
> Ann Arbor on every occasion and at every opportunity where it can be done
> without being too open and with many of the Conference schools awed by
> Mr. Crisler, et al ... about our only chance to rise is through the good graces
> of your University.[81]

The president was requesting help from the University of Minnesota. Plan B once again appeared to be the only viable option for the college as long as Michigan was in control. Hannah wanted the Golden Gophers on his football schedule to complement the Fighting Irish of Notre Dame.

Lew Morrill agreed to assist his friend. The Buckeye distrusted the Wolverine athletic leaders as much as John Hannah did.[82] Morrill's only request was to "keep me in touch with any developments at your end." He shared Hannah's letter with Frank McCormick, who promised to do his best to accommodate Michigan State.[83]

John Hannah kept his end of the bargain with Morrill by keeping him "in touch" with developments back in Michigan while the two worked diligently during the early fall to prepare for a December application. In late November the president wrote to his friend expressing frustration, once again, in dealing with Fritz Crisler. He charged the Michigan athletic director with "brow-beating our people into agreeing to playing all of the Michigan-Michigan State games in Ann Arbor for an indefinite period and insisted upon an answer before the coming Conference meetings [in December]."[84] In response to the Michigan leader's aggressive antics, President Hannah would relieve his athletic director, Ralph Young, of his negotiating responsibilities. Faculty Representative Lloyd Emmons was assigned the task. Fritz Crisler would finally meet his match in the long-running scheduling debate!

Hannah was fairly confident that his college would be admitted into the Western Conference by December. He had President Alexander Ruthven's assurances that the

---

[81] Hannah to Morrill. 2 June 1948. University of Minnesota, President's Office; Box 238, folder: Physical Education and Athletics 1948-49

[82] Morrill to Rottschaefer. 16 September 1948. University of Minnesota, President's Office; Box 238, folder: Physical Education and Athletics 1948-49

[83] Morrill to Hannah. 15 June 1948. University of Minnesota, President's Office; Box 238, folder: Physical Education and Athletics 1948-49

[84] Hannah to Morrill. 23 November 1948. University of Minnesota, President's Office; Box 238, folder: Physical Education and Athletics 1948-49

University of Michigan would fully support his initiative.[85] Many other schools were lining up behind the Spartans as well. Hannah sensed that Crisler knew it was inevitable–and that Michigan's dominance over the college was diminishing. The current actions by the Wolverine director, and his board, were seen as one final attempt at maintaining control over the Spartans, for at least the short term.[86] Crisler did not want to lose that season-opening date with Michigan State in Ann Arbor. No other school, after all, could provide a comparable return on investment for the scrimmage game before the start of the Big Nine season in October.

JOHN HANNAH wrote to Lew Morrill in late September of 1948 just after the Spartans had lost to the Wolverines by a narrow margin in the stadium-expansion dedication game. "Our boys at least deglamorized them, and from now on out instead of being the great Rose Bowl team of 1947 they will be a team that was almost matched by the little stepbrothers from East Lansing,"[87] "little stepbrothers" being his version of "weak sisters." It was evident, by the misquote, that by now, one year later, he too shared Munn's conviction that Michigan–Fritz Crisler–was the author of the "weak sister" comment shared with the press in June of 1947.

Both Hannah and Morrill were making significant progress toward conference membership by the time of the the historic game in East Lansing. A strategy devised back in the late spring, following the fifth rejection, was moving forward just as planned. December–and success–was only 10 weeks away.

---

[85] Hannah to Morrill. 23 November 1948. University of Minnesota, President's Office; Box 238, folder: Physical Education and Athletics 1948-49

[86] Ibid.

[87] Hannah to Morrill. 27 September 1948. University of Minnesota Archives, President's Office; Box 138, folder: Michigan and Michigan State 1948-59

A Revised Strategy, a Realized Dream

THE MCCORMICK Miscue, rejection five, failed to discourage James Lewis Morrill. His East Lansing counterpart might have been frustrated with the apparent antics of the University of Michigan, but Morrill had another game plan certain to gain a rare victory for the Spartans over their rival from Ann Arbor. The traditional approach to achieving membership–a right provided the faculty representatives since 1896–would never work as long as the Wolverines had any say in the matter.

Morrill and John Hannah still viewed Ralph Aigler as the most powerful conference leader. His presence and rhetoric clearly influenced the five new and inexperienced faculty representatives who had joined the exclusive club in the past five years.[1]

Assuming Michigan was honest in its professed support of the Spartans, what frustrated Hannah and challenged Morrill was its inability to deliver a favorable vote for Michigan State–as the decision of May 1948 illustrated. Morrill was convinced Professor Aigler was not truly committed to the Spartan cause. A man of his stature could have used his pro-Michigan State stance to impact the views of a faculty committee in transition. Away from the conference rooms–where the real decisions are made–the Minnesota president suspected "skullduggery over Scotch and soda" had contributed to the recent rejection.[2]

John Hannah, on the other hand, was suspicious of Fritz Crisler. In his view, the Wolverine had displayed his true convictions two weeks prior to the joint gathering of the faculty and directors in late May. At the time of the McCormick Miscue, Hannah felt the highly regarded Crisler could have easily swayed his colleagues in supporting the college's plan.[3] Lacking any favorable directive from the athletic directors–assured by Crisler's lack of support–the faculty representatives merely deferred making a decision on the Rottschaefer motion.

---

[1] Richart to Pollard. 11 March 1949. University of Illinois Archives. Series 4/2/12; Box 3, folder: Western Intercollegiate Conference 1948-49

[2] Morrill to Rottschaefer. 16 September 1948. University of Minnesota, President's Office; Box 238, folder: Physical Education and Athletics 1948-49

[3] Hannah to Morrill. 2 June 1948. University of Minnesota, President's Office; Box 238, folder: Physical Education and Athletics 1948-49

These apparent maneuvers by the Michigan leaders were what ultimately prompted Morrill to revise the original plan that he had inadvertently failed to share with Hannah and his staff. His solution to the controlling influence held by the Wolverines was simple: He would manipulate the Handbook rules on applying for membership.

Back in February, Morrill had received a copy of Henry Rottschaefer's "Statement and Codification and Amendments to the Conference Code" in anticipation of the meeting of fellow presidents, faculty representatives, and athletic directors a week later. He had proposed this meeting in December with an eye toward the presidents taking a more proactive role in oversight of the conference. Morrill was troubled by trends developing within the conference, and Ralph Aigler was troubled by Morrill's grab for more presidential power, which he saw as contrary to the Handbook.[4] The professor of law had little recourse but to support the initiative. The presidents, after all, had created the conference in 1895; it was within their purview to redesign it as well.

Rottschaefer's four-page document provided the specific revisions, as outlined by Morrill, to strengthen enforcement and adjudication within the conference. But as he scanned the draft, Morrill's attention must have been caught by Article I, section 1.

> The Western Intercollegiate Athletic Conference shall consist of the
> universities now members and such other universities or colleges as may
> hereafter be admitted to membership by majority vote of the Intercollegiate
> Conference of Faculty Representatives.[5]

This might have been his first realization of the requirements for admission into the Intercollegiate Conference. The process, it appeared, was quite simple. Contrary to recently adopted practices, the athletic directors held no role in determining membership. This was a right reserved only for the faculty representatives. The fifth rejection of May 1948 was accomplished in violation of Handbook policy. And Michigan–the trumpeter of rules and regulations–appeared to be the source of that action.

Lew Morrill decided two could play at this game. During the early summer of 1948, shortly after the Spartan rejection, he drafted a multifaceted strategy to counter the Aigler-Crisler control over the current admission process. Morrill's new plan involved the staffs of both Minnesota and Michigan State working together for a common goal; communication was critical to avoiding another McCormick Miscue.

Due to his background in journalism, Morrill maintained a good working relationship with the press. He would seek its help as a public-relations resource in promoting Hannah's college. And as a leader of the Council of Nine, he would openly solicit the support of fellow presidents. Finally, the Minnesotan would encourage the Spartan faculty representative to travel about the conference and cultivate good will by interacting with his cohorts.[6]

Phase one involved Morrill's key associate William Nunn. He encouraged his

---

[4] Aigler to Richart. 14 December 1948. Bentley Historical Library, University of Michigan. Ralph W. Aigler Papers, 87406 Aa 2; Box 10, folder: correspondence 1946-52 "R" misc.

[5] Rottschaefer to Morrill. 26 February 1948. University of Minnesota Archives, President's Office; Box 238, folder: Physical Education and Athletics 1948-49

[6] Denison, James H. 5 November 1969. "Intercollegiate Conference." Michigan State University Archives. Hannah Papers, UA2.1.12; Box 80, folder: 12

executive assistant to meet with James Denison, Hannah's counterpart at the college. The two were instructed to coordinate his revised strategy. Collaboration and effective communication between the staffs of both administrations were essential for success in December.

Minneapolis Star sports editor Charles Johnson would play a critical role in phase two of the Morrill plan. The journalist was a good friend of the president's.[7] He would encourage editors at various Midwest newspapers to publish favorable articles regarding the college during the months leading up to the election.[8] [9]

The third component of Lew Morrill's plan, perhaps the most controversial, involved the power of the presidency. He was convinced that colleagues about the conference could easily influence their faculty representative's vote through persuasive means.[10] [11] He personally had asked Henry Rottschaefer and Frank McCormick to support Michigan State's cause one year earlier.

> I am very sympathetic with the plea [of Hannah]–for two reasons: (1) the Michigan State athletic plant, which I recently visited, is one of the finest in the nation, and (2) I am completely convinced of the soundness and integrity of President Hannah's views and influence upon the administration of athletics at Michigan State[12] ... I want very much, if you [both]agree, to get this proposition off dead center and to bring it to a vote in the Western Conference upon our initiative ... [13]

A decade ago Rottschaefer had voted against Michigan State College being admitted as an eleventh member. Backroom politicking by Aigler may have played a role in that decision–the General College fiasco and treatment of President Lotus Coffman notwithstanding. Rottschaefer ultimately agreed with his fellow faculty representatives that there was no reason to expand at the time. But by midsummer of 1948, he had lined up behind his boss's plan.

The president would actively seek the support of his eight colleagues on the Council of Nine for his friend's cause.[14] It would be an easy sell for Morrill. Hannah was already

---

[7] Morrill to (Nunn). 19 February 1948. University of Minnesota Archives, Morrill, J.L.; Box 2, folder: 50 Mpls. newspapers re. Chas. Johnson

[8] Thomas, David A. *Michigan State College: John Hannah and the Creation of a World University, 1926-1969.* East Lansing: Michigan State University Press, 2008, p. 290

[9] Linton, Ron. "Officials Keep Mum As College Awaits Big Nine Decision." *State News* 3 December 1948. Michigan State University Archives. UA12.107, Madison Kuhn Collection; Scrapbook 108, folder: 5

[10] Aigler to Richart. 14 December 1948. Bentley Historical Library, University of Michigan. Ralph W. Aigler Papers, 87406 Aa 2; Box 10, folder: correspondence 1946-52 "R" misc.

[11] Thomas, David A. *Michigan State College: John Hannah and the Creation of a World University, 1926-1969.* East Lansing: Michigan State University Press, 2008, p. 295

[12] Morrill to Rottschaefer. 9 July 1947. University of Minnesota Archives, President's Office; Box 238, folder: Physical Education and Athletics 1948-49

[13] Morrill to Rottschaefer. 16 September 1948. University of Minnesota Archives, President's Office; Box 238, folder: Physical Education and Athletics 1948-49

[14] Aigler to Richart. 14 December 1948. Bentley Historical Library, University of Michigan. Ralph W. Aigler Papers, 87406 Aa 2; Box 10, folder: correspondence 1946-52 "R" misc.

well connected with most members of that group. He was a actively involved with an informal organization of 13 midwestern universities that met periodically to discuss challenges in managing large institutions in the aftermath of the war. All Big Nine presidents routinely attended the sessions.[15] Seven of those Intercollegiate Conference leaders were also on his "blueberries and maple syrup" list: they were close friends.

Howard Landis Bevis of The Ohio State University, despite participating in the association of universities focused on "cooperation, coordination and regionalization in education," was the only leader John Hannah did not know well. Lew Morrill, who remained in contact with his former boss, would address that matter. He planned to visit with Bevis in Columbus during October, well before the annual December meeting.[16]

The final phase of the revised Morrill Plan involved Michigan State's Professor Lloyd Emmons. The dean of liberal arts was assigned the task of selling the college to certain faculty representatives about the conference. From August 23 through September 2 he visited Madison, Evanston, Urbana, Bloomington, and Columbus.[17] Henry Rottschaefer, in the spirit of collaboration, probably facilitated many of those encounters. It is noteworthy that Iowa City was not included. As will be seen, there may have been reasons for the apparent Hawkeye snub.

Dean Emmons proved to be quite effective at his job.[18] He gained assurances of support from representatives at every program other than Northwestern.[19]

The strategy was brilliant and effective. But one problem still needed attention: the influence of Ralph Aigler and Herbert Crisler. Morrill had to find a way to counter their control of due process. By September, his friend from East Lansing had an answer.

Michigan State required only five votes, a simple majority, to achieve admission into the conference. Minnesota was a certainty. And Lloyd Emmons was confident that he had four nods after his recent travel. Realizing how critical it was to assure that those votes remained committed, in mid-September President Hannah proposed an amendment, of sorts, to the Morrill Plan. It was a rather devious scheme. Enacting it merely required the cooperation of Henry Rottschaefer as a voting member of the Faculty Representatives Committee. In a letter to Professor Rottschaefer, Morrill outlined the Hannah amendment that would almost certainly preclude any Aigler-Crisler counter move behind closed doors.

> By reason of my sympathetic interest in the matter, it was quite logical that
> President Hannah should ask me whether it would be possible for the
> University of Minnesota to initiate definite action on the pending
> application. If we should, Michigan would have to support it and there
> would be four additional supporting votes if the other institutional
> representatives meant what they said to the Michigan State faculty

---

[15] "Conference of Representatives of Thirteen Midwestern Universities on Cooperation, Coordination and Regionalization in Education." 16 March 1946. University of Wisconsin-Madison Archives. E.B. Fred Papers, General Correspondence Files, Series 4/16/1; Box 64, folder: Mi misc. 1945-46

[16] Morrill to Rottschaefer. 16 September 1948. University of Minnesota Archives, President's Office; Box 238, folder: Physical Education and Athletics 1948-49

[17] Minutes of the State Board of Agriculture. 16 September 1948. www.onthebanks.msu.edu.

[18] Denison, James H. 5 November 1969. "Intercollegiate Conference." Michigan State University Archives. Hannah Papers, UA2.1.12; Box 80, folder:12

[19] Minutes of the State Board of Agriculture. 16 September 1948. www.onthebanks.msu.edu.

chairman.[20]

Ralph Aigler would be placed in a predicament. Since March of 1946 he (and Crisler) had openly professed allegiance to President Ruthven's politically astute commitment to support John Hannah's cause. In private, however, Aigler maintained that no sponsorship would be given the college application by Michigan until the school was in full compliance with conference standards. Without a sponsor there could be no vote. But now, with Hannah gaining a confidential commitment from Minnesota to nominate Michigan State, a decision among the faculty regarding the Spartan application would have to take place.

For weeks in advance of the December meetings, the press had been speculating on how members might vote. Assuming Emmons' count was accurate, a rejection, in Morrill's opinion, would indicate that Professor Aigler had sided against Michigan State.[21] [22] [23] But the university president, in his letter to Rottschaefer, had overlooked the fact that, regardless of how Michigan cast its vote behind closed doors, Minnesota's support gave the college the simple majority necessary for admission. Leaks, following certain meetings held in 'executive session,' however, were becoming quite common in the conference, much to the frustration of Ralph Aigler.[24] [25] If the Wolverine professor, behind closed doors, were to cast a nay vote and it was later revealed to the press, he would be hung in effigy back in the state of Michigan. So it would appear that Hannah, in proposing his amendment to the Morrill plan, was less concerned with how Michigan might vote in "confidence." His focus was on simply assuring that a vote take place.

THE WARM Friend Tavern was the only hotel in downtown Holland, Michigan. Its interior elegance contrasted with the ascetic traditions of the Dutch populating much of the area.

Henry Rottschaefer grew up in Holland. Upon graduating from the University of Michigan Law School in 1915, he returned to West Michigan on occasion to spend time with family. He maintained little contact otherwise with the community. Hope College even lost track of its celebrated alumnus, despite his accomplishments as a professor of tax and constitutional law[26] and his distinguished service as faculty representative to the Western

---

[20] Morrill to Rottschaefer. 16 September 1948. University of Minnesota Archives, President's Office; Box 238, folder: Physical Education and Athletics 1948-49

[21] "M.S.C. Seen Sure Spot in 'Big Ten.'" *Chicago Daily News* 20 November 1948, University of Minnesota Archives, President's Office; Box 238, folder: Physical Education and Athletics 1948-49

[22] Linton, Ron. "Officials Keep Mum As College Awaits Big Nine Decision." *State News* 3 December 1948. Michigan State University Archives. UA12.107, Madison Kuhn Collection; Scrapbook 108, folder: 5

[23] "Opposition to Michigan State's Bid Seen Growing." *Lansing State Journal* 11 December 1948, Michigan State University Archives. UA12.107, Madison Kuhn Collection; Scrapbook 108, folder: 5

[24] Aigler to Spoelstra. 27 May 1949. Bentley Historical Library, University of Michigan. Ralph W. Aigler Papers, 87406 Aa 2; Box 10, folder: correspondence 1946-52 "B" misc.

[25] Spoelstra to Aigler. 2 June 1949. Bentley Historical Library, University of Michigan. Ralph W. Aigler Papers, 87406 Aa 2; Box 10, folder: correspondence 1946-52 "B" misc.

[26] "A Tribute to Professor Henry Rottschaefer." November 1957. *Minnesota Law Review*, volume 42, no. 1

Conference. [27] [28]

But on Friday, September 17, 1948, Rottschaefer was in Holland visiting family. While staying at the Warm Friend, he received an airmail special delivery letter from his president. The three-page communiqué outlined Morrill's strategy regarding Michigan State's application process. He wanted to be certain that the faculty representative was agreeable to his role in the revised Morrill Plan, as recently amended by John Hannah. The December meetings were only a few months away.[29]

Rottschaefer penned an airmail reply–on Warm Friend stationary–professing his commitment. He also shared comments heard at a recent conference gathering in Chicago. Spartan Faculty Representative Lloyd Emmons' visits to conference schools–one aspect of the Morrill Plan–had been quite successful. By Rottschaefer's canvass of colleagues at the meeting, Michigan State was assured a simple majority of favorable votes.[30]

He then referred to comments in Morrill's letter regarding Ralph Aigler and Fritz Crisler. The president was privy to some gossip that both leaders were opposed to the Spartan application; they had shared their opinions in confidence with a few conference colleagues.[31] Somebody in that small core of confidants had leaked word to Minnesota. "I agree that Michigan's stand puzzles me … a couple of years ago it was represented to me as favorable, but I've heard their sincerity questioned."[32]

Irrespective of the gossip, Lew Morrill was satisfied with the response he got from Holland. Henry Rottschaefer was committed to the cause. The Minnesota president's scheme was right on schedule.

JOHN HANNAH completed much of his assignment in the revised Morrill Plan during September. He invited all conference athletic directors and faculty representatives to the stadium-expansion dedication game between Michigan and Michigan State on September 25, 1948. The Spartans lost 13-7. The defeat was irrelevant. Hannah used the opportunity to showcase the college to people critical in the voting process.

Ohio State faculty representative Wendell Postle returned to Columbus thoroughly impressed. The dental school professor reported to the athletic board on October 20 his recollections of the weekend in East Lansing. The board then discussed the Spartan application. "The general opinion seemed to be that, if the Conference felt it desirable to enlarge, the logical school to add was Michigan State."[33] Only three years earlier, while

---

[27] The Hope College Joint Archives had one biographical file on Henry J. Rottschaefer: a reprint dated 4/1957 from the University of Minnesota Law School announcing his retirement.

[28] Aigler to Owens. 24 September 1938. Bentley Historical Library, University of Michigan. Ralph W. Aigler Papers, 87406 Aa 2; Box 7, folder: correspondence 1934-39 "O" misc

[29] Morrill to Rottschaefer. 16 September 1948. University of Minnesota Archives, President's Office; Box 238, folder: Physical Education and Athletics 1948-49

[30] Rottschaefer to Morrill. 17 September 1948. University of Minnesota Archives, President's Office; Box 238, folder: Physical Education and Athletics 1948-49

[31] Morrill to Rottschaefer. 16 September 1948. University of Minnesota Archives, President's Office; Box 238, folder: Physical Education and Athletics 1948-49

[32] Rottschaefer to Morrill. 17 September 1948. University of Minnesota Archives, President's Office; Box 238, folder: Physical Education and Athletics 1948-49

[33] Four Hundred and Ninety Second Meeting of the Athletic Board of The Ohio State University. 20 October 1948. The Ohio State University Archives, Athletic: Director of (RG 9/e-1/1), "Athletic

Lynn St. John was still in command, the group had favored the University of Pittsburgh.[34] Acknowledging Lloyd Emmons' favorable visit with Dr. Postle back in late August, the change in allegiance among the leadership probably reflected some adept politicking by OSU graduate Lew Morrill.

On October 13, one week in advance of that monthly Ohio State Athletic Board meeting, Morrill had traveled to Columbus to visit some old Buckeye friends. In point of fact, he was on a mission.[35] His personality and persuasive talents most likely swayed the opinions of those he visited, including athletic board members and President Bevis.[36]

But influencing the Ohio State vote was not the only task James Lewis Morrill took upon himself in aiding John Hannah. He had previously petitioned President Fred Hovde of Purdue for support.[37] As it turned out, Hovde was already fully committed.[38] His friendship and respect for the college president dated back a few years.[39]

But regardless of Hovde's relationship with Hannah, it would have been an easy sell for Morrill. Hovde remained quite upset over "the actions, procedures and tactics used by [the] Faculty Conference Committee throughout the spring and summer ..."[40] The former Minnesota engineering professor probably had an axe to grind with Ralph Aigler in particular. The Michigan faculty representative's motion to more severely penalize the Boilermakers–passed during the joint May meetings through his influence and power of persuasion–was galling to the president.[41]

Fred Hovde was the assistant director of the General College at Minnesota during the controversial–at least in the minds of Minnesotans–Aigler investigation of Lotus Coffman's novel experiment in transitional education back in 1936.[42] A number of years later, now as president of Purdue, Hovde would again cross paths with the law professor over his proposal to harshly reprimand the Boilermakers for institutional violations of an evolving, unofficial academic scholarship policy for athletes. And adding to his ire, Hovde

---

Board: Minutes: June 1946-June 1951."

[34] Four Hundred and Forty Fourth Meeting of the Athletic Board of The Ohio State University. 4 April 1945. The Ohio State University Archives, Athletic: Director of (RG 9/e-1/1), "Athletic Board: Minutes: September 1940-May 1946."

[35] Morrill to Rottschaefer. 16 September 1948. University of Minnesota Archives, President's Office; Box 238, folder: Physical Education and Athletics 1948-49

[36] Hannah to Morrill. 23 November 1948. University of Minnesota Archives, President's Office; Box 238, folder: Physical Education and Athletics 1948-49

[37] Morrill to Hovde. 4 October 1948. University of Minnesota Archives, President's Office; Box 238, folder: Physical Education and Athletics 1948-49

[38] Hovde to Morrill. 29 September 1948. University of Minnesota Archives, President's Office; Box 238, folder: Physical Education and Athletics 1948-49

[39] Hovde to Hannah. 12 September 1952. Michigan State University Archives. John A. Hannah Papers, UA2.1.12; Box 90, folder: 27. Hovde, as expected, was on the "blueberries and maple syrup" list; the land-grant university president shared a special relationship with Hannah.

[40] Hovde to Morrill. 29 September 1948. University of Minnesota Archives, President's Office; Box 238, folder: Physical Education and Athletics 1948-49

[41] Minutes of the Intercollegiate Conference Joint Meeting of the Faculty Representatives and Athletic Directors. 29 May 1948. University of Illinois Archives. Series 4/2/12; Box 3, folder: Western Intercollegiate Conference 1947-48

[42] "Coffman Sees Change of Grid Rules in Line With Education Shifts." *Minnesota Daily* 18 February 1936, University of Minnesota Archives, President's Office; Box 4, folder: 120

also knew that Michigan was one of three schools considering a boycott of Purdue at the upcoming scheduling meetings in December.[43] The president had access to all conference minutes!

The ultimate decision to censure Purdue by the faculty committee, kept confidential due to Hovde's threat to go public, was finally handed down to the land-grant university in mid-September. Morrill's contacting the former Minnesota academician, shortly thereafter, could not have occurred at a more opportune time. Hovde guaranteed his colleague from Minneapolis Purdue's unequivocal support.[44]

President Morrill had been advised previously by his athletic director, Frank McCormick, that the "Faculty Conference Committee is not likely to act without the advice of the directors, or at least not likely to act against the advice of the athletic directors [regarding a replacement]."[45] He felt his boss should personally meet with the commissioner to discuss ways of influencing the directors' votes on expansion. Kenneth Wilson might prove a valuable asset for the Morrill Plan. The commissioner would encounter most of the directors at some point during the upcoming football season.[46]

His backing a plan to add a tenth member to ease the biennial scheduling morass might prove invaluable. Neither McCormick nor Morrill had any suspicion of Wilson's covert support of the University of Pittsburgh over the past few years. Morrill took heed of McCormick's advice. He would ultimately "work out a quick trip to Chicago for the purpose of seeing Wilson about this ... [he] seem[ed] the best channel to get it under way."[47]

A few months later, in mid-November, John Hannah would also meet with Wilson. He openly revealed the Morrill strategy of politicking the presidents, rather than the faculty representatives, for the Spartan cause over the preceding few months. He wanted to assure Wilson that he, as an outsider, had not violated protocol. Hannah would not seek the support of any member of the Council of Nine presidents.[48] His only request, however, was that the commissioner assure him that the college receive "fair and adequate consideration" when it came time for the directors to consider expansion.[49]

All Kenneth Wilson could do, in reply to the Hannah appeal, was "extend [his] courtesies and sympathetic interest to the college's cause."[50] He essentially declined intervening for Michigan State. His job description precluded involvement in membership politics. Reality, however, proved otherwise for the commissioner of the Western Conference. Over the past few years Wilson had frequently offered insider information to the Panther leadership. But with Pitt athletic director James Hagan out of office since June,

[43] Minutes of the Intercollegiate Conference Meeting of Athletic Directors. 30 November 1948. University of Wisconsin-Madison Archives. The University Faculty Athletic Board, Series 5/21/6; Box 1, folder: Western Conference minutes 1947-51

[44] Hovde to Morrill. 29 September 1948. University of Minnesota Archives, President's Office; Box 238, folder: Physical Education and Athletics 1948-49

[45] Morrill to Rottschaefer. 16 September 1948. University of Minnesota Archives, President's Office; Box 238, folder: Physical Education and Athletics 1948-49

[46] Ibid.

[47] Ibid.

[48] Hannah to Wilson. 15 November 1948. University of Minnesota Archives, President's Office; Box 238, folder: Physical Education and Athletics 1948-49

[49] Ibid.

[50] Ibid.

he had no one with whom to share strategic plans gained from his conversations with Morrill and Hannah. That would soon change, however.

KENNETH WILSON started out his career as track coach and athletic director at Drake University. In 1925, at the age of 29, he became the youngest athletic director in the history of the Intercollegiate Conference. After 20 years in that position at Northwestern, he was ready for a change.[51] The commissioner's job would offer him not only prestige but also more money.[52][53]

Tug Wilson had not been the first choice of his peers to replace John Griffith; Fritz Crisler was. Many of the faculty questioned the decision to tender the job to the Northwestern administrator.[54] William Lorenz, a professor of psychiatry at the University of Wisconsin, felt that Wilson was easily manipulated by strong personalities.[55] A few years later Lynn St. John may have proved the psychiatrist's assessment accurate. Following Wilson's promotion, St. John, seeking an insider willing to provide the same service as Griffith had, would successfully recruit his old friend for the Pitt cause.[56][57] It was likely a calculated move on his part–since December of 1944 St. John had been the principal advocate for Wilson.[58][59] He was probably convinced that the Michigan director would turn down the job. Crisler's present position, after all, offered him a far greater opportunity to impart a lasting mark on amateur athletics.[60] As Wisconsin's Lorenz shared with Ralph Aigler a few weeks later, "I believe the commissioner's job is a poor second to that which [Crisler] now holds [in Ann Arbor]."[61]

With St. John's retirement in June of 1947, the lone insider aiding the Panther cause was Ken Wilson. He had very little time, however, to confidentially collaborate with Pitt during that year. The conference faculty leaders were focused on policies to ensure a legitimate academic scholarship program for student-athletes. They anticipated the Sanity Code being passed in January of 1948 at the NCAA annual convention. The Big Nine wanted to be proactive and have a compatible policy on record prior to the New York

---

[51] Schultz, Kay. "Tug Wilson, A Giant Among Greats." *Pioneer Press Suburban Newspapers* 8 February 1979. Northwestern University Archives; Biographies: Kenneth Wilson

[52] Aigler to Lorenz. 19 February 1945. Bentley Historical Library, University of Michigan. Ralph W. Aigler Papers, 87406 Aa 2; Box 10, folder: Wilson, Tug

[53] Lorenz to Aigler. 23 February 1945. Bentley Historical Library, University of Michigan. Ralph W. Aigler Papers, 87406 Aa 2; Box 10, folder: Wilson, Tug

[54] Ibid.

[55] Lorenz to Aigler. 2 January 1945. Bentley Historical Library, University of Michigan. Ralph W. Aigler Papers, 87406 Aa 2; Box 12, folder: correspondence A-Z misc.

[56] St. John to Wilson. 13 May 1946. The Ohio State University Archives, Director of Athletics (RG 9/e-1/10), "Intercollegiate Conference: Commissioner: Correspondence (Wilson): 1945-47."

[57] Wilson to St. John. 20 May 1946. The Ohio State University Archives, Director of Athletics (RG 9/e-1/10), "Intercollegiate Conference: Commissioner: Correspondence (Wilson): 1945-47."

[58] Lorenz to Aigler. 2 January 1945. Bentley Historical Library, University of Michigan. Ralph W. Aigler Papers, 87406 Aa 2; Box 12, folder: correspondence A-Z misc.

[59] St. John to Crisler. 27 December 1944. Bentley Historical Library, University of Michigan. Board in Control of Intercollegiate Athletics, 8729 Bimu F81 2; Box 30, folder: papers 1944 January

[60] Lorenz to Aigler. 23 February 1945. Bentley Historical Library, University of Michigan. Ralph W. Aigler Papers, 87406 Aa 2; Box 10, folder: Wilson, Tug

[61] Ibid.

meetings.

Debates regarding controversial aspects of the scholarship proposal continued into the early fall. A tentative plan was put in place by September of 1947. The commissioner was asked to monitor compliance with the policy, Rule 6, section 4, by using the Highland Park yardstick. As a consequence of all these activities, Wilson had no time to devote to the University of Pittsburgh cause. He could only advise Hagan not to proffer an application that year; the directors and faculty had little time to contemplate expansion issues. It would be far better for the Panther leadership to focus on earning good will while playing six Western Conference schools during that autumn campaign.

As it turned out, the strategy to stack Pitt's schedule with Big Nine competition was a major mistake. By June of 1948 Hagan would be without a job. Regardless of the plight facing Wilson's friend, there were no new developments in conference politics worthy of sharing with Pitt leaders during the first half of the year. In addition, Wilson was consumed with Purdue's President Fred Hovde questioning his qualifications as commissioner in the aftermath of the suspect investigation of his university.[62]

Since Pitt had yet to hire a new athletic director, Ken Wilson had no one in the athletic department to share insider information gained from his meeting with Morrill in mid-October.[63] It was probably irrelevant. The conversation centered on the role of the athletic directors in a Spartan membership application. But the meeting with John Hannah, one month later in Chicago, was different. The president shared some data with the commissioner that, as a friend of Pitt, was shocking news. Wilson realized that Michigan State was about to pull off a major victory if left unchecked.[64]

The following day, he probably made some phone calls to Pittsburgh regarding Hannah's confident projections.[65] [66] Two weeks later the university leadership, a few months in advance of its previous intentions, announced that Captain Tom Hamilton of the US Naval Academy would be its next athletic director as of February.[67] [68] [69]

The highly regarded director of athletics at Annapolis was updated on the significant advances made by Michigan State over the last few months, in large part due to Ken Wilson's recent discovery. A commissioned officer until January 31, 1949, Hamilton voluntarily agreed to coordinate a response to the Spartan strategy over the next few days. On the seventh anniversary of Pearl Harbor, he telephoned Pitt Chancellor Rufus Fitzgerald

---

[62] Hovde to Morrill. 29 September 1948. University of Minnesota Archives, President's Office; Box 238, folder: Physical Education and Athletics 1948-49

[63] Morrill to Rottschaefer. 16 September 1948. University of Minnesota Archives, President's Office; Box 238, folder: Physical Education and Athletics 1948-49

[64] Hannah to Wilson. 15 November 1948. University of Minnesota Archives, President's Office; Box 238, folder: Physical Education and Athletics 1948-49

[65] Ibid.

[66] Hannah to Morrill. 23 November 1948. University of Minnesota Archives, President's Office; Box 238, folder: Physical Education and Athletics 1948-49

[67] The Tenth Meeting of the Athletic Committee. 29 November 1948. University of Pittsburgh Archives. 2/10; Box 2, folder: FF 19

[68] "Rating On Gridiron Seen Goal of Pitt-New Athletic Head Who Will Seek Better Material to Be Considered Monday." *New York Times* 26 November 1948. University of Pittsburgh Archives. 2/10; Box 2, folder: FF 19

[69] Fitzgerald to Leib. 8 December 1948. "Telephone: Karl Leib of State University of Iowa." University of Pittsburgh Archives. 2/10; Box 2, folder: FF19

and revealed his plans to counter what appeared to be a Spartan surprise attack at the Sherman Hotel in Chicago.[70]

Hamilton laid out a very extensive scheme. Everyone involved accomplished their tasks as commanded. The final order was to have Fitzgerald write the conference expressing Pittsburgh's ongoing interest in membership.[71] The chancellor composed a very diplomatic letter to Kenneth Wilson in line with the Hamilton strategy; he expressed appreciation to Wilson and the conference for allowing Pitt representatives to attend the meetings.[72] The Navy captain had responded decisively under fire. Was it sufficient to forestall the Spartans?

THE VOTES tallied by Henry Rottschaefer, while at the Warm Friend Tavern back in September, suggested that many schools were supporting the Spartan initiative. Even the University of Michigan–despite some questioning of its sincerity–publicly approved the application.[73] [74] For the time being it appeared that the Wolverines were backing John Hannah.

Following Lew Morrill's communiqué with Fred Hovde in late September and his visit with Ohio State athletic leadership–as well as President Howard Bevis–in mid-October, it appeared only Northwestern and Iowa remained in doubt by the third week in November.[75] [76] [77] John Hannah, by that time, wanted nine favorable votes. A simple majority would not provide him the "feeling that [Michigan State was] welcomed by all of the universities involved."[78] Only unanimity among the membership could erase the humiliation of five rejections over the past decade.

Despite being aware of the wavering stances of Northwestern and Iowa, Hannah chose to follow traditional protocol, as he had promised Ken Wilson a week earlier, and not communicate with the presidents of those schools.[79] He would rather have Dean Lloyd Emmons visit both campuses one more time in early December. The faculty representative was charged with ensuring those votes.[80]

---

[70] Fitzgerald to Hamilton. 7 December 1948. University of Pittsburgh Archives. 2/10, FF19; Box 2

[71] Ibid.

[72] Fitzgerald to Wilson. 9 December 1948. University of Pittsburgh Archives. 2/10, FF19; Box 2

[73] Linton, Ron. "Officials Keep Mum As College Awaits Big Nine Decision." *State News* 3 December 1948. Michigan State University Archives, Madison Kuhn Collection, UA17.107; Scrapbook 108, folder: 5

[74] Morrill to Rottschaefer. 16 September 1948. University of Minnesota Archives, President's Office; Box 238, folder: Physical Education and Athletics 1948-49

[75] Hovde to Morrill. 29 September 1948. University of Minnesota Archives, President's Office; Box 238, folder: Physical Education and Athletics 1948-49

[76] Morrill to Rottschaefer. 16 September 1948. University of Minnesota Archives, President's Office; Box 238, folder: Physical Education and Athletics 1948-49

[77] Hannah to Morrill. 23 November 1948. University of Minnesota Archives, President's Office; Box 238, folder: Physical Education and Athletics 1948-49

[78] Hannah to Bevis. 22 November 1948. University of Minnesota Archives, President's Office; Box 238, folder: Physical Education and Athletics 1948-49

[79] Hannah to Wilson. 15 November 1948. University of Minnesota Archives, President's Office; Box 238, folder: Physical Education and Athletics 1948-49

[80] Minutes of the State Board of Agriculture. 16 December 1948. www.onthebanks.msu.edu.

Hannah's promise to the commissioner, however, would soon be broken. On November 20, 1948, an article in the *Chicago Daily News*, sent through the Associated Press wire service to newspapers around the Midwest, "declared that Ohio State, Iowa, Northwestern, and 'oddly enough,' Michigan, are lined up in opposing Michigan State's bid." The *Daily News* never mentioned its source. It did acknowledge, however, that "political pressures in Michigan will force the Wolverines to change to the affirmative."[81]

John Hannah was particularly disturbed by the Ohio State reference. Lew Morrill had assured him of a favorable Buckeye vote back in October. So Hannah decided to take action and write President Bevis; he sent the same letter to Presidents Snyder of Evanston and Hancher of Iowa City. He was cautious in his direct sales pitch. The college leader informed all three that his faculty representative would make a site visit to each campus to address any remaining questions about Michigan State and its application.[82] As it turned out, the Associated Press statement on the Buckeye stance was totally wrong. The views from Evanston and Iowa City, however, may have been accurate. There appeared to be a real threat to the Morrill-Hannah success. As reported by the press on December 11, "It has become apparent that somebody has been working feverishly against the Spartans within the last couple of weeks [before the conference meetings]."[83] Might that "someone" have been Ken Wilson?

There was no reason for a wavering Wildcat stance in late November of 1948. President Franklyn Snyder's name was included on the "blueberries and maple syrup" list dating back to the early 1940s.[84] In June of 1945 the Northwestern leader was asked by John Hannah to deliver the spring commencement address.[85] He departed East Lansing impressed with Hannah's accomplishments in improving academics.[86] [87] President Alexander Ruthven of Michigan sanctioned support of a Spartan application in March of 1946. Shortly after, Snyder wrote his friend in East Lansing that "[you] can count on me to do anything I can to get your application approved … the Conference would be better in every way if Michigan State College were a member of it."[88]

Commissioner Ken Wilson, now privy to the impending success of the revised Morrill Plan–conveyed by John Hannah one week earlier in Chicago–maintained an office only a few miles from the Evanston campus. A brief meeting with the current Northwestern athletic leadership might have been all he needed to cast some doubt with them on the

---

[81] Hannah to Morrill. 23 November 1948. University of Minnesota Archives, President's Office; Box 238, folder: Physical Education and Athletics 1948-49

[82] Hannah to Bevis. 22 November 1948. University of Minnesota Archives, President's Office; Box 238, folder: Physical Education and Athletics 1948-49

[83] "Opposition to Michigan State's Bid Seen Growing." *Lansing State Journal* 11 December 1948. Michigan State University Archives, Madison Kuhn Collection, UA17.107; Scrapbook 108, folder: 5

[84] Snyder to Hannah. 30 July 1945. Northwestern University Archives, Franklyn Snyder Papers; Box 3, folder: 1

[85] Geil to Snyder. 14 June 1945. Northwestern University Archives, Franklyn Snyder Papers; Box 3, folder: 1

[86] Hannah to Snyder. 18 June 1945. Northwestern University Archives, Franklyn Snyder Papers; Box 3, folder: 1

[87] Snyder to Hannah. 19 June 1945. Northwestern University Archives, Franklyn Snyder Papers; Box 3, folder: 1

[88] Snyder to Hannah. 19 March 1946. Northwestern University Archives, Franklyn Snyder Papers; Box 13, folder: 20

merits of a Spartan membership. A confidential leak to a few friends at the *Chicago Daily News* suggesting Wildcat skepticism regarding the college's application was sufficient for citing Northwestern in that article. Hannah's letter to Franklyn Snyder prompted the Evanston leader to intervene. "No one has talked to me about it, and I am inclined to think the report is without any merit." He promised to "look into the matter."[89] Snyder imposed his will on his faculty representative: Northwestern fully supported Michigan State on December 12, 1948.

President Virgil Hancher of Iowa was also on John Hannah's "blueberries and maple syrup" list.[90] They had been friends since the fall of 1942.[91] As a favor to Hannah, the legal scholar investigated the charges made by the Chicago sportswriter regarding Iowa's uncertain position. His athletic director, Paul Brechler, "knew of no reason why any newspaper man should have reported that Iowa was lined up against Michigan State."[92]

As it turned out there were a number of compelling reasons. Iowa's evasive stance on a replacement for the Chicago Maroons–as will be seen–may have been politically as well as strategically motivated. In addition to the Spartans' application, there were a few other highly contentious issues requiring debate during the December meeting. The State University of Iowa athletic leaders–Paul Brechler, in particular–appeared to have some plans in place for the upcoming December gathering at the Sherman Hotel. The Hawkeyes were no longer going to defer to the sentiment of the majority on matters significantly impacting Iowa City.

THE AGENDA for the annual meeting of the Intercollegiate Conference was completed a few weeks in advance of the December 10 weekend gathering. As scripted by Lew Morrill, Henry Rottschaefer of Minnesota contacted Chairman Frank Richart requesting a spot on that agenda to discuss "Michigan State."[93] The notice of intent assured him time to make a motion for the admission of the college into the Western Conference. It was consistent with the revised Morrill Plan, as amended by Hannah in September, to force a vote on the application. The University of Michigan's Ralph Aigler would have no way to block the process since Minnesota was sponsoring the Spartans.

The athletic directors had already met in late November to bring closure on the 11 scholarship violations by five schools revealed to the public in mid-September. Commissioner Wilson was satisfied with the actions taken by each institution to comply with conference regulations. He then discussed the Purdue reprimand. The university had completed an admirable corrective action plan in his opinion. Fritz Crisler was pleased; there was no longer a need for Michigan to boycott the Boilermakers. But Ohio State and Illinois were unimpressed. "For certain reasons" they would not sign contracts with the

---

[89] Snyder to Hannah. 24 November 1948. Northwestern University Archives, Franklyn Snyder Papers; Box 13, folder: 20

[90] Hancher to Hannah. 12 April 1947. University of Iowa Archives, Iowa City, Iowa. Virgil Hancher Papers, RG 05.01.11; Box 171, folder: 122

[91] Hancher to Hannah. 31 December 1942. University of Iowa Archives, Iowa City, Iowa. Virgil Hancher Papers, RG 05.01.11; Box 60, folder: 91

[92] Hancher to Hannah. 29 November 1948. University of Iowa Archives, Iowa City, Iowa. Virgil Hancher Papers, RG 05.01.11; Box 227, folder: 98-100, 1948-49

[93] Rottschaefer to Richart. 2 December 1948. University of Illinois Archives. Series 4/2/12; Box 3, folder: Western Intercollegiate Conference 1948-49

West Lafayette land-grant for three years.[94] Purdue had been caught breaching the borders of both states while recruiting football talent a year earlier, which was a clear violation of the old "Buckeye Rule" that was now officially codified in the Handbook.[95] The disciplinary action imposed on Purdue would have profound financial repercussions during the three-year boycott,[96] but there would be no public disclosure.

Also on the agenda for directors during their two-day meeting in Chicago, held in advance of the annual December get-together scheduled in two weeks, was a planned debate on whether to offer a recommendation for expansion of the conference to the faculty. Due to protracted discussions on complex scheduling for 1950-52, the athletic directors ran out of time to address that question on the second day.[97] The agenda item was of critical concern for Michigan State and John Hannah.[98]

The president contacted Tug Wilson on the 2nd of December "to find out what happened in Chicago at the [athletic directors'] meeting which was supposed to decide Michigan State's entry into the Western Conference."[99] He had to know whether the directors supported expansion of the group. Without their nod, as Frank McCormick previously shared with Lew Morrill, the faculty representatives would table the Rottschaefer motion. Wilson's responses to Hannah were evasive. Hannah then asked his executive assistant, James Denison, to contact Bill Nunn at Minnesota. Morrill's right-hand man could get the inside scoop from Director McCormick. Nunn promised a quick phone call to Denison once McCormick returned to Minneapolis.[100] The following day Hannah had his answer: The athletic directors had never discussed expansion.

Lacking a decision on whether the directors wanted to replace the Maroons, John Hannah could not predict the outcome of the upcoming weekend meeting. He was virtually assured admission, but only if those nine athletic department administrators had agreed it was "expedient" to add a tenth member. That question would now need to be addressed at the December meetings prior to the Rottschaefer motion.

BACK IN May of 1948, during the spring joint conference in Madison, Frank Richart had moved that the Big Nine not take action on Michigan State's application until "it can be shown that [it] is adhering to the spirit and wording of all phases of the Conference Rules."[101] This motion, tactfully stated by the Illinois representative, was probably penned

---

[94] Minutes of the Intercollegiate Conference Meeting of the Athletic Directors. 30 November 1948. Bentley Historical Library, University of Michigan. Board in Control of Intercollegiate Athletics, 8729 Bimu F81 2; Box 84, folder: Big-10 records 1941-52

[95] Four Hundred and Ninety-First Meeting of the Athletic Board of The Ohio State University. 12 October 1948. The Ohio State University Archives, Athletics: Director of (RG 9/e-1/1), "Athletic Board: Minutes: Jun 1946-Jun1951."

[96] The eventual boycott lasted only two years (1950-51).

[97] Minutes of the Intercollegiate Conference Meeting of the Directors. 1 December 1948. Bentley Historical Library, University of Michigan. Board in Control of Intercollegiate Athletics, 8729 Bimu F81 2; Box 84, folder: Big-10 records 1941-52

[98] Nunn to Morrill. 2 December 1948. University of Minnesota Archives, University Relations; Box 64, folder: J.L. Morrill 1945-48

[99] Ibid.

[100] Ibid.

[101] Minutes of the Intercollegiate Conference Joint Meeting of the Faculty Representatives and Athletic Directors. 29 May 1948. Bentley Historical Library, University of Michigan. Athletic

by Ralph Aigler.[102] Two weeks in advance of Richart's proposal, somewhat similar verbiage was used by the athletic directors in turning down Frank McCormick's request "to consider Michigan State College's pending application for membership..."[103] At that time, "it was the sense of the Directors that the Conference should determine in what manner Michigan State is adhering to Conference regulations before final action be taken on the application."[104] It was probably not coincidental. Fritz Crisler may very well have influenced the anonymous recommendation as stated in the minutes. After all, he had participated in the February 1946 meeting involving Ralph Aigler and John Hannah. During that discussion, Aigler emphasized to the president that Michigan State must be fully compliant with the Intercollegiate Handbook before Michigan would approve a Spartan application.[105]

But based on politics in the state of Michigan, there was no way Professor Aigler could have had his name, let alone the university's, associated with both similarly worded motions. President Alexander Ruthven had announced his support for Michigan State's petition in March of 1946. He would later reaffirm that commitment to President Hannah in November of 1948.[106] The University of Michigan representative needed someone else to make the motion at the faculty meeting. If a leak to the press occurred following confidential debate, suggesting Aigler was the source of the latest proposal opposing action on a Spartan application, Ruthven's integrity would have been seriously questioned.

The law professor convinced Richart to propose the stonewalling maneuver well in advance of the May meetings at the Madison Club.[107] He must have shared his convictions on questionable activities taking place in the athletic department in East Lansing. Otherwise there appeared to be no reason for the engineering professor to make the motion. In March of 1946 Richart confidentially offered his opinion regarding the Spartans' application with President A.C. Willard. He was impressed with the school, its facilities, and the leadership. Richart felt that the Spartans were a logical choice for membership should the need arise.[108]

Despite approval of the Richart-Aigler Motion, circumstances within the conference at the time prevented the faculty from devising a process to verify Spartan compliance with the Handbook. Commissioner Wilson's report on violations of Rule 6, section 4 proved a major distraction throughout the summer and early fall for the nine faculty leaders. In the meantime, the revised Morrill strategy proceeded on schedule. By early December

---

Department, 943 Bimu 2; Box 84, folder: Big-Ten directors meeting 3/41-7/52

[102] Aigler to The Members of the Board. 16 December 1948. Bentley Historical Library, University of Michigan. Ralph W. Aigler Papers, 87406 Aa 2; Box 10, folder: correspondence 1946-52 Wilson, K.L. 2/2. Richart's motion was very similar Aigler's amendment to the Rottschaefer motion of December 11, 1948 admitting MSC into the conference.

[103] Minutes of the Intercollegiate Conference Meeting of the Athletic Directors. 16 May 1948. University of Wisconsin-Madison Archives. The University Faculty Athletic Board, Series 5/21/6; Box 1, folder: Western Conference minutes 1947-54

[104] Ibid.

[105] Aigler to Richart. 21 December 1948. University of Illinois Archives. Series 4/2/12; Box 3, folder: Western Intercollegiate Conference 1948-49

[106] Hannah to Morrill. 23 November 1948. University of Minnesota Archives, President's Office; Box 238, folder: Physical Education and Athletics. 1948-49

[107] Aigler to Richart. 21 December 1948. University of Illinois Archives. Series 4/2/12; Box 3, folder: Western Intercollegiate Conference 1948-49.

[108] Richart to Willard. 25 March 1946. University of Illinois Archives. General Correspondence, 1934-1946, Series 2/9/1; Box 104, folder: Mi

Richart's proposal, prompted by his Wolverine colleague, appeared to be a moot point. As time would soon bear out, however, Ralph William Aigler was always ahead of the game!

THE FIRST session of the annual meeting took place on Saturday December 11 at the Sherman Hotel. Representatives of both Michigan State and the University of Pittsburgh were present outside the conference room. The meeting was called to order at 2:15 pm. After cleaning up some minor business matters Secretary G.R. Lundquist of Northwestern addressed item 6 on the agenda. Pittsburgh professor and dean W. Vincent Lanfear was invited into the room. He addressed the group, expressing a desire to renew the Pitt application.

Lanfear followed the script as precisely drawn up by Captain Tom Hamilton. He cited six reasons supporting the Panthers as the logical choice for membership, but "no action was taken upon [the] application."[109] This decision was no surprise for the Panthers. Hamilton wanted to cast doubt on a Michigan State membership. His delay tactic was intended to buy him time until he could prepare a counteroffensive for the spring of 1949.

The second session took place that evening at the University Club over dinner and cocktails. The meeting concluded at 10:45 pm. Michigan State was not invited into the closed-door dining room. The Spartan faithful back in East Lansing would face one more night of uncertainty.

The following morning a joint session of faculty and directors met. Professor Frank Richart, as chairman of the faculty committee, opened the discussion on the application for membership of Michigan State College of Agriculture and Applied Science. But before proceeding, he "also called attention to the University of Pittsburgh's application for membership."[110]

The University of Nebraska was not mentioned. Unlike two years earlier, the Cornhuskers now lacked an advocate: former faculty representative Karl Leib had resigned in the spring of 1947 in order to serve as president of the NCAA. It appeared Nebraska had finally lost interest in conference membership.

Kenneth Wilson "reviewed the history of Michigan State's application and reported [answers to] certain questions [which had been submitted by faculty and directors] regarding that institution's athletic practices."[111] President Hannah had provided his responses in writing to Wilson a few weeks earlier.[112] [113] Pittsburgh was offered an equal opportunity to reply.[114]

Following completion of that task, the first order of business during the joint

---

[109] Minutes of the Intercollegiate Conference of Faculty Representatives. 11-12 December 1948. Bentley Historical Library, University of Michigan. Athletic Department, 943 Bimu 2; Box 84, folder: Faculty Representatives minutes 1941-57

[110] Ibid.

[111] Ibid.

[112] Hannah to Wilson. 15 November 1948. University of Minnesota Archives, President's Office; Box 238, folder: Physical Education and Athletics. 1948-49

[113] Hannah to Morrill. 23 November 1948. University of Minnesota Archives, President's Office; Box 238, folder: Physical Education and Athletics. 1948-49

[114] Minutes of the Intercollegiate Conference of Faculty Representatives. 11-12 December 1948. Bentley Historical Library. University of Michigan Archives. Athletic Department, 943 Bimu 2; Box 84, folder: Faculty Representatives minutes 1941-57

session was to decide whether the conference should expand back to 10 members. The athletic directors had not addressed the question two weeks earlier. Rather than take a tally, faculty committee chairman Richart decided to ask each director to openly express his opinion.[115] Frank McCormick was the most vocal and enthusiastic; Fritz Crisler was the most objective and thorough.[116] The discussion centered on current scheduling challenges encountered with an odd number of institutions. The 9/6/2 rule, approved in December of 1945, did not solve the problems experienced by Iowa, Indiana, and Purdue in contracting with tier-one schools capable of filling their stadiums and coffers. Would adding a tenth member simplify the arduous task facing the directors since the end of the war?

No definitive conclusion came out of that meeting. No vote took place. Frank Richart's recollection of the process was surprising and revealing.

> In trying to reconstruct [the directors'] comments, I would say that there
> were two or three favorable, two or three against, and the rest non-
> committal. I left the meeting feeling that the general tone … was somewhat
> against the proposal [for expansion], and even more definitely against
> Pittsburgh than Michigan State [as a new member].[117]

The chairman failed to call for a motion. His oversight would profoundly impact not only Michigan State but the University of Pittsburgh as well.

In the absence of a show of hands, most of the nine faculty representatives interpreted the response by the athletic directors as favoring expansion.[118] By essentially bypassing their input–through an official tally–Richart allowed Lew Morrill's plan to move forward unabated. The faculty could no longer dodge its role. John Hannah's modification of his friend' strategy, back in September, was rolling out just as planned. And there appeared nothing Ralph Aigler could do to stop it.

The nine representatives regrouped at the University Club Sunday afternoon for a working lunch. Agenda item 2 for December 12, 1948, pertained to an application by Michigan State College of Agriculture and Applied Science for admission to the Western Conference. After 12 years and five rejections, the college was finally within reach of an institutional goal first proposed by Robert Sidey Shaw and the State Board on November 23, 1936.[119]

In advance of the meeting, Dean Lloyd Emmons had requested an opportunity to make a brief statement regarding the college's application.[120] Chairman Richart had no choice but to honor the request. Professor Lanfear of Pittsburgh had been granted a similar

---

[115] Minutes of the Intercollegiate Conference Joint Meeting of the Faculty Representatives and the Athletic Directors. 12 December 1948. Bentley Historical Library, University of Michigan. Athletic Department, 943 Bimu 2; Box 84, folder: Big-Ten directors 1941-52

[116] Aigler to Richart. 14 December 1948. University of Illinois Archives. Series 4/2/12; Box 3, folder: Western Intercollegiate Conference 1948-49

[117] Richart to Aigler. 17 December 1948. University of Illinois Archives. Series 4/2/12; Box 3, folder: Western Intercollegiate Conference 1948-49

[118] Aigler to Richart. 14 December 1948. University of Illinois Archives. Series 4/2/12; Box 3, folder: Western Intercollegiate Conference 1948-49

[119] Minutes of the State Board of Agriculture. 23 November 1936. www.onthebanks.msu.edu

[120] Richart to Aigler. 17 December 1948. University of Illinois Archives. Series 4/2/12; Box 3, folder: Western Intercollegiate Conference 1948-49

opportunity one day earlier. Following his comments, Emmons answered all remaining questions and then departed. His performance was graded exceptional by many in attendance.[121] It reassured most, but not all, of the remaining skeptics.

Professor Henry Rottschaefer of the University of Minnesota Law School then moved "that Michigan State be admitted, the admission to take effect at such time as a Committee of the Faculty Representatives shall have certified to the conference that the rules and regulations and other requirements of the conference are completely in force at that institution."[122]

The motion was seconded by Dean Vincent Freeman of Purdue University.[123] President Hovde, since September, had been more than willing to aid the Spartan cause[124] but he also had a personal vendetta with the Faculty Representatives Committee regarding the reprimand announced at around the same time.[125] Freeman's support of the proposal, thereby assuring a vote, may have been at the request of his president. Perhaps it was a subtle way for Hovde to strike back at some powerful leaders, including one man from the University of Michigan.

The official minutes of the Sunday afternoon session state that the Minnesota representative's motion was unanimously approved. President John Hannah had not only achieved a seat in the conference, he had done so with a resounding tally.[126] But was it truly a vote of confidence?

ON NOVEMBER 23, John Hannah wrote to President Virgil Hancher of Iowa. He was concerned about a newspaper account indicating that Iowa was opposed to a Spartan admission. Hannah and his friend Lew Morrill had kept a tally of supporters throughout the fall.[127] It seemed certain that Michigan State had the simple majority necessary for admission.[128] But Hannah, having experienced five rejections from either Michigan or the Faculty Representatives Committee since 1937, wanted a unanimous vote. He included in his letter a copy of the article from the *Lansing State Journal* mentioning the rumor about the Hawkeyes' voting plans.

> We should like to be admitted with the feeling that we are welcomed by all
> of the universities involved. If there is any information that you or your
> faculty representative in the Western Conference or your athletic people

[121] Richart to Aigler. 17 December 1948. University of Illinois Archives. Series 4/2/12; Box 3, folder: Western Intercollegiate Conference 1948-49

[122] Minutes of the Intercollegiate Conference of Faculty Representatives. 11-12 December 1948. Bentley Historical Library, University of Michigan. Athletic Department, 943 Bimu 2; Box 84, folder: Faculty Representatives minutes 1941-57

[123] Ibid.

[124] Hovde to Morrill. 29 September 1948. University of Minnesota Archives, President's Office; Box 238, folder: Physical Education and Athletics 1948-49

[125] Ibid.

[126] Hannah to Hancher. 22 November 1948. University of Iowa Archives. Iowa City, Iowa. Virgil Hancher Papers, RG 05.01.11; Box 227, folder: 98-100 1948-49

[127] Hannah to Morrill. 23 November 1948. University of Minnesota Archives, President's Office; Box 238, folder: Physical Education and Athletics 1948-49

[128] Aigler to Richart. 15 May 1946. Bentley Historical Library, University of Michigan. Ralph W. Aigler Papers, Aa 2; Box 9, folder: correspondence 1946-52 "H" misc.

would like before the Conference meetings are held, we shall be glad to furnish it ....[129]

President Hancher, on November 29, wrote back to Hannah. "I spoke to Paul Brechler, our Director of Intercollegiate Athletics, about the clipping in your letter of November 22nd. He knew of no reason why any newspaper man should have reported that Iowa was lined up against Michigan State."[130]

Brechler's comments may have been a clever play on words that dodged Hannah's concern. Rather than merely stating that the press statement was inaccurate, the athletic director questioned where the reporter could have obtained such information. As it turned out, Brechler (and the complicit Paul Blommers) had quite a few reasons for opposing the Spartan admission. But no one else, including President Hancher, knew of their plans for December 12, 1948.

Hancher then stated that it was his athletic leadership's opinion that the Western Conference was the right size. "There is no magic in the number ten, and although we regretted the withdrawal of Chicago from intercollegiate competition, there has seemed to us no compelling reason for finding a substitute."[131] He closed by stating that "if it is the majority opinion of the members of the Conference that another institution should be added, our representatives expect to vote for Michigan State College."[132] The school, in the opinion of Hancher and his athletic leaders, was the "logical choice."[133]

President Hancher, however, was not privy to discussions between Paul Brechler and Paul Blommers over the past seven months. Michigan State was of great concern; the school's reputation bothered both leaders. But the athletic director, in particular, was also disturbed by some political developments within the conference. The two decided, as of late November, to use the Spartan vote to make a political statement. But, as it turned out, Iowa may not have been the only school challenging the application behind closed doors.

On December 21, 1948, Lew Morrill wrote to John Hannah congratulating him on the college's success. Since the two shared a mutual distrust for the University of Michigan, Morrill wanted to inform him what had really transpired in the confidential meeting.

> I haven't yet had a chance to hear the "inside story" of the Chicago meeting–except that George Hauser, our assistant football coach, who represented [Bernie] Bierman at the [coaches] meeting, told me that the University of Michigan people worked very hard undercover to block the admission. This makes it all the sweeter, so far as I'm concerned.[134]

Ralph Aigler, intimately involved with the critical vote that Sunday afternoon, had a somewhat different version of what transpired. He shared his recollection of events to the members of his Board in Control a few days after the election. His confidential memo

---

[129] Hannah to Hancher. 22 November 1948. University of Iowa Archives, Iowa City, Iowa. Virgil Hancher Papers, RG 05.01.11; Box 227, file: 99-100

[130] Hancher to Hannah. 29 November 1948. University of Iowa Archives, Iowa City, Iowa. Virgil Hancher Papers, RG 05.01.11; Box 227, file: 99-100

[131] Ibid.

[132] Ibid.

[133] Ibid.

[134] Morrill to Hannah. 21 December 1948. University of Minnesota Archives, President's Office; Box 238, folder: Physical Education and Athletics 1948-49

revealed what really happened leading up to the "unanimous" decision.

> When we came to the Michigan State matter, Henry Rottschaefer moved that Michigan State be admitted to membership. After the motion was seconded and no one else made any further move, I proposed an amendment ... it was almost exactly these words: "Such membership to take effect at such time as a [three man] committee of this conference shall have made a thorough investigation of Michigan State, and certified to the Conference that she is then complying in all respects with the rules, regulations and other requirements of the Conference." That motion was seconded and then, to simplify the matter, ... the original motion [was combined] with the amendment. After a lot of discussion the motion was carried, with Iowa being the only one to cast a negative vote. The Iowa representative then withdrew his negative vote so as to make the vote unanimous.[135]

Based on his account, Ralph Aigler had gotten what he wanted since the spring meetings. The Richart-Aigler Motion of May 1948,[136] mandating Spartan compliance with the Handbook before acceptance as a member was not overlooked after all.[137] He was not going to let the distractions of the summer months—the Wilson investigation debate—detract from his parochial concerns with the suspect practices taking place in East Lansing.

Iowa's Professor Blommers was asked to be a member of the special Committee of Three charged with investigating the Spartans. That request, in addition to the law professor's comment that "a lot of discussion" followed his amendment to the Rottschaefer motion, implied that there was much more to the nay vote than Iowa's opposition to expansion—despite what President Hancher stated in his letter to John Hannah two weeks earlier. It appeared that there was something about Michigan State that troubled Iowa's athletic leadership—and Paul Brechler in particular.

So, as it turned out, John Hannah did not achieve an initial vote of confidence after all. It was probably irrelevant, however. The following day newspapers would proclaim that Michigan State had been unanimously elected into the Intercollegiate Conference.[138]

TWO DAYS following the Chicago meetings, Virgil Hancher sent a congratulatory letter to his friend in East Lansing. His comments suggested that John Hannah was already aware of events leading up to the final vote on Sunday. But Hancher, in defense of Paul Blommers, pointed out that Iowa's initial stance opposing expansion and its ultimate decision supporting the majority were consistent with his November 29 letter.[139]

---

[135] Aigler to Members of the Board. 16 December 1948. Bentley Historical Library, University of Michigan. Ralph W. Aigler Papers, 87406 Aa 2; Box 10, folder: correspondence 1946-52 personal

[136] Minutes of the Intercollegiate Conference Joint Meeting of the Faculty Representatives and Athletic Directors. 29 May 1948. Bentley Historical Library, University of Michigan. Athletic Department, 943 Bimu 2; Box 84, folder: Big-Ten directors meeting 3/41-7/52

[137] Aigler to Richart. 21 December 1948. University of Illinois Archives. Series 4/2/12; Box 3, folder: Western Intercollegiate Conference 1948-49

[138] Devine, Tommy. "Conference Backing Unanimous." *Detroit Free Press,* 13 December 1948. Michigan State University Archives. Madison Kuhn Collection, UA17.107; Scrapbook 108, folder: 5

[139] Hancher to Hannah. 14 December 1948. University of Iowa Archives, University of Iowa, Iowa

Lew Morrill, of Minnesota, mailed his official note of congratulations on the 21ˢᵗ of December. Obligations in Washington the previous week prevented his writing sooner. He hadn't yet heard the "inside story" of the Chicago meeting. Professor Rottschaefer, however, had sent his personal copy of the meeting minutes to the old Buckeye. He informed his boss that "much of what occurred is concealed in the formal action recorded."[140] He and Frank McCormick would meet with him in the near future. Morrill promised to share their stories with the college president.[141] Surprisingly, unlike Hannah, Morrill was not yet aware of the confidential Iowa scheme. His two athletic leaders would update him on that in short order.

One day following receipt of the Morrill letter, President Hannah wrote Virgil Hancher thanking him for his explanation of the Iowa vote. No hard feelings were implied. "We are all happy that [Paul Blommers] could vote to admit Michigan State College when the matter came to a final decision, and we are looking forward to a long and pleasant relationship with your institution."[142] Hannah, of course, had no idea of Paul Brechler's role in this football game played off the gridiron.

RALPH AIGLER was disturbed by the official conference press release. He felt it misrepresented the facts. In the interest of accuracy, he wanted his board to be aware of what was now in store for the Spartans–a formal inspection as mandated by his amendment to the Rottschaefer motion. "You will thus see that Michigan State, despite newspaper reports to the contrary, is not now a member of the Conference."[143]

Aigler pointed out that Dean Emmons had been notified that "they would have to drop all [financial aid for] the 71 members of their various varsity squads who are holders of the Jenison scholarships, with the exception of those who qualify for such financial aids under the current Conference rules [involving the Highland Park yardstick and Rule 6, section 4]."[144] He also stated that the college must "stop using her training table in the sports other than football."[145] Illegal recruiting activity would cease; "'bird dogs' ... coaches who sit on boys' doorsteps ..." hounding prospective candidates must be kept on a leash.[146] Finally, the State Board of Agriculture would have to revamp its policies to ensure complete faculty control of all athletics at the institution.[147]

The Jenison Awards were a very powerful recruiting tool for certain programs at Michigan State. Coaches used them to entice highly talented athletes to the school. Aigler

---

City, Iowa. Virgil Hancher Papers, RG 05.01.11; Box 228, folder: 115 "M" misc. 1948-49 MSC

[140] Rottschaefer to Morrill. 22 December 1948. University of Minnesota Archives, President's Office; Box 138, folder: Michigan and Michigan State 1948-59

[141] Morrill to Hannah. 21 December 1948. University of Minnesota Archives, President's Office; Box 238, folder: Physical Education and Athletics 1948-49

[142] Hannah to Hancher. 22 December 1948. University of Iowa Archives, Iowa City, Iowa. Virgil Hancher Papers, RG 05.01.11; Box 228, folder: 115 "M" misc. 1948-49 MSC

[143] Aigler to The Members of the Board. 16 December 1948. Bentley Historical Library, University of Michigan. Ralph W. Aigler Papers, 87406 Aa 2; Box 10, folder: correspondence 1946-52 Wilson, K.L. 2/2

[144] Ibid.

[145] Ibid.

[146] Ibid.

[147] Ibid.

questioned how those students would now finance their education in the absence of the controversial grants. The professor then shared a prediction that would one day prove him prescient.

> It is, of course, possible that in cutting off those [coaches] from their
> Jenison awards, they will devise some sub-rosa scheme, the existence of
> which will be difficult to detect. I am satisfied that both the Conference and
> the NCAA will have to be on the alert with reference to Michigan State.[148]

He closed his confidential memo to the Board in Control by emphasizing that the inspection by the ad hoc committee was not a mere formality. Michigan State must be in full compliance with conference rules before being formally accepted into the elite group of institutions. The faculty representatives decided to have the special committee visit East Lansing after the college had reasonable time to put its house in order.[149] Ralph Aigler predicted it would take at least a few months to address the four demands imposed on the college before official acceptance might be granted.

AFTER THE December 12 meeting Professor Aigler needed the opportunity to revisit the circumstances leading up to the vote with a confidant. A number of letters passed between Ann Arbor and Urbana over the next few days.

On December 14, Aigler offered Frank Richart his thoughts on the historic weekend for Michigan State. He expected the vote would go the Spartans' way. All he really wanted was assurance that the college was entering the exclusive club on equal footing with other members. Aigler noted that the university's position regarding Michigan State had been consistent since March of 1946–and he expressed his frustration with the constant questioning in the press of Michigan's support. Both he and Fritz Crisler, in particular, were taking a verbal beating by writers swayed by untruths emanating from East Lansing.[150] [151]

Aigler called "specious" Henry Rottschaefer's argument that adding a tenth member would solve the complex scheduling problem. Michigan State, in the law professor's opinion, would not be satisfied with playing just Indiana, Purdue, Iowa "and to a somewhat lesser extent, Wisconsin ..."[152] He anticipated that the Spartans would aggressively posture for more attractive competition among the tier-one programs.[153]

What Aigler failed to address in his first letter, however, was the major role Michigan had held in making that contracting process so complicated over the preceding decade. Had Fritz Crisler agreed to end the practice of scheduling non-conference schools years in advance of the biennial May meetings–clearly in violation of Handbook policy–

---

[148] Aigler to The Members of the Board. 16 December 1948. Bentley Historical Library, University of Michigan. Ralph W. Aigler Papers, 87406 Aa 2; Box 10, folder: correspondence 1946-52 Wilson, K.L. 2/2

[149] Ibid.

[150] Aigler to Emmons. 6 December 1948. Bentley Historical Library, University of Michigan. Ralph W. Aigler Papers, 87406 Aa 2; Box 9, folder: correspondence 1946-52 "E" misc.

[151] Aigler to Richart. 21 December 1948. University of Illinois Archives. Series 4/2/12; Box 3, folder: Western Intercollegiate Conference 1948-49

[152] Aigler to Richart. 14 December 1948. University of Illinois Archives. Series 4/2/12; Box 3, folder: Western Intercollegiate Conference 1948-49

[153] Ibid.

there might not have been the support necessary for adding a tenth member. More weekends would have been available for the tier-two programs.

But what really bothered Aigler was Hannah's "high-pressured" approach to gain admission. He noted that it was "a most vigorous campaign, and that campaign was picked up and pushed along conspicuously by Minnesota."[154] He felt Rottschaefer was blindly promoting a Morrill agenda without considering the consequences.[155]

Aigler pointed out that the vote on December 12 had challenged the "basic anchor of the Conference ... full and complete faculty control."[156] Henry Rottschaefer and a few other faculty representatives had turned over that responsibility to the presidents. He feared the committee might never regain what the Intercollegiate Conference Handbook granted to them alone.[157] [158]

> I have had the feeling for some time that Lew Morrill wants to manage rather than merely help (in advising the faculty leadership). I am satisfied that Hannah has precisely that same disposition, though in an exaggerated form. These are the reasons why I have felt during the last day or two no little concern about the future of the Conference ... I think the interest and support on the part of the presidents, due largely to the pressures put upon them by Morrill and Hannah, was without much thought about the real nature of the problem.[159]

Aigler viewed John Hannah as "supremely ambitious for his institution ..."[160] While he respected that character trait, he also felt that it might one day get the college in trouble through a "willingness, and perhaps even an urge, to cut corners."[161] President Hannah, in his opinion, was "not going to be satisfied with Michigan State as merely a member of the Conference."[162] Tier-one status was his goal.

Professor Frank Richart responded three days later. He was more concerned with his own treatment of the athletic directors during the joint Saturday evening dinner meeting with the faculty representatives. He commented on the fundamental question that he had posed to the directors on whether expansion back to 10 members was in order. Richart expressed disappointment that "they did not give us a definite recommendation." He worried that he might have placed the nine administrators on the spot by going around the.

---

[154] Aigler to Richart. 14 December 1948. University of Illinois Archives. Series 4/2/12; Box 3, folder: Western Intercollegiate Conference 1948-49

[155] Ibid.

[156] Ibid.

[157] Ibid.

[158] Aigler's prediction proved accurate. As noted in the epilogue, by 1987 the Council of Ten would assume responsibilities previously granted to the faculty by the presidents!

[159] Aigler to Richart. 14 December 1948. University of Illinois Archives. Series 4/2/12; Box 3, folder: Western Intercollegiate Conference 1948-49

[160] Ibid.

[161] Ibid.

[162] Ibid.

table and requesting an opinion from each in front of 20 attendees.[163] [164] Perhaps a private vote would have been more appropriate.

Richart honestly felt that "the chances of admitting either school were not very good" regardless of the athletic directors' ambivalence.[165] He noted, however, that Dean Emmons' speech before the faculty had effectively presented the Spartan cause. "I think [Emmons] answered all questions in such a sincere and positive fashion that he removed some of the doubts raised by the directors."[166]

Richart questioned Aigler for altering the original Rottschaefer motion. He felt that the amendment had influenced the voting of a few skeptical representatives. "The qualification that was added, I believe, satisfied some of those present that we would be complying with the resolution passed at the [May] meeting regarding a thorough investigation."[167] Richart was referring to the motion that he had made on Aigler's behalf. Nonetheless, he was surprised by the ultimate vote in response to Aigler's modification of the Rottschaefer proposal.

The engineering professor felt a need to defend Henry Rottschaefer. He noted that there had been no lobbying on his part. "Our group has been conspicuously free from the cloakroom type of political log-rolling and I think it should remain so ..."[168] Based on Lew Morrill's December 21 letter to John Hannah, the Minnesota contingency could easily take issue with that assessment![169]

Richart concluded his first letter by indicating he was more optimistic that the Spartans would comply with the amended Rottschaefer motion than his associate from Ann Arbor was.[170]

Aigler wrote back to his colleague on December 21. He questioned Richart's optimistic assessment of Spartan compliance with the Handbook. However, if the aggressive program was forced to abide by conference rules and regulations, he felt that the University of Michigan would stand to benefit from the college's presence in the conference. Lacking the Jenison Awards as an enticement, the Wolverine leader was confident most quality athletes would choose Ann Arbor over East Lansing.[171]

He closed by emphasizing the need for vigilance in monitoring the practices of the Spartan coaches. He feared subsidizing would go "underground," implying that boosters would assume the financing role vacated by the college. Athletes not academically

---

[163] Richart to Aigler. 17 December 1948. University of Illinois Archives. Series 4/2/12; Box 3, folder: Western Intercollegiate Conference 1948-49

[164] Minutes of the Intercollegiate Conference Joint Meeting of the Faculty Representatives and Athletic Directors. 12 December 1948. Bentley Historical Library, University of Michigan. Athletic Department, 943 Bimu 2; Box 84, folder: Conference Directors 3/7/41-7/1/52

[165] Richart to Aigler. 17 December 1948. University of Illinois Archives. Series 4/2/12; Box 3, folder: Western Intercollegiate Conference 1948-49

[166] Ibid.

[167] Ibid.

[168] Ibid.

[169] Morrill to Hannah. 21 December 1948. University of Minnesota Archives, President's Office; Box 238, folder: Physical Education and Athletics 1948-49

[170] Richart to Aigler. 17 December 1948. University of Illinois Archives. Series 4/2/12; Box 3, folder: Western Intercollegiate Conference 1948-49

[171] Aigler to Richart. 21 December 1948. University of Illinois Archives. Series 4/2/12; Box 3, folder: Western Intercollegiate Conference 1948-49

measuring up to the Highland Park yardstick would be aided through alternative means.[172]

Open and honest in his impressions of the school, he nonetheless reminded the Illinois representative that all communiqués between them must remain confidential.[173]

ON DECEMBER 14, 1948, Chairman Frank Richart wrote President John Hannah welcoming him into the Intercollegiate Conference of Faculty Representatives. He reminded him that the recent vote had qualifications. The college must demonstrate complete compliance with all Handbook rules before the faculty leaders would approve its admission into the Big Nine. He pointed out that the provisional action was not unique to Michigan State College. Similar tactics were "taken in 1917 on the occasion of the petition of the University of Michigan for re-admission to the Conference."[174] Professor Aigler may have reminded Richart to include that bit of Wolverine history in the letter to Hannah. The shrewd suggestion offered him legitimate cover, especially if there were a leak to a reporter about his confidential amendment to Henry Rottschaefer's proposal. Aigler could now argue that Michigan had to do the same 31 years earlier following its Decade of Defiance.

Hannah replied in kind to the gracious letter from the chairman of the Faculty Committee. The college president emphasized that "it is our hope that the certifying committee will be able to come at an early date and that we can be formally admitted to the Conference at the earliest possible time."[175]

While Professor Richart, on behalf of the conference, was composing his letter to Hannah, the Michigan State leader was working on a special note to James Lewis Morrill.

> First of all, I want to tell you again in writing what I told you over the telephone Sunday evening. All of Michigan State College is deeply grateful to you, Professor Rottschaefer, and Director McCormick for the leading part that you played in our admission to the Western Conference. We know well that without your help we would not have succeeded, and we shall not forget it.[176]

While writing his memoirs in the late 1970s, almost 30 years after Michigan State University was accepted into the Big Ten, John Hannah noted that "if I were to identify a single individual to whom I think is due as much or more credit than any other single person for his contribution to making Michigan State ... the institution it is today ... I would put [Professor] Floyd Reeves at the head of the list." His role in development of the curriculum and organization of the college was critical during a time when accreditation was in jeopardy.[177]

The accolade for the University of Chicago consultant was well deserved. But Lew

---

[172] Aigler to Richart. 21 December 1948. University of Illinois Archives. Series 4/2/12; Box 3, folder: Western Intercollegiate Conference 1948-49

[173] Ibid.

[174] Richart to Hannah. 14 December 1948. University of Illinois Archives. Series 4/2/12; Box 3, folder: Western Intercollegiate Conference 1948-49

[175] Hannah to Richart. 17 December 1948. University of Illinois Archives. Series 4/2/12; Box 3, folder: Western Intercollegiate Conference 1948-49

[176] Hannah to Morrill. 15 December 1948. University of Minnesota Archives, President's Office; Box 238, folder: Physical Education and Athletics 1948-49

[177] Hannah, John A. *A Memoir*. East Lansing: Michigan State University Press, 1980. pp. 48-49

Morrill merited consideration too. His dogged commitment to the vision of his friend allowed Michigan State to expand beyond a regional college serving its state into a land-grant institution with extension services about the globe.

The "final Morrill" of this story was revealed by President Hannah, somewhat in jest, many years later. At the time, he was asked why his counterpart from Minneapolis had been so supportive of the college's plans.

> [Morrill] had at one time been an alumni executive at Ohio State University
> where there was no love for the University of Michigan, and he had said
> frankly that the people at Minnesota were convinced that they would have
> better success in their traditional [Little Brown Jug] games with Michigan
> if Michigan State were in a position to compete with Michigan for athletes
> and athletic support.[178]

Of course any strategy that might also impact the outcome of the annual Ohio State-Michigan rivalry was just and honorable for an old Buckeye!

---

[178] Denison, James H. 5 November 1969." Intercollegiate Conference." Michigan State University Archives. John A. Hannah Papers, UA2.1.12; Box 80, folder: 12

Why the Iowa "No" Vote?

IN APRIL of 2008 a stack of boxes were gifted to the Bentley Historical Library at the University of Michigan by the estate of Mrs. Eileen Aigler. A treasure of documents dating back 100 years was sorted by student volunteer Marc Levitt. Seventeen linear feet of archival shelf space, with boxes full of folders exposing the amazing 47-year career of a legal scholar and indefatigable leader, were the end result of his painstaking efforts.[1] Five months later, a physician/amateur historian visited the Bentley in search of the role his alma mater had played in the evolution of Michigan State College into a university. Through the Notre Dame graduate's endeavors, a puzzle–containing thousands of pieces spread among 13 archives–was discovered. Three years later, the puzzle lacked one final part.

Newspapers reported that the vote to admit Michigan State into the Western Conference had been unanimous. But, as the Aigler collection reveals, those reports were incorrect because of inaccurate information that the conference had given to the press. The truth was that one school had in fact opposed the Rottschaefer-Aigler motion to approve the Spartans as the newest member of the association. The researcher was left with one obvious question: Why had the State University of Iowa cast that lone nay vote? Until that piece was found, the puzzle would remain incomplete.

A MAJOR transition in the athletic leadership in Iowa City took place during the summer of 1947, when Faculty Representative Karl Leib tendered his resignation to assume the presidency of the NCAA. University Registrar Paul Blommers, with no experience serving on the Board in Control of Athletics, was asked by the Faculty Senate to assume the position–a surprising choice. President Virgil Hancher, in a letter to Commissioner Ken Wilson, however, felt that the "Dutchman from Pella, Iowa" would prove his worth.[2]

Athletic Director Ernest Schroeder retired for health reasons at the same time. Hancher, on the advice of his Board in Control, appointed Paul Brechler as the next

---

[1] Levitt, Marc. University of Michigan Archives, Ralph W. Aigler Papers, 87406 Aa 2; processed by Marc Levitt: May 2008

[2] Hancher to Wilson. 28 August 1947. University of Iowa Archives, Iowa City, Iowa. Virgil Hancher Papers, RG 05.01.11; Box 194, folder: 93

Hawkeye athletic director. He was considered "extraordinarily able, energetic, and mature." The president felt that Brechler had a "combination of intelligence, strength, and reasonableness which is quite rare" for a young leader.[3]

Sixteen months later, Hancher's assessment of his new director's character would prove accurate as the department administrator spearheaded a defiant stance by the State University over the admission of Michigan State College into the Western Conference.

THERE APPEARED to be no obvious reason for Iowa to oppose a Spartan application for the vacated University of Chicago spot–at least at the highest levels of leadership. John Hannah was very good friends with President Virgil Hancher. Their relationship dated back to the early 1940s. And Hancher was also quite close with Lew Morrill of the University of Minnesota.[4] [5] Despite their shared friendship, Hancher never bought into Morrill's plan to aid Hannah's quest. He would not influence the vote of his faculty representative on a selection process which was well-defined in the Intercollegiate Handbook. His background as a prosecuting attorney in Chicago and later a professor of law at Iowa probably played a role in his maintaining that position.

Acknowledging Hancher's respect for the letter of the law, there are four plausible explanations for why Paul Blommers cast the lone "nay" vote in December of 1948:

1. the decline in equality among membership in conference governance, as best exemplified by the 9/6/2 scheduling morass
2. the "value" to Iowa's football program of a Spartan membership
3. the implications of accepting a reprobate into a highly respected conference
4. Iowa's inability to find an end-of-season rival after Chicago's withdrawal from football participation

THE IMPACT of the subsidy scandal of 1929 on the State University of Iowa would extend far beyond a one-year probation and a collective scheduling boycott. During the 1930s the school continued having problems contracting with those powerful programs controlling large gate returns. Although the Hawkeyes were convinced that these difficulties were related to an unforgiving membership,[6] both Indiana and Purdue faced a similar plight despite being free of cardinal sins.[7] Regardless of Iowa's convictions, the reason the three were mistreated at scheduling meetings was their inability to draw crowds. The powers of the Western Conference needed money to meet stadium bond payments during the Depression. It was more lucrative for a school such as Michigan to compete against Northwestern or Illinois than one of the tier-two schools.

Chicago's withdrawal from football in late December of 1939 only made matters

---

[3] Hancher to Wilson. 28 August 1947. University of Iowa Archives, Iowa City, Iowa. Virgil Hancher Papers, RG 05.01.11; Box 194, folder: 93

[4] Morrill to Hancher. 10 September 1946. University of Iowa Archives, Iowa City, Iowa. Virgil Hancher Papers, RG 05.01.11; Box 176, folder: 169

[5] Hancher to Morrill. 9 October 1947. University of Iowa Archives, Iowa City, Iowa. Virgil Hancher Papers, RG 05.01.11; Box 209, folder: 171

[6] Hancher to Leahy. 3 December 1953. University of Iowa Archives, Iowa City, Iowa. Virgil Hancher Papers, RG 05.01.11; Box 338, folder: 163 ND

[7] Bachman, Charles. "The Athletic Side of John A. Hannah." Circa 1970. Michigan State University, Hannah Archives Project, UA2.1.12.2; Box 34, folder: 2 Bachman

worse for the "weak sisters." The odd number of football participants created a scheduling conundrum. Ralph Aigler's motion of May 1940–the temporary and experimental 9/6/2 scheme for the 1943-44 seasons–was intended to accommodate dissension in the ranks following the Maroons' decision.[8] [9] [10] The professor wanted to avoid any further embarrassing press. Robert Maynard Hutchins had done enough, as the anonymous source, in the aftermath of the Blackstone Hotel cocktail party just a few months earlier.

The Intercollegiate Conference of Faculty Representatives traditionally limited its season to eight weekends. By Handbook mandate, a minimum of four games were to be held with the membership. Competition was to end the Saturday prior to Thanksgiving.[11] The short gridiron campaign was intended for one reason: to minimize the impact of practice, game day activity, and travel time on the student-athlete's performance in the classroom.[12] [13]

The problem with the 8/4 commitment lay in actions by certain powers to contract with non-conference schools well in advance of the biennial scheduling meeting. This allowed for fewer weekend dates to accommodate Indiana, Purdue and Iowa. In May of 1940, the long-term solution agreed to by the directors was an 8/6 format; only two games could be held with non-members.[14] But with Michigan and a few others having already signed up non-conference teams for 1943-44, Professor Aigler's temporary fix was to add one game, thus the 9/6/2 rule. Six of those weekends had to be with conference schools; moreover, every member was obligated to host two home games.[15] But Aigler's motion also included the word "experimental." Other conferences were taking on more than eight opponents a season. The faculty probably wanted to assess the impact of an added game on

[8] Minutes of the Meeting of the Directors of Athletics of the Intercollegiate Conference. 24-25 May 1940. Bentley Historical Library, University of Michigan. Athletic Department, 943 Bimu 2; Box 84, folder:Faculty Representatives minutes 3/41-7/52 (AD), 1947-57 (FR)

[9] Northshore Hotel, Evanston, Illinois. (Faculty Representatives Meeting). 24 May 1940. Bentley Historical Library, University of Michigan. Athletic Department, 943 Bimu 2; Box 84, folder: Big Ten Faculty Representatives minutes 1918-46

[10] Bachman, Charles. "The Athletic Side of John A. Hannah." Circa 1970. Michigan State University Archives. Hannah Archives Project, UA 2.1.12.2; Box 34, folder: 2 Bachman

[11] Rules, Regulations, and Opinions of the Intercollegiate Conference of Faculty Representatives-Revised 1930. University of Minnesota Archives, University of Minnesota Athletic Papers; Box 13, folder: small handbook 1895-1908, 1930, 1941

[12] Minutes of the Meeting of the Board in Control of Physical Education. 29 January 1940. Bentley Historical Library, University of Michigan. Board in Control of Intercollegiate Athletics, 8729 Bimu F81 2; Box 49, folder: Board in Control minutes Feb 1938-June 1950. Coach Crisler's comments on scheduling a game out west with California reflected this concern; at the time, the board was debating the impact of travel time on classroom obligations.

[13] Crisler to Aigler. 22 April 1940. Bentley Historical Library, University of Michigan. Ralph W. Aigler Papers, 87406 Aa, Box: 12, folder: athletics 1939-41 A-Z misc. Crisler suggested that the Big Ten forego its ban on post-conference play and contract with the Pacific Coast Conference to compete in the annual Rose Bowl game. But to protect the student's study time prior to final exams, he proposed that practice be limited to two weeks before the New Year's game.

[14] Minutes of the Directors of Athletics of the Intercollegiate Conference. 24-25 May 1940. Bentley Historical Library, University of Michigan. Athletic Department, 943 Bimu 2; Box 84, folder: Athletic Director's office, Big Ten committee minutes 1932-40

[15] Ibid.

the academic well-being of the student. Following the 1944 season, the leadership could evaluate how one additional week of practice affected classroom performance.

That experiment never took place. Within months the conference leadership would meet with military brass and offer their services for the war effort. By 1943, most Big Ten schools were aiding the war effort by training young men for combat duty overseas. As part of that commitment, military athletic rule assumed control over the conference. Schedules were expanded to ten games, contrary to Handbook policies, to accommodate make-shift football teams from midwest naval bases and pre-flight schools. As a consequence, the 9/6/2 format was never tested in 1943-44.

The Second Great War was declared over on September 2, 1945. The Intercollegiate Conference, in anticipation of this historic event, opted for a gradual transition back to conference rule.[16] The 1945 gridiron campaign would be its first relatively normal season in almost four years. The 9/6/2 proposal could now be tested. The two-year experiment, however, ended up lasting one season.

In December of 1945, during the annual conference meetings, Fritz Crisler of Michigan declared the Aigler 9/6/2 plan a resounding success. His motion to officially adopt the format, based on that one season, was approved by the directors;[17] the tally was not mentioned in the minutes.

It was unclear how Crisler arrived at that conclusion. There was no comment in the minutes on whether the proposal was even debated. And somewhat surprisingly, the faculty representatives rubber-stamped the directors' request.[18] [19] There was no study on the impact of the added game on student academic performance.

It would appear that the Crisler motion passed for one reason: money. The added Saturday meant more revenue for six programs capable of attracting decent crowds even during the war years. And for Fritz Crisler, faced with a bond debt of almost $786,600 in 1943 on a stadium completed back in 1927, the income allowed him to retire some obligations.[20] But in addition to the dollars, the Wolverine also liked the scheduling format for another reason: It made signing up two intersectional games each season–a demand placed on him by the national Michigan alumni network–that much easier.[21] His only

---

[16] Minutes of the Meeting of the Board in Control of Intercollegiate Athletics. 21 January 1946. Bentley Historical Library, University of Michigan. Board in Control of Intercollegiate Athletics, 8729 Bimu F81 2; Box 49, folder: Board in Control minutes Feb 1938-June 1950

[17] Minutes of the Joint Meeting of the Intercollegiate Conference of Faculty Representatives and Athletic Directors. 6 December 1945. Bentley Historical Library, University of Michigan. Athletic Department, 943 Bimu 2; Box 84, folder: Big 10 records 1941-52

[18] Minutes of the Intercollegiate Conference, Meeting of Athletic Directors. 6-7 December 1945. Bentley Historical Library, University of Michigan. Athletic Department, 943 Bimu 2; Box 84, folder: Big 10 records 1941-52

[19] Minutes of the Joint Meeting of the Intercollegiate Conference of Faculty Representatives and Athletic Directors. 8 December 1945. Bentley Historical Library, University of Michigan. Athletic Department, 943 Bimu 2; Box 84, folder: Big 10 records 1941-52

[20] Crisler to the President, the Honorable Board of Regents and the University Council. January 1944. Bentley Historical Library, University of Michigan. Alexander Ruthven Papers, 86550 Aa, Uam; Box 36, folder: 22

[21] Minutes of the Meeting of the Board in Control of Intercollegiate Athletics. 8 December 1948. Bentley Historical Library, University of Michigan. Board in Control of Intercollegiate Athletics, 8729 Bimu F81 2; Box 49, folder: BIC minutes Feb 1938-June 1950

obligation was to accommodate six conference members every year.

With the Crisler motion now sanctioned by the faculty, the directors and coaches met in May of 1946 to make arrangements for a three-year schedule. But only the 1947 season could be drafted to the satisfaction of all participants. The 9/6/2 format, originally proposed to aid scheduling for the tier-two programs, was clearly not working out as planned;[22] and somewhat ironically, the main reason appeared to be the University of Michigan.

Dating back to at least 1934, the Wolverines had signed up two intersectional schools well in advance of the scheduling meetings.[23] At the time, an athletic director's only obligation was to contract a minimum of four conference contests during the eight-game season.[24] Fielding Yost had to guarantee two dates with rivals Ohio State and Minnesota every year. He was also required to ink Michigan State on his schedule; a nifty agreement with Ralph Young assured him that the Spartans would always accept the season opener.[25][26] And with demanding alumni wanting to see their Wolverines in action, he contracted home-and-home series with two schools from either coast up to a year prior to the scheduling meetings. That left three weekends on Michigan's schedule for the seven remaining members to compete for behind closed doors. Yost would generally accommodate one tier-two program per year. The other Saturdays were offered to those conference schools capable of generating a good-sized crowd.

Other prominent schools, including The Ohio State University, soon adopted Yost's practice. It was understandable why Indiana, Purdue, and Iowa were upset with the scheme by the late 1930s. There were few weekend dates left after the powers made promises to non-conference teams.[27] Aigler's 1940 plan to expand the season by one game to accommodate the impotent three seemed to be a viable short-term solution to their frustrations until the 8/6 format could be implemented. And in a gesture of support for the tier-two programs, the revised 1941 Handbook included what might be considered the "Michigan Rule." The policy allowed no more than one contract date with a non-conference program in advance of the scheduling meetings.[28] Despite the proscription, Fritz Crisler

---

[22] Joint Meeting of the Western Conference Football Coaches and Athletic Directors. 30 May-1 June 1946. Bentley Historical Library, University of Michigan. Athletic Department, 943 Bimu 2; Box 84, folder: Big Ten Directors' Committee minutes 1941-52

[23] Yost to Griffith. 22 May 1934. Bentley Historical Library, University of Michigan. Ralph W. Aigler Papers, 87406 Aa 2; Box 7, folder: correspondence 1934-39 "X-Y-Z" misc.

[24] Rules, Regulations, and Opinions of the Intercollegiate Conference of Faculty Representatives-Revised 1930. University of Minnesota Archives, University of Minnesota Athletic Papers; Box 13, folder: small handbook 1895-1908, 1930, 1941

[25] Michigan State Football Date. February 1949. Bentley Historical Library, University of Michigan. Herbert Orin Crisler Papers, 85823 AC UAm Aa 2; Box 1, folder: topical correspondence, MSU 1947-49

[26] Young to Yost. 8 July 1940. Bentley Historical Library, University of Michigan. Herbert Orin Crisler Papers, 85823 AC UAm Aa 2; Box 1, folder: topical correspondence, MSU 1943-46

[27] Bachman, Charles. "The Athletic Side of John A. Hannah." Circa 1970. Michigan State University, Hannah Archives Project. UA2.1.12.2; Box 34, folder: 2 Bachman

[28] Handbook of the Intercollegiate Conference of Faculty Representatives, Revised 1941. University of Minnesota Archives, University of Minnesota Department of Intercollegiate Athletics Papers; Box 13, folder: small handbook 1895-1908, 1939, 1941.

would continue the old Yost practice,[29] much to the exasperation of members desperately needing shared revenue gained from contests with the elite programs.[30] [31] [32]

So in an attempt at easing the current scheduling impasse for the 1947-49 seasons, Frank McCormick of Minnesota proposed changing the format temporarily to 9/5/2. One less contract with a member might solve the dilemma brought on by Crisler's actions. The Michigan athletic director, as might be expected, seconded the motion. And much to the dismay of Iowa, Indiana, and Purdue, the McCormick solution was approved 5-4, subject to faculty consent. Illinois, for unknown reasons, sided with the tier-two schools in opposing the motion.[33]

The State University of Iowa, following passage of the McCormick motion, decided it was time to speak up. Athletic Director Ernest Schroeder, frustrated for years over the humiliating scheduling process,[34] [35] offered his solution to the problem. Why not expand the season to 10 games and mandate that all members play each other annually? In a show of support, Purdue's Guy Mackey seconded the motion. The ruling powers, however, defeated the motion 5-4 without an explanation. Illinois again sided with the impotent three. Undeterred, Schroeder then proposed a round-robin rotational schedule. Indiana and Purdue, but not with Illini support, joined Schroeder in backing the concept–his motion was again vetoed by the tier-one powers.[36] The scheme, in the opinion of the dominant directors, would limit dates for non-conference competition. But in a small victory for the tier-two programs, the Faculty Representatives Committee overruled the McCormick-Crisler recommendation.[37] The 9/6/2 format remained Handbook policy.

Despite the temporary success, it was now obvious how politics played out among the directors. Subservient to the majority in control–a trend dating back at least 15 years–the three schools agreed to work with the other directors during the summer months to make the 9/6/2 scheme work. The schedules would be ready for faculty approval in December.[38] But at that annual meeting in Chicago, perhaps in a gesture of support for the Hoosiers,

[29] Minutes of the Meeting of the Directors of Athletics of the Intercollegiate Conference. 24-25 May 1940. Bentley Historical Library, University of Michigan. Athletic Department, 943 Bimu 2; Box 84, folder: Faculty Representatives minutes 3/41-7/52 (AD), 1947-57 (FR)

[30] Wilson to Crisler. 28 October 1948. Bentley Historical Library, University of Michigan. Board in Control of Athletics, 8729 Bimu F81 2; Box 31, folder: papers 1948

[31] Wilson to Crisler. 3 November 1948. Bentley Historical Library, University of Michigan. Board in Control of Athletics, 8729 Bimu F81 2; Box 31, folder: papers 1948

[32] Bachman, Charles. "The Athletic Side of John A. Hannah." Circa 1970. Michigan State University, Hannah Archives Project, UA2.1.12.2; Box 34, folder: 2 Bachman

[33] Joint Meeting of Western Conference Football Coaches and Athletic Directors. 30 May 1946-1 June 1946. Bentley Historical Library, University of Michigan. Athletic Department, 943 Bimu 2; Box 31, folder: Big Ten Directors Committee minutes 1941-52

[34] Devine, Tommy. "Big Ten a Real Exclusive Club." *Detroit Free Press* 13 December 1948. Michigan State University Archives. Madison Kuhn Collection, UA12.107; Scrapbook 108, folder: 5

[35] Bachman, Charles. "The Athletic Side of John A. Hannah." Circa 1970. Michigan State University. Hannah Archives Project.,UA2.1.12.2; Box 34, folder: 2 Bachman

[36] Joint Meeting of Western Conference Football Coaches and Athletic Directors. 30 May 1946-1 June 1946. Bentley Historical Library, University of Michigan. Athletic Department, 943 Bimu 2; Box 31, folder: Big Ten Directors Committee minutes 1941-52

[37] Ibid.

[38] Ibid.

Boilermakers, and Hawkeyes, Commissioner Wilson cautiously admonished Fritz Crisler for his past practices. He affirmed that the 1941 Michigan Rule "that no more than one commitment for the date of a non-Conference game shall be permitted in advance of the schedule meeting" must be respected and practiced by all.[39]

Two years later, in the spring of 1948, the directors, including Ernest Schroeder's replacement, Paul Brechler, and the nine football coaches met in Madison to arrange the 1950-52 schedules. The 18 participants failed to arrive at a plan.[40]

The finger was again pointed at the 9/6/2 rule–and also at Fritz Crisler, who continued to defy the Michigan Rule.[41] [42] [43] A possible boycott of Purdue by Ohio State, Illinois, and the Wolverines further complicated the horse-trading that weekend.

The May 1948 gathering of directors held at the Madison Club had been an awakening for Iowa's Paul Brechler. Two years earlier he had been promoted to business manager of the athletic department.[44] Shortly after Schroeder returned from the scheduling meetings held in Urbana, the two probably discussed the contracting impasse. Now as the Hawkeye athletic director (since Schroeder's retirement in 1947), Brechler could fully appreciate his mentor's frustrations regarding disturbing trends in conference politics–and power.[45] [46]

Unsuccessful in drafting schedules back in May, the directors met in late November to once again try to work out arrangements for the upcoming three seasons. Following Commissioner Wilson's report indicating that Purdue was now fully in compliance with the conference Handbook, the nine were ready for some serious discussions. Fritz Crisler started off by declaring his satisfaction with the Boilermakers' corrective actions. Michigan would not boycott them. Ohio State and Illinois, however, opted to exercise vigilante justice for three years. Recognizing how complicated scheduling would now be with the boycott in place, Frank McCormick proposed the 9/5/2 concept, as he had done two years earlier, to

---

[39] Minutes of the Intercollegiate Conference of Faculty Representative. 27-29 May 1948. University of Wisconsin-Madison Archives, The University of Wisconsin Athletic Board, Series 5/21/6; Box 1, folder: Western Conference minutes 1947-51

[40] Joint Meeting of Western Conference Football Coaches and Athletic Directors. 30 May 1946-1 June 1946. Bentley Historical Library, University of Michigan. Athletic Department, 943 Bimu 2; Box 84, folder: Athletic Director's office, Big-Ten Director's committee minutes 1941-52

[41] Crisler to Fairman. 24 February 1947. Bentley Historical Library, University of Michigan. Board in Control of Intercollegiate Athletics, 8729 Bimu F81 2; Box 35, folder: football schedules 1944, 1946, 1947

[42] Crisler to Fairman. 4 April 1947. Bentley Historical Library, University of Michigan. Board in Control of Intercollegiate Athletics, 8729 Bimu F81 2; Box 35, folder: football schedules 1944, 1946, 1947

[43] Crisler to Wilkinson. 8 September 1947. Bentley Historical Library, University of Michigan. Board in Control of Intercollegiate Athletics, 8729 Bimu F81 2; Box 35, folder: football schedules 1944, 46, 47

[44] Board in Control of Athletics. 4 June 1946. University of Iowa Archives, Iowa City, Iowa. Board in Control of Athletics, RG 28.03.05, Series II; Box 3, folder: BIC minutes 1942-48

[45] Brechler to Crisler. 18 May 1948. Bentley Historical Library, University of Michigan. Board in Control of Intercollegiate Athletics, 8729 Bimu F81 2; Box 31, folder: papers 1948

[46] Crisler to Brechler. 31 May 1948. Bentley Historical Library, University of Michigan. Board in Control of Intercollegiate Athletics, 8729 Bimu F81 2; Box 31, folder: papers 1948

simplify the onerous task confronting all of them.[47]

The following day Ohio State's Richard Larkins moved that the McCormick proposal become permanent legislation. Fritz Crisler, as expected, seconded the motion–he had always been in favor of the five-game commitment. To no one's surprise, Iowa, Purdue and Indiana continued to oppose manipulation of the scheduling format at their expense. And to avoid rejection of the proposal by the Faculty Representatives Committee (as had occurred two years earlier, in defense of the impotent three), the powers decided to let both sides present their case to the faculty charged with approving any new legislation. Fritz Crisler would argue for the majority. Paul Brechler would offer the minority position opposing the reduction in number of conference games.[48]

Finally, Brechler had an opportunity to plead his case. A scheduling shenanigan, such as the 9/5/2 ploy, was not the real issue after all. It was merely a symptom of a far more serious problem. Equality no longer existed among the membership. The dominant programs ruled and dollars were the main reason. In his presentation, the young Brechler argued that the inability to make the 9/6/2 work would suggest a schism within the conference that could very well harm its reputation as a cohesive group.[49] [50] If the powers wanted only a five-game commitment, only they would benefit. Iowa, Indiana, and Purdue gained nothing.

As it turned out, Brechler won the debate. The faculty decided that "they [were] not satisfied that the Directors have exhausted every possibility to make a six game schedule." But acknowledging the challenges currently facing the administrators, the academicians stated that "in case it become[s] impossible to reach such schedules, the six-game requirement may be waived … [for those three years]."[51] And in a statement of support for the tier-two schools, long held hostage by the dominant programs, Athletic Director Douglas Mills of Illinois emphasized that all must abide by the de facto Michigan Rule in planning outside commitments in advance of future scheduling meetings.[52] He wanted to make sure that Herbert Orin Crisler heard those words loud and clear.

Paul Brechler's impassioned plea for equality and fairness in governance and legislation was well-received. It was critical, in the opinion of the faculty leadership, that future decisions be made for the good of the conference and not just for an individual program.

---

[47] Minutes of the Intercollegiate Conference Meeting of the Athletic Directors. 30 November 1948. University of Wisconsin-Madison Archives. The University Faculty Athletic Board, Series 5/21/6; Box 1, folder: Western Conference minutes 1947-51

[48] Minutes of the Intercollegiate Conference Meeting of the Athletic Directors. 1 December 1948. University of Wisconsin-Madison Archives. The University Faculty Athletic Board, Series 5/21/6; Box 1, folder: Western Conference minutes 1947-51

[49] Annual Minutes of the Stockholders and Directors of the Intercollegiate Conference Athletic Association. 11 December 1948. Bentley Historical Library, University of Michigan. Athletic Department, 943 Bimu 2; Box 84, folder: Big 10 records 1941-52

[50] Brechler to Crisler. 18 May 1948. Bentley Historical Library, University of Michigan. Board in Control of Intercollegiate Athletics, 8729 Bimu F81 2; Box 31, folder: papers 1948

[51] Minutes of the Intercollegiate Conference of Faculty Representatives. 11-12 December 1948. Bentley Historical Library, University of Michigan. Athletic Department, 943 Bimu 2; Box 84, folder: Faculty Representatives meetings 1941-57

[52] Ibid.

The certain selection of Michigan State as the next member of the Intercollegiate Conference was not popular with the coaches, directors, and a few representatives. The college succeeded in large part due to the political machinations of one very powerful university president.[53] Perhaps the Hawkeye director's opposition to a Spartan admission lay with that conviction. He was making a statement to the faculty leadership.

IN JUNE of 1947, Iowa was implicated by an anonymous Big Nine leader as one of three institutions currently offering no added value to the Western Conference. The Spartans would merely join their ranks as another "weak sister" if granted membership. The denigrating statement by Ohio State's Lynn St. John undoubtedly embarrassed three proud programs all struggling to develop or regain a football tradition. Despite proving to be humiliating for the State University, the comment did raise an important question for Paul Brechler shortly after assuming the athletic directorship in Iowa City: Just what value would a Spartan admission bring to the conference, and perhaps more importantly, to Iowa?

Part of the challenge facing four Iowa athletic directors since 1929 had been how to revive a listless Hawkeye program. With the exception of an occasional winning season, its victories were few and far between during those 18 years. Unsuccessful in landing "Sleepy Jim" Crowley from Michigan State in the early 1930s, the State University had hired three different coaches. In March of 1945 Clarence "Biggie" Munn was offered an interim head coaching position, but the Michigan assistant coach wanted nothing to do with a temporary job.[54] It would ultimately require Paul Brechler hiring Forest Evashevski in 1952 before a winning tradition would resume in Iowa City.

One year after the "weak sister" incident, John Hannah wrote to Iowa's President Virgil Hancher in early June requesting a home-and-home series with the Hawkeyes. Hannah was looking for a season finale with a Big Nine school.[55] Paul Brechler, as director of athletics, declined the offer.[56] Signing up Michigan State would not benefit a program still searching for success on the gridiron. The two schools had no past football relationship. The contest would generate no interest among fans or sportswriters to justify a contract.

But of greater concern for the Iowa director a few months later were reports in the press about how close the Spartans were to achieving their December goal of a seat in the Intercollegiate Conference. As rumors mounted, Brechler became aware that Michigan State would not be satisfied with playing just Iowa, Purdue, and Indiana, despite what sportswriters were opining.[57] [58] The Spartans, in the minds of some conference leaders, would settle for nothing less than tier-one competition–the same programs Brechler and his

---

[53] Crisler to Little, Blommers, Wilson. 30 March 1949. Bentley Historical Library, University of Michigan. Ralph W. Aigler Papers, 87406 Aa 2; Box 9, folder: correspondence 1946-52 "E" misc.
[54] Board in Control of Athletics. 5 March 1945. University of Iowa Archives, Iowa City, Iowa. Board in Control of Athletics, RG 28.03.05, Series II; Box 3, folder: BIC minutes 1942-48
[55] Alderton, George S. "The Football Future." *The Lansing State Journal* 14 December 1948. Michigan State University Archives. Madison Kuhn Collection, UA12.107; Scrapbook 108, folder: 5
[56] Connell, Phil E. 4 June 1948. University of Iowa Archives, Iowa City, Iowa. Virgil Hancher Papers, RG 05.01.11; Box 194, folder: 93
[57] Aigler to Richart. 14 December 1948. Bentley Historical Library, University of Michigan. Ralph W. Aigler Papers, 87406 Aa 2; Box 10, folder: correspondence 1946-52 "R" misc
[58] Devine, Tommy. "Big Ten a Real Exclusive Club." *Detroit Free Press* 13 December 1948. Michigan State University Archives. Madison Kuhn Collection, UA12.107; Scrapbook 108, folder: 5

predecessor had struggled to sign up every few years.[59][60]

And so, if there was little value for the Hawkeyes in contracting with Ralph Young in June for a two-game series, there was absolutely no value for the State University in supporting Michigan State College for membership in December.

THE SPARTANS' reputation for circumventing the amateur code might have been another reason for Paul Brechler declining to contract with Ralph Young in June and encouraging Paul Blommers to cast a nay vote in December. There was no reason to add a reprobate to an honorable conference that set the amateur benchmark for others to follow.

Professor Blommers, lacking any athletic-board experience in Iowa City before becoming the university's faculty representative, probably had no knowledge of the loan guarantees, Jenison Awards, recruiting tactics, and suspect eligibility requirements in practice in East Lansing. Paul Brechler may have gained some background on these Spartan ploys while serving in Ernest Schroeder's athletic department. But most of their appreciation of alleged past and present Spartan transgressions probably derived from discussions between meetings with colleagues. Opinions were easily influenced through interactions with nationally respected conference leaders such as Ralph Aigler and Herbert Crisler.[61][62][63]

The Aigler Boycott of 1935 was a classic example. Michigan State, despite offering huge guarantees to certain Big Ten schools, was unable to consummate a contract with any program. The confidential disciplinary action against the Spartans ultimately broke down in 1939 when Indiana and Purdue signed contracts with Michigan State.[64][65] They needed competition and dollars.

In July of 1940, following its success with the Hoosiers and Boilermakers, Michigan State's Athletic Council offered the State University of Iowa a surprising guarantee of $12,500 plus 50 percent of gate receipts for a home-and-home contract during the 1943-44 seasons.[66] But Athletic Director Ernest Schroeder turned it down. Board in Control minutes fail to even mention the proposal.[67] He may have had reasons for failing to

[59] Aigler to Richart. 14 December 1948. Bentley Historical Library, University of Michigan. Ralph W. Aigler Papers, 87406 Aa 2; Box 10, folder: correspondence 1946-52 "R" misc.

[60] Devine, Tommy. "Big Ten a Real Exclusive Club." *Detroit Free Press* 13 December 1948. Michigan State University Archives. Madison Kuhn Collection, UA12.107; Scrapbook 108, folder: 5

[61] St. John to Crisler. 27 December 1944. The Ohio State University Archives, Director of Athletics (RG 9/e-1/10), "Intercollegiate Conference: Commissioner: Correspondence (Griffith and St. John): 1940-46."

[62] Aigler to Owens. 23 January 1945. Bentley Historical Library, University of Michigan. Ralph W. Aigler Papers, 87406 Aa 2; Box 8, folder: correspondence 1940-45 "N-O" misc.

[63] Hannah to Morrill. 2 June 1948. University of Minnesota Archives, President's Office; Box 238, folder: Physical Education and Athletics 1948-49

[64] Minutes of the State Board of Agriculture. 1 January 1939. www.onthebanks.msu.edu

[65] Bachman, Charles. "The Athletic Side of John A. Hannah." Circa 1970. Michigan State University Archives. Hannah Archives Project, UA 2.1.12.2; Box 34, folder: 2 Bachman

[66] Hannah to Young. 6 July 1940. Michigan State University Archives. Board of Trustees Records, UA1.0. Supplementary Material; Box 1885, folder 15 7/5/40.

[67] McCartney, David F. "RE. thank you." E-mail to David J. Young. 7 June 2010. The archivist paged through the BICOA minutes from 7/17/40 through spring of 1945 and found no mention of an

mention the generous proposal at those meetings.

A month after Schroeder was named athletic director in January of 1937, Professor Ralph Huston of Michigan State visited Iowa City to meet with Faculty Representative Clarence Updegraff. Schroeder was probably included in the discussions. Huston's intent was to dispel mistruths, at least in his opinion, being spread by Ralph Aigler about the Spartan program. He had been mandated by the State Board to gain votes for a planned Spartan application to the Western Conference in May.[68] Following Huston's departure, Updegraff probably informed the rookie director about the Spartan's reprobate reputation and the Aigler Boycott. As a likely consequence of this discussion, in July of 1940, Schroeder had no interest in contracting with a school that openly violated Handbook rules on subsidies, eligibility, and proselyting.

Regardless of past ploys by Michigan to influence conference decisions on the Spartans, Paul Blommers (and Paul Brechler) required no counsel from either Fritz Crisler or Ralph Aigler while reading a letter sent to him from President John Hannah in January of 1948. In the brief note mailed to all nine faculty representatives, he announced that the State Board of Agriculture had decided to rescind its Jenison Awards;[69] [70] the grants were clearly in violation of the recently passed Sanity Code. Although it was portrayed as an honorable move, it still begged the question: why did the college even have a subsidy program in the first place? Financial aid of any sort, prior to the fall of 1947, was contrary to the Western Conference Handbook. All schools competing against conference members were obligated to abide by those rules. The Spartans, in maintaining the Jenison Awards since 1941, were violating that policy while continuing to compete against the University of Michigan. The Spartan scheme, tolerated by the Wolverines only because state taxpayers had demanded that the schools annually compete on the gridiron, was undoubtedly offensive to the current Hawkeye athletic leadership. The take-home message for Blommers and Brechler was clear: Michigan State could not to be trusted.

The May 1948 Richart-Aigler Motion requiring the pioneer land-grant college to be fully compliant with conference rules and regulations before the faculty representatives would consider any application may have been the final wake-up call for the two Hawkeyes.[71] [72] Back in Iowa City, Blommers and Brechler probably compared notes on what they heard about Michigan State between meetings. Financial aid to athletes was not the only violation occurring in East Lansing!

But what might have sealed the decision by Iowa to oppose Henry Rottschaefer's motion of December 12 was an unanticipated telephone call from the chancellor of the

---

MSC offer. On 3/10/41, the board approved a nine-game schedule for the 1943 and 1944 seasons. The board later revised the schedules, due to the war, on 4/19/43.

[68] Minutes of the State Board of Agriculture. 18 March 1937. www.onthebanks.msu.edu

[69] Hannah to Richart. 23 January 1948. University of Illinois Archives, Series 4/2/12; Box 3, folder: Western Intercollegiate Conference 1947-48

[70] Hannah to Aigler. 23 January 1948. Bentley Historical Library, University of Michigan. Ralph W. Aigler Papers, 87406 Aa 2; Box 9, folder: correspondence 1946-52 "H" misc.

[71] Minutes of the Intercollegiate Conference Joint Meeting of the Faculty Representatives and Athletic Directors. 29 May 1948. Bentley Historical Library. University of Michigan. Athletic Department, 943 Bimu 2; Box 84, folder: Big-Ten directors meeting 3/41-7/52

[72] Aigler to Richart. 21 December 1948. University of Illinois Archives. Series 4/2/12; Box 3, folder: Western Intercollegiate Conference 1948-49

University of Pittsburgh. Rufus Fitzgerald, prior to moving to Pittsburgh in the late 1930s to become provost–and later chancellor–at the university, had been a faculty associate of Professor Karl Leib at the State University of Iowa. The chancellor was under instructions from Captain Tom Hamilton, his new athletic director, to contact his old colleague who was now president of the NCAA. Pittsburgh wanted to delay the selection process until the spring of 1949 when it might be better prepared, under Hamilton's guidance, to offer an alternative proposal to Michigan State's application. During their confidential discussion Leib informed Fitzgerald that the conference leadership had no immediate plans to enlarge the Big Nine–at least in his opinion. But he promised to "pass the word along to the Iowa adviser, Paul Breckler [sic]" about Pitt's intentions.[73] [74]

Professor Leib no doubt fulfilled his promise to an old friend. What gossip he shared with Brechler about Michigan State, based on his decade serving alongside Ralph Aigler on the Faculty Representatives Committee, remains speculation.

Perhaps the "no" vote reflected Iowa's concerns with the integrity of the athletic program at Michigan State. With so many questions about its past and present practices, why offer a seat to an institution that might harm the honorable reputation of the Intercollegiate Conference of Faculty Representatives?

CONFERENCE RIVALRIES and season finales, in the aftermath of The (Chicago) Announcement, may provide one final explanation for the Iowa "no" vote. It might also offer a reason for Paul Brechler refusing to honor John Hannah's summertime request for a home-and-home series with Iowa in the near future.

William Nunn of the University of Minnesota met with James Denison of Michigan State at the annual American College Public Relations Association convention held in Denver in early June. With explicit instructions from his boss, Nunn revealed for the first time Lew Morrill's revised plan to assist the college in attaining a seat at the Sherman Hotel conference rooms. Following the meetings in Colorado, Denison would return to East Lansing and advise President Hannah about the clever scheme.

At the same time that Nunn and Denison were having confidential discussions in Denver, John Hannah was reassessing his strategy for gaining admission into the Western Conference. Plan A had been a failure. He would now focus all his attention on Plan B. On June 2nd of 1948, shortly after the fifth rejection, he wrote two letters, one to Lew Morrill and the other to Virgil Hancher, requesting gridiron relationships with both Minnesota and Iowa.[75] [76] Notre Dame and Michigan assured two nationally renowned programs on the schedule each year. Adding the Golden Gophers and Hawkeyes could provide Hannah– perhaps now more accepting of an independent fate–a few more Big Nine competitors certain to grab headlines in major newspapers about the Midwest.

Consistent with his aggressive practices as president of Minnesota, Lew Morrill

---

[73] "Telephone: Captain Hamilton and RHF." 7 December 1948. University of Pittsburgh Archives. 2/10; Box 2, folder: FF19

[74] "Telephone: Karl Leib of State University of Iowa." 8 December 1948. University of Pittsburgh Archives. 2/10; Box 2, folder: FF19

[75] Hancher to Hannah. 5 June 1948. University of Iowa Archives, Iowa City, Iowa. Virgil Hancher Papers, RG 05.01.11; Box 194, folder: 93

[76] Hannah to Morrill. 2 June 1948. University of Minnesota Archives, President's Office; Box 238, folder: Physical Education and Athletics 1948-49

asked Frank McCormick to find a few Saturdays for the Spartans on the Golden Gophers' schedule within the next few years.[77]

Virgil Hancher, however, approached the Hannah letter differently. Mindful of institutional protocol, the Iowa president asked his executive assistant, Phil Connell, to deliver the communiqué to Paul Brechler. Hancher accepted his director's terse reply without question.[78] The president had no idea what was taking place in his Hawkeye athletic department over the spring and summer of 1948. His leadership style was to delegate responsibility to trusted administrators–in this case, Brechler.

Ever since Robert Maynard Hutchins' announcement of 1939, the Hawkeyes lacked a legitimate conference rival to close out the Big Nine campaign.[79] Illinois had maintained an intrastate rivalry with the University of Chicago until Hutchins' December press conference. As a logical alternate, the Illini quickly signed up the Wildcats of Northwestern. The domino effect from that action profoundly impacted the low-flying Hawkeyes. Over the previous decade Iowa had been sharing the official conference closing date with Northwestern and Nebraska.

But now, without a conference member to end the season prior to the Thanksgiving holiday, Ernest Schroeder turned to Lincoln, Nebraska for help. The Cornhuskers were more than willing to accommodate him during the early 1940s. The gesture, after all, might aid their own ultimate goal: admission into the conference. But by the spring of 1944 it had become apparent to Nebraska's athletic leadership that the faculty representatives had no interest in expansion or replacement for the foreseeable future. The Cornhuskers agreed to compete against the Hawkeyes one more time early in the 1946 season. Late November dates would now be reserved for Big Six members. The season-ending rivalry was over–at least for the next 65 years![80]

Schroeder looked to numerous regional programs for help but was unsuccessful. Even Pittsburgh, despite having signed up just about every Big Nine school over the past few years to enhance its chances for admission into the conference, was no option for him. In 1939 the Panthers had begun competing against Pennsylvania State College on the Saturday before Thanksgiving. The tradition continued throughout the 1940s. As a consequence of his inability to sign up any program, the final weekend of conference play for the Hawkeyes was left blank for 1946-47.[81] Although in violation of Handbook policy, Commissioner Wilson tried to mitigate Iowa's predicament by gaining faculty approval for the school to begin its football season one week in advance of the traditional last Saturday in September. But it was a hollow accomplishment for the Hawkeye athletic director.[82]

---

[77] Morrill to Hannah. 15 June 1948. University of Minnesota Archives, President's Office; Box 238, folder: Physical Education and Athletics 1948-49

[78] Hancher to Hannah. 5 June 1948. University of Iowa Archives, Iowa City, Iowa. Virgil Hancher Papers, RG 05.01.11; Box 194, folder: 93

[79] Wilson to Faculty Representatives. 5 August 1947. University of Illinois Archives. Series 4/2/12; Box 3, folder: Western Intercollegiate Conference 1946-47.

[80] Nebraska was admitted into the Big Ten on 1 July 2010. Conference play began in the fall of the following season, 102 years since the first Nebraska Response.

[81] Alderton, George S. "The Football Future." *The Lansing State Journal* 14 December 1948. Michigan State University Archives. Madison Kuhn Collection, UA12.107; Scrapbook 108, folder: 5

[82] Memorandum. Wilson to Faculty Representatives. 5 August 1947. University of Illinois Archives. Athletic Committee Chairman and Faculty Representative's File 1907-1949, Series 4/12/12; Box 3,

With Schroeder's retirement in June of 1947, Paul Brechler was left with the major challenge of finding and promoting a fan-pleasing rivalry. But within months of assuming the athletic director's office in Iowa City, he experienced (like John Hannah one year earlier) some Irish luck that would help solve his problem.

Since 1939 Iowa and Notre Dame had competed four times during midseason. The contractual agreement was one of the final acts of athletic director Oscar Solem before he turned the department over to Ernest Schroeder in January of 1937.[83] [84] The series was critical to a program in dire straits. President Hancher summed up just how important it was to Iowa in a letter to Frank Leahy in 1953. "We at Iowa have appreciated the fact that Notre Dame stood by us during some of our lean years when we were trying to re-establish ourselves after the Big Ten had taken such drastic action against us in the early thirties."[85]

Solem had found the Holy Cross priests to be tough negotiators. In contrast to the traditional Western Conference practice of splitting gate receipts, the Irish received 50 cents more than the Hawkeyes for every $3.00 ticket sold in South Bend.[86] That was actually a small price to pay for having the Irish on the schedule. And more important than gate receipts, the State University received national exposure on those Saturdays in the fall–news coverage critical for rebuilding a winning tradition.

In January of 1946 Schroeder announced to his Board in Control of Athletics that Notre Dame had asked to continue the relationship through the 1947-48 seasons.[87] Before his retirement in the summer of 1947, the Iowa director revealed another extension of the contract: The Hawkeyes were officially inked on the Irish schedule through 1951.[88]

Paul Brechler recognized the value the Irish-Hawkeye relationship as well. Eight months into his tenure as athletic director, in March of 1948, he announced to his Board in Control that Notre Dame was willing to reserve the weekend before Thanksgiving for the Hawkeyes beginning in 1949.[89] It was a major accomplishment for the new director. As it turned out, his achievement may have correlated with a gracious letter he had penned to Father John Cavanaugh following his first visit to South Bend on October 25, 1947. Two weeks after that loss to Frank Leahy's lads, Brechler had written to President Cavanaugh stating "it is our feeling that the football relationship between Iowa and Notre Dame is on a very high plane, and that it should be continued for many years to come."[90] The letter led to

folder: Western Intercollegiate Conference 1946-47

[83] Board in Control Meeting. 10 June 1936. University of Iowa Archives, Iowa City, Iowa. Board in Control of Athletics, RG 28.03.05; Box 3, BIC Minutes 1934-36

[84] Board in Control Meeting. 18 January 1937. University of Iowa Archives, Iowa City, Iowa. Board in Control of Athletics, RG 28.03.05; Box 3, BIC Minutes 1937-41

[85] Hancher to Leahy. 3 December 1953. University of Iowa Archives, Iowa City, Iowa. Virgil Hancher Papers, RG 05.01.11; Box 338, folder: 163ND.

[86] Board in Control of Athletics. 1 May 1939. University of Iowa Archives, Iowa City, Iowa. Board in Control of Athletics, RG 28.03.05; Box 3, BIC Minutes 1937-41

[87] Board in Control Meeting. 16 January 1946. University of Iowa Archives, Iowa City, Iowa. Board in Control of Athletics, RG 28.03.05, Series II; Box 3, BIC Minutes 1942-48.

[88] Lysy, Peter J. "Re: Paul Brechler." E-mail to David J. Young. 7 May 2010. The Notre Dame Faculty Board in Control agreed to a long term contract with Iowa at its meeting on 1/23/1947.

[89] Board in Control of Athletics. 11 March 1948. University of Iowa Archives, Iowa City, Iowa. Board in Control of Athletics, RG 28.03.05, Series II; Box 3, BIC Minutes 1942-48.

[90] Brechler to Cavanaugh. 6 November 1947. Archives of the University of Notre Dame, [UPCC 13/2], "General Correspondence series"

renewed negotiations. The end result was Iowa gaining a season finale with the Irish for the next 14 seasons. The only break occurred in 1950 when the Hawkeyes opted for sunshine and a game with the Hurricanes of Miami in late November.

With Brechler hiring Forest Evashevski in 1952, the State University was on the verge of regaining football prominence in the Western Conference. Although he would win only three of eight games against Notre Dame during his stay in Iowa City, Evashevski claimed the Big Ten title for Iowa in 1956 and 1958. A Rose Bowl victory over California on January 1, 1959, confirmed the resurrection of the program. The mythical national championship was bestowed on the Hawkeyes in the 1958 season.

Looking back, it appears that the contract with Notre Dame for a season-ending contest might have been the most significant reason why Paul Brechler dodged John Hannah's request to visit Iowa City every other year in late November.[91] The president was not privy to Brechler's contract with Notre Dame when he wrote to Virgil Hancher in June. With the Irish signed up for that final Saturday before Thanksgiving beginning in 1949, Brechler's fear of having to compete against Michigan State in the season finale was ended.

Shortly after Hannah's college was voted into the conference, the *Lansing State Journal's* George Alderton–a trusted friend of the president and the first sports information director at the college–gave some validity to Brechler's concerns about a potential season-ender with Michigan State. In his commentary, Alderton acknowledged Hannah's achievement and speculated about the implications it held for the school. "It is quite likely that Michigan State College and the University of Iowa will find it possible to get together for a closing football game for both their schedules in the new Big 10 picture. The Hawkeyes are the only member of the old regime without a traditional closing game."[92]

The well-connected sportswriter continued, "It is well known in building the 1948 schedule that Spartan officials attempted to persuade Iowa to play the [college] on the late November date. The Hawkeyes demurred, however, and turned to Boston University for a game."[93] And to validate the challenges faced by Hawkeye athletic directors over the past seven years, Alderton noted that "while the game would lack any traditional background, it … would find newcomer Michigan State stepping into a vacant berth and at the same time solve Iowa's last game problem."[94] He was, like President Hannah, unaware of Iowa's March 1948 agreement with the Fighting Irish as well.

What George Alderton also failed to appreciate, was just how much the current athletic director of the State University disliked Michigan State. That conviction had been apparent during the scheduling meetings that took place just prior to the Spartans' tentative acceptance into the conference. Although the college, as will be seen, would be denied official recognition of its football accomplishments until completion of the 1952 season, conference directors were welcomed to book games with the Spartans in the interim. Five programs agreed to short-term contracts; the other four, including Iowa, declined any relationship. Despite struggling to complete its 9/6/2 obligations for those three seasons, the State University of Iowa would not sign up the Spartans. The Brechler Boycott, part of a

---

[91] Alderton, George S. "The Football Future." *The Lansing State Journal* 14 December 1948. Michigan State University Archives. Madison Kuhn Collection, UA12.107; Scrapbook 108, folder: 5
[92] Ibid.
[93] Ibid.
[94] Ibid.

grander scheme to impose vigilante justice on the Spartans, would finally end with a gridiron contract in 1953.

FOLLOWING COMPLETION of the contentious spring meetings of 1948, Paul Brechler returned to Iowa City. A few days later, on June 4, he was handed a letter that needed a response. It was addressed to President Virgil Hancher, from John Hannah. Hancher's friend was making a personal plea for a home-and-home football contract with Michigan State.[95] The Spartan president was circumventing institutional protocol by appealing directly to Brechler's boss. Hancher asked executive assistant Phil Connell to hand deliver the request to his athletic director.

Later that same day, Connell typed a brief note to his boss summarizing the interaction. "Dr. Brechler states that they are not interested in this series for two or three reasons–which I did not ask him to divulge to me."[96] It's unfortunate that Hancher didn't ask his athletic director what those reasons might be. The answer to why the Iowa "no" vote of December probably lay hidden within those three responses. As a consequence, a complex puzzle pieced together by an amateur historian will remain unfinished.

---

[95] Hancher to Hannah. 5 June 1948. University of Iowa Archives, Iowa City, Iowa. Virgil Hancher Papers, RG 05.01.11; Box 194, folder: 93
[96] Connell, Phil E. 4 June 1948. University of Iowa Archives, Iowa City, Iowa. Virgil Hancher Papers, RG 05.01.11; Box 194, folder: 93

IF RALPH Aigler viewed Michigan State College as "outlaws" in 1935,[1] there's no telling what derogatory title he might have given to the University of Pittsburgh at about the same time. Under the coaching direction of John "Jock" Sutherland, the Panthers had dominated college football for almost two decades. Dr. Sutherland, a member of the dental school faculty during the off-season, found gridiron success through dollars. In other words, he hired athletes. By the late 1930s his reputation for buying top talent was the reason that prominent programs, including Notre Dame and many Western Conference members, had quietly severed relationships with Pitt.[2] The resulting financial impact on a school still making bond payments for its $2.1 million stadium was profound. Pitt's debt burden by 1939 remained at $1.5 million on a structure completed 14 years earlier.[3]

Sutherland's downfall came about in the late 1930s as Pittsburgh's chancellor became painfully aware of the reason for the de facto boycott.[4] Pitt needed Ohio State, Minnesota, and Notre Dame to fill its 67,000 seat facility.[5] The athletic director could not count on subsidies from an administration struggling to raise monies to finance the enormous $10 million "Cathedral of Learning" being constructed nearby.

JOHN GABBERT Bowman, born and raised in Iowa, graduated from the State University of Iowa in 1899 with a master's degree. He eventually received his doctorate from Columbia. After a brief stint as president of Iowa, he was hired as chancellor of the University of Pittsburgh, where he was charged with resurrecting the academic reputation of an institution that author Upton Sinclair had derided in 1919 as "the only high school in the

---

[1] Aigler to Long. 7 October 1935. Bentley Historical Library, University of Michigan. Ralph W. Aigler Papers, 87406 Aa 2; Box 12, folder: athletic correspondence 1933-36 "L" misc.

[2] Wallace, Francis. "The Test Case at Pitt-The Facts about College Football Play for Pay." *The Saturday Evening Post*, 28 October 1939. The University of Pittsburgh Archives, 9/10-A, FF 772; Box 1

[3] Ibid.

[4] Ibid.

[5] Alberts, Robert C. *Pitt: The Story of the University of Pittsburgh 1787-1987*. Pittsburgh: University of Pittsburgh Press. p. 158

country that gives a degree."[6]

But it was football that ultimately led to Bowman's reputation as a reformer. By May of 1937, the chancellor had finally heard enough about Jock Sutherland's antics. After verifying those accusations, he decided to "begin a definite retreat from an athletic position that was not only threatening Pitt's desirable schedules but which was smearing its academic reputation."[7] Bowman first forced the resignation of the current athletic director. He then hired a former Sutherland player, James Hagan, to lead the reformation. Hagan, however, was no Martin Luther. While he never nailed his plan to the front doors of the Cathedral of Learning, he did upset many alumni!

As the new athletic director, Hagan assumed control of schedules and modified Sutherland's subsidy policy. Known as the "Hagan Plan," it still recompensed athletes but it did so as part of a work-study program.[8] Such reforms, however, were inadequate in the eyes of a muckraking press.

In response, on February 9, 1938, the chancellor announced "Code Bowman," which essentially adopted the rules and regulations of the Western Conference. The faculty would assume control of athletics at Pittsburgh. Subsidies would cease. Athletes would be obligated to demonstrate advancement toward a degree or be declared ineligible.[9] The ultimate goal was to lure back those schools capable of generating revenue to cover the stadium bond debt. The problem with the Bowman strategy, however, was Pitt's inability to attract athletic talent in the absence of a payment scheme. Crowds were not inclined to buy tickets to watch their Panthers go down in defeat.[10]

At about the same time, Chancellor Bowman turned to the State University back in Iowa City in search of a provost to resurrect the tarnished academic reputation of the school. Rufus Henry Fitzgerald, invaluable assistant to President Eugene Gilmore of Iowa, was chosen chief academic officer of the University of Pittsburgh in 1938.[11]

In February of 1939, shortly after Fitzgerald's arrival, Hagan, with the administration's approval, persuaded Western Conference Commissioner John Griffith to assist him in cleaning up the athletic mess at Pitt. Acting as a consultant for the school, Griffith was charged with assisting the athletic director in implementing and enforcing the Intercollegiate Conference's amateur ideals.[12] The fees for Griffith's services were not incidental; the conference gained over $11,000 for his services in 1939 alone. Hagan planned to continue the arrangement for the foreseeable future.[13]

---

[6] Wallace, Francis. "The Test Case at Pitt-The Facts about College Football Play for Pay." *The Saturday Evening Post*, 28 October 1939. The University of Pittsburgh Archives, 9/10-A, FF 772; Box 1

[7] Ibid.

[8] Ibid.

[9] Ibid.

[10] Ibid.

[11] Gilmore to Aigler. 23 November 1939. Bentley Historical Library, University of Michigan. Ralph W. Aigler Papers, Aa 2; Box 8, folder: correspondence 1940-45 "G" misc.

[12] Wallace, Francis. "The Football Laboratory Explodes-The Climax in the Test Case at Pitt." *The Saturday Evening Post,* 4 November 1939. The University of Pittsburgh Archives, 9/10-A, FF 772; Box 1

[13] Griffith to St. John. 1 March 1940. The Ohio State University Archives, Director of Athletics (RG 9/e-1/9), "Intercollegiate Conference: Athletic Director's Correspondence: 1938-1940."

ONE OF Rufus Fitzgerald's first tasks as provost was to address problems in the law school. Its accreditation was in jeopardy.[14] New leadership was needed. Fitzgerald searched for a legal scholar with integrity and a national reputation to return the graduate program to respectability. The provost consulted with two former colleagues at Iowa, President Gilmore and his predecessor, Walter Jessup. Both highly recommended Ralph William Aigler of the University of Michigan Law School.[15] Based on their response, Fitzgerald was convinced that Aigler's credentials, impeccable reputation as an educator, and penchant for leadership would bring credibility to the troubled program.[16]

In preparing for the initial interview the law professor read a two-part article regarding the controversial football program at Pittsburgh that had appeared in *The Saturday Evening Post* on October 28 and November 4 of 1939.[17] The information from the muckraking article educated Aigler on the serious problems facing the institutional leadership at Pitt.

In mid-January of 1940 Aigler declined the Pitt offer.[18] Despite that rejection, Fitzgerald probably felt the interviews with the influential professor might some day prove advantageous for the University of Pittsburgh.

LYNN ST. John of Ohio State, as a director in the Western Conference, was fully aware of the consultative services being provided the University of Pittsburgh by John Griffith. As a good friend of the commissioner, he was also aware that the chancellor wanted to reestablish relationships with those who had abandoned Pitt due to its indiscretions. An improved reputation, in part gained through a contractual association with a man of John Griffith's stature, might lure some of those programs back–and help the school fulfill its financial obligations to bond-holders.

Beginning in the fall of 1940, Ohio State would end the Big Nine boycott, essentially in force since the mid-1930s, and agree to compete against Pittsburgh. Commissioner Griffith, having forged a close friendship with Pitt director James Hagan since taking on the challenge in February of 1939, probably had a role in convincing "Saint" to resume gridiron competition with the Panthers. A home-and-home series would benefit Hagan's efforts at fulfilling Bowman's mandate. But St. John, like any good athletic director, never signed a contract without an ulterior motive. He knew a relationship with the Panthers would one day translate into large gate receipts regardless of venue.

On February 6, 1941, the commissioner inquired whether the OSU director would like to accompany him on a trip to the University of Pittsburgh to meet with Hagan. He was evasive about the purpose of the visit.

---

[14] Aigler to Gilmore. 13 January 1940. Bentley Historical Library, University of Michigan. Ralph W. Aigler Papers, Aa 2; Box 8, folder: correspondence 1940-45 "G" misc.

[15] Goodrich to Aigler. 20 November 1939. Bentley Historical Library, University of Michigan. Ralph W. Aigler Papers, Aa 2; Box 8, folder: correspondence 1940-45 "G" misc.

[16] Fitzgerald to Aigler. 16 December 1939. Bentley Historical Library, University of Michigan. Ralph W. Aigler Papers, Aa 2; Box 8, folder: correspondence 1940-45 "G" misc.

[17] Aigler to Goodrich. 20 November 1939. Bentley Historical Library, University of Michigan. Ralph W. Aigler Papers, Aa 2; Box 8, folder: correspondence 1940-45 "G" misc.

[18] Aigler to Goodrich. 15 January 1940. Bentley Historical Library, University of Michigan. Ralph W. Aigler Papers, Aa 2; Box 8, folder: correspondence 1940-45 "G" misc.

> For reasons which I would like to give you the next time I see you, I think it is wise for me to run over to Pittsburgh for a talk on general matters with Jimmie Hagan and some of the men over there. I have no one item that is tremendously important but I would like to get Jimmie's slant and that of the other men at the University regarding some of these questions.[19]

In a follow-up letter one week later, Griffith still remained vague. He did not want anything leaked to the media. And, as recent history bore out, he had his reasons for remaining evasive.[20]

Only a few years earlier the University of Pittsburgh Varsity Club had hounded John Griffith about discussions he supposedly had had with Provost Fitzgerald. The communiqué mailed out to over 800 Panther Lettermen was embarrassing to the consultant. It was fed to the press by club leaders.

> An announcement is expected shortly of Pittsburgh's election to membership in the Big Ten and it is supposed that Nebraska will also be a member. Our congratulations to Provost Fitzgerald who as a former Iowa man had much to do with this ...[21]

The commissioner vehemently denied the rumor. In a memo to the nine athletic directors that employed him, he commented that "for your information, neither Provost Fitzgerald, Chancellor Bowman, Director Hagan nor anyone else at the University of Pittsburgh ever indicated to me that the University of Pittsburgh would like to become a member of the Big Ten Conference."[22] He had to save face. Recruitment of an institution for membership, after all, was not in his job description.

The claim by the Panther Varsity Club letter was not factually based. For years the Western Conference had declined offers from a number of institutions. The Cornhuskers in 1908 and 1912, Notre Dame in 1912, 1919, and 1926, and Michigan State in 1937 were just a few of many schools rejected.[23] The Nebraska Response remained the standard reply. There was simply no apparent reason for adding a new member. Robert Maynard Hutchins and his board at the University of Chicago had not even begun discussions on the future of

---

[19] Griffith to St. John. 6 February 1941. The Ohio State University Archives, Director of Athletics (RG 9/e-1/9), "Intercollegiate Conference: Commissioner: Correspondence (Griffith): 1940-41 (Folder 1 of 2)."

[20] Griffith to St. John. 12 February 1941. The Ohio State University Archives, Director of Athetics (RG 9/e-1/9), "Intercollegiate Conference: Commissioner: Correspondence (Griffith): 1940-41 (Folder 1 of 2)."

[21] Griffith to The Directors of Athletics of the Conference. 30 September 1939. The Ohio State University Archives, Director of Athletics (RG 9/e-1/9), "Intercollegiate Conference: Commissioner: Correspondence (Griffith): 1939-40 (Folder 2 of 2)."

[22] Ibid.

[23] Kryk, John. "The Door Opens." *Maple Street Press*, July 2011: 117-19. Kryk's research indicates that Nebraska, Notre Dame and others schools applied annually to the conference beginning in 1899. As reported by sportswriters, the faculty felt ten members would make the conference "unwieldy." Following Michigan's withdrawal in January of 1908, the Cornhuskers tried a different strategy and applied for the vacated Wolverine spot. At the spring meetings, the faculty leaders used the Nebraska Response for the first time while turning away the suitor.

Maroon football until November.[24] So in the early fall of 1939, the conference leadership, if confronted with a Pitt application, would have decided that it was "not expedient to expand at this time."[25]

Having been embarrassed by the Pittsburgh press two years earlier, it was understandable why Griffith was being very cautious in his statements to Lynn St. John. At the same time, including the Buckeye director in strategic discussions regarding a highly confidential matter was a very wise move–it offered him cover should his employer, the Western Conference, suspect he was exceeding his bounds as commissioner.

> If we spent Sunday afternoon and part of Sunday night with Jimmie we
> could, in my judgment, accomplish some good. I hope that by all means
> that when I see Jimmie you can sit in with me. I have written him that I
> have nothing of any tremendous importance to discuss with him but a
> number of minor items, the sum total of which may be of some
> importance.[26]

The three met at the Schenley Hotel in the early afternoon of Sunday, February 16, 1941[27] and returned to Columbus the following morning. What they discussed was never revealed. Developments over the next several months offered some clues, however. As it turned out, they may have been scheming for a Pitt application to join the conference in the aftermath of The Announcement of December 1939. Scheduling was proving to be a major challenge for the membership with the Maroons out of action. The 9/6/2 experiment in contracting, promoted by Michigan's Aigler and Crisler and tentatively adopted by the others, was not felt to be the answer. Expansion remained the only logical solution.

One month after the meeting, Pitt faculty representative R. E. Sherrill contacted Ralph Aigler. His intent was to discuss the "functioning of our Faculty Committee on Athletic Policy." The meeting was arranged at the request of his athletic director, James Hagan.[28]

The committee, by providing faculty oversight, was trying to emulate practices within the Western Conference. The program, with Griffith's guidance, was already up and running. The timing of the planned meeting with Aigler would suggest that there was more to Sherrill's agenda than discussing the ongoing role of faculty in monitoring athletics.

Griffith and St. John, however, both knew that admission to the conference required Faculty Representative Committee approval by a simple majority vote. It was also understood that to succeed, any applicant needed the support of Ralph Aigler, the most influential member of that select group of academicians.

The Michigan professor had been in Pittsburgh a little over a year earlier to

---

[24] Lester, Robin. *Stagg's University: The Rise, Decline & Fall of Big-Time Football at Chicago.* Urbana and Chicago: University of Illinois Press: Urbana and Chicago, 1995 p. 183

[25] Aigler to Rottschaefer. 18 February 1944. Bentley Historical Library, University of Michigan. Ralph W. Aigler Papers, Aa 2; Box 8, folder: correspondence 1940-45 Rottschaefer

[26] Griffith to St. John. 12 February 1941. The Ohio State University Archives, Director of Athletics (RG 9/e-1/9), "Intercollegiate Conference: Commissioner: Correspondence (Griffith): 1940-41 (Folder 1 of 2)."

[27] Ibid.

[28] Sherrill to Aigler. 19 March 1941. Bentley Historical Library, University of Michigan. Ralph W. Aigler Papers, Aa 2; Box 8, folder: correspondence 1940-45 "S" misc.

interview for the position of dean of the law school. He was well aware of "Code Bowman."[29] The commissioner was performing an admirable job advising the athletic leadership in Pittsburgh. So it seemed odd that Professor Sherrill felt a need to travel up to Ann Arbor to discuss faculty oversight; communication by letter would appear to suffice. As Ralph Aigler soon learned, however, the Pitt representative had a very different agenda for that one hour meeting at Hutchins Hall in mid-April.

In December of 1942 President Virgil Hancher of Iowa revealed to John Hannah that "at one time it was said that the University of Pittsburgh proposed to apply for admission ..."[30] Hancher's comment suggested that Pitt may have had a dalliance with the conference sometime during the preceding few years. John Griffith's confidential meeting with Hagan and St. John in Pittsburgh, away from public scrutiny, as well as Sherrill's visit with Aigler in April, quite possibly substantiated Hancher's recollection.

The Schenley Hotel gathering may have served another purpose as well. In addition to Ohio State, Hagan needed other prominent programs on his schedule to rebuild the football fortunes of the Panthers. With St. John's influence at biennial contracting meetings, the University of Pittsburgh soon became a regular opponent on the schedules of most conference schools. Even the University of Michigan contracted one game with the Panthers–Chicago's withdrawal made available an unexpected date for Hagan in 1941.[31] John Griffith might have convinced director Fielding Yost during the 1940 scheduling meetings to take a chance on the Panthers as Jimmie Hagan struggled to clean up the mess in the Iron City.

By the fall of 1946, Fritz Crisler had a developed a good working relationship with Pitt's athletic director. He no longer viewed Pittsburgh as a renegade. Crisler had an available date for the following year and eagerly offered it to Hagan.[32]

Illinois, Minnesota, and Northwestern all agreed to compete with Pitt at various times during the 1940s. The second-tier schools helped out as well. Both Indiana and Purdue inked Pittsburgh on their respective schedules for seven seasons. The State University of Iowa, however, failed to offer even one contract with Pittsburgh during the decade. The school remained the lone holdout during Ernest Schroeder's tenure in the athletic department.

On the surface, the absence of a Pittsburgh-Iowa relationship was puzzling. There was a very strong Hawkeye influence at the University of Pittsburgh. Both Chancellor Bowman and Provost Fitzgerald were former State University of Iowa leaders. Fitzgerald, in particular, maintained contact with many of his former colleagues. He wrote to Iowa

---

[29] Wallace, Francis. "The Test Case at Pitt–The Facts about College Football Play for Pay." *The Saturday Evening Post*, 28 October 1939. The University of Pittsburgh Archives, 9/10-A, FF 772; Box 1

[30] Hancher to Hannah. 31 December 1942. University of Iowa Archives, Iowa City, Iowa. Virgil Hancher Papers, RG 05.01.11; Box 60, file: 91

[31] Minutes of Joint Meeting of Football Coaches and Athletic Directors. 19 May 1938. Bentley Historical Library, University of Michigan. Athletic Department, 943 Bimu 2; Box 84, folder: Athletic Director's office Big Ten committee minutes 1932-1940

[32] Crisler to Hagan. 7 October 1946. Bentley Historical Library, University of Michigan. Herbert Orin Crisler Papers, 85823 AC UAm Aa 2; Box 35, folder: football schedules 1944, 46, 47.

president, Virgil Hancher.[33] [34] The provost and eventual chancellor also recruited law professors Eugene A. Gilmore and Charles B. Nutting to serve in various administrative capacities at Pittsburgh.

Regardless of Iowa's reasons for failing to contract with Pitt while Schroeder held office, it was clear that his colleagues had embraced the Panthers and Jimmie Hagan by the spring of 1944 when schedules for the 1946-47 seasons were being drafted. The Griffith-Hagan-St. John scheme, devised during the Schenley Hotel meetings of February 1941, appeared to be working out well for the University of Pittsburgh.

IN EARLY October of 1946, the University of Pennsylvania cancelled a date with Michigan for the upcoming year. As a consequence, Fritz Crisler, in need of a replacement, contracted with Jimmie Hagan of Pittsburgh. The decision to offer the Panthers the third weekend of the 1947 gridiron campaign, as it turned, was quite disturbing for one man in Ann Arbor. Ralph Aigler had actually been troubled by the slight his athletic director and the Board in Control had shown Michigan State during the scheduling talks that began in September of 1946.

For years the college had been petitioning Fritz Crisler for a Saturday later in the season. But once again the Spartans were offered only the opener–on September 27, 1947. Pittsburgh, however, was given the more favorable weekend in mid-October. In making Michigan State first on the schedule, Crisler was following the 1932 Yost-Young understanding[35] that became official university athletic policy only three days before he contacted Hagan.[36] [37] He knew that the Spartans would almost fill his stadium on the opening weekend. The Panthers, however, could not possibly achieve comparable ticket sales if asked to take on the scrimmage game. But the fallacy in Crisler's argument lay in the team he asked to assume that vacated weekend. Since 1940, Pitt had won only 19 times while competing in 53 contests. Regardless of which weekend was offered Jimmie Hagan's program, fan interest about Ann Arbor and Detroit would have been marginal.

In a letter to Homer Hattendorf of the *Chicago Tribune*, Aigler commented on Crisler's political oversight. It was a surprising statement coming from the professor. He had made the motion, approved by the Board in Control a few weeks earlier, that essentially codified the old Yost-Young agreement. Unbeknownst to the Spartans, the scrimmage game weekend now belonged to them indefinitely.

[Michigan State is] pretty hurt, and frankly … between you and me, I think

---

[33] Hancher to Fitzgerald. 5 September 1951. University of Iowa Archives, Iowa City, Iowa. Virgil Hancher Papers, RG 05.01.11; Box 229, folder: 156F, Pittsburgh.

[34] Hancher to Fitzgerald. 8 April 1953. University of Iowa Archives, Iowa City, Iowa. Virgil Hancher Papers, RG 05.01.11; Box 320, folder: 154, Pittsburgh.

[35] "Michigan State Football Date." circa 1946. Bentley Historical Library, University of Michigan. Herbert Orin Crisler Papers, 85823 AC UAm Aa 2; Box 1, folder: topical correspondence Michigan State University 1940-42

[36] Minutes of the meeting of the Board in Control of Intercollegiate Athletics. 4 October 1946. Bentley Historical Library, University of Michigan. Board in Control, 8729 Bimu F81 2; Box 49, folder: minutes Feb 1938-June 1950

[37] Crisler to Hagan. 7 October 1946. Bentley Historical Library, University of Michigan. Herbert Orin Crisler Papers, 85823 AC UAm Aa 2; Box 35, folder: football schedules 1944, 46, 47.

they have some reason for it. I believe we handled the matter rather badly, considering the relationships between these two state institutions. If we had been able to fill that October 11th date with a team like Army, Navy, Harvard, Yale, or Princeton–or even Pennsylvania–we would have been on some much more defensible ground than we are, filled as it is, with Pittsburgh. While it is not my field of concern–namely the relationships between the University and Michigan State–I do feel that it could be bad for this institution to have anything like a split between us.[38]

So it appeared, despite his role in the recent board policy, Ralph Aigler felt that the Spartans deserved the right of first refusal for this unique opportunity to play the Wolverines a few weeks later in the season. Perhaps he was softening his hard-line stance towards the college![39] In the aftermath of Alexander Ruthven's directive of March 1946, it also appeared to be the politically correct thing to do.[40]

Regardless of whether Ralph Aigler was a changed man or merely toeing the political line, Michigan crushed the Panthers 69-0 the following year on its way to winning the mythical national championship. The Spartans fared no better. In the annual scrimmage game, begrudgingly accepted by the college for that last weekend in September, the squad from East Lansing lost 55-0 to the Wolverines. It was Biggie Munn's first game as head coach.

The trade-off for Crisler's political slight was Michigan's willingness to visit East Lansing in September of 1947 for the opener. It required some very intense negotiations a year earlier, however, to accomplish that major victory off the gridiron.

BACK IN November of 1943, Professor Ralph Aigler was approached by a former student now practicing law in Pittsburgh. As it turned out, the young attorney was an emissary for the director of the Pittsburgh athletic department.[41] He was laying the groundwork for a meeting between James Hagan and Aigler in February of 1944.

Hagan was seeking Professor Aigler's opinions on whether another attempt at applying to the conference in the near future was in order. Although the law professor made it clear he could not speak for others, he assured the athletic director that "everybody in the Conference was friendly to Pittsburgh and even admired her for her efforts to clean house." He then commented "that if [an] application [was] made and it [was] to meet the fate that other applicants had met, they certainly should not consider that we thought they were unfit." Nonetheless, he encouraged Pitt to apply. He advised Hagan that over the previous 25 years many schools had sought admission. The answer was always the same: the Nebraska Response of 1908.[42] But if Pitt were to apply, the law professor reminded Hagan,

[38] Aigler to Hattendorf. 7 November 1946. Bentley Historical Library, University of Michigan. Ralph W. Aigler Papers, 87406 Aa 2; Box 9, folder: correspondence 1946-52 "H" misc.(HA-HN)
[39] Aigler to Wilson. 8 August 1945. Bentley Historical Library, University of Michigan. Ralph W. Aigler Papers, 87406 Aa 2; Box 8, folder: correspondence 1940-45 misc. "Wilson"
[40] Ruthven to Hannah. 23 March 1946. Bentley Historical Library, University of Michigan. Herbert Orin Crisler Papers, 85823 AC UAm Aa 2; Box 1, folder: MSU correspondence 43-46 topical
[41] Aigler to Rottschaefer. 18 February 1944. Bentley Historical Library, University of Michigan. Ralph W. Aigler Papers, 87406 Aa 2; Box 8, folder: correspondence 1940-45 Rottschaefer
[42] Aigler to Rottschaefer. 18 February 1944. Bentley Historical Library, University of Michigan. Ralph W. Aigler Papers, 87406 Aa 2; Box 8, folder: correspondence 1940-45 Rottschaefer

the soonest it could be considered would be December of 1944.[43]

Pitt was clearly excited over the encouraging comments from the politically influential leader. Was Ralph Aigler a convert to the cause? In late July, a Pitt troika of two Pittsburgh faculty members and a trustee visited room 320 Hutchins Hall in Ann Arbor. Their intention was "to discuss the … proper contents of an application for membership in the Conference." Aigler acknowledged "that the personnel of the Conference [had] changed rather radically in recent years and that it was, of course, within the realm of possibility that the present membership might feel differently" about adding a school to replace Chicago on the football schedule.[44]

The membership had indeed changed. With the unexpected death of Thomas French on November 2, 1944, only four out of 10 members from the 1937 club that had rejected a Michigan State application were still active in conference politics.[45] They included Aigler, Henry Rottschaefer of Minnesota, Frank Richart of Illinois, and William Lorenz of Wisconsin.[46] Aigler accurately confessed that he could no longer predict outcomes.

The comment by the law professor about new conference leadership possibly having different ideas on expansion was viewed in a positive light by James Hagan when he huddled with the troika after its return from Ann Arbor. It now appeared to Hagan that the two most powerful men in the conference, Lynn St. John and Ralph Aigler, might support a Pitt initiative. Consequently, an application was advanced on December 8, 1944, at the annual faculty representatives' meeting in Chicago.[47]

> The usual order of business was changed to permit a short conference
> requested by two members of the faculty of the University of Pittsburgh.
> These gentlemen, Professors R.E. Sherrill and H.L. Mitchell gave
> information in some detail regarding the athletic organization and policies
> at their institution. Upon leaving, the business meeting was resumed.[48]

The presentation could not have occurred at a more inopportune time. With the deaths of Buckeye leader Thomas French in mid-November and John Griffith one day before the meeting commenced, the faculty representatives were in no mood for discussing expansion of the conference. The Pittsburgh initiative was tabled. The application would be reconsidered at the May 1945 meeting of the faculty representatives.[49]

As it turned out, regardless of the unfortunate developments of the late fall, Pittsburgh may have misinterpreted Ralph Aigler's comments to Hagan in February and the

---

[43] Aigler to Rottschaefer. 18 February 1944. Bentley Historical Library, University of Michigan. Ralph W. Aigler Papers, 87406 Aa 2; Box 8, folder: correspondence 1940-45 Rottschaefer

[44] Aigler to Rottschaefer. 31 July 1944. Bentley Historical Library, University of Michigan. Ralph W. Aigler Papers, Aa 2; Box 8, folder: Correspondence 1940-45 Rottschaefer

[45] Minutes of the Intercollegiate Conference of Faculty Representatives. 22 May 1937. Bentley Historical Library, University of Michigan. Ralph W. Aigler Papers, Aa 2; Box 14, folder: Athletics 1937-39, Meetings Minutes

[46] Minutes of the Intercollegiate Conference of Faculty Representatives. 8 December 1944. University of Illinois Archives. Series 4/2/12; Box 2, folder: Conference Minutes 1944-45

[47] Sherrill to Richart. 23 May 1946. University of Pittsburgh Archives. Collection 9/2, FF1; Box 1

[48] Minutes of the Intercollegiate Conference of Faculty Representatives. 8 December 1944. University of Illinois Archives, Series 4/2/12; Box 2, Folder: Conference Minutes 1944-45

[49] Ibid.

troika in July. In a letter to Henry Rottschaefer of the University of Minnesota Law School, Aigler expressed concerns about taking on a new member. He feared that acceptance of Pitt would lead to "similar requests from two or three other institutions."[50] The "others" included Nebraska, Notre Dame, and Michigan State.[51]

Admitting the Cornhuskers made good sense for the State University of Iowa in December of 1944. It would partially solve Ernest Schroeder's frustration with a scheduling process that would eventually preclude the Hawkeyes from competing on the last weekend for the 1946-47 campaigns. Nebraska was a logical choice to complement the popular end-of-season rivalries in existence about the conference.[52]

Notre Dame had applied for membership only to be rebuffed on at least three occasions.[53] [54] It did not help their cause that both Fielding Yost and Ralph Aigler, for various reasons, lacked any respect for the Irish and their athletic leadership.[55] [56] [57] [58] But the Irish drew big crowds, as Friz Crisler learned in October of 1943, wherever they suited up. Their presence on schedules would benefit the coffers of every program in the conference.

But perhaps Ralph Aigler's greatest concern was Michigan State College. (Alexander Ruthven's mandate of March 1946 was still a few years away.) The last thing Professor Aigler wanted was state politicians promoting a Spartan application. It was far easier to maintain the 32-year tradition of declining all applications with the Nebraska Response than dealing with impassioned legislators and voters.

Henry Rottschaefer concurred with Aigler's reasoning. But the Minnesota tax law specialist had no concern about institutional politics back in his home state. That was Ralph Aigler's problem. Rottschaefer was more troubled "that the admission of one new member would be bound to produce many more applications and increase the difficulty of graceful refusal of any or all of them."[59] He was quite sensitive regarding the impact of rejection on applicants passionate about gaining membership within the Intercollegiate Conference.

---

[50] Aigler to Rottschaefer. 31 July 1944. Bentley Historical Library, University of Michigan. Ralph W. Aigler Papers, 87406 Aa 2; Box 8, folder: Correspondence 1940-45 Rottschaefer

[51] Leib to Hancher. 8 January 1943. University of Iowa Archives, Iowa City, Iowa. Virgil Hancher Papers, RG 05.01.11; Box 60, file: 91

[52] O'Brien, Jack. "Munn's the Word." *Esquire*, November 1953: 132. Michigan State University Archives, Ralph Young Papers, UA 17.114; Box 903, folder: 71.

[53] Minutes of Intercollegiate Conference of Faculty Representatives. 6 December 1919. Bentley Historical Library, University of Michigan. University of Michigan Athletic Department. Bimu 2; Box 84, folder: Athletic Director's office, Faculty Representatives Minutes 1918-1940

[54] Minutes of Intercollegiate Conference of Faculty Representatives. 28 May 1926. Bentley Historical Library, University of Michigan. University of Michigan Athletic Department. Bimu 2; Box 84, folder: Athletic Director's office, Faculty Representatives Minutes 1918-1940

[55] Kryk, John. *Natural Enemies: Major College Football's Oldest, Fiercest Rivalry – Michigan vs. Notre Dame.* Lanham: Taylor Trade Publishing, 2007. pp. 85-92.

[56] Aigler to Griffith. 13 January 1932. Bentley Historical Library, University of Michigan. Ralph W. Aigler Papers, 87406 Aa 2; Box 3, folder: correspondence Griffith

[57] Aigler to Long. 12 May 1936. Bentley Historical Library, University of Michigan. Ralph W. Aigler Papers, 87406 Aa 2; Box 12, folder: athletic correspondence 1933-36 "L" misc.

[58] Aigler to Griffith. 26 October 1932. Bentley Historical Library, University of Michigan. Ralph W. Aigler Papers, 87406 Aa 2; Box 3, folder: correspondence Griffith

[59] Rottschaefer to Aigler. 13 September 1944. Bentley Historical Library, University of Michigan. Ralph W. Aigler Papers, Aa 2; Box 8, folder: Correspondence 1940-45 Rottschaefer

Despite their opposition to expansion in 1944, both legal scholars suspected that the man promoting Pitt's agenda throughout the year was John Griffith.[60] What they failed to realize, however, was that the commissioner had a confidant–Lynn St. John of Ohio State.[61] The dean of athletic directors had steadfast reasons for supporting the Panther's plan. But the three other schools rumored to have an interest in joining the Big Ten would offer little to benefit his athletic program.

Notre Dame would have no place in St. John's conference. His anti-Catholic convictions notwithstanding,[62] [63] the Irish posed a recruiting challenge for his coaches. The state parochial school system had been responsible for sending many outstanding athletes to The Ohio State University.[64] The "Buckeye Rule" on recruiting would be difficult to enforce with Catholic high school coaches steering kids towards South Bend. As a consequence, other than a two-game series in the mid-1930s to appease alumni, he avoided contracting with the Irish.

St. John had little concern for the plight of the tier-two schools in the Big Nine, including Iowa.[65] The Cornhuskers might fill the Hawkeyes' need for a regional rival, but Ohio State would gain little in added revenue by adding the current Big Six member.

And if Nebraska lacked value for the athletic director from Columbus, Michigan State offered even less. Due to its small stadium capacity, St. John saw absolutely no financial benefit for his Buckeyes to travel to East Lansing every other fall.[66] In addition, the college had dropped intercollegiate football in August of 1943 due to War Department rules. Despite recently announcing plans to resume competition in the fall of 1944 with a makeshift group of players, it would be years before the Spartans could pose a team befitting membership in the Western Conference.[67] [68]

---

[60] Rottschaefer to Aigler. 13 September 1944. Bentley Historical Library, University of Michigan. Ralph W. Aigler Papers, Aa 2; Box 8, folder: Correspondence 1940-45 Rottschaefer

[61] Four Hundred and Forty-Fourth Meeting of the Athletic Board of The Ohio State University. 4 April 1945. The Ohio State University Archives, Director of Athletics (RG 9/e-1/1), "Athletic Board: Minutes: September 1940-May 1946."

[62] St. John to Griffith. 7 July 1939. The Ohio State University Archives, Director of Athletics (RG 9/e-1/9), "Intercollegiate Conference: Commissioner: Correspondence (Griffith): 1939-1940 (folder 2 of 2)."

[63] St. John to Wilson. 1 May 1945. The Ohio State University Archives, Director of Athletics (RG 9/e-1/10), "Intercollegiate Conference: Commissioner: Correspondence (Wilson): 1944-1945."

[64] Porretta, Dan. 5 November 2009. Personal communication. Porretta was a two-way lineman for Wayne "Woody" Hayes from 1962-1964. According to Dan, Coach Hayes "steered" Catholic high school recruits, more interested in playing for the University of Michigan than Ohio State, toward Notre Dame. He would rather have Ohio boys play for the Irish than dress in Maize and Blue and compete against his Buckeyes. Shortly after my visit with him, Dan passed away.

[65] St. John to Wilson. 13 May 1946. The Ohio State University Archives, Director of Athletics (RG 9/e-1/10), "Intercollegiate Conference: Commissioner: Correspondence (Wilson): 1945-1947."

[66] Ibid.

[67] Alderton, George. "Spartans Return to Grid Saturday." *Lansing State Journal,* 29 September 1944: Sports Section. Michigan State University Archives. UA12.107, Madison Kuhn Collection; Scrapbook 108, folder: 5

[68] Alderton,, George. "State Resumes Football-Bachman has 60 Candidates on 1944 Squad." *Lansing State Journal*, 10 September 1944. Michigan State University Archives. UA12.107, Madison Kuhn

IN MARCH of 1945 the faculty representatives chose Kenneth "Tug" Wilson, former athletic director at Northwestern University, to fill the position vacated by the death of Commissioner John Griffith. Wilson picked up where Griffith left off in supporting a Pittsburgh membership.[69] St. John was successful in selling the strategy to his friend of 20 years.

On June 4, 1945, Professor Frank Richart delivered the disappointing news to Professor Sherrill that "it was not desirable at this time to increase the number of members."[70] The fact that two strong-willed leaders–Aigler and Rottschaefer–were opposed to expansion may have contributed to the rejection. The faculty representatives and presidents were anticipating major changes in the operation of intercollegiate athletics following the end of the war and military rule on campuses.[71] Debate on expanding to 11 was not a priority at the time.

Despite the rejection, Pittsburgh remained focused on eventually achieving admission into the conference. The Faculty Committee on Athletic Policy felt that there was much to be gained by affiliation with the group of highly regarded academic research institutions.[72] Pitt would try again at a later, more appropriate, time.

Rufus Fitzgerald assumed the chancellorship of the university in July of 1945 with John Gabbert Bowman's retirement. In early March of the following year, the new Pitt leader telephoned an old colleague from his days in Iowa City. Professor F. G. Higbee had been a member of the State University of Iowa Athletic Council since the late 1920s. During the 1929 Iowa subsidy scandal, Fitzgerald–President Walter Jessup's right-hand man–was asked to personally investigate the Western Conference charges filed against the institution.[73] As part of that assignment, while working closely with the council, he probably developed a friendship with Higbee. Now, many years later, the chancellor sought some advice from his old friend in the aftermath of the second Chicago Announcement.

Fitzgerald was renowned for keeping thousands of meticulous notes over his long tenure at the university.[74] He would later have those notes transcribed and filed for future reference.

> … [Higbee] asked what we were going to do about the Big Ten. I said that
> had not been determined, but that I personally was very much interested.
> He said that they had been notified definitely that Chicago was out. He
> stated that Nebraska, Pitt, Notre Dame, and Michigan State were being
> discussed for the vacancy. He made it clear that no institution would get in

---

Collection; Scrapbook 108, folder: 5

[69] Wilson to St. John. 20 May 1946. The Ohio State University Archives, Director of Athletics (RG 9/e-1/10), "Intercollegiate Conference: Commissioner: Correspondence (Wilson): 1945-1947."

[70] Sherrill to Richart. 23 May 1946. University of Pittsburgh Archives, Collection 9/2, FF1; Box 1

[71] Sherrill to Fitzgerald. 10 April 1946. University of Pittsburgh Archives. Rufus Henry Fitzgerald Papers, Collection 2/10, FF24; Box 4

[72] Ibid.

[73] Persons, Stow. *The University of Iowa in the Twentieth Century: An Institutional History.* Iowa City: University of Iowa Press, 1990. p. 98

[74] Alberts, Robert C. *Pitt: The Story of the University of Pittsburgh 1787-1987.* Pittsburgh: University of Pittsburgh Press, 1986. p. 195

unless they went after it, that there was a feeling in some places that the Big Ten would reach out and tag someone. That is incorrect. He said he thought St. John had considerable influence in the Conference. He also made it clear that the leaders in the Mid-Western institutions would want to know what I thought about it personally.[75]

In response to Professor Higbee's advice back in March, the university began pursuing the seat soon to be vacated by Chicago. But Fitzgerald wanted to avoid the mistakes made with the unsuccessful application one year earlier. That presentation, in his opinion, had failed to show that the entire Pitt community–trustees and faculty–was committed to joining the conference. Some remained skeptical of the benefits, both academic and athletic, from an affiliation with the Big Ten.[76]

By early May, two months after the second Chicago Announcement, James Hagan had learned from Commissioner Wilson that "officials of the conference were of the opinion that it would be advisable for the university to refrain from making a formal application for membership at this time." He added, however, that Pittsburgh should express an interest in ultimately gaining admission to the association.[77] Faculty Representative Sherrill, after being informed of Hagan's findings, shared that insider information with his chancellor on May 20, 1946. "Mr. Wilson had ... been checking with the faculty men of the Conference and would recommend that we write Professor F. E. Richart about our desires for Conference membership."[78]

At the May 23, 1946, meeting of the Faculty Committee on Athletic Policy, Hagan reported that the Spartans of Michigan State were planning to make a presentation for admission at the upcoming spring meetings. He noted that neither Ralph Aigler nor Herbert Crisler was planning to influence the outcome of any vote. Hagan had acquired this information from the commissioner.[79]

Wilson was uncertain how to advise the university "in its dealing with the Western Conference officials."[80] The Michigan State application complicated matters. Instead of recommending any change in direction, he suggested that Pitt merely restate its interest in maintaining an application for membership. Hagan also pointed out that Lynn St. John of Ohio State "thought that some members of the Faculty Committee on Athletic Policies might advantageously be present at the June meeting of the Conference."[81] But Wilson let Hagan know that "other Conference officials were of the opinion that the presence of

---

[75] Fitzgerald to Higbee. 10 March 1946. University of Pittsburgh Archives. Rufus Henry Fitzgerald Papers, Collection 2/10, FF24; Box 4

[76] Fitzgerald to Sherrill. 8 April 1946. University of Pittsburgh Archives. Rufus Henry Fitzgerald Papers, Collection 2/10, FF24; Box 4

[77] Minutes of the Meeting of the Faculty Committee on Athletic Policies. 2 May 1946. University of Pittsburgh Archives. Collection 9/2, FF1; Box 1

[78] Fitzgerald to Sherrill. 20 May 1946. University of Pittsburgh Archives. Rufus Henry Fitzgerald Papers, Collection 2/10, FF24; Box 4

[79] Minutes of the Meeting of the Faculty Committee on Athletic Policies. 23 May 1946. University of Pittsburgh Archives, Collection 9/2, FF1; Box 1

[80] Ibid.

[81] Minutes of the Meeting of the Faculty Committee on Athletic Policies. 23 May 1946. University of Pittsburgh Archives, Collection 9/2, FF1; Box 1

Pittsburgh [leaders] at the Conference meeting might be misinterpreted."[82] It was never revealed who those "officials" were but evidence would support that either Ralph Aigler or Frank Richart was involved.

The two faculty representatives had just recently debated whether to offer John Hannah a spot on the agenda for the May meetings. Richart argued that the directors must first decide whether they even wanted to expand.[83] Once that decision was made, opportunities for presentations could be offered suitors, such as Hannah, at a later date.

Aigler liked that argument.[84] He admitted having no personal desire for Hannah to attend the meeting.[85] His "magnificent speaking voice and imposing presence" were powerful attributes that only a lawyer could fully appreciate.[86] John Hannah could command an audience–and the professor was wary of that gift.

Aigler's and Richart's letters were copied to committee chair Lawrence Kimpton of Chicago. He concurred with their logic. Hannah was kindly denied a presence at the May 1946 gathering of conference leaders.[87]

Based on that series of letters, it appeared Ralph Aigler was most likely one of those "other conference officials" Wilson had referenced in his communications with Hagan. An innocent phone call to the professor in mid-May, perhaps to discuss the meeting agenda, might have led Wilson to inquire about whether a Pitt representative could attend the gathering at the Urbana-Lincoln Hotel. Just recently informed of Kimpton's confidential discussion with Hannah, Aigler probably advised against the visit. With Hannah being denied admittance to the meeting, allowing Pitt a presence in Urbana might be "misinterpreted" by Michigan State. And to substantiate that likely statement to Wilson, in a letter to Larry Kimpton a few days later, Aigler commented that "...I did want to avoid giving [Hannah] and his institution any ground for saying or thinking that the Conference had not been as gracious to them as it has been to [Pittsburgh]."[88]

Aigler never revealed to Ken Wilson the scheme involving Dean Larry Kimpton. But he did answer, perhaps unwittingly, the commissioner's most pressing question. There would be no vote on a Spartan application at the May meetings despite Michigan having made a public statement of support for the college in March.[89] Jimmie Hagan would share that "insider" scoop, provided by the commissioner, on the 23rd of May with the Faculty Committee on Athletic Policy. The group respected the advice from the dean of faculty

---

[82] Minutes of the Meeting of the Faculty Committee on Athletic Policies. 23 May 1946. University of Pittsburgh Archives, Collection 9/2, FF1; Box 1

[83] Richart to Aigler. 14 May 1946. Bentley Historical Library, University of Michigan, Ralph W. Aigler Papers, 87406 Aa 2; Box 9, folder: correspondence 1946-52 "H" misc

[84] Aigler to Richart. 15 May 1946. Bentley Historical Library, University of Michigan, Ralph W. Aigler Papers, 87406 Aa 2; Box 9, folder: correspondence 1946-52 "H" misc

[85] Aigler to Kimpton. 25 May 1946. Bentley Historical Library, University of Michigan, Ralph W. Aigler Papers, 87406 Aa 2; Box 9, folder: correspondence 1946-52 "H" misc

[86] Denison, James H. Untitled. Michigan State University Archives. Hannah Archives Project, UA2.1.12.2; Box 34, folder: 8

[87] Kimpton to Aigler. 20 May 1946. Bentley Historical Library, University of Michigan, Ralph W. Aigler Papers, 87406 Aa 2; Box 9, folder: correspondence 1946-52 "H" misc

[88] Aigler to Kimpton. 25 May 1946. Bentley Historical Library, University of Michigan, Ralph W. Aigler Papers, 87406 Aa 2; Box 9, folder: correspondence 1946-52 "H" misc

[89] Minutes of the Meeting of the Faculty Committee on Athletic Policies. 23 May 1946. University of Pittsburgh Archives, Collection 9/2; Box 1, folder: FF1

representatives and stayed at home.

Reassured by Ken Wilson's espionage, Rufus Fitzgerald decided to have Professor Sherrill send a letter that very day to the conference reaffirming Pittsburgh's continued desire to become a member some day.[90] It was more honorable than the aggressive tactic of seeking out the position–a recommendation provided by Iowa's Professor Higbee to Fitzgerald a few months earlier. But the chancellor wanted it clearly understood that Sherrill's confidential letter was not an application.[91] Politics back in Pittsburgh among students, fans, and alumni were still too contentious to run the risk of another embarrassing leak to the press about the university's strategic plan.

Michigan State was in the early phases of Plan A, first conceived in January of that year. John Hannah wanted desperately to meet with the Faculty Representatives Committee and bring closure on the application process, especially since Michigan had recently professed allegiance to his cause. But having experienced the third Spartan rejection–in large part due to the recent Aigler-Richart-Kimpton collaboration–it appeared that he would have to wait for another opportunity. In the meantime, feeling let down by both Aigler and the conference, Hannah would turn his attention to Plan B and contact another old friend, Frank Leahy of Notre Dame. Rufus Fitzgerald, at least for the time being, could take a big sigh of relief. His insider connections, both Ken Wilson and Lynn St. John, were still very reliable sources.

IF THE 1939 football season was utter humiliation for the University of Chicago, the 1947 gridiron campaign for the University of Pittsburgh was an absolute calamity. Pitt would close out the season with only one victory. Adding to its woes, early in the season the Panthers would lose on successive weekends to Notre Dame (40-6) and Michigan (69-0).[92]

Following the Michigan debacle, Rufus Fitzgerald concluded that strict compliance with amateur rules, surpassing what was practiced among the membership in the Western Conference, was not conducive to winning football. James Hagan became the scapegoat for years of defeat on the gridiron.[93] The chancellor "concluded that what the athletic situation needed was a strong athletic director, a man of experience and stature in his own right, a leader who could take charge, work with the faculty and the alumni, and free [him] from the turmoil of the past seven seasons."[94] The chancellor's decision proved to be one of three strategic blunders made by the university administrative and athletic leadership that year. Those tactical mistakes may very well have cost the Panthers a seat in the Intercollegiate Conference of Faculty Representatives.

The timing for a change in leadership of the athletic department was terrible. Hagan quietly stepped down in June of 1948. In his absence, sports information director Frank Carver was asked to manage the department. The publicist had no knowledge of the former director's significant role in Pitt's highly confidential plan to gain membership in the Western Conference. The chancellor and the Faculty Committee on Athletic Policy merely wanted Carver to maintain the status quo until a new athletic director was hired.

---

[90] Sherrill to Richart. 23 May 1946. University of Pittsburgh Archives, Collection 9/2, FF1; Box 1

[91] Sherrill to Richart. 24 May 1946. University of Pittsburgh Archives, Collection 9/2, FF1; Box 1

[92] Alberts, Robert C. *Pitt: The Story of the University of Pittsburgh 1787-1987*. Pittsburgh: University of Pittsburgh Press, 1986. p. 222

[93] Ibid., p. 223

[94] Ibid., p. 224

So while the University of Pittsburgh athletic department lacked someone to orchestrate a strategy for admission during the summer and fall of 1948, Michigan State was making major advances with its revised Morrill Plan. In fact, the only achievement the university made following Jimmie Hagan's departure, occurred on July 12. Behind closed doors, the Faculty Committee affirmed Captain Thomas Hamilton as their "number one choice" for athletic director.[95] Due to his remaining military commission, the committee decided to refrain from making the official announcement until January of 1949.[96] The chancellor and his team anticipated the press release would be major news at the time. Hamilton's affiliation with the university would reassure skeptics within the conference about the Panther's intentions following the release of Hagan. Hiring the highly respected athletic leader could almost guarantee a vote of confidence during the May 1949 meetings. But in the meantime, their selection of a director would remain confidential.

The decision to withhold that announcement was Pitt's second major miscue of 1948. Had the Western Conference athletic directors and certain skeptical faculty representatives been made aware of the Hamilton appointment in July, the Morrill Plan may not have succeeded.[97]

On November 14 John Hannah met with Ken Wilson in downtown Chicago at the Sherman Hotel. Hannah innocently shared with the conference leader Lew Morrill's strategy. The president felt that he was merely keeping the commissioner updated on the status of Michigan State's application. Hannah was confident that the college had enough votes to assure membership, but he wanted a unanimous pronouncement after being subjected to so many rumors and rejections over the years. "If there is a serious division of opinion, I hope that you will present our case not as a supplicant, but as a great public university ... if elected, we expect to be fully credible members in every respect."[98] Wilson listened but was noncommittal. He was more preoccupied with the implications of the college president's statements. A phone call to Pittsburgh followed their encounter.

Two weeks later, on Monday November 29, the University of Pittsburgh athletic leadership met during the evening hours. The urgent gathering at the Cathedral of Learning, held shortly after the Hannah-Wilson meeting in Chicago, would suggest the commissioner's complicity in sharing Hannah's data.[99] A strategy to counter the Spartans was already in progress by the time the doors opened in the Pitt conference room. A few days earlier, word had been leaked to the *New York Times* that Hamilton held the "inside track" for the directorship.[100] The Faculty Committee on Athletic Policy, following its evening meeting, officially confirmed that rumor by announcing the hiring of Captain

---

[95] The Tenth Meeting of the Athletic Committee. 29 November 1948. University of Pittsburgh, Collection 2/10, FF19; Box 2

[96] Kerr to Fitzgerald. 14 February 1949. University of Pittsburgh Archives, Collection 2/10, FF19; Box 2

[97] Hamilton to Fitzgerald. 9 December 1948. University of Pittsburgh Archives, Collection 2/10, FF19; Box 2

[98] Hannah to Wilson. 15 November 1948. University of Minnesota Archives, President's Office; Box 238, folder: Physical Education and Athletics 1948-49

[99] The Tenth Meeting of the Athletic Committee. 29 November 1948. University of Pittsburgh Archives, Collection 2/10, FF19, Box 2

[100] "Rating on Gridiron Seen Goal of Pitt." 26 November 1948. *New York Times.* University of Pittsburgh Archives, Collection 2/10, FF19; Box 2

Hamilton. It was intended to gain additional publicity on the heels of the recent leak. The committee also planned to send a representative to the Western Conference meetings in a few weeks to again express interest in membership.[101] [102]

Fully aware of Michigan State's recent progress, Chancellor Fitzgerald, also in attendance, decided that the university must pursue everything within reason to forestall the Hannah blitzkrieg. He would avail himself of Tom Hamilton's good name. A special telephone hook-up with Hamilton was arranged on December 7, 1948, after which the Navy captain officially took over control of the wayward ship. Hamilton quickly proposed a strategy to counter the anticipated Spartan attack, insisting that Pitt "should make all the games it can arrange with Big-Nine teams at this time." Regardless of the humiliating autumn campaign of 1947, the seaman wanted to maintain relationships with conference schools. He assigned various Pittsburgh faculty and administrators critical tasks to perform over the next few days. Time was running out. The Western Conference meetings were only four days away.[103]

Captain Hamilton also requested approval from the chancellor to "make some phone calls to some of the Big Nine people whom he knows asking that they give consideration to Pitt."[104] He was quite familiar with Ralph Aigler of the University of Michigan. Ten years earlier, as a young lieutenant coaching at the academy, he was briefly the leading candidate for the head job in Ann Arbor. The law professor, at the time, had been quite impressed with his leadership skills and integrity.[105] Hamilton very likely contacted the faculty representative for advice. Any support from Michigan would be valuable.

Because Fitzgerald had been affiliated with the State University of Iowa before taking the provost position at Pitt in 1938, Hamilton asked him to contact President Virgil Hancher. Although Fitzgerald was acquainted with the current Hawkeye leader, he said that he would be more comfortable seeking out insider information from his very good friend, Professor Karl Leib. Captain Hamilton concurred. He wanted the chancellor to encourage Leib, the current president of the NCAA, to advocate for Pittsburgh. The former faculty representative, with nine years of experience in conference politics, could offer persuasive counsel to Iowa's current athletic leaders.[106]

Hamilton also asked Fitzgerald to telephone Tug Wilson and request a Pitt presence at the Chicago meetings to "reaffirm" its application.[107] The commissioned officer, by this time, was well aware of Wilson's past involvement with James Hagan and the Panther Faculty Committee on Athletic Policy. The commissioner, it was hoped, would find a spot

[101] Fitzgerald to Leib. 8 December 1948. "Telephone: Karl Leib of State University of Iowa." University of Pittsburgh Archives, Collection 2/10, FF19; Box 2

[102] The Tenth Meeting of the Athletic Committee. 29 November 1948. University of Pittsburgh Archives. Collection 2/10, FF 19; Box 2

[103] Fitzgerald to Hamilton. 7 December 1948. University of Pittsburgh Archives. Collection 2/10, FF19; Box 2

[104] Ibid.

[105] Aigler to Ruthven. 5 February 1938. Bentley Historical Library, University of Michigan. Ralph W. Aigler Papers, 87406 Aa2; Box 7, folder: correspondence 1934-39 Ruthven

[106] Fitzgerald to Hamilton. 7 December 1948. "Telephone: Captain Hamilton and RHF." University of Pittsburgh Archives. Collection 2/10, FF19; Box 2

[107] Ibid.

on the weekend agenda for Pittsburgh.

On December 8 Fitzgerald called Karl Leib in Iowa City. The professor confessed he was not privy to current conference politics, but he did promise to "pass the word along" to athletic director Paul Brechler. Leib also mentioned in confidence that "he thought the newspapers had overplayed the whole situation and he was doubtful that there was any real intention to enlarge the Big Nine at this time."[108] The chancellor was relieved to hear those words.

Captain Hamilton's decision to allow Fitzgerald to contact Leib rather than Hancher would prove to be Pitt's third tactical error in 1948. President Hancher could have provided Fitzgerald with a far more accurate assessment of current affairs within the conference. His relationship with John Hannah and their recent sharing of letters regarding Iowa's voting plans would have been valuable information for Hamilton to contemplate while assessing Pitt's chances in forestalling Michigan State. Instead, he was given misleading advice by Iowa's former faculty representative.

The following day, less than 48 hours before the conference room doors opened at the Sherman Hotel, Hamilton and Fitzgerald had another long-distance conversation. The Navy leader expressed optimism. He had successfully contacted all schools except Iowa and had found "a pretty favorable reaction." He added that all the athletic directors had "seemed glad that Pitt was taking this action." The commissioner, also contacted by Hamilton, had offered cautious words of encouragement.[109] Fitzgerald then shared Leib's assessment. Hamilton concluded the telephone conversation with his future boss by emphasizing "he didn't look for any action, but that this was a delaying action."[110]

His strategy was a defensive tactic. Once Hamilton assumed his new position in February the university could proceed with a counteroffensive against the college at the annual spring meetings a few months later.

PITTSBURGH SHOWED up for the December meetings relatively confident that it could delay an election until the spring gathering. Captain Hamilton and his shipmates from the Pitt administration had appeared brilliant under fire a few days earlier. Commissioner Wilson, needing to maintain cover, could no longer assist his Panther friends. But if the university could survive this attack, he would be ready to serve as a counterintelligence agent for Pitt as it prepared for a May offensive on Evanston.

On December 11, 1948, during the first day of faculty representative meetings, the commissioner introduced Dean Vincent Lanfear to the committee. The professor indicated that Pitt wished to renew its application for membership and offered reasons for the Panthers being a logical selection next spring. As anticipated, the faculty took no action on his comments.[111] His presence was intended only to cast doubt on the Spartan initiative.

The following day, Dean Lloyd Emmons of Michigan State was center stage for a

---

[108] Fitzgerald to Leib. 8 December 1948. "Telephone: Karl Leib of State University of Iowa." University of Pittsburgh Archives. Collection 2/10, FF19; Box 2
[109] Hamilton to Fitzgerald. 9 December 1948. University of Pittsburgh Archives. Collection 2/10, FF19; Box 2
[110] Ibid.
[111] Minutes of the Intercollegiate Conference of Faculty Representatives. 11-12 December 1948. Bentley Historical Library, Athletic Department, Bimu 2; Box 84, folder: Athletic Director's Office, Faculty Representatives Minutes 1941-57

brief performance in front of the faculty. His role, unlike Lanfear's, was to offer reassurance about the Spartans and answer any remaining questions. Subsequently, the faculty representatives met in executive session.[112] Ralph Aigler did not recuse himself as he had done during the 1937 decision on a Michigan State application. Henry Rottschaefer moved for the admission of MSC into the Western Conference. Aigler then proposed his highly confidential amendment to verify Spartan compliance with conference policies.[113]

After "a lot of discussion" the amended Rottschaefer motion carried. Shortly after, the commissioner of the Intercollegiate Conference of Faculty Representatives made an announcement to the press waiting outside the board room that Michigan State College had been unanimously selected to fill the spot vacated by the University of Chicago two years earlier.

BACK IN September of 1944, Professor Henry Rottschaefer, in a letter to Ralph Aigler, commented on the unpleasant task the faculty committee had in gracefully refusing honorable applicants seeking admission to the conference.[114] The responsibility for notifying the suitor was traditionally reserved for the chairman of the conference Faculty Representatives Committee. For the year 1948, that task fell to Frank Richart. On December 15 he officially informed Pitt's Vincent Lanfear of the committee's decision to accept Michigan State into the conference. He went on to state that "no further action was taken regarding your application." The faculty had decided, after admitting the Spartans, not to expand beyond ten. He then indicated that the "possibility seems very remote" for expansion any time soon. "I have long had a high regard for your institution and for Tom Hamilton, your new athletic director. I can only offer my regrets that the circumstances that have taken place recently could not be favorable to you."[115]

Delaying the announcement of Captain Thomas Hamilton as the new athletic director, combined with two other miscues by Pitt leadership during the summer and fall of 1948, may well have cost the University of Pittsburgh a reserved seat in the Sherman Hotel boardroom every December. The Ralph W. Aigler papers, as well as various documents from Iowa City, Minneapolis, and Pittsburgh,[116] reveal just how close Pitt came to gaining membership in the Intercollegiate Conference of Faculty Representatives.

---

[112] Rules, Regulations and Opinions of the Intercollegiate Conference of Faculty Representatives – revised 1930. University of Minnesota Archives, Department of Intercollegiate Athletics Papers; Box 13, folder: 1930

[113] Aigler to Smith. 17 December 1948. Bentley Historical Library, University of Michigan. Ralph W. Aigler Papers, 87406 Aa 2; Box 10, folder: correspondence 1946-52 "B" misc.

[114] Rottschaefer to Aigler. 13 September 1944. Bentley Historical Library, University of Michigan. Ralph W. Aigler Papers, Aa 2; Box 8, folder: Correspondence 1940-45 Rottschaefer

[115] Richart to Lanfear. 15 December 1948. University of Illinois Archives, Series: 4/2/12; Box 3, folder: Western Intercollegiate Conference 1948-49

[116] Alberts, Robert C. *Pitt: The Story of the University of Pittsburgh 1787-1987*. Pittsburgh: University of Pittsburgh Press, 1986. p. 222

WITHIN THE next few months the Committee of Three, as mandated by the Aigler amendment, would visit East Lansing. The ad hoc group was asked to verify "complete compliance" with the conference Handbook on four items of major concern to the nine faculty representatives. The list included the usual issues raised by Ralph Aigler and Fritz Crisler over the past decade:

1. Complete faculty control of athletics
2. Discontinuation of all scholarships contrary to revised Rule-6 as of January 1, 1949
3. Use of an autumn "training table" only for athletes on the traveling football squad
4. Termination of recruiting practices by coaches involving travel[1]

Professor Lloyd Emmons, John Hannah's right-hand man delegated with the task of preparing for the investigation,[2] was given notice that "all other phases of [your] athletic program and procedures will also be investigated by the Committee." The date of the investigation was left open; Chairman Frank Richart felt "[you] may need a little time to familiarize [yourself] with our requirements and to make adjustments ..." He concluded by mentioning that "when you feel that you are ready, we can consider arrangements for the visit of the Committee" to East Lansing.[3] Richart was anticipating it would take a "couple of months" before the college would be prepared for the unusual investigation.[4]

Each member of the ad hoc committee brought certain skills necessary for an efficient and effective investigation. Kenneth Wilson, as current commissioner and former coach and athletic director, represented the interests of directors actively involved with

---

[1] Richart to Emmons. 21 December 1948. University of Illinois Archives. Series 4/2/12; Box 3, folder: Western Intercollegiate Conference 1948-49

[2] Hannah to Richart. 17 December 1949. University of Illinois Archives. Series 4/2/12; Box 3, folder: Western Intercollegiate Conference 1948-49

[3] Richart to Emmons. 21 December 1948. University of Illinois Archives. Series 4/2/12; Box 3, folder: Western Intercollegiate Conference 1948-49

[4] Richart to Little, Blommers, Wilson. 11 January 1949. University of Illinois Archives. Series 4/2/12; Box 3, folder: Western Intercollegiate Conference 1948-49

athletic operations at the nine institutions.[5] His office would also assist in coordinating the investigation. Having two experienced registrars–representatives Paul Blommers of Iowa and Ken Little of Wisconsin–review the academic records of almost 100 student-athletes would prove invaluable with the time constraints imposed on the group.[6] The faculty wanted the State University of Iowa leadership, and Paul Brechler in particular, to be on board with any final decision on the admission of the Spartans. This was another reason the faculty chose Blommers.[7] Professor Little was asked to chair the committee.[8]

RALPH AIGLER opted to provide historical background, pertinent opinions, and advice, as well as legal counsel for the committee. On January 28, 1949, responding to recent actions by both the State Board of Agriculture and the college Faculty Senate in rescinding the Jenison subsidies, he wrote the first of three letters to the Little Committee members.[9] [10]

> I need not emphasize to you three men what a drastic step that [has been]
> … particularly by the young men who have been enjoying that easy income
> and then find it taken away from them. I have some evidence that a
> considerable dispute has arisen on the campus over at East Lansing in this
> respect. It must be perfectly obvious that the pressure to find some
> alternative way of taking care of these athletes will be tremendous. You
> men on the committee can easily learn whether they have been taken off the
> Jenison list. It will not be so easy for you to learn whether the aids have
> been continued in some more subtle form.[11]

Six weeks earlier, Chairman Frank Richart wrote John Hannah welcoming Michigan State into the conference. He reminded the president that the invitation was predicated on the college undergoing an investigation. Within days Hannah optimistically wrote back to Richart–he was confident that the task of meeting the four requirements would be achieved in short order. "It is our hope that the certifying committee will be able to come at an early date and that we can be formally admitted to the Conference at the earliest possible time."[12] On January 7, 1949, Lloyd Emmons notified Richart that the Little

---

[5] Report of the Special Committee on Admission of Michigan State College. Circa May 1949. University of Wisconsin-Madison Archives. Faculty Athletic Board, Series 5/21/6; Box 1, folder: Western Conference Minutes 1947-51

[6] Ibid.

[7] Brechler to Richart. 20 January 1949. University of Wisconsin-Madison Archives. The University Faculty Athletic Board, Series 5/21/7; Box 1, folder: Western Conference General files

[8] Richart to Little, Blommers, Wilson. 11 January 1949. University of Illinois Archives. Series 4/2/12; Box 3, folder: Western Intercollegiate Conference 1948-49

[9] Minutes of the State Board of Agriculture. 13 January 1949. www.onthebanks.msu.edu

[10] Report of the Special Committee on Admission of Michigan State College. Circa May 1949. University of Wisconsin-Madison Archives. Faculty Athletic Board, Series 5/21/6; Box 1, folder: Western Conference Minutes 1947-51

[11] Aigler to Wilson, Blommers, Little. 28 January 1949. University of Wisconsin-Madison Archives. The University Faculty Athletic Board, Series 5/21/7; Box 1, folder: Western Conference General files

[12] Hannah to Richart. 17 December 1948. University of Illinois Archives. Series 4/2/12; Box 3, folder: Western Intercollegiate Conference 1948-49

Committee could begin its investigation at any time.[13]

Frank Richart was taken aback that Emmons accomplished his task in only three weeks. The conference chairman anticipated that it would take "reasonable time,"[14] perhaps a couple of months, before the college would be ready for an investigation by the Little Committee.[15] [16] He informed Emmons that, due to the challenge of coordinating the calendars of the three investigators, a visit was unlikely "[within] the immediate future."[17] Two weeks later, Emmons again wrote the engineering professor. "We are as anxious as a ten year old boy anticipating the arrival of a circus and, therefore, hope that the visit may not be delayed any longer than necessary."[18]

If Richart was surprised by Emmons' achievement, Ralph Aigler was flabbergasted. The legal scholar questioned whether "[President] Hannah and his associates at Michigan State realize just what it means for them to live up to Conference rules."[19] The haste with which the college sought official approval, he implied, reflected misaligned goals emanating from Hannah's office. "Their attention was [totally] centered upon the prestige that they thought would come from being made a member of the Conference."[20]

In his letter to the committee he offered an analogy to support his hunch. "It has been often pointed out that a new pair of shoes is most apt to hurt only after they have been worn for a while. I have a notion the frantic calls that Tug [Wilson] had from Hannah in San Francisco [during the recent NCAA annual meetings] were due to the shoes beginning to pinch."[21]

Aigler then referenced Fritz Crisler's comments "that Tug had reported to him the people at Michigan State were manifesting impatience in wanting the committee to make its visit over there in the very near future."[22] The law professor had anticipated this action from the leadership in East Lansing.

> I should not be at all disturbed or distressed by their impatience. After all, their election to membership, in so far as that has yet been accomplished, is something that is being done for them rather than for us. Knowing the

---

[13] Emmons to Richart. 7 January 1949. University of Illinois Archives. Series 4/2/12; Box 3, folder: Western Intercollegiate Conference 1948-49

[14] Richart to Hannah. 14 December 1949. University of Illinois Archives. Series 4/2/12; Box 3, folder: Western Intercollegiate Conference 1948-49

[15] Richart to Emmons. 21 December 1948. University of Illinois Archives. Series 4/2/12; Box 3, folder: Western Intercollegiate Conference 1948-49

[16] Richart to Little, Blommers, and Wilson. 11 January 1949. University of Wisconsin-Madison Archives. The University Faculty Athletic Board, Series 5/21/7; Box 1, folder: Western Conference General files

[17] Richart to Emmons. 11 January 1949. University of Illinois Archives. Series 4/2/12; Box 3, folder: Western Intercollegiate Conference 1948-49

[18] Emmons to Richart. 24 January 1949. University of Illinois Archives. Series 4/2/12; Box 3, folder: Western Intercollegiate Conference 1948-49

[19] Aigler to Wilson, Blommers, Little. 28 January 1949. University of Wisconsin-Madison Archives. The University Faculty Athletic Board, Series 5/21/7; Box 1, folder: Western Conference General files

[20] Ibid.

[21] Ibid.

[22] Ibid.

situation as I know it, there are going to be strong pressures at East Lansing to cut corners, particularly in such things as these Jenison scholarships. As I said at the meeting when we were considering their application, I, for one, am not satisfied with their statements, even promises that they will comply … It is much better for our Conference that we be sure that they are doing this before their membership takes effect, rather than to have to contemplate possible disciplinary measures after they are in.[23]

So in response to pleas for an early visit by the Committee of Three, Ralph Aigler proposed a stonewalling strategy. The investigation should be delayed, he asserted, "long enough so that it may be demonstrated that they are actually abiding by the rules and not merely saying that they will do so."[24]

A few days later, in a candid letter to Kenneth Wilson, the professor shared his greatest concern regarding the election of Michigan State.

The truth of the matter is, Tug, that we have a problem child on our hands and that is the reason why I wrote you [three] men on the committee expressing the views I did [earlier in the month] … You may wonder in the light of this why it is that Michigan supported her application for membership. There were really two reasons. The first one had to do with state relationships. The other was purely selfish, in that it was my firm conviction that the members of the Conference and Michigan in particular would be better off if Michigan State were inside the fold, where we had some measure of control over her activities. We have looked down our noses at the southern schools. Michigan State has been as bad or worse. Let us act as cautiously regarding Michigan State as if we were considering an application for membership from one of the southerners.[25]

It appeared that Aigler's opinion of the Spartans had not changed over the past 15 years after all. The Spartans were still the same "outlaws" (outside the laws of amateurism) he described to confidants back in 1935.[26] And one decade later, in March of 1946, he had no choice but to stand behind President Alexander Ruthven's political decision to support John Hannah's quest. Professor Aigler's only satisfaction at that time was in knowing that the Spartans, if one day elected into the conference, would be forced to finally abide by all Handbook policies.

But the Wolverine from Bellevue, Ohio later admitted that there was another reason for supporting his boss's edict. "On purely selfish grounds, speaking institutionally, I have been for [the college's] admission … you have, of course, no way of knowing how much good athletic material has chosen Michigan State under the influence of her program in

---

[23] Aigler to Wilson, Blommers, Little. 28 January 1949. University of Wisconsin-Madison Archives. The University Faculty Athletic Board, Series 5/21/7; Box 1, folder: Western Conference General files

[24] Ibid.

[25] Aigler to Wilson. 31 January 1949. Bentley Historical Library, University of Michigan. Ralph W. Aigler Papers, 87406 Aa 2; Box 10, folder: correspondence 1946-52 Wilson, K.L. 2/2

[26] Aigler to Long. 7 October 1935. Bentley Historical Library, University of Michigan. Ralph W. Aigler Papers, 87406 Aa 2; Box 12, folder: athletics, correspondence 1933-36 "L" misc.

financial aids."[27] Aigler was confident that high school seniors, no longer tempted by Jenison dollars, would opt to play at Michigan Stadium rather than the recently expanded Macklin Field.

FOLLOWING THE tentative approval of Michigan State in December, Frank Richart asked the athletic directors to send comments regarding any questionable Spartan practices that their coaches might be aware of to Iowa's athletic director.[28] Including Paul Brechler was a savvy move by Richart. Now both Iowans were involved in the process, prompted by their initial vote on the Rottschaefer-Aigler motion.

Much to the surprise of Brechler, however, the directors had little to reveal about Spartan infractions.[29] He shared the disappointing news with Professor Richart on January 20, 1949. The skeptic from the State University was "sure that some [evidence of wrongdoings] must be available but that the schools hesitate to put it down on paper."[30] Michigan had yet to reply. Brechler was confident that Fritz Crisler would have "a good deal of information" for the committee to investigate.[31] But for unclear reasons, the Wolverine director would refrain from providing comment until late March.

Lacking any solid proof from the athletic directors regarding Michigan State shenanigans, the faculty representatives were in a real predicament. The Little Committee needed hard evidence, not just accusations provided by an intrastate rival, to guide its investigation. In response, the nine decided to hire a private investigator, by the name of McClendon, who would report to Commissioner Wilson.[32] [33]

The sleuth was asked to interview athletes no longer receiving Jenison Awards to determine how they planned to finance their remaining years of college. He was also encouraged to investigate Michigan State's work-study program: Had staff been assigned to oversee it? Had records been kept verifying actual participation by student-athletes in legitimate jobs? In response to Coach Munn's recent off-season success in signing a number of highly talented high school seniors (despite the absence of the Jenison Awards), McClendon was challenged to find out whether boosters–some perhaps members of the old Downtown Coaches Club–might be illegally offering financial aid. And finally, Wilson requested that the agent "quietly visit around with some of the athletes at their hangouts on campus to see if any information can be picked up about their attitude towards [conference] rules."[34]

---

[27] Aigler to Richart. 21 December 1948. University of Illinois Archives. Series 4/2/12; Box 3, folder: Western Intercollegiate Conference 1948-49

[28] Little to Blommers, Richart, Wilson. 15 January 1949. University of Illinois Archives. Series 4/2/12; Box 3, folder: Western Intercollegiate Conference 1948-49

[29] Richart to Little. 28 January 1949. University of Illinois Archives. Series 4/2/12; Box 3, folder: Western Intercollegiate Conference 1948-49

[30] Brechler to Richart. 20 January 1949. University of Wisconsin-Madison Archives. The University Faculty Athletic Board, Series 5/21/7; Box 1, folder: Western Conference General files

[31] Ibid.

[32] Wilson to Little. 17 March 1949. University of Wisconsin-Madison Archives. University Faculty Athletic Board, Series 5/21/7; Box 1, folder: Western Conference General files

[33] Wilson to Little. 20 April 1949. University of Wisconsin-Madison Archives. University Faculty Athletic Board, Series 5/21/7; Box 1, folder: Western Conference General files

[34] Wilson to Little. 17 March 1949. University of Wisconsin-Madison Archives. University Faculty Athletic Board, Series 5/21/7; Box 1, folder: Western Conference General files

In an effort to be fair to Michigan State, the commissioner agreed to notify Ralph Young of the committee's plan. He told the Spartan athletic director that the practice of hiring an investigator, often a retired FBI agent, was not unique in the history of the conference. Commissioner John Griffith had often used them to verify grievances filed by member institutions.[35] [36] His reassurances, however, were merely a decoy. Wilson promised Chairman Ken Little that he would "not tell [Young] what … investigations this individual will do so there will be no opportunity for them to alert the athletes ahead of time."[37] The former University of Pittsburgh advocate, personally well versed in covert activities over the past three years, was confident that a considerable amount of material would be forthcoming as a result of McClendon's poking around East Lansing in early April.[38] [39]

RALPH AIGLER, a participant in the mid-March discussion to hire a private investigator, decided it was now the proper time to write his final letter to the Little Committee. In the professor's opinion, the people who ran the school and the athletic program were dishonorable. He noted that even though "on innumerable occasions in the last few years, the statement has come from Michigan State officials, from the President down, that Michigan State was 'scrupulously observing Conference rules,'"[40] the college had failed to abide by them during the previous two decades. "We certainly can formulate opinions as to the kind of people they are and the sort of athletic administration they [have] by looking at past practices."[41] Furthermore, Aigler wrote, "I think past practices mean a great deal more than present assertions and promises as to what is going to be done in the future!"[42]

In early January of 1949 a *Detroit Free Press* reporter had announced that the Spartans were "now 'putting their house in order' preparatory to the visit of the inspection committee."[43] The claim was pure hypocrisy in Aigler's opinion. The professor noted that the registrar at the college was still allowing athletes to maintain eligibility despite classroom failures and delinquencies. "If they were speaking frankly and truthfully when they insisted and advertised that they were in all respects observing Conference rules, then such practice regarding eligibility is difficult to understand. Their own rules would have forbidden it."[44]

Aigler then addressed financial aid inconsistencies referenced in a letter he sent to the committee eight weeks earlier. He argued that Michigan State was currently practicing

---

[35]Griffith to Aigler. 6 August 1941. Bentley Historical Library, University of Michigan. Ralph W. Aigler Papers, 87406 Aa 2; Box 8, folder: correspondence 1940-45 Griffith

[36] Griffith to Aigler. 14 August 1941. Bentley Historical Library, University of Michigan. Ralph W. Aigler Papers, 87406 Aa 2; Box 8, folder: correspondence 1940-45 Griffith

[37] Wilson to Little. 17 March 1949. University of Wisconsin-Madison Archives. University Faculty Athletic Board, Series 5/21/7; Box 1, folder: Western Conference General files

[38] Ibid.

[39] Wilson to Little. 20 April 1949. University of Wisconsin-Madison Archives. University Faculty Athletic Board, Series 5/21/7; Box 1, folder: Western Conference General files

[40] Aigler to Little, Blommers, and Wilson. 25 March 1949. University of Wisconsin-Madison Archives. University Faculty Athletic Board, Series 5/21/7; Box 1, folder: Western Conference General files

[41] Ibid.

[42] Ibid.

[43] Ibid.

[44] Ibid.

duplicity. What John Hannah wrote to the conference leadership, in mid-January of 1948, immediately following approval of the Sanity Code by the NCAA was not consistent with evidence obtained by Professor Aigler.[45]

> I am satisfied that you will find that as recently as 1948, though perhaps not late in the year, the Jenison awards were being freely made, and made to men in amount and number that could not possibly be deemed permissible under the rules of our Conference ... I think you will find that they were commonly awarding these financial aids on the basis of tuition and maintenance to practically all men of varsity caliber, many of whom presented high school entrance credentials that were of even dubious quality for mere admittance.[46]

The legal scholar never understood the rationale behind the Jenison Awards. His hospitalization for a severe respiratory illness in early December of 1941 forced the cancellation of a meeting with Hannah to discuss the grants before seeking board approval a week later. As a consequence of his protracted hospital stay, the Wolverine faculty representative would learn of the controversial subsidy program secondhand months later.

The professor emphasized to the Committee of Three that the varsity teams in most major sports were composed of young men receiving financial aid from Fred Jenison's bequeathal to the college. The list exceeded 70 by his count. Aigler felt it critical that the ad hoc committee fully investigate how these students were now financing their college education. "If there has [sic] been no substitutions of other, perhaps more subtle, aids, I cannot believe that that number of men at Michigan State on that basis could possibly have gone without a ripple."[47]

With apparent assistance from informants in East Lansing, Aigler claimed knowledge of the academic records of all Jenison athletes. He encouraged the committee to review those files.

> You will find that virtually none was [sic] entitled to financial aid of the sort they have been getting, if the requirements of our current rules were observed.[48]

In fairness to John Hannah, however, the Spartan practice of continuing to honor the Jenison contracts signed before January of 1948 was consistent with NCAA policy passed down following approval of the Sanity Code.[49] [50] Michigan State, prior to being elected into the conference, had every right to maintain the grants until those students had completed their eligibility. Assuming the last group of athletes to receive the Jenison Awards enrolled

---

[45] Hannah to Aigler. 23 January 1948. Bentley Historical Library, University of Michigan. Ralph W. Aigler Papers, Aa 2; Box 9, folder: correspondence 1946-52 "H" misc.

[46] Aigler to Little, Blommers, and Wilson. 25 March 1949. University of Wisconsin-Madison Archives. University Faculty Athletic Board, Series 5/21/7; Box 1, folder: Western Conference General files

[47] Ibid.

[48] Ibid.

[49] Minutes of the State Board of Agriculture. 1 January 1948. www.onthebanks.msu.edu

[50] Bulletin No. 2. 12 July 1948. University of Wisconsin-Madison Archives. The University Faculty Athletic Board, Series 5/21/6; Box 1, folder: Western Conference minutes 1947-51

as freshmen in the fall of 1947, their three years of varsity competition would end with completion of the 1950-51 academic year. But with adoption of the Code, the only legitimate assistance the college could provide future athletes was based on scholastic achievement rather than athletic skill.

Regardless of Michigan State's good intentions to honor contracts with Jenison awardees, as of January 1, 1949, the newest member of the Western Conference was now obligated to abide by standards actually exceeding the benchmark 1948 Sanity Code. The NCAA executive committee ruling of June was irrelevant.[51]

Only athletes meeting the rigid academic standards of the 1948 Handbook–defined in Rule 6 and measured by the Highland Park yardstick–could be given financial aid. The State Board of Agriculture officially adopted the conference requirement at its mid-January meeting. The governing body of the college "specifically rescinds and revokes any previous athletic scholarship program that may have been in effect."[52]

The mistake in the meeting minutes–confusing Jenison Awards with athletic scholarships–was never corrected by the man who originally proposed the grants for non-scholastic attributes. Four months later, that misquote would be included in the "Report of the Special Committee on Admission of Michigan State College" for the faculty and directors to peruse during the joint meeting on the fate of the Spartans. Ralph Aigler probably gained a sense of personal satisfaction in the oversight by the college president.

No matter how Michigan State worded a subsidy for athletes, Aigler continued to doubt whether the college could provide legitimate financial assistance, in the form of work-study programs, to former Jenison athletes. The professor suspected overzealous alumni and fans would intervene with "alternative way[s] of taking care of these athletes."[53] To Aigler, it was the perfect set-up for booster activities like those offered during the "Sleepy Jim" Crowley tenure in East Lansing.

Aigler was also suspicious of the curriculum requirements for many physically talented Spartans enrolled in the school. "Are they registered in the solid courses of the institution calling for honest, intellectual endeavor, or are they in the police school, etc.?"[54] More than a little bit of Ann Arbor arrogance was evident in that comment. Michigan State, as a land-grant institution, was mandated to offer utilitarian degrees consistent with Justin Morrill's philosophy on education. As it turned out, by the early 1950s the Police Administration program would gain a national and international reputation for excellence.[55]

PAUL BRECHLER had been waiting since January to receive word from Fritz Crisler about

[51] Report of the Special Committee on Admission of Michigan State College. Circa May 1949. University of Wisconsin-Madison Archives. Faculty Athletic Board, Series 5/21/6; Box 1, folder: Western Conference Minutes 1947-51

[52] Ibid.

[53] Aigler to Wilson, Blommers, Little. 28 January 1949. University of Wisconsin-Madison Archives. The University Faculty Athletic Board, Series 5/21/7; Box 1, folder: Western Conference General files

[54] Aigler to Little, Blommers, Wilson. 25 March 1949. University of Wisconsin-Madison Archives. The University Faculty Athletic Board, Series 5/21/7; Box 1, folder: Western Conference General files

[55] Thomas, David A. *Michigan State College: John Hannah and the Creation of a World University, 1926-1969.* East Lansing: Michigan State University Press, 2008. p. 160

unscrupulous practices in East Lansing. His seven other colleagues had offered no incriminating actions–much to his disappointment. The Hawkeye was anticipating that his Wolverine counterpart would provide worthwhile evidence for the Little Committee. He never received that note from Ann Arbor. Crisler opted instead to write directly to the committee in late March.

> First, let me say I do not envy your assignment. It is a most difficult one. We have a situation of a new member coming to our Conference with an athletic philosophy quite apart from that which has been identified with the Conference for years. The authorities adopted a policy of a paid-player basis and operated under it for years. As a matter of fact, they conducted their athletics much the same as some institutions in the South. In a lot of respects they even excelled the practices of some of those institutions in the number of boys who were given aid and the total amount allotted to tuition and maintenance. If a Southern institution had applied for admission to the Conference, we would have thrown up our hands in horror. Now we have an institution (that) pressured its way into the Conference. It wasn't invited.[56]

Crisler acknowledged that he had little information to share. In his opinion, the Spartans were very good at covering up their tracks. "For example, it is perfectly apparent they have very carefully briefed prospective athletes as well as their parents on what to say if questioned. We have had boys come to our campus and all their answers are standard ones and the same is true of any parents we have questioned."[57]

It seems evident that he and Aigler had shared notes before writing their letters in March. For some time Ralph Aigler had predicted that the Spartans, in pursuit of athletic excellence, would eventually get caught violating the Handbook. Crisler seemed to concur. "It is my conviction that even after the investigation and their formal admittance, they will have loose administration in their athletics. It is far better to try and close any loopholes now rather than later."[58] He clearly questioned the oversight provided by Ralph Young and his department. "I only wish that their administration in athletics was as sound and thorough as we are led to believe."[59]

Crisler then raised concerns voiced by the conference coaches during the December meetings. He noted that Michigan State was not a "popular choice" to replace the University of Chicago. The coaches were upset with having to compete against a school that acquired talent in the open market. "I will hazard a guess that if a vote were taken among all coaches in the Western Conference, it would be almost unanimous against their admission."[60]

The Wolverine athletic director closed his remarks by expressing to the three

---

[56] Crisler to Little, Blommers, Wilson. 30 March 1949. Bentley Historical Library, University of Michigan. Ralph W. Aigler Papers, 87406 Aa 2; Box 9, correspondence 1946-52 "E" misc.
[57] Ibid.
[58] Ibid.
[59] Ibid.
[60] Ibid.

investigators his "earnest hope that you will have a fine visit at East Lansing."[61] Based on that final comment and the overall tone of his letter, it appeared that Fritz Crisler truly wanted the Spartans to be found in compliance. But in the spring of 1949, he maintained a sense of skepticism just as Ralph Aigler did.

IN FEBRUARY, Commissioner Ken Wilson developed the format for the investigation. Assigned specific tasks while in East Lansing,[62] [63] the three members of the committee began their review of the athletic program on April 14, 1949. Their job was completed two days later.

Upon his return to Chicago, Wilson was besieged with phone calls from several directors around the conference. Each caller was "intensely interested" in what had been discovered in East Lansing. Declining to reveal any findings, he told them that the report would be available for all to review before a final vote on the fate of Michigan State.[64]

Two prominent leaders within the conference, however, would be informed well in advance of the printed summary. A number of weeks prior to his visiting the Red Cedar campus with Little and Blommers, Wilson had planned a trip to Ann Arbor. He probably intended to review some agenda items with the Michigan athletic leadership in advance of the annual spring conference meetings in Evanston. Though the special committee report was not on his agenda that day, the commissioner anticipated "a lot of direct questioning from Ralph and Fritz" regarding its investigation of the Spartans two weeks earlier.[65]

The three met in Ann Arbor in early May. It was no surprise to Crisler and Aigler that the Committee of Three had discovered incongruities in East Lansing. Its final task was to "decide whether … as a whole, 'the rules and regulations and other requirements are completely in force' at Michigan State."[66] According to Wilson, the investigators concluded that the college was essentially in compliance. Only the Michigan leaders were privy to that assessment. The report would be held in confidence for the next three weeks in the commissioner's office. Now aware of the committee's findings, Fritz Crisler, in particular, had time to focus his thoughts in advance of the Evanston meetings. The Crisler Scheme would profoundly influence debate in two weeks.

The athletic director was very sensitive to Paul Brechler's concerns about discord within the conference. They had shared thoughts about this subject a year earlier in a few letters.[67] [68] Both agreed that it was critical that the Western Conference remain resolute in its

---

[61] Crisler to Little, Blommers, Wilson. 30 March 1949. Bentley Historical Library, University of Michigan. Ralph W. Aigler Papers, 87406 Aa 2; Box 9, correspondence 1946-52 "E" misc.

[62] Wilson to Little. 10 February 1949. University of Wisconsin-Madison Archives. The University Faculty Athletic Board, Series 5/21/7; Box 1, folder: Western Conference files

[63] "Report of Special Committee on Admission of Michigan State College." Circa May 1949. University of Wisconsin-Madison Archives. The University Faculty Athletic Board, Series 5/21/7; Box 1, folder: Western Conference files

[64] Wilson to Little. 19 April 1949. University of Wisconsin-Madison Archives. The University Faculty Athletic Board, Series 5/21/7; Box 1, folder: Western Conference files

[65] Ibid.

[66] Little to Blommers, Wilson. 23 April 1949. University of Wisconsin-Madison Archives. The University Faculty Athletic Board, Series 5/21/7; Box 1, folder: Western Conference files

[67] Brechler to Crisler. 18 May 1948. Bentley Historical Library, University of Michigan. Board in Control of Intercollegiate Athletics, 8729 Bimu F81 2; Box 31, folder: papers 1948

[68] Crisler to Brechler. 31 May 1948. Bentley Historical Library, University of Michigan. Board in

actions. And in the second year of the Sanity Code, it was even more crucial that the association that proudly promoted that legislation speak with unanimity in all decisions.

The conference, for years, was viewed by the press as "[giving] off a holier than thou aroma" for its rigid stance on amateurism.[69] Any action–including the admission of a college with a reputation for committing cardinal sins–had to be presented adeptly to a skeptical national press.

Aware that Michigan State did not meet all the criteria for compliance, Crisler planned to take command of a potentially contentious meeting among his colleagues and manipulate the vote on a motion that would not only be acceptable to the directors and their coaches but also fair to the college as a new member. The Faculty Representatives Committee, with Ralph Aigler's power of persuasion, would act favorably on that advice. The professor would assure that the vote would be reported as unanimous to the press.

AT THE joint dinner meeting of the faculty representatives and athletic directors on May 19, 1949, the report of the "Special Committee on Admission of Michigan State College to the Conference" was presented. As Herbert Orin Crisler had anticipated, a heated discussion followed. "Several Directors stated that it was their opinion that the coaches ... did not feel that they should be required to compete in Conference competition against Michigan State until at such time as the athletes recruited under the Jenison scholarship plan were no longer eligible."[70] The question needing an answer, however, was when that would take place. Injuries that might delay completion of eligibility for some in the final group of Jenison awardees (fall of 1947) were unpredictable.

The athletic directors then met in executive session later that evening to address that question. Crisler immediately took charge. His awareness of the Little Committee findings, gained from that meeting with the commissioner two weeks earlier, allowed him ample time to contemplate an equitable motion for all concerned. He suggested three options they might offer to the college. His proposal, based on the anticipated remaining years of eligibility for Jenison athletes, was as follows:

1. Allow Michigan State to enter into conference competition in all sports just as rapidly as conference schedules permit.
2. Permit that institution to begin competition in all sports, [except] football, in the school year of 1952-53.
3. Allow Michigan State to enter into conference competition as rapidly as schedules permit provided [that] all athletes who previously held Jenison scholarships are declared ineligible to compete.[71]

Validating Crisler's impact on his audience, Richard Larkins of Ohio State proposed

Control of Intercollegiate Athletics, 8729 Bimu F81 2; Box 31, folder: papers 1948

[69] Griffith to Directors of Athletics. Memorandum. 17 October 1940. The Ohio State University Archives, Director of Athetics (RG 9/e-1/9), "Intercollegiate Conference: Commissioner: Correspondence (Griffith) 1940-1941 (folder 2 of 2)."

[70] Minutes of the Intercollegiate Conference Joint Dinner Meeting of the Faculty Representatives and Athletic Directors. 19 May 1949. University of Illinois Archives. Series 4/2/12; Box 3, folder: Conference minutes 1948-49

[71] Ibid.

a motion almost identical to Crisler's. It was seconded by director Douglas Mills of the University of Illinois.

> [It is recommended] that the Faculty Representatives be advised that it is the feeling of the Directors that two alternatives be offered to Michigan State College: (1) that Conference competition shall not begin for Michigan State until the academic year of 1952-53,[72] or (2) that all members of Michigan State athletic squads who held Jenison scholarships be withheld as ineligible and Michigan State enter into the Conference competition just as rapidly as schedules permit.[73]

In deference to the directors and coaches, Crisler's option (1) was not even a consideration. The politically wise Wolverine knew both groups would oppose allowing the Spartans to "enter into ... competition in all sports just as rapidly as ... schedules permit." Thus, the Larkin Motion that was approved pertained only to options (2) and (3). In a gesture of fairness to Michigan State, it essentially offered the college the opportunity to choose its own fate over the next three years. If the institution felt that it was unjust to penalize its Jenison athletes (for contracts now null and void), then its official participation in conference football would be deferred until all past recipients had either graduated or used up their eligibility.

Fritz Crisler's scheme, scripted in Ann Arbor a few weeks earlier, was working out just as he had planned for that evening. Back on December 13, anticipating that the college would be admitted into the Big Nine following the Committee of Three investigation, the Wolverine had proposed to his fellow directors "that Michigan State's football competition with Conference schools shall not be counted in Conference standings through the season of 1952."[74] In other words, the Spartans would begin official Big Ten play in September of 1953. His motion was not intended to be a disciplinary action–Crisler was not vengeful towards the college for its past actions.[75] And he certainly did not want to compromise the eligibility of good kids caught up in an illegal subsidy scheme no longer in practice. He merely wanted to place a de facto "asterisk" next to all games the Spartans played with conference members for three years.[76] It was a gesture of support for the coaches asked to field teams against an incredibly talented football squad that, some would say, had been acquired with dollars.

The Michigan athletic director offered his Asterisk Proposal shortly after he and his colleagues completed football contracts for the 1950-52 seasons. The meeting was

---

[72] Larkins' option (1) differed from Crisler's option (2) in that all sports, not just football, would be denied competition for conference titles until the academic year 1952-53.

[73] Minutes of the Intercollegiate Conference Joint Dinner Meeting of the Faculty Representatives and Athletic Directors. 19 May 1949. University of Illinois Archives. Series 4/2/12; Box 3, folder: Conference minutes 1948-49

[74] Minutes of the Intercollegiate Conference Meeting of the Athletic Directors and Head Football Coaches. 13 December 1948. Bentley Historical Library, University of Michigan. Athletic Department, 943 Bimu 2; Box 84, folder: Big 10 records 1941-52

[75] Crisler to Little, Blommers, Wilson. 30 March 1949. Bentley Historical Library, University of Michigan. Ralph W. Aigler Papers, 87406 Aa 2; Box 9, correspondence 1946-52 "E" misc.

[76] Aigler to Schmidt. 5 July 1951. Bentley Historical Library, University of Michigan. Ralph W. Aigler Papers, 87406 Aa 2; Box 10, correspondence 1946-52 "B" misc.

challenging for the administrators. The faculty representatives, in the aftermath of the Brechler-Crisler debate a few days earlier, obligated the directors to abide by the 9/6/2 rule for those three years. They would waive the mandate in favor of a five-game format only if scheduling for those seasons proved untenable.[77] Due to Crisler's defiance of the Michigan Rule as well as Ohio State's and Illinois's plans to boycott Purdue, only the 1952 schedule fulfilled that six-game requirement.

The implications for Michigan State, following approval of Fritz Crisler's December motion, were profound. Regardless of whether Ralph Young could muster up five contracts for 1950-51 and six for 1952 to fulfill the minimum number of games needed to qualify for a conference championship run, the Spartans would be declared ineligible. And, as Ralph Young would soon discover, regardless of de facto asterisks, the college struggled to find members even willing to compete against them during those three years. Michigan maintained its intrastate rivalry dates. Indiana had non-conference vacancies–it could accommodate the school each year. Purdue, another "weak sister," found a spot on its schedule for 1952. Minnesota, due to a previous commitment, was already inked on the Spartan schedule for 1950. And Ohio State, perhaps in deference to Lew Morrill, assured Ralph Young of one Saturday to compete against Biggie Munn's powerhouse. But that was it. The Spartans, like Purdue, were clearly facing a scheduling boycott. Despite not yet being an official member of the conference, vigilante justice was being served Michigan State. The college turned elsewhere for contracts during those years spent in waiting.

So, by late May, what ultimately took place in executive session among the athletic directors was probably irrelevant to John Hannah. Michigan State's short-term fate had been decided five months earlier. The Larkin Motion, allowing the college to choose one of two options, was merely a means to appease some angry football coaches not willing to compete against hired talent. Hannah had no real choice. Should he pick the second option and begin competition in the conference later that fall, Coach Munn would be left with no student-athletes to field a team.[78] The young men previously promised Jenison money would forego remaining eligibility.

The first option was essentially a restatement of the Asterisk Proposal of December. Ironically, had Crisler not made the motion, the de facto boycott now in force by a few schools would have accomplished the same result. With its athletic director able to sign-up only three conference teams each season, by default the Spartans would have been ineligible for Big Ten championship competition. So John Alfred Hannah, as anticipated by the Michigan Men, chose the just option–based on his creedal convictions–and allowed the Jenison athletes to complete their remaining years of eligibility in East Lansing. Michigan State's inaugural season in Big Ten football action would begin with the 1953-54 academic year. Ralph Young could start signing contracts for that historical campaign–at least for Spartan faithful–during the December 1949 conference meetings in Chicago.[79]

Crisler's brilliant Asterisk Proposal, accepted at the directors' meeting one day

[77] Minutes of the Intercollegiate Conference of Faculty Representatives. 11-12 December 1948. Bentley Historical Library, University of Michigan. Athletic Department, 943 Bimu 2; Box 84, folder: Faculty Representatives meetings 1941-57

[78] Most football players were Jenison Award recipients.

[79] Minutes of the Intercollegiate Conference Meeting of the Athletic Directors and Head Football Coaches. 13 December 1948. Bentley Historical Library, University of Michigan. Athletic Department, 943 Bimu 2; Box 84, folder: Big 10 records 1941-52

following Aigler's amendment to the Rottschaefer motion, ultimately proved that the University of Michigan did get the final say in this story after all. John Hannah and Lew Morrill could celebrate the "sweet" success of out-smarting–at least in their minds–the powerful tandem from Ann Arbor,[80] but the Wolverine leadership got what it really wanted. Michigan State was given a blunt message: Membership carried with it certain obligations. And to prove how serious the faculty representatives were about this matter, their rubber-stamping the Asterisk Proposal would deny Michigan State three shots at conference gridiron titles. For a very talented Spartan football team, that was a major disappointment. During those three years, Biggie Munn not only led the college on a 24-game winning streak, he also claimed for the school the mythical national championship in 1952. His overall record was 26 wins against one defeat to Maryland in early October of 1950.

But perhaps of greater satisfaction for both Ralph Aigler and Fritz Crisler during that evening dinner meeting at the Orrington Hotel was a statement on the second page of the Little Report, under the section addressing faculty control, noting a motion by the Michigan State Faculty Senate. "Effective January 1, 1949, the regulations and agreements governing the conduct of athletics at M.S.C., eligibility of athletes for unearned financial aids, practices of staff members in respect to the recruiting of students, and eligibility of students for participation in intercollegiate athletics shall be the same as the rules and regulations of the Intercollegiate Conference of Faculty Representatives."[81] With that one sentence, the Michigan athletic leadership was vindicated. After two decades of claiming compliance with the Intercollegiate Conference Handbook–a contractual promise necessary to compete against the membership of the Big Nine–Michigan State College appeared to finally admit its guilt.[82] [83]

The committee members then addressed remaining questions and concerns regarding their eight-page report. At 11:15 pm the athletic directors convened in executive session and approved the Larkin Motion as shrewdly proposed by Fritz Crisler. The meeting was adjourned within 30 minutes.[84]

The next afternoon the nine faculty leaders reconvened for the fourth session of the two-day meeting. Of the five remaining agenda items, number 17 was the most significant. Having been informed of the two Larkin options earlier that day, Michigan State chose the first. Now aware of John Hannah's decision, Henry Rottschaefer proposed a motion that was seconded by Wendell Postle of Ohio State. It read:

> That the report of the special committee certifying that the rules,
> regulations and requirements of the Conference are now substantially in
> force at Michigan State College be accepted; and that Michigan State

---

[80] Morrill to Hannah. 21 December 1948. University of Minnesota Archives, President's Office; Box 238, folder: Physical Education and Athletics. 1948-49

[81] Ibid.

[82] Aigler to Richart. 21 December 1948. University of Illinois Archives. Series 4/2/12; Box 3, folder: Western Intercollegiate Conference 1948-49

[83] Aigler to Long. 7 October 1935. Bentley Historical Library, University of Michigan. Ralph W. Aigler Papers, 87406 Aa 2; Box 12, folder: correspondence 1933-36 "L" misc.

[84] Joint Dinner Meeting of the Faculty Representatives and Athletic Directors. 19 May 1949. Bentley Historical Library, University of Michigan. Athletic Department, 943 Bimu 2; Box 84, folder: Big Ten Directors minutes 1941-52

College be declared a member of the Conference. Conference competition by Michigan State College will not begin before the academic year of 1950-51, and in the case of football at the expiration of schedules heretofore drawn [through the 1952-53 academic year].[85]

The Larkin Motion as presented to the Faculty Representatives Committee had been revised during debate. There was no mention of any role Ralph Aigler might have played in that discussion. But it was evident that the "asterisk" provision–originally proposed by his athletic director–remained as Crisler had intended: only football would be impacted. The college could commence competition for titles in all other sports within the year since few of those student-athletes had received Jenison money.[86] The final tally was not mentioned in the minutes. It was probably irrelevant. The Spartans were now recognized as members of the Big Ten.

ON MAY 27 Professor Kenneth Little, as chairman of the special committee, wrote President John Hannah regarding the faculty decision from one week earlier. He cited the Rottschaefer motion and noted that the vote was unanimous.[87] As it turned out, his statement was inaccurate and misleading.

A motion, based on conference tradition, was designated in the minutes as either "voted" or "lost" based on a simple majority count. An outcome was documented as "unanimously voted" if all members approved. The Rottschaefer proposal was not unanimous. The minutes for agenda item 17 indicated that the motion was only "voted."[88] There were some faculty representatives who did not agree with the majority. In an apparent cover-up, the conference announced a unanimous decision. Consistent with the concerns of Fritz Crisler and his faculty representative, however, it was critical that the conference speak as one, especially in such a high-profile story as the Spartan admission.

But a few days after President Hannah received Little's letter of congratulations, *Detroit News* sports columnist Walter ("Waddy") Spoelstra reported that the outcome of the vote was actually 5-4.[89] Ralph Aigler was livid. Someone within the exclusive club had violated "executive session"[90] rules and leaked information to the press. Michigan and the law school professor were both implicated by the news media as casting one of the four

---

[85] Minutes of the Intercollegiate Conference of Faculty Representatives. 19-20 May 1949. Bentley Historical Library, University of Michigan. Athletic Department, 943 Bimu 2; Box 84, folder: Faculty Representatives minutes 1941-57

[86] Hannah to Young. 19 May 1945. Michigan State University Archives. Hannah Presidential Papers, UA2.1.12, Box 63, folder 7: Scholarships-Jenison 1942-45

[87] Little to Hannah. 27 May 1949. University of Wisconsin-Madison Archives. The University Faculty Athletic Board, Series 5/21/7; Box 1, folder: Western Conference files

[88] Minutes of the Intercollegiate Conference of Faculty Representatives. 19-20 May 1949. Bentley Historical Library, University of Michigan. Athletic Department, 943 Bimu 2; Box 84, folder: Faculty Representatives minutes 1941-57

[89] Spoelstra to Aigler. 2 June 1949. Bentley Historical Library, University of Michigan. Ralph W. Aigler Papers, 87406 Aa 2; Box 10, folder: correspondence 1946-52 "B" misc.

[90] Handbook of the Intercollegiate Conference of Faculty Representatives-Revised 1941. University of Minnesota Archives, Department of Intercollegiate Athletics Papers; Box 13, folder: small handbook 1941

opposing votes.[91]

Professor Aigler had experienced a few public-relations nightmares during his long, distinguished career in conference governance. The Iowa scandal of 1929 and the Blackstone Hotel cocktail party incident of December 1939 were two glaring examples. The Spartan election, in the context of the Spoelstra revelation, could be added to that list. Shortly after Michigan State gained tentative approval for admission into the Western Conference back in December, Frank Richart had shared with Aigler his greatest fear: "the embarrassing position we might all be in if the investigation [by the Committee of Three] shows an unsatisfactory condition continuing at the institution ..."[92] Due to a decision by an irate representative to leak confidential information, that "embarrassing position" was now a reality for Ralph Aigler.

It was again time for damage control. The conference's good name was in jeopardy. The integrity of Ralph Aigler and the University of Michigan was also on the line. Upset, he wrote back to Spoelstra in confidence.

> Where, in the name of heaven, Waddy, do you get your purported
> information? The truth of the matter is that there was no dissent on
> anybody's part to the acceptance of the report of the Little Committee,
> which made Michigan State a member ... As you know, the votes in the
> executive sessions of the Faculty Representatives are not given to the press,
> and I am therefore stating this to you not for publication, but the simple fact
> is that the one person responsible for Michigan State not having to wait two
> more years than the one decided upon [academic year 1950-51] before her
> official competition begins [in all sports but football], is the person writing
> this letter. I have no doubt that if other Faculty Representatives felt free to
> talk about this subject, they would confirm completely what I have just told
> you ... You can thus see why I am getting to be sick and tired of this
> constant misrepresentation of Michigan's position. Back in December,
> when the action of that meeting was taken, after the meeting was adjourned
> Dr. Postle of Ohio State said to me almost exactly these words: "Michigan
> State owes the favorable action today to the fact that you supported them,
> and I have told Dean Emmons precisely that." I must confess to a little
> additional irritation that no one at Michigan State seems to have been
> moved to make any effort whatever to correct the general misunderstanding
> regarding the position of this university.[93]

As it turned out, Aigler was absolutely correct regarding his role in the confidential discussions. In mid-December of 1948 the professor maintained that in fairness to those schools currently penalized for violating Rule 6, the Highland Park yardstick should apply

[91] Spoelstra to Aigler. 2 June 1949. Bentley Historical Library, University of Michigan. Ralph W. Aigler Papers, 87406 Aa 2; Box 10, folder: correspondence 1946-52 "B" misc

[92] Richart to Aigler. 17 December 1948. University of Illinois Archives. Series 4/2/12; Box 3, folder: Western Intercollegiate Conference 1948-49

[93] Spoelstra to Aigler. 2 June 1949. Bentley Historical Library, University of Michigan. Ralph W. Aigler Papers, 87406 Aa 2; Box 10, folder: correspondence 1946-52 "B" misc.

to all Spartans receiving aid through the Jenison program at the same time.[94] In many ways, the institutional reprimand passed down on Purdue was equally appropriate for Michigan State. By March of 1949, however, Aigler had softened his stance. At that time he was advising the Little Committee on how to objectively evaluate past versus current practice of Michigan State. "To be sure, we could not in any sense mete out any punishment for violations of Conference rules prior to the time they become a member, but we certainly can formulate opinions as to the kind of people they are and the sort of athletic administration they had by looking at past practices."[95] That statement cleared his name and that of the university of having any plans to penalize the college. The Asterisk Proposal accomplished much more than any disciplinary action on the school and its student-athletes could have.

But Aigler, with his guard uncharacteristically down, may have confirmed Waddy Spoelstra's source as being reliable. There appeared to be a faction within the conference ruling body wanting to deny all Spartan athletic teams, not just football, from official competition until the academic year 1953-54. The professor recognized this as inherently unfair to students not tainted by Jenison dollars. And Ralph Aigler's defensive stance regarding debate held in executive session appeared to substantiate the *Detroit News* columnist's claim that there was not unanimity among the nine members. The voting outcome might very well have been 5-4 had the persuasive Michigan representative not intervened on behalf of the Spartans.

Regardless of the controversy over the tally, Professor Ken Little's May 27 letter to President Hannah led him to believe that all faculty representatives had approved the report of the special investigating committee as modified by the directors. It was the second time in five months that the college had gained what Hannah thought was a unanimous vote of confidence by the Western Conference.[96] In his note Little also graciously welcomed Michigan State on behalf of his colleagues. He then went into detail about the two remaining issues needing attention for the college to be in full compliance.[97] The Wisconsin registrar expected Michigan State to accomplish the task in short order.

John Hannah responded to the letter a few days later. Michigan State, he announced, "will try to be a worthy member in every way."[98] It is not known whether Henry Rottschaefer shared the "inside" story with Lew Morrill back in Minneapolis.

ON MAY 20, 1949, it became official: Michigan State College of Agriculture and Applied Science was finally a member of the Intercollegiate Conference of Faculty Representatives. Within six years it would be designated a university by legislative act. And with that acknowledgement, John Alfred Hannah, the former poultry specialist, would soon achieve his grand vision–a land-grant research institution providing extension services to the world.

---

[94] Aigler to Richart. 14 December 1948. University of Illinois Archives. Series 4/2/12; Box 3, folder: Western Intercollegiate Conference 1948-49

[95] Aigler to Little, Blommers, and Wilson. 25 March 1949. University of Wisconsin-Madison Archives. The University Faculty Athletic Board, Series 5/21/7; Box 1, folder: Western Conference General files

[96] Hannah would learn from President Hancher hours later how Iowa cast its votes earlier that day.

[97] Little to Hannah. 27 May 1949. University of Wisconsin-Madison Archives. The University Faculty Athletic Board, Series 5/21/7; Box 1, folder: Western Conference files

[98] Hannah to Little. 27 May 1949. University of Wisconsin-Madison Archives. The University Faculty Athletic Board, Series 5/21/7; Box 1, folder: Western Conference files

IN 1990 Pennsylvania State University was "invited" into the Big Ten. Two decades later, the chancellors and presidents of the conference finally found it "expedient" to welcome the University of Nebraska into the Intercollegiate Conference of Faculty Representatives.[1] Expanding the membership, in each instance, appeared to be financially motivated. The decision by the Council of Ten also resolved, once and for all, an old debate among academicians, the public, and the press regarding the ultimate purpose of institutions of higher learning.[2] [3] [4] [5] In addition to educating students and promoting faculty and graduate research, entertaining the masses–as orchestrated through athletic departments– was finally acknowledged as a valid function of the university. The dollar-driven decision confirmed what had been understood by athletic directors and coaches since the early 1920s: Intercollegiate athletics was big business.

The Council of Ten, in the late 1980s, knew that adding Penn State would expand the conference's influence–and revenue-generating potential–eastward. The enhanced market share would also strengthen the membership's negotiating position when ABC's contract with the Big Ten came up for renewal in a few years.[6] But as a decade passed, that television bonus was no longer sufficient to help balance the athletic budgets of 11 Big Ten universities. The Council's response was to sign a joint venture with Fox Cable Network in 2007. The conference leadership, overnight, became majority shareholders in a huge

---

[1] The name was officially changed to the Big Ten Conference in 1987.

[2] Savage, Howard. *American College Athletics*. Boston: D.B. Updike-The Merrymount Press, 1929. p. v-xxi

[3] Lester, Robin. *Stagg's University: The Rise, Decline & Fall of Big-Time Football at Chicago*. Urbana and Chicago: University of Illinois Press, 1995. pp. 127-28

[4] Ruthven to Griffith. 19 December 1930. Bentley Historical Library, University of Michigan. Ralph W. Aigler Papers, 87406 Aa 2; Box 4, folder: correspondence 1929-33 Ruthven

[5] Aigler to Pollard. 19 June 1945. Bentley Historical Library, University of Michigan. Ralph W. Aigler Papers, 87406 Aa 2; Box 8, folder: correspondence 1940-45 "P" misc.

[6] Murphy, Austin. "Out of Their League?" SI.com. 1990. SI Vault–Your Link to Sports History. 7 May 1990 http://sportsillustrated.cnn.com/vault/article/m.

entertainment subsidiary,[7] better known as The Big Ten Network. It has access to over 75 million households and an outreach overseas.[8]

The addition of Nebraska allowed the conference to create two six-team divisions; a playoff between the winners of the Legends and the Leaders extended the season by one weekend into December.[9] New rivalries were anticipated. But of greater significance, the financial success of the network and its shareholders was assured by the brilliant marketing scheme. The Cornhusker admission also exposed, once again, the limited role that the faculty representatives held in conference governance. That transformation took place in 1987, when the Big Ten presidents and chancellors "incorporated the conference and vested absolute power in themselves as part of a long overdue move … to take control of their athletic departments."[10] Ironically, that grab for controlling influence had its origins in 1948, when President Lew Morrill of Minnesota, in a clear violation of Handbook protocol, advanced the cause of John Hannah's college to the Council of Nine presidents–men capable of influencing the votes of their respective faculty representatives.

WHILE DOING research for this book, I came across a 1954 letter written by Professor Hugh Gardner Ackley of the University of Michigan to President Harlan Hatcher. The highly respected Keynesian economist was essentially submitting his resignation from the Michigan Board in Control of Intercollegiate Athletics. He began his letter by noting the role of free market practices in acquiring high school talent for institutions of higher learning.

> You are well aware … of the concern … the Board … and the Director of Athletics have felt over postwar trends in intercollegiate athletics. During this period, the amateur principle has been largely replaced by a system in which promising high school athletes are put on the auction block (often by their parents) and sold to the highest bidder. The Western Conference has not escaped this trend.[11]

He pointed out that rules regarding recruiting and subsidizing were being ignored by conference members. And despite valiant attempts by Ralph Aigler and Fritz Crisler, there was no groundswell of support for correcting the problem. With Michigan remaining the lone school adhering to the Handbook, it was only a matter of time before the

---

[7] "Big Ten Network to Officially Launch August 30th." IU News Room. 2 July 2007. http://newsint.iu.edu/new/page/normal/5936

[8] "About Us–Big Ten Network." Big Ten Network. 11 June 2010. http://www.bigtennetwork.com/subindex/about_us

[9] The decision by the Council effectively voided the March 10, 1906 rule mandating that the season end the weekend prior to Thanksgiving. Precluding December play was intended to emphasize academics (and the well-being of the student) over athletics in the aftermath of the deadly 1905 campaign.

[10] Murphy, Austin. "Out of Their League?" SI.com. 1990. SI Vault–Your Link to Sports History. 7 May 1990 http://sportsillustrated.cnn.com/vault/article/m.

[11] Ackley to Hatcher. 2 July 1954. Bentley Historical Library, University of Michigan. Herbert Orin Crisler Papers, 85823 AC UAm Aa2; Box 6, folder: UM BIC of Intercollegiate Athletics Papers 1953-54

Wolverines would be "destined for 'second division' status."[12] The once-proud athletic tradition was in peril with the decline in the amateur code. "We therefore faced a choice between losing teams or swallowing our scruples and doing a better job of meeting the competition for athletes."[13] The board chose the latter. In doing so, academic grants, intended for qualified students, were now being offered to any athlete regardless of scholastic acumen. The University of Michigan had finally embraced the concept of an athletic scholarship.

A few months following that decision, Ralph William Aigler would retire after 38 years of dedicated service to his university and intercollegiate athletics. With his departure, the demise of amateurism and the advance of semi-professionalism in the college ranks was inevitable.

The implications of the Board in Control "swallowing [its] scruples" were profound. Acknowledging the honorable intentions of financially assisting kids "who [might] not otherwise be able to attend college," the economics professor noted that "this ignores completely the real fact that universities seek these men not through any desire to educate the underprivileged or the promising but as part of a vast and thoroughly commercialized business operation. Any educational benefits are quite incidental."[14] He argued that the reputation of Michigan was at risk.

> Not only these boys but others who become associated with them and with college athletics must receive a distorted sense of educational values, and a cynical view of an educational system which still pretends that its athletic program is designed to build sound bodies and to provide outlet for youthful exuberance–just good clean fun. Further, the flattery and cheap salesmanship exerted by university representatives to induce high school athletes to attend their institutions degrades the university, and gives the boy, his parents, his high school, and his townsmen a distorted idea of what universities consider important.[15]

The board's decision, soon to be presented to the regents for approval, would effectively compromise the integrity of the university. The "distorted idea" given the public, in Ackley's opinion, was that to sustain a winning tradition, the amateur ideal had to be sacrificed. It was all about the money.

And now, 60 years later, talented athletes, essentially employees of the entertainment division of universities,[16] provide over 40 hours a week to the product line. The obligation, however, does not end with the last game of the season. Coaches, whose job security rests in gaining victories, not admirable graduation rates, demand a yearlong commitment to the program. Ultimately these kids are exploited for the benefit of a very big

---

[12] Ackley to Hatcher. 2 July 1954. Bentley Historical Library, University of Michigan. Herbert Orin Crisler Papers, 85823 AC UAm Aa2; Box 6, folder: UM BIC of Intercollegiate Athletics Papers 1953-54
[13] Ibid.
[14] Ibid.
[15] Ibid.
[16] Sperber, Murray. *Beer and Circus: How Big-Time College Sports is Crippling Undergraduate Education.* New York:Henry Holt and Company, 2000. p. 235

business.[17]

Part of the problem, as Gardner Ackley suggested, may be the pressure placed on coaches (and administrators) to enroll academically unqualified students at the university level. The pursuit of victories and inherent financial gains justifies their actions.

As a way to address this injustice, one might look to the two-year General College program that Minnesota President Lotus Coffman instituted during the early 1930s. Consistent with Justin Morrill's philosophy of utilitarian education, it was intended for a different type of student.[18] Football Coach Bernie Bierman's staff adapted the program to attract talent to Minnesota that might not otherwise qualify for admission to the university. Bierman won a lot of football games. But Ralph Aigler's Eligibility Committee soon caught on to the ploy and declared the students ineligible. The General College, in its opinion, was not a part of the University of Minnesota.

But today, Coffman's educational model might offer an honorable solution to the hypocrisy that still exists in revenue-generating amateur sports. As a colleague of mine (who tutored Michigan State Spartans during the great football years of the mid 1960s) has argued, universities should affiliate with regional trade and technical schools. As contractual subsidiaries, these training centers (divisions) could offer an alternative education to athletes not qualified for admission to the university–and still allow them to participate in intercollegiate sports.[19] [20]

On paper the Coffman concept has promise; in practice it would probably fail. During the debate regarding the Wisconsin Reynold's proposal[21] of 1936, that allowed well-defined recruiting and subsidizing of gifted students also skilled in athletics, Ralph Aigler argued that "... the same people who will cheat when no [financial-aid is] permissible will cheat when we allow it to [exist under strict guidelines]."[22] Unscrupulous coaches would eventually find ways to manipulate the rule to their advantage. "We may bend our most earnest efforts toward the elimination of the evils and problems [of intercollegiate athletics with novel plans like Wisconsin's], but with human nature as it is the hope that we shall attain complete success is in my humble opinion a vain one."[23]

Aigler's comment on "human nature" still applies today. The NCAA, while

---

[17] Sperber, Murray. *Beer and Circus: How Big-Time College Sports is Crippling Undergraduate Education.* New York:Henry Holt and Company, 2000. p. 270

[18] Cullum, Dick. "Big Ten Questions Eligibility of Gopher Stars." *Minneapolis Journal* 16 February 1936. University of Minnesota Archives, President's Office; Box 5, folder: 120

[19] Thomas D. Burns, M.D., PhD. Circa 1989. Personal communication.

[20] Savage, Howard J. *American College Athletics.* Boston:D.B.Updike-The Merrymount Press, 1929. In the preface to Savage's survey, Carnegie Foundation President Henry Pritchett argued that most young people, including many athletes, did not qualify for higher education. (xviii) Their "usefulness and happiness would be best served in a commercial or industrial trade...." (xvii) His solution to the hypocrisy in amateur athletics, unlike my colleague's, was not to accommodate athletes. Pritchett would rather bring back "inter-college and intramural sports...to a stage in which they can be enjoyed by large numbers of students and where they do not involve an expenditure of time and money wholly at variance with any ideal of honest study." (xxi)

[21] Lorenz to Aigler. 2 June 1936. Bentley Historical Library, University of Michigan Archives. Ralph W. Aigler Papers, 87406 Aa2; Box 12, correspondence 1933-36 "L" misc.

[22] Aigler to Lorenz. 1 July 1936. Bentley Historical Library, University of Michigan Archives. Ralph W. Aigler Papers, 87406 Aa2; Box 12, Athletic Correspondence: 1933-36 "L" misc.

[23] Ibid.

maintaining a $757 million budget funded by contracts with various networks, has recently stepped up its enforcement activities. It has no choice. There is too much at stake. Thousands of jobs depend on those dollars; member schools from all three divisions benefit from splitting the profits. At the time of publication of this book, a number of prominent schools are being disciplined for infractions against complex rules intended to uphold a perception of pure amateurism still existing in the college ranks. A few more programs are rumored to soon face disciplinary action as well. Regardless of the "get tough" public-relations gesture by the national association, nothing really changes. Money will still rule the day in amateur intercollegiate sports.

THIRTY YEARS ago, our neighbor Jack Breslin watched my two brothers and me play a game of commando basketball. During a break in the action, prompted by word of brother Mike's recent acceptance into Notre Dame, he shared a truncated story of the roles Notre Dame and Michigan had in Michigan State gaining admission into the Big Ten. In September of 2008, out of curiosity, I decided to research his comments. What started as a passion quickly evolved into an obsession. The project proved to be an exhausting experience; as a full-time physician I had no business trying to research and write a book in my spare time. There were many nights during the week that I would continue writing into the early morning hours. And weekends were marathons. I often devoted up to 14 hours each day typing on my laptop. Some patients expressed concerns about their physician's health. Many commented on how tired I appeared. Their clinical assessment was quite accurate. But the three-year task is now complete, much to my relief!

Before I began this work I shared many of John Hannah's convictions on the role team sports play in unifying the college community of students, faculty, administrators, alumni, and fans. The athlete, having to balance academics, practice, and game-day activities, seemed to learn life lessons that the non-athlete did not. I viewed college athletics, and football in particular, as honorable undertakings for institutions of higher learning. But now, after all the books I read, all the documents I uncovered, and all the interviews I conducted, I have lost my passion for college football. Gardner Ackley's sobering letter, in the context of recent developments in Big Ten operations, was a major factor in that change of heart. My love for the game–the excitement and splendor of spending an idyllic autumn afternoon in Spartan or Notre Dame Stadium–is now, disappointingly, past tense.

Alberts, Robert C. *Pitt: The Story of the University of Pittsburgh 1787-1987.* Pittsburgh: The University of Pittsburgh Press, 1986.

Behee, John R. *Fielding Yost's Legacy to the University of Michigan.* Ann Arbor: Uhlrich's Books, Incorporated, 1971.

Brewer, Gordon. *"But How You Played the Game!"–A History of Intercollegiate Athletics at Hope College 1862-1955.* Holland: Hope College Publising, 1992.

Celizic, Mike. *The Biggest Game of Them All: Notre Dame, Michigan State and the Fall of '66.* New York: Simon & Schuster, 1992.

Chernow, Ron. *Titan: The Life of John D. Rockefeller, Sr.* New York: Random House, 1998.

Crowley, Joseph N. *In the Arena: The NCAAs First Century.* Indianapolis: The NCAA, 2006.

Duderstadt, James J. *Intercollegiate Athletics and the American University: A President's Perspective.* Ann Arbor: The University of Michigan Press, 2000.

Duderstadt, James J. *The View From the Helm.* Ann Arbor: The University of Michigan Press, 2007.

Falla, Jack. *NCAA: The Voice of College Sports–A Diamond Anniversary History 1906-1981.* Mission, Kansas: National Collegiate Athletic Association, 1981.

Hannah, John A. *A Memoir.* East Lansing: Michigan State University Press, 1980.

Hesburgh, Theodore M. *God, Country, Notre Dame.* New York: Doubleday, 1990.

Kryk, John. *Natural Enemies: Major College Football's Oldest, Fiercest Rivalry–Michigan vs. Notre Dame.* Lanham, Maryland: Taylor Trade Publishing, 2007.

Kuhn, Madison. *Michigan State: The First One Hundred Years 1855-1955.* East Lansing: Michigan State University Press, 1955.

Lester, Robin. *Stagg's University: The Rise, Decline & Fall of Big-Time Football at Chicago.* Urbana and Chicago: University of Illinois Press, 1999.

McNeil, William H. *Hutchins' University: A Memoir of the University of Chicago 1929-1950.* Chicago and London: University of Chicago Press, 1991.

Niehoff, Richard O. *Floyd W. Reeves: Innovative Educator and Distinguished Practitioner of the Art of Public Administration.* Lanham, Maryland: University Press of America, Incorporated, 1991.

Persons, Stow. *The University of Iowa in the Twentieth Century: An Institutional History.* Iowa City: University of Iowa Press, 1990.

Pollard, James E. *Ohio State Athletics: 1879-1959.* Columbus: The Athletic Department of Ohio State University, 1959.

Ratermann, Dale. *The Big Ten: A Century of Excellence.* Champaign, Illinois: Sagamore Publishing, 1996.

Savage, Howard. *American College Athletics.* Boston: D.B. Updike/Merrymount Press, 1929.

Siebold, Jack. *Spartan Sports Encyclopedia: A History of the Michigan State Men's Athletic Program.* Canada: Sports Publishing, L.L.C., 2003.

Soderstrom, Robert M. *The Big House: Fielding H. Yost and the Building of Michigan Stadium.* Ann Arbor: Huron River Press, 2005.

Sperber, Murray. *Onward to Victory: The Crises That Shaped College Sports.* New York: Henry Holt and Company, 1998.

Sperber, Murray. *Beer and Circus: How Big-Time College Sports is Crippling Undergraduate Education.* New York: Henry Holt and Company, 2000.

Stabley, Fred W. *The Spartans: Michigan State Football.* Tomball, Texas: Strode Publishers, 1988.

Thomas, David A. *Michigan State College: John Hannah and the Creation of a World University, 1926-1969.* East Lansing: Michigan State University Press, 2008.

Watterson, Jack Sayle. *College Football: History, Spectacle, Controversy.* Baltimore and London: The Johns Hopkins University Press, 2000.

Widder, Keith R. *Michigan Agricultural College: The Evolution of a Land-Grant Philosophy, 1855-1925.* East Lansing: Michigan State University Press, 2005.

Album of Portraits

Law professor Ralph William Aigler: his leadership was critical to Michigan regaining membership in the Western Conference following it's 'Decade of Defiance'.
Bentley Historical Library, University of Michigan

Early in his teaching career Professor Aigler could claim Henry Rottschaefer and John Hannah as his students. The Minnesota faculty representative and the college president would one day challenge his influence and leadership within the Big Nine.
Bentley Historical Library, University of Michigan

For over four decades, the most powerful man in all of college sports, Ralph Aigler, worked out of this simple faculty office on the third floor of Hutchins Hall in the Law Quadrangle at the University of Michigan.
David J. Young

With the University of Chicago announcing plans to withdraw from the Big Ten in June of 1946, Wolverine President Alexander Ruthven decided it was politically correct for Michigan to finally support a Spartan application for membership.
Bentley Historical Library, University of Michigan

Despite expressing no interest in the Wolverine coaching position, Princeton's Herbert "Fritz" Crisler (shown here with mentor Amos Alonzo Stagg) was still placed on the short list of two for the job in December of 1937 - within a decade Crisler would become a Michigan legend.
Bentley Historical Library, University of Michigan

Not only one of the greatest college coaches of all time, Athletic Director Fielding Yost was also the visionary behind a stadium that still symbolizes a tradition of athletic excellence.
Bentley Historical Library, University of Michigan

Long-serving MSC Athletic Director Ralph Young would reach an understanding with Fielding Yost in 1932 that all future games between the state rivals be held the first weekend of the season and always at Michigan Stadium. The agreement assured him of dollars necessary to balance his athletic budget. As a consequence, Young viewed the Ann Arbor site as a "home game for both of us." Those words would come back to haunt him in December of 1942.
Michigan State University Archives and Historical Collections

Minnesota President James Lewis Morrill, a Buckeye-by-birth, drafted the critical strategy that earned John Hannah a seat in the Western Conference. Four decades later the Council of Ten would essentially adopt the '48 Morrill Plan. As of 1987, the presidents would assume responsibilities regarding conference size previously granted the faculty since 1896.
University of Minnesota Archives
University of Minnesota – Twin Cities

Notwithstanding his May 1948 "miscue," Minnesota Athletic Director Frank McCormick ultimately collaborated with Faculty Representative Henry Rottschaefer in carrying out Lew Morrill's revised plan to aid a Spartan admission.
University of Minnesota Archives,
University of Minnesota – Twin Cities

Law Professor Henry Rottschaefer, originally from Holland, Michigan, played a major role in advancing Lew Morrill's plan to assist John Hannah's application for membership in the Western Conference. The crafty scheme for the December 1948 meeting of the faculty representatives, an amendment of sorts to the Morrill Plan, was devised by Hannah to circumvent the powerful influence of the University of Michigan on controversial votes.
University of Minnesota Archives
University of Minnesota – Twin Cities

Former Minnesota lineman and Wolverine assistant coach Clarence "Biggie" Munn's tenure at MSC included a 28 game winning streak, a mythical National Championship in 1952, a conference championship in its inaugural season of competition (1953), and a Rose Bowl victory over UCLA in January of 1954.
Michigan State University Archives and Historical Collections

Frederick Cowles Jenison, graduate of The State Agricultural College and later successful insurance agent in the greater Lansing area, would bequeath to MSC his estate. The gift, in part, would be used to finance the controversial Jenison Awards.
Michigan State University Archives and Historical Collections

John Alfred Hannah's grand vision, a concept in evolution since assuming the presidency of MSC in 1941, was to have the pioneer land grant institution provide extension services to the world.
Michigan State University Archives and Historical Collections

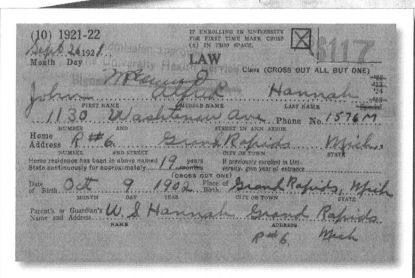

Following two years at Grand Rapids Community College, John Hannah enrolled at the University of Michigan in September of 1921 to study law (LLB). He later transferred to Michigan Agricultural College to pursue a degree in poultry sciences. By 1923 Hannah was employed as an agricultural extension service agent for the institution.
Bentley Historical Library, University of Michigan

Reverend John J. Cavanaugh, president of Notre Dame, was actively involved in negotiations leading to the "Spaghetti and Meatball" contract of October 1946. Cavanaugh is shown with his successor Reverend Theodore M. Hesburgh.
University of Notre Dame Archives

Governor Harry Kelly (ND '17) played a critical role in reassuring his friend, Father John Cavanaugh, that President Hannah's promise (despite lacking board approval) to expand Macklin Field by the fall of 1948 was a certainty. The "Spaghetti and Meatball" contract was consummated over lunch at the governor's home in Lansing.
University of Notre Dame Archives

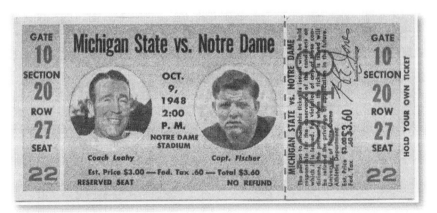

Following the 1921 ND-Michigan Agricultural College game held in South Bend, the Irish ended the long-running series with the Aggies. There was no return-on-investment for the private school to travel to East Lansing and play in a facility seating only 4,000. Twenty five years later Notre Dame agreed to resume the series based on a promise to expand Macklin Field to 52,000 seats by September of 1948.
University of Notre Dame Archives

With the University of Chicago no longer participating in Big Ten football as of December 1939, Ohio State Athletic Director Lynn St. John, the most powerful director in the conference at the time, sought out a program capable of assuring sell-outs at home and on the road for his Buckeyes. That program was a few hours east of Columbus.

The Ohio State University Archives

Commissioner John Griffith was consulted by the University of Pittsburgh in 1939 to assist its athletic director, James Hagan, in cleaning up the tarnished reputation of the Panthers. Shortly after, he became involved in a confidential scheme to promote a Pitt application for membership in the Western Conference. His actions were in violation of a very well-defined job description!

Courtesy of the Big Ten Conference

Northwestern Athletic Director Ken Wilson was a very good friend of the influential, but aging, Lynn St. John of OSU. Through some backroom politicking, St. John successfully got his colleague elected as commissioner of the Big Ten following the untimely death of John Griffith. The Buckeye appeared to have his reasons for manipulating that outcome.

Courtesy of the Big Ten Conference

Despite being a good friend of John Hannah, State University of Iowa President Virgil Hancher opposed the Morrill Plan. He would not use his office to influence decisions regarding membership —a right traditionally reserved for the faculty representatives.

F.W. Kent Collection, University of Iowa Archives, The University of Iowa Libraries; Iowa City, Iowa

Paul Brechler orchestrated the Iowa "no vote" of December 1948. The recently appointed athletic director appeared to have concerns about admitting a school with MSC's suspect reputation. He was also using the vote to make a political statement about disturbing trends in governance within the Western Conference.

F.W. Kent Collection, University of Iowa Archives, The University of Iowa Libraries; Iowa City, Iowa

Handcuffed by his president's public support of the Hannah cause, Ralph Aigler needed an accomplice to carry out a plan to prevent or forestall a Spartan election. Illinois Professor Frank Richart agreed to carry out that role for his colleague.
Courtesy of University of Illinois at Urbana-Champaign Archives

Commando basketball was THE game back in 1976. Due to aging, the brothers (l to r: David, Tim and Mike) now compete on the golf course instead.
David J. Young

Made in the USA
Lexington, KY
23 July 2012